THE DOG BIBLE

THE

DG

BIBLE

Everything Your Dog Wants You to Know

TRACIE HOTCHNER

GOTHAM BOOKS

GOTHAM BOOKS
Published by Penguin Group (USA) Inc.
375 Hudson Street, New York, New York 10014, U.S.A.
Penguin Group (Canada), 90 Eglinton Avenue East, Suite 700, Toronto, Ontario, Canada M4P 2Y3 (a division of Pearson Penguin Canada Inc.); Penguin Books Ltd, 80 Strand, London WC2R 0RL, England; Penguin Ireland, 25 St Stephen's Green, Dublin 2, Ireland (a division of Penguin Books Ltd); Penguin Group (Australia), 250 Camberwell Road, Camberwell, Victoria 3124, Australia (a division of Pearson Australia Group Pty Ltd); Penguin Books India Pvt Ltd, 11 Community Centre, Panchsheel Park, New Delhi - 110 017, India; Penguin Group (NZ), 67 Apollo Drive, Mairangi Bay, Auckland 1311, New Zealand (a division of Pearson New Zealand Ltd); Penguin Books (South Africa) (Pty) Ltd, 24 Sturdee Avenue, Rosebank, Johannesburg 2196, South Africa

Penguin Books Ltd, Registered Offices: 80 Strand, London WC2R 0RL, England

Published by Gotham Books, a division of Penguin Group (USA) Inc.

First printing, November 2005

10 9 8 7 6 5 4 3

LIBRARY OF CONGRESS CATALOGING-IN-PUBLICATION DATA

Hotchner, Tracie.
    The dog bible / Tracie Hotchner.
        p. cm.
    ISBN 1-592-40132-5 (alk. paper)
    1. Dogs. I. Title.
    SF427.H79 2005
    636.7—dc22
            2005004043

Printed in the United States of America
Set in ITC New Baskerville
Designed by Liney Li

For My Father

Who Inspired This Book

and My Love for Dogs

CONTENTS

FOREWORD

Dogs are such a part of my life that I cannot imagine being without them. There are those days, while cleaning up the vomit on the Moroccan rug, or protecting the UPS guy from attack, that my devotion is tested. But one walk with my dog, Haggis, and all is forgiven. The expression on her face when she runs to catch up with me on the beach will get me out of any self-absorbed bad mood. She seems to reach a state of suspended animation over the sand as her back legs reach under and ahead of her front legs, her nose jutting forward like a fighter jet.

Because I'm a veterinarian, I have the pleasure (and sometimes pain) of dealing with dogs and their guardians every working day. There has been a recent flurry of press clippings, television shows, and veterinary journal articles suggesting a new level of connection between dogs and humans. The only part that is new is the press's interest. People and dogs have had such an intimate connection from the furthest reaches of archaeology to the present day that it is impossible to separate our common histories. Did a woman on a farm in rural America 300 years ago love her dog less than a woman living today? Our lives and stresses have changed over time, but our dogs' loyalty has remained constant. One of the secret pleasures of my job is to observe this bond between my clients and their dogs. It stretches from the lady who requests that her dog be bathed in Evian water to the dog who provides direction for the blind man.

A common element of our association with dogs is this simple, unwritten contract: The dog provides the devotion, love, companionship and work, while we accept the responsibility for providing food, water, shelter, healthcare in life and death, and hopefully some love in return. Unfortunately, we as people often fall short. Dogs rarely do. Tracie Hotchner has written a book that will help us keep up our side of the bargain.

When I first met Tracie, she was surrounded by a mad flurry of three dogs. They all seemed to move as one unit. I was not surprised to learn later that she was writing a book about dogs. While reading one of the chapters of this book, I found out why she always brings the whole gang to the vet (you will have to read it to find out!). I wanted to suggest that that sentence be omitted from the book—because my practice would quickly be overrun with every vet visit—but her advice made too much sense. Many vets, breeders, pet-store owners, and people on the street believe so strongly in supporting and promoting their particular belief that it can be hard to wade through the conflicting advice while making decisions for our dogs' care. It seems as if no two people can ever agree on how to care for a dog. Tracie puts forward a refreshingly common-sense approach. There will always be disagreement and a different way to do things. On the balance, though, this book will ride that line of providing the most up-to-date, mainstream thinking without being afraid to challenge the status quo. Tracie has that special quality of having strong thoughts and ideas but also the ability to remain completely open to new information that makes sense.

While talking with Tracie a few days ago, she mentioned to me that she wanted to empower people with information about dog care so that they may make informed choices. This is exactly how I feel. My job as a vet is to give people all the information I have, put it together in a plan of action with options and possible outcomes, and then let the client decide what is best. The paternal, secretive approach to veterinary medicine rarely results in the best care. You are your dog's advocate. Your dog lives with you, not Tracie, me or the breeder. This book will give you what you need to make your life together with your dog the best it can be.

Barry C. Browning, BVM&S, MRCVS
Sag Harbor, NY
November 17, 2004

INTRODUCTION

THIS BOOK IS GOING TO CHANGE YOUR DOG'S LIFE.

It will explain how she thinks, feels, develops and communicates, so you can get the most out of each other's company . . .

It will give you the truth about the different ways and places to get a dog, so when you make a decision it is a fully informed one . . .

It will give you all of the most reliable information about health care, nutrition, training and everything else that pertains to the practicalities of a dog's life, so that you can make good decisions for your dog based on your own situation . . .

It will cover every possible problem you might encounter with your dog and give you choices in how to handle it . . .

It will help you safely introduce your dog to new situations and people, to babies and children, to other dogs and to cats . . .

This book is going to change *your* life.

If you've picked up *The Dog Bible,* then you have a dog, you want to get a dog, or you're close to someone who falls into those two categories. You may already have discovered that no book exists that covers everything a dog-lover needs to know.

I wrote this book because I went looking for it and couldn't find anything like it. I wanted a book I could reach for when I had any questions or problems with my dogs, to find quick ideas and suggestions, remedies and advice. There's never been a book like this, and we dog people needed it. So I embarked on the research of every aspect of a dog's life and covered all the bases. I read the latest medical and nutritional journals. I interviewed vets and dog trainers, consulted breeders and pet-store owners and dog owners, asking them what they would want to find in an encyclopedic book about dogs. And here it is.

When I was researching this book, people frequently assumed I was relying on the Internet for information, but the opposite was true. Even though there are dozens of sites affiliated with dogs on the Internet—and what seems like a river of information—much of it is superficial and/or unreliable. Every so often I'd come upon something interesting, however much of it was simplistic and the origin of the information was unclear. We all tend to forget that the Internet is not just a free encyclopedia or Yellow Pages in cyberspace: it's a place where money changes hands at various levels. Many canine sites are venues to sell dog-related merchandise. There is nothing inherently bad about that—after all, commerce makes the world go around—but you certainly wouldn't want to make any important decision about your dog's life based on anything you surfed on the Net. Having said this, there are some good Internet sites for canine health and wellness issues: any address with ".edu" means a site is affiliated with a university or veterinary school.

You're going to want this book because it has in-depth, objective, thorough facts; because it understands the different ways that dogs are dear to all of us and our desire to get the most out of sharing our lives with them; because it gives you an encyclopedic tool you can reach for when you want information about anything to do with your dog. With all due respect to the late great Benjamin Spock, MD, you can think of this as the "Dr. Spock" for your dog, the has-it-all book that you reach for in times of need or curiosity.

Until *The Dog Bible* came along, there was no reliable place to turn with questions and concerns about pooches. The typical dog owner knows so little about this creature who basically lives for us, yet there is a mountain of information about every aspect of humans sharing their lives with canines. Researchers are discovering nuances about the nutritional, developmental and emotional needs of dogs. Our devotion to our dogs means that the standard of luxury and care for dogs is constantly being raised. Scientists and doctors are developing medical tests and treatments for dogs that were unimaginable a decade ago. In this book you can find out the latest information about what makes dogs tick; how to enhance the human-dog connection; learn the optimal conditions in which to raise a dog; advances in medical care; what choices you have in feeding a dog; the special needs of very small and very large dogs; healthy living with a dog in the city; how to manage canine health for maximum happiness and longevity; and, eventually, how to deal with the options available for bringing a dog's life to a dignified and serene close.

My goal in researching and writing *The Dog Bible* was to improve every aspect of the life you share with your dog. I was already immersed in it, having been a three-dog woman for years now, although not always with the same three dogs. I have never lived without a dog: I was born into a home with a puppy already waiting for my arrival—a fluffy Bedlington Terrier named Pango who shared my life until we were both sixteen. He was my first sibling, and that first year I spent on all fours on the floor with him left me with a compassion for the dog's point of view that I have never lost. I held onto it for Pango's daughter Pandora and then the pair of Bedlingtons we had after them—Mistress Quickly and Falstaff—and then the Golden Retriever Roma; the Cocker Spaniel Amalfi; the Rottweilers Brutus and Yogi Bear; the Corgi/Jack Russell Lucca; the Weimaraners Lulu, Billy Blue and Scooby Doo; and Miss Jazzy, a smooth Collie/sled dog mix. And that doesn't count the dozens of dogs belonging to friends and family who have shared my life and taught me so much.

There is so much more that dog lovers need to know today—so many more choices about what to do with and for our dogs. With most issues about canines there is rarely an absolute—to each his own. If you are a first-time dog owner, you will soon find that almost everyone has opinions about dog ownership. That age-old wisdom not to give people advice about their pets or children is ignored by lots of folks who want to tell you what to do with your dog. Once you have the facts, you can weigh the information and advice you get and be free to make an informed decision for yourself. But without an objective reference source to begin with, you are at the mercy of secondhand advice and hearsay, which you cannot evaluate intelligently.

How to Use This Book

Any way you want, basically. Don't let its size put you off. It's there for as little or as much as you need. You can read all of it or only snippets; the part you need today and the part leading up to it another. The front of each chapter has a list of its subjects to help you navigate, but I've tried to make it as logical and user-friendly as possible. There's a massive index so you can find and cross-check absolutely everything that interests you. Some day, at some point, you may have flipped this book open to most of the entries and gotten the direction you needed. Just knowing it's all there should be a comfort: you're not alone and you're not in the dark. This book will fortify you with enough information to help you determine whether you can handle things alone or need professional assistance.

Dogs are so deeply important to so many people in our world. In fact, a dog is front and center in so many households (sixty million in the United States alone) that collectively we don't even feel the need to defend how shamelessly in love many of us are with our dogs. We don't need to explain the huge amount of time and energy we devote to our canine companions. There are so many reasons that dogs are vitally important to us.

As dog owners we all want to take the best care of our pets. To do that, we need to arm ourselves with information, and *The Dog Bible* presents you with objective information as simply as possible.

I wish a long and happy life to each of you with your dogs. I hope you are able to give them as much pleasure as I'm sure they give you.

I hope that when people see you with your dog they say the same thing that they say to me: "Boy, when I come back, I want to come back as *your* dog."

Tracie Hotchner
East Hampton, New York, 2005

Chapter 1

MATCHMAKING YOU
AND A DOG

 In this chapter you'll find ways to discover the dog that is right for you. Use what you learn here as a jumping-off point into a fun, loving and fascinating relationship with a four-legged creature. Keep in mind that just as there is not "one right person" for each of us—some are just more suitable than others—so it is with people and dogs.

People often pick their dogs for all the wrong reasons—or for no particular reason at all—yet a dog becomes a member of your family for anywhere from eight to eighteen years, depending on the breed, his health and good luck shining on you both. Wouldn't it be nice to know some of the qualities that could be relevant in choosing the dog with the best chance of being appropriate for you? And wouldn't it be nice to have that information *before* you bring that pooch into your home? You really want to avoid winding up in a mismatch with an individual dog just because you followed an impulse or listened to someone else's affection for a particular breed. If you know the ways that the more than one hundred existing breeds of dog can be compatible with all the ways that people want to live with them, it will help you make the best possible choice. If you're getting a mixed-breed dog and can get a sense of what the dominant breed(s) is/are that influence the dog's behavior and/or temperament, you'll be able to eliminate the guesswork. By comparing your dog's head shape, ear type, color and type of coat, and some of her natural inclinations, you can make some good guesses about what breeds contributed to the final outcome.

If you are drawn to a particular breed, ask yourself some questions about why that kind of dog appeals to you before you act on your emotion. This section will help you figure out whether, for example, your attraction to the large, willful, athletic Afghan Hound would be better transferred to a small, lovey-dovey Maltese, a humorous Pug, or an even more humorous English Bulldog. You may be drawn to a particular breed by nothing more than purely a feeling, an instinct.

Maybe you feel nostalgic about a breed of dog you once had or knew, or maybe you just love the look of a particular breed. Did you see an appealing dog passing you on the street? Does a friend have a breed that caught your fancy? Do you have fond memories of a dog you had in childhood?

Before you act on any impulses, do yourself (and your future dog) the favor of learning something about the breed that appeals to you: how much exercise and grooming they require, whether their general temperament suits your lifestyle, whether that breed would be a good a match with your personality. Impulse puppy-buying and uninformed decision-making have caused headaches and heartaches that were avoidable—and that left too many nice dogs abandoned at animal shelters and breed-rescues.

Would you marry someone you'd caught no more than a glimpse of in a park?

Would you spend a decade of your life with someone because they look like someone you used to know?

Would you share your home and hearth with a person who is not compatible with your lifestyle and energy levels?

Would you adopt a baby only because you want a playmate for your other child?

These are roughly equivalent to some of the reasons that people pick dogs, and you need more than that for your decision to make sense and turn out all right for everyone.

The Practical Demands of Dog Ownership

Many of the dogs given up for adoption (or euthanasia) come from people who incorrectly assume that getting a dog is sort of like getting a new treadmill or mountain bike. These same people were surprised to find that having a dog join their lives was more like adding a new family member, with a lot of practical chores and demands but also an emotional give-and-take that they were not expecting.

An average day with most dogs requires feeding the dog twice, taking her on three walks (at least two of them somewhat lengthy, depending on the breed of dog and the weather), playing, and light grooming every few days (again depending on the individual needs of the dog's coat). For a younger dog you'd also have to consider time devoted to training and socialization. Since this is only a conservative time estimate—and one that doesn't consider the downside of medical problems or the upside of just hanging out with the dog and keeping each other company—you really have to ask yourself whether making that kind of commitment to an animal is appealing to you or realistically out of the question.

Some people can feel guilty or resentful toward a dog they perceive as an impediment to their personal freedom; those negative emotions take the fun out of it. That sense of obligation can even interfere with the person's attachment to the pet. Realizing too late that you don't really have (or want to give) the needed time for a pet can also lead to a dog being given up to the shelter, a traumatic failure for the animal that could have been avoided by a realistic assessment beforehand of how much time and energy a dog requires.

And what if something happens to you? You need to think about what will become of your dog if you can't take care of him over the short term or the long term. Having a contingency plan ready in case something prevents you from getting back to your dog—such as sickness, travel or the need to work extended hours—is a practical necessity that is often overlooked. If only for your own peace of mind, it's important to plan backup care to doggie-sit or board your dog. You'll need to plan ahead so there is someone in the wings to take care of the dog when you cannot. You need to start cultivating these services well in advance of need or emergency, so that everyone involved knows the dog and her particular needs.

IMPROVING YOUR ODDS OF A GOOD MATCH

The information in this section should illuminate for you which parts of your daily routines and personality traits may enhance or diminish the quality of your interaction with a particular kind of dog, while helping you to better understand and anticipate your dog's behavior.

Don't worry if you got a dog before you had a chance to read this. Don't fret if you've had a dog for years and wish you'd had this knowledge all along. Better late than never that you learn all you can about the inborn tendencies of your dog's breed.

Organizations like the American Kennel Club (AKC) that dominate dog-breeding and dog shows have traditionally placed the many different breeds of dogs into seven categories. This was probably done for consistency in dog-showing. Even though these seven groupings have limited practical application in real life, dog charts still tend to cluster them in those same groupings. Categories like "Non-sporting" or "Working" are not really relevant to the practical realities of whether a certain breed would be a good fit for a single apartment-dweller or a family of five in the suburbs. It may be meaningless to the modern pet owner whether a dog was originally bred to jump into freezing water after ducks (Labs and Retrievers), or hunt lions in the jungle (Rhodesian Ridgebacks). Since few people have large flocks of sheep that need herding, or the need for a terrier to help eliminate rats down in the coal mine, what matters are the canine qualities that actually apply to a dog's interaction with people in the modern world. Maybe the dog who has staked a claim to your once-beige sofa is from a breed originally meant to bound across frozen tundra with his team, pulling a sled laden with supplies, but that doesn't mean that some individuals from this breed might not be just as content to stretch out on that couch with you.

How can you know whether the life you are offering to share with a dog will be mutually satisfying? The general personality and energy level particular to a breed can affect your compatibility—once you have a realistic expectation of what a particular dog needs from you, then what it boils down to is whether you can offer that dog the kind of attention and exercise that he needs.

THE WORKSHEET

There is a crucial issue in matchmaking you and a dog that many books and trainers do not even address: the human part of the equation, the who-what-where of *you* as the future owner.

You can divide the kind of attitudes that owners can have about a dog's place in their lives into three basic categories. The quiz below allows you to take an honest look at yourself from these perspectives, because before you think about what qualities in a dog are most important to you, you have to think about what makes you tick as a potential owner.

WHY TAKE A QUIZ?

The following worksheet is designed around two extremes of self-description in areas that have some relevance to dog ownership. On some traits or adjectives you will be solidly one way or the other, while for most aspects you'll probably fall somewhere between the two. Be honest with yourself about where your personality fits in the spectrum of possible attitudes.

The intent of this worksheet is to stimulate you to think about yourself from various perspectives, so that when you are considering the size, energy level and requirements of different dogs you will have the best shot at making a good match for yourself. There is no way to predict with certainty how the qualities listed in the quiz will affect your behavior with a dog, but most dogs generally behave best when you train and interact in a consistent manner, instituting the boundaries and routines you choose and then maintaining them. Therefore, if more of your personality traits fall on the right side of the chart, it seems logical that you would do better not to choose a hard-to-train breed of dog that is generally known to be stubborn or very independent. A smaller, people-oriented lapdog or companion dog might be just the ticket. However, this doesn't mean that if your personality traits are mostly on the left column you will necessarily be a good match for an active breed with tendencies to stubbornness. On the contrary, it may even be a *bad* idea for a strong-willed owner to be paired up with a "tough" dog, because their personalities may clash if both decide to stand their ground.

◆ What the Worksheet Tells You

The human qualities based on the worksheet all have some bearing in training a dog and cohabiting with her; knowledge about yourself can lead you to discover what sort of dog would be a good fit for your life. If you feel like it, circle the number from 1 to 5 that best describes you. The evaluation is not black and white, and there is no value judgment intended in any of the adjectives. You may very well have a number of traits from both columns, all of which can give you a more accurate description of your personal style or that of other family members who will be interacting with the dog.

Worksheet:

Evaluating Yourself and Your Family

PART ONE: PERSONALITY AND PHYSICAL TRAITS

	1	2	3	4	5	
Physically Strong	1	2	3	4	5	Not Physical
Outdoors/Sporty	1	2	3	4	5	Indoors/Nonathletic
Active/Energetic	1	2	3	4	5	Sedentary/Meditative
Assertive/Outspoken	1	2	3	4	5	Low-key/Soft-spoken
Rushed/Impatient	1	2	3	4	5	Calm/Patient
Leader/First in line	1	2	3	4	5	Hang Back/Waits one's turn
Demanding/Bossy	1	2	3	4	5	Easygoing/Non-disciplinarian

PART TWO: ATTITUDES TOWARD DISCIPLINE AND ORDER

Follows the rules	1	2	3	4	5	Undisciplined
Disciplinarian	1	2	3	4	5	Inconsistent/Laissez-faire
Patient teacher	1	2	3	4	5	Impatience during learning process
Willing to be tough	1	2	3	4	5	Can't put one's foot down
Set ideas	1	2	3	4	5	Open to new methods/ideas

PART THREE: WHERE THE DOG FITS INTO YOUR LIFE

Which scenario most applies to your idea of a dog's place in your household?

Scenario One

Main reason for the dog is practical: it'll be fun for your child(ren).

Dog's routine of eating/walking is fairly consistent.

Dog viewed as part of the household rather than a member of the family.

Dog goes on some trips and outings with you, in the car or on a leash.

Dog sleeps in a family bedroom, on the floor or in a dog bed.

Dog is included when visitors are around.

Scenario Two

Primary motive for a dog is as a companion for you personally.

Dog is perceived as a cohabitant whose needs are considered alongside your own.

Dog accompanies you on errands/social events/jogging/car outings.

Dog travels with you when possible.

Dog sleeps in your bedroom—maybe on the bed.

Dog has an eating/exercise schedule that people accommodate.

Dog is taught manners necessary for him to participate socially.

Dog is not left completely alone for long periods of time or overnight.

You communicate with the dog by responding to each other's nonverbal signals.

Scenario Three

Motive for dog is practical: to discourage burglars, go hunting.

Dog is perceived as useful: she is there for people's needs and/or pleasure.

Human needs always supersede canine needs.

Dog spends time only at home (usually his only car trip is to the vet).

Dog is not permitted to sleep in a bedroom.

Dog is shut in a room, crate or outside when there are visitors or workmen.

Dog is alone a lot: while you work and/or at night when you go out.

If a country dog, his only exercise is in his own backyard—no walks or outings.

Dog kept solely outside or has limited house privileges.

Special Considerations about Children

(This topic is covered briefly here, but for a more in-depth look at kids and dogs, see chapter Fourteen, which begins on page 468).

You need to find out whether the breed of dog you want is compatible with children, because most children can be counted on to be unpredictable and rambunctious, as well as effusive with their affection or frustration. For some dogs the loudness and quickness of children makes no difference at all, while for other breeds, small children push all the wrong buttons. You should be able to trust a good breeder to give you the truth about whether the breed you're interested in is generally a good one for kids. A breeder with a conscience will not say her dogs are child-friendly just to make the sale—especially because she doesn't want the puppy to wind up in a situation where he could cause trauma and physical jeopardy for the child, not to mention possible relinquishment or euthanasia for the puppy.

Many breeds are too jumpy and sensitive to be comfortable around the noise and unpredictability of children. Kids move quickly and in unexpected ways—their voices can be high and shrill, they can yell or scream in pleasure or in pain, their explosive crying and often surprisingly rapid motions can be alarming to some dogs.

Of course, if you raise a dog around children and carefully teach the children to respect the dog—also showing the children the appropriate body language to use with dogs—you can generally be assured of a good outcome.

SMALL DOGS NOT USUALLY RECOMMENDED WITH CHILDREN

Some canine experts believe categorically that toy breeds are not child-appropriate. They say the little dogs are too small and delicate and can be easily injured by children's actions—and small dogs can also be snappy, these experts contend. But people often report that their little dogs have halos over their heads because they allow themselves to be treated like stuffed animals by small children. So who's to say, really, what kind of dog will or will not work with children? You need to evaluate your individual dog, expose her to babies and the sights and sounds that accompany children and note how she handles it. So while there are exceptions to every rule—I have known a Yorkie and Rottweiler who were the most child-friendly dogs I ever met—do you really want to challenge the evaluation of a breeder who is honest enough to tell you that her animals are *not* great with children!?

Choosing a Breed to Suit You

The big secret about choosing a dog is that it's basically a gamble—you cannot positively predict how any individual dog will turn out. With purebred dogs you can improve your odds, but there really is no guarantee that you'll be getting a dog that fulfills your personal ideal. Having *realistic expectations* goes a long way in promoting a good foundation for any relationship (between humans or between humans and animals).

Because people have manipulated the genetic makeup of different breeds, the dogs have fairly predictable differences in how fierce or loud or outgoing they are. Their stamina, sensory perceptions, agility and emotions vary breed by breed, too. Two characteristics that can make a huge difference in your experience of a dog are its *trainability* and **obedience.** German Shepherds have done guard work and aided handicapped people and worked with the military and police forces since the beginning of the breed; it would be hard to accuse Scottish Terriers or Jack Russell Terriers of ever aspiring to such lofty tasks.

By choosing one breed over another, what you are buying is predictability in a variety of areas—size, temperament, specific instinctual drives, type of coat.

BREED PERSONALITIES (OR NOT)

Don't think that because you like a dog of a certain breed, all members of that breed—even another member of that breed, or even another from the same litter—is going to be just like that dog. Every dog has an individual personality, which may or may not be representative of his breed (or, in the case of a mutt, the dominant breed).

Think of how many differences there are in look and disposition and intelligence among human children who share the same two parents—not even counting other members of the same extended family. (They broke the mold with you, too: have you ever met someone exactly like you?)

Every dog is one of a kind. That's part of what makes living with dogs such an adventure and a mystery.

THE HUMAN ELEMENT TO CANINE PERSONALITY

Although each dog is born with a predisposition toward a certain emotional makeup, the ways in which people interact with dogs have a lot to do with their personalities. Just like with people, a dog's personality may seem to change depending on the different ways that humans may perceive and behave with them.

Regardless of what a dog's breed is supposed to be like, an individual dog can be overconfident or fearful; hyperactive or sluggish; reserved or outgoing.

DESIRE FOR PHYSICAL AFFECTION

The desire for physical affection varies with individual dogs, just as it does with people. Some dogs want to snuggle up with you, others don't want much physical contact.

Mismatches of dog and human personalities can happen on several levels, but display of affection is certainly an important area.

◆ Dealing with Differences

If you and a dog are on different wavelengths about affection, it doesn't have to become a problem unless you ignore the signals your dog is giving you. If you pay attention to your dog's interaction with you, it's possible to read his desires through his physical reaction to people's actions (see page 68 for a "Dictionary of Body Language"). Where you can get into problems is when you have a big, noisy extended family that does not pay attention to the feedback a dog gives them about her need for space, privacy and less physical interaction. If you can see when enough is enough for a dog and respect that, you'll have true compatibility with her.

✦ Head Patting

Many dogs hate being patted on the head. You have to look at their facial contortions to see this, or the way they shrink away from an oncoming hand. If you give a head pat to a dog like that as a reward for obedience, you are sort of punishing them—at the very least it will make them less responsive or obedient.

When a dog is agitated or aroused, happily or otherwise, it's normal not to want to be patted. She just can't take any more sensory stimulation.

✦ Showing Affection to a Big Dog

How about the way you pat your dog? Is it an anxious "pat-pat-pat"? Have you watched to see how he feels about it? Do you play the drums on his back—and how does he react to that? Or do you have a big dog that you give the big, open-handed horse-slap/pat on the back, shoulders or hindquarters? Does he lean against you for more, look back dreamily at you in gratitude for the attention—or does he kind of cringe and lean away? Just because a dog is large doesn't mean he appreciates big thumping patting. Pay attention: the dog will make clear what he likes and what he doesn't.

DIFFERENCES IN TEMPERAMENT
(See also Chapter Three, "Picking a Puppy," page 62)

Dogs are individuals and should be viewed as such—each dog is a product of the personality she was born with and her experiences so far in life. It is not useful to make assumptions about a particular dog as a representative of her breed or cross-breed—in other words, don't write off every Pit Bull or Rottweiler as potentially dangerous. But even more importantly, do not assume that a cute Cocker Spaniel or a frisky little Yorkshire Terrier is safe. Cockers are renowned for having one of the worst bites in dogdom—and a frequency for using their teeth against people—while Yorkies can get very nippy. My Rottweiler, Yogi Bear, was possibly the most profoundly affectionate and imperturbable dog anyone has ever met.

✦ How's His Noise Sensitivity?

This is a little test you can do to test noise sensitivity. (NOTE: Do not do this between the ages of eight and eleven weeks, a development period known as the "fear imprint stage," when sudden scary noises or events can be so traumatic for a puppy that the experience leaves a permanent emotional scar.) You can also do this with an adult dog.

When the puppy's attention is elsewhere, drop something clattery—a noisy item like a metal pan on the kitchen floor—but not too close to the puppy. Do this from behind your back so the puppy doesn't see where it came from.

A dog's reaction to noise can be a harbinger of self-confidence. If the puppy is startled—but then curious—that's good. A quick recovery and then wanting to check out the object is the sign of a well-adjusted puppy with healthy self-confidence.

A puppy who is freaked out—running away, vocalizing fear, perhaps urinating or defecating and unable to calm herself down—may be a high-strung dog without self-confidence who may have trouble around loud noises, at the very least.

THE "PERFECT" BREED FOR YOU

In trying to figure out what kind of dog will best suit you, you may have invested in one or more dog books with elaborate charts and graphs comparing all the breeds from every possible angle and giving them a rating on each element.

There are shiny-cardboard-covered books about each breed that are usually on revolving racks in pet stores. Don't be in a rush to buy one! The books claim to have specialized, comprehensive information that is unique to that breed, but there are very few, if any, characteristics that are always going to show up in any one breed. Even though breeders have been trying for decades to establish solid profiles of their particular dogs—and those breed descriptions are part of the reason that people would buy that breed—new evidence shows that these results are not so dependable. You can pretty much toss those books now!

For example, people generally believe that Golden Retrievers are sweet-natured, and most do have nice temperaments. However, it isn't realistic to assume that every individual dog of a breed will embody the standard characteristics. Quality and consistency in every puppy is a fundamental purpose of any breeding program, but that goal is not reliably achieved.

Another problem with these breed books is that looking at most of them is like looking at the files in a dating agency: every photo shows off each "candidate," and the descriptions always accentuate the positive and underreport or neglect to include health and behavioral problems. The AKC's own breed book is guilty of having an attitude that all breeds are great, every dog is wonderful—as if they were trying to keep all breeders happy or not show favoritism by giving one breed a more positive description than another. But obviously there are breeds that *are* more trouble on various levels. If you are still attracted to the breed once you know the challenges, imagine how helpful it will be to know ahead of time what you may be facing.

It's nearly impossible to make sense of graphs when they cover a hundred breeds of dogs: they show obvious differences in size and energy levels and numerous other characteristics that you have to factor in to determine your "perfect" breed. It's unwise to depend on a particular breed to *guarantee* you a long list of specific qualities, because to a great extent all dogs share the same fundamentals: they can bark as watchdogs, they will respond to affection and enjoy human company, and they can be trained and socialized. And besides, every dog is an individual, not a cookie-cutter representative of an ideal. So you wind up choosing a dog for a whole slew of reasons (or none at all, if it's an impulse), but no matter how you get there don't be too discouraged if your dog does not behave according to the detailed breed description—respect and celebrate the unique individual in every dog, and you'll rarely be disappointed.

Behavior Traits

The categories that follow give you an unconventional way to categorize dog behavior, by dividing it into six groups: Intelligence, Independence, Determination, Dominance, High Energy and Prey Drive.

Under each behavior category are the characteristics that describe it. So when you are considering which breed of dog might be good for you, or you want to evaluate an individual dog who is available, the following list may help you make a good match.

INTELLIGENCE

❏ has the natural ability to find an exit despite a barrier
❏ is creative and resourceful when looking for ways to amuse herself
❏ tailors her response to a command from us by evaluating our moods
❏ quickly understands what words mean when directed at her
❏ has an innate curiosity—to explore, to watch us, to be on the alert

INDEPENDENCE

❏ shows indifference to people and other animals
❏ dislikes physical affection shown to her
❏ dislikes being groomed
❏ prefers to be alone
❏ turns away when scolded
❏ has her own agenda independent of the one we had in mind

DETERMINATION

❏ is single-minded in returning to a task even after you have diverted attention
❏ is oblivious to physical corrections
❏ displays obsessive behavior, like chasing a ball fifty times
❏ gets his own way regardless of how long it takes

DOMINANCE

❏ guards food, territory
❏ growls and/or snaps when he doesn't get his way
❏ stands his guard in a public place
❏ stands his ground in a new or frightening situation

HIGH ENERGY/HYPERACTIVE

❏ doesn't sleep much
❏ gets overexcited from even slight stimuli
❏ always ready for action
❏ initiates action, makes the "call to arms"

PREY DRIVE

❏ frequently sniffs the air and ground, and even your feet
❏ shakes and "kills" stuffed animals by shaking them in his teeth
❏ stalks cats, birds, squirrels, etc.
❏ bites your feet when you start to move

Breed Groups—General Observations

One of the main reasons that people gravitate toward one breed or another has to do with the way the dog looks—and perhaps its size. Although part of you may think it is wrong to make a decision based on superficial looks, there's nothing to be ashamed of when you realize that many of the things we are drawn to in life begin with a visual attraction, whether it is a partner or objects that we purchase.

However, it is possible for people to get into a serious bind if they base the acquisition of a dog solely on her looks without learning more about the temperament and the physical needs of the breed. You can educate yourself beforehand by finding out what the dog was originally bred to do (if anything at all) and then learn how this can impact the disposition of each individual as a pet. It's kind of a "form vs. function" issue, because if you choose a dog on the basis of her *form* rather than equally considering her intended *function,* you may turn out to be ill-suited to each other's natural energy level and style of living.

I probably don't need to point out that a frail, book-by-the-fire kind of person may admire the elegant looks of a Rhodesian Ridgeback, but the person needs to know that they're probably going to be miserable with a powerful, independent dog bred to hunt big game. By the same token, think how miserable *a dog* would be if mismatched with the wrong kind of owner—what would happen if an outdoorsy person wanted a gorgeous little Maltese with her flowing white coat? A jogger/hiker/beach person would probably not be the right "designated human" for a lapdog that's most happy indoors, out of the elements.

◆ **Training Challenges** *(Usually in the Terrier and Nonsporting Hound Groups)*
Very independent breeds can be tough to civilize and control, yet their value is in their determination and ability to initiate their own actions. Afghan Hounds, Beagles, Bulldogs, Chow Chows, Corgis, Dachshunds and Rhodesian Ridgebacks are just a few breeds intended to do a job without dependence on their person or even an attachment to the person while working. These breeds are less interested in what you think and are not dependent on your approval for them to carry on.

DIVIDING BREEDS INTO CATEGORIES

The groupings that follow are somewhat different than how the American Kennel Club (AKC) categorizes dog breeds: their standard for dividing dogs into groups was created primarily for the purpose of dog shows. I've tried to group similar breeds together in a way that may be more relevant if you're trying to decide on a kind of dog that might suit you. The categories should give you a chance to really consider the practical aspects of living with each type of breed, taking into account what the particular breed's original purpose was before its main "job" was transformed into becoming the family pet.

Obviously, these groupings can't specifically mention all of the breeds that could possibly belong in each category, but if the breed you're interested in is not mentioned, you can probably figure out which group it would fall into.

SPORTING DOGS

Retrievers, Spaniels, Setters, Pointers, Weimaraners, Vizslas
This group was bred to work alongside man, so they take well to training and they make great family dogs. But they do need a lot of exercise—preferably opportunities to run off-leash. You need to make time to play fetch with a ball or a dog-safe Frisbee (made of softer material that won't hurt their teeth). If given a chance to retrieve, the breeds with "retriever" in their name thrive on playing games with you.

If there's a way to incorporate swimming, most retrievers go nuts for the water. Whatever you do to satisfy their need for exercise, make time to give these dogs a chance to use their bodies and minds so that the "hunting drive" in them will not be displaced into other (possibly destructive or neurotic) behavior.

Some of these breeds were developed to work at a distance from the hunter, so they have a strong drive to roam or hunt on their own. If you want the dog to be off-leash in woods or wide-open spaces, teach and practice the recall at home first.

HERDING DOGS

Australian Cattle Dog, Border Collie, Briard, Collie, Old English Sheepdog, German Shepherd, Shetland Sheepdog, anything with "shepherd" in the name
These dogs were developed to herd and protect. They make great family dogs—your family makes a nice little flock for them to protect and herd. If these dogs circle around you at the front door and nip at your heels to keep you in a tight group, you should understand that it's just their genetic tendency.

WORKING DOGS

Bernese Mountain Dog, Boxer, Doberman Pinscher, Rottweiler, Saint Bernard
These dogs are highly intelligent, so keep them interested when training and keep them on their toes with a change in routine. They are devoted to their people, but their protective instincts have to be shaped by you: you have to be in command of the natural inclinations of these often large and powerful dogs. Decisions have to come from you throughout their life so they never start to believe that they are "the alpha"—or things could get unpleasant or even dangerous (more on this on page 153 in Chapter Seven.)

SPITZ DOGS

Akita, Alaskan Malamute, Chow Chow, Finnish Spitz, Pomeranian, Shiba Inu, Samoyed, Siberian Husky
The AKC puts these dogs in the "working dog" category, but they have characteristics quite specific to their type. Spitz dogs exist around the world and are charac-

terized by a wedge-shaped head; small, pointed, erect ears; a tail curled over the back and a double coat.

Strength, independence and courage are their primary qualities—obedience or compliance are not programmed in. Malamutes and Huskies, among others, pull sleds through polar conditions—the desirable attitude in such brave and hardy workers is that there's a job to be done, so get out of my way. Dogs in this category are fast learners but not interested in your approval of their obedience. Despite the hard work and patience they require, these breeds can be especially affectionate and devoted. These breeds are also runners that can just take off and never look back, so forget strolls in wide-open places—it's unlikely that you can ever safely walk them off a leash if you want to see them again!

TERRIERS

Airedale, Australian, Bedlington, Border, Bull, Cairn, Irish, Jack Russell, Kerry Blue, Miniature Schnauzer, Norfolk and Norwich, Scottish, Skye, Smooth Fox Terrier, Soft Coated Wheaten and others with "terrier" in their names

These high-energy dogs are supremely cheerful, feisty with other dogs, stubborn and "forgetful" about obedience issues. Great fun and sometimes infuriating, these dogs are long-lived, so you'll have years to try to iron out their rough edges while they try to train *you* to obey!

The smaller of the dogs in this group were bred to chase rodents and tunnel down into holes to go after them, which is what gives them a cocky attitude. Terriers can be aggressive toward other dogs, and hardheaded and relentless about what they want; people who love them love that about them.

SIGHT HOUNDS

Afghan, Basenji, Borzoi, Greyhound, Ibizan, Irish Wolfhound, Pharaoh, Saluki, Whippet

Dogs in this group are generally gorgeous, graceful and blisteringly fast. They originally hunted in packs, so they get along well with other dogs. These are generally not dogs to trust off the leash, because they keep an eye on what might be out there and can be off in a flash. They are responsive to training with a light hand—these are sensitive, gentle dogs that you need to teach with equal gentleness, never being rough or loud.

SCENT HOUNDS

Basset Hound, Beagle, Bloodhound, Coonhound, Foxhound

Most scent hounds are hard to housebreak, in part because they were bred to live outdoors in kennels and be part of a hunting pack—they do not have the inbred instinct to keep clean. They're low to the ground (the better to sniff it), and while they can be noisy barkers or howlers, they usually have no instinct to put that vocalization to work as watchdogs. Getting along with other dogs is what they are all about; they make lovely, gentle members of the human family. Practice obedience work indoors to build a foundation, because once outdoors, they are easily distracted by scents.

TOY DOGS

Chihuahua, Maltese, Papillon, Pug, Silky Terrier, Toy Poodle, Yorkshire Terrier (would be a true terrier except for size)
Bred solely as companions to people, these dogs are devoted, funny and bright. Although they are small and portable, people need to take their housebreaking and obedience training seriously, because otherwise these little dogs can be frustrating. Despite their small stature, many of them have huge personalities.

Qualities of Some Breeds

What follows are a few lists of dogs that share qualities that might appeal to you about a breed— or might turn you off to a breed that you were considering.

SOME SLOW-MOVING BREEDS

Basset Hound
Clumber Spaniel
English Bulldog
English Mastiff
Great Dane

Greyhound
   (ironically also the fastest)
Newfoundland
Sussex Spaniel

SOME ZIPPY BREEDS

Most herding breeds, such as the
Australian Cattle Dog,
Border Collie, Shetland Sheepdog, etc.
Dalmatian

French Bulldog
Jack Russell Terrier
Siberian Husky

SOME VERY BRIGHT BREEDS

Border Collie
Doberman Pinscher

Golden Retriever
Poodle

American Staffordshire Terrier   German Shepherd
Belgian Malinois   Giant Schnauzer
Border Collie   Jack Russell Terrier
Boxer   Labrador Retriever
Flat-Coated Retriever   Rottweiler

The Most Popular Purebred Dogs

There are more than 300 different breeds of dogs in the world—many of which have never been seen in the United States—of which approximately 150 are registered with the American Kennel Club (AKC). The number of officially recognized dog breeds is constantly fluctuating as more breeds become recognized by the organization. There are some breeds that are not yet accepted by the AKC and are recognized only by the UKC (United Kennel Club), which is a smaller group that registers dogs and sponsors shows.

There are about fifteen dogs that are the most popular in the U.S. year after year. One amazing fact is that for many years the Labrador Retriever has not only been the most popular dog in the country, it has been more plentiful than the next dog (the Golden Retriever) by more than *double*. So if you think you see Labs everywhere you turn, you're probably right.

After those two dogs, the breeds in the following box are the next most popular, in descending order of number of registrations with the AKC. From year to year one of these breeds may go up or down a notch on the list, but these are basically the breeds that have maintained their positions on the "Popularity Chart." If any of these breeds are ones that interest you, keep in mind that there are two sides to popularity. The good side is that there should be a ready supply of dogs—either puppies from breeders, or those same puppies a few months later when they've been abandoned to a breed-specific rescue organization. The bad side is that the demand for the breeds means that unscrupulous breeders—and particularly the "big business" wholesale puppy breeders—start churning out litters, perhaps with even less regard than usual for the welfare of the mothers and the well-being of the puppies. The breeds that go through phases of enormous popularity generally pay a high price for the increased demand on the gene pool. Cocker Spaniels—and then Golden Retrievers—were at one time the all-American dog that the Labrador Retriever has now become. Let us hope that overbreeding and inbreeding (mating dogs too closely in a family tree) of Labradors does not create the health and temperament problems that affected those other two once-popular breeds.

16 Most Popular Breeds in the U.S.

Labrador Retriever	Chihuahua
Golden Retriever	Shih Tzu
German Shepherd	Rottweiler
Dachshund	Pomeranian
Beagle	Miniature Schnauzer
Yorkshire Terrier	Pug
Boxer	Cocker Spaniel
Poodle	Shetland Sheepdog

Exercise Needs Based on the Dog's Size

The size of a dog doesn't necessarily correlate with her energy level—you might be surprised to learn that, as a group, the smallest dogs are by far the most high-energy. But the little dogs get most of the activity they need indoors, so you aren't obligated to take them on planned walks.

At the other end of the spectrum, many very large dogs need hardly any exercising since they tend toward being lethargic. Some of the biggest giants—Saint Bernards, Greyhounds, Great Danes and Newfoundlands—are content to lie about like royal pashas.

In the sporting dog breeds, the breeders either concentrate on "show dogs," which are bred to shine in the ring and are more laid-back at home, or "field dogs," which are bred for actual hunting and generally require more exercise and activity for the high energy and stamina that have been bred into them.

TINY & SMALL DOGS

This size dog is easy to travel with but hard to house-train (see the "Small Dogs" section, page 618). Many of them don't need much outdoor exercise, if any—indoor running around can often satisfy them. Owners often forgo obedience training (little dogs get away with murder!), which is also covered in the "Small Dogs" chapter.

Life expectancy: Twelve to sixteen years.

MEDIUM DOGS

One good walk a day is enough for most of these pooches; some off-leash running is good when and if possible.

Life expectancy: Twelve to fourteen years.

LARGE DOGS

Depending on the breed, a generous amount of exercise is needed for the bigger dogs, although there are lots of exceptions (see the "Slow-Moving" list, page 18). But for many of the sporting/working dogs, if you don't burn off their energy outdoors you'll live to regret it, because they'll find a way to do it in your house or yard!

Life expectancy: Eight to fourteen years.

GIANT DOGS

Many don't need much exercise because of their bulk and slower metabolism. Life expectancy: Seven to ten years.

Nature or Nurture: What Shapes a Dog?

The old debate in the human world about "nature vs. nurture" is not usually considered in the dog world. Is the early environment in which a pup is raised more or less important than what he is born with, than the cards he is dealt by the luck of the genetic draw? Is a dog's temperament influenced by his genetic background as much as the environment in which she is raised in the first few months of life? You also have to consider that added to the effect of the puppy's earliest environment will be the influence of the home in which the dog is going to grow up and grow old, and how it will affect her if during her lifetime she is "re-homed" (the politically correct phrase that means "given up for adoption"). However you cut it, all these factors have to influence a puppy's eventual personality. Each dog is the product of heredity, the mother's health during pregnancy, conditions at birth, the parents' temperaments and the environment in which the puppy is raised (diet, health, socialization). Then, of course, there's also the JPL factor: Just Plain Luck.

The best thing you can do for yourself and your dog is to let go of any unrealistic expectation of what your dog's personality or temperament "should" be. Each dog is a distinct individual who may be a better or worse representative of a particular breed, but at the end of the day what it's really all about is the connection that you (and your family) form with that particular dog, regardless of how much she conforms to an arbitrary list of ideal breed characteristics.

A Word about Certain Breeds

There are a few areas about breeders and purebred dogs (which are covered in depth in Chapter Two) that need to be discussed here, in case it makes a difference to the choices you make about a dog. Numerous breeds of popular dogs are becoming predisposed to serious health problems and life-threatening conditions, and the only protection you have against this is if the breeder willingly has genetic testing done on her breeding dogs to reduce the chances of problems in her puppies.

From the physical health point of view, genetic testing of the puppy's parents—which would lower her chances of getting any of the medical conditions that can be passed on in the genes—can be beneficial. In dogs, important medical problems like hip dysplasia (and to a lesser degree elbow and knee problems) are passed on through the parents. If a breeder is highly responsible she will have X-ray tests done on any breeding pair to be sure they aren't passing on those joint problems. When a dog has been tested in this way and given a clean bill of orthopedic health, he is certified as having "clear hips" (or whatever the breed-specific genetic risk may be). If the breeder uses a female that is also certified as clear, then the litter should be free of joint problems.

However, without being too cynical, you have to question whether that genetic testing was actually done. How can you be sure that a breeder is telling you the truth? This question of a breeder's honesty is not intended to cast doubt on all dog breeders, but the reality is that you have to be careful in any aspect of life where there is a monetary value to paperwork that can be forged or doctored. Horse breeding is a perfect example of this: there are layers of safeguards in the breeding process and its documentation (while there are none to speak of in dog breeding). Yet in the horse world there are still fiddles and switches in what paperwork goes with which horse, even to prove its age or color.

Think about it: Even though dog breeding can bring in a tidy sum to those breeders who manage their program well and ask top dollar for their dogs, there are still a lot of expenses. If you're running a business, especially a small one, you obviously want to limit costs to maximize profit. Realistically, how many breeders will take the time to go through the added expense of having each of their breeding dogs x-rayed under anesthesia to be sure their hips/knees/etc. are "clear"? How many breeders are going to pay the high laboratory fees for genetic blood tests of each of their breeding stock? Other than having a conscience, what stops the breeder from producing one such document and using it for all puppies? Who would be the wiser? Breeders might think, Why go to this significant expense and trouble when other breeders are not doing it—and dogs generally sell just as well with little more than a verbal guarantee of the health of the puppy's parents?

Cautionary Tips about Some Breeds

WARNING ABOUT PIT BULLS

Pit Bulls were developed to fight other dogs in cruel contests that have been illegal for decades—but that are still held in rural areas as well as inner cities. These dogs have enormous physical strength and aggressiveness that have been encouraged through breeding—which means the dog may include people as its targets. Pit Bulls—especially those living in pairs or in multi-dog households—have been known to randomly attack people, even the people closest to them. Sometimes attacks occur over food or affection being shown to another dog; other attacks have no clear provocation. It's essential to understand that these are not just growly squabbles—people and other dogs have died as a result. The Pit Bull's history as a fighting dog and its record as one of the breeds responsible for the most human dog-bite fatalities have made the breed a topic of intense debate over its suitability as a companion animal.

Pit Bulls can be good family pets if raised properly from puppyhood, and many owners are proud, protective and defensive about the breed. However, given the knowledge of why Pit Bulls were developed as a breed—and given the potential jeopardy to people inside and outside the

Pit Bull's home, as well as the fact that there are more than 200 other breeds of dogs—you might wonder why some owners would place themselves and others around them at that kind of risk. Having said that, of course, there are people who adore each and every breed for all sorts of emotional reasons. A poor choice or decision in picking a Pit can result in tragedy, even death. These dogs are so strong and have such potential to do damage that you have to be careful in selecting and raising one. You also have to be on the defensive with other people because the reputation that Pits have gotten makes other people wary of them.

If you own, or are looking to own a Pit Bull, do not take the responsibility lightly. You may want to search out an eighty-minute video by Sue Sternberg called *The Controversial Pit Bull,* which explores the differences between Pits, Pit-Mixes and most non-Pit shelter dogs. The video emphasizes observing and temperament-testing Pit Bulls in a breed-specific way, so as to identify a potentially dangerous dog compared to one that will make a good household pet.

"At first glance there may not be any discernible differences between a Good Pit and a Scary Pit," Sternberg says. "The average owner will think that both dogs are just being effusively friendly. Most Pit Bulls will greet you by wriggling all over and wagging their tails exuberantly, their tongues hanging out with big grins. A temperament problem is more evident in most other dogs. In Pit Bulls it's very hard for the average person to appreciate—until it's too late."

Here are just a few of Sternberg's tips about how to distinguish a Good Pit from one that has latent aggressive tendencies:

SIGNS OF A SCARY PIT BULL

- ❏ A dog that arouses quickly—gets all wound up and competitive immediately when playing
- ❏ A dog that does not calm down easily from that arousal state
- ❏ A dog that avoids petting, that moves away from you to avoid your touch
- ❏ A dog that avoids mild restraint—he shakes you off or uses his mouth (even gently) to escape your touch if you hold his collar

All Pits love tug-of-war, but beware of Pits who quickly and repeatedly "re-grip" up the rope or leap at your arm or hand to get control of the game. You shouldn't be playing tug-of-war with any aggressive dog anyway (see page 160). For more information on the controversy please go to www.thedogbible.com, click on "Inside the Book," and go to "Pit Bulls."

WARNING ABOUT FRENCH BULLDOGS FROM RUSSIA

The French Bulldog Rescue Network has been following bad news about these Russian-bred dogs, and has found they are often taken from their mothers at four to five weeks (instead of the eight to twelve weeks that the smaller breeds need). This could explain, at least in part, the serious health and temperament problems that have been surfacing with "Frenchies," as French Bulldogs are affectionately nicknamed.

Many of the puppies are sold on the Internet; others are sold through ads placed through "brokers" in newspapers; many of the Frenchies found in pet stores come from disreputable breeders in Russia.

The dogs have been collapsing and dying. The Russian French bulldogs are also unnaturally aggressive, which is even more disturbing since French bulldogs are normally docile. These Russian "Frenchies" have a long list of serious and expensive illnesses—from throat infections to the need for hip replacement surgery at a young age.

BREEDS DISCRIMINATED AGAINST BY INSURANCE COMPANIES
(See Chapter Seventeen on "Dogs and the Law," page 644, for more on this topic.)

Some insurance companies will not write homeowner's insurance for households that contain the following breeds:

- ☐ Pit Bull
- ☐ Rottweiler
- ☐ German Shepherd
- ☐ Mastiff

It is true that some breeds have been statistically involved or implicated in dangerous situations. Despite the possibility that your own dog from one of these breeds is well-behaved and trustworthy, you may have to pay a steep price for owning one.

The breeds above—as well as others, which may be added as time goes on—are considered grounds by some insurance companies for refusing to sell insurance to their owners. If you are a fan of the Pit Bull or any of the "outcast" breeds, you can contact the SPCA in your area to learn how you may be able to contribute to reverse the trend toward breed discrimination. The SPCA's Web site also has a letter that you can download and send to your state senator or representative. The SPCA also suggests contacting your state insurance commissioner to inform them of your difficulty in obtaining homeowner's insurance based on the dog breed you own. The commissioner may be able to give you names of insurance companies that are not discriminatory.

Chapter 2

WHERE TO GET YOUR DOG

This chapter shows you the options you have in finding a dog. If you already know the breed of dog you want, the explanation of the differences in breeding operations will help you to decide where and how you want to purchase a puppy.

However, you may feel it is preferable *not* to purchase a dog when there are so many homeless dogs already. You also may not want to participate in the economic circle of pet stores after learning the disturbing facts about where and how they procure puppies (pages 27–29). Instead of getting a purebred puppy, you may want to explore alternative ways of having a dog join your home: buying from a private breeder, getting a pooch from an animal shelter or from one of the volunteer organizations for specific breeds, or adopting a dog directly from a person.

In Chapter Two you will find:

- ❏ *Wholesale breeders* (also known as "puppy mills") and the *pet stores* that sell the pups
- ❏ *Private breeders* (who raise show dogs and sell the "pet-quality" dogs to individuals)
- ❏ *"Backyard" breeders*—uninformed owners of one or two dogs
- ❏ *Genetic testing of parents*—?
- ❏ *"Second-chance" dogs*—a puppy, "near-puppy" or an adult dog
- ❏ *Animal shelters*—making the most of the system
- ❏ *Breed-rescues*—finding the breed you want and saving a life

Wholesale Breeders, AKA "Puppy Mills"

According to the Humane Society of the United States, there are about 4,000 puppy mills, most of which operate in the Midwest, although there are also a significant number in Pennsylvania. Many of the farms were previously pig or chicken farms. Many of the volume dog breeders have attitudes that reflect those barnyard origins—which would explain why there is no "quality of life" for the moms and pups and no attempt to breed for genetic health. Mother dogs churn out litter after litter—mating pairs are kept together so there is no time for the mother to recover and rest between pregnancies—and they are bred nonstop, often inbred with dogs related to them. There is minimal veterinary care, poor-quality food and little, if any, interaction with humans. The dogs often live stacked in crowded wire cages on top of each other, with urine and feces falling down onto the dogs below them. Dogs are killed when they become critically ill or too worn out to keep producing constant, plentiful litters. It is common practice at some kennels to feed the bodies of deceased dogs to the survivors.

Puppies from mills are raised in an environment without enough human handling and stimulation. They are taken away from the litter at far too young an age for proper development, and they lose important socialization time. These barely weaned puppies are emotionally frightened and often physically sickened by their dispersal and journeys to pet stores across the country—and once there, they will go into small wire and glass cages to await purchase.

When people talk about laws to improve conditions for breeding bitches and young pups at puppy mills, what they don't seem to understand is that these "dog factories" are governed by the rules and regulations of the USDA, the same as the wholesale pig or chicken operations that used to occupy these farms. The government acknowledges that it lacks the necessary number of inspectors to oversee puppy farms—just a handful of employees for the hundreds of thousands of puppies born yearly—but in any case the USDA regulations they are enforcing were originally intended to apply to animals destined to be killed and consumed.

Another issue with puppies from wholesale producers is the complexity of transporting thousands of tiny puppies across a vast country so that they reach pet stores when they are still only eight weeks old. Optimally, puppies should remain with their litters until they reach that age. However, to be most saleable, pups need to be in the retail destinations while they are still very young—which means they'll have missed the essential developmental period of six to eight weeks when they should be interacting with their littermates, learning how to behave with other dogs throughout their lives (see page 72 for more on this). Consumer demand pushes these tiny pups out of the nest, which is just dandy for the farmers because the less time the "stock" spends at the farm, the less expense for the producers and the greater the profit per unit. Remember, just because they have the cute word "puppy" in front of their description, these are just businesses like any other. Whether making widgets or eggs, they are looking for the greatest profit margin.

What buyers don't consider when they "oooh" and "aaah" over the puppies in a pet store's window is what went into getting "their" puppy into that cage: the complexity of getting the right puppy to the right pet store across a vast nation is almost a canine version of a troop movement. There are numerous logistics involved in filling the requests of individual pet stores (which might need one or a dozen puppies of different breeds) and then transporting thousands of these little dogs. The process is streamlined because puppy farmers do not deal directly with pet stores: there are middlemen, the puppy brokers who organize and disperse the truckloads of puppies that constantly arrive at their holding facilities. These brokers organize birth documents (their phone number appears as the "breeder" on the AKC registration form of most pet-store puppies—which is why those buyers can never reach their dog's actual breeder) and then the broker coordinates transportation. The Hunte Corporation is the dominant puppy broker in the country, but they do not speak to the press or public—why should they be put on the defensive and hassle with questions since their business keeps humming with strong supply and demand (which is to say, every single person who buys a pet store puppy)? To give an idea of the volume of puppies being processed just at Hunte, the corporation employs *seven* full-time veterinarians to fill out health certificates for interstate transportation of the puppies.

Another example of the staggering volume of these operations is what was known as the "Missouri Five" puppy-mill auction held in Montgomery City, Missouri, on November 19, 2000. Rescue volunteers for several breed-rescue groups went there to buy the freedom of dogs by posing as commercial breeders looking to acquire breeding stock. Volunteers from the local Weimaraner rescue went to the liquidation sale of one commercial breeding facility that had *more than 3,000 registered dogs*. Many of the dogs were closely related; many of the breeding bitches had been born at the mill and bred nonstop for five years. Each dog cost $75 to buy out. Most were so unaccustomed to being with people that it took years to socialize them enough to be adopted into normal homes.

PET STORES AND YOUR PART IN THE EQUATION

Puppies from "the mills" are the end product of an assembly-line mass production of dogs: 300,000 to 400,000 puppies a year are sold to pet stores, which are the only sales outlet for these operations. People opposed to commercial dog breeding say that if you are a softhearted person you should never set foot inside a pet store, because you'll feel sorry for the dogs and think they're so cute that you'll just have to take one home. People mistakenly think they are "saving a puppy's life" by buying it, when what they are actually doing is personally supporting puppy mills and encouraging and extending the suffering of the puppy's mother by perpetuating the cycle of mass puppy production.

It is bad for a puppy's health and emotional well-being to be stuck in a tiny area behind glass. It is lonely and traumatic to be alone in a shop window with people banging on the glass. It is equally unhealthy to be one of twenty-five puppies in one glass room, a central problem being that the most aggressive puppies eat too much while others get no food at all.

I do understand the convenience of being able to go to a store and buy the exact kind of dog you want, right when you want it—sort of like going into a car dealership and wanting the model, color and options on a car that you can drive right out of the showroom. As you probably know, that's not always easy, even with a car. Impulse buying is a common phenomenon, and impatience about getting what we want, when we want it, is something we should probably guard against in general. Even when you're shopping for a new sofa you go around to a few stores; once you see one you like, you'll probably have to wait months before they can deliver it. Surely you should be willing to do at least that much where buying a dog is concerned? No matter how enthusiastic you or other family members may be, take a deep breath and realize that a dog is not an object you're collecting, but a living, feeling being who will become part of your family for years to come. You owe it to yourself and to the little critter to invest the time and make the effort to make a careful decision.

If you are disturbed by what you've learned about puppy mills and wonder how wholesale "dog farming" continues, the answer turns out to be quite simple: supply and demand. Business is driven by economics: puppy mills are profitable because the markup is gigantic on an "in-demand commodity." There would be nothing more to make a fuss about if people were to buy puppies from private breeders instead of supporting the system that puts puppies in pet-store windows.

QUESTIONABLE CLAIMS MADE BY PET STORES

♦ "Our Puppies Come from Good, Reputable Breeders."

It cannot be true when a pet store assures you that its puppies are from "good" breeders, because responsible breeders belong to the nationally recognized organization of their breed. And the fact is that all members of those groups sign an agreement when they join vowing that they will *never sell a puppy to a pet store.* Good breeders would never subject their offspring to a pet-store setting and the unpredictability of where their puppies can wind up. This should tell you everything you need to know about the relationship between commercial breeders and pet stores.

♦ "We Buy Only from USDA-licensed Brokers."

This is a pointless claim since the USDA is the department of agriculture, a government agency that oversees livestock—generally that are destined for the dinner table. As mentioned before, there is an insufficient number of inspectors, but in any case their criteria for evaluating a facility are not applicable to pets. USDA rules and licenses have nothing to do with conscientious breeding practices for companion animals, nor with humane and beneficial puppy-rearing techniques.

♦ "Health Guaranteed"

This sounds like a reassuring promise to offer: that if anything should be physically wrong with the puppy they will pay for its care or replace it. However, there are now "doggie lemon laws" in twenty states that have laws or regulations that allow consumers to be reimbursed for vet bills or receive a full refund for a puppy that was sick when purchased, so this promise is pretty much required by law. Instead of offering to "swap" a defective puppy like it's a piece of equipment, what pet stores should be doing is avoiding puppies unless they have certifiable proof that the breeding parents were free of genetic defects or are not carriers of them. You want genetic testing *before* breeding—not a guarantee after the fact for problems that could have been prevented.

♦ "I'll Bring the Puppy to Your Door."

Avoid anyone offering to "bring a puppy to your door direct from the breeder." This is some version of a middleman who has found a way to bypass the pet store to bring you a "puppy mill" puppy, keeping the substantial profit for himself but denying you the recourse and backup of buying from an established retail outlet.

ILLNESSES COMMON IN PET STORES

Puppies are vulnerable to a number of serious illnesses when they are kept in close quarters with many other fragile puppies in a pet-store setting. There are very few pet stores with a general knowledge of puppy health care and the resources to promptly and aggressively treat common but potentially fatal illnesses in young pups. Instead of making frequent emergency trips to the local veterinarian, a well-informed and -stocked pet store should have general knowledge of the health risks to puppies. Under a vet's supervision a pet store should stock antibiotics, nebulizers for breathing treatments and fluids for intravenous feeding.

Kennel cough (also known as "bordatella") is common and highly contagious to dogs of any age.

Hypoglycemia (low blood sugar) primarily affects puppies of toy breeds and can be a life-threatening condition. Caretakers of very young and delicate puppies need to know the risk of hypoglycemia in toy dogs and be certain that the young ones are eating at frequent intervals.

Pneumonia and its attendant breathing problems can also threaten a puppy's life.

Private Dog Breeders

Dog breeders who work on a small scale—as a hobby on the side or as their only business—are known as "noncommercial" breeders. I like to call them "private breeders" to contrast them with large-scale commercial dog farmers.

Keep in mind that dog breeding is a business—a business in which some breeders are more savvy salespeople than others. You need to be aware of a good salesperson, one who has learned to tell the customer what she wants to hear. For example, many puppy buyers ask about temperament, about whether the breeder's dogs have nice dispositions—which is like asking the deli counterman whether the food is fresh before ordering it! What would you expect a breeder to say? No breeder who wants to sell puppies is going to admit what might be the truth: "Our puppies' personalities don't really matter much to us. We ignore disposition and concentrate on getting a good coat on our dogs."

FINDING BREEDERS

There are a number of ways listed below to find breeders of the kind of dog that interests you. Probably the most efficient and rewarding way is to go to a dog show, if there is one anywhere near where you live. But even if you do go to one, you can still explore some of the other options, as well.

◆ Benched Dog Shows

"Benched" shows are those in which the breeders and handlers are required to sit on raised platforms (benches) with their dogs except when they are showing in the ring or grooming their animals. This gives spectators a chance to talk to hundreds of breeders and handlers of the breed(s) that interest them and visit with some dogs, learning more in a short amount of time than they could any other way. If you have no idea what kind of dog appeals to you—or if you are certain of the one you want or curious about a few others—a benched dog show is the perfect place to see many of those dogs up close.

There are very few benched shows anymore. The most famous one is the Westminster Kennel Club show, which takes place in New York City every year on the second Monday and Tuesday of February. There are only five other benched shows—two in Chicago, one each in Detroit, San Francisco and Philadelphia—but if you can get to any of them, you should make the effort.

◆ Breed Clubs

There is a club somewhere in America for every breed. Contact the club and they should be able to tell you which breeders are closest to you.

Buying from a breeder who belongs to a club gives you an extra perk: members have to adhere to a code of ethics. It encourages honesty and adds incentive to do the best they can for their dogs and potential customers.

◆ Ask a Friend or Acquaintance with a Great Dog.

If you know someone who owns the breed that you like, ask for a recommendation. Maybe you even like the breed because you love your friend's dog, but if that is the case keep two things in mind:

1) Dogs are individuals, and even with the same parents you may never get another dog like your friend's—just look at human families and whether any two kids are even close to alike in personality, abilities, etc. 2) The dog you admire may be great because of the excellent way he has been raised and trained—don't give credit to a breed of dog for what may simply be the great environment in which he was brought up.

◆ Contact AKC/UKC to Find Shows.

To find out where non-benched dog shows are in your area, you can go to the AKC Web site at www.akc.org. or get a sample copy of its publication, the *AKC Gazette,* by calling 919-233-9767.

The "alternate" (more than "rival") dog-registering organization to the AKC is the UKC, or United Kennel Club, which is much smaller. Some breeds of dogs are recognized only by this organization and not by the AKC. Their phone number is 616-343-9020. You can get information from them and request their magazine, which is called *Bloodlines.*

◆ National Clubs of Individual Breeds

Clubs and even some individual breeders are listed online. Even if you're not the quickest student of the Internet, you can just type in the breed of dog you're interested in and lots of choices appear. But don't be taken in by a slick Web site—just because a breeder has good sales instincts and can have a great site designed tells you nothing about her puppies.

◆ Other Breeders

Breeders of each breed tend to be clannish, with an informal network of information about what litters other breeders have or are expecting. If breeders don't have a litter or the puppy you want, they are usually generous in sending you to a breeder they know who might be able to fill your request.

Because you are asking a favor of someone, be thoughtful about when you call—figure out the time difference if there is one and avoid calling at dinnertime or too late or early. Do not leave your number on their answering machine unless you tell them to reverse the charges and return your call collect. You are asking for a recommendation of another breeder for which they will have no personal gain.

◆ Dog Magazines

Dog World, Dog USA and *Dog Fancy* are the big dog magazines that come out every month. Strangely enough, they are all published by the same company, with a slightly different emphasis in each one. You can pick up copies at a newsstand and find a listing of virtually every show being held anywhere.

There are also advertisements in the back of those magazines with classified and attractive display ads for breeders. Call to find out whatever you can about the dogs they have, using the recommendations of "Questions to Ask a Breeder" in this section on page 34. NOTE OF CAUTION: Although the majority of breeders advertising in these magazines are reliable professionals, there are some breeders who advertise to sell guard dogs or very small toy breeds who are *not* responsible and ethical. Have your antennae up when you speak to them on the phone, and use the list of questions for breeders to determine whether they are just trying to make a quick buck or are dedicated to turning out quality examples of their breed.

◆ Newspaper Ads (Be Suspicious)

Many of the ads you'll see in the paper are placed by irresponsible breeders. High-quality, successful breeders very rarely take ads in the paper. You can check it out, but be aware of what you're dealing with. There are phrases and buzzwords that can be clues that an ad has been taken by an unknowledgeable or unreliable "backyard" breeder. If you see one or more of these phrases in an ad, it is a tip-off that you are not dealing with a good, well-informed breeder and should not respond to the ad.

Buzzwords to Watch Out for:

☐ *"Shots and wormed"* It is assumed that all puppies should have this done. Bragging about a basic health safeguard is hardly impressive.

☐ *"AKC Registered" or "Purebred" or "Pedigreed"* All these words refer to the same thing— only a purebred dog with a pedigree can be AKC registered. See page 35 for an explanation of why AKC registry doesn't necessarily confer any stamp of approval on a dog anyway.

☐ *"Champion Lines"* This can mean that the dog's grandfather or maybe only one or two other ancestors was a champion—meaning the breeder hasn't shown the puppy's parents. It has to say "champion parents" or "champion sired" to show that the breeder has been taking her dogs to shows and they have been judged as good quality.

- **"See Both Parents"** You should always be able to see the mother, although you may not be able to meet the father. It may even be a good sign if the father is owned by another breeder and that dog lives elsewhere, since it would indicate that time and money were spent to breed to that dog. A good breeder makes informed choices about the best sire to enhance the qualities of his female and goes out of his way to breed to the right male—unlike a breeder who has males and females that he breeds because it's free and easy, even if that union might not result in the optimal offspring.
- **"Extra" or "Giant-sized"** Protection breeds like Rottweilers that are already large should not be pushed to develop into even larger sizes—but unscrupulous breeders may claim to have produced an even larger version of a breed that may already be impressive and intimidating. The truth is that over-large dogs are usually outside the breed standard and would not even qualify for dog shows, but more importantly, that increased size can cause health problems, especially bad hips and knees, to which many large breeds are already prone.
- **"Teacup" or "Pocket-sized"** Where toy breeds are concerned, any term that indicates ultra-small dogs is unwise: when small breeds are forced to become even smaller, it can cause a mountain of physiological problems for the dog.
- **"Rare Color"** This a tip-off that the puppies may be from a careless breeding that resulted in colors that are unusual and not accepted in that breed's standards. Even if you don't intend to show your dog, the goal for any breeder is to conform to the breed standards.
- **"Rare"** A meaningless adjective, since dogs like Shar-Peis were once rare, back when they were first brought to this country years ago. Shar-Peis have now been around for years, while a dog like the Tibetan Terrier, for example, is new to the American dog scene and thus unusual—which anyone trying to buy one has already discovered.

VISIT A LOT OF BREEDERS.

Try to visit as many breeders as you possibly can. Educate yourself. Comparison shop, which is something you'd do with any important decision or purchase in your life—in this case, not for the price so much as for the right attitude. Getting information from a breeder lets you compare the physical qualities of their facility for cleanliness, roominess and whether the dogs seem relaxed and happy in their environment. You need to visit a few breeders, if possible, because without a point of comparison it's hard to gauge what you are seeing and make an intelligent evaluation. You'll probably make a good decision if you trust your gut reaction, especially when something doesn't look or sound right to you.

Even the most successful breeders don't have a big, formal breeding facility—it is often just their home, where they often have the dogs right inside their house. Don't be alarmed if the house itself is untidy or a downright mess, because "dog people" often put their animals' housing before their own. What matters is whether the dogs' environment is clean and pleasant and equipped with toys, beds and clean water. Nothing should look dirty or broken or potentially hazardous in the equipment or surroundings.

Trust your intuition—if the place strikes you as not clean or safe, or if it's a place you'd never want to send a puppy back to—then be on your way. No matter how far you might have come, you should turn around now and leave. It might seem rude not to be polite and at least go through the motions of looking at the puppies, but it's only going to make you feel worse if you spend time with the puppies and then leave them in a place that seems awful to you.

The following qualities won't all apply to every breeder—but when you are choosing the breeder of your future dog a lot of these points should apply.

QUALITIES OF "PROPER" BREEDERS

- ❐ They breed only a few litters a year.
- ❐ They breed a female no more than once a year.
- ❐ They breed only one or two breeds.
- ❐ They ask you a lot of questions about your lifestyle and expectations of the dog.
- ❐ They want to meet your preexisting dog or know about her beforehand.
- ❐ They require you to sign a spay/neuter contract if buying a "pet quality" puppy.
- ❐ They want the puppy back if you can't keep her anymore for any reason. They tell you they will take the puppy back if he develops any health issues. (That is *not* a promise the breeder makes *instead of* genetic testing of the parents—this means she will take back a puppy if it develops a serious health problem(s) despite good results on the genetic tests and her best intentions in the decisions she made in breeding.)

QUALITIES OF BREEDERS TO AVOID

- ❐ Raises puppies outdoors in a kennel or garage instead of socializing them indoors.
- ❐ Makes little or no attempt to introduce puppies to a wide variety of stimuli.
- ❐ Produces more than three litters a year.
- ❐ Raises more than two breeds of dogs.
- ❐ Breeds to one or another size extreme (not desirable)—boasts that a large dog is a "giant" or a small one is a "teacup."
- ❐ Allows puppies to leave the litter before seven to eight weeks of age (see page 62 for age issues—with small breeds it should never be before ten to twelve weeks). NOTE: *If you really want the puppy despite a breeder telling you to take it early, give him a deposit and ask him to keep the pup with her family for another two weeks.*
- ❐ Makes excuses for not doing genetic testing: claims that "the tests are not reliable" (false); "the disease/defect is not proven to be passed along in the genes" (false); "puppies are too young to be certified" (irrelevant, since it's the *parents* you want to test beforehand); "testing was done but not sent for official clearance" (why not—unless they fear the results?).
- ❐ Pressures you to make a decision about a puppy and buy it right away (pressure sales tactics such as "Three other people are coming later to look at her" should be saved for car sales!).

ASKING QUESTIONS OF A BREEDER

The following is a list of questions to ask a breeder. Some breeders will be chatty and happy to answer a bushel of questions, others will be annoyed if you bug them with too many. So start with questions that interest you the most, see how the breeder responds and go from there. How the breeder answers the questions tells you a lot about her as a person and as a businessperson. A breeder may not have thought about some of these questions before, but even the way she answers can reveal a great deal about how she views breeding and the puppies that result from it. You want to discover what level of docility or compliance the breeder expects from the dogs she breeds.

QUESTIONS TO ASK A BREEDER

- ❏ "Can I meet the puppy's parents?"
- ❏ "Have the puppies been handled a lot? Groomed? Nails cut?"
- ❏ "Is the mother friendly to familiar dogs? To unfamiliar ones?"
- ❏ "How much exercise does this breed need to keep them relaxed?"
- ❏ "What tests have been done on the parents? And what about the grandparents?" NOTE: You will have checked the "Genetic Testing" chart in the appendix, page 53, so you'll know which genetic problems apply to this breed. Because testing for hips and eyes has been going on for the longest time, if these tests are recommended for your breed, then all four grandparents should be certified as clear for at least those two items.
- ❏ "Do you have the vet's report of the official rating of their clearance status?"

✦ Questions to You from the Breeder

Below are some questions you might expect to hear from a breeder who takes seriously the kind of home his puppy is going to live in. Do not be offended by these questions, even if they make you feel defensive—they are the sign of a breeder who really cares. In fact, be wary of a breeder who does not ask you *some* questions about the life you have planned for his precious little pup. If more breeders spent time educating and interviewing prospective owners, it could help eliminate people who abandon a puppy to the pound after a few months because they had no idea what to expect. Sadly, rescue organizations are sometimes more vigilant about "vetting out" prospective homes for the dogs they have rescued than many breeders are in the first place.

QUESTIONS A BREEDER MAY ASK YOU

- ❏ "Have you got a crate or are you going to borrow one?"
- ❏ "Why did you pick this breed?"
- ❏ "Have you owned this breed before? Any other breed(s)?"
- ❏ "What has happened to other dogs you have owned?"
- ❏ "Do you have any pets at home now?"
- ❏ "How many hours will the dog be left alone at home? Who is home during the day?"
- ❏ "Do you have children? What ages? Have they been around dogs?"
- ❏ "Where will the dog sleep?"
- ❏ "Do you have a yard? Is it fenced?"

- ❒ "Could I come visit your home?"
- ❒ "If you rent can you get a letter from your landlord okaying a dog?"

DOCUMENTS FROM THE BREEDER

◆ A Word of Caution about Documentation

A certain amount of importance is placed on the paperwork that proclaims the ancestry of a purebred dog; a breeder or pet store will usually make a big deal about AKC papers, even when selling a "pet-quality" pup destined for neutering. There are also vital health issues that can be resolved with the results of genetic testing of a puppy and her parents. However, there is a fundamental problem in the dog-breeding and -selling world that no one wants to admit but that you need to know: it is not that difficult for registration papers and testing documentation "proof" to be switched and doctored. And it isn't all that rare.

Think about it: dog breeding can bring in a tidy sum to those breeders who manage their programs well and get top dollar for their puppies. But there are a lot of expenses, and when running a small business every dollar you lay out is one you aren't banking, so limiting costs maximizes profits. Other than honesty and a well-developed conscience, what is there to stop a breeder from "recycling" some AKC documents so that the ones you get are actually those of another dog? The same goes for medical records showing "clear hips, knees" etc. Genetic testing is time-consuming and expensive—realistically, what would stop a breeder from paying the high lab fees and X-ray costs on one dog and then using it for many others, instead of incurring the same costs many times over? How can you be sure that a breeder is honest, that the genetic testing was really done on your dog, and that you aren't being given the documentation for some other dog's ancestry?

There need to be rigorous standards in any human endeavor where there is monetary value to paperwork that can be forged or doctored. This is true of the world of show horses, where paperwork is taken more seriously—yet it is still not uncommon for false documents to accompany a horse, for example, fiddling its age to be lower than is the case.

I'm not trying to be a killjoy, but it's better to be alert, cautious and safe—check and double-check—than to be trusting and wind up with medical records that don't really pertain to the puppy you're taking home.

DOCUMENTS YOU CAN EXPECT TO RECEIVE

◆ Sales Contract

This spells out the understanding between you and the breeder about this puppy. It defines what is expected of you, which in a "pet-quality" (also referred to as "companion-quality") puppy is pretty straightforward. You agree to spay or neuter the pup and to tell the breeder if you can no longer keep the dog. The breeder's responsibility is a guarantee of the puppy's health and temperament (and how that is defined or determined) and what she agrees to do if the puppy falls short in either department (like replacing the puppy or returning your payment).

If you want to show or breed the dog (in which case you obviously would not spay or neuter it) the breeder will often not give you full ownership of the dog and will expect to have a significant voice in the showing plans, as well as when and to whom the dog might be bred. A breeder's reputation is driven by how her progeny do in the show ring, so it is essential for her to be involved in the decisions about the dog's life. If you have no experience but want to get into the world of dog showing, having the breeder as a partner is a good place to start.

◆ Pedigree

This is your puppy's family tree, a diagram showing the names of ancestors for three generations with the titles they won beside their names. "Ch." stands for "champion," which is the highest award a dog can get for conformation and movement, based on a system of accumulated points from shows. "Working titles" are awarded not for the way the dog looks but for performance in obedience, herding or hunting, depending on the breed.

◆ Registration Application

The puppy may already be registered by name, which many breeders do in order to include their kennel name in the dog's official name. They will give you that form to mail back to the AKC (American Kennel Club) with a place to add your name as the buyer/owner. If the breeder has not already registered the name it will be blank for you to fill in with your own information.

But the real truth is that there is really no practical reason to send in those registration papers at all. Unless you intend to breed or show the puppy, then having an AKC registration does not benefit you or the puppy in any way.

◆ Health Record

This shows the dates on which the puppy was wormed and vaccinated by the breeder, so that your vet will know when the pup is due for her next inoculation(s). (Since breeders often do the puppy shots and worming themselves, don't worry if there's not a vet's name next to those vaccination dates.)

"Backyard" Breeders

[*Neutrality is a goal of this book, but there are times when common sense calls out for criticism. Breeding dogs is something best left to those who do it responsibly, as a vocation, not on a lark.*]

"Backyard breeders" is the phrase commonly used to identify people who are breeding and selling dogs with no plan in mind. Let's call them "BYBs" for brevity's sake. They are dog owners who just decide to mate their dog with another dog for the fun—or profit—they assume will result. Some will say it's so their "children can see the miracle of birth" or some such—but that may just sound like a more acceptable reason than wanting to make money off their dog. Certainly there are enough nature programs on television to satisfy any young person's curiosity—and in any case if BYBs want to teach their children something of value it should be that it is not morally correct to bring four to ten new puppies into a world where there are thousands who are already here without homes. But I digress.

The basic problem with BYBs is that they tend to be uninformed about the potential for genetic problems in all purebred dogs and the unnecessary pain that their own ignorance may cause in dogs with genetic problems. People who choose to breed without knowing how to make good breeding decisions or even how to find an appropriate mate for their dog are not doing anyone a favor by turning out untested puppies. BYBs generally aren't bad people—they can easily be people who love dogs, enjoy puppies or want to make some extra money—but they are making a bad decision. Nonprofessionals have no business making a business of something that requires the careful planning and attention to detail that they don't even aspire to.

One of the reasons that professional breeders demand that their offspring who are "pet-quality" puppies be neutered is just for this reason: so owners don't suddenly decide they're going to breed on an impulse of "I love my dog" (or "I'd love to make a few thousand dollars off my dog").

ATTRIBUTES OF BACKYARD BREEDERS

✦ No Involvement in Dog Sports
Participation in dog shows and/or competitions is a test of a breeder who takes what she is doing seriously. If a breeder is completely uninvolved in the dog-show world—often true of BYBs—then she is not showing much interest in top-quality breeding and the concerns of those who are doing it professionally.

✦ No Knowledge of Genetic Defects
All breeds have defects they can pass on, especially the more popular breeds (see Appendix on page 53). A sloppy breeder or a BYB may claim there are no defects in his breed, or that his dogs are free of them, but without testing and documentation this is an empty claim (actually, often more like a *lie!*). All purebred dogs are becoming increasingly at risk for horrible defects or life-threatening illnesses, many of which are not immediately discernible in puppies—the problems of joint disease or deformity and cancer are at epidemic levels in many breeds. You don't want to take on the heartbreak of these painful problems if you can avoid it—nor would you want to encourage BYBs to breed their pets by buying from them.

✦ No Documentation
If a puppy has been advertised as AKC-registered, then the breeder should produce that paperwork. Both of the parents' AKC documents should also be available. The same goes for health claims: there has to be documentation from a vet that both parents are genetically "clear" of the congenital health problems common to that breed. BYBs will sometimes have none of those documents or partial versions of them (which are useless). BYBs will rarely have gone to the trouble and expense of genetic testing, and they may even chide you for being "a stickler" for asking for proof of their documentation.

- ◆ **No Introduction to the Puppy's Mother**

At the very least you should be able to meet any puppy's mother. It would tell you a lot more if you could meet both parents and/or the rest of the litter. It would be highly informative to see where the puppy has been living and under what conditions.

- ◆ **No Socialization of the Puppy**

The most important thing a breeder can do for puppies once they're born is to spend time every day handling and talking to them and exposing them to as many different stimuli as possible. The important time for the puppies to learn from their littermates is in the sixth to eighth weeks. You want to avoid any breeder who does not know the importance of systematically socializing puppies from the earliest age or does not know how to stimulate them—all of which can be true of BYBs.

Purchasing the Dog

HOW MUCH DOES A PUPPY COST FROM A PRIVATE BREEDER?

The price of a dog is a question best saved for last. It is not the most important piece of information in dog buying—yet there are people who ask it right away. This can bother breeders, many of whom feel that anyone immediately asking the price of a puppy is putting the emphasis on the wrong thing. Asking about cost right up front gives the impression that the price of a puppy matters to you more than other aspects that a breeder has often worked hard to develop in his line.

Don't worry too much about the price: you don't have to worry that a breeder is going to get rich off you. Even if a breeder has a high price tag on his pups, rest assured that dog breeding is not a highly profitable venture. Let's put it this way: it isn't a business you'd go into to get rich! For most of those in the field it is a passionate hobby. Breeders can make some money, but the more seriously they take it, the more they spend to improve their puppies with every litter. Genetic testing of the parents and X-rays of their joints are just two of the high costs that are included in pricing puppies.

HOW DO PET STORES SET PRICES?

Puppy mills sell puppies for $50 to $200 a puppy to pet-store owners. These are the same puppies that you *then* buy in a pet store for $500 to $2,000 (which is why a pet shop can have supposedly great sales to get rid of puppies as they grow, and still make obscene profits).

The "proper" price should be between $300 and $600 for most breeds, but not more than that unless it is a rare breed (see page 39, "High-priced dogs.")

"PET QUALITY" VS. "SHOW QUALITY"

"Pet quality" versus "show quality" would alter the price, but that's not relevant when you consider that most puppies are going to be pet quality. All it takes is a few white hairs or an ear that doesn't sit at the precise angle and there's no chance of stardom for that pooch in the show ring.

Steer clear of a breeder who justifies a high-priced puppy by saying, "She'd be twice as much if she were show quality." (Well, obviously—and if I were Venus Williams I'd be playing at Wimbledon—but what's that got to do with anything?)

Beware breeders who sell females at one price and males at a lower price—the quality of each dog is what should determine the price, not the gender.

It is common practice to pay in cash or with a cashier's check; it's unlikely that anyone will accept a personal check.

There are a few cases where there are legitimate reasons that puppies are more expensive. For example, English Bulldogs are a breed that requires artificial insemination (meaning everything that humans go through for infertility treatments) to reproduce. In addition, the puppies then have to be delivered by cesarean because of physical limitations. The price will be higher because the cost to the breeder is so much higher. $1,000 or more is standard.

Do not attempt to negotiate—each breeder has a set price based on what the breed generally goes for, or even what the market will bear. Obviously, you can try to negotiate if you insist, but it's considered an offense to the breeder. A dog is not viewed as a car. And even if a dog were a commodity, would you try to bargain for the price of a dress in a store? Would you try to negotiate the price of a meal in a restaurant?

Dog breeds that are not yet recognized by the AKC, or are only recently recognized in this country, may cost more. Once again, this is understandable, since it is costly for breeders to import breeding stock from the country of origin in order to eventually build up good breeding stock here. There are any number of breeds from Switzerland, France, China and Tibet that will take years to build up to the level of popularity that previously foreign breeds (for example, the Bernese Mountain Dog, the Shih Tzu or the Chinese Shar-Pei) have developed in America.

HIGH-PRICED DOGS

There is a small number of breeders who have overpriced their puppies, seemingly for no reason other than that they can! Their "what the market can bear" attitude may strike you as a touch unethical, but these breeders do well. The fairly pathetic fact is that there are people who actually want to brag about how much they spent for a dog—or believe that if a dog is priced higher it is somehow a better animal. There are greedy breeders with slick Web sites and good sales techniques who can command astronomical prices for their puppies based on their claim that their line of dogs is competing in field trials instead of ring shows, the kind we usually see on television.

But unless you are a hunter or shepherd yourself, why would you need a dog from a line that has been pumped up to compete in the field? Some of these breeders may claim that their Labrador or Border Collie is "smarter" than those bred for the show ring, but the truth is that field dogs are not necessarily smarter: what they are is "higher drive"—meaning more motivated to work. Therefore these field dogs often make worse pets, because they are bred to work long hard hours in the field and there just isn't enough for them to do in the family life in a modern home.

Why are people paying $1,300 and $1,400 for Labrador Retrievers when Labs are the single most popular and readily available dog in America—and like any non-rare breed should cost around $500 from a private breeder? Unless you're looking for a potential show champion, why would you pay more than twice the going rate? Is it a status symbol to overpay and brag about it—or is it that theory that anything that costs more must be better?

LOW-PRICED DOGS

Just as a high-priced dog does not mean you are getting a better animal, neither is a low-priced dog necessarily a bargain. It is fair to surmise that a breeder must be cutting corners if she is selling puppies at below the going rate. A responsible breeder spends time and money to do genetic testing to eliminate the risk of congenital defects being passed along from his breeding stock—it is expensive and time-consuming to protect the next generation. So if puppies are priced below market value, that breeder cannot be spending what she needs to in testing a puppy's parents.

If you need one reason to buy a purebred puppy from a private breeder, it is for honest genetic testing. BYBs generally do not know much about the importance of genetic testing, much less make it a rule to do so. A pet store may claim that the breeder/supplier of the puppy has paperwork "proving" that the puppy's parents are genetically clear of defects, but one would be naive to think that in wholesale breeding operations with upward of 1,000 dogs, every breeding pair has honestly been x-rayed and otherwise tested, or that documentation cannot be easily forged, copied, etc. Forgive the cynicism, and my apologies to the one-in-a-million backyard or wholesale breeder who genuinely has followed testing guidelines, but this book has to be the "watchdog" for the all the dogs and owners out there.

Second-chance Dogs

There are a number of ways to find dogs looking for a new home. Read on and see whether any of these options is appealing to you as a way to bring a dog into your life. Animal shelters are probably the most common way that people find dogs that need a second chance in life. There are also breed rescues for specific breeds of dog, and then there's word-of-mouth placement, where someone is asking around or has posted notices about a dog needing new people to share his life.

In my experience, the gratitude these dogs will show you—the profound attachment they make so wholeheartedly to their new owners—is a connection that can feel more intense than the one you make with a puppy you've raised from puppyhood.

ADOPTION FROM AN ANIMAL SHELTER

If you like the idea of saving a dog that has been abandoned or given up by his original human family, consider going to your local shelter (what used to be called the "dog pound"). Animal shelters are filled to bursting with "orphans," and there are some wonderful mixed-breed dogs there ("Heinz dogs" they used to be called, when Heinz advertised its fifty-seven varieties). Since Labradors are the most popular dogs in America—twice as popular, in number, as the next most-owned breed—many of the mixed-breed dogs you meet will probably be some part Lab, which can be a nice piece of any "combination dog." Unfortunately there are also a disproportionate number of Pit Bulls and Pit Bull mixes in the shelters, because these volatile, powerful and dangerous dogs have often not been neutered and have been permitted to run free.

People may ask or you may wonder, "Why take on a problem dog—someone else's problem?" The answer is that many of those dogs are not at fault and many of them have been abandoned because of changes or complications in their people's lives. People change their minds about dogs when they find out how much trouble and work it is to raise one well. People get divorced. They move. They get sick. They have financial problems. Someone in the family becomes allergic. There are more reasons than you can think of that people no longer can care for their dogs—and many of them have nothing to do with the dog herself.

◆ Choosing a Good Animal Shelter

There are many versions of animal shelters—there's the gloomy old run-down building and there's the clean, new cheerful facility, but just as important is what the staff is like.

CHECKLIST FOR AN ANIMAL SHELTER STAFF

- ❏ Are they pleasant and welcoming?
- ❏ Does the staff or volunteers seem interested in helping you find a pet, or do they make you feel like you're just interfering with their job?
- ❏ Do they have a trainer/animal behaviorist who evaluates and socializes dogs to make them more adoptable?
- ❏ Is there some kind of veterinary care readily available?
- ❏ Does the staff seem dedicated to the animals and interested in what they are doing, or do they seem burned-out and disinterested, waiting to punch a time clock?
- ❏ If they give you a questionnaire and then ask you questions, do you feel you are being harshly judged or encouraged to adopt?

In order to have a positive experience when making a decision, you need to feel you and the other humans are all on the same page: working to find a home for one of the orphan animals. If you feel you are being given the third degree, or the atmosphere is adversarial, you should feel free to leave and look for your dog elsewhere. And if you feel strongly enough about the treatment you received, consider telling the people at the shelter that one of their dogs has missed a chance at a loving home because they made you so uncomfortable. Maybe they'll be more pleasant to the next person.

◆ Picking a Dog at the Shelter

Here's a simple way to pick out a dog from all those heartbreaking faces "behind bars" at the shelter: walk past the rows of cages. Stop when you see a dog that appeals to you; if the dog comes up to the door to sniff your hand and greet you, that's a good sign. Dogs locked in cages in a shelter are emotionally deprived, so when human contact is offered they should gravitate toward it. On the other hand, some dogs need more leeway in judging their caged response because they might have a personality that is more depressed by institutional living. If you were in their place, wouldn't you like to get the benefit of the doubt?

Some dog trainers have their own "mini-tests" of shelter dogs, but they get complicated and require experienced judgment. Here is something you can try before you even take a dog out of her cage to get useful feedback: while speaking gently and encouragingly to the dog, move your hand back and forth slowly in front of her face. A well-socialized, outgoing dog will follow your hand. A dog that jumps or barks at you or retreats to the back of the cage is a dog with problems—and therefore not worth considering. That may sound too harsh as a rule of thumb—to eliminate a dog because of an apparent personality flaw (probably caused by whatever she's already suffered in life)—but you need a firm resolve to find the best adoptable dog and enjoy a positive outcome. Many animal-lovers identify with the least lovable or most problematic candidates for adoption, but (being one myself!) I'd suggest that you not be so softhearted that you wind up soft-*headed*! Why create a nightmare for yourself or rob another more well-adjusted dog of a chance to share your life? For every damaged/neurotic/unpredictable dog, there are so many sweet-natured candidates who have had sad pasts of their own and are every bit as worthy—if not more so—of the wonderful life you are offering.

◆ Background Information about Adult Dogs

If a dog does have problems, you should know that most dog problems can be overcome (outside of serious aggression, which may result in having to put a dog to sleep). Most behavior problems in dogs are the result of mistakes by people—cruelty, neglect, ignorance and/or violence by the previous owner. But it may also be that those dogs were puppies who were not well-socialized by greedy, unscrupulous breeders—and that they were then bought by innocent people who did not know the responsibility involved in successfully raising a dog.

The current estimate is that three to four *million* dogs are euthanized every year in the United States. These dogs are often put to sleep after they are returned to the shelter more than once, having gone through the stress of not being able to adjust well to several homes—where those families suffered, too, trying to deal with the dog's problems and then making the painful decision to give up.

There are several areas of personality and behavior that it's helpful to know about ahead of time when considering a dog past puppyhood. The more you know about a dog you are considering adopting, the better you can anticipate if she will be a good fit in your life. The only problem is that with most dogs that are up for adoption there is either no information, or the facts are unreliable.

Below is a quick assessment of some things to keep in mind when determining the reliability of whatever information may be available.

QUESTIONS ABOUT A DOG'S HISTORY

- ❑ What behavior issues does the dog have?
- ❑ How does he behave around other dogs?

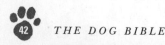

- ☐ Has he lived with or around cats (if applicable)?
- ☐ How about his interaction with children? (This is good to know even if you have no kids, since children may be part of your extended family or come with visitors.)
- ☐ What is his energy level?
- ☐ Does he have any health problems—or if he's a purebred, are there health issues specifically connected to that breed?

PERSONALITY ISSUES WITH "DISCARDED DOGS"

Generally, you know nothing about the history and background of a dog you want to adopt, except for the rare case in which you are getting a dog directly from someone. The reason this is relevant is because when a dog "with a past" first comes to you, she may do things that seem terrible or terribly pathetic. It helps with the transition and encourages patience if you see things from the dog's perspective and can help her overcome problems.

Any dog that has led a "narrow" life will probably surprise you with a lot of overreactions to normal household life. This is true for a dog who was a stray living on the street, for a dog whose previous owner never let him in the house, or for a dog who stayed too long in a "puppy mill" and never got properly socialized as a youngster.

Try not to judge a dog too harshly for any of the behavior discussed in this section; refrain from making a snap negative judgment. The dog is going through a form of culture shock, trying to find a way to fit into a home that may be nothing like he has ever seen or smelled before. What if you were set down on a strange planet or desert island? It may not be much different for a dog who lived in an entirely different environment before, maybe even incarcerated in the pound for weeks or months. The dog's reactions to your life and home will mellow before long. The spookiness—or clinginess, or whatever it is—will fade as you give the dog positive reinforcement and she begins to feel like she belongs to you.

◆ What to Expect in a "Secondhand Dog"

Expect an anxious, jumpy dog, and notice what triggers her fears so that you can gently and slowly expose her to the "terrifying thing" and desensitize her. Expect the dog to be confused, disoriented and depressed, looking around for the familiar sounds and smells of the people and places that were her life before. Even if you've gotten her from a shelter—and it seemed no better than a prison to you—that was still the world she knew and the people and routines she had gotten used to. Change is difficult and frightening to all living beings, so be patient and understanding of your new pooch. The basic period of adjustment is estimated at anywhere from six to twelve weeks, so if your new dog settles in within days you'll know she is way ahead of the pack.

◆ Fearfulness in the Adopted Dog

Some reactions that you might see in your newly adopted dog include pacing, whining, flinching or cringing, rolling on her back submissively, urinating in fear, hiding, exhibiting startled jumpiness, etc.

Things That Can Scare a "Secondhand" Dog

- Loud indoor sounds (stereo system, trash-can lid, banging screen door)
- Hair dryer
- Vacuum cleaner
- Obedience commands (might have been harshly punished?)
- A hand reaching out (flinches because he has been hit in the past?)
- Sticks, umbrellas, garden hose (been hit with them in the past?)
- Stairs (won't walk past or go up or down)
- Running water from faucet (was sprayed?)
- Garage or garage doors (was locked in there?)
- Car ride (only place he went in a car was to the vet?)

What the dog needs is socialization—the chance to get out and about with you, to see and hear things and discover that there is no bad outcome for him. Starting slowly, expose him to as many sights and sounds and smells as you can manage and he can tolerate. Before long the world will seem a friendlier place to him.

◆ Finding Particular Breeds at a Shelter

If you're looking for a particular breed, call the local shelters in nearby large cities and towns and ask them to tell you if that breed turns up. Ask for the name of the person you've spoken to so you can develop some phone rapport and have an individual looking out for you. Call periodically to remind them that you are still interested. Ask the shelter if it knows of a *rescue group* for that breed anywhere in your area (although the efficient way to find a rescue organization near you is through www.petfinder.com).

Individual Breed-rescue Groups

A "breed-rescue" is usually the personal creation of one individual (who may gather others) with the goal of being a social safety net for dogs of the breed they love. This person dedicates his own money and time to finding good new homes for the chosen breed when things no longer work out with the dog's original human family. These organizations vary enormously in how large they are and how well they are organized. A group can be as ambitious as Friends for Pets in California (where my Weimaraners came from), which takes in Weims (and a couple of other hunting breeds) from people who can no longer keep them, buys the breed out of animal shelters and has raised money for a facility where they care for the dogs and work with them until the right new home appears.

If a rescue "group" consists of one overwhelmed person, then she will be less efficient and effective in her ability to make plans for abandoned dogs than a bigger group that has successfully fund-raised and may have a network of "foster homes" where volunteers keep the dogs, get to know them and evaluate them for eventual permanent placement.

If you think that there must have been something wrong with a purebred dog in order for the people who bought her to be getting rid of her, think again. All the reasons that drive people to abandon their mixed-breed dogs mentioned earlier in this chapter apply equally to an expensive purebred. The abandonment may just seem harder to understand when the owners went to considerable expense to get the dog in the first place.

CONTACTING A BREED-RESCUE GROUP

These groups are run by extremely dedicated individuals who volunteer massive amounts of time and often their own money (or money they've raised) to find homes for whichever breed interests them. Since this volunteering is very demanding—and since circumstances change in people's lives and they suddenly cannot devote themselves in the same way to their volunteer efforts—there is often turnover in who is running a breed-rescue. Therefore do not be impatient or discouraged if you don't succeed with the first contact numbers you find on the Internet or elsewhere. Don't give up—try other avenues to find the breed you want, because somewhere out there your dog is waiting for you.

When you do reach the breed-rescue, keep in mind that while you may be pleased with yourself for doing what you consider a good deed (giving a home to a dog), the person you are talking to has been doing that good deed on behalf of many dogs for a lot longer! Have reasonable expectations of the people you come into contact with: they are usually volunteers with full lives of their own, so don't be impatient no matter how long it takes them to contact you or to generate paperwork, etc.

Breed-rescue organizations and individuals are going to ask you a lot of questions. Don't be offended, don't get defensive or resentful of specific information they want about the home you can offer one of "their" dogs. Their commitment is to those dogs; if any of them seems a little fanatic, maybe they are. Rescue volunteers can be forgiven any excesses because their devotion is so tiring and thankless. Basically they want to know what kind of "dog person" you are and what kind of life you are offering a dog. They certainly don't want to put a dog into a home situation they don't think will suit the breed—and they don't want you to be disappointed, either, because that would mean taking the dog back and finding yet another placement, which can devastate the dog.

◆ Greyhound Rescue

Greyhounds give people a chance to be heroes. Retired racing greyhounds are definitely headed for a horrible death or old age if no one steps in to give them what will probably be the first loving home they've ever had. This is a really special opportunity to not just save the lives of horribly mistreated animals, but to have a kind, elegant, mellow pet share your life. Despite their size and speed, greyhounds are actually one of the most sedentary of all breeds.

The plight of racing greyhounds has been publicized nationally, and there is a raised awareness of the horrible future that awaits the dogs of this breed who are no longer fit to race.

There are several dozen greyhound rescues in the U.S., and a group called Greyhound Pets of America has nationwide affiliations. (800-366-1472, or visit www.greyhoundpets.org to get all the info you need.) [Note: greyhounds often have dental problems.]

THE NEW "COMBO-BREEDS"

Crossing purebred dogs to make new breeds with catchy names is not just a passing fad. Their popularity is increasing, with breed clubs and even an official organization—the American Canine Hybrid Club—to register the dogs. Go to www.thedogbible.com, "Inside the Book" for more on this.

◆ The "Poo" Breeds

Cockers and Poodles were crossed to come up with the Cockapoo . . . Pekingese and Poodles were joined to create Peek-a-Poos . . . and more combinations are being "invented" all the time. But these mutts-on-purpose are not what is meant by a "breed" of dog, even though people may think so. What they are is mixed-breed mutts that happened randomly at one point in time and looked appealing, which gave some greedy people the idea to cross these breeds on purpose under the delusion of creating a so-called "breed."

These "poo" breeds come from two breeds, each of which has its own health problems—and mixed together, these problems can possibly *all* appear in a "poo" cross. There is no predicting with these mixes what you will come out with health-wise or temperamentally. It's a better gamble to take $25 to your local animal shelter and find a purebred dog or a nice little mixed-breed pooch. In any case, people paying hundreds of dollars for these so-called "poo breeds" are encouraging the purposeful creation of more mutts in an already overcrowded dog population. The result of this cross-breeding is basically a random mix of characteristics of two breeds with nothing in common. Why mess around when there are already more than 150 breeds to choose from that have been carefully bred for years with serious attention to retaining desired qualities? For a few dollars more you could go to a breeder and get an actual breed of dog.

◆ Personal Cross-breeding Experiments

People should not be dabbling in breeding dogs at all—and they certainly should not be playing with the idea of mixing two breeds. The weaknesses and problems of both breeds may be emphasized when two breeds that were never meant to intermingle are allowed to do just that.

For example, I thought I was doing my sister a great favor when I bought her the cutest puppy I had ever seen—he was half Jack Russell, half Welsh Corgi and had been bred on purpose. I took him out of the owner's arms and even paid a fair amount of money for him. However, Lucca seemed to have inherited difficult breed attributes from both parents: he was feisty to the point of aggressiveness and stubborn to the point of disinterest in pleasing anyone. My sister loved him unconditionally and people stopped her on the street, wanting an adorable dog that looked just like him, but why make life harder? And to prove that random cross-breeding can bring a mountain of trouble, his littermate got a deadly cancer to which he succumbed when he was only four.

◆ Who's Your Mutt's Mommy?

People with purebred puppies know just what their dog will look like when grown and in many cases may have dogs that are so close to breed type that they can barely be told apart from others of their breed. People with mutts love having unique dogs—one of a kind—"broke-the-mold" special dogs—yet they can be curious what combination of breeds went into the special mix that became their dog. Most people with a mixed-breed dog eventually wind up trying to guess their dog's ancestry.

Note about the heading: I apologize for being sexist. The mystery of your mutt's daddy is equally intriguing, and while both parents contribute their DNA, it's a dog's mother who determines the size of the mixed-breed result. In cross-breeding, the offspring's size is determined by the size of the mother's uterus, while the other characteristics come equally from both sides of the parental family.

The information below considers some common physical traits and temperament characteristics corresponding to the most popular breeds which, just because they are most plentiful, have a greater chance of being the dogs out there breeding on their own. When you consider that Labrador Retrievers have been far and away the most popular and plentiful breed for years, it's fair to assume that many mutts will have some Lab in them so you would look for those qualities first. German Shepherd dogs (often referred to as GSDs) had enormous popularity for many years, so the markings, longer coat, taller ears and feathered tail can still be seen in earlier generations of mutts. A great number of the dogs up for adoption in shelters are Pit Bulls and Pit mixes. This is a breed being propagated by a segment of society that does not neuter or spay and lets dogs run free, often using these powerful and devoted dogs for "security" purposes (often related to less-than-desirable activities and locations). In some tough urban geographic areas, this scenario also applies to Rottweilers.

The breeds listed below are just a sampling of the popular breeds that you should consider in unraveling the unique "cocktail" of breeds that went into making your once-in-a-lifetime dog. However, if your dog has a highly unusual characteristic like a ridge of hair growing against the grain down the middle of his back, you can be sure there's some Rhodesian Ridgeback in his history; if your dog has a dark purplish/black tongue, it's likely he has some Chow Chow in his blood. If your dog doesn't correspond to the breeds listed below, you can do your own detective work studying photos in a dog breed book, then compare your dog's features and qualities with the descriptions you find.

Some of the qualities to consider when evaluating the ancestry of your pooch are: physical characteristics like head, ears, tail and coat type (see below); energy level; sociability; intense drive (to herd, retrieve, guard) or laid-back and playful.

LABRADORS

COLORS: yellow (honey to platinum blond); black; brown
COAT: smooth, dense coat that water rolls off
HEAD: two styles: *square* (chiseled forehead and jaw, deep-set eyes) and *tapered* (smaller head with long narrow snout, sloping forehead)

EARS: smallish flap ears set high on head

TAIL: long, medium-thick straight tail, expressive sweeping wag

PERSONALITY: easygoing, love water (expert swimmers), addicted to retrieving

GOLDEN RETRIEVERS

COLORS: reddish; honey; platinum blond

COAT: thick, luxurious, flowing coat with feathers (longer hair) on legs and tail

HEAD: varies from square to narrow (as in Labs above); expressive face, often appears to be smiling with eyes and corners of mouth

EARS: smallish flap ears with some hair on them

TAIL: long, thick, feathered, tapering at tip, always wagging

PERSONALITY: sweet-natured, easygoing, playful; sometimes the distinctive gait of a side-to-side waddle with the back end, especially when wagging and walking

COCKER SPANIELS

COLORS: honey (and other shades of blond); black; black and white

COAT: thick, dense coat; heavy feathering on legs and underside

HEAD: very deep-set eyes behind pronounced "stop" in the snout; some heads small in proportion to body; loose upper lip overhangs lower

EARS: very long flaps covered in thick hair, ears can drag on ground when dog is sniffing

TAIL: docked in purebreds

PERSONALITY: very affectionate; can be intense and yappy, highly reactive or carefree to the point of head-in-the clouds spaciness; originally bred for hunting but often show no practical doglike qualities

GERMAN SHEPHERD DOGS

COLORS: tan with black markings (legs, ears, face, tail); black; white

COAT: medium-thick, rough double coat (undercoat, heavy shedder)

HEAD: long large face; large, wide-set attentive eyes that miss nothing

EARS: large, upright and expressive, frequently moving, picking up information

TAIL: feathered and held in a low sweep; distinctive gait is a low-slung back end with slinking/gliding motion

PERSONALITY: attentive; goal-oriented, obedient; intelligent; herding; guarding

SPITZ DOGS (SLED-PULLING TYPE)

COLORS: white; gray and white; variations

COAT: thick, dense double coat (especially around neck and chest); heavy shedding

HEAD: foxy, triangular, tapered to narrow snout

EARS: small, upright, alert to information

TAIL: thick like coat, often curls up above or over back

PERSONALITY: high-drive: intense, focused on tasks; physically powerful and tireless; limited guarding inclination; devoted; often howls instead of barks; barks when playing

ROTTWEILERS

COLORS: black with tan/honey markings on legs and feet, above eyebrows and on cheeks, chest and underside
COAT: medium-thick with under coat
HEAD: square, chiseled jaw or longer and narrower muzzle
EARS: small, high on head, tip may flap over
TAIL: docked in purebreds; if untouched, similar to a Labrador's
PERSONALITY: intense guarder *or* outgoing and sociable; affectionate; rarely barks

PIT BULLS

COLORS: tan; brindle; many variations of solid and marked
COAT: short, smooth
HEAD: very distinctive, square-jawed, wide from eye to eye; eyes sometimes almond-shaped, almost Asian
EARS: small, high flap-over ears; sometimes only one flaps over
TAIL: long, whiplike, curled
PERSONALITY: high-drive, high-energy, task-oriented; can be playful, affectionate; prey-driven with animals (can be misdirected to people); powerful jaw

Private Placement of a Dog

There are many sad reasons that people have to give up their dogs: people lose their jobs or homes and cannot afford a dog anymore; people get divorced or change jobs and move into housing that doesn't allow dogs; people suffer fatal illnesses. But there are many people who decide to discard their loyal companions because the dogs are an inconvenience—they're "more trouble than they're worth." Others give up their dog because someone in their household is allergic to dogs (they may not know that there are remedies to this, such as weekly bathing, anti-allergen sprays for the dog, allergy shots and pills for the person, etc., see page 172).

People who are willing to give up a puppy or dog they have paid for and raised must be highly motivated to give up that dog—and therefore less inclined to be brutally frank and tell you the downside of this dog. You'd think that someone offering you a puppy or dog of their own would shower you with a wealth of information, but that is not always the case.

THE OWNERS REALLY DON'T WANT THIS DOG.

Unless the owners seem heartbroken about giving up their family pet—and are only doing so because they are relocating to a country with a six-month quarantine or one where dogs are in jeopardy of being kidnapped and eaten—you can assume they really want to get rid of this dog for reasons of their own. This means they are going to play up the good qualities and play down the negative side. Selfishly speaking, that would be in their best interest—and it certainly puts you at a disadvantage if you mistakenly believe you have been fully informed. However, full disclosure is in everyone's best interest, even the dog's.

Obviously it would be immoral to withhold information about a dog that could cause harm to someone or ultimately send the dog unnecessarily to his death. For example, let's say the dog cannot handle small children but winds up being taken in by an unknowing young family, where he snaps at a child and is therefore euthanized. If the truth had been known about the dog's unreliability around kids, then people with children would never have considered taking the dog. This lack of appropriate information happens more often than we'd like to think. For these reasons, you want to encourage the previous owners to give full disclosure about the dog they are giving up.

The point of all this is that you must beware of what *isn't* being said about the dog in question and read between the lines of what you are being told. *Caveat emptor*—"buyer beware"—because even if you are technically a "recipient" and not a buyer you have to be wary because other people have their own agendas. They are trying to find a new home for their dog, and although there's no reason to distrust a person relinquishing a dog, you have to remember their motivation and how it affects their choices.

SOME PROBLEMS WERE THE OWNER'S FAULT—NOT THE DOG'S.

If possible find out if there were problems with how a dog behaved with children. Just imagine all the startling and painful things a small child can do to a dog if that child is not taught how to touch and move around a dog and *constantly supervised*. The previous owners may not have known what all canine experts agree about: that pre-school children and dogs should never be left alone together (see page 481 in "Dogs and Children"). So while the dog you are considering may have a less than great "rating" with children, that doesn't mean you should reject her. At least consider giving that dog a trial run, because it may only be a matter of erasing some of the dog's bad memories and having your child(ren) give her a positive experience.

"Behavior problems" in a dog that you are offered should not be a deterrent to considering that dog, certainly not until you learn more about these problems.

A dog can get a bad reputation when it was really something lacking in his environment. Problems often stem from either not enough exercise or not enough human company, both of which are the cause of a host of problems in dogs. In fairness to the previous owners, they may not have understood how much time and energy a dog requires and simply did not have enough of either to give the dog, which is why they're trying to re-home him. Complaints about the dog's energy level, destructiveness or other personality defects may be forgotten once that dog gets into a stable, consistent and satisfying home—he will probably be a very different animal. A dog's behavior is influenced by what is going on around him, and he can change in response to changes in his environment.

CAN THE OLDER DOG REALLY BOND WITH YOU?

There is an age bias against adopting an adult dog because people believe (incorrectly) that only a puppy can form a bond with you during a vulnerable developmental stage. People also assume that a dog will remain forever attached to its original owners and not be able to make the emotional transition to a new owner. Dogs generally adapt amazingly well to new homes and new owners. I've owned a succession of re-homed dogs, all of whom seem to worship the ground I walk on (as they must have with their previous owner).

A wonderful "dog woman" (Diane Monahan, who established Friends for Pets in Sun Valley, California, and devoted herself to the rescue of Weimaraners, Golden Retrievers and other sport dogs for decades) once explained to me about re-homed dogs: "It takes them about three days to transfer their affection and attachment to their new family—the first day they're depressed and may be confused or not eat, the next day they are figuring out their new environment, and by the third day they won't leave your side. It's not that they're fickle, it's part of the canine survival mechanism: dogs depend on humans for all their basic needs, so for their species to survive they have to be adaptable to whatever humans dole out, including abandoning them to other humans. I've watched hundreds of dogs make this reattachment."

So I've come to think of dogs' total loyalty and total transference of loyalty sort of like "The king is dead. Long live the king!"

"Homeless" dogs may also be more appreciative: they remember what it feels like to have *lost* their warm, safe bed inside their previous home as part of a family—and then have the relief and joy of finding a home again.

◆ Adoptable Dogs Are Most Often Adolescents.

Puppies who have just become teenagers are the ones most often abandoned or relinquished to shelters. It is often when the pup reaches the six-month mark that her owners realize they've taken on more than they can handle. The reasons are pretty predictable: people got a cute fuzzy puppy without having a clear picture of what was going to happen—and the jeopardy that all their belongings faced.

The puppy required bottomless patience and energy from them to fulfill her needs and protect their possessions against her. Then, around five or six months, the puppy lost her baby-cuteness and began to be an even bigger handful—maybe rebellious, certainly destructive in some areas and more demanding for exercise, training time, etc. This is when many people part company with their pet.

They may not have originally considered the full dimensions of the breed when it is fully grown. The dog may have had a strong personality or breed type that requires a firm hand in training that they could not supply. The puppy may not have been trained or well-socialized and is now the proverbial bull in the china shop (who is probably just lacking some boundaries and basic obedience work). But most dogs can make a complete turnaround with the restorative power of love and a firm hand in making rules.

Giving Up Your Dog

There are many reasons why people have to give up their beloved dogs. It is an agonizing decision but almost always for the best, because if you have decided to re-home your dog then your life is probably going through some major changes. Although there are people who just ditch a dog because they didn't realize the time and energy required, for the most part people will do everything in their power not to lose their pets. The list that follows can make people feeling terrible guilt about giving up their dogs realize they are not alone—and it can encourage compassion from people who adopt abandoned dogs and feel indignant that these beautiful dogs could have been given up.

WHY PEOPLE GIVE UP THEIR DOGS

- ❏ A move somewhere that doesn't allow dogs, or a trip that's too arduous.
- ❏ A breakup in a relationship, after which neither person will be settled for a while.
- ❏ Two dogs in a household that don't get along, to the point of deadly fights.
- ❏ A household in which someone has developed severe allergies to the dog.
- ❏ The arrival of a new baby, with a dog that is too jealous or possessive of you.
- ❏ Financial hardship that doesn't allow for proper care of the dog.

HOW THE DOG HANDLES BEING RE-HOMED

It takes a dog about two to three days to begin to bond to her new owners. First there's a day of restlessness, then one of being picky or not eating. By the third day a dog is usually showing signs of attachment and affection to her new owners. It is estimated that a dog needs about two weeks after that to figure out what the routines are in your household and where she fits in the hierarchy.

HOW YOU DEAL WITH GIVING UP YOUR DOG

Re-homing your dog is heartbreaking for you, but the dog will do fine. Dogs are able to switch attachments to people quite easily, and it is no reflection on how much they loved the first owner. Even though your dog may love you forever, a canine's ultimate survival depends on how well he can bond with the next human who holds the keys to his basic needs.

It's important for you to help choose the dog's next owners. It's especially important to choose the next home well so that the first try is a successful switch. Dogs cannot successfully make new attachments over and over—there is a limit.

✦ Some Feelings about Giving the Dog Away

Guilt, ambivalence, self-doubt, self-consciousness, profound sadness, blaming yourself and obsessing about your former dog's welfare are just some of the emotions you can expect to experience when you choose to give away your dog.

If you, or anyone in your family, becomes overwrought with disturbing feelings about letting your dog go, there are avenues to explore for help and guidance.

See the section on "Grief" (page 662) to learn about some hotlines and other outlets for grieving and counseling. Even though your dog has not died, there is a similar effect for some people who have to give up their dog.

Other people may not understand what you have done or be able to sympathize with your pain, which can just make the pain that much more bitter.

Finding a Stray Dog

Maybe someone found a stray and told you about it.

Or maybe the dog came up to your car or house.

Even without a collar and tags, that dog may still very much belong to someone. Even if the dog is skinny and scruffy, that can happen in just a few days on the loose. Don't judge the owner for the dog being lost—the owner is not necessarily to blame if the dog is either a veteran escape artist or ran away when startled by noise like fireworks or loud construction sounds nearby.

DOING THE RIGHT THING

If you really like this dog and your other family members and/or other dogs love her, it's easy to tell yourself that "fate" brought her to you and you should just keep her. But you know that the right thing is to give her a decent chance to be reunited with whatever family she had before. That way if she *does* become yours, it will be the "legitimate" adoption of an orphan.

WAYS TO FIND THE RIGHTFUL OWNERS

- ❑ Post "Dog Found" signs in the neighborhood and at local veterinarians' offices.
- ❑ Take advantage of your local radio station or newspaper's free "Dog Found" services.
- ❑ Call animal control in your town and tell them you have the dog.
- ❑ If you don't want to get too attached until you know you're free to keep the dog, you can give the dog to animal control to hold in case the owner does appear. However, that usually means trauma for the dog.

Look for those "Dog Lost" notices on trees or in the local paper; give it about a week so that everyone has a fair shot.

If you keep the dog for that week, it gives you a good chance to get to know her well enough to decide whether or not she'll fit in with your family, should no one claim her during that time.

Appendix to Chapter Two: Genetic Testing

What follows at the end of this section is a list of the most popular breeds and the health clearances that are recommended for them by the responsible proponents of those breeds. Do not buy a puppy of any breed without seeing proof that both of his parents' names on the registration match the names on the certificate.

BREEDERS TO AVOID

◆ Defensive Breeders
The health problems that have become so common in various breeds have made some breeders really jumpy and defensive. They will claim that there are no such problems in their breed, will refuse

to test for it and so on. They may claim that their own line of the breed has never had a problem, but it is wishful thinking to imagine that a widespread, breed-specific problem does not exist for them.

If you are buying a breed that is known to have genetic defects, you have all the more reason to seek out a breeder who fully acknowledges that this problem exists and explains what she has done to guard against it.

◆ Dishonest Breeders

Where health certificates are concerned it is unfortunate that there are breeders who lie about having the documents. They will tell prospective buyers to "just take their word for it"—when their dogs do not actually have the certificates. Your protection against this is to carefully check that the sire's and dam's (father's and mother's) names on the registration papers are *the same exact names* on the health document. Be aware that many dogs from one kennel can have similar-sounding names with the same words or variations on them, making it hard to distinguish among them.

GENETIC TESTING FOR PROBLEMS

There are a number of standardized tests that can be done on the parents of puppies to help prevent the passing along of genetic weaknesses that can result in serious problems for the offspring. There are also less common problems that crop up, primarily in a few breeds, that are every bit as serious and important to guard against before breeding takes place. These conditions are noted below. You need to ask the individual breeders what tests exist for the conditions potentially affecting their breed and whether they have used them.

Specialists in canine genetics now predict that the average purebred dog is carrying at least four to five defective genes. This is a chilling fact, since those defects are likely to cause misery for you and your dog in some way.

The Institute for Genetic Disease Control in Animals (GDC) at the UC Davis School of Veterinary Medicine (www.vetmed.ucdavis.edu/gdc/gdc.html) has established an all-breed open registry based on the success of the Swedish model (where they reduced hip dysplasia by fifty percent in all breeds just by encouraging the elimination of the dogs with hip problems from the breeding ranks).

What the Certificates Mean

When the breeder's veterinarian takes the hip X-rays, she sends them to one of several places to be evaluated. The breeder then receives an official rating and a clearance certificate.

There are four different rating centers with the following acronyms:
OFA: Orthopedic Foundation for Animals
PennHIP: University of Pennsylvania Hip Improvement Program

GDC: Institute for Genetic Disease Control in Animals

OVC: Ontario Veterinary College (Canada)

OFA (HIPS)

Hip dysplasia is a serious problem in purebred dogs. The ball of the hip does not fit properly into the socket and causes varying degrees of lameness, pain and arthritis in the joint. This is a developmental disease, which means that it is not present at birth but can appear as early as five to twelve months of age (in severe cases), or, in milder cases, not until eighteen months or even later.

Some researchers believe this problem is completely genetic; others say the cause is a deficiency of vitamin C and improper nutrition; others claim that too much early exercise for puppies of large breeds along with high-protein puppy kibble encourage overly rapid growth. Obviously several of these causes may conspire to cause the alarming frequency of hip dysplasia in dogs, with all breeds of purebreds being susceptible but the large and giant breeds especially so.

Because a young puppy may seem fine and then suffer terribly for the rest of her life—or a breeding adult may have only a mild touch of these problems but can pass on a more serious condition to offspring—the only hope is pretesting of parents. It is not a guarantee that your puppy won't develop dysplasia, but if both the parents have had their hips x-rayed by a veterinarian and declared clear, your chances of a healthy puppy are much improved.

OFA (ELBOWS)

Elbow dysplasia is a catchall term that covers a number of elbow-joint problems. Some of these orthopedic disorders are UAP (ununited anconeal process), FCP (fragmented coronoid process) and OCD (osteochondritis dissecans).

If you are considering a puppy from a breed of dog prone to elbow dysplasia, then the elbows of the parents should have been certified at the same time the hips were x-rayed.

OFA (PATELLA)

A dog with this condition is prone to having the kneecap dislocate from its socket. It is seen most often in the smaller breeds but can occur in any size dog that is prone to it. The official name for these bad kneecaps is "luxating patella."

The official clearance certificate for this condition is very new, so even the more conscientious breeders depend on a physical exam of the dam and sire by their vet. However, you should be able to see a letter stating that the parents' knees are stable.

CARDIAC

There are two common heart defects in dogs that can be screened for with an EKG: cardiomyopathy and subaortic stenosis (SAS).

A responsible breeder of a breed prone to these conditions should have a vet's letter stating that the EKG was successfully performed. There is a cardiac certification program like the programs for hips and elbows—see page 55—but because it is fairly new, many breeders are not yet sending for that official document.

CERF (EYES)

There are several serious eye diseases present in some breeds that can eventually cause blindness: progressive retinal atrophy (PRA), juvenile cataracts and retinal dysplasia.

The parent dogs' eyes cannot just be examined by a general vet—they have to be seen by an ophthalmologist board-certified by the American College of Veterinary Ophthalmologists (ACVO). The breeder then sends the results of that examination to the Canine Eye Registration Foundation (CERF) for an evaluation and official clearance certificate.

NOTE: *The certificates are valid only for one year. Check the date on the document you are shown and make sure it is current.* Because eye diseases can start at a variety of ages— some can be detected in six-week-old puppies while others don't start for years—the CERF certificates have to be repeated every year.

A DNA test has been developed for a few breeds prone to PRA that can give total accuracy about whether a parent is affected, is a carrier (does not have it herself but can pass it along to offspring) or is clear (neither has it nor is a carrier). As research discloses more about DNA markers, more breeds will be covered by this test.

BAER TEST (HEARING)

Deafness is a major problem in some breeds, the Dalmatian being notorious— more than twenty percent are born with hearing in only one ear and more than ten percent are born deaf.

This is not a test for the parents—it is a test of a puppy to find out if he is afflicted with congenital deafness. The BAER (Brainstem Auditory Evoked Response) test can be administered starting at six weeks of age.

In some areas of the country BAER testing is not available, so you would have to buy an at-risk breed of dog without being able to test it, or choose a different breed.

vWD CLEAR

Von Willebrand Disease (vWD) is a blood-clotting disorder similar to hemophilia in humans. It can result in hemorrhaging from a small cut externally or minor surgery internally.

A DNA test has been developed for only a few at-risk breeds (as with PRA), and this can show with total accuracy whether a dog is affected, is a carrier that can pass it on, or is clear (is not affected and is not a carrier).

This disorder is not widespread—maybe only a half dozen of the popular breeds on the list that follows are known to be afflicted. Until more breeds can be covered by the DNA test, people interested in breeds that have not yet been identified as at risk for vWD have nothing to turn to except a simple blood test (called the ELISA assay), which unfortunately cannot give a reliable result.

THYROID PROBLEMS

Many purebred dogs have problems with a thyroid gland that does not produce enough hormones to maintain normal metabolism. The result is hypothyroidism, which causes weight gain, skin and hair abnormalities and low energy.

All breeds can suffer from it, but some are more prone than others. In those breeds it is wise to get a complete blood workup that includes T3, T4, free T3 and free T4. It is less expensive to test only for T4, but that is not enough information. (Although it is not important for dog owners to know what these values stand for, any person with thyroid problems has been tested for them).

Genetic Defects by Breed

The screening symbols below that you will see next to the breed names indicate a higher risk of that breed developing or being born with those conditions. For the most part, those will be the only known inbred defects to guard against with each breed.

As an interesting side note, there are three breeds with absolutely no tendencies to genetic problems: one of the largest, the Scottish Deerhound; one of the smaller breeds, the Skye Terrier; as well as the Irish Terrier.

What the Symbols Represent
ACVO (eyes checked by an ACVO-certified ophthalmologist at six to eight weeks)
AD (axonal dystrophy, a serious nerve disease)
BAER (hearing)
CARDIAC
CERF (eyes checked by an ophthalmologist, yearly)
CHD (for chondrodysplasia, or dwarfism)
CT (copper toxicosis—a buildup of copper in the liver that can be fatal)
GCL (global cell leukodystrophy, a fatal enzyme deficiency)

Hips
Knees (luxating patella)
OCD (elbows)
PFK (phosphofructokinase deficiency)
PNA (progressive neural abiotrophy, fatal nerve disease of very young pups)
PRA (eye disease causing blindness)
SA (skin biopsy for sebaceous adenitis)
TT (temperament-testing for dominant breeds)
vWD (blood disorder)

AFFENPINSCHER	knees, cardiac
AFGHAN HOUND	hips, CERF
AIREDALE TERRIER	hips
AKITA	hips, elbows, CERF
ALASKAN MALAMUTE	hips, CERF, CHD
AMERICAN BULLDOG	hips
AMERICAN COCKER SPANIEL	hips, CERF, knees
AMERICAN ESKIMO	hips, CERF
AMERICAN FOXHOUND	hips
AMERICAN HAIRLESS TERRIER	knees
AMERICAN PIT BULL	hips, TT
AMERICAN STAFFORDSHIRE	hips, TT
AMERICAN WATER SPANIEL	hips, CERF
AUSTRALIAN CATTLE DOG	hips, CERF, BAER
AUSTRALIAN KELPIE	hips, CERF
AUSTRALIAN SHEPHERD	hips, elbows, CERF, ACVO
AUSTRALIAN TERRIER	knees
BASENJI	CERF
BASSET HOUND	hips, CERF
BEAGLE	CERF
BEARDED COLLIE	hips
BEDLINGTON TERRIER	CERF, CT
BELGIAN GROENENDAEL	hips, elbows, CERF
BELGIAN LAEKENOIS	hips, elbows, CERF
BELGIAN MALINOIS	hips, elbows, CERF
BELGIAN TERVUREN	hips, elbows, CERF
BERNESE MOUNTAIN DOG	hips, elbows, CERF
BICHON FRISE	hips, knees, CERF
BLACK AND TAN COONHOUND	hips, elbows, CERF

BLOODHOUND	hips
BOLOGNESE	knees, CERF
BORDER COLLIE	hips, CERF, ACVO
BORDER TERRIER	hips, CERF
BORZOI	hips, CERF
BOSTON TERRIER	knees, CERF
BOUVIER DES FLANDRES	hips, cardiac, CERF, thyroid
BOXER	hips, CERF, cardiac
BRIARD	hips, CERF
BRITTANY SPANIEL	hips, CERF
BRUSSELS GRIFFON	knees, CERF
BULLDOG	cardiac, thyroid
BULLMASTIFF	hips, elbows
BULL TERRIER	knees, BAER
CAIRN TERRIER	CERF, GCL
CANAAN DOG	hips, CERF
CAVALIER KING CHARLES	hips, knees, CERF, cardiac
CHESAPEAKE BAY RETRIEVER	hips, PRA, CERF
CHIHUAHUA	knees
CHINESE CRESTED	CERF
CHINESE SHAR-PEI	hips
CHOW CHOW	hips, elbows, knees, thyroid
CLUMBER SPANIEL	hips, CERF
COLLIE	hips, CERF, ACVO
CURLY-COATED RETRIEVER	hips, CERF
DACHSHUND	thyroid, cardiac
DALMATIAN	hips, CERF, BAER
DANDIE DINMONT TERRIER	thyroid
DOBERMAN PINSCHER	hips, cardiac, thyroid, vWD
ENGLISH COCKER SPANIEL	hips, CERF, BAER
ENGLISH FOXHOUND	hips
ENGLISH SETTER	hips, CERF, BAER
ENGLISH SPRINGER SPANIEL	hips, CERF, PFK
ENGLISH TOY SPANIEL	knees, cardiac, CERF
FIELD SPANIEL	hips, CERF
FINNISH SPITZ	hips, knees, CERF
FLAT-COATED RETRIEVER	hips, CERF
FOX TERRIER	hips, CERF
FRENCH BULLDOG	hips, knees, cardiac, vWD, CERF
GERMAN POINTER	hips, cardiac, CERF

GERMAN SHEPHERD	hips, knees, cardiac
GIANT SCHNAUZER	hips
GOLDEN RETRIEVER	hips, elbows, CERF, cardiac
GORDON SETTER	hips, CERF
GREAT DANE	hips, cardiac, thyroid, CERF
GREATER SWISS MOUNTAIN DOG	hips, elbows, knees, CERF
GREAT PYRENEES	hips, knees
GREYHOUND	CERF
HARRIER	hips, CERF
HAVANESE	knees, CERF
IBIZAN HOUND	hips, CERF, AD
IRISH SETTER	hips, PRA, CERF
IRISH TERRIER	None
IRISH WATER SPANIEL	hips, CERF
IRISH WOLFHOUND	hips, CERF
ITALIAN GREYHOUND	knees, CERF
ITALIAN SPINONE	hips, elbows, CERF
JACK RUSSELL TERRIER	CERF, BAER
JAPANESE CHIN	knees, CERF
KEESHOND	hips, knees, CERF
KERRY BLUE TERRIER	hips, PNA
KOMONDOR	hips
KUVASZ	hips, CERF
LABRADOR RETRIEVER	hips, elbows, CERF
LAKELAND TERRIER	CERF
LHASA APSO	knees, kidneys
MALTESE	knees, thyroid
MANCHESTER TERRIER	vWD, CERF
MASTIFF	hips, elbows, cardiac, thyroid, CERF
MINIATURE BULL TERRIER	knees, cardiac, BAER
MINIATURE PINSCHER	knees, CERF
MINIATURE SCHNAUZER	CERF
NEAPOLITAN MASTIFF	hips, elbows, CERF
NEWFOUNDLAND	hips, elbows, CERF
NORFOLK TERRIER	knees
NORWEGIAN ELKHOUND	hips, CERF
NORWICH TERRIER	knees
OLD ENGLISH SHEEPDOG	hips, elbows, CERF
OTTERHOUND	hips
PAPILLON	knees, CERF

PEKINGESE	knees
PETIT BASSET GRIFFON VENDEEN	hips, CERF
PHARAOH HOUND	hips, CERF
POINTER	hips, CERF
POMERANIAN	knees
POODLE	hips, thyroid, vWD, CERF, knees (min)
PORTUGUESE WATER DOG	CERF, PRA
PUG	hips, knees, CERF
PULI	hips
RHODESIAN RIDGEBACK	hips, elbows
ROTTWEILER	hips, elbows, cardiac, CERF
SAINT BERNARD	hips, elbows
SALUKI	cardiac
SAMOYED	hips, CERF
SCHIPPERKE	CERF
SCOTTISH DEERHOUND	None
SCOTTISH TERRIER	vWD
SEALYHAM TERRIER	CERF, BAER
SHETLAND SHEEPDOG	hips, CERF, ACVO
SHIBA INU	hips, knees, CERF
SHIH TZU	hips, CERF
SIBERIAN HUSKY	hips, CERF
SILKY TERRIER	knees
SKYE TERRIER	None
SOFT COATED WHEATEN	hips, CERF
STAFFORDSHIRE BULL TERRIER	hips, CERF
STANDARD SCHNAUZER	hips, CERF
SUSSEX SPANIEL	hips, cardiac, CERF
TIBETAN SPANIEL	hips, elbows, knees, CERF
TIBETAN TERRIER	hips, knees, CERF
TOY FOX TERRIER	hips, CERF
VIZSLA	hips, SA, CERF
WEIMARANER	hips, elbows, CERF, vWD
WELSH CORGI	hips, CERF, ACVO, PRA
WELSH SPRINGER SPANIEL	hips, CERF
WELSH TERRIER	CERF
WEST HIGHLAND WHITE TERRIER	knees, GCL
WHIPPET	CERF
WIREHAIRED POINTING GRIFFON	hips, CERF
YORKSHIRE TERRIER	knees

Chapter 3

PICKING A PUPPY

 This chapter gives you the scoop on what makes puppies tick—and ways to evaluate the best possible puppy for you. In Chapter Three you will find:

❑ *Timing*—when to look at a litter, when a puppy can go home with you and whether two puppies are a good idea.
❑ *Picking a puppy*—going in person and all the considerations that can help you make a good choice, along with tips on how to evaluate a puppy's personality.
❑ *Picking and shipping a puppy long-distance*—things to know if you send for a puppy from out-of-state.
❑ *Developmental periods*—how a puppy develops to the twelfth week and how that affects the kind of dog she will become.

Timing

AGE TO TAKE A PUPPY HOME

There is a general agreement that between six and eight weeks is the best age—right in the middle of the socialization period. There is a general consensus that six weeks is too young because it interrupts the puppy's socialization to other dogs by removing him from the litter. At seven weeks old a puppy has already formed his personality. Some experts say that exactly forty-nine days of age is the perfect moment for a puppy to leave his nest. While I don't think people should be marking their calendars and getting too crazy about this, it is true that the forty-ninth day comes up again when personality testing is assessed, so there really may be some essential developmental milestone for a young dog on that day.

Many canine experts feel that taking a puppy younger than eight weeks away from his litter can be a problem because that puppy will miss out on essential interactions with his littermates. Every young dog needs time to learn basic social-pack skills from his brothers, sisters and mother, but if a puppy goes home with you too young, the main deficit is that he will not learn how to modify his bite strength by having practiced with a littermate. This means that when playing with you, your children or other dogs later in life, he may use too much jaw pressure and cause damage without knowing it.

Puppy's Age at Homecoming

SEVEN- TO TWELVE-WEEK-OLD PUPPY (DELICATE BABY STAGE)

Advantages:

Adorable ball of fluff

Has no bad habits, is a blank slate for you to fill

Easily introduced into your life and to the people/other animals in it

You can watch her grow up

Disadvantages:

No way to predict her final personality and looks

Needs constant vigilance, correction

Needs protection from other dogs, children

Everything goes in the mouth—lots of destruction

Housebreaking hell: bladder or bowel control for only a few hours

TWELVE-WEEK AND OLDER PUPPY (FRUSTRATING TEENAGER)

Advantages:

Less fragile than the younger puppy, can exercise and play more fully

Housebreaking easier, greater physical control

You can see what he'll eventually look like

May have had some training so should be easier for you to train

Disadvantages:

No longer the cute stage, may even be going though a gangly phase

A teenager now, dog can be emotionally flighty, insecure

Physically gawky, bounding around clumsily, knocking into things

Leadership issues: testing you; rebelliousness may begin

If he's been raised at the breeder's, he may have "kennel syndrome" (deep fear of everything new: people, objects, noises)

GETTING TWO PUPPIES AT ONCE

Plain and simple, this is a bad idea that sounds good. One puppy at a time is about all that any household can successfully civilize. And if two puppies is bad, two from the same litter is even worse because although the idea sounds warm and fuzzy, you will run the risk of having *two* dogs who never really shape up. Littermates bond very closely, so if you take two at once it will be a constant struggle to get their attention, get them focused on you instead of each other, and keep them from inciting each other into "illegal activity."

Ask people with twins what it's like to have a pair of toddlers in the "terrible twos"! Except with dogs, the terrible twos can last *the whole two years* from when you get them until about their second birthday—generally speaking, small dogs exit from puppyhood at about a year but the larger breeds take at least two years to really mature. Two puppies at once is a recipe for disaster and destruction: if you think one puppy can do a number on a sofa cushion, you've never seen two go at it from opposite corners!

If you want two dogs, then your best bet is to first get one puppy and concentrate on molding that dog into a delightful companion who respects the limits you place on his world. You can get another puppy after about two years—most experts say to not get a second dog any sooner than the second birthday of the first puppy, since he will just be emerging into adulthood by that age.

The first dog will show the ropes to the younger one, who will learn by example. Turn your first puppy into a stellar role model and take half the work out of raising the second puppy.

Picking a Puppy

MEET THE PARENTS

Many experts say you should meet a puppy's parents, since purebred dogs are selected genetically for temperament. They advise that you can learn about your puppy's probable disposition by watching her mother and father. The only problem with this is that it is not realistic or helpful, because what you see in a parent is not necessarily what you are going to get in the next generation. Another reason that visiting a puppy's parents may not be advisable is because it can give the false impression that if you do enough homework you have control over what you'll be getting in a puppy—and just as with other creatures, each dog is an individual with a unique set of pre-wired attributes.

Those same canine experts who emphasize the predictive nature of a pup's parents also claim that, because a mother dog's genes make up half of the puppy's gene pool, the first thing you should do when visiting a litter is to focus on the mother, not the litter of cute babies. The theory is that her puppies have a fifty percent chance of turning out like their mother, so you should pay attention to how she reacts to new people and other dogs. Although it sounds dense to me, I include this theory here since you may come across it elsewhere—but even as a *non*expert you can see the fallacy in this reasoning, since the mother dog's personality is obviously not set in stone or predetermined by her genetic makeup. Her responses to the world around her have been formed as much by events in her own environment as by the way she is naturally put together—much like the rest of us!

If you want to meet the father—who is responsible for the other half of your puppy's personality genes—to see how *he* handles new people and children, just keep in mind that his own upbringing and current life are entirely different than your puppy's are going to be. Meeting the parents really doesn't have much practical application, since the way that parental traits are passed down to offspring is random and unpredictable. This is generally true: Man O'War's parents didn't have any foals just like him—and none of Mozart's children were musical geniuses, either!

If you are getting your puppy directly from a breeder, then a chance to meet the pup's parents can be interesting—but realistically it has nothing more to offer you than a point of interest. Take a deep breath and accept fate—that's what I would say to anyone who hopes that by researching the daylights out of a puppy's heritage they'll have any guarantee about how their puppy will turn out.

Basically, the home you'd like to see a puppy come from would feature a friendly, well-fed mother who is attentive to her pups in a healthy, well-socialized litter.

MALE OR FEMALE PUPPY?

The generalizations that follow are about the theoretical differences between male and female dogs. In my own experience, most of these gender differences have not held true—perhaps with the exception that females can seem more emotionally aware and connected to their people. But for what the gender comparison is worth, here goes:

 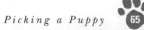

Males are:
- larger
- more dominant
- more likely to fight and roam
- less moody
- better workers
- do not come into season
- less expensive to neuter

Females are:
- smaller
- less dominant and defiant
- less likely to fight
- less likely to roam
- moodier than males if not spayed (they come into season twice a year)
- more sensitive to people's emotions

Picking a Healthy Puppy

COAT

Free of parasites (part the hair and look for a pepper-like substance, which is actually flea droppings). He shouldn't be scratching or biting the base of his tail or rear end (parasites). The skin should not be dry, white or flaky.

EYES

Bright and clear, not watery. Whites should be white—not watery or yellowish or streaked with red. No tearstains down the face. Depending on his age, eye color may still be blue, which changes to brown in most breeds.

TEETH

Straight and white, no undershot bite (except for a few breeds like Bulldogs, which require it) and no overshot bite where upper teeth jut over the lowers.

EARS

Should not be smelly or have discharge. Dog should not be shaking his head or scratching at his ears, which is a sign of ear mites.

PUPPY PERSONALITY TESTING

The idea of giving a puppy a few simple tests has gained popularity in the dog world. The best known series of tests is called "Volhard testing," named after the couple who standardized their own testing techniques to identify a dog's personality. However, there are any number of similar canine tests aimed at the same goal: devising a yardstick to be a reliable predictor of a puppy's current and future personality.

The reasoning behind such tests is the practical purpose of finding out a puppy's "dominance level," or how headstrong he is by nature. An extremely bold dog is going to be a handful to train, while at the other end of the spectrum the very shy puppy—who can be startled by his own shadow—will be difficult to train for different reasons. The tests also give a sense of a puppy's level of interest in people, which will affect his trainability and how easily he'll become a member of your family.

• Age for Testing

Seven weeks—forty-nine days to be exact—is considered to be the ideal age for a puppy to be evaluated away from the litter. Except for a small amount of learned behavior, a seven-week-old puppy is thought to be a clean slate, meaning that testing at this time is supposed to give a true reading of his nature.

Take a moment to watch the whole litter without interacting with them. Are most of them uncomfortable with you being there—are they barking or running away? That would be such a bad sign that you should just walk away from the whole litter, since it indicates that this is a line of breeding that turns out suspicious dogs or that this breeder hasn't socialized the puppies. In either case, it makes it an uphill situation for you and that puppy—and why load the dice against yourself going in?

• Puppy-testing Scenarios

There are many variations on how puppies may respond to any of these "pop tests," but I include only two ends of the spectrum: anything in between is your judgment call. But in the case of very dominant or very submissive dogs, you can predict that they will behave almost the same way in every situation. The independent dog will ignore most of what you're doing and go her own way; the very shy dog will tremble, pee and/or cringe submissively. Avoid both these extremes, because otherwise you could have a lifetime of extra effort dealing with the simplest issues. You can try some or all of these experiments, but don't get too serious about them. Unless a puppy is consistently off the chart at either end of the spectrum (in which case you have to hope there's *someone* out there who will love her), you can do a fine job raising any puppy.

Common wisdom is that you should avoid any personality extremes in a pup: not the laid-back puppy, but not the most forward and pushy one, either. Other than that, try some of the little tests that follow—"Pop Tests for Pups," you might call them—and see which appeals to you as a way to get to know a puppy quickly.

- The person doing the testing should be a stranger to the puppies.
- The tester should be confident about executing the exercises that follow and feel he knows what he is doing.
- The test area should be a room unfamiliar to the pups.
- The test time should be when the puppies are at their most active.
- Puppies should be tested individually so that the results aren't skewed by the confidence-boost of having littermates there.

Test #1: Hold the puppy in your arms.

Shows whether a dog accepts social domination.

Bend down and firmly stroke from the puppy's head down to the top of his shoulders. A dog's head, neck and shoulders are dominant areas: when two dogs meet, the higher-ranking one will often put his paw or chin across the withers (the ridge between the shoulder bones) of the other.

An ideal puppy will probably not object to this. He might whine, wiggle or stiffen for a moment, but then he'll relax and even lick you.

A dominant puppy will likely object to your dominating stroking of him—he may growl or try to jump on you. He may panic, struggle or freeze and not snap out of it.

Test #2: Pet the puppy but don't hold him: speak warmly.

Measures for curiosity and eagerness about people. Does he enjoy human affection enough to work for it in training?

Bend down, clap your hands, but don't call to the puppy right away—just watch.

An ideal puppy comes right over, will stay with you, wagging his tail.

A dominant puppy may bite at you or wander away disinterested.

Test #3: Call the puppy to you: crouch down, clap your hands, whistle, sound encouraging.

Bend down, open your arms for the most welcoming position.

An ideal puppy will come over with tail wagging, confident, cheerful.

A dominant puppy might ignore you, or come straight at you and nip, jump or bump into you when she gets there.

Test #4: Will he follow you?

Stroke the puppy, walk away, then see how readily he follows.

An ideal puppy follows you.

A dominant puppy follows, but so closely that he gets underfoot and might even try to bite at your feet or clothes.

Test #5: Hold the puppy off the floor: cradle your hands under his stomach.
What does the puppy do when she has no control and you have total control? Gently lift her a few inches off the ground and hold the position for fifteen seconds.
An ideal puppy struggles a little, then relaxes in your hands.
A dominant puppy will struggle and fight and may bark, whine or try to bite your hands.

Test #6: Sit down and hold the puppy on her back in your lap: stroke her belly, speak reassuringly.
What is her reaction to being gently restrained?
An ideal puppy will struggle briefly then relax.
A dominant puppy will thrash around to get off her back and may vocalize or bite.

Test #7: Retrieving. Set the puppy on the floor, get her attention by waving a ball or toy, and then roll it across the floor. Make enthusiastic, encouraging, "Come on girl!" noises to bring it back.
An ideal puppy will chase the object, play with it and maybe even bring it back to you if you clap your hands and whistle. She'll let you take it away without too much objection.
A dominant puppy will chase the object and take off with it, ignoring you when you try to recall her. If you try to take it back she won't relinquish it and may growl.

Picking and Shipping a Puppy Long-distance

If you cannot find a litter of the breed you want anywhere near where you live, you might want to consider buying a puppy long-distance and letting the breeder ship the pooch. This is especially true of less-popular breeds, where you really don't have many options, unless you have the time and money to fly or drive to wherever the breeder is located. It is certainly preferable to deal with a reputable breeder sight-unseen than to deal with someone closer who is less impressive just for the geographic convenience.

VIDEOTAPE THE LITTER PLAYING
Although it would be nice to just take the breeder's advice on which puppy to get from his litter, the more prudent choice would be to ask him to videotape the puppies at play. Choosing a puppy is so subjective, and you may not even be able to say what it is that draws you to one puppy or another. But you could make a decision based on watching a video.

DOCUMENTATION FOR SHIPPING

Before any long-distance transaction is complete you'll need all the documentation for the puppy and especially the results of any OFA or CERF tests recommended for that dog's breed (see pages 54–57 of the appendix to Chapter Two for an explanation and a list of tests by breed).

Shipping can be expensive, it takes coordination, and there is some risk for the puppy, due to the mechanical problems that can arise with airplanes and the emotional effect on the dog of losing his littermates and the breeder's human family.

What the breeder will do is put the puppy into a shipping crate and put him on a plane, contacting you with the luggage tab number so you can meet the plane on the other end. You often can make an arrangement so that if the puppy doesn't work out—especially if you have other dog(s) to introduce him to—you are free to ship him back.

Stages of Puppy Development

You will find that several of the following stages in the puppy's growth will overlap, which reflects the different ways that individual dogs mature. The information is a roughly chronological look at the stages that puppies go through and the issues they experience as they grow.

CANINE SOCIALIZATION (FOURTEEN TO FORTY-NINE DAYS) (TWO TO SEVEN WEEKS)

Learns how to regulate strength of bite, how to socialize with other dogs and establish a pecking order—and has a positive experience with human contact.

Teeth cannot yet be used for tearing meat, chewing bones or any adult activity—but they are needle-sharp and can get her in trouble with other dogs.

Play, play-fighting and biting teach a pup how hard to bite to cause pain. Hearing a littermate's yelp of pain when she bites his ear teaches her she has bitten too hard. Getting bitten in return teaches a puppy what that pain feels like. A puppy's jaw muscles are weak and underdeveloped at this stage, and this period is when she learns how to regulate her strength of bite.

Puppies need to stay with littermates during this period to become well-balanced dogs. By the fifth week, they move together as a group. This is the beginning of pack behavior as adults.

Dominance and Submission During the Learning Stage

During the socialization period, a puppy learns how to display dominant characteristics—and also how to show submission—with his littermates. He experiments with both in discovering his own personality. The list of these behaviors can be useful to you in understanding—and not misinterpreting—these activities when you see them.

Learning Dominant Activities
Chasing, ambushing and pouncing on littermates
Stalking other puppies with lowered head and tail
Circling another pup with stiffly wagging tail
Standing over littermate with neck arched, head and tail high
Hackles up, hair erect on shoulders or along backbone
Displaying teeth and growling
Biting around face and neck
Shoulder slams
Front paws on other pup's back or shoulders
Direct penetrating stare
Mounting from behind with or without pelvic thrusts
Standing on hind legs, boxing with front legs

Learning to Display Submissive Behavior
Staying still while dominant puppy circles
Accepting another pup putting paws on shoulders
Not moving while another pup mounts
Tail tucked between legs
Head held low, ears down, eyes averted
Submissive grin, with lips pulled back to show teeth
Licking lips, yawning, sneezing, sometimes showing incisor teeth at same time
Rolling onto back
Lying on side, lifting uppermost leg to expose belly and genitals
Urinating, defecating

♦ Between Four and Seven Weeks the Puppy's Brain Is Growing.
At an incredible rate. By seven weeks the brain is transmitting adult brain waves and a puppy is capable of learning by example, and will often mimic its mother and littermates.

♦ Weaning Starts in the Sixth Week.
By the sixth week weaning begins: the mother refuses to let the puppies near her breasts and threatens them when they try to nurse. To back the puppies off, the mother usually gives a low warning growl. If a puppy does not respond to her warning, she snarls at him and makes piercing eye contact. She may stand over the puppy, who by now is usually lying on his back, squealing. The next time she growls, he'll respond immediately. This is how a puppy learns the meaning of discipline. Especially with a puppy of dominant character, the mother needs to discipline him properly at this point or he'll grow up to be a nightmare for his future owners. By the seventh week, the puppy is weaned. It is at this critical point that humans need to enter the picture and "socialize" the puppies (see below).

♦ Puppies Taken Away Early from Their Mothers

"Puppy mill breeders" are guilty of removing pups from their litters sometimes as early as four and five weeks of age in order to send them to the brokers who handle their dispersal to pet shops all over the country. These little creatures are subjected to stressful transportation conditions and at least two changes of environment when they are shipped first to dog dealers and then to a pet shop. The unsuspecting buyer does not stop to realize that in order for them to find that puppy in a pet store at eight weeks of age the little pup had to be taken away from his mother and litter at a much-too-young age. And what the buyer does not know is that these dogs have never learned how to be dogs—that by leaving the litter so young they've missed out on the essential *canine socialization period*. This means they often can't get along with other dogs; they can also be hard to train because they didn't receive their mother's discipline in the critical early weeks.

♦ Sick Puppies Up to Sixteen Weeks Old Also Suffer.

If a puppy gets ill between birth and the fourth month he can wind up with some of the negative behavioral changes associated with restricted early socialization. Puppies that are sick in their early development, especially during the normal socialization period of ten to twelve weeks, show more aggression, fear of strangers and children and separation-related barking than dogs who remain healthy.

♦ Some Breeders Sell Puppies at Six Weeks—a Big Mistake!

The puppy at six weeks still needs time with her mother to learn how to respect authority, and time with littermates to learn how to interact appropriately with other dogs. It is disturbing to informed dog enthusiasts to learn of supposedly responsible breeders letting puppies go immediately after weaning. The assumption is that they must be doing this for economic reasons (they want the money sooner) or for their own convenience (to have two fewer weeks of feeding, cleaning up and dealing with inoculations and other medical issues). In any case, information about the developmental growth of puppies has been around long enough that a professional breeder should know better than to send puppies out of the nest at six weeks—and they should know that they are doing the puppy and its new owners a disservice.

SOCIALIZATION TO PEOPLE (FIVE TO TWELVE WEEKS)

Before the pups are weaned at seven weeks, they need to be handled by people. Puppies not exposed to people from five to twelve weeks of age will have over-socialized with dogs and undersocialized with humans. This is called the "sensitive period" for dog-human bonding. Dogs that do not meet people until after the socialization period can be antisocial, hard to train and spooky. Some dogs will never be able to react normally to people throughout their lives; others may even develop a lifelong fear of humans if they are not properly exposed to us during these critical weeks.

♦ Physical Contact with People

In order for puppies to adapt to living in human families, people should touch them starting at five weeks—but only for short periods. It is extremely important that the affectionate handling by people only happen *once a day, briefly,* so that the puppy can remain with her litter the rest of the time. This ensures that she will be well adapted to both people and other dogs.

The delicacy of timing and intensity of these human interactions with puppies are two of the many reasons that puppies born in huge breeding facilities are at a distinct disadvantage: "puppy-mill puppies" do not get these important benefits.

◆ The "Sensitive Period" Cannot Be Made Up Later.

Once gone, that five-to-twelve-week window is gone forever. The loss of the individual development that comes during this period is probably going to leave a dog with behavior problems. It is believed that environmental circumstances explain most canine behavior—that means that the nature vs. nurture question falls heavily on "nurture" where dogs are concerned. Experts do not believe that a puppy's personality problems can be inherited or that a puppy's genes determine his temperament—his character is shaped by the environment he grows up in, particularly during this crucial sensitive period. A pup's temperament is not "written" in his genetic code. Puppies are known to *copy* their mother's behavior; they may mimic a growling or overly assertive mother, but the undesirable traits they mimic can be unlearned.

◆ Between Three and Eight Weeks a Puppy Needs Exposure.

During these weeks a puppy needs to be exposed to a wide variety of things that she will encounter later when she has left her canine family. Puppies from mass-production breeders have no prayer of being shown potentially frightening objects and noises. With a responsible breeder you can hope that the litter has been exposed to stimuli such as vacuum cleaners, aerosol sprays, children, mail deliverers, cats, vehicle noises, etc. (More on socialization issues later, page 111.)

This exposure should optimally continue up to twelve weeks of age and then on into the juvenile period.

◆ Taking a Puppy Home at Around Eight Weeks

A puppy taken home at eight to twelve weeks has the best chance of fitting right into the new human family he is joining. By sixteen weeks it is already a more difficult transition, and eight weeks is considered the prime time—a puppy has the best chance of becoming a well-adjusted adult dog at this age. Human socialization begins during the end of the canine socialization period. During this time any good breeder knows the importance of handling the puppies frequently, showing them that contact with humans is a pleasurable event. Handling also lowers the puppy's level of stress with new sensations and experiences, which helps prepare him for stressors in later life.

SOCIALIZATION WITH LITTERMATES (EIGHT TO TWELVE WEEKS)

Combative play gets more intense among siblings, which helps develop a ranking order within the litter. These interactions have a lasting effect and help shape a puppy's permanent personality into a dog who falls somewhere in the middle of the spectrum of timid, even-tempered or overtly aggressive.

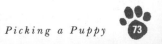

Puppies do best in adapting to their new homes if they are removed from their litters between eight and twelve weeks. The benefit of this is that you avoid developing a puppy with a personality extreme from the effects of a dominance order from rough play—other littermate(s) dominate him into subordination—which is not helpful to living with people. It is for this reason that researchers have determined that when people are socializing puppies, the dogs should be removed from the litter to be handled (see below, under "Fear-Imprint Period").

◆ **Staying with the Litter Past Twelve Weeks of Age**
Puppies kept in a kennel by a breeder until they are twelve weeks and older can suffer from "Kennelosis" or "Kennel Syndrome." Staying too long with his littermates can be a problem for a dog who is naturally shy. Staying with the litter past twelve weeks can actually have a downside for any dog: even three weeks past this time can result in dogs that lack confidence. This was proven by a study of guide dogs for the blind, which showed a disproportionate failure rate in those puppies who were left with their litters past twelve weeks: the dogs did not have the self-confidence to make independent decisions necessary to protect a blind person, who might give a command that could endanger him.

Being kennel-bound also means the dog has missed her socialization period with people: she will never really learn to fully identify with humans. Kennel Syndrome can also make a dog unable to handle stressful situations later in life. These dogs will most likely develop a general fearfulness of strange environments and new situations and be overly excitable or overly withdrawn. You can eventually overcome some of this deficit, but it takes patience, persistence and buckets of time and love.

Puppies that remain in the litter from the twelfth to fifteenth weeks develop into a dog pack, with their positions and a dominant-subordinate pattern established. If a puppy who is naturally not as strong and assertive as her littermates stays in the litter during this period—and if the others bully her and force her into a subordinate position—she may develop a shyness that will stay with her for life. To avoid the problem of chronic shyness in an adult dog, steer clear of any puppy who remained with the litter past sixteen weeks of age.

◆ **Eight to Twelve Weeks Is the Fear-imprint Period.**
This period is an especially sensitive stage of the puppy's growth: it is called the "fear-imprint" stage because if the puppy has a frightening experience now, the circumstances leading up to the scare will become deep-rooted, with the fear often staying with the dog for life. For this reason you should avoid even the possibility of the puppy having traumatic experiences during this month.

During this four-week fear-sensitive period, most puppies (and especially those that are particularly sensitive to new and "scary" things) should stay home, rather than run the risk of encountering something especially spooky. That may sound extreme, but whatever frightens a young dog during the fear-imprint period may very well frighten her for the rest of her life, so you might want to give her the extra measure of security by staying on familiar turf.

These four weeks are usually a puppy's first weeks in her new home. Stay home and let her continue to play with you, your family and friends, and whatever dogs you already have that are the puppy's new pack.

It is important that all contact with humans—including social visitors and service providers—be positive experiences. Avoid giving any corrections or reprimands to the puppy in these early weeks. Under no circumstances should you hit or even threaten to strike the little pup. Physical punishment of a dog is *never* a solution to a problem with a dog of any age, but it can be especially harmful at this stage of a puppy's development.

The First Vet Visit

The first vet visit should fall within these important weeks (see page 118), giving you a good chance to let the puppy have a positive experience with the vet, who you hope will be especially warm and gentle with a little pup. If you aren't happy with how the doctor treats you or the puppy, then this is a good time to find another health provider, before there is a medical emergency (more on choosing a vet on page 287).

Obviously the puppy fears will be more pronounced in some individuals than others. If you have a puppy who seems to spook and startle at every strange noise or new sight, then it may be worth the time for you to help her overcome some of those fears.

Chapter 4

THE HOMECOMING

Your New Dog's First Days with You

Let the adventure begin! It's great that you've decided to open your heart and home to a dog. This chapter walks you through some of the things you may want to consider and plan for during the early days of introducing a new dog into your life. If you're prepared for the transition, you'll be better equipped to deal with the ways that it can affect both of you.

As with many topics in this book, there can be a difference in how homecoming relates to the puppy versus the mature dog. When I refer to a "mature dog," I mean over a year old, while "puppy" means anything up to that age. One year is the generally accepted cutoff for puppyhood, even though puppies of very large breeds can take twice that long to mature and will act like puppies until about two years of age. Unless you see either the term "puppy" or "mature dog," then any other reference—pooch, pet, dog, canine, companion—applies to dogs of all ages. Some of the topics you'll find in this chapter include:

❏ The emotional aspect of bringing the dog home
❏ Practical suggestions about the homecoming and preparations for it, including a basic gear chart
❏ The puppy's first days at home, including puppy-proofing; the puppy layette; and special tips on the pup's first night
❏ Sleeping arrangements for now and later
❏ Introduction to other dogs including planning ahead for the introduction; the logistics of the meeting; possible fighting; temporary loss of housebreaking
❏ Introduction to cats and children

The Emotional Components of "The Homecoming"

"MAIL-ORDER MARRIAGE"

The getting-to-know-you stage with a dog or puppy can be as intense and rewarding as the courtship period between people. A dog can pack a wallop to your heart before you know what's hit you! It's good to be reminded of that in case you weren't expecting the possibility of an intense emotional experience. For those people who have never "fallen in love" with an animal, you may have a wonderful surprise coming your way. If you've had a dog in the past or even have one now, it's easy to forget how intensely you can feel about a new dog in the early stages. Dogs and people must be wired to connect this way after centuries of being together—we worm our ways into each other's hearts in record time and bingo! we're hooked.

You could think of the first few days with a new dog as sort of like the beginning of an arranged marriage. With the arrival of the "mail-order bride" (your dog) both of your hopes are high but neither of you knows very much about the other yet. It's really not far-fetched to compare getting a dog and marrying a virtual stranger. In both cases you decide to spend a lifetime together based on little more than a quick meeting. Sometimes there isn't even a face-to-face if you're getting a purebred dog that's being shipped long-distance from a breeder. The decision may even be based on not much more than a conversation with an out-of-state breeder who sends you a photo of the puppy. But even if you get a puppy in person from the breeder, it's not as though you can learn a whole lot about the dog you're choosing from a brief visit with a puppy's whole litter (see "Picking a Puppy," page 64). If you're adopting from a breed-rescue or shelter, you may have little more to go on than a photo from a Web site, followed by a meeting under less-than-optimal circumstances at the place where the dog has been locked up.

All in all, accepting a dog into your life is a leap of faith. When you think about it, isn't it amazing how well people/dog relationships do turn out, considering that we have so little to go on before deciding to share our lives (and often our beds) with a four-legged member of a different species?

There's a magical glue that bonds us to dogs. The deep connection that has always existed between man and dog can transform us and a new canine from strangers into inseparable companions within days.

THE ULTIMATE GOAL IS TO FIT THE DOG HARMONIOUSLY INTO YOUR LIFE.

As long as he is clear about what to expect—and his needs are considered, too—then a dog can fit into whatever life you have. Dogs have been bred for centuries to accommodate human needs. To put it bluntly, dogs are here mostly for our comfort and delight. Generally we have made dogs into what they are to make us happy. Obviously there are true working dogs who perform useful tasks, but for the most part none of us is a Basque shepherd with an unruly flock of sheep that we could never manage without our devoted little herding companion.

You may really want a dog but wonder if you should even have one—you or those around you may question if it will be fair to the dog. But then you have to ask whether any alternative homes for that dog are so much better or different. Aren't there millions of dog owners who live in apartments? Have busy professional lives? Are single and go out a lot at night? Are married with children and have limited time or energy? What makes them so much more deserving or worthy than you are of a dog's love and companionship—and vice-versa?

Dogs enrich our lives—that's why they mean so much to us. It's easy to feel guilty about how the time constraints in our lives seem to shortchange the time we can spend with our dogs. You may look at people who have dogs but don't have much time for them and be tempted to feel critical, to make a value judgment about the owner for leading a life that may seem selfish. But the truth is that not all dogs can live in a perfect dog-oriented environment with hours to run free and play and acres to do it on—but nevertheless they are happy and give happiness. Dogs are about their people—and as long as they have the affection and attention of their masters, they can enjoy their lives.

WAYS TO VISUALIZE YOUR NEW DOG.

✦ Think of the New Puppy as a Newborn Infant.

It should help you accept the huge burden of a puppy by perceiving him as a lonely, frightened baby. Think how shocking the move to your house must be for a young pup, suddenly removed from a warm bed full of squirming siblings and a mommy full of tasty milk. Suddenly he's all alone—and you're the new parent bringing him to his new home, where he'll probably sleep alone in a crate. It's quite an adjustment! So if in the early days the puppy cries or whines or gnaws on things, try to be patient and compassionate. He's not doing it to irritate you, or because he's "spoiled." Remember, he's only a baby.

✦ Think of a New Older Dog as a Foster Child.

If you got the dog from a rescue organization or county shelter, you may not learn much about her past. The dog may have already been in multiple homes or other institutions (shelters, breed-rescues). She cannot know whom she belongs to or what's expected of her or what's going to happen next. That doesn't mean you feel sorry for the dog and let her have free rein without imposing any rules. On the contrary, knowing that someone is in charge and is consistent is part of what will make her feel secure in her new environment. Showing her what the boundaries are and creating some sort of predictable schedule will help her make a successful transition into your home.

The Emotional Roller Coaster of the First Days

THE FIRST WEEK CAN BE THE BUMPIEST TIME, SO BE PATIENT.

As you and the pooch adjust to this new living arrangement and get to know each other, things should smooth out. If you have prepared yourself and your family for what to expect in the early days with a new dog, you'll be ready for whatever happens. For example, if you don't want a dog on the furniture or begging from the table, then everyone should be clear about that and respect the rules right from the start. It's harder to undo a bad habit then to never let it begin in the first place.

Begin the relationship right by making clear what you expect of the dog. You also want it to be clear how she can expect the people in the household to be with her. Remember, you're building a solid foundation for the best possible life with the four-legged addition to your family.

YOU MAY SUDDENLY FEEL YOU'VE MADE A MISTAKE IN GETTING A DOG.

Feeling unsure about having gotten a dog—or *this* dog—is not unusual. But just because you have doubts doesn't mean that you have to *do* anything about the feelings. Why *wouldn't* you feel apprehensive about having made the decision to take full responsibility for another being's welfare? Those negative feelings should diminish in the early days as the attachment process begins and the positive feelings crowd out the doubtful ones.

Embarking on what is going to be a lifetime with an unknown companion can seem overwhelming: if you view the new pooch as being like an arranged spouse, you can understand that it's not that unusual to get cold feet at the altar. Getting a dog is a big decision—and having last-minute doubts doesn't mean there's something wrong with you or that you should bail out of ownership. It probably means that you're realizing the importance of the commitment. It's okay to feel overwhelmed by the changes and responsibilities that come with getting a dog. But it can make it easier to deal with if you realize that's what you're feeling.

YOU MAY FEEL REALLY CRITICAL OF THE DOG.

If you have feelings of ambivalence about getting a dog, it may cause you to be unfairly critical of her. If you're having second thoughts (which are quite normal) then that part of your brain has figured out that if you can find enough fault in the dog, it could be grounds for giving her back.

It really isn't fair to judge a dog *at all* right at the beginning: she isn't settled down enough in the early days to be her true self with you yet. Although it's honest to admit to the doubts you're feeling, your qualms probably aren't about this individual dog but about the whole event of having a dog join your life. Don't place blame on the dog, who deserves a fair chance to fit into your life before being evaluated.

THE DOG IS HAVING A ROUGH TIME, TOO.

It may help you to know that your new dog is experiencing her own emotional challenge. For you *and* the dog, moving in together is a big step on both sides of the equation. She, too, is probably feeling a combination of excitement mixed with anxiety. If she's a puppy, there's the giant step of going from her own litter to being the sole four-legged creature in a house full of two-legged ones. If she's an older dog, she has all the bittersweet memories of the place(s) she's lived before—and then lost. Now she has the worry of wondering how it will turn out with you.

Practical Suggestions

STAY HOME FOR A COUPLE OF DAYS WHEN YOU FIRST GET THE DOG.

For most people, the best time to devote a couple of days to the new pup will be the weekend. It would be great if you could take a couple of days off work—say a Friday and Monday—to give you and the pup a four- to five-day window of getting to know each other. Or take a day and a half so that the day you go back to work is only a half day and you can get home to spend the other half with the pup, who has spent what are probably his first hours totally alone.

You don't have to focus on the dog, but just your presence can make him feel secure. Extended time spent together will give you information about his temperament. This doesn't mean you can't go out, but try to spend as much time around the house as possible so there's a chance for low-key bonding to take place. One of the most important things for a puppy to learn, aside from house-training, is to feel comfortable with your coming and going from the house.

AVOID A BUSY WEEKEND FOR THE HOMECOMING.

If there's a lot of confusion and excitement in the house and lots of people coming and going, it can raise the stress level during the dog's transition into your family. Of course, if all that activity is normal for you—if your household is normally like Grand Central Station—then maybe the dog had better get a taste of it right off the bat! However, it would be best to keep strangers to a minimum in the beginning and give the new dog time to settle down and settle in. It's really not necessary for all your friends and your children's friends to pay a visit to meet the new arrival in the first forty-eight hours.

DON'T OVERSTIMULATE THE NEWCOMER ON THE FIRST DAY AND NIGHT.

Keep it cozy and relaxed without letting the dog spin out with excitement. This is especially true for puppies, who tire quickly and can get too worked up. You wouldn't pass an infant hand to hand to be dandled by a bunch of people. Keep it simple. Family members only at first. And no matter how excited or happy the people may be, try to save shrieks and shouts of delight for after the dog has had a chance to settle in.

COME AND GO WITHOUT DRAMA.

Right from the beginning it will make life easier for both of you if your dog accepts your departures and returns. If you don't make any fuss about it, neither will the puppy.

Use a catch phrase like "See you later" and just leave. Go out for a minute or so, then return. Give the pup a brief pat on returning—no big fanfare—and then leave again, using the "See you later" phrase. Stay out for longer this time before coming back inside. Once again, make sure your return is no big deal.

Tips for the First Week

There is no "right way" to introduce a dog into your life. Each person has to find his own way of weaving the canine arrival into the rhythm of his household. There are practical considerations covered in this chapter, but then you're on your own: take what applies to you, use what works for you. Beware of people or publications telling you what you "have" to do; avoid the mind-set that the whole experience is some kind of test, just another thing in life at which you can "fail" or "succeed." You are not being graded here. Being a dog owner isn't something that has a test at the end. Adding a dog to your life is supposed to be fun and pleasurable for all concerned—otherwise, what's the point, right?

Personalize your choices: there are as many different possibilities for handling the first few days and nights with your dog as there are differences in people. There is rarely an absolute "right" or "wrong." Keep in mind that dogs basically exist to please us. They have evolved over centuries to be companions to people: it's what they are wired to do. Make your dog as happy as you can, but remember that the love and company of their "people" is generally what means the most to dogs. Trust yourself—go with whatever works for you and your particular dog.

Based on your personality and lifestyle, and the age and attitude of your new dog, you will find your own way. Trust your instincts to find the most satisfying way to incorporate a dog into your home. Your dog is a one-of-a-kind individual, too, with her own personality—whether she's a little puppy or a more mature dog with "emotional baggage." She is her own special self: half the fun of dog ownership is discovering that uniqueness. Together you will discover a harmonious way to share your lives.

Adding a dog to your life is decidedly different than getting a lovely object you've wanted. Although a material acquisition may give you a certain kind of pleasure, acquiring a beautiful new couch is obviously an entirely different experience than acquiring a dog, a living being who comes into your home with her own unique personality and emotional depth. Another difference, of course, is that you don't have to housebreak the couch.

TAKE LOTS OF PICTURES!

One "dog essential" often forgotten is an easy-to-use camera and extra film. Keep the camera loaded and accessible so you can create lots of mementos of the puppy or dog sleeping or at play. Taking pictures might not be the foremost thing on your mind during the new dog's first days with you, but he'll never seem so cute and new and amazing as he does at the beginning. If the camera is lying around you'll be more likely to pick it up. Puppies grow so fast that there's no way you'll remember the smallness and clumsiness of his roly-poly self a year from now. And no matter how old the new dog is, in years to come you'll be glad to have the recorded memories.

PUPPY-PROOFING THE HOUSE

You want to pick a few rooms that the puppy can be in with you without too much danger to his health or your home. The kitchen is always a logical room. It can be made safe and cleaned fairly easily, and there is generally a lot of activity in and around the kitchen, which is perfect for a puppy who is trying to acclimate to life with you.

Depending on your personal lifestyle and decor, there may be other rooms that you can safely make puppy-friendly. Areas that are closed off from the rest of the house, like the garage or basement, are not a good choice. These are unkind locations for a little dog, and do nothing to help integrate him into the life of the household.

Look at things from a puppy's point of view and remove or protect anything reachable that he could chew—ties on chair cushions, electric cords, tassels on carpets . . . even the carpets themselves.

◆ Preparation for the Puppy's Arrival

Put away any object or aspect of your decor that could be destroyed by the puppy and any item that could be dangerous to him.

Think of a human toddler and how everything goes in his mouth—it's the same with a puppy when it comes to protecting the youngster from dangerous substances (except with the puppy those sharp little teeth will chew through anything you leave in his path).

Put human baby-proofing latches on low cabinets—some pups can open these doors.

Any electrical or phone wires that you can't tuck out of the way should be treated with Bitter Apple cream (the spray is too messy for thinner wire).

Any object that smells like you is a magnet for a puppy.

◆ Creating a Safe Space for the Pup

Set aside a confined area if you will be going out for longer than the puppy should be confined to her crate (her age in months plus one for the acceptable number of hours).

If you have a really big kitchen, you'll need to enclose only part of it or choose a bathroom instead.

Get a baby gate to close the doorway—try to find a wire one, since pups will chew on wood and/or plastic.

Planning the Trip Home and First Hours

Bringing your dog home is exciting, but it can be stressful if you don't anticipate what you'll need ahead of time. It may be stressful for the dog in any case, but for you it will be a lot easier if the dog throws up on a towel rather than in the crevices of your car upholstery.

🦴 *The Car Trip Home*

- Have someone else drive so you can hold the puppy or sit with the older dog.
- Bring the whole family, as long as children understand to keep it low-key so the dog stays calm.
- Bring old towels and/or blankets to cover the seats or put in your lap.
- Bring paper towels in case there's an accident.
- Bring with you a blanket or piece of a blanket that was in with the litter—the familiar smell of his dog family on the blanket will be comforting, and it should go into his crate at your house.

WHAT TO DO WHEN YOU GET HOME

✦ Give Her a Small Amount of Water (One Cup) When You Get Home.
If she doesn't throw that up after fifteen or twenty minutes (from the excitement and car travel), you can leave water down for her.

✦ Give a Small Bowl of Food at Her Normal Feeding Time.
Ask the breeder (or wherever you got her) when she is accustomed to eating. Also find out the brand of kibble she has been eating and ask the breeder (or shelter) for a couple of days' supply to give you time to purchase some, if it happened to be one of the preservative-free healthy brands (it's unlikely that either a breeder or shelter would spend that extra money on the premium brands). If the puppy has not been fed a high-quality brand like Innova or California Natural, then mix some of the kibble she is used to with the new brand you'll be feeding. Ask if there is any special way the food has been given to the dog (with or without water, a bit of meat, etc.). For some dogs it is more important than others to feel comfortable with food. For a sensitive dog like that you can avoid an upset stomach from "new home stress" if the puppy gets food that is familiar in the unfamiliar setting of your house. By mixing the two foods she can gradually get used to the new brand.

✦ Adjust the Dog's Feeding Schedule over the Next Few Days.
It is fine to slowly change the times the dog will eat to make the hours more compatible with your schedule. Any dog's feeding routine can be reprogrammed to accommodate your life. This is true of every dog except the young puppy, who still needs to continue the three or four daily feedings she is used to and that her growing body needs. However, at least you have the option of slowly changing the hours of her meals to coincide with when you or someone else can get there to feed her. ("Free-feeding" [see page 443] is not an option for a young puppy if you hope to have any success with house-training.)

YOUR DOG NEEDS A NAME.

✦ We Speak a Dog's Name to Get His Attention.
A dog's name is his primary way of being alerted that you are trying to communicate with him. In the training chapter of the book (page 235) and the section on communication between man and dog (page 148), you will discover that we say a dog's name before any command, before anything we want to give him, even to warn him of danger. So it puts both you and your dog at a disadvantage not to have a name ready to start applying as soon as he enters your life.

✦ Try Out a Few Different Names and See Which One Suits Him the Best.
Experiment with two or three names that you think might work and see which one you feel suits him best. With a puppy you can call him by absolutely anything you want—it's more the way you call him that will get the response. With a youngster his response to a name is really not as important as it is for an older dog whose name you may be changing (see chart below

on "Naming Tips"). It is your tone of voice—the energy and up-inflection when saying his name—that will catch his attention. If you give the puppy a treat when he looks up or makes eye contact or comes over when he hears his name, then you are teaching him that his name is a good thing.

✦ If the Dog Comes with a Name, You Can Change It.

If you are inheriting, adopting or rescuing an older puppy or mature dog, don't feel obligated to keep his name unless you like it. If you know the dog's name—and do not like it—before you adopt him, then you may want to choose two or three possibilities for a replacement name. You can test which one suits him best, or which one he seems to respond to more. Let's say he was called Killer before and you like the name Satchmo (after considering the name-choosing tips in the chart below). In order to switch him over to the new name, you call him with a hyphenated name: you simply say Killer-Satch, putting emphasis on the "Satch." Reward him with a treat when he responds to the new, hyphenated name. If you're using a bright cheery tone it shouldn't take more than a few days for the dog to look up at you when you say just "Satchmo"—and when he does, give him a ticker-tape parade. You want to give a *jackpot treat* when you get a quick response in a challenging learning situation like this. "Jackpot" is part of a theory of *training reinforcement,* which is described fully on page 240 of the training chapter, but basically it's a high-value treat plus several more as booster treats.

✦ Move On if You Don't Get a Fairly Fast Response to the New Name.

It could be that the replacement name you've chosen does not resonate with the dog—which you'll know because he doesn't put one and one together and come alive to the sound of that name. If that is the case, then try your second choice in the same way—say it by hyphenating it with the dog's old name. You'll soon see if he responds to your second choice.

🦴 *Naming Tips*

- If you have other dogs, make this name completely different.
- Make it no more than two syllables—anything more is awkward.
- Avoid names that sound like basic obedience commands.
- If you love a name that sounds like "come" or "stay," then simply choose a different word for the obedience command.
- Use the new name whenever you talk to your dog (more on verbal interaction, page 244) to get him tuned into it.

Things You'll Need for the New Dog

There are quite a few things you need to get before you bring your new dog home. Some of them are fairly obvious; others might not have occurred to you. Some items you may be able to borrow from friends (for example, you could borrow a small crate for your puppy, who will quickly grow into a much bigger fellow). The same goes for a collar. A puppy who is going to become a large dog will need at least three sizes of collars that he will grow out of until he reaches his full size. You may have a friend who saved her puppy's outgrown collars and will pass them along to you to use during the growth spurts of the first year.

COLLARS

Collars come in dozens of materials and shapes. What you pick will be influenced by your personal taste, your budget and your dog's neck. There is rolled leather, which can be good on a long-haired dog because it doesn't get stuck in the fur. Flat leather collars come in many widths, with an endless variety of adornments attached. There is every imaginable hue and thickness of collars in nylon webbing, cloth, needlepoint, ribbon, rhinestone, etc.

Some people opt for a nylon collar that has your name and telephone number stitched right into the nylon, so that there's no tag to struggle with or lose.

◆ Your Dog's Collar Is His Only Link to You If You Are Separated.

Your dog needs to be wearing a collar at all times. With his name tag, he can always be returned to you. Without it, you may never be reunited. Even if your dog never runs away or has no opportunity to get lost, there are other ways that he can be separated from you. For example, your dog may be inside a car in an accident and not even be injured, just get spooked and take off.

Fireworks or lightning storms can frighten a dog so much that he runs away from home and becomes so disoriented that he forgets where he lives. The people who find him won't know, either.

See "Lost Dogs" in Chapter Eight ("Everyday Life") on page 209 for more on collarless ID options.

ID TAGS FOR COLLARS

Many vet's offices and pet stores can order ID tags for you. The tags generally come within two weeks. See the "Lost Dogs" section of Chapter Eight about the importance of having a temporary identification on your dog from the first minute you bring her home.

If you have no intention of moving in the next year or two, have an extra tag or two made up, because most dogs lose their tags or collars at some point.

◆ Metal or Plastic?

All the tag companies seem to sell both metal and plastic tags. The metal tags are often harder to read and can make a clanking sound against the dog's license. The plastic ones can wear out against the metal license, but most of the tag companies have a lifetime replacement guarantee.

There are some fancier or more unusual tags available from a number of companies, all of which have Web site listings: doggieid.com, planetdog.com, goodmangries.com, finearf.com, georgesf.com, bellatoccatags.com, fetchingtags.com.

You need to check the tag from time to time to make sure it is still attached, and to see that the information is still readily visible.

◆ What to Put on the Tag?

The tag companies expect you to put your name, the dog's name and your address and phone number on the tag.

One problem with this method is that there really isn't room for two phone numbers because the tags were designed before cell phones became so prevalent.

Another problem in putting all your personal information on a tag is that it can make you or your house a target. I have also heard a warning that if you put your dog's name on a tag, anyone who wants to steal him can get the dog to respond as though he were his own. These seem unlikely eventualities to me, but these precautions would clearly be an issue in some locations more than in others.

One solution to these problems is to put the word REWARD on the hang-tag and then put as many telephone numbers as you can fit on there: your home, office and cell at the least. The dog license has a phone number, but no one answers it after hours. Imagine how awful you would feel if you lost your dog, someone found him and generously tried to contact you—but could not reach you.

◆ Digital Dog Tags

The information age has caught up with dog tags, and now you can get a Dog-e-Tag that digitally stores up to forty lines of information. You can put your phone numbers, license and vaccine numbers, destination phone number if you're traveling, medications she's taking and the number of the dog's veterinarian, etc.

The tag can be updated when traveling or moving, or for changes in your dog's health and medical condition. The high-resolution digital display is easy to read and can be programmed in English, French, German, Italian and Spanish. The cost is $40, and the tags are available at (866) DOG-ETAG, or www.dog-e-tag.com.

◆ Safety Collars

There are collars that glow in the dark, which could save your dog's life if you live in the country or suburbs and there's even the remotest chance that your dog might be out in the dark without you. If you walk your dog at night anywhere but in a brightly lit city, there are also leashes that have built-in reflective strips.

One such product is the "Co-Leash Night-Lite," which is a collar with a leash attached (both of which feature a wide Scotchlite reflective strip) that runs about $20 in various sizes and colors. Go to www.co-leash.com for more information, or check out similar products on any of the dog-product Web sites or catalogs.

Another product is the waterproof "Night Light Collar" from American Leather Specialties Corp. It can be set to slow flash, fast flash or continuous shine. The lights are visible from a mile away. The batteries included provide 125 hours of service, and the collar runs about $25. (718) 965-3900.

SIZING A COLLAR

The collar should be loose enough that when she's lying down it doesn't dig into her neck but tight enough so that she can't pull backward and pull the collar right off over her head.

To get a neck measurement, put a flexible tape measure around the neck and then add two inches to that number. If you have a really small dog, add only one inch to the actual measurement to get the collar size.

Basic Gear for the New Dog

- Crate for training (see page 218 in Chapter Nine, "House-Training")
- Collar with temporary name tag and six-foot leash (see page 209 in Chapter Eight, "Everyday Life")
- Gentle Leader TM or harness for walks (see page 272 in Chapter Ten, "Teaching Manners"), unless the dog already walks obediently in a flat collar
- Dog bed (see page 179 in Chapter Eight, "Everyday Life with Your Dog")
- Brush, comb, toenail trimmer (see page 404 in Chapter Twelve, "Grooming Your Dog")
- White vinegar and cotton for ear cleaning (see page 422 in "Grooming Your Dog")
- Dog shampoo(see page 417 in "Grooming Your Dog")
- Old bath towels for bathing and seat covering
- Dog food and treats (see Chapter Thirteen, page 433, "Nutrition")
- Bowls for food and water (see page 443 in "Nutrition")
- Car safety belt/car gate (see page 504 in Chapter Fifteen, "Traveling with a Dog")
- Toys (see page 193 in Chapter Eight, "Everyday Life with Your Dog")

A Puppy's Homecoming

When we talk about a new dog's first days at home with you, there are a variety of issues that affect only a puppy. Issues that can surface immediately include chewing things, digging things up and other forms of destructiveness that are limited only by the strength of the individual puppy's inborn imperative to "rearrange" his environment!

In some cases, grown dogs have puppy-type problems when they first get to their new homes, due to high anxiety or stress about adjusting. But for the most part, it is the puppies who demand the most of your time and patience when they come home with you.

WHAT YOU NEED TO DO FOR THE NEWCOMER

◆ Take It Easy the First Day.

Keep it mellow and quiet in the first few hours home, at the very least. All family members have to be made to understand that this is a big transition for a baby dog, and that lots of noise and commotion make it even tougher for her.

Sit on the floor and watch her explore the space you've set aside for her. Give her a chance to meet her new people—at her own pace. When she comes over to any of you, use a calm, friendly voice to greet her and give her a gentle scratch or stroke on the chest or back (don't reach right for her head).

◆ Decide on a "Potty Area."

The puppy's "go to" area can be outside if you have a yard or on papers if you don't or live in an apartment. First thing in the morning, when you take her out of the crate, immediately place her in the potty area. Do the same thing after every play session, after she eats or drinks, and first thing when you get home. It doesn't matter whether she goes or not. Housebreaking is probably the biggest challenge with a puppy—not just training her to relieve herself outside, but the fact that you have to take her outside frequently to do so, sometimes in the middle of the night. However, don't even try to house-train the puppy for the first day or two. Give her a chance to settle in before tackling that challenge.

◆ Start to Learn Your Puppy's "Language."

Puppy behaviors such as crying, whining or barking are all forms of communication—it's up to you to try to figure out whether she really needs to go out, wants to be let out of her crate (if she's in one) or is being playful. Like human babies, it seems that puppies are each quite different in their sleep patterns and the related frequency with which they have to relieve themselves. So your first weeks may be fairly restful at night or fairly hellish, but at least puppies grow up a lot faster than human babies do, so it shouldn't be long before the pup outgrows her immature bladder and sleep cycles.

PUPPY-PROOFING

Puppy-proofing your house is only important if you value any of your belongings . . . because *everything* a puppy can reach is fair game! Puppies are like babies—they put everything in their mouths. However, unlike a toothless human baby, a puppy has a full set of razor-sharp teeth that can destroy pretty much anything.

◆ Think of a Puppy as a Toddler.

Just as parents child-proof a house to protect children as they begin to walk, you need to puppy-proof for the puppy's sake. Evaluate every room your puppy will go into: put away anything breakable to keep the little critter from ingesting bits and pieces of things that can make her sick. The puppy's well-being and safety are often overlooked as people worry about protecting their belongings. As much as you need to puppy-proof for your own benefit, your little pup is as vulnerable and foolish as a toddler when it comes to the dangerous things she will put in her mouth.

- Put away anything that's loose. Think of it as battening down a ship before a storm: a puppy can be like a gale wind that blows through the premises.
- Take a "puppy-eye view" of your rooms and remove anything that looks enticing.
- Remove carpets with fringe borders, tassels on anything, decorative pillows.
- Tie up pull-cords for blinds; tuck drapery above puppy level.
- Electric and phone cords should be out of your dog's reach.
- Keep all slippers, shoes and clothing off the floor.
- Keep children's toys out of reach.

◆ Puppy-proof Before You Bring the Puppy Home.

You don't want to make the first days miserable by dashing from room to room, snatching objects out of the puppy's mouth and reprimanding her for doing what comes naturally—which is to taste everything.

Although the checklist covers the major temptations to puppies, don't think your house is safe just because you've removed the most desirable items. Even in an empty room, a puppy with the craving to chew is going to do so, especially if he's teething. Some puppies are demolition experts: they will gnaw on baseboards (where your walls meet the floor); others have been known to eat right through Sheetrock on the walls. This is not good for the long-term stability of your house, but it is also dangerous for the dog, who will be swallowing substances never meant to enter an alimentary canal.

◆ Get a Chew-deterrent Spray.

There are nasty-tasting liquids that can be sprayed as a deterrent on almost anything that the puppy has already tasted—or might taste next. "Bitter Apple" and similar products are sold in pet stores.

You can also mix up your own version of bitter-tasting spray by filling a squirt bottle with rubbing alcohol and adding some drops of Angostura Bitters and Tabasco or other hot sauce. Remember to test the spray on a small patch of the surfaces you want to protect, since this concoction may stain. But don't expect these sprays to be some sort of guarantee that an item is now safe from the pup—some dogs have much less sensitive taste buds and/or a much higher drive to chew and will do so no matter how foul the object tastes.

◆ Use a Crate for Both Your Sakes.

Crate-training takes on a new meaning when you have a chewing-aggressive puppy. It will no longer seem cruel or unfair to have the puppy confined in the crate. A variety of puppy-safe chew toys will satisfy his urges and keep your possessions intact.

A little puppy cannot "hold it" for more than a few hours, so she can't stay in the crate for more than three hours at a time when she is very young. That means that if there isn't going to be someone at home who can take her out every three hours or so, then you'll either have to come home within that time frame or have a friend, neighbor or pet-sitter come in to take her out. In the early weeks her life is basically going to be potty-play-potty-sleep-potty-eat-potty-play-potty-sleep, etc. She needs a chance to relieve herself before and after everything she does, and her small bladder (a tiny bladder if she is a small-breed dog) has an extremely limited capacity.

If there isn't any way to have someone take the puppy out of her crate at least every three hours, then you have to set up a puppy playpen with her crate in it as a sleeping den, which must also include a potty area with newspapers and some toys and water. The house-training chapter on page 215 goes into this in detail.

Puppy Layette

- Small crate for house-training (see note on crate size, page 219)
- Pet stain–removal products for accidents
- Chew-proof baby gate for room confinement (page 82)
- Puppy-safe plush toy
- Radio for nighttime comfort and company (see page 207)
- Puppy-size chew toys (softer and smaller)
- Puppy brush (softer than for adult coat)
- Puppy food and water bowls (smaller than adult)

TIPS ON THE PUPPY'S FIRST NIGHTS

- ☐ The puppy won't be sleeping much, so you shouldn't expect to, either.
- ☐ Sleep in sweat-clothes, or keep them beside your bed in case the puppy wakes you up by crying, scratching and/or walking around in his crate.
- ☐ Tire out the puppy before bed by playing with her about an hour before you expect to be going to sleep. Let her wind down and mellow out before you put her into the crate. A tuckered-out puppy is generally more relaxed.
- ☐ Try different comfort items in the crate. Put in a hot-water bottle (or microwaveable heating pad) wrapped in a towel—the warmth is a reminder of the coziness of his lost littermates. A loudly ticking clock can achieve the same result, and a piece of real or synthetic lambskin, or a toy made of the same, can also be soothing company.
- ☐ If you have a wire crate, try putting a big towel or blanket over the top and down two sides. This can make the crate seem cozier, more den-like.

- Ask the breeder for a piece of cloth from the bedding the puppy has lived in with her littermates. The familiar smell will provide a security blanket when the young pup feels most insecure those first few nights on her own.
- Keep the crate by your bed so you can hear when the puppy gets restless and needs to go out.
- The puppy will probably cry several times during the night. This is normal: there is nothing wrong with him, he just feels vulnerable.
- Do not verbally try to soothe a whining, crying puppy in a crate. If you say, "Good boy, that's okay," you are praising and reinforcing the whining.
- Don't yell at the puppy, either. Raising your voice and sounding angry will only make an anxious puppy more nervous.
- Take the puppy out to pee if he cries or whines, but keep it low-key: no playing, no festivities, just business. Praise the peeing but put the puppy right back into the crate.
- Do not reprimand the puppy for crying in the early days. It's a big thing to be taken away from your litter and left to sleep all alone in the dark. You'd probably cry a little, too.
- The puppy has to go out to pee the VERY first thing in the morning. Before you pee, she pees. You have better bladder control at this point.

GENERAL SLEEPING ARRANGEMENTS

• A Dog Should Sleep in the Bedroom with His "People."
This is the general agreement among the dog experts, based on the current understanding of the canine/human bond. Dogs are "pack" animals: in the dog's eyes you are now the leader (alpha) of that pack, so it follows that you should all share the same "den" at night.

• Sleeping in the Same Bedroom Promotes Closeness.
The dog's bed should be near yours to encourage attachment to you. While the puppy is young and you are using the crate for training you can put the crate in your bedroom at night to enhance the bonding between the puppy and his new family. If space permits and it isn't otherwise a burden on you, having two crates would mean you could keep one crate in the bedroom and one in the main "hanging out" space in the house. The latter should be positioned so that the puppy can see you in bed and doesn't feel abandoned.

• Let the Dog Stay in the Bedroom for at Least the First Few Nights.
If you have doubts about your bedroom being the dog's bedroom, keep an open mind. Depending on how it goes you may change your mind. Even if you decide later that you want the dog to sleep elsewhere, it is recommended that you give it a try for a little while, because it promotes closeness and a sense of security for the dog. Also realize that the more the pup feels bonded to you, the greater her desire will be to protect and defend you. Many people sleep more soundly knowing that their dog is the best alarm system they can get.

◆ **Dogs Generally Don't Care about Our Sex Lives.**

Some people worry that if the dog is in the bedroom he will be bothered by or interfere with their lovemaking. In asking around, it seems as if dogs ignore people's sexual encounters—even noisy ones!—no matter how exciting they seem to us. This is usually true whether you have a dog from puppyhood or adopt an adult from an unknown background.

The possible interference with your sexual activity is a different story if you've allowed the dog to sleep on the bed . . . since he'll be right in the middle of it. (Perhaps this is a good reason *not* to teach your dog to sleep with you?) People who are adamant about their dogs "needing" to sleep on the bed with them may live alone and not be sexually active, or they may be in a relationship but have an inactive sex life. Or perhaps they may not realize that the dog(s) sleeping on their bed could be a contributing factor to sex not taking place in either case. (Obviously these are people-to-people issues, not dog-to-people issues, and would need to be addressed in a different forum.)

◆ **The Dog's Bed Needs to Be Cozy and Comfortable.**

In order for a dog to want to sleep on his bed, it needs to be inviting. The cover should be frequently washed and turned over for even wear. If the bed has loose fill rather than a solid piece of foam inside, many fussy dogs won't lie down on it if you don't shake the bed to even out the fill. Choose a bed for the size and type of your dog based on the criteria you'll find under "Basic Gear for the New Dog" on page 87.

Introductions to Other Pets

If you have realistic expectations of how the resident animal occupants of your home will probably react to a new dog, then you won't be dissuaded from enlarging your canine family. This section can help prepare you for what's going to happen when you introduce the new dog or puppy to other dogs or cats you may have.

RESENTMENT FROM THE RESIDENT ANIMAL(S).

The incoming dog may be viewed by other dogs, at least at first, as an interloper—intruding on territory that's already been staked. Consider it unlikely that you're going to have an immediate lovefest between the pet(s) you already have and the pooch you're bringing home—that way, you can be pleasantly surprised if it turns out to be easy. However, be prepared for your existing pet to embarrass you and be a lousy host.

The probability of a rocky transition certainly shouldn't discourage you from bringing home that new dog—far from it. The dog(s) you already have will be delighted, sooner or later, with their new canine companion. After all, dogs are pack animals by nature. However, the first response to the new dog can often include one or many of the not-so-wonderful reactions on page 97.

I refer to "pets" in this section rather than just previous dogs, because even though canines are probably the most frequent preexisting animals in a home that's adding a new dog, it is also true that people have cats, ferrets, birds, miniature horses, potbellied pigs, snakes—you name it—as household companions. I also use "pets" in the plural because it's easier, although obviously you may have only one other nonhuman household resident.

CONSIDERATIONS BEFORE INTRODUCING TWO DOGS

There are a number of things to consider when bringing home a new dog. Following some of these suggestions can make life easier, although there are some issues that may not arise until the new dog has actually joined your personal animal kingdom. Making the best possible match is what you should aim for, while avoiding areas that are known to cause conflict.

◆ Avoid Choosing Dogs with Equally Strong Temperaments.

Two strong characters are sure to wind up locking horns with each other. If both dogs have dominant personalities, you may find yourself running a canine United Nations, constantly trying to resolve issues between them. The dogfights you try to avert by intervening will probably happen anyway when your back is turned. By avoiding dogs of similar temperaments, you may also avoid a constant knot of worry in your own stomach, as well as all those pricey vet visits to patch up the warriors.

◆ Try Matching Your Current Dog's Size and Activity Level.

It can make sense to look for another dog of your dog's same or a related breed—not only will they be of a similar build, but a breed sometimes has its own inborn style of play. Some breeds stand on their hind feet and "dance/box" with each other. Other breeds use a lot of open-mouthed teeth play (you can actually hear their teeth clack together like castanets). There are dogs who prefer to wrestle on the ground and "chew" each other's faces. Obviously, individual dogs have their own style of play, which has often come from experimentation. Most dogs will eventually alter their play style to suit another dog's way of having fun.

Be careful if your older dog is much larger than a new puppy. The bigger dog can accidentally hurt the puppy if they start to play. Don't scold the older dog—you don't want any negative association with this new relationship. Just separate the dogs so they can settle down, remain calm yourself and then give them another chance to have fun.

Assuming that both dogs are healthy and relatively matched in age—young or middle-aged—you want them to be able to play safely and happily with each other. Compatibility is difficult if two dogs have great differences in height, weight, fitness or even their sense of humor when playing games like "keep-away" and "tag."

◆ Should the New Dog Be Male or Female?

Generally speaking, grown dogs are more likely to tolerate an interloper of the opposite sex. However, given individual personalities, there are exceptions to this rule. It used to be taken as an absolute rule that you should never get two dogs of the same sex: it was believed that a fight would inevitably break out between any two females or two males. There was also the opposite assumption: that dogs of the opposite sex will automatically fit right in with each other. There are many exceptions there, too.

A dog's gender can certainly play some part in the introductory process. There's no doubt about the possibility of flying fur if your adult male or female is a strong alpha personality and you bring them a dog of their same sex who is also a dominant personality. However, compatibility between dogs can often have more to do with the personality and maturity level of the individuals than their gender.

A young puppy of either sex is rarely seen as any kind of challenge by most dogs. Even an older puppy or adolescent dog of either gender will tend not to threaten most mature dogs.

✦ Don't Assume All Females, or All Males, Are Alike.

Beware of sexist stereotyping—dogs probably don't like it any better than their human counterparts! Preconceived notions about how males or females "always act" can interfere with distinguishing your dog's individual personality. And make no mistake: dogs really do have distinct personalities and preferences, if you take the time to understand them.

Female dogs are generally characterized as being submissive and gentle, but there are females who can be tough, feisty and dominating. Just as there are human girls who don't play with dolls and won't wear frilly dresses—because they get in the way of climbing trees—so are there female dogs who don't have what are considered "feminine traits."

Not all male dogs are put-your-dukes-up, macho guys, either. The flip side of rough-and-tumble females is those male dogs who are not aggressive (a dog like that is sometimes referred to as "soft" by trainers, meaning that it takes less intensity from the owner or trainer to get a point across to the dog). This atypical kind of male generally follows rather than leads, waits and watches instead of instantly reacting, and basically doesn't fit the standard idea of how a tough male dog behaves.

Knowing your own dog is probably the most useful tool to have when introducing your dog to another. Stay tuned to your dog, and pay attention to the subtle clues you can pick up from him about how he's feeling in an introductory situation. By knowing his idiosyncrasies in dealing with new dogs, you can facilitate a good introduction with the newly arrived pooch.

Even so, you may have an older dog who views a little puppy as an alien and freaks out over the baby dog's roly-poly antics and sharp, nipping teeth.

THE FIRST MEETING

✦ Both Dogs Should Already Be Spayed or Neutered Before They Meet

For both males and females, the tendency to be aggressive is linked to sex drive, and neutering lessens or eliminates that sex drive. Neutering also eliminates the hormonal scent, which can trigger a variety of reactions in other dogs of both sexes.

✦ Try to Bathe the New Dog Soon Before the First Meeting.

There is an "unfamiliar odor" aspect to new encounters between dogs, and by eliminating it, you lower the tension level a few notches. The other dog will be less threatening to your existing dog, because a recent bath will have washed away her personal odor.

◆ Bring Treats in Your Pocket.

Have super-delicious goodies in your pocket or "bait bag" (see chapter Thirteen, "Nutrition"). You want to have a way to reward the dogs right away for anything they do that shows acceptance of each other, and little bits of cheese, small pieces of cut-up hot dog or strips of beef jerky made for dogs (which you can break up into small pieces beforehand) will all inspire them.

Plan ahead to reward all good behavior between the dogs—whether it is tail-wagging, playfulness, face-licking—and remember that when you see it, you need to give the treat immediately so that you precisely reinforce the good behavior (see "The Learning Process" on page 236). As soon as the dogs wag their tails and display body language showing that they want to play, give each of them a food treat to encourage that attitude.

You should be aware that *neutral* behavior is also a sign of acceptance between them. Anything that is not hostile is good—so neutrality should be praised and well-rewarded, too.

◆ Concentrate on Staying Mellow Yourself.

The dogs will pick up any anxiety or excitement you're feeling. Remind yourself beforehand that you need to keep a cool head, because you'll be setting the example for everyone involved—the dogs and any of your family members who might be there. If you feel frightened or panicky at any point during the introduction, a good way to calm yourself down is to concentrate on your breathing and take in deep, slow breaths.

Speak calmly and do not raise your voice, no matter what the dogs do. Your own dog is already able to read your emotions from even the slightest change in your tone of voice—you certainly don't need to raise it for him to notice. You especially need to avoid getting loud or shrill in a way that sounds frightened or angry. Your dog could read your distress as a cause for alarm—and turn on the new dog. Or your agitation could frighten the new dog.

◆ Stay Aware of Your Part in the Dogs' Interaction.

Don't think of yourself as an "innocent bystander" in this meeting between dogs—you are very much a part of it. Don't underestimate how influential you are. Stay conscious of your voice and body language, both of which send messages to the dogs about how to behave.

◆ Meet on Neutral Ground.

Unless you feel really sure that your dog will warmly accept an unknown dog on your own property, plan to make the introduction on a friend's fenced property or in a quiet public park, beach or wooded area, or even in your front yard if your present dog is always in the back—whatever is available to you. This will remove your current dog's territorial protectiveness from the equation.

If your dog is territorial (also known as "turfy") he may not be very welcoming to other dogs on his territory. This makes a neutral meeting-ground even more important. If you were to have the first meeting in your own yard, there's a good chance your dog would act defensively or aggressively on ground he considers his own.

◆ Meeting on Your Own Property

If you want to use your fenced yard, first give the new dog a few minutes outside in the yard with you to get oriented. Then let the other dog(s) out. You should keep the new dog on a leash, for his safety. A leash may actually make him feel more secure because it's attached to you, and this way he won't bolt if he gets spooked when your dog(s) comes outside to meet him. By doing the introduction outdoors, you give the animals more room to maneuver, rather than bringing the newcomer directly into a house, which is a more cramped space and can also stimulate more territoriality in the resident dog.

◆ Two Handlers May Be Necessary.

You should be the one to bring the new dog to the neutral meeting point. Your attachment to the new dog will be influential in your current dog's reaction. Ask a friend or relative who is savvy about dogs in general and, if possible, knows your other dog well to bring him to the meeting point.

SIBLING RIVALRY

If the new dog is still a little puppy, you can imagine how the homecoming might feel to the dog you already have. Compare it to the arrival of a new baby into a family that already has a toddler. His parents bring home a newborn and present her with a triumphant flourish. The little one who was there first may share his parents' beaming delight—or he might burst into tears for the number-one position he has just lost. It's quite normal for children to respond negatively when a new baby comes home—they are jealous of all the attention the infant gets, especially from what used to be exclusively *their* parents. If you can empathize with that kind of hurt/displaced human scenario, you know it can be a transition that's fraught with emotion, and you can be compassionate toward your existing pets. If the new puppy gets lots of attention—and what puppy doesn't?—the resident dog may feel jealous on top of feeling invaded or displaced.

If you're bringing home an older puppy or more mature dog, both the resident dog and newcomer are likely to have "issues." In order to understand what the canines are going through, compare it to what it can feel like to both children when a foster child joins a preexisting family. There are often rough patches in which everyone involved feels awkward and unsure of where they fit in the new picture. Insecure about their place in the family hierarchy, they can have a bumpy ride until things get sorted out. Since the animals will be looking to you for leadership, it will make the transition smoother if you are clear about how to handle the issues that arise between the dogs.

To make the transition smoother, it helps to maintain a realistic expectation of how your existing pets will react to the newcomer. If you know what to expect, you won't be alarmed or discouraged. Don't worry that you've made a terrible mistake in bringing home a dog, or that the mistake is the one you chose to bring. Avoid feeling annoyed or disappointed in either animal. Some of the normal responses that current pets can feel toward a new canine arrival are listed in the chart on page 97—so you'll know that there's nothing wrong with your current dog if she experiences any of these reactions.

- Jealous
- Threatened
- Offensive/aggressive
- Frightened/intimidated
- Withdrawn/depressed
- Possessive of you
- Territorial about bed/toys

- Suspicious/anxious
- Urinating/defecating in house
- General disobedience/ignoring commands

If you anticipate some of these normal adjustment reactions, and understand that they are generally short-lived, then the transition will be less stressful for you. It can be frustrating to feel so happy and excited about bringing home the new bundle of joy, only to be met by growls and hisses from the resident pet(s). But what can you do? You can accept your resident dog's behavior without judgment, because the crabby attitude will pass. As a friend likes to say in defense of her dogs: "Hey, they're only human."

LOGISTICS OF THE FIRST MEETING

✦ Give the Dogs Time to Relieve Themselves and Run Around a Little.
Do this before the two dogs meet and their adrenaline starts to flow in the excitement of the introduction. Burning off some steam beforehand lowers the stress level for "the meeting."

✦ Both the Newcomer and the Resident Dog Should Be on Leashes.
Those who advocate leashed introductions think that if one dog were to get aggressive the leash would give you a way to intervene. However, other trainers point out that just being leashed can make some dogs more aggressive, possessive and/or protective of you. You might want to consider using the leash only at the very beginning, for the first few sniffs—especially for dogs unaccustomed to being on a leash in the first place because they live out in the country or in a fenced environment where a daily leash is unnecessary. If the opening moments between the dogs seem civilized, then consider letting your original dog loose.

There can be problems with leashes, but that is often because people misuse them: they may yank or pull on the leash because they anticipate trouble between the two dogs. Putting any tension on the leash sends the message to the dog to be on high alert. A taut leash will telegraph your nervousness: you are sending a warning signal to the dog and he will respond to it. Both handlers have to keep slack in the lead: fight the impulse to yank or pull on the leash.

Keep moving so the leashes don't get tangled. Instead of standing in one spot, move around. Let the dogs circle each other: keep moving with them so you don't get wrapped up. Don't pull or yank on the leashes to maneuver the dogs—let them dictate the rhythm of their "first dance."

DOMINANCE: WHO WILL BE "TOP DOG"?

Food, toys and the attention of their master are the pivotal issues that the dogs will be negotiating for at least the first few days. Your best bet is to remove yourself from the process of sorting out who will wind up on top—the dogs have to work it out in their own way. Think of yourself as a neutral "UN advisor." Only step in between the dogs if it looks like it's leading to war.

◆ It's Quite Natural for One of the Dogs to Be Dominant.

The dog world (the whole animal kingdom, really) is not a democracy. Dogs do not have our human ideas about "fairness." Yes, you can teach them to share—you can even teach them to take turns or wait their turn for your affection or treats. But at the end of the day, one dog will come out on top as Numero Uno: it's the way dogs are wired. It is not helpful to your dogs if you project human ways of thinking onto them. Perhaps to you "dominant" means something good, like "best" or "the winner" (and, by inference, those who aren't dominant are automatically "losers" or "inferior"). Or, for you, "dominant" may have a negative implication—it may mean pushy or bossy or greedy. But in the dog universe "dominant" has no value judgment, it just means that one of them has been elected "Top Dog."

◆ What If Your Dog Is a Dominant Female?

A strong female may do best with a submissive type of either gender—a "whatever you say, boss" kind of personality. In this situation, the dogs should meet on neutral turf *twice* before the homecoming to give them ample opportunity to iron out any differences—and then they should return home together.

◆ The Resident Dog Will Probably Be in Charge.

It's likely that your resident dog will be dominant over the new dog, but if it doesn't turn out that way, leave the situation alone. If you try to keep your resident dog on top, imposing your idea of "fair play," it will only increase any conflict that the dogs would otherwise have worked out naturally. Canines have their own way of holding elections; we cannot interfere and try to stuff the ballot box.

DOGFIGHTS ARE SCARY, BUT NATURAL

The way that dogs work out their issues is that they first use eye contact and body language signals to each other—but if these are ignored or challenged, the issue can escalate into growling, showing teeth and sometimes using teeth. The hard thing for many people is to not interfere with dogs when they're trying those earlier, nonviolent ways of working out who is going to be where in the pecking order. For you to understand what's really going on, see the section on "Aggression Between Dogs" (page 540). But the best rule of thumb is to back off: control your misguided impulse to "fix" things by intervening (which will only exacerbate and escalate problems) and let the dogs do it their way. Unless you're trying to protect a very young or very old dog from a dangerous situation that he himself does not comprehend, trust in the natural canine process of communication.

✦ Do Not Get in the Middle of a Squabble.

If a dogfight starts, or there is a standoff with teeth bared in which neither dog moves, you need to step back. Anything you do could trigger a worse outcome than what might have happened without your provocation. If a conflict is broken up too soon—or before one of them emerges as the victor—it will leave unresolved tension between the dogs, which can brew into a bigger problem down the road.

When dogs start growling, it may sound worse to you than it really is. These moments usually blow over in a matter of seconds, at which point the issue is resolved between them. You need to back off, no matter how scary it seems, unless it is a full-fledged battle and one dog is really getting hurt (in which case you have to think of your own safety first, anyway—see page 540 on "Dogfights" for more on this). If you must do something, resist the instinct to reach between the dogs (which could leave you with hands like Swiss cheese). Turn a garden hose on the dogs at full pressure (if you are inside and in the kitchen, use the sprayer attachment from the sink), or get a pot or bucket of cold water and dump it on their heads.

✦ Let the Dogs Work It Out on Their Own.

Everyday life will present inter-dog issues we don't even recognize; the dogs will be guided by whatever power balance they work out now. Depending on your personality and how compulsive or controlling or dominant *you* are, it may take some self-control for you to let the dogs work it out unimpeded by you. Stepping aside is easier for some people—for others, it's agony not to monitor or arbitrate any potentially nasty moments between the dogs. However, it may be easier to keep yourself out of the middle of it if you trust that the dogs have their own language and will sort it out themselves.

✦ When the Conflict Is Over, Pay Attention to the Winner First.

This may seem unfair, unless you remember that dogs don't abide by the human concept of "fairness." Your attention to the winner will reinforce the dominance hierarchy that the dogs have just established. Once that hierarchy is in place, there should be no more fighting.

✦ Continue to Reinforce the Balance of Power.

Once the dogs are living together, you must maintain the power structure that they've established. You should always greet and give affection to the dominant dog first; her food should always be served first; she should be allowed first into the car; she should have her leash put on first and be allowed out the door in front of the other dog. These are the natural "perks" of being Top Dog; both dogs will feel best if you respect that hierarchy.

At the same time, regardless of who's on top, it is considered wise to continue giving the resident dog at least the same amount of affection that he got before the new dog came along, regardless of which dog won the position of Top Dog. You would not want to give your first dog reason to be jealous or resentful of the newcomer. If there are no power issues between the resident dog and the newcomer, then your first dog should remain first in everything—sort of the first-come, first-served theory. The resident dog gets treats first, goes out the door first, gets his dinner bowl set down first and is greeted first by you.

FOOD FIGHTS

Food is a volatile issue between dogs, especially dogs that are strangers to each other. You may have two dogs that are getting along fine, but when a dish of food or even a hand-delivered treat comes along they may go after each other.

◆ No Free-feeding during the Introduction Period.

If you have been "free-feeding" your current dog—leaving a dish of dry dog food out at all times—you may have to change that routine at least for a while. The new dog may not be used to having unlimited access to food and may be greedy about the "free" food and want to eat all of it. Your resident dog may be possessive of his food dish and not want the new dog to go near it. It's easier all the way around to just remove the provocation for now.

◆ Keep the Dogs' Food Bowls Separate.

When you serve the dogs their meals, put their dishes down at a distance from each other. Stay with the dogs while they eat so that neither dog tries to go to the other's dish. It only takes a few minutes for most dogs to eat, so you staying there as a silent monitor is the best insurance against "food fights."

A dog is not usually possessive about his water bowl, but if you see your dog acting in any way possessive of his water dish (standing by it and guarding it in a defensive stance, growling when the other dog comes near it), find another spot to put down a second water dish so that the new dog has an alternative.

HOUSEBREAKING ACCIDENTS DURING THE INTRODUCTION PERIOD

Don't be surprised if you discover that one of the dogs is peeing in the house. You probably can't be sure which dog it is, or even if it is only one of them—although the most likely occurrence is that the new dog is having trouble adjusting to her new environment. In all likelihood, a break in house-training is only going to be a temporary problem.

◆ If Either Dog Has an Accident in the House, Don't Make a Big Deal of It.

In fact, don't show any reaction at all if you find urine anywhere in the house, or even a "bigger" accident. Under the pressure and excitement of the new arrangement, accidents can happen to either dog.

However, if either dog starts urine-marking in the house, you have a more complicated territorial issue that is probably best handled by a professional. In the first day or two you may not be able to distinguish between an accident and purposeful urine-marking. However, since the anxious/confused accidents usually stop after the first day or two, it will be clear if urine is reappearing in one location, or there are signs of several wet spots after that.

You might consider contacting a dog trainer/behaviorist as soon as you become aware that this is a urine-marking problem, because you want to stop it before it becomes a habit that is much harder to break.

◆ **Clean Up the Urine with an Enzymatic Cleaner.**
You should have on hand any of the liquid products—such as Simple Solution or Nature's Miracle—that clean bodily fluids and are marketed for house-pet accidents. These products neutralize the urine (or feces, blood or vomit), rather than simply cleaning superficially. Do not use any product containing ammonia, since it smells like urine (more on general cleanups on page 228).

◆ **The New Dog Needs Time to Get Used to Her New Surroundings.**
Your resident dog takes your lifestyle in stride and anticipates what is going to happen, but keep in mind that the routines and schedule of your house are mysteries to the new dog. Because she will be disoriented as she tries to figure them out, give her more chances to relieve herself outdoors, either by taking her out or making sure she knows how and where to exit on her own, if there is an open door or a dog door.

Dogs and Cats

You know the expression "It's raining cats and dogs"? If you've never stopped to wonder what it means, just remember that it does not refer to a gentle spring drizzle but a torrential downpour.

On some level your cat will probably never fully forgive you for polluting her world with a canine. (If, on the other hand, you already have a dog, then introducing another one to your cat may simply be an increase in the same torture she's already been enduring.) There are some rare cats who actually like dogs, but more frequently they will come to accept one dog—usually with comments on the side—but probably not the canine species as a whole.

Cats can even go past tolerance to actual friendship with a dog, but that is pretty rare. Anyone who has had a mixed dog/cat household can tell you that cats are discerning about their interspecies friendships. They definitely know one dog from another—you only have to see one go from sharing a bed with "their own" dog to flying up a tree if a strange dog comes into view to understand this.

◆ **Take It One Cat at a Time.**
Cats are at least as unique in their personalities as dogs are, so each one will have his own tolerance level and timetable for coping with a dog entering the household. Of course, how that goes will have a lot to do with how the dog handles it—whether she is respectful and lets the cat call the shots, or whether she is spring-loaded to take chase as soon as the cat jumps off the counter. One thing is for sure: it is usually a very slow process, and it may be months before your cat accepts the presence of the new dog sufficiently to walk around without looking like he is being hunted.

Just don't expect to come home some evening anytime soon and find the kitty and pooch snuggled together on the couch watching *Seinfeld* reruns.

✦ Some Breeds of Dogs View Cats as Potential Snacks.

These are technically known as "prey-driven" dogs, meaning that when a smaller animal takes off, they take off after it. It would be foolhardy to consider bringing a grown dog like that into a home that already has a cat. If you are a cat owner, you need to find out as much as you can about a dog's attitude to cats before you bring such a dog home.

Dog breeders generally know whether this hunting aspect is true of their breed and will usually be honest about it. They don't want an interspecies tragedy to happen. If you are adopting a dog, the shelter or breed-rescue may have information about the cat-friendliness of a dog whom you are considering for adoption.

You can consult the chart below to at least eliminate any dogs that are strongly prey-driven. However, keep in mind that just because a dog breed is *not* on this list doesn't necessarily mean it is cat-friendly, either. Remember that every dog is an individual and may not fit any particular mold. Don't assume anything—negative or positive—until the dog has been watched (on a leash) around a cat over a period of several days.

The breeds mentioned are just a sampling, and being on the list does not mean that these breeds are vicious or bad—they are just following an instinct to chase prey. Prey-driven dogs are basically hardwired to chase anything small that runs away from or past them—look at racing Greyhounds, who run like the blazes after a fast-moving mechanical rabbit. Some breeds also have the instinct to kill that prey if they do catch it. However, all dogs have a prey drive, it is just stronger in some breeds and some individuals. Most terriers were bred to chase and kill rodents, so any smaller animal is fair game for them. Many of the hunting breeds are also prey-driven, and those that have been bred specifically for fieldwork have it to an even higher degree—although there are many working field dogs that live lovingly with cats.

You can help determine whether your dog has a strong prey-drive by referring to the chart below: if your dog has more than one of these qualities, there's a good chance she will go after a moving cat.

🦴 *Signs of Prey-drive in a Dog*

- Excited by moving objects
- Sniffs the air and/or ground frequently
- Stalks birds and small animals
- Shakes and "kills" toys or other objects
- Hunts or bites at your feet when you walk

Some Dogs Incompatible with Cats
- Pit Bulls
- Weimaraners
- Most terriers
- Greyhounds
- Akitas
- Field hunting breeds

♦ More Than Two Dogs Spells Trouble.

There is a terrible phenomenon that can happen with dogs and their behavior toward cats (and other prey) when there are more than two canines around: a bloodthirsty pack mentality can take over. Unfortunately, human beings are vulnerable to this, too: when people are in groups they will do horrific things that they would never even contemplate if they were on their own or with only one other person.

So nobody else suffers the horrible experience of jeopardizing your cats' lives, it's worth telling how my two dog-trusting cats were almost killed when I added a third dog to my canine family. I had previously had a Golden Retriever and a Cocker Spaniel with several household cats—there was peace on Earth—but when the Golden died, I went to Friends for Pets, the Golden Retriever rescue in Los Angeles. I wound up adopting my first Weimaraner, Lulu (because it was also the Weimaraner rescue) and even though I said I had cats they did not dissuade me from taking the dog. However, when I got Lulu home I didn't like the expression with which she regarded the cats: licking her chops with narrowed eyes. The usually trusting cats were on guard. When I called the rescue to report this worrisome behavior, they did acknowledge that some Weimaraners were cat-chasers, and that I'd just have to see if this was true of Lulu.

Fortunately, with close supervision and obedience work, I got to the point where Lulu learned to ignore the cats and I felt the kitties were not in jeopardy. So then I got a second Weimaraner from Friends for Pets as a companion for Lulu. It turned out that Billy Blue did not pose a threat to the cats, because all he lived for was meals and he was not interested in food unless it was already cooked and in a can. The trouble started when I rescued a two-month-old Rottweiler puppy who had been thrown away on the roadside in a cardboard box. From the moment the Weimaraners accepted the new youngster into their pack, the older dogs began to harass the cats, chasing and cornering them. Within a week both cats had made emergency visits to the vet and two dear friends each gave a new home to one cat—who, by the way, have outlived two generations of dogs in my home.

The point is this: if you have three or more of a laid-back, non–prey driven breed, it's probably not going to be an issue, but otherwise, either live a feline-free life or wait until you're down to fewer than three dogs and then see what you want to do.

◆ Put Your Cat's Food and Water Up High on a Counter.

Some people always keep their kitty's food up high so there is nothing you need to change when a dog arrives, but if it isn't already there, then you need to move it up. Even the most cat-loving, respectful dog in the world cannot pass up that delicious, smelly cat food that goes down the hatch in two quick gulps. If you are going to change the location of the food and water, then do it a few days before the dog arrives so the cat gets used to where her things are before the dog walks in and she has everything else to adjust to.

◆ The Dog Has to Be on a Leash for the First Introduction.

If the dog is not restrained there's a good chance the cat will bolt, the dog will chase, all hell will break loose and the future of their relationship will be grim. If the cat does take off at the sight of the dog, the dog's natural instinct will be to chase. That's why you have a leash on him. By the way, just because he chases does not mean he is necessarily "prey-driven," which is something more intense than the general canine instinct to chase.

◆ Expect a Traumatized Cat When the Dog Is First Introduced.

If there has never been a dog in the household before, be prepared for your cat to freak out when you bring in the dog. The cat will probably hiss and spit, her hair will stand on end and she'll take refuge in some unreachable spot. She may hide under a bed. She may even go on a hunger strike and not show up for meals, either. Being a cat, she'll show up again when she's good and ready.

◆ Have Some Treats in Your Pocket to Reward the Dog for Not Chasing.

Do not yell at your dog or use an angry, harsh tone to correct his natural impulse to chase. One of the first commands you'll want to teach the dog is "Leave it." Use the command at a time like this, then give him a treat for turning his attention to you and away from the cat.

◆ Don't Worry about the Cat—She Can Take Care of Herself.

A cat with claws can go on the offensive and take a swipe at the dog's face, but even a declawed cat can escape unscathed. A feline is rarely in serious jeopardy, because she can usually jump up onto something to get away from a dog or hide underneath furniture where the dog can't reach her. However, there is still the possibility that this can be traumatic for the cat. You really don't want to let the dog develop a chasing/hunting habit.

◆ Your Dog Might Get Scratched in the Face If He Doesn't Step Back.

It shouldn't take long for a dog of even average intelligence to learn that the "Flying Furball" can be dangerous and should be shown some respect. If your cat does have a face-to-face with the dog she will appear quite fearsome—she'll arch her back, hiss and lash out with a clawed paw. Most dogs will back right off when a cat does her display. Puppies might not get the cat's message if they are still too sweet and dumb, but a swipe of the paw across the nose will smarten them up real quick. However, if you have a grown dog who does not shrink from the cat's display—who shows no fear and wants to keep on coming—you may have a possible cat-killer on your hands. This might be a situation in which you want to bring in a professional dog trainer to evaluate the situation.

✦ Keep a Gentle Leader or a Short Leash on the Dog.
When the dog is loose in the house with you in the first few days, have him drag a short leash at all times so you can grab the leash or step on it should he decide to take off after the cat. A sharp verbal reprimand of "No!" as you step on the leash should get the idea across. If you prefer, you can keep a Gentle Leader on him with a hanging tab (see page 272 in "Training Equipment"). With luck, any chasing behavior can be nipped in the bud.

✦ Don't Leave Them Alone Together in the Beginning.
Do not leave the dog and cat loose and alone together in the house until you are certain that they have developed at least a grudging mutual respect and can fend for themselves. Dogs and cats can learn to share the same space in friendship or at least a truce, but the peace needs to be negotiated by you from the start. The cat can fend for herself, but what you can help with is setting boundaries for the dog and gently correcting him for any aggressive tendencies toward the cat or for encroaching on her territory.

DOG MEETS CHILD(REN)

This important topic is covered thoroughly in the chapter on "Dogs and Children" (page 468), which is where you should look for guidance in handling the often delightful but potentially dangerous combination of children and dogs.

Keep in mind that it isn't just the children in your own household who will be meeting the new dog, but also their friends and other visiting children. It is important for both the children and the dog to learn about each other in a controlled environment, so that accidents don't happen and there isn't a chance to establish bad habits.

Chapter 5

RAISING A GREAT PUPPY

This chapter is an essential tool for anyone getting a puppy of any age—there is so much to plan for and deal with that it can seem overwhelming at times. Puppy-rearing can be fun, but it is also hard, frustrating work. This chapter should help you over the rough spots and clarify the confusing ones.

So many dogs abandoned at shelters are purebred puppies who were once the apple of someone's eye—until one day those people just couldn't imagine dealing with the "puppy stuff" for a year or more in order to one day wake up to the dog of their dreams. If there's an overall wish for this book, it's to help people *really* understand everything that goes into sharing our lives with dogs, so that we can all feel part of an amazing interspecies adventure and not just the unwitting recipients of puppy chaos. This chapter is dedicated to explaining what is happening with a young dog every step of the way, and breaking down the huge experience of bringing a puppy into your home into manageable bits.

Even if you already have a dog, or are bringing a mature dog into your life, it can still be pretty interesting to find out what goes into a puppy's development and how it affects the dog that youngster becomes. In this chapter you will find:

❏ *The Developmental Stages*—a detailed description of what is happening in various stages of a puppy's physical and emotional growth that will enable you to understand and effectively work with your little pooch.

❏ *Puppy Peculiarities*—some of the odd little things puppies can do that might alarm or confuse you if you didn't know about them.

❏ *The Puppy and the Vet*—What to expect on the first vet visit, with suggestions about ways to make going to the vet a pleasant experience for all of you. Includes the customary inoculation schedule and the facts you need to know to decide whether you should follow it.

❏ *Puppy Training*—Some basics to get you started on the right foot with the pup; common puppy misbehavior and how to deal with it.

Puppy Developmental Stages from Eight Weeks

THE FIRST VET VISIT

The first vet visit should fall within the formative weeks during the fear-imprint period (eight to twelve weeks), which will give you a good chance to let the puppy have a positive experience with the vet, who you hope will be especially warm and gentle with a little pup. If you aren't happy with how the doctor treats you or the puppy, then this is a good time to find another health provider, before there is a medical emergency (more on "The First Vet Visit" later in this chapter, on page 118).

BONDING TO PEOPLE: THREE TO FIVE MONTHS (TWELVE TO TWENTY WEEKS)

This is the precise period when the closest bond is formed between dogs and their people. If your behavior with the youngster is that of a loving, sensitive and reasonable leader, it will have a positive influence on how he turns out. Your effect on your pup is enormous: you *are* your puppy's world. Puppies are fascinated by their human family and everything in their new home; they also have a strong desire to play.

◆ Kids Compared to Dogs

People often compare children to puppies, which is a mistake in my view, because few of the similarities are actually relevant and the dissimilarities are numerous. But if making a comparison is appealing, you can get a rough idea of the equivalent maturity between puppies and children by translating "weeks" into "years." That would mean that this puppy developmental age of twelve to twenty weeks is like human adolescence—a time in human development when kids act out, test boundaries and do all the things that require adults to set limits and enforce them.

TWELVE TO SIXTEEN WEEKS: BECOMING A YOUNG ADULT

We tend to view dogs in this age group as still being puppies—which can be a big mistake. If you demand too little, that's what you can expect from your dog. We continue to cut a lot of slack to a dog in this age group, permitting her liberties that her own mother and siblings never would if she was still living with her "original pack." Even though your dog is still puppy-cute, don't smile on misbehavior and let it slide. You can't laugh off poor behavior in your puppy any more than a responsible parent would tolerate a prepubescent child "copping an attitude" and thinking they can get away with it. Anything you wouldn't want a full-grown dog to do, don't allow your puppy to do—or you will live to regret it or work yourself ragged trying to undo it.

The pup's personality can go through big (although usually temporary) changes during this period. For a week or two at a time he'll suddenly seem shy or unsure. You need to be the rock: stay predictable, be consistent in what you expect of him and how you expect him to behave. Just as your parents survived your teenage years and all that they entailed, so you will live through your puppy's adolescence.

◆ Obedience Training Now! Puppy Classes from Twelve Weeks

As the puppy enters the "juvenile period" by end of the twelfth week, he is ready for obedience training. Dogs mature at a much faster rate than humans: if you view this age-group as representing the early teen years, you'll know by comparison how firm and clear you need to be with a puppy at this age. Some people believe that the twelve-to-eighteen-week age is an optimum learning time for a puppy, who will develop into a better dog by participating in puppy classes. If such classes are offered in your area, it may be a good investment in your dog's future and in your relationship with him.

Most puppy classes encourage the whole family to attend so that everyone can be aware of basic health-care issues and simple training. Children can be guided in how to handle themselves and their puppy, getting that relationship off to a good start.

The classes should be aimed at having fun and meeting other puppies and their owners—a training system based on positive praise and rewards will make the class enjoyable for both of you. Getting used to other dogs is an important part of the puppy's socialization, and doing so in a group under a watchful eye is a good place to start. This is the age when most puppies should have gotten all of their vaccinations, which makes it safe to mingle with other dogs.

SIX TO FOURTEEN MONTHS: PUBERTY AND ADOLESCENCE

Hormonal changes take place in both the male and female during this time that are similar to the changes that human beings go through during puberty. The surge of hormones can be as dramatic for some dogs as it is for some children. The body has to cope with the changes brought on by the new hormones, while the mind has to cope with the side effects that often accompany the physical upheaval. Like teenagers of any species, the puppy will have mood swings and will at times be distracted, confused and difficult to communicate with. There's nothing wrong with your dog—he's just a normal teenager.

◆ Showing Independence at Eighteen Weeks (Four-and-a-half Months)

By this point, the emotional umbilical cord that has kept the puppy quite tied to you—and willing to stick by your side—begins to break. By five months the pup is ready to take off by himself, often without a backward glance. Obviously this is a generalization, and there will always be individuals who do not fit this age-related description.

This is why it's important that you train your dog before eighteen weeks to follow you, to be aware of where you are. Think of it as "looking over his shoulder to keep you in his rearview mirror." Unless you already have this thought process programmed into the puppy's busy little brain, by the time he has reached five months he may well be oblivious to your location when he's ready to have a good time. For more about training your dog, see Chapter Ten. By the time he is eighteen months old, a puppy is going through big physiological changes—if the puppy is not neutered, then the testosterone level in a male starts to rise and, with it, the dog's attitude can become bolder and more feisty.

FIVE TO SEVEN MONTHS—BIG PHYSICAL DEVELOPMENT

This is the time when a puppy's body is still growing, and for many breeds the time of greatest physical development. But the process is ongoing, even past the pup's first birthday. Do not think that a puppy's social education stops at any point. There's no stopwatch for when a puppy has grown up, or when he has learned all that he needs to know. As with children, there are differences in how individual puppies develop and mature, but you should not doubt that your input is making a positive difference.

During this period, puppies can learn basic commands if you teach them in a relaxed and cheery atmosphere. Think of this as "puppy kindergarten" and make it fun. (For more on "Puppy Classes," see page 116.)

Consider how important it is for children to enjoy and look forward to school when they first start—the same is true for teaching dogs. Make the process entertaining and satisfying and you will have an eager student for life.

For the whole first year of life, a puppy is being socialized and is maturing. If he is one of the giant breeds, he won't mature until around eighteen months, so his juvenile stage may last a lot longer.

◆ Instinct to Run Off (Four to Eight Months)

At some point during this period, most puppies develop the urge to take off. Until this stage, most puppies happily come back to their owners when they are called. Now you may be shocked to discover that your obedient little pup suddenly has wanderlust and is deaf and blind to your calls. The puppy's desire to hit the road and explore may last a few days or even as long as a month, but it is a natural part of growing up and an important part of canine development.

There is one problem, however. If your dog should get away and have a terrific time while she's out and about, that memory will stay with her a long time—and that happy memory can influence her readiness to respond to your calls to her in the future. This natural inclination to take off is something you need to be on the lookout for at this age. When you're walking her during this period, pay attention to whether she's acting differently, whether she seems oblivious to you and ready to run off. If you have any suspicions about whether she is feeling newly emboldened, put her on a long line or retractable leash until she settles back down again, whether that's in a couple of days or weeks. You do not want to let your dog take charge of the situation and run the risk of her having such a fun time being out and about in the world that she thinks twice about obeying your commands later on.

AT AROUND NINE MONTHS AGGRESSION CAN BEGIN TO DEVELOP

Between nine and twelve months may come the first sign of aggression, which develops in stages with puppies. Aggression usually emerges in a puppy after nine months and before a year, which is when sexual maturity begins, along with all the hormones that make it happen.

Then, when the dog hits eighteen months and late adolescence, there's another round of assertion, independence (which you may view as disobedience) and aggression. By about two years of age, many dogs have reached the full extent of whatever aggression they have in them, and there may be a dogfight or biting incident around this time.

You need to be on alert for the emergence of aggression if your puppy has already shown signs of being aggressive—because it takes very little time for him to go from disobedience, to growling, and then to biting. And unless you pay close attention to the signals that he gives off, you can go from a having a darling little puppy (aggression comes in all breeds and sizes) to having a tragedy on your hands.

Aggression problems do not "just happen"—they usually brew for a while, like a volcano before it erupts—so you have to know what markers to look for and how to deal with them. If you ignore the first growl or any other aggression, you can be certain it will escalate to the next level. A growl is a warning—you have to take it seriously. You can't make excuses for it or hope it was a one-time thing. A growl is the first symptom of an aggressive pattern that will inevitably escalate and have a terrible outcome if you don't nip it in the bud. But dogs will sometimes develop aggression in a tidy progression, while at other times they may show only a minor warning sign before erupting into full-blown aggression. So no matter how your dog expresses that aggression, **take it very seriously and deal with it on the spot**. For more on dealing with aggression see page 124 later in this chapter in "Puppy Misbehavior."

The bottom line is that if a puppy is born with aggression there's not much you can do about it. Some breeds have an inborn tendency toward aggression. If a puppy six months or younger growls or snaps or bites, then he's either got a strong genetic tendency or has been badly abused. Whatever the case, puppies like this often have to be euthanized because you can't safely keep them and it would not be moral to try to give them away.

Showing aggression before six months old means that the puppy has got it "in his blood," and sadly, these puppies do not have a high probability of becoming safe, reliable pets. If you have a puppy who is leaning in this direction, get a professional trainer right away because training can't start too young—even at two months of age. You have a dog who may become a dominant, assertive adult who will need obedience training to put him in his place.

Aggressive behavior and attitudes are not things that a puppy outgrows—in fact, if you don't curtail those instincts, the puppy will grow into a dog who feels free to act on aggressive impulses. A puppy has to learn that you will not tolerate any aggression by him against other dogs or smaller animals. Your puppy must be raised to understand that every human is above him in terms of "the pack." (The whole idea of viewing domestic dogs in terms of the wolf packs from which they evolved is explained in detail later in this section and in "Obedience and Other Training." Briefly, all dogs expect a leader in their pack: they will take a backseat and chill out if you take the leadership role according to the wolf modality, which is about being in charge without taking charge.)

◆ **Teen Fears**

Don't be surprised by sudden changes in your dog's reactions. The "fear of the familiar" is not an uncommon syndrome: suddenly, something the dog has seen many times seems frightening to him. Your dog may suddenly develop "teenage shyness," or what seems to be a phobia, in which he growls or barks at a new object. This is probably a result of adolescent hormones galloping through his system.

Teenage shyness can lead to fear-driven aggression in some dogs, so you need to continue his socialization education so that he can overcome a cautious, worried attitude toward new experiences.

◆ Your Reaction Matters.

The way you react to any inexplicable behavior on your dog's part has a direct effect on his developing personality. You will only serve to reinforce his bizarre fears if you are solicitous and reassuring. When the dog is acting out this new terror, your positive attention for a negative action is a reward for it. Instead, just go about things as normal. Use a pleasant, conversational tone to tell him to knock it off if he barks or whines at some familiar object. Your casual attitude neither punishes his irrational behavior nor rewards it with comfort or praise. Dog owners need to ignore the canine melodrama of puberty and look forward to the return of normalcy.

THE IMPORTANCE OF SOCIALIZATION

Early socialization of puppies—getting them exposed to as many sights and sounds as humanly possible—is fundamental to raising a well-balanced dog. A puppy who is kept isolated will miss that developmental period and may grow up fearful of strangers and the world around him.

There is also an entirely canine form of socialization that needs to take place at this tender age. Appropriate positive socialization has to happen during the window that opens at three weeks and is at its peak between twelve and sixteen weeks. It is known that between the twelfth and sixteenth week the puppy's short-term memory starts crossing over to long-term memory and the puppy begins to retain what he is taught—which makes that period the perfect time for puppy kindergarten. There are many behavioral skills that dogs can only learn from other dogs, so puppies need to hang out with others of their own kind. Meeting members of his own species is vitally important before sixteen weeks of age, because those weeks are followed by a "fear period" in dog development that interferes with adaptation and learning.

◆ Pet Store Pups

The puppies that have the most to gain from puppy classes are those purchased at pet stores, which come from wholesale brokers and breeders who raise them like livestock in puppy mills (for more on puppy mills, see page 26). A puppy raised in that environment has rarely been touched by a person, and if so, it was certainly not with the gentle care that pups need and deserve. Employees cleaning and feeding hundreds of puppies in a farm environment are neither taught nor motivated to treat the dogs any differently than they would chickens or pigs—and yet there is a delicate foundation that must be laid for the powerful relationship these puppies will one day have with people. So if the pups miss it in those vital early weeks, it has to be made up as soon as possible.

ONE TO FOUR YEARS—MATURING AND REACHING ADULTHOOD

Dogs reach maturity at different times, ranging from one year up to four years depending on their size. The smaller the dog, the sooner he enters each phase of maturity. Until dogs are four months old they all follow pretty much the same growth patterns. After that the periods of development vary slightly, with smaller dogs graduating to the next phase of development before the larger ones.

Once a dog reaches full maturity, there is a reorganization of the pecking order: during this final phase of growth the dog tries to show her identity within the pack once and for all. The way your dog reacts when she reaches full maturity will be the sum total of how you and she have handled issues and perhaps confrontations in the stages that led up to full maturity. If you have allowed a dog to reach a "high rank" during the first stage of classification (twelve to sixteen weeks), then you now face the ultimate test: any challenge between you and the dog over who will ultimately have "alpha status" can become aggressive.

The alpha figure in a wolf pack disciplines all lower-ranking individuals who try to take benefits they did not earn. If your dog acts aggressively when you challenge him and you have had him since puppyhood, his personality is a result of how you allowed him to mature. Whether or not there are confrontations between you and the dog at this juncture depends entirely on the type of dog you are dealing with and how you have responded in the past to his demands. If your dog's instinct is to be passively defensive, then when you confront him he will display total submission—or he may display silly puppy behavior.

If you have a dog who, when challenged, responds with aggression, don't think of him as being a "bad" or "difficult" dog—he is a high-ranking dog behaving in an aggressive style, protecting his turf. But if he respects you as the pack alpha figure, then you're home free. For more on how to become the alpha figure in your dog's life, see page 152.

Socialization Issues in Puppy Development

There are distinct "socialization periods" in a puppy's development that have been studied and agreed upon by most dog behaviorists and trainers. It makes your interaction with the dog so much easier if you know when these stages occur—and what takes place when they do.

THE IMPORTANCE OF PLAY ACTIVITY

Pups that are denied play activity until they are twelve weeks old can develop strange behaviors such as self-mutilation (licking until there is a sore, etc.) to relieve their tension. The further price these puppies have to pay (besides missing out on playing!) is that they learn less well, are more insecure and antisocial, are often afraid of people, noises and other animals and are reluctant to explore.

Play activity during the socialization period teaches a pup to have a soft mouth (the "inhibited bite" learned from his littermates' squeals when he bites too hard) and how to greet an unknown dog. If puppies don't play with other pups at this stage, they may become too attached to people and be fearful of other dogs.

ISOLATION CAUSES PERMANENT HARM.

A puppy that is isolated at any point during the socialization period will have an impaired learning response: his ability to learn is damaged for the rest of his life. Studies have shown actual changes in the growing brain of a puppy that is cut off from his littermates and people for even one week. Puppies should not be left alone for long periods. They should not be shut away in isolation as a form of punishment when they are developing, because it will stunt their emotional growth.

SOCIALIZATION RECOMMENDATIONS AND TIPS

• The Value of Meeting Strangers

When dogs meet people other than their owners—especially children, if there aren't any in your household—it sets a good foundation for being comfortable around humans. Puppies should meet men, women and children, as well as people of a race different from your own. Some dogs may seem "racist" because they growl or behave otherwise aggressively toward people who are different from those they've been exposed to at the breeder's or your house. A dog will do this if he has not met a wide range of people—and whatever smells or looks unfamiliar will usually bring about a negative reaction.

Even though the pup hasn't had all her vaccinations yet, you can go to a willing "dogless" friend's house—if they have a fenced backyard, so much the better—at least until she's had her second set of immunizations at nine or ten weeks.

Then, after ten weeks, you can have friends visit at your house—so much the better if they have immunized, gentle dogs and/or children (the children should be gentle ones, too—although *their* immunizations are not as relevant!). Before ten weeks there is no good reason to expose your little pup to other dogs, who, even though they themselves may be healthy and immunized, may have come into contact with ill dogs or bacteria that could compromise a very young puppy.

• New Situation Equals Treats.

Shower the dog with treats when he's faced with new people, places or things. Make all experiences fun and positive. Expose him to lots of friendly humans: give treats while waiting on lines at shops or banks, and enlist strangers to hand the treats to the dog when possible.

When at home, keep a stash of tasty dog treats somewhere near your door (inaccessible to the pooch, of course) and hand a treat to anyone who comes around—visitors, the mailman, deliverymen, service people. Ask them to hand it to the puppy so she associates a good treat with anyone who comes to your house. The puppy should sit first for the stranger before getting the treat.

• Carry a Treat Tube.

Invest in a squeeze tube for cheese or organic peanut butter and try to keep it close at hand during the socialization period. These tubes are fabulous ways to give your dog a mouthful of something heavenly when there is something threatening coming his way—a big lumbering truck, shopping cart, bicycle, skateboarders, etc. Just open the top and squeeze a small amount directly into the dog's mouth—no need to even get your hands dirty. A treat squeeze tube is an especially useful tool to help socialize a particularly jumpy, nervous, easily spooked dog. Everything is less scary when you have a mouthful of peanut butter!

NOTE: Skippy squeezable peanut butter in a tube sounds like a great quick food reward, but it is not a recommended food for dogs (it isn't all that good for kids, either). Peanuts are one of the most chemically treated crops in America: unless they are grown organically they are covered with pesticides.

Furthermore, the sugar and salt content of Skippy and other commercial brands are not good for dogs' teeth and digestive systems. They are also fattening and thus a poor choice for overweight dogs. For dogs with delicate stomachs and tendencies to diarrhea, peanut butter can act as a laxative.

◆ Borrow Children.
Find a friend who'll "loan" you a small child or two—and then give the children bits of cheese to feed the dog. Accustoming a puppy to children is one of the most important steps in socializing a pup, because, let's face it: children are everywhere. And the problem with kids is that they look, act and sound so different from adults: they are louder, faster, and higher-pitched and make unpredictable noises and motions. Some dogs have a really hard time getting used to the little humans, so the sooner they get started, the better for all concerned. However, before starting your child/dog experiments, read Chapter Fourteen on "Dogs and Children" so you are well prepared for how to keep the child(ren) safe and happy while teaching them and the dog to become friends.

◆ Make Your Own Puppy Play Group.
If you can't find any puppy classes near where you live, or you don't want to do the legwork of finding an acceptable puppy kindergarten, you have the option of creating a do-it-yourself puppy social group. Many professional breeders recognize the importance of "civilizing" their puppies, but there's no way they could take eight puppies to a class. Many of the more dedicated breeders have come up with their own versions of puppy education, and there's no reason you can't follow their lead. Come up with a plan that gives your puppy a good exposure to a variety of adults, children and other dogs.

WHAT ABOUT PUPPY SHOTS AND COMMUNICABLE ILLNESS?
The paradox is that the most critically sensitive developmental weeks in a puppy's life—when some say it is best to introduce him to places and things—are the very weeks when others recommend keeping your puppy physically isolated because he is most vulnerable to getting illnesses from other dogs.

Standard medical advice suggests that a puppy should not be exposed to other pups until two weeks after the puppy vaccine is given. The earliest that shot is given is at twelve weeks. But what becomes of a puppy who is isolated for that long at such a crucial period? How is his development stunted? Generally speaking, dogs with this isolation grow up oriented and attached to people much more than to other dogs. For most people this is an acceptable outcome, since a dog that is more responsive to them is easier to train and relate to—even if he may be awkward around other dogs, or downright antisocial to them.

Your puppy isn't fully immunized until sixteen weeks, but the critical socialization period ends around week twelve or thirteen. Some experts would tell you to keep puppies away from all other dogs and public places until their puppy shots are finished at sixteen weeks; others claim that your puppy will be emotionally stunted unless she meets lots of dogs and experiences loads of social situations by the time she reaches her sixteenth week. As noted earlier, you can never recapture that super-sensitive period; many canine behaviorists believe you need to expose the young dog to lots of experiences, protecting her health as best you can but not being so protective that she misses out on the interactions. It's a risk/reward decision you have to make for yourself, and there are suggestions later in this section on how to walk that line.

✦ What's the Worst That Can Happen, Medically Speaking?

Most of the infectious diseases that puppies are vaccinated against have fortunately become rare, or even extinct (in good part because of aggressive vaccination programs in the past). Parvovirus and distemper are two of the most common and dangerous diseases that can affect puppies: distemper has been almost entirely wiped out, and parvovirus ("parvo") doesn't occur often. Rabies is rare, and "canine infectious hepatitis" is practically unheard-of, although it can be deadly to an entire litter.

Kennel cough (also called Bordatella) is probably the most dangerous illness that's out there for all dogs, which means it can be even more serious for little puppies. It is a highly infectious airborne disease that a dog can spread by coughing or even just breathing—and it's an illness that is contagious before the carrier dog even has symptoms himself (for more on Bordatella see "Vaccinations" on page 120).

Veterinarians' waiting rooms are notorious places for the disease to spread—certainly never let a small puppy down on the floor at the vet's. Do not let him sniff or play with any other dog in there. Puppies are physically vulnerable and their immune systems are not fully up and running yet. It doesn't matter whether people tell you their dog has had vaccinations or is in good health—that dog can be carrying an infectious disease that does not bother his strong, adult constitution, but could lay your little puppy flat.

✦ So Should Your Puppy Socialize or Be a Hermit?

What is the truth? Which side of this issue is "right"—or *more* right? As with so many black-or-white controversies, both sides have a point, but the gray area is where the answer lies.

How to resolve this dilemma for yourself? How precise are those critical weeks in a puppy's emotional development? How essential is it for her to get out and about—and on the other hand, is the physical risk of mingling with other dogs that great?

Talk to your vet about it, but understand that there are doctors who may know less about the social development of dogs than they do about "disease process," so their point of view may be skewed toward the physical health considerations. This conservative approach on the part of some vets may be weighed in favor of safeguarding puppies from infectious disease, but it disregards the importance of how a dog can suffer lifelong damage from early social isolation.

For most people the answer will be moderation: don't live locked away but do be careful where you take the puppy. That doesn't just mean choosing a puppy kindergarten carefully, it means you need to think twice about taking the puppy into *any* public place where other dogs will be or have been. Avoiding heavily dog-trafficked areas like parks and sidewalks, doggie-day-care facilities and the vet's office (unless medically necessary, obviously) will go a long way toward lowering your risk.

Puppy classes, also known as "puppy kindergarten," can be an extremely positive part of your puppy's development, but the setting needs to be reliably safe and clean. Try to get recommendations from dog-oriented people like groomers, your vet, dog trainers, other dog owners and the owners of small pet stores (preferably those that only sell food, supplies and grooming services, not puppies). Unless you live in a big city, it's unlikely that you'll have a choice of more than one puppy class, but at least you can get feedback about the class(es) available in your area.

If the timing works out you can check out the puppy kindergarten when your puppy is really small or even before you get your puppy. (Why not? Don't some mothers check out preschool before their babies are even born?) If you can, visit a puppy kindergarten while a class is going on. That will tell you so much more than interviewing the owner over the phone and asking a lot of questions. Make sure that the teacher demands proper proof from all participants that their puppies have been immunized, which ensures the health of all members. When you see the participants in the class, it will be clear whether the puppies come from homes where they are kept clean, and whether the owners are the kind of people who have their pups on a dependable vaccination schedule (for more on "Vaccinations," see pages 120/296).

Puppy classes are held before the traditional age of six months, and can begin as early as twelve weeks. The point of these classes is to socialize the puppy to other youngsters. It also gets her used to the idea of being in a class with everyone doing something together. Most trainers recommend the socialization benefits of these get-togethers.

For suggestions on other considerations when picking a puppy kindergarten, refer to Chapter Ten.

Puppy Peculiarities

Hiccups
Puppies get hiccups after eating, drinking or play. No cause for alarm. (Quite normal, quite funny.)

Craziness
Puppies can go into a hypercharged energy state in which they run, jump, bark and spin as though jet-propelled. These episodes can last a few minutes and happen a few times a day. (Also quite normal—and funny!)

"Buddha Bellies"
Puppies' bellies can distend dramatically after they eat. This is not related to the dangerous bloated stomach of an adult dog suffering from "bloat" after eating. It is no cause for alarm if you notice a bulging little "Buddha Belly." (Quite normal and adorable.)

Eating Feces
Eating dog poop—their own or others—is probably the grossest thing that some puppies will do. (Quite common and revolting.) There are a few theories about why they do it—nutritional defi-

ciencies is one—but for you the main thing is not *why* they do it but *how* to stop them. The simplest way is to clean up after your dog every time he poops, even if you happen to live in the country—just the way people do in a city. This lack of poop on the ground will also save you from the odor and the flies—and save people from eventually stepping in the stuff.

The other suggested remedy is to put something in the dog's food that makes his poop unappetizing to him (you'd think it wouldn't need any help, wouldn't you?). The suggestions are to sprinkle either Adolph's Meat Tenderizer or a vet-supplied product called For-Bid on the puppy's food. These apparently make otherwise delicious-tasting poop not so tasty . . . but who are we to judge?

If you have multiple dogs and the puppy seems interested in eating any feces on your property, then all the above suggestions still apply.

Puppy Won't Go Down/Up Stairs

Puppies don't have good enough depth perception to see the individual steps—the stairs look like one long slide to them. Some puppies just figure it out, one step at a time—other pups put their front feet one step down but then don't seem to be able to figure out how to get their back feet down to join the front end—they just stretch way out across the steps.

To help your pup understand how stairs work, sit at the bottom of the stairs and put her on the first step. Clap your hands and when she jumps off, give her lots of praise. Next put her on the second step from the bottom and clap and call until she comes down the two steps to you. Then the third step up and so on, until she gets the hang of it.

If going up the stairs poses a problem for your puppy, do the same exercise in reverse.

Physical Issues in Development

TEETHING

By four months of age a puppy's sharp little teeth have been replaced by adult ones—twenty-eight puppy teeth become forty-two permanent ones.

This time can be difficult for him, because it can be painful when his adult teeth come in, and they can drive him crazy. Chewing is one way to relieve the pain and tension, so most puppies want to chew nonstop to feel better. To ensure that he has lots of "legal" options, see page 459 for suggestions on chew toys and teething toys.

There can be problems with teeth, such as baby teeth being retained after the adult teeth come in—the new teeth erupt but the baby teeth do not fall out. This can cause problems like infection, misalignment of the permanent teeth or problems with jaw development.

You need to check your puppy's mouth regularly while the new teeth are coming in. If you see a double row of teeth—it is easiest to see this in the front teeth—or anything that looks fishy to you, have your vet check it out. Retained baby teeth have to be surgically removed, as they do with people.

THE PUPPY'S COAT

Even by the seventh or eighth month the puppy's fur has not fully grown in, so if you live in a cold climate you might want to protect him with dog clothing of some kind. He's still a growing baby: dry the puppy off when he gets wet so he doesn't get a chill.

The exception to this is breeds similar to Siberian Huskies, Alaskan Malamutes and Samoyeds, whose fur is fully developed at an early age. This is probably because in their native environments these breeds were subjected to below-freezing temperatures before their first birthday. In the summer, don't clip these thick-furred breeds, which have double coats. Just as it functions against the cold, their long hair provides insulation against the heat.

Puppy Vet Visits

No matter where you got your puppy—from a friend, a breeder, a rescue or a shelter—you should visit the vet who will be your puppy's doctor within *a couple of days* of bringing that puppy home. It doesn't matter whether this puppy was just seen by a vet connected with the puppy's origins—you still need the seal of approval from your own vet, who is an objective third party.

In the vast majority of cases, this visit is going to be a quick, pleasant outing, but in the event that there may be something wrong with your puppy, it's important for both of you to find this out right away while you can be objective—before you have grown attached—and can think clearly about what options you have. I once had to give back to the breeder within days a gorgeous little Rottweiler puppy who leaked pee, because I couldn't face the expense, uncertainty of outcome and pain of major surgery for an eight-week-old puppy.

Another reason to bring the puppy in to your vet for a checkup is for her to have a positive early experience with the doctor, who also gets to know her—and you—a little bit. Most vets understand the importance of this first visit, because they know it sets the tone for the friendly, trusting relationship they hope to have with your pup during a long, healthy lifetime.

If the puppy acts frightened or aggressive at the vet's, don't make excuses for him or try to soothe him. Patting or "cooing" to a dog translates to him as reinforcement of the very behavior you want him to stop. Be upbeat and matter-of-fact in the way you handle and talk to your puppy from the moment you go into the vet. Don't allow your own apprehensions about going to the vet—or your projected fears on the puppy's behalf—diminish the calm confidence you should be showing your dog.

WHAT HAPPENS AT THE FIRST VET VISIT?

Before you go, ask whether the vet offers a "puppy plan" or some "wellness package." With this, all the shots, exams and worming needed for a pup are typically covered by one fee.

The vet's office will probably tell you to bring two things with you:

❏ A record of whatever inoculations the pup has already had
❏ A fresh stool sample

(To get the stool sample, just take a plastic baggie, turn it inside out and put your hand inside it. Then, when the puppy has moved her bowels, pick up her offering with your hand protected by the plastic bag, turn it right side out again, and seal it. There is no need to refrigerate or otherwise conserve it—but it should be taken on the day of the appointment for the best chance of finding parasites like worms, if there are any.)

You should bring these two items even if they forget to remind you.

◆ The Dangers of the Waiting Room

You should be cautious about where your puppy walks and sniffs when he is still very young and doesn't yet have his full immunity against disease. This means he shouldn't walk into the vet's office, where there has been a steady flow of sick dogs. Carry him. Do not let him interact with any other dogs, especially other young ones who have also not finished their full set of inoculations against disease. This ban against interaction means *especially* not touching noses.

Don't put your puppy on the table in the examination room until you are sure it has been wiped down with disinfectant. Puppies are vulnerable to many diseases and are easy hosts for parasites—don't take this lightly. We Americans are so accustomed to dogs being vaccinated that most of us haven't had the occasion to see the misery and often death that a common disease like distemper can wreak on an unsuspecting little puppy.

🦴 *What Happens at the First Vet Visit*

- Weigh puppy (for a base weight to compare to over time).
- Listen to heart and lungs for pulse and breathing rate and heart or lung abnormalities.
- Feel puppy's belly to check internal organs.
- Take temperature—normal is 100°F to 102.5°F. (Ask the vet to show you how to use a rectal thermometer, so you can do this if your puppy is ever feeling under the weather.)
- Check male's testicles to be sure two testicles are present and descended; in any case, discuss when/if neutering is planned (see "Neutering," page 391).
- Check female's genitals for discharge or other signs of infection.
- Check skin, eyes, ears, anal region for normalcy and good health.
- Check mouth for signs that teeth and gums are healthy.
- Vaccinate depending on what puppy has already received (see page 120).
- Start heartworm preventive tablets (see page 121 about need to pretest; also see page 121 for the new concerns about the dangers of injectable heartworm medication.)

◆ **Vaccinations/Inoculations**

Vaccinations against common diseases are usually given in combinations of at least three and as many as five at two- to four-week intervals.

Canine distemper can be passed simply by sniffing an infected animal's urine. Parvovirus is passed in other dogs' stool. However, active immunity to these diseases does not develop until about twelve weeks of age. Until that time, your puppy should not be exposed to other dogs.

Puppy shots usually begin at six weeks, and the boosters follow every few weeks. These vaccines are intended to protect against six diseases, based in part on where you live and what your vet recommends.

As with any immunization—such as those given to children—they contain weakened doses of the actual diseases they protect against. This stimulates the puppy's immune system to create antibodies against that illness, so that if he's exposed to the disease, his immune system will recognize and destroy it.

The rabies vaccination isn't given until sixteen weeks of age (see page 122).

Born with immunity When puppies are drinking their mother's milk, they're protected against the diseases to which she has immunity (just like with people and breast-feeding babies). However, since this protection declines in the first few weeks of a puppy's life, the shots to pick up where the mother's milk left off are given over several weeks.

If your puppy came from a breeder, they'll often give the whole litter their first series of shots. However, many vets will repeat a vaccination given by a breeder in case the vaccine was given when the puppy was too young (in which case it won't work) or wasn't handled properly (not kept consistently cold, the expiration date wasn't carefully watched, etc.). For example, one of the Bedlington Terriers I had while growing up came down with distemper when he was about ten weeks old; the only explanation was that the vaccine given by the breeder was ineffectual. Falstaff survived, by the way—after days spent in a hot, steamy bathroom to help him breathe—but he never matured properly.

Is there danger in clustering inoculations? There is common experience and anecdotes that suggest some dogs may be in jeopardy if they are given all their shots at one time. Some breed advocates have said for a long time that their breed (for example, Weimaraners) can be sickened or even killed by having all their vaccinations at one time. Most vets are accustomed to giving the puppy vaccinations in a combined cluster, but there are also doctors who are open to the idea of spreading out the vaccinations. This requires more visits to your vet, but it may save your pet's life if he has a bad reaction from receiving the usual dosage of several immunizations all at one time.

If you do choose to separate the inoculations by a few weeks, most vets will not require you to pay for a separate visit each time. To save you money and keep the vet's schedule clear for other patients, when it is time for another inoculation you can bring your dog to the vet without an appointment and do what is called a "pass back"—a technician takes the puppy back into the treatment area and a vet, vet tech or nurse gives the next injection in the sequence.

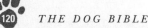

◆ Internal Parasites (Worms)

Puppies are born with worms—an unappealing thought, but that's the way it is! The worms that puppies are born with are roundworms (ascarids), although there are other intestinal parasites that can infest puppies: hookworms, whipworms, tapeworms and single-celled parasites called *coccidia* and *giardia*. Puppies should be wormed at birth and every two weeks after that, until stool samples show there are no more parasites.

Intestinal parasites must be eliminated because they can weaken young animals and stunt their growth. They can also be passed to humans from the puppies, especially to children. The best insurance you have is to remind everyone around a young puppy to wash their hands after having contact with her—especially after picking up dog droppings.

How to know what parasites your puppy has You cannot know what worms may be in your puppy's gut without having a stool sample examined by your veterinarian's office. Bring a stool sample to his first vet visit. Based on what is found, your puppy will receive the necessary treatment.

How do you rid the puppy of worms? Worming medication—which usually consists of a pill or pills—is something that only a vet should give, because it must be specific to the worms that are there. Some intestinal parasites can be treated only by a prescription medication. There are also over-the-counter worming medications, but you wouldn't want to do that because the product may be aimed at a variety of parasite(s) that your puppy doesn't have—and therefore would not eliminate the parasites that the puppy *does* have.

Heartworms are internal parasites that are much better to prevent than to try to treat. It didn't used to be treatable once a dog was infested, but medical advances have now made it more feasible to eliminate the worm.

This sickness is carried by mosquitoes that pass it to the dog when they bite her. True to its name, the worm can literally get into the heart and kill the animal. However, there are no early symptoms, so you wouldn't know the dog was infected until it was too late. There are monthly tablets and biyearly tablets—Heartgard is one such brand—that your veterinarian can sell you to protect against this illness. However, there is a newer injectable medication called ProHeart 6, which is given twice a year but that has caused serious (sometimes fatal) reactions in dogs. Many vets have stopped prescribing this treatment—or never even offered it—because of the adverse reactions.

Your puppy is safe for a while if his mother was on a heartworm preventive medication when she was pregnant, which any responsible breeder would have made certain she was.

You can consider having your puppy take preventive medication at the time of his first vet visit, but only after discussing it with your vet and careful consideration. You don't have to worry about your dog having this illness or protecting against it if you live in an area where there are no mosquitoes (or climate conditions that could attract them).

THREE WARNINGS ABOUT HEARTWORM MEDICATION

1. The dog needs a blood test before taking the tablets to be sure that no infection has occurred—UNLESS the puppy's mother was on preventive medicine and the puppy

was started on the medication by twelve weeks of age. Taking the tablet can kill a dog that has already been infected.

2. Once you start the dog on medication, you have to give it every month, even during periods when there is no possibility of mosquito activity. If you do stop, you'll have to have the dog blood-tested before starting the medication again, so it's easier on you and the dog to just get in the habit of taking the pill year-round if the dog will encounter mosquitoes at any point.

3. Avoid the injectable medication until it is proven safe.

◆ Rabies Vaccine

The rabies vaccine protects you *and* your puppy (or dog as she gets older) against this deadly disease. Rabies is fatal to humans and dogs once symptoms of the disease appear (interestingly, it may be a year before a person who has been exposed shows such symptoms). It is in our best interest to make sure that all dogs are vaccinated, which is why rabies vaccinations are required by law. If an infected animal bites an unvaccinated dog, she will get the disease—and she will die from the rabies if she isn't treated before symptoms appear.

It's unlikely that people would get close enough to the wild animals that pose the greatest threat of rabies (including skunks, raccoons and bats) to be bitten by them. But our pets can get mixed up with any of these carrier animals and get bitten—and then pass the rabies on to humans.

General Puppy Training Advice

THINGS TO DO WHILE GETTING TO KNOW YOUR PUPPY

Don't start off the relationship by being tough and critical. Harsh discipline has no place here; you're a teacher, not a cop. The pup has to feel he is a member of the family.

Affection first, rules later. Establish a loving bond, and trust will come from the sense of security he gets.

◆ Sound Levels

Keep your tone of voice soft, soothing and calming. When the puppy first comes home keep the lights low; keep the noise level low, too—no high-pitched, screechy excitement about the dog from children or adults following the puppy's arrival. A high-pitched tone of voice is arousing. Using a high, falsetto voice will get the puppy's attention, but right now you don't want to rev him up.

◆ Cuddle the Puppy.

All puppies like physical contact and stimulation, so hold, rub and scratch them. Physical contact is important to convey to the puppy how you feel about him.

◆ Handling, Grooming
If you have a pup that loves to be stroked, brushed, etc, just keep it coming. If anything happens that makes her resist, give her lots of treats while slowly continuing the handling.

Common areas of sensitivity include the ears, mouth, neck, hindquarters, tail and feet. Desensitize her to such areas by going slowly, giving praise for her cooperation with verbal encouragement and delicious bits of cheese. If feet are a problem, for example, then at the point on her leg where she gets nervous as you approach, give her the cheese (or chicken). Keep touching that place and giving treats until she is okay with it. Then make your way down the leg—stopping when she gets nervous and giving her mega-treats until she's relaxed and you can keep heading south.

◆ Many Small Training Moments
You can train a puppy by asking for a response in ordinary situations many times a day. This method of getting the idea across and making good behavior an ingrained habit is more pleasurable and effective than drilling it in with practice sessions.

◆ Expect the Puppy to Do Most Things Wrong in the Beginning.
Don't adopt the attitude that you can never let a puppy "get away" with anything, when all he's doing is just trying to figure out what you want.

◆ Make a Rule, Stick to Your Guns.
Consistency is vital to a well-raised puppy. Don't let the puppy get away with a forbidden behavior because you're tired or in a rush, or because right now it doesn't seem so important.

You cannot allow something like paws on the counter one day and then get furious the following day when the pup does it again.

Everyone who comes into contact with the puppy needs to follow those same rules—for example, you can't have some family members or friends allowing the dog to jump up, because it undermines whatever rules you have laid down.

Praise profusely when the puppy does anything right, especially something new that he might not have fully understood. Your praise helps reinforce the behavior.

◆ Sit.
A puppy should be expected to sit before dinner or any treat and before getting groomed or patted. Sit should be the "please" and "thank you" that people work so hard to drill into their children—which makes polite kids so pleasant to be around.

Sitting before any greeting is really a helpful habit, because it means the dog is not in a position to jump and accidentally scratch with his claws.

◆ Go to Your Bed.
A puppy should be pleasantly sent to a bed that is near the door or near the dining table, and then praised generously and quite quickly released with an "Okay!" This makes it enjoyable to

"go to your bed"—it's almost like a game the puppy is learning while developing a quick response to being told to chill out and back off.

Anything you let the puppy get away with she will continue to do when she is full-grown. You have to ask yourself: how cute will it be then? Letting a puppy get away with murder means you are setting the stage for an adult dog who is constantly being yanked and yelled at and made to feel like a delinquent. It's much harder to undo bad habits than to go out of your way to avoid forming them early on.

THINGS NEVER TO DO TO A PUPPY

◆ Never Yell at a Puppy for Making a Mistake.

"Learning" means you are *in the process* of learning something. Being harshly and loudly reprimanded can drive it right out of your head.

◆ No Corporal Punishment

Never hit a puppy—with your hand, a rolled newspaper or anything else. This used to be the accepted way of training a dog, but it harks back to the not-so-distant past when the physical abuse of wives and children by their spouses and teachers was commonly accepted. "Spare the rod and spoil the child" was engraved on many a school paddle—and dogs were trained with similar harsh attitudes, with pronged choke collars and objects used to strike a dog. Physical punishment of wives and children is no longer tolerated in the modern world, and we're finally catching up in the animal world, too. It would be hard to find an animal behaviorist today who would justify the old-fashioned barbaric custom of hitting a puppy to "teach it a lesson."

CURES FOR COMMON PUPPY MISBEHAVIOR

◆ Preventing Puppy Aggressiveness

(Note: the following comments refer to puppies only. Aggression issues with grown dogs are best handled by an experienced trainer.)

Neuter your puppy. The most frequent dogfights happen to young, intact (which means not neutered) males. Simple solution: neuter your dog at six months of age. If he is exhibiting numerous incidents of aggressive or dominant behavior, talk to your vet about neutering the puppy even earlier. See page 394 about "neutering" to learn about the hormonal odor that an intact dog gives off that can incite fighting.

All humans are above the puppy. Explain to everyone in your family (or anyone who spends a lot of time in your house) that they have to take a superior position to the dog—something as simple as all people in the household asking the dog to sit before any treat or meal, or even just requesting a sit and then giving the dog generous praise as a reward.

Humans control all the food. Your puppy has to learn this. Get the puppy used to activity near his food dish by having the adults add a handful of dry food to the puppy's bowl as he is eating. Move slowly, and make sure he sees you coming. The idea isn't to startle him, it's for the puppy to learn to tolerate activity near his bowl. Once the adults have done this without incident and the puppy is clearly unthreatened, allow the child(ren) in the family to add a handful of kibble to the pup's bowl.

Give a toy to the dog, then take it away, then give it back. The point of this is to create another area in the dog's head in which humans rule. You can go a step further and teach the dog to give the toy to you, rather than you taking it back. Put your open palm under his mouth and say "Out" or "Let go" or "Give." As soon as he starts to relax his hold on the toy, encourage him verbally ("Good boy" or "That's it") and give him lots of praise.

Do not play rough with the puppy. Avoid all games that get a puppy roughed up or riled up—no tug-of-war, keep-away or monkey-in-the-middle. Also avoid any version of those games that could encourage an aggressive reaction from the puppy. Don't let children wrestle or tumble around with him on the ground. Instead, choose games like hide-and-seek or find-and-fetch (see games, page 160).

Do not let the pup play rough with you. No biting—not ever, not at all. Be consistent. Don't let the puppy chew on your fingers or anywhere else on you. Correct the chewing with a deep, growly "Nooo," and then immediately give the puppy a toy that he *is* allowed to chew on.

Growling is never acceptable. It has to be stopped from the first noise in a puppy's throat. You need to cut that right off by using a deep, stern voice to react to any deep-throated protest or commentary by the dog.

◆ Begging (See the Section in the "Problems" Chapter (page 588) for More on Begging.)

The basic idea is that people create begging dogs, and if you start it when she is a puppy, you'll have set her on the wrong course yourself and encouraged a dog to stare at you—hovering and panting at your feet while you eat. As with everything concerning a puppy, habits learned early will make both of your lives easy for a lifetime.

Do not feed tidbits from your hand at the table. Dropping bits of food on the floor is the exact same thing, so don't kid yourself.

You can put the puppy in her crate or tether her to a bed near the table and give her a nice chew toy. As soon as the meal is finished, you can release her and put a small bite of something down on the floor in the kitchen as a reward for being quiet and patient during your meal. This was a plan I stumbled on thanks to my habit of letting my dogs lick the dinner plates before putting them (the plates, that is) in the dishwasher. I discovered that the dogs went right to their beds or chewed a toy during our meal, in part because they knew that there was something in it for them at the end.

◆ Chewing Shoes, Furniture, etc.

Give the puppy something to put in his mouth to replace whatever item you find yourself rescuing. Think of it as a barter system—you relinquish my shoe and I replace it with a plastic squeaky-toy lamb chop. It is crucial that when the puppy releases your property and takes the bartered item in its place, you praise the dickens out of him for doing so.

♦ Start Gently with Corrections.

Use a lower-impact correction first, give it a chance to sink in and then move to a stronger correction. A simple verbal "no" may interrupt the puppy enough that you can steer him away from the unwanted behavior. You don't want to raise your voice or clap your hands or whatever you might do to loudly get his attention if softly calling his name is effective.

If the puppy begins to go for the undesirable action again, keep your voice low (reminiscent of his mother's growl) and make a short, sharp "Anh!" sound (like the first half of "uh-uh"—as if to say, "Oh, no you don't."). It's amazing how effective this sound can be: all you have to do is make the sound and he will look up at you. By doing so, he has stopped doing or trying to do the forbidden act, and now you can praise him up and down, or perhaps give him something else to chew or chase instead.

The secret squirt Fill a squirt gun or squirt bottle with water and a splash of something unpleasant like lemon juice or vinegar, and keep it handy. Try just plain water if you want first, which works fine without "additives" for most dogs.

When the dog is doing something you don't want, say "No" firmly but unemotionally and give him a good squirt in the face. Hold the bottle next to your side so the puppy will not see where the stinging water is coming from. Let the squirt do the work. Just go on about your business as if you know nothing about it.

Time-Out Just as with children who misbehave, it is acceptable to try a "time-out" to reinforce the point you are teaching. However, there are three caveats here:

- ❏ You cannot reinforce a rule that the puppy does not yet understand or remember.
- ❏ You should not shut a puppy into a space behind a closed door. Being shut out of sight causes many puppies to panic. It can be frightening and confusing, and is equivalent to locking a child in a closet to reprimand him. A puppy needs to be confined behind a safety gate or in a crate where he can see where you are, or else, in the throes of a panic attack, he may hurt himself or scratch and bite at the door or other objects, etc.
- ❏ You should not shove your puppy into his crate as though it is jail—whenever he goes into his crate it has to be a neutral place. So if you place him there, make it a firm but gentle placement, because you don't want a puppy to ever have a negative impression of the crate itself, which is his den and needs to always be a safe place for him regardless of why he's in it.

Chapter 6

UNDERSTANDING YOUR DOG

Considering how deeply dogs and people become attached to one another, it's surprising how many people often don't know what is going on in their dog's head. People frequently make assumptions and judgments about their dogs' actions based on human behavior, which really has no application in the canine experience of life.

This point in *The Dog Bible* is as good a time as any to get a dog's perspective of the world. The better you understand dogs in general, the better you can read your own dog's behavior and reactions. You can learn to pick up clues about what she's thinking and even what she is planning on doing.

This chapter should help explain all dogs—from a physical and a mental perspective—so you'll have realistic expectations of what a dog is capable of doing and where his limitations lie. If you have a dog who is in some way a difficult or complicated individual, then the more you can understand the whole species, the better time you will have together. Knowing what dogs are all about can help you function as a better buffer or interpreter between your dog and the outside world.

SOME OF THE TOPICS COVERED IN THIS CHAPTER INCLUDE:

- ❑ The dog's senses—sight, hearing, smell and taste
- ❑ Relationships between and among dogs, including play and aggression
- ❑ Charts on dominant traits and submissive traits in body language
- ❑ Dog body language—the dog's state of mind as revealed by every part of his body: torso, ears, tail, facial expression, even the hair on the back of his neck
- ❑ Dog vocal communication, including sounds dogs can make and in what situations they use them

❑ Dog stress, with charts of factors contributing to stress, signs of stress in a dog and a section on ways to give relief to the dog

❑ Why do dogs do that?—a look at some of the weird (to us) things that dogs do or eat or react to, and what causes this behavior

The Dog's Senses

SIGHT

A dog is ten times more sensitive to peripheral movement than we are. He picks up movement on either side of him better than we ever could, in part because most dogs' eyes are closer to the sides of their heads than ours are. A dog's vision is poor up close, but he can see quite well at a distance.

◆ Anatomy of the Eye

The dog's eye is different from ours. Our eyes are better at defining detail in bright light. The dog's eye has a reflective layer that intensifies light and helps the dog (as it did his predecessor, the wolf) to see more when he needs it most: for hunting at dawn and dusk. At night, when you see a car's headlights reflect brightly off a dog's eyes, what you are seeing is that reflective layer. Dogs can see in low light but they cannot see in the dark—they do not have the mechanisms that a cat does to allow that.

Dogs see in black and white when there is low light, but when it is brighter they do see some color.

◆ Sight Hounds

Some dogs have very good eyesight because the work for which they were originally intended required great vision. Many retrievers and the so-called sight hounds—for example Salukis and their descendants like Afghan Hounds, Borzois and Greyhounds—have amazing vision. These dogs have frontally placed eyes, as people do.

Many terriers have slanted eyes—they're physically frontal, but the slant allows them to see around corners.

Guardian dogs like German Shepherds and Akitas have more laterally placed eyes.

There are also many breeds that depend much more on their sense of smell and even on their hearing, so their vision is unremarkable.

◆ Blindness

"Progressive retinal atrophy" is an inherited blindness that can strike dogs in breeds that are at risk for it. There are times when people think an otherwise healthy dog is going blind because they notice that she cannot see a toy "right in front of her." However, the inability to see something "right in front of her nose" is not a cause for concern, because due to where a dog's eye is placed on her head, the toughest place to see anything is directly in front.

HEARING

Dogs' hearing is more acute than ours. They can hear high-pitched noises that are inaudible to us—this may have allowed their wolf ancestors to pick up the high-pitched squeaks of small mammals such as mice. However, their hearing ranges over eight and a half octaves, just like ours, while a cat can hear more than ten octaves.

It is the *pitch* that dogs are able to discriminate that makes their hearing abilities seem so impressive, which also explains how they are able to pick out the sound of their mistress' car engine as it approaches home. More of the dog's brain is devoted to sound than ours—plus they have mobile ears that scan and then collect the sound waves.

A dog's acute hearing explains why a sudden loud noise can be upsetting to him, although as with everything in the dog world, these are individual issues. Some dogs hate the suddenness of noise and others cannot stand loudness—and yet there are plenty of dogs who seem oblivious to a racket. For example, it isn't clear why some individual dogs become terrorized by the sound of gunfire or thunder, while others don't even raise their heads although they have perfectly good hearing. It may be that hunting dogs from breeds originally raised to accompany men with guns may be somewhat genetically desensitized to the loud cracking report of a gun.

SENSE OF SMELL

Dogs are among several animals that have an extra organ in the nasal cavity called the *Jacobson's organ*. These animals can literally smell the air—which is why you often see a dog tip his nose up into the air and see his nose twitching to "read" the smells wafting on the breeze. What the dog is actually doing has been described not so much as smelling the air but "tasting" it. This is a concept that is hard for creatures like us to really understand, since we're so limited in the olfactory department.

The dog's nose has sensory tissue that is directly exposed to the world around her. It is made up of three different kinds of cells, one of which is the sensory receptor. There are tiny, hair-like "cilia" on those cells that pick up the chemicals that make up a smell. The amount of cilia per cell is connected to the acuteness of an animal's sense of smell.

A comparison of the cilia in a dog vs. that in the human nose shows that people have six to eight cilia per cell, while dogs have 100 to 150.

Sensitivity to odors is partly inherited and can be increased by selective breeding and training. Examples of this selection for "great noses" are the Beagles that sniff at airports for contraband, and the Bloodhounds that are used to track criminals and lost people.

"Air-scenters" include dogs like Collies, which run along a scent trail in the air, weaving back and forth with their heads held high. They circle when they lose the scent and go in widening circles until they pick it up again.

SENSE OF TASTE

People have a more refined sense of taste than dogs do, which seems contradictory when you consider that their sense of smell is so much more powerful and complex than ours. Humans have about 9,000 taste buds on their tongues—dogs have less than twenty-five percent of that.

Dogs do register salt, sugar, sweet and sour, but these do not register as they do in people. The odor of food is what first attracts a dog, but after she starts eating, the smell has no effect on her more limited sense of taste. Lab tests on dog's taste preferences have shown some surprising results:

DOGS' TASTE PREFERENCES

- ❏ Canned meat over fresh
- ❏ Cooked meat over raw
- ❏ Meat over cereal
- ❏ Warm food over cold

◆ Water Flavor

Dogs have additional primary taste receptors that respond to water (cats and pigs have these, too). So if you've noticed your dog being picky about the water in his bowl, it may be that his "water sensor" is on the job. It is thought that dogs may actually be able to taste the differences between types of water from different sources or from different receptacles. Not much is known about this sensitivity, and it's not really feasible to set up a test to determine levels of sensitivity, since each dog has varying degrees of sensitivity and might very well not show a measurable response to the differences that he tastes.

Relationships between and among Dogs

PACK BEHAVIOR

All dogs originate from one standard blueprint: a single species from northern Europe that lived more than 10,000 years ago. All the evidence indicates that the domestic dog originally descended from the wolf. Wolves are pack animals that live in a strong social structure with a clear hierarchy; understanding wolf-pack behavior helps us understand what makes our dogs tick. This inborn drive to be a social pack animal is what makes it natural for a dog to fit right into a human family—provided that the leadership chain is clear.

All breeds of domestic dog have brains that are approximately the same size, so they have more in common than their physical differences would make it appear. Therefore, the difference between a huge hairy Newfoundland and a tiny hairless Chihuahua is mainly the outside packaging. This means that no matter what kind of dog—or mixture of dog breeds—you have, once you understand the concepts of wolf packs and how they work, you will have the necessary information about your own dog.

◆ How a Pack Functions

Dogs expect to live within a pack; it's where and how they're comfortable. A pack has a hierarchy: the dominant dog is the pack leader, there is a number-two member, then a number-three and so on. Dogs feel safe and comfortable with a clearly established pecking order. Knowing exactly where he stands in relationship to the other pack members makes a dog feel secure. Every dog does not have the desire to be on top, but he does need to know who falls where on that family ladder.

◆ General Pack Rules

The rules in a pack are generally easy to understand, but it can get confusing for our dogs, who live in a "mixed-species" pack (them and us). Since we are the superior species (at least intellectually), we need to take responsibility for seeing things from the dog's quite different perspective. Deference to an alpha male is a basic foundation of pack life; that is a role that the human leader *must* take to ensure a harmonious living situation with dogs. But more on that later.

If you ever feel frustrated or confused by your dog, keep in mind that a pack animal has joined your household: she is operating on a different set of rules and assumptions than you are. A dog can only understand canine rules and values about what matters and what is acceptable conduct. We make a fundamental error if we assume that a dog is capable of comprehending our way of thinking and our human value system. If we can get away from that people-centered view—and the burden it places on our companions—life will be simpler for dogs and their people.

SOME PACK ACTIVITIES

- ❏ Sleeping together
- ❏ Eating together
- ❏ Walking, running and investigating together
- ❏ Sitting or lying together
- ❏ Barking or howling together
- ❏ Mutual grooming, licking
- ❏ Hunting, digging, stalking together

◆ People Are Evaluated, Too.

A dog will test any new human who enters the family circle to see where that person fits in the hierarchy; some dogs may test or challenge your guests or friends. You may think your dog is just being an annoyance when he checks out new people, but he is really just doing what his brain is programmed to do: place everyone up or down on the ladder.

If there are multiple humans in a dog's home life, he will try to sort out the dominance issues there, too—and he may test the human(s) beneath the leader to determine where they fit. It is important that you make it clear to the dog that *all* humans are higher on the scale than he is— and that includes children (more on them in the "Dogs and Children" chapter).

THE SOCIAL HIERARCHY IN A DOG PACK

Social rank works very simply: a dog respects, obeys and follows those above him—and has pretty much the opposite attitude toward those beneath his rank. In dog terms, dominance can surface over food, toys, the most desirable bed and even closeness to favorite people.

✦ Dominant or Submissive?

Social standing and status among dogs is often misinterpreted by people as a dominance struggle, as though this is something negative or destructive. We worry about dogs being dominant and equate it with aggressiveness, which we also deem negative. We think that jockeying for position is somehow a potential problem, when in fact, based on their wolf origins, it is quite natural and necessary for dogs to clarify their pecking order.

Nearly ninety percent of what dogs do is connected to their wolf heritage. An essential component of that hardwiring concerns rank within the pack. When two dogs meet for the first time, there are two types of signals they can display: dominance or submission. Dominance and submission are not good or bad. There is no value attached to either behavior, which can be hard for humans to understand. They are the only two ways of acting and/or reacting, nothing more.

However, a dog cannot be dominant in a vacuum: he can only be dominant vis-à-vis another dog, and that dog must display submissiveness, accepting the dominant dog's claim to higher rank.

You can learn to read a dog's personality and frame of mind by understanding her body signals.

Going back to wolf origins, dominance is a behavioral trait that ensures the survival of an individual. There are two ways in which dominance is expressed: one is competition over resources (also called "possessiveness") and the other is self-protection. Self-protection can mean a response to gestures that the dog finds threatening—actions that invade the dog's personal space, such as bending over or reaching out to pat his head, which you (or a dog more submissive by nature) would never think of as a threat.

✦ The Alpha

Every pack needs a leader, referred to as the "alpha," who leads and rules the pack—but he does not accomplish this through constant aggression or displays of power. His position of authority is upheld by the constant displays of deference shown to him by the others.

Rank is about who gets what privileges. However, this is not an across-the-board ranking. In a multi-dog household, for example, the dominant dog gets to decide how he wants things vis-à-vis the other dog(s) (see the section on "Multi-dog Households" on page 624). No individual is king forever, nor does every issue have equal importance. So while the alpha dog may eat first, another dog gets the bed he chooses. Either of the two (or another dog if you have more than two) will go out the door first. Not everything has equal importance, and certainly none of it fits into our human way of thinking.

Dogs are not comfortable in a leaderless situation: they want a leader to please. Whether you have more than one dog or it's just you and a dog, *you* need to assume the position of pack leader. If you don't take that role, the dog will be genetically driven to fill the space.

✦ Pack Rules: the Privileges of Rank

While all members of the pack can read and display the same body postures and signals, if a lower-ranking individual tries to take a privilege reserved for the higher-ups, order is restored with a gesture from the alpha dog. That gesture can be as small as a curled lip or a withering glare.

The rest of the pack constantly shows deference to the alpha in many small ways: the subordinates keep a low head carriage and avoid eye contact, and they allow the alpha to go first through doorways. Food is important as a means of maintaining the social order, and the alpha figure has first pick of what he wants.

DOMINANCE IN ACTIVITIES
(See also "Dog Meeting Dog" section for more on dominance issues.)

There are a number of dog behaviors that are directly related to the issues of dominance and submission. These concepts are not necessarily logical to the human way of thinking, but we need to understand them because these actions directly affect how dogs interact with each other.

✦ Mounting Another Dog
When a dog mounts another dog, he often makes a thrusting motion that appears sexual to the human eye, but mounting is actually a sign of dominance over the other dog.

✦ Going through Narrow Openings
If a higher-ranked dog occupies a doorway, lower-ranked canines don't approach until the passageway is clear.

✦ Putting Paws on Another Dog's Shoulder
This is considered a pretty intense challenge to another dog. If a younger puppy were to try this, he would probably be pinned to the ground or growled off by his elders; if the dog doing it is no longer a pup, then he'd better be ready to back up his overt challenge.

✦ Dog Rolling Over, Belly in the Air
This is a sign of submission. If your dog does this to other dogs, he is showing that he is beneath them, that he is not a challenge, that he is even afraid of them. (When a dog puts his belly in the air for a *human,* it can be out of submissiveness or apprehension—or just because he's hoping to get his belly rubbed!)

THE UNDERDOG IN A MULTIPLE-DOG HOUSEHOLD
(See also Chapter Nine, "House-training")

If you have more than one dog in your family, don't make the mistake of thinking you are supposed to be judge and jury. The dogs will sort things out by themselves. In fact they MUST sort them out their way, or there will be lingering resentments and issues that can escalate into serious fighting in which the dogs may get injured.

Squabbles and spats arise among dogs. Generally speaking, our sense of fair play and fair fighting does not apply to the dog mentality—dogs always have an alpha. Naturally, there is also a low man on the totem pole. This is the way dogs perceive the world, so you'll be doing yourself and your dog a big favor by remembering to factor it into your understanding of him.

◆ **People Need to Stay Out of It.**

It is part of being human to root for the underdog, to protect the weakest link. A dog does not mind being lower on the ranking scale—each dog needs to know what her standing is within the context of your family. Don't try to protect the dog that's relegated to the bottom rung by the other dog(s). It can cause deathly fights between dogs if we try to alter the balance that has evolved naturally among them.

◆ **Support the Alpha Dog.**

The *people* in the household need to support and reinforce the position of the alpha dog, just as the other dogs do. The top dog gets patted first, fed first, given first and best choices of toys, beds, etc. This may not appeal to your sense of fair play, but it is about the dogs' perceptions. Call it sibling rivalry, but you have to support the decision of the pack as to which of them is the alpha. If you aren't sure which dog has been anointed leader, then just watch which dog is allowed to go to the food bowl first . . . to push in for your affection first . . . to exit the house or enter the car first. . . .

◆ **Meddling Can Cause Serious Damage.**

Even if you wanted to play God and rearrange the hierarchy that has evolved naturally on canine terms, no self-respecting alpha dog is going to accept your attempt. All you'll do is stir up resentment from the alpha and confusion from the other dog(s) before they revert to the order they had developed on their own.

If, for example, you reprimand the alpha dog for putting a lower-ranking dog in her place, you are upsetting the natural order of things. Your intervention will create a grudge, a wrong that must be righted. This can wind up setting in motion a bloody fight, when as little as a curled lip from the alpha dog could have made it all crystal clear, and they could have all lived in peaceful harmony.

Dog Body Language

All dogs, regardless of their breed or size, will go through and display the same development patterns as their distant wolf ancestors, even though our breeding has emphasized some characteristics as being more desirable in their breeds.

The body posture of dogs and wolves is nearly identical. We can read obvious signals of fear, aggression, pleasure and submission, but we're not often aware of the more subtle dog-to-dog signals. Dogs display their rank in the pack through their body carriage. They also establish their standing in the way they hold their heads, bodies and tails. In fact, dogs show their state of mind through the position of every part of their bodies: ears, tail, facial expression and hair.

DECIPHERING BODY LANGUAGE

A dog's emotional state can usually be figured out with the clues outlined below . . . *but not always.*

Some breeds are easier to read and understand, while other breeds can be considered unreliable or even dangerous because they do not signal their intentions with the same body language.

This is true of Rottweilers, for example, which generally don't signal with their bodies when they have a change in mood or intention.

What complicates our understanding is that with the wide variety of dog breeds, the happy, low-tail wag of a Golden may seem the same as the high-tail carriage and tip-of-the-tail wagging of the German Shepherd. So if you live with a Golden who wags every time you look at her, it can be a shock to discover that with a German Shepherd, her waving tail carriage indicates a clear threat that "If you come any closer, I'll bite."

Canine Body Language

Once you learn how to "read" your dog's body language, there is so much you can figure out about what she is thinking, which instincts are being triggered and what she might do next. People sometimes ignore very clear warning signs of a dog's increasing tension, anxiety or aggression: if they were looking and knew what it meant, many problems could be nipped in the bud. Other times people may misinterpret what their dog's physical cues mean, so they act on false assumptions—thinking, for example, that their dog is being passive/aggressive by freezing with another dog when it could actually be her attempt to lower tension. What follows is a chart that can help you decipher what is going on in the mysterious mind of your dog.

Head to Tail Body Language (When in Doubt, Choose the Most Aggressive or Fearful Response)

EYES
- Direct staring = confident, challenging or dominating
- Blinking, looking away = yielding
- Soft, warm = content, relaxed
- White in corner of eye, sideways glance = tension, insecurity
- Casual eye contact = relaxed, interested
- Dilated (large) pupils = fearful or aggressive

EARS
- Erect, forward-leaning = challenging or interested
- Relaxed muscles around ear = content, calm
- Back flat against head = fear, submission or worry
- Moving, not as a pair = gathering information
- Sideways = uncertainty

MOUTH
- Yawning=stress (lowers the blood pressure)
- Tongue flicking=insecurity, tension, submission
- Lip curling, exposing teeth=happy or submissive grin, or aggressive
- Snarl with teeth=threat
- Turn snout away=yielding
- Mouthing (with teeth)=warning or challenging
- Mouthing (no teeth)=greeting, excitement
- Face licking=subordination

BODY POSTURE
- Raised up on stiff front legs=assertive, challenging
- Scratching=tension, insecurity
- Trembling=excitement, fear or anxiety
- Frozen in place=yielding or threatening
- Mounting=domination
- Moving slowly=yielding, fearful
- Lying on back=playful or submissive
- Turning away=yielding
- Approaching at an angle (arcing)=yielding, deferring
- Muscle tension in head and shoulders=frightened or aggressive
- Hair raised (piloerection)=involuntary response to perceived threat
- Approach and retreat=uncertainty

GESTURES
- Play bow=happiness, invitation to play
- Nose nudging=attention seeking
- Pawing a person=attention seeking
- Scratching after elimination=visual marker for other dogs

TAIL
- Up, wagging=happiness
- Up, wagging very quickly=excitement, anticipation
- Straight out, wagging steadily=cautious, worried
- Relaxed, at ease=contented
- Up, quivering=nervous but friendly
- Broad sweep=pre-attack, anticipation
- Tucked between legs=fear, submission

◆ The Body Language of an Aggressive Dog

(Note that "aggressive" and "dominant" are two different things.)

The direction in which a dog's body is shifted tells a lot: if she is snarling and growling but leaning a bit backward, she's on the defensive and not looking to attack.

If you do not keep advancing toward that dog—if you don't pressure her—nothing more will happen. However, if you push her into a corner—physically or psychologically—there will be trouble.

If the dog is shifting backward and forward he is undecided: conflicted between wanting to attack and wanting to flee. With no extra pressure from you, nothing will happen. A quiet, stiff-legged dog, shifted slightly forward—standing still, staring directly into your eyes—is definitely reason to worry for your safety.

◆ Beware of a Frightened Dog.

A fearful dog can react unpredictably—and maybe even dangerously. Some signs of a frightened dog include ears flattened back, tail between the legs and overall cringing.

◆ Handling Dogs at Emotional Extremes

With a dog who is either shy or aggressive, do not push her. Do not even advance toward these dogs, because they often cannot tolerate the stress of your proximity.

Even when holding your ground, avoid leaning forward. Don't put all your energy and weight forward: it may cause the dog to perceive you as a threat. It will be less threatening to a dog like this if you shift onto your back foot and turn slightly sideways.

DOG MEETING DOG

The body language of two dogs approaching each other establishes their rank immediately—often imperceptibly to us.

◆ Head Carriage Is the Prime Issue.

The dog holding his head higher as they approach each other is the higher-ranked dog—*if* the other dog lowers his head and does not make eye contact. However, if the second dog does *not* submit in this way but keeps his head high, too—and goes even further to make direct eye contact—then you have a standoff that will lead to a dogfight unless one of the two backs down. All this happens within seconds and without any visible aggression or dramatics.

Accidentally interfering with a leash If a person has the submissive dog on a leash and tightens it up when they see another dog, this can inadvertently lift the dog's head. This artificially raised head gives an aggressive posture message to the other dog—"I'm not backing down"—even though that is the last thing on the subordinate dog's mind. At the same time, the more assertive dog is waiting for the submissive one to submit with lowered head and averted eyes, but the owner's tight leash does not leave room for the natural lowering. So the dominant dog keeps on coming, not knowing it is the human's leash holding his (actually meek) adversary's head up in that offensive posture.

✦ A Direct Stare Between Two Dogs (see "Dominance in Activities" on page 133)

There are some misconceptions about what eye contact means between dogs. Unblinking, unwavering eye contact is in some sense a gauntlet thrown down. The implied message is, "Either accept me as your superior or we'll have to duke it out."

The dominant dog stares down the less dominant dogs; the submissive dog avoids direct eye contact by averting his gaze and exposing his neck. The dominant stare is usually accompanied by a motionless body and a head held high on a rigid neck; as the staring continues, the body language results in one dog standing even taller.

If the other dog gives back as hard and unblinking a stare, then he has taken it as a challenge. It now becomes a waiting game of which one will look away first. If the other dog looks away, especially if he lowers his head and keeps his ears low, then he has submitted and life goes on. That hard stare from one dog to another is a statement of superiority (in an "alpha dog" sense); the less important dog must avert his eyes as an admission of his lower ranking. If neither dog backs down, the stage is set for a dogfight.

✦ Dominant Body-language Traits

Dominance and submission are attitudes and behaviors that function to keep the peace whenever two or more dogs meet or relate. As long as one dog responds more submissively to the other dog's dominant display, there will be no fighting. This matters to you not as an anthropology lesson but because if you can read your own dog's body language, you can prepare for what it signifies and intercede as you see fit. You can avoid the other dog or you can interrupt a potentially negative interaction with another dog by stepping in as the idea is still unfolding in their minds.

DOMINANT DISPLAYS

- Holding the tail erect
- Holding the ears erect/pricked
- Staring directly at the other
- Muscles tensed
- Circling and sniffing the other
- Growling/snarling if the other whimpers or moves
- Marking the area with urine
- Putting chin on the other's shoulders
- Putting paws on other's back

SUBMISSIVE DISPLAYS

- Tail lowered or even curled between back legs
- Ears flat against the head
- Eyes looking away
- Licking or swallowing nervously
- Cringing, shaking
- Rolling over, hind leg lifted, exposing the belly
- Submissive urination

Chemical Communication between Dogs

Scent is the dog's most highly developed sense, and dogs use it when encountering another species. Dogs produce chemicals called "pheromones" that greatly affect other dogs: one dog can identify another dog's sexual status and rank within his pack just from picking up the scent. Pheromones are present in a dog's saliva, urine, vaginal secretions, feces and anal and tail glands. The scent of these chemicals influences the way one dog responds to another.

SNIFFING ANOTHER DOG'S BUTT

We may think it is "rude" or vulgar for our dog to run right up and stick her nose under another dog's tail, but it's actually the dog equivalent of shaking hands. The anal glands are bulb-like reservoirs that are paired on either side of the anus. The substance they produce ranges from clear to white to brown.

After the anal area is sniffed, dogs then move to other areas where pheromones may be present, such as the lips.

◆ Sniffing Another Dog's Feces

A dog's feces is a Post-it note left for other dogs: it tells the sniffer all about the dog whose anal glands have secreted on the feces.

◆ Sniffing Another Dog's Urine

Urine contains sex hormones. It leaves information from the female about her reproductive status and confirms the authority and power of the male.

◆ Over-peeing Another Dog's Urine

Over-peeing is status, too. The last one to pee is highest in the pecking order. If you have a clear top dog, you will see a definite need to over-pee any time he sees one of his pack peeing.

Vocal Communication

Dogs have some basic sounds that they can all make, but each dog is quite unique as to when and how he uses his vocal repertoire to make himself understood. By paying close attention to your dog you can come to understand how he is feeling and/or what he wants, based on the sounds he makes.

A human mother learns to distinguish what her baby is trying to communicate from the short list of vocalizations that a baby can make: laugh, giggle, cry, wail, gurgle, scream, etc. For example, a mother learns when a cry is for hunger or pain, and when fussiness is from fatigue, discomfort or hunger. The mother's response to all the different sounds that her baby makes is part of what establishes and reinforces the bond and communication between them.

Vocal communication with your dog can deepen your attachment to each other and enrich the experience of dog companionship. The more you respond to your dog's vocalizations, the more you may find her attempting to get her ideas across. This depends on the individual dog, of course. Some dogs will barely utter a peep throughout their lives, while others of the same breed will develop a whole mini-language with their people: several different ways of barking or crying or moaning, directed right at their owner. I have found that the more you verbally respond to your dog's vocalizations, the more frequent and varied her verbal style will become.

THE SOUNDS DOGS MAKE

Dogs can bark, growl, whimper, whine, moan, yelp, yip, cry and howl. Each of these vocalizations is used to get across different emotions or information.

If you take note of what your dog is doing when he vocalizes, you can begin to distinguish the different occasions that elicit the different tones and pitches in his vocalizations.

◆ Barking

Barking is the most common dog noise, and it can telegraph a variety of emotions. The alert and observant owner can tune in to the different tonalities of her dog's bark and be able to pick out which of the different kinds of barking her dog is displaying.

A FEW KINDS OF BARKS

- ❏ The deep *"warning"* bark that sounds the alarm: someone or something is approaching or encroaching on the dog's territory
- ❏ The loud, neutral *"come tend to me"* bark used when the dog wants to be let in
- ❏ The short *to-the-point* bark used when the dog needs to be let out
- ❏ The shrill, happy *"please play with me"* bark directed at you or another dog
- ❏ The furious, excited *"oh-my-god-it's-another-dog-out-there"* bark
- ❏ The incessant, pointless *"another dog is barking so I'd better, too"* bark

◆ Growling

A warning growl is used to serve notice that the object of the growl had better change his behavior or suffer more serious consequences. Common wisdom says that a growl is always a frightening sound signifying a potentially dangerous situation.

However, there are a variety of growls—one is a serious warning that emanates from deep in the chest, while another is a throaty growl that is generally considered lower on the "jeopardy" scale.

Some dogs growl playfully as a way to elicit play with another dog. Even though dogs are supposed to understand each other's signals, there are times when this playful and good-natured use of the growl can be misinterpreted by other dogs and elicit a hostile response from them or a defensive response from people. One example is Yogi Bear, a gorgeous, huge Rottweiler of mine who had a growl of such enthusiastic greeting it that seemed to rumble from deep in his innards and exit out through the tips of his perky little ears. Coming from a 120-pound Rottweiler, however, it was often misunderstood.

◆ Howling

A dog may howl for many reasons: to communicate with others, to signal daybreak or moonlight, to proclaim his location or to express emotions.

Howling in the wolf pack serves to coordinate how the pack members are spaced—their comings and goings—in their territory. For dogs that hunt with people, howling serves many of these same purposes.

Howling is also the vocalization used by dogs that "sing"—it is how some dogs react to certain types of music. Some breeds are more prone to howling, typically the pack-hunting dogs such as Beagles and Hounds, and wolf-type breeds such as Huskies and Malamutes.

◆ Moans and Groans

Dogs often moan and groan with pleasure when you stroke or scratch some part of them that is particularly pleasing. These sounds are used by dogs toward their people, not toward other dogs. These are pleasure sounds, something like the purring of a cat.

The way in which some dogs make long, low sighing sounds can sound almost like a low growl—except that the dog's body language is far from aggressive. When a dog moans she is usually totally relaxed with her eyes closed or lidded, or even looking at you adoringly—not with the hackles raised and a stiff body.

◆ Whining and Crying

Whining, whimpering and crying are inter-dog sounds that dogs usually outgrow as they reach maturity—these are juvenile communication sounds that adult dogs rarely use with each other. However, mature dogs do use these sorts of noises when interacting with their people.

Dogs learn that whining and whimpering get them the attention of humans. These sounds are not part of an adult dog's natural repertoire: they are a learned response.

If you don't mind—or may even enjoy—your dog communicating with you using these tones, that's fine. But if you don't like the whiny noises, then you can do something to help your dog unlearn them: stop rewarding the whine or cry with food, affection or attention.

◆ Yelping

This is the most common withdrawal sound. It means either distress or actual pain, and it's what you hear if you step on a sleeping dog's ear or paw, or a bee stings her.

Stress in Dogs

The way people live—the way we dash around the modern world with barely enough time for all of our "multitasks"—has an effect on the emotional state of the dogs who share our lives. There are some dogs who are naturally laid-back; they live alongside our raised voices, frustrated phone conversations and high-speed comings and goings seemingly unaffected. However, many high-strung dogs are sponges or magnets for our emotional states, and they pay a price for what we put ourselves through. They pick up on our frenetic way of life and the stress it causes us. Of course, we humans pay our own price for rushing and stress, but (theoretically, at least) we have some choice in the matter. The dogs are victims trapped on our carousel, and some of them really feel the effects.

While it is universally accepted that stress causes physical and emotional problems in people, owners rarely consider what the cost of their lifestyle may be on their animal companions.

CAUSES OF STRESS

- Speedy human lifestyle
- Lack of mental stimulation
- Insufficient physical exercise
- Loneliness
- Discord among human family members
- Sudden family changes: death, divorce, child going away to school

SIGNS OF STRESS

- Licking (self, floor, walls, furniture)
- Tail-chasing
- Pacing
- Running back and forth along a fence
- Panting or drooling excessively
- Lying flat and completely still
- Excessive hair loss
- Pooping symbolically (owner's bed, middle of living room)

Human family problems—silent anger, tension, yelling and screaming—can make a dog feel trapped between his two people. If there is a toxic relationship in the household—parent/child, children with each other, parent/parent—it can adversely affect a dog, especially if he is a highly sensitive creature.

This tension can lead to house-soiling by the dog. In some instances, the dog may even defecate on the warring couple's bed.

METHODS AND PRODUCTS TO RELIEVE CANINE STRESS

◆ TTouch System

This is a system of massage-like methods to therapeutically touch animals and to relieve tension by opening neural pathways and unblocking emotional issues such as fear and aggression.

TTouch is short for "Tellington touch." It was developed by Linda Tellington-Jones, and has been popular with horse owners. Many of the areas that TTouch addresses correspond with Chinese acupuncture and acupressure points, particularly the "ear work" done in TTouch, which concentrates on the acupoints in the ear, a location that Chinese medicine designates as corresponding to areas on the whole body.

I have no experience with my horses or dogs and thus can't comment personally about it but if this kind of theory appeals to you there are TTouch books, videos and a directory of practitioners of this system at available at www.lindatellingtonjones.com.

◆ Anxiety Wrap

This is a product that uses the principle of applied pressure—sort of like the idea behind swaddling infants to calm them. Information about this ACE-style bandage is available at www.anxietywrap.com.

◆ Comfort Zone

This is a room atomizer made by Farnam Pet Products that emits a substance the manufacturer calls "dog-appeasing pheromone" ("DAP" for short). The company claims that DAP releases a natural stress-reducing hormone similar to what a mother dog emits while nursing her puppies. It has reportedly been used successfully in Europe for some time to reduce or eliminate stress-related barking, destructiveness, whimpering and whining, urination and defecation in the house, etc.

The Comfort Zone atomizer plugs into an electrical socket the way a room deodorizer does and releases the DAP substance. One atomizer is supposed to cover an area of 500 to 650 square feet for about a month. The substance has been deemed safe for puppies, dogs and people.

People have reported success with DAP in the house, and vets find customers reordering it. The manufacturer suggests that if you keep your dog(s) in proximity to this remarkable little gizmo, you could be one of the lucky ones whom DAP may help with arousal barking, thunder phobia, separation anxiety, noise phobia, aggression, etc. Personally, I could not see a difference in Jazzy, my very nervous traveler, when I used the spray version in the car.

If your dog has stress-related personality issues, it seems well worth it to spend $25 and give it a try. NOTE: If you try Comfort Zone and your dog's behavior or stress gets worse, the manufacturer advises to unplug the atomizer immediately. A bad result does not turn into a positive result—it just isn't going to work for that dog. Save it for another dog, give it to a friend to try on his dog or just throw it away.

Odd Things Dogs Do

There are any number of strange—or at least strange to us—behaviors that don't necessarily have explanations. But if your dog does any of these things, at least you'll know there's nothing wrong with her—she's just following some ancient script in her genes.

CROTCH-SNIFFING

Dogs greet each other by sniffing each other's private parts. Some dogs extend this habit to include humans.

The natural reaction of many people to being sniffed is to back away—but the better fix is to step right at the dog, pushing toward his offending nose and forcing him to step back. Correct him in a serious but not angry tone—say anything you want but just sound fed up: "Get off, go find someone your own size," for example. You need to correct your dog so this dog-appropriate behavior becomes limited to dog encounters. With a leash on the dog, when he puts his nose toward a person's crotch, say "leave it" and jerk the leash to the side. Ask the dog to sit, and praise him if he does.

REACTIONS TO UNUSUAL VISUALS

Some dogs notice when a person's shape is different, and they can't make a mental adjustment. For example, a person wearing a hat or a baseball cap turned backward or a pencil behind the ear, or someone carrying a cane or an umbrella, or wearing a jacket hood or sunglasses or a backpack, or someone walking in with their arms full of packages can elicit growls, barking or running away. If you have a hyperalert dog, or a very shy one she may react to a change in what people normally look like. Get her more accustomed to visual differences by wearing straw hats and carrying unexpected objects around the house.

ELIMINATION ISSUES

◆ Peeing on Top of Another Dog's Pee

This is called "overmarking" the urine of other dogs; it's a social-status thing. Higher-status individuals overmark—or "over-pee"—lower-status dogs.

The law in the dog world seems to be: whoever pees last is top Dog.

◆ Female Dog Lifts Back Leg When Peeing

This is a sign of a dominant personality. It shows a female who has the boldness and assertiveness of a male.

◆ Scratching with Hind Legs After Defecating

Many people think dogs do this to cover up their poop, but it's actually done to call attention to it. When dogs pee and defecate they often do it in the same area, which is part of how they mark their territory—it's called "scent posting." Those scratch marks are actually like arrows in the ground that point to the dog's posted scents as a warning to any other dogs (potential rivals and adversaries) who might enter that territory.

There is also the possibility that another scent is left at the site from the sebaceous glands between the dog's toes, which also leave their individual "calling card."

ROLLING IN SMELLY STUFF

There are many theories about why dogs roll in things like maggoty carcasses, decomposing fish on the beach, feces, etc.

Some people think dogs view these stinking items as "doggie perfume" that smells good to them and other dogs. Others think that rolling in such smells tells a story—that when returning to the pack it sends a message to the others that the dog has discovered a "gold mine" somewhere nearby. Still other people think dogs roll in order to cover up their own odor by camouflaging it with the stench they've rolled in. This theory makes very little logical sense: why would any other animal trust a dog that smells like a dead rabbit?

The final answer is: we don't know why dogs do this.

DOG MOUNTS YOU DURING TRAINING

Some trainers believe that mounting is not a sexual behavior, that it's about dominance. Others believe that with puppies it's practice for sex later on.

The dog is asserting a leadership position—which you are attempting to take when you train him. Some female dogs do it, too—generally the more macho ones. By mounting you, a dog is trying to put you down—put you in your place. He considers himself the Top Dog.

If he has not yet been neutered, now might be a good time.

From now on, clarify who's in charge by demanding something of the dog ("sit," "down," "wait") before the dog gets any affection, treats or fun activity. Don't push the dog off—that just affirms that there is a power struggle between you. Instead, let the leash make the correction (see "Teaching Manners" page 235).

EATING GRASS

Is it used as a digestive aid? Is it due to a nutritional deficit or imbalance? Do they have an upset stomach and want to make themselves throw up? Or is it that they just enjoy it? Or all of the above? No one really knows.

DIGGING HOLES

This drive is hardwired in dogs, more so in some dogs and breeds. Terriers and other British breeds, for example, were developed to "go to ground" during the hunt and ground game. They are generally expected to leave no hole in the ground unexplored.

BURYING BONES OR TREATS

This is called "caching," and wolves do it, too. But what does it mean that some dogs never try to hide a treat, while others do so consistently? Are the dogs saving up for a rainy day—an emergency fund for the future? We really don't know.

CIRCLING BEFORE LYING DOWN

Some dogs scratch and make digging motions and rebuild the entire dog bed, while others never engage in this odd ritual. Wolves flattened the grass to make a more comfortable nest. Perhaps it was also done to drive out snakes or other pests in the den.

HACKLES RAISED (PILOERECTION)

When the hair stands up on the back of a dog's neck (above his shoulder blades and down his spine) it is thought of as an offensive threat because it makes the dog appear larger (many species have this automatic response to danger).

However, piloerection is sometimes also seen when a dog is being defensively threatening; less often, it can happen when a dog is extremely aroused or agitated.

PANTING

Generally speaking, panting is a normal type of respiration for a dog. Dogs have poorly developed sweat glands, so they can't cool off through pores in their skin the way we (or other animals, like horses) do. This means that when it's hot and you're grateful for a cooling breeze, your dog does not feel that cool air on his skin.

A dog pants to provide what is called "evaporative heat loss": panting increases evaporation from the respiratory tract, which the dog needs when the temperature in the environment gets close to his body temperature. When the outside air gets hotter than his body temperature, panting is the only way that a dog can get cooler.

Individually, each dog pants more or less than others in response to panting triggers such as the ambient temperature, exercise and/or excitement or nervousness. Some dogs just naturally pant more than others. It may be that they have thicker coats and therefore get hotter and need to lower their temperature more than other dogs. My huge Rottweiler, Yogi Bear, panted like a steam engine for thirty to sixty minutes after a big run in the woods in warm weather; although it seemed alarming, that was normal for him. It also may be that—just as with people—there are some dogs who are just naturally warmer than others and feel the heat more.

Since panting is generally such a normal behavior for dogs, you should be able to tell whether your dog is panting a lot for him and whether there are other symptoms that are unusual for him. If that is the case, take him to the vet.

DOGS EATING FROM THE CAT LITTER BOX

For most dogs, there are no more delicious snacks than the ones in the cat's litter box. For most of us, nothing seems more disgusting than our dog's breath smelling . . . well, never mind.

There is only one sure way to solve this: make the cat's box inaccessible to the dog. Depending on your household setup, there are a number of possibilities. One is to keep the litter box in the basement and keep the basement door open just enough to allow the cat to go through (a nail in the door molding and a string that attaches it to the doorknob can work). You can do the same thing with a bathroom door, although that can be awkward for human use unless you happen to have an extra bathroom that is rarely used. Putting the litter box inside a bathtub works for some situations, although if the tub is low and the dog is tall, he might find a way to just reach his head over to get into the "snack bin."

The litter boxes that have lids on them, with only an opening for the cat, may be a very good solution. Get a model with clamps on either side that hold the lid on, in case the dog is so highly motivated that he still looks for a way to get into the box.

DOG EATING DOG POOP

This is a totally gross habit, which fortunately only some dogs indulge in.

There isn't much known about why some dogs do it—perhaps some nutritional need, or something in their genes—or why they often grow out of it.

There are several known ways to change this habit. Putting Adolph's Meat Tenderizer or Accent (or a product sold by vets called For-Bid) on the dog's food makes his feces taste really bad.

Apparently, these products take up to three days to work, but if you see no change in the dog's behavior after that time then this remedy is not going to dissuade him.

There is also a natural way to make a dog's feces especially unappetizing: put pineapple or zucchini in the dog's food.

Some advocate changing the diet to a less rich food, but there is not much success with that method.

Some people try to spray the poop with Bitter Apple immediately after the dog defecates, so that presumably he won't go after it later.

As with so many bad habits and problems, prevention is the best solution. Picking up after the dog even in your own yard is the surest, simplest way to avoid the problem. You're going to pick up the poop eventually anyway, so it might as well be right away.

DOG EATING HUMAN FECES

No one likes to admit that this goes on, but you'll see it happen if you've ever taken your dogs on long walks in the woods or along trails where people have jogged or biked or camped— or even if you come upon a construction location where workers may have relieved themselves outside. If you see a pile of crumpled toilet paper or tissue that your dog makes a beeline for, that's probably what is attracting him.

It seems to be a natural desire to the dog, so keep your dog leashed anywhere that you suspect this enticement might be available. If it's an area where you go often with your dog, such as a park or hiking trail, you can try contacting whatever local officials might have jurisdiction about supplying a Porta-Potty in areas where people relieve themselves publicly.

DOGS EATING DIRT

Some dogs eat dirt (technically it's called "geophagy"). It is not good for a dog's digestive tract. People worry that the dog is doing this because he may be hungry or has a vitamin/mineral deficiency, but no research supports this claim. You may be able to stop geophagy by increasing fiber in the dog's food with a "Senior" or "Light" variety, always using one of the high-quality kibbles like California Natural or Innova (see "Canned Food or Dry?" in the nutrition chapter, page 440).

Do not punish or scold the dog over this. Some dogs experience your concern and punishment as attention—and just like some children, they would rather have negative attention than none at all.

Don't allow the dog to go outside unsupervised until this problem has been resolved. However, you want to give the dog as much exercise as you possibly can, because a tired dog gets into less mischief.

Chapter 7

COMMUNICATION BETWEEN DOGS AND PEOPLE

In this chapter you will find topics that relate to understanding the wolf background of all dogs and the way it affects communication and understanding between our two species.

- ❏ The dog/wolf connection and how it affects everything our dog does and thinks
- ❏ Dealing with dominant dogs
- ❏ The body language of dogs—clues to what dogs are feeling
- ❏ Our body language—and how dogs perceive us
- ❏ Differences in communication styles between dogs and people
- ❏ Good ways to caress dogs

There has been a breakthrough in the understanding of what makes dogs tick, as scientists have confirmed the connection between dogs and their direct ancestor, the wolf. Canine anthropologists have concluded that their studies of wolves teach us everything we need to know about the dogs who share our lives.

Our pet dogs—from the tiniest Pekingese to the largest Deerhound—all have the same number of chromosomes that a wolf does. People have been manipulating what dogs *look* like for thousands of years, and yet all dogs continue to have the same wiring in their brains: the mind of a wolf. By some calculations, people have been breeding and domesticating dogs for 8,000 years, and yet no matter what we have done to alter the outside of the "package," the inside of a dog's mind is unchanged. From the study of wolf behavior has come a "new and improved" understanding of our constant companions—and ideas about how to communicate with them.

There has been a gradual but significant evolution in the understanding of the interaction and how to ensure that the human is in charge of that relationship. Th ior of wolves is what has given dog trainers/behaviorists their understanding of ho maintain a harmonious balance between dogs and between dogs and their peopl

The most current beliefs about living with and training dogs is that we humans "powerful" ones in those relationships, but that we should not have an adversarial relationship with our dogs based on domination.

The Dog/Wolf Connection

Jan Fennell, who wrote *The Dog Listener,* does a beautiful job of explaining her theory about the wolf origins of dogs and how this affects our relationship to them. There has been a fair amount of research on this subject over the last decade, but Fennell's brilliance is to describe with great simplicity how to turn your unruly pack of dogs (or even a solo dog) into mellow, attentive canines.

To follow this wolf-oriented line of thinking about dogs, you may have to suspend preconceptions about how your pooch thinks and what motivates her actions. But once you open yourself to these revolutionary ideas and begin to experiment with these techniques, your interaction with your dog(s) will become so easy that it will seem like magic.

I recommend Fennell's book to anyone who has the time and desire to read the whole saga of how she came to her theory, but like any truly great idea, the practical aspects of playing alpha wolf to your dog(s) can be boiled down to a simple formula, outlined below.

THINK LIKE A WOLF

First and foremost, we have to embrace the concept of just how differently dogs process relationship dynamics. Humans are verbal, whereas dogs rely on body language. In order for us to understand and to be in control of the dog's place in our lives, we need to understand the nonverbal messages of wolves and dogs. For us, tapping into that system is like plugging into the motherboard of a dog's computer, rather than fooling around with hit-or-miss software that we try to develop.

Wolf packs are hierarchies with one "alpha pair." They get the first and best of everything—food, bed, etc.—in return for taking responsibility for the group. The word "alpha" has been misused and misunderstood by dog trainers for years: they have been interpreting the term as *humans* understand it (power and control by intimidation and force), whereas leader may be a better word. Dogs are not similar to people, who are taught to surpass others, to be on top. In the animal kingdom there are many creatures, along with dogs, who neither want to be nor are equipped to be the "alpha." In fact, they are content and even relieved to have a clearly designated leader so that they can stop worrying about all the questions answered by his leadership. In the wolf/dog universe there is no value judgment for dogs about where they fall on the spectrum—there is no shame in being third from the top, or third from the bottom—as there

...uld be in human society, where being number one is given immense importance. Dogs just need to know where they fall in the family or pack. We have to keep that in mind when trying to understand our dog—and in every single thing we do with her.

Research into how wolves live and communicate with each other has revealed that in wolf terms, there are a few central areas where there is a clear role for the leader. We humans have to play the role of leader with our dogs—with whom we create an interspecies pack—because in dog terms there has to be a leader. Some pack member has to assume that place, so if you don't step in—in terms the dog can understand based on her wolf origins—the dog will worry and try to fill that leadership place herself. This can lead to nervous, neurotic behavior in a dog—barking, destructiveness, being clingy—all ways of expressing anxiety over the fact that no one is in charge and keeping the den safe.

What we need to learn is in which areas a wolf leader, the "alpha," naturally asserts himself. By knowing what those areas are with our dog(s), we can take them over. We don't want to fight the dog's inborn tendencies; we want to go with the dog's instinct.

◆ Better Yet, Think Like a Bee.

The social structure of beehives can help us understand the position we need to assume with our dogs. There is only one queen: all the drones and workers accept her importance, are happy to do their bit in her service and are not challenging her for that position. With dogs, if they know who is in charge, it frees them to relax, play among themselves and work better. With our dogs we need to become the queen bee.

FOUR THINGS THAT MATTER TO WOLVES AND DOGS

There are four areas of wolf-pack behavior that Fennell claims can be applied to our relationship with our dogs to bring about startling changes in communication and understanding. The four are seemingly mundane events: leaving home, returning home, feeding and dealing with visitors. But to the wolf mentality, these moments are highly important. Just by altering the way you handle yourself in these situations, you "train" your dog(s)—without any active lessons—to respect you and honor your wishes.

◆ One: Leaving the House (Hunting)

The alpha always goes out of the den first, as the most courageous and the best decision-maker. So it's okay to let your dog precede you through interior doorways, but when you are exiting the house through a main door, you should *always* tell the dog(s) to wait and let you go first, after which you can release them with an "okay" so they can follow you out.

Instead of trying to stop them from getting all wound up before going out, look at the principles of the wolf pack: leaving the den is prelude to a hunt—and they are hardwired to get their adrenaline pumping so they are "up" to hunt well for food. The alpha in a true wolf pack lets the others bounce around like rubber balls. If you have more than one dog you may have noticed heightened emotions and behavior whenever you leave the house with them—it is because of their wolf origins. Eventually your dog(s) will settle down to the job at hand: "hunting."

◆ Two: Coming Home (Reuniting the Pack)

Whenever a pack is reunited after being apart a ritual takes place: the alpha reasserts his dominance. The alpha has a personal space that has to be respected: no other pack member can approach that private space unless invited to do so.

Because in the true wolf world it is possible to get injured or killed while out hunting, upon the alpha's return the pack makes a huge fuss over him to reassure themselves that he is okay. Is he still the boss? Who will protect them if danger arises? Who will lead the hunt?

If you have more than one dog, you may face pure histrionics from your dogs when you come home from the outside world—jumping, barking, etc. You have to ignore them the way the alpha ignores his pack upon returning.

If you do take the alpha role and give your dogs the cold shoulder for the first few minutes when you come through the door, you will all be happier. But that means *no* reaction from you. You cannot even turn around to say "Stop" or "Off" because then you would be giving the dogs attention. If a dog puts his feet on your lap or jumps up, you have to gently push him down by his chest. No words, no emotion. Even saying the word "Off" aloud breaks the spell of aloofness that is central to the dog perceiving you in this new, powerful role.

I decided to try Fennell's methodology with some skepticism. My three dogs were always so obnoxiously wound up when I returned home that I had abandoned my generally high standards for mannerly obedience. Was Jan Fennell right that they could become laid-back just by my *totally ignoring them* as I came into the house? Sure enough. Dogs who ordinarily spent four to five minutes on my return home holding toys, crying/whining, nibbling at my jacket sleeve, pressing against me and carrying on with each other for my attention—all acted in less than a minute as though they had been shot with tranquilizer darts, and calmly lay down on their beds. This dramatic transformation came about simply because I did not acknowledge the dogs' existence in words, touch or eye contact when I walked in the house. It was mind-blowing. I would have thought it was a parlor trick if I hadn't set it up myself and seen the difference between the previous hopped-up greetings and the new, mellow ones.

When the dog relaxes and wanders off to lie down somewhere, that is his signal that his resistance is over. By deferring, he is showing respect for your space and your position.

◆ Three: Eating

The alpha always eats first, and he eats his fill of the best portion before others can eat. Therefore, don't feel sorry for your dog if you eat before he has been fed—in fact, it's a relief for him because it reassures him that you are in charge, which means he doesn't have to be. By putting on a charade of eating right before you put down the dog's dish, you are sending a strong message about being in charge—in nonverbal terms that the dog reads immediately.

In her book, Jan Fennell maintains that you may need to reinforce the concept that you are the alpha. One way to drive this point home is to make a dramatic event of eating before the dog does. Prepare a cracker or other edible item next to the dog's dishes. Before putting the dog's dish on the floor make a big drama out of lifting the cracker or snack for yourself as though it is coming right from the dog's dinner bowl. After eating the cracker you can put the dog's bowl down. You will have made your point. You may feel foolish but some dogs need the point rubbed in.

◆ Four: Danger (Visitors)

Whenever there is the possibility of danger, it is the alpha's role to protect the pack. Once you recognize that, then dealing with your dog's reaction to those "intruders" makes more sense. There are specific suggestions on how to handle this in Chapter Ten, "Teaching Manners," page 235, but what follows are a few shorthand suggestions for handling your dog's sometimes unruly reaction to people arriving at your house.

The arrival of strangers to the pack—visitors or delivery people coming to the door—is an event of perceived danger to a dog. They leap around the visitor, sniffing and barking, which can make you feel like an idiot for having such wild dogs. If your dog barks madly and generally freaks out when visitors arrive outside the door, calmly tell the dog "Thank you," and then firmly say, "Enough." The dog has recognized the potential danger and alerted you—but then you need to take over from there, much to his relief! Relieved of responsibility, he can relax; many dogs seem calmer after being taken "off duty."

Put the dog on a leash with a head collar, if necessary, before the people come in. This gives you some control without raising your voice and escalating tension. You can also tell your visitors (whether friends, family or delivery people) to do exactly what you do: ignore the dog(s). Do not make eye contact. Do not touch them. Do not talk to them. This can be really hard for some people, especially the hard-core dog lovers, but you should insist upon it.

What to do with visitors who won't cooperate If there are people who refuse to get with the program (or those too young or too old to understand) then you need to shut the dog(s) away before those people arrive. You will get dramatic relief from dog madness if all people entering the house give those dogs a cold shoulder. That is what alpha wolves do upon returning to the den: aloofness is their body language, which says that they have returned safe and sound and are still the leader.

Obviously, your visitors can do anything they want with your dog(s) after the first few minutes. It is only that initial wound up greeting that needs correction.

How to Assert Your Authority as Top Dog

Over centuries of domestication, dogs have become generally subservient to man. The domestic dog depends on her human mistress to be the leader. This symbiotic bond of people with dogs is not just passively inherited by the dogs—puppies need to be socialized with humans before fourteen weeks or the chance of making a close connection is diminished, if not ruined (see "Puppy Development," page 107).

If we look at the rights and privileges of the alpha and the mistaken way many of us have come to live with our mutts—as though there is some kind of democracy between us, or our dogs are even given royal status—it's no wonder that communication breaks down. Chaos ensues, and we wind up calling the poor confused beast a "problem dog" or "disobedient." The root of many dog problems is often that humans don't take responsibility for their basic entitlement to a higher rank, which is the natural order of things from the canine point of view.

This is not a call to arms. No one is suggesting that you should be at war with your dog or push her around. Go ahead and love your dog up one side and down the other. A huge part of the dog population has operated for hundreds of years enjoying profuse privileges and indulgences from humans without spoiling their temperaments or behavior. However, if you have a dog with a behavior or control issue, look at the way you cohabit with the canine. Without realizing it, you may have been handing over a higher rank to the dog than the one you should claim for yourself.

What follows is a list of the things that a dog of lower rank would never do to a superior dog in the pack—and certainly never to the alpha dog. These instinctive rules are built into all dogs—which means your dog is wired this way, too. (She learned these lessons as a little puppy at seven weeks of age . . . before you took her home and scrambled all the natural signals!)

THINGS A LOWER-RANKING DOG WOULD NEVER DO

- ❏ Try to take a bone or toy from a higher-ranking dog
- ❏ Try to eat before the alpha, who gets the pick of the food
- ❏ Go through a narrow opening before the higher-ranking dog
- ❏ Greet a higher-ranking dog by placing its chin on his shoulders or touching him with its paws or teeth
- ❏ Disturb the alpha dog when he is resting

Compare this chart with the one that follows, which shows the ways that we unwittingly act submissive to our dogs.

HIGH-RANKING PRIVILEGES WE GIVE OUR DOGS

- ❏ We show deference to the dog, validating his "superiority."
- ❏ We feed him before ourselves—"first pick" of food is the sole privilege of the alpha.
- ❏ We let him sleep on our furniture and bed—but we never invade his bed.
- ❏ We let him go first through doorways.
- ❏ We accommodate his sleep by not disturbing him.
- ❏ We respond immediately to the dog's demands for attention, or allow him to push or lean or head-butt for it—yet we accept his choice not to respond to our overtures.
- ❏ We let him win strength games like tug-of-war and "keep-away."
- ❏ We allow him to "mouth" our arms, hands, clothing, his leash, etc.

WHAT DOMINANCE MEANS WITH YOUR DOG

Establishing the right dominance/submission level between you and your dog is necessary in order for him to accept your training requests and social expectations. "Getting dominance over your dog" is a dangerous concept because it is so often misunderstood. You want to establish yourself as the pack leader, the "alpha," without physical roughness.

What you'll learn in this section is what rank and dominance mean in dog/wolf terms so you can make adjustments in the way you live with your dog. Once you understand which seemingly insignificant actions signify dominant behavior to a dog, you'll see how many of us make it nearly impossible for our dogs to look up to us and follow our orders. If you allow a dog to lean against you, or to pull on your sleeve or paw at your pants leg, or to lie in doorways blocking your passage, you have indicated to the dog that he is in charge of you.

But all it takes is removing a few privileges from the dog, inviting him *off* that sofa, and you may get better results in obedience work.

◆ Identifying Dominance

There are a number of things you can try to reduce your dog's dominant tendencies. First you have to identify which behaviors have to do with dominance. The chart below has some signs that would show that your dog has dominance issues.

Signs of Dominance Issues

Toy Guarding: Dog snaps or growls when you come close (throw away that highly guarded object).

Food Guarding: Dog snarls, snaps or growls before chasing you away from his bowl.

Furniture Guarding: Dog claims one or more pieces of furniture or parts of them and will not get off when asked to.

Attention Demanding: Dog begs, whines, barks or paws at you, and you can't stop him.

Dinner Interrupting: Dog barks, whines or paws when you're at the table and won't stop when told. May even try to take food from you.

◆ Behavior Problems

Many of the serious problems that dogs have stem from their misconception about their rank within your family (pack). Biting people, chasing joggers, going after bicycles and attacking other dogs are all symptoms of a dog who has been led to believe that she is leader of the human pack she lives with. This usually happens with owners who unknowingly lead their dogs to think they are the alpha in the family, which forces the dog by its very nature to protect against all intruders or perceived threats. As soon as the dog's ranking is lowered into a better perspective (the human is alpha), the aggressiveness is reduced or ends.

◆ What Can Lessen Dominant Tendencies in Aggressive Dogs?

Medications are being used to try and change the brain chemistry in aggressive dogs. Just as antidepressants work for millions of people, so can they improve a dog's life. Ask your vet for more information about prescriptions—but for goodness' sake don't attempt to medicate your dog yourself with human prescriptions.

Serotonin is a neurotransmitter that is central to the dominant states—in people and dogs. Fluctuating levels of serotonin are thought to contribute to dominance-related aggression. As a result, serotonin-enhancing medications have a pronounced antiaggressive effect.

Prozac increases serotonin levels and can be effective in reducing dominance-related aggression in some dogs. Once the dog is on the medication, the owners can be more effective in their training and behavior-modification exercises.

◆ Dealing with Dominance

1. Avoid any situations with the potential for confrontation between you and the dog.

2. Do not give the dog any opportunities to reinforce his aggressive response. In time, that reaction will disappear or at least diminish.

3. Steer clear of the dog if he begins any dominant, growling behavior. Steer clear, stay out of his way.

4. Do not crowd a dominant dog. Give the dog space, since feeling cornered can bring out aggression.

5. Any toy or chew items that elicit intense guarding from him should be permanently removed.

6. Don't allow the dog to be at your eye level. Dominant dogs will be more aggressive when their eyes are on the same level as a person's.

7. Don't let the dog up on any furniture, because it raises his eye level (and his ego along with it). Order the dog off any furniture he gets on: have no emotion in your voice, no anger. Point to the ground and say "Off." If he gets right off, praise him with chest scratching and make a fuss. If he won't obey, you have to get him off without dragging him off. Try calling with "Come" or "Let's Go" and give him some encouragement, such as a food treat or toy he loves. After that, see #8, below.

8. Discourage furniture guarding by making the furniture that he guards inaccessible: tip the chair up, remove the sofa cushions, place mousetraps underneath layers of newspaper (lots of layers so dog can't get hurt) as a shocking deterrent to climbing up the next time, use barriers like baby gates propped against the furniture.

9. Avoid all rough games (see page 160 in this chapter) such as wrestling, tug-of-war or slap-boxing (which is slapping the dog gently on either side of his face, a gentle "ear boxing" motion that some men seem to think is the way to play with dogs). All these games stimulate aggressive tendencies in a dog already headed in that direction.

10. Don't play on the ground with a dog that has dominance issues. There are cases in which dominant dogs have attacked and seriously injured owners who did not take dominance issues seriously enough.

DOMINANCE AND FOOD

k, the most important issue is food: who gets first crack at it, and who
mestic dog gets a couple of free meals a day, but her wolf heritage is still
es around food. For many people the wolf in their dog's background
onship or does so in an enjoyable way—but for others it can turn nasty.
ea with the most potential for problems with a dominant dog, it is also an
ct an improvement in your dog's behavior.

If you have a dog with borderline aggression issues such as food-dish guarding, the most important action you can take is to control the dinner hour. You are already in charge of the food because you dispense it, and that has importance to the dog. You need to turn the feeding process into even more of an advantage.

Anytime he gets a meal, it has to be directly from you, on your terms. Make the dog do something for you before you offer the food dish—for example, obeying a simple command such as "sit." It would be even better if he took the more submissive "down" position, but that command inspires resistance in dominant dogs. Decide for yourself if you think you can achieve the "down" without a big hassle—otherwise, go for the sit.

Once the dog executes the command, put down the food bowl without any drama. Let him eat without interruption. When he finishes eating you can pick up the bowl after he leaves the room—there's no point in running the risk of a confrontation over the empty dish.

NOTE: If the dog does not execute the "sit" or "down" commands, the dog does not get that meal. After you give the command you need to wait to the count of ten—do not repeat the command—and then put the dish away and leave the room with no drama or second chances. Your actions get the point across. Don't worry about him skipping a meal—none of us needs to eat as much as we do anyway, and if your hardball tactics work, you have probably kept that dog from becoming more aggressive.

◆ Diet Can Make Dominance Worse.

There are some dietary theories about the role of food in aggressive behavior problems.

High protein in a dog's diet is blamed by some experts for causing increased activity and impulsivity. Low-protein diets are thought to reduce territorial aggression in dogs who also suffer from fearfulness.

Ethoxyquin is an artificial preservative used in many dry dog foods, and it is often blamed for bad behavior in dogs, although nothing has been proven. To be on the safe side, use preservative-free foods such as Innova or California Natural.

Being Tough Is No Longer Recommended.

What scary person thought this one up, anyway: flipping a dog onto her back and pinning her there by the throat? And fortunately, grabbing a dog by the scruff of the neck and shaking her isn't championed anymore, either. Didn't your common sense tell you there was something amiss with this way of thinking? In a training situation, trust your instincts—if a trainer has you doing something that feels wrong, just think of that sixties bumper sticker that read, QUESTION AUTHORITY. Just because a book extols it, or a trainer you're paying demands it, do not do anything to your dog that doesn't feel right to you.

It used to be thought that being firm to the point of roughness with a dog would teach her who was boss, but the days are long gone when trainers suggest coming down hard on dogs—either verbally, with harsh choke chains or by pinning them by the neck to the floor. Those concepts went out with the "spare the rod, spoil the child" kind of thinking. Corporal punishment of children is outdated and offensive; similarly, violent treatment of dogs is now called "animal abuse." Yet until very recently there were nationally recognized dog trainers who advocated throwing a ring of keys right at a dog or hanging them by their collar (the latter was the Monks of New Skete, by the way). That belongs to the bygone (thank goodness) era of paddling schoolchildren and wife-beating.

Roughness is not called for in dealing with dogs, and with some it will backfire, possibly frightening a "soft" dog (one who is timid or fearful) and putting an intense dog on high alert. Being physically harsh with a dog who can't cope with being backed against a wall can cause defensive aggression. Overtly dominant behavior does not exist in a wolf pack, it is not part of a dog's hardwiring, so if you behave that way, it will just disturb a dog.

◆ Don't Be Rough with a Laid-back Dog.
If your dog is content with being a middle-management kind of gal, not a queen bee, then any kind of rough, tough attitudes in training are especially inappropriate, since all the dog wants is to be a team player, a part of a family.

TRIGGERS LEADING TO AGGRESSION
There are a number of things you can do that, instead of putting an assertive dog in her place, as you intended, could actually push her over the edge. This dangerous possibility is another reason to avoid being threatening and intimidating with *any* dog.

◆ Being Told Off
The person yells or hits or raises his hand, or raises a rolled-up newspaper or other "weapon."

◆ Physical Challenges
Being pulled back by the scruff of the neck or collar, being lifted off his feet, being stared at ominously—and for some dogs already close to that edge—even being hugged, patted or groomed, or having his nails cut or ears cleaned.

◆ Confrontation
The person corners the dog or tries to force him to do something he does not want to do.

SAFE ACTIVITIES THAT REINFORCE YOUR AUTHORITY

There are any number of ordinary, everyday activities that you can emphasize to get the idea across to your dog that you are the one in charge of things. Some of these actions are simple; what matters is that you realize the impact of many commonplace events on your relationship with your dog.

LITTLE WAYS TO STAY ON TOP

❑ Frequently practice obedience exercises such as sit, stay, down, come
❑ Avoid aggressive tugging-type games (that he might think he won)
❑ Use an assertive, deep tone of voice when giving a command
❑ Be generous with praise—even for just lying quietly with you
❑ Be consistent—always correct any unwanted behavior *every* time it occurs
❑ Correct misbehavior *at the moment* it happens, or it means nothing
❑ Request a "sit" before patting or giving a treat—make it on your terms
❑ Put a stop to any display of canine dominance (see below)

✦ Dog to Human Dominant Actions

Unless you know which behaviors spell "dominance" to a dog, you could be constantly reinforcing your dog's superiority over you without knowing it. The list below will help you see which of your actions are considered submission by dogs—many of which you probably didn't even know.

Just a reminder, in case it isn't already clear: if you do not have problems with your dog, then this is not really relevant. The dominance issues covered in this section are intended for situations where people are having trouble with their dog's assertive or aggressive behavior. However, even if you have a timid or nervous dog, it can be reassuring for him if you confirm that you are the alpha figure in charge.

DOG DOMINANT BEHAVIOR

❑ Pushing his ball into your lap/hand to throw (high-ranking dogs initiate play)
❑ Pushing his head into your hand/lap to be patted
❑ Leaning against you (canine way of showing strength)
❑ Barking back at you when you give a command
❑ Growling even slightly when touched during chewing/eating/sleeping
❑ Refusing to release a toy or bone
❑ Mouthing your hand when you brush/toenail clip/leash/bathe him
❑ Pulling at your clothing
❑ Pushing past you in a doorway (higher rank goes first)
❑ Lying across a doorway (controlling it)
❑ Lying in a hallway watching human activities (guarding his territory, surveying his pack)

USING AFFECTION TO YOUR ADVANTAGE

There is a way to pat or stroke your dog that reinforces your superior position to her at the same time you are giving her your affection. What you basically need to do to enhance your dominance is ridiculously simple: stroke your dog, beginning just behind her eyes, running your hand slowly and firmly across the top of her head and down her neck, and then finishing at her shoulders.

This stroking across the top of the dog's head and neck—called the "top line"—uses the area that a mother dog uses to get control over her pups. The neck and shoulder are also the areas where dogs exert dominance over each other—in play and attack—with their mouths or paws.

You may think this "dominating affection" is irrelevant to you if your dog is not assertive but actually happens to be timid or shy. However, using techniques that incorporate dominant messages can give a dog confidence she might otherwise lack. An insecure or anxious dog often may be calmed and reassured by knowing that you are in charge: amazingly, she can feel that instinctively simply because of the way in which you stroke her across the top line.

POSITIVE REINFORCEMENT

A new point of view now favored for teaching children (not just dogs!) is to not criticize or try to correct the negative, but instead just ignore it and accentuate the positive. Heap lots of praise when your dog does what you want, and even lots of praise for the dog doing nothing—things such as sleeping at your feet or chewing her bone—when sometimes that is what you want most of all. You can even get down and cuddle or caress her when you're especially grateful that she's being so quiet and good. The best way for her to know what you want is through positive reinforcement.

Dog-Human Play

Playing with a dog has a lot more instinctive importance for the dog than for you. A ball is just a round rubber object to you, but to a dog playing with it, that ball can be symbolic. Bringing a ball back to you—or holding onto it—can be quite a trophy.

In a wolf pack or a situation between dogs, playing is an important way for a dog to test where he stands in the pack hierarchy. If you allow a dog to win a tug-of-war—if you permit him to keep possession of a toy that has become all-important—then that dog will have an inflated opinion of where he stands in your household.

WHERE THE TOYS ARE

The dog should never be the one to initiate play—she should not be coming over to you, pushing her muzzle against your hand and demanding that you play. This is the kind of behavior that only the alpha leader dog should be permitted, and it should be firmly discouraged by any other pack member. Instead, the person should keep the play toys in a separate place. The person decides when and where play will happen: this is part of assuring that a dog does not believe she is above the human in the house. If the dog believes that she is stronger and in charge, that dog may begin challenging human authority.

GAMES TO AVOID

Some of the most common games people play with dogs are ones that teach the dog behavior you wouldn't really want him to engage in. What you think of as just a game may actually be reinforcing natural and instinctive dog behavior that is not appropriate or safe for interaction with people.

Do not play the games listed below, and don't allow children or guests to engage in any of these games or activities, either. And don't bend these rules for anyone: be firm with other people who want to play with your dog, even if they try to convince you it's okay, perhaps because they say their own dog is fine with it or they've had dogs forever.

Dogs have teeth and basic instincts to use them—play is one of the rehearsals they have as pups to use the same techniques later for defense, aggression and feeding. Do not give them more opportunities to practice these techniques.

◆ Chasing the Dog

You may see two dogs playing chase or tag or catch-me-if-you-can. But this game is a poor idea for you and your dog because it teaches him to run away from you, to elude you. There are too many times in everyday life when you do not want this attitude/tendency reinforced in your dog: for example, when he has something in his mouth you want to remove (a dead animal or someone's discarded steak bone) or when you're in a rush and want him in the car or back in the house.

You should not be chasing your dog any more than he should be chasing you. He is not your prey, even in play, and you (or any other person) are not his quarry.

◆ Wrestling, Rough Physical Games

A lot of people—men in particular—like to encourage a dog to wrestle with them. A man will get the dog up on his hind legs and then playfully rough him up around the head and neck, growling and making other noises.

People sometimes encourage dogs, especially large dogs, to come leaping at them in a football tackle sort of way.

Dogs do not understand what people intend in these interchanges. Dogs use their teeth for much of their play, and even if they are well-mannered and try to keep their teeth out of it, eventually in the heat of the moment there can be a slip.

Once a dog's adrenaline is up, there is not an off/on switch you can flip when you want the game to end. It is unfair—even cruel—to wind a dog up and then think you can shut him off like a machine when you've had enough.

When you teach a dog that wrestling and body blocking are a way to play with people he will take you at your word—and he may very well choose a child or older person to leap at or knock over.

If you have the need to wrestle, go to a gym and find someone with two legs.

◆ Chasing Laser Lights

It is entertaining to watch a dog chase a laser beam, but it is not worth the risk: the personality of a dog who gets frantic about chasing light is the kind of dog who is likely to turn the game into an obsessive/compulsive behavior called "shadow-chasing."

Shadow-chasers become fixated on any movement of light and will compulsively chase any reflections, lights or shadows that cross their path of vision. Once this kind of obsessive/compulsive behavior starts it can be disturbing in intensity and very hard to cure. Avoid light-chasing or any similar game that can bring out intense compulsive reactions in a dog.

GOOD GAMES

The desirable games are ones that are fun for you and the dog, encouraging communication between you. They engage the dog's mind and sense of humor. They can tire him out in ways that straight exercise cannot.

◆ Tug-of-war

This game is misunderstood: people are often told to avoid playing it, even though they and their dogs enjoy it. It is mistakenly believed that playing tug with your dog can make her aggressive and that if she wins the tug it encourages her to be dominant or aggressive. But in truth, all you have to do is stop the game if the dog gets too wound up.

Some benefits of tug-of-war:

It is a great release of energy or tension, playing this way with your dog creates a pleasurable bond between you, and it is a valuable tool to distract your dog if you need to redirect her attention from some temptation. It is also a good tool to teach your dog manners because she has to play by your rules.

Set some "house rules" for tug:

❑ The tug toy(s) should be set aside and brought out only when you choose to play. This makes tug-of-war a special occasion and puts you in control.

❑ The dog must not jump up or grab the toy from your hand. You teach this by ending the game: put the toy behind your back if she grabs and say "Ooops!"

❑ When you offer the toy again, say "Take it" or "Tug" and start to play.

❑ Always stop the game a few times during each play session to maintain your controlling position. Have delicious treats in your pocket that you offer and say "Give" or "Out." As soon as the dog lets go of the tug, give a treat and start the game again. This keeps you in charge.

◆ Fetch

This is the most obvious game, but throwing a ball or stick or toy can turn into tug-of-war, which you do not want. This game gives a dog a great, quick workout; it takes very little time and virtually no effort from you—which can sometimes be a good thing.

Not all dogs want to play fetch, however. Some have the desire and instinct to chase an object and bring it back to you. Others have no interest in this game. Some of it has to do with the breed—Labradors and other retrievers are obviously named for this skill—but in some cases it is the individual dog's desire or lack of it. You can try to encourage a dog to fetch who is disinterested by lavishing any attempts with lots of enthusiastic praise from you. But if you have a dog that just stares at you when you toss a toy, then accept that throw-and-retrieve is not going to be a feature of your time together.

If a dog doesn't bring the ball or toy back to you because he does not want to let go of it, you can change this by not paying any attention to the toy. When the dog does come over to you, give him loads of verbal praise and patting and ignore the toy in his mouth. Give him a few moments of paying no attention to the toy he's so proud of and the dog will often then drop it, or release it if you hold your hand near or under his mouth and say "Drop it." If the dog does let it go, give lots of verbal praise and quickly toss it off again, so the reward is the continuation of the game.

If the dog will not let go no matter what, try having two of the same toy or ball so that when he comes back and gets praised, you throw the second object. Most dogs will drop the first one to get the second and you can pick up the just-dropped one to continue the "bait and switch." (Then again, you may wind up with a less-than-Einstein-like dog like my Cocker Spaniel, Amalfi, who would try to pick up toy number two with toy number one still in his mouth. Then he would just sit beside toy number two staring mournfully at it with toy number one in his mouth. These play sessions wound up being relatively short.

◆ Hide and Seek

This is another great game to play with your dog, especially if you have children. You need at least one person in addition to yourself, but you can also have as many people as there are in your household. Dogs can distinguish among different names and make a correct choice when given certain names—as long as when you're sending him you say the name clearly and give huge celebrations when he finds the right person.

Hold the dog while the person who's about to hide gives the dog lots of hugs and kisses. Then that person goes and hides nearby, someplace the dog can clearly see her going. Then you release the dog and cue him: "Sarah. Go get Sarah."

When the dog goes to where he has seen Sarah hide, make a huge fuss over him and how clever he is.

Then do it again, making Sarah's hiding place more difficult each time.

If the dog is not a good searcher—or does not bring enough enthusiasm to the game—have the person who is hiding call the dog's name and make a big fuss over him when he finds them.

◆ Shake Hands

This is a fun one to teach your dog, because giving a paw or pawing is a gesture of submission. You want to take every opportunity to reestablish the dog's subordination to you so there's no doubt in her mind who is boss. Tap your leg and hold out your palm, then tap on the dog's upper leg/shoulder and hold out your palm again. You can even tilt the dog a little off balance and then take hold of his paw to get the idea across. Give lots of vocal and physical encouragement until he gets the point.

A "Dictionary" of Body Language

When you have two different species living as closely together as we do with our dogs, it's important to know if you're sending physical signals that you may be unaware of but that have meaning to the dog. This section covers many physical movements that dogs use to get across important information to other dogs. It also explores the different ways that dogs interpret their species' behavior and ours.

We may wonder how dogs seem to know what we are planning to do way before we ever do it. Is it mind reading? No, they're reading our physical messages, the ones we don't even realize we're sending.

A dog's cognitive powers are very sharp. She sees bags being packed—or even the behavior that precedes getting the bags out—and begins to mope. She sees a stack of towels in your arms and she'll run and hide from the bath you have planned.

READING A DOG'S BODY LANGUAGE

Dogs communicate their state of mind through the position of their body and the expressions on their faces. This section is an attempt to explain many common canine physical attributes and behaviors.

Canine Body Language

HAPPY DOG: *ears relaxed or half back, mouth relaxed and slightly open, eyes relaxed*
CONFIDENT OR AGGRESSIVE DOG: *ears erect, mouth closed, eyes alert*
WORRIED DOG: *ears held to the side, forehead wrinkled with anxious eyes*
FRIGHTENED DOG: *ears back, head down, eyes averted*

If you are unsure of a strange dog's state of mind, this is a quick checklist of how to evaluate a few positions that can reveal the dog's mental state if you want to make a snap judgment.

3 VERSIONS OF CANINE BODY LANGUAGE

- ❏ A dog trying to appear larger is confident, with her tail straight up, ears erect and eyes making direct contact.
- ❏ A threatening dog stands tensely, head held high and forward, neck arched, eyes locked on what he's looking at.
- ❏ A dog who is scared is trying to seem smaller: cowering, ears folded back, tail tucked under, eyes averted.

SIGNS OF HAPPINESS IN DOGS

Tail-wagging, licking and jumping are the three behaviors that we associate with a dog showing love and contentment. Although it often seems to us that there is no doubt about these things, many dog behaviors have no emotional component but go back to wolf behavior that was practical in the wild. However, there are many clues to be gathered from the way your dog exhibits any of these three behaviors, so what follows is some information that may help you understand.

◆ Tail Wagging

Tail position is an indication of how a dog views his own position in any given setting. If the tail is up that means dominance, while a tucked tail means submission.

The tail-wagging tendency varies widely among breeds. How a dog uses its tail "emotionally" depends somewhat on what the intended activity of that breed originally was—or, if you have a mixed breed, the most dominant breed in his makeup. However, much of a purebred dog's tail activity is not so much individual as it is a reflection of the inherited characteristics of that breed. As you will see, in the breed standards for showing, some breeds have docked tails that they use to point in hunting, some shepherd dogs have plumed tails that they hold perfectly still while working, and others hold their tails erect without wagging at all.

◆ Wagging Differences in Breeds

Depending on your dog's heritage, he may be more or less prone to tail-wagging. You should not judge a dog as too reserved or too enthusiastic based solely on that tail activity, because it may be his genetic history being acted out and not his personal reaction to a situation.

- ❑ *Hunting Dogs (Spaniels):* Tend to wag constantly, then hold rigid when prey is found.
- ❑ *Hunting Dogs (Pointers):* The whole body stands still upon locating prey, but the tail wags intensely.
- ❑ *Sled Dogs:* Tail held high to show attentiveness to driver and signal any inter-canine problems.
- ❑ *Herding Dogs:* Tail held low so that movement does not distract herd as it is moved around with nips and the dogs' own body motion.

◆ Jumping Up

Some people think that when their dogs jump all over them when they get home, it's an expression of love and how much they were missed. Those owners might be disappointed to learn that the paw prints the dog inflicted on his owner's clothes had nothing to do with love: in dog language, jumping up is an assertion of dominance over a lesser creature. In the dog-human relationship, people have speculated that jumping up may be an attention-getting device. So if you thought that your dog jumping up on you was a good thing, it might be worth rethinking your dirtied clothes and the things knocked out of your hands.

Trainers agree that the best way to handle a dog's annoying bid for attention is to ignore him. Turn away. Don't react. That means that when your dog jumps up on you, don't yell or pull the dog off or push him away. Simply give him the cold shoulder, and remember that any attention— even negative attention—is still attention, so don't reward him with it. Eventually, a dog who is being ignored will go and lie on his bed. When he does this, go right over and praise him for being a gentleman.

◆ Licking People's Faces

Licking means many different things to dogs and to people. Even experts contradict each other about inter-dog licking. Some experts say that the more dominant dog licks its own nose and sometimes that of the other dog—while the submissive dog nervously flicks his own tongue. But other experts say that the submissive dog licks the lips of the dominant one. This is presumed to come from a wolf cub's habit of licking his mother's mouth when she gets back to the den, in order to stimulate her to regurgitate whatever she's eaten so that her lunch becomes his. (Ah, mother nature.)

Many dog owners encourage their dogs to lick them on the face. If you like being licked, then praise your dog for it. This won't cause any problem from the point of view of who's in charge but I hope you wouldn't go so far as to throw up your lunch for him.

There are some dog lovers (I am at the top of that list) who cannot stand to be licked on the face by a dog—or by anyone, really. Teaching a dog not to lick the face is easy. Just turn your face aside, firmly say "No" and ignore the dog for a moment. If he stops trying to tongue your face, praise him and play with him. If he persists in wanting to lick you, repeat the steps above and give him a toy instead. I've never had a dog or even a puppy continue trying to lick me for long. If the licking attempt happens when the dog is greeting you, then have something to put in his mouth like a toy or a "towel burrito" (see page 193 in Chapter Eight, "Everyday Life with Your Dog") so he isn't tempted. For the most part, it should be enough to just turn your face away, and then pat and praise the dog when he stops licking.

DIFFERENCES IN HUMAN/DOG COMMUNICATION STYLES

There are big differences in how humans and canines communicate through body language. If you know what the differences are, you can modify your behavior or at least learn what your dog is interpreting from the signals you are sending, usually unintentionally.

◆ Making Eye Contact

Humans think that it is polite and a sign of good manners to look someone in the eye. However, eye contact between dogs is a sign of dominance: the more assertive dog will stare down the lesser one, and whichever dog can hold a stare longer is the victor.

Most well-socialized dogs eventually learn that when a human makes eye contact, they are not being threatened. When dogs watch us, they watch our eyes—because to dogs, eyes are an important means of communicating authority. Dogs who are insecure and submissive by nature can be frightened by human attempts to establish eye contact.

Use eye contact for power. You can use eye contact to establish or reestablish your higher rank. Just stare at a dog.

Warnings about eye contact Never stare into the eyes of a dog you don't know—an assertive dog can view this as a challenge and become defensive or offensive with you. An unknown dog may even attack, feeling provoked by your staring

Withholding eye contact to dismiss your dog Stop looking at a dog that pesters you for attention. Break off visual contact for the ultimate snub in dog language. Turn your head away in a "snobby" position—with your chin raised, your head turned to the side. Although snubbing someone may go against our instincts when dealing with other people, doing so will drive a dog away faster than anything else.

◆ Your Body Language Interpreted by the Dog

For dogs, standing over another dog is the way they establish and maintain dominance. When humans bend over a dog and reach toward him, some dogs view this action as a threat—and many dog bites occur because of this misunderstanding. So if you are standing above a dog you don't know, especially a fearful or aggressive one, don't be surprised if you get a snarl or worse. Pay attention to any such noise that a dog makes: this is intended as a warning, to make you back off. If you don't heed the warning, you could become the victim of a dog bite—one that never needed to occur.

If you stand right over a shy or frightened dog, she may submissively urinate or "submit" to you by rolling over on her back with her legs in the air.

◆ Noticing Dogs' Visual Signals to Us

Dogs are sending us signals all the time about how they're reacting to us or other stimuli in the environment. Despite what you hear, very rarely does a problem with a dog come out of nowhere in either dog-to-dog aggression or dog-to-human problems. Dogs give signals with every part of their anatomy: ears, tail, body stance, eyes, even lips. You just have to learn how to read the information and decipher the code.

◆ Greetings—the Approach

Dogs do not approach head-on and they do not look directly into each other's eyes the way people do. If two dogs were to come at one another head on, eye-to-eye, it would cause tension that could result in aggression. Dogs greet from the side, and they avoid direct eye contact. Looking directly into a dog's eyes is like a slap in the face to some dogs; for shy dogs the head-on approach is even worse.

The best way to greet an unknown dog It's much safer to stand sideways and let a dog come to you. When you're going to make initial contact with a dog, the least threatening way to do so is to squat down, turn sideways and let the dog come to you.

Try this: stop a few feet from a new dog. Stand sideways. Don't look directly into her eyes. Wait for the dog to come all the way to you. If she doesn't, then she doesn't want to be petted, and you should respect that.

If the dog approaches with a stiff body, stay still. If the dog is relaxed, hold your hand low (not over her head, which can be threatening) and let her sniff it with your palm closed.

When you do pat an unfamiliar dog, do so beneath the chin or on the chest—never on top of the head.

◆ The Dog "Smile"

A dog can pull back the corners of her mouth, which to us may look like a smile, but do not be misled: a "smile" in a dog is not a good sign. When the corners of a dog's mouth pull back it's often from submission or fear—such a facial expression is a big indicator of a dog's state of mind. You will see the corners pull back even in an aggressive dog that is growling and showing teeth. If the corners go backward it's a defensive grin. If the dog is also growling it means she's afraid of losing something of value to her and is guarding it with her growl and expression. If the corners of her mouth are forward it can be a serious threat: this dog can be dangerous. Dogs with either expression can bite, so if it is your own dog exhibiting this so-called "dog smile," you need an experienced trainer who is humane yet firm to help you evaluate the dog and devise a plan.

Miscommunication in Physical Displays of Affection

There are substantial differences between dog (wolf-pack) behavior and human/primate habits where affection is concerned. Knowing these areas should improve communication with your dog.

HUGGING

Humans love to hug, but dogs have no such activity. The closest behavior in the canine repertoire is to paw at another dog to get her to play. A dog can also place a paw on the shoulder of another to show dominance and establish social status, but there is no equivalent to human hugging. In fact, many dogs will growl if hugged. Hugging is perceived as a domineering, threatening display. Hugging a dog can trigger an attack, it's that alien to them.

Individual dogs may react differently. Your own dog may permit you to hug her, but not because it's pleasurable to her, just to show you respect. As long as you know what a hug means to most dogs, you can understand that some will react more negatively than others.

PATTING ON THE HEAD

Many dogs interpret being patted on top of their head as a threatening gesture. Instead, you might want to try reaching under the dog's chin and scratching him there. You can also pat him on the shoulder.

Many dogs find "head pats" an aggressive move by a person—and they can react defensively. I'm referring to the short, staccato, bang-bang-bang taps with rigid fingertips that many of us use on dogs without stopping to wonder how it feels. (If you want to know how uncomfortable that is, try it on your own head, or ask someone else to tell you what it feels like when you do it to them.) Most dogs learn to put up with patting as a display of affection from people, but it can be pretty unpleasant, and discomfort is obviously the last thing you want your dog to feel.

A person reaching his hand over the top of the dog's head can be hard for some dogs to tolerate. However, you can turn the way you stroke your dog's head to your advantage when communicating with your dog.

VERBAL VS. VISUAL

Humans are verbal—we don't just talk, we tend to talk even more when we are anxious, excited or happy.

Dogs are visual. They pick up hundreds of subtle physical signals that we're constantly giving, most without being aware of what we're doing. Dogs notice everything we do. They react to us. Dogs assume that the small changes in our face and body actually mean something, since in dog language, all movement means something. Small things we do can have a big effect on what our dog does. We're communicating with our bodies all the time—so why not put that to use?

We raise our voices and speak louder when we're not understood, because that's what humans do. But words—and especially loud words—mean nothing to dogs. Becoming aware of what we do—paying attention to our motions, our head movements, our shifts in weight forward or backward, the stiffening or relaxing of our bodies—will improve our dog relationships and the understanding between us. Some people are naturals at this. The rest of us just have to learn and then practice.

GOOD WAYS TO TOUCH DOGS

For most dogs, petting is pure pleasure. The motion of scratching or stroking is their favorite, not the pat-pat motion we are taught as children to use with animals and carry forward into life, thinking we're doing the right thing.

✦ Ears

Dogs *love* to have their ears stroked—it appears to be sensual for them and has a calming effect on most dogs. Take the whole flap of the ear between your thumb and finger where the ear is attached to the dog's head and stroke gently down. When the dog is lying down you can stroke the ear flap down against the dog's cheek, smoothing it with a light, firm touch.

Scratching a dog behind the ears where the ears attach to the head—either both ears at once or one at a time—also makes dogs happy.

✦ Chest

Dogs love to have their chest scratched or rubbed, right between the front legs.

✦ Head

If you watch a dog's expression and body language, you will often see him duck his head down or recoil from a human hand coming right at his head. Try the shoulder or chest for a loving pat instead.

✦ Cheeks

Dogs love to have their cheeks stroked and scratched, from the corner of their mouths to their ears. Some people think there may be glands in the cheeks that enhance the pleasurable feeling, but whatever the reason, you can certainly endear yourself to a dog by working that area with your fingers.

✦ Stifle Area

There is an area of taut skin right where the hind leg fits into the torso called the *stifle*. In a horse, this is such a sensitive area that you know to avoid it or groom very gently, because horses will often kick or bite if you apply too much pressure there. It's not clear how that sensitivity corresponds to a dog's anatomy, but apparently, a mother dog nibbles on a puppy is that area getting out of line and it settles him down.

The stifle area is the stretched skin that connects the dog's back leg to the torso around the ribs. Roll the skin between your fingers, massaging it. Your dog's expression should be pure bliss.

◆ **Face/Muzzle Cupping**

Cup your hands around your dog's muzzle. In wolf language, when two wolves meet, the lower-ranked wolf will put her mouth inside the mouth of the more dominant wolf. The lower-ranked animal then licks the alpha wolf under his chin. Sometimes you'll see dogs who live together doing some version of this. And if you cup your hand over the top of a dog's nose and give it gentle pressure, most dogs will wag their tails and relax.

(NOTE: Do not scratch or stroke a potentially dominating dog underneath the chin, because this is a subordinate gesture—beneath the chin is where the lower-ranked dog licks a higher-ranked one, so it's an area already designated for a certain message.)

Introducing Your Dog to a New Partner

If you are a single person, you need to appreciate the difficulty your dog may have when you start seeing someone—or even the threat that is posed by a really close friend or a relative who has come to live with you. It is not unusual for a dog who has had you all to himself to resent and reject a new person in your life.

THE NEW PERSON AS A "TREAT MACHINE"

During the adjustment period, the new person should give the dog an occasional biscuit and a nice chest or tummy rub. The new arrival should also ask for a "sit" before giving the biscuit, to establish a pecking order with the new person higher on the ladder than the dog.

CREATING A BOND

Another way to build your dog's rapport with the new person is to treat your dog as a "third wheel." Go out of your way to include him in everything so that he doesn't feel left out. If he is treated like an outsider, he'll "blame" the newcomer for that. Resentment and jealousy are easier to avoid than to overcome.

For example: if you and the new person are talking animatedly, laughing or horsing around and the dog starts to bark, instead of yelling at him to be quiet, clap your hands and praise him for asking to be included . . . which might be the case.

CONNECT THE NEW PERSON WITH GOOD TIMES.

Include your dog in everything that you and the newcomer can do that involves fun—beach walks, swimming, even just a car ride. You want the dog to associate the new person with good times.

Let the newcomer give the dog her meals and play the dog's favorite games with her.

LET THE DOG SET THE PACE.

Some dogs are slower to warm up than others; some don't like someone coming at them with hands, face, voice, etc. So unless your dog is especially gregarious (in which case you probably won't have any adjustment problems), don't force the bonding with your new friend. Let the dog keep whatever distance makes her happy. Curiosity will eventually bring her closer.

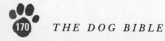

Chapter 8

EVERYDAY LIFE WITH YOUR DOG

This chapter is a practical one, covering many of the day-to-day issues and choices you may have about how you cohabitate with your dog. Some of the topics covered in this chapter are:

☐ *What to expect*—having realistic expectations of your dog
☐ *Human allergy to dogs*—ways to lessen allergens; charts of breeds that are considered "hypoallergenic," or not likely to cause an allergic reaction
☐ *Sleeping arrangements*—the choices of where, with whom and on what
☐ *Equipment and products*—dog doors, ramps, cleaning products, toys
☐ *Your dog's daily schedule*—organizing your dog's life
☐ *Daily exercise*—for the country dog or the city dog
☐ *Water safety and emergency first aid*
☐ *City dogs*—their special needs and the burden of guilt on the working owner
☐ *Lost dogs*—how to prevent this tragedy (including types of fencing), and what to do if it happens
☐ *Disaster preparedness*—planning for your dog in case of a general catastrophe or your own personal crisis (such as an injury or delay in getting home)

Your Dog Is Not a Person

Unrealistic expectations are the cause of much unhappiness in our lives, particularly where relationships are concerned. It is worth keeping that idea in mind when you think about your expectations of what of a dog's place should be in the human home, whether it's perfect obedience and control, an animal in place of a child, companionship instead of loneliness, or the adventure of living in symbiotic harmony with another species.

As you set out to plan your cohabitation with a dog, please keep in mind that underneath it all, a dog is really a dog—and that is the true beauty of sharing your life with her. Think of a clichéd phrase like "Dogs will be dogs" and realize that it's just a simple truth that affirms the inherent "dogness" of the animal. There are people who become so attached to their dogs that they stop thinking of them as canines and begin to think of them as four-legged little people (with different "hair issues" than ours).

There is no value judgment intended about people who are deeply attached to their dogs and live with them always by their side. It's great to adore your pet, for him to be your "best friend" and go everywhere with you—but fussing over a dog and pampering him is not always kind. Treating a dog like a human child can be an unfair burden because there is still that basic wolf-pack background in every dog. A four-legged animal can suffer from stress if he is expected to conform to expectations of human behavior and human responses. Some dogs will be confused and not feel comfortable being waited on by humans. No matter how loving and generous you are to your dog it is thoughtless to assume that he understands concepts that are beyond his ability.

Human Allergy to Dogs

People usually think that dog hair causes their allergic reaction, but there are actually three ways in which people can be allergic to dogs: to their fur, their dander or their saliva. In the case of saliva, people can have allergic symptoms when a dog licks them, but they may often not realize the cause and continue to let dogs touch their skin with saliva. Even when a dog is pretty hairy and sheds a lot, what most people who are allergic are reacting to is the dead skin cells flaking off.

You can have a dog for years and then seem to suddenly develop an allergy, but it does not actually happen immediately. The development of an allergy can take from weeks to years: once there are enough antibodies in your system, you will begin to have the allergic symptoms, generally in your nose, eyes, lungs and and/or digestive system.

PERSONALIZED INDIVIDUAL REACTIONS

Allergies can vary greatly between one person and another, and your reaction can even vary from one dog to another within a breed.

If you know you are allergic, then visit a few different breeds and see whether there's a difference in your reaction. You owe it to a potential dog to make sure that your allergy doesn't wind up punishing her so that she can't be in rooms with you. This would not be anything a dog could understand or, in some cases, even tolerate.

Before making a final breed choice, have your allergies tested by a doctor who specializes in allergy treatments. With a series of shots spaced out over many months, you can lessen your allergic reaction to dogs or eliminate it entirely.

CHILDREN'S ALLERGIES TO DOGS

Doctors often tell parents of children who have allergies that they should not have pets. Until recently, most research on allergies focused on reducing the amount of allergens—such as pet dander—that a person is exposed to. Newer research suggests that early exposure to pets might actually help a child's immune system build defenses against allergies and even asthma.

One research study involving nearly 1,000 one-year-old children showed that those who were exposed to two or more cats and dogs were less susceptible to other allergens by the time they were seven years old. Other studies have shown that early exposure to cat dander decreased the risk of asthma in children aged twelve to fourteen. Asthma rates have doubled in the United States since 1980 and have become a huge health concern among affected children.

Another study of nearly 300 kids tracked from birth to five years of age showed that those who had a dog were much less likely to develop allergic skin rashes, a sign that the immune systems of such children are stronger than those of children who don't have a dog in the home. There is speculation that it may not be the dog herself but the dirt that she tracks in that primes the child's immune system and helps infants develop a stronger immune response.

CHOOSING DOGS THAT ARE LESS ALLERGY-PROVOKING

◆ Non-shedding Breeds

There is really no breed of dog that doesn't shed at all; the skin and hair of all dogs is constantly flaking off and being replaced by new growth. Some breeds are referred to as "dander-free," such as Bedlington Terriers and Poodles, but they are really just a few of the low-dander, low-shedding breeds (see next page). However, if it is dog *saliva* that causes your allergy, it would make no difference if a low-dander dog were to lick you: it might as well be a hairy Old English Sheepdog, you'd still have an allergic reaction.

People with allergies are told to find a non-shedding breed, which generally means any breed with hair that keeps growing unless it is clipped (as opposed to breeds that "shed out," or drop those hairs that you're allergic to). Non-shedding breeds are curly-coated breeds such as the Poodle, Bichon Frise, the Portuguese Water Dog; and "minimal shedders" are terriers such as the Bedlington, Kerry Blue, Soft Coated Wheaten and both sizes of Schnauzers. Lastly there are low-shedding or single-coated dogs such as Basenjis, Italian Greyhounds, Chihuahuas and Maltese. Another reason that non-shedding dogs may be less allergy-provoking is that these breeds require more frequent grooming, which can decrease the amount of dead skin cells you are exposed to.

However, it is a myth that non-shedding breeds are less likely to trigger allergies. Dander has to do with the skin—not the hair—and even *hairless* dogs have skin that is constantly renewing itself and dropping dead cells in the process. Also, if canine saliva is the true cause of your allergic reaction, those hairless dogs are just as likely to lick themselves and then lick you as any other kind of dog.

Most Hypoallergenic Breeds

Basenji	Irish Water Spaniel	Shih Tzu
Bedlington Terrier	Kerry Blue Terrier	Soft Coated Wheaten
Bergamasco	Lowchen (Little Lion Dog)	Terrier
Bichon Frise	Maltese	Spanish Water Dog
Bolognese	Native American	Tibetan Terrier
Border Terrier	Indian Dog	West Highland White
Cairn Terrier	Poodles (all sizes)	Terrier
Coton de Tulear	Portuguese Water Dog	Wirehaired Fox
(a kind of Bichon)	Puli	Terrier
Havanese	Schnauzer (all sizes)	Yorkshire Terrier

♦ **Hairless Dogs**

There are only a few breeds of hairless dogs, but having allergies is no reason to choose these breeds. Keep in mind that these dogs may not have fur coats, but they still have skin and saliva, which are the primary causes of allergies in people. Therefore, choosing these breeds solely for their nonallergenic qualities would be foolish unless it is a breed you are already attracted to (or you want a rare breed of dog because you like having a dog that you can be pretty sure no one else has). These are some exotic- sounding (and -looking) pooches: the American Hairless Terrier, the Chinese Crested, the Hairless Khala, the Peruvian Inca Orchid and the Xoloitzcuintle—and yes, that is the correct spelling.

High(er)-dander Breeds

In these breeds the top layer of skin—the epidermis—is replaced more rapidly. Since that dead skin is what causes most human allergic reactions, these breeds would be the ones to avoid. These are dogs that are prone to dry or oil seborrhea (scaling), which causes rapid epidermal turnover—their skin flakes off in a matter of days instead of weeks.

Afghan Hound	Doberman Pinscher
Bassett Hound	German Shepherd
Chinese Shar-Pei	Irish Setter
Cocker Spaniel	Springer Spaniel
Dachshunds	

REDUCING YOUR ALLERGIC REACTION

There are ways to live with your dog and minimize your allergies. The suggestions below should help you to live more comfortably with your dog.

◆ Dander and Dry Skin

When a person is allergic to dogs, the reaction is usually to the dander on the dog's skin. Dander consists of dead skin cells and other microbiotic waste matter. Think of it as dandruff. If the dog's skin is dry, it can cause itchiness and irritation, which spreads more dander because the dog scratches himself more. You need to determine why the dog's skin is so dry, correct the problem and then minimize the presence of dander.

COMMON CAUSES OF DRY SKIN

❑ Dermatological reasons such as mange, hormone or thyroid imbalance, flea-bite allergies or bacterial dermatitis

❑ Poor nutrition can result in an imbalance in the essential fatty acids in the dog's diet, causing dry, flaky skin

❑ Not bathing the dog frequently enough

❑ Using the wrong shampoo, which can dry out a dog's skin (See below under "Bathing.")

❑ If a dog is not brushed frequently, the natural oils in his skin will not be distributed to the coat.

◆ Bathing to Reduce Allergens

Just bathing your dog on a weekly basis may give you the best result of all. People generally don't know that baths are good for dogs (and good for anyone who gets itchy, sneezy, drippy or "hivey" around dogs). The frequency with which you can and should wash your dog is often misunderstood: people think that bathing a dog can dry out her coat and skin, but it actually reduces the amount of dander. You will benefit from bathing your dog every week, and if you are really allergic, you can wash her as often as twice a week, always using good dog shampoos.

Skin problems from bathing can occur when dog owners make the mistake of using shampoo meant for people: even the highest-quality human shampoo has a pH factor that is wrong for dogs. People can also use a medicated shampoo for dogs too often, which can cause the skin to dry out (see page 404 under "Grooming" for more on this). Use a gentle, high-quality dog shampoo for regular baths. If there is still flaking, using conditioner (made for dogs) after the bath can help control dander.

If you are so allergic that your symptoms get worse during the actual bathing process, enlist a family member or friend to do the honors, or have a mobile dog bathing service come to the house if it's available in your area. Failing any of that, bite the bullet and make a weekly appointment at the local groomer or at your vet's, if he offers bathing services.

✦ Larger Dog=More Skin=More Allergies

There is an almost simpleminded logic to determining which dogs are going to cause you the least allergic reaction: it has to do with their size more than breed or coat type. The larger the dog, the more skin surface he has, and therefore the more dander he produces and the worse the allergic reaction. However, that doesn't mean that smaller is necessarily better. The very smallest of all dogs, the Chihuahua, is *not* considered a low-allergen breed.

✦ Topical Products That Can Help

DanderFree is one of the brands of probiotic sprays that claim to contain "friendly" microbes that feed on the dander. It sounds kind of creepy—the idea of a "carnivorous" spray!—but whether or not that's really how it functions did not interest me as much as the results. I am allergic to dogs. A couple of weekly sprayings of DanderFree followed by a brushing of my short-haired, dandruff-prone Weimaraners eliminated the white flakiness on their skin and reduced my allergic reactions. You can find DanderFree (or similiar products like Nature's Miracle Dander Remover & Body Deodorizer) in pet stores or at www.heredog.com.

✦ Eliminate Carpeting Where You Can.

Carpets are great collectors of all allergens, particularly animal dander since the pets are always down there at carpet level. Wall-to-wall carpeting is toughest, but large area rugs can also harbor all sorts of allergens. Eliminate carpets wherever you can.

✦ Put an Electrostatic Air Filter on Your Heating System.

The central-heating (and air-conditioning) system in your house needs a special filter to help clean the air that is circulating through the house.

✦ Keep Your Dog Off Furniture, Your Bed or Certain Rooms.

If you allow your dog to get up on chairs and sofas, it will increase the amount of allergens you're exposed to, because she will sprinkle them right where you will later sit. There's no good reason to allow even the smallest dogs up on furniture, where they can leave footprints, hair and dander (see page 179 on "Dog Beds" for suggestions on the many comfortable choices available). If your dog is accustomed to getting up on furniture and you actually like it, use washable slipcovers or cover the furniture the dog gets on with a throw or sheet that you can wash often—and wash those throws as often as possible.

Your dog should definitely not be on your bed, where you will be breathing in the debris that settles off your dog's coat and skin for eight hours. If you are both in this habit already and are unable or unwilling to give it up, then wash your bedding constantly to remove the allergens that the dog deposits there every night.

If you are willing to keep your dog out of your bedroom entirely, you should keep your bedroom door shut at all times so that you can breathe more freely when sleeping and waking.

❖ Wash Your Hands After Touching Your Dog.
Allergens on our dogs can be absorbed through our skin as well as inhaled, so any direct contact with them can increase our allergies. The more you wash your hands after patting or playing with your dog, the more you can reduce your allergic response.

❖ Wash the Dog's Bedding and Soft Toys.
Wash everything that the dog comes into contact with on a frequent basis, using hot water.

❖ Get a Great Vacuum Cleaner and Use It Frequently.
You might think that vacuuming frequently would be a good idea, but if you don't have a really great vacuum it can make things worse by stirring up the dust and allergens that settle in the carpets. One thing you need on your vacuum is a HEPA filter that you change frequently: make the investment in a high-quality vacuum cleaner intended for people with environmental allergies. Then you can vacuum every day and know that you are getting in deep where allergens can settle in carpets and crevices.

❖ Buy Electric/Electronic Room-air Cleaners.
There are dozens of air cleaners/purifiers/filters on the market; many are expensive, some work wonders, some are noisy, others are unobtrusive and many are ineffective. Most claim to have a HEPA filter, but I've found it's more about how they work. The ionizers from Sharper Image are advertised a lot and are all about style, but the one I had just stopped working and they wouldn't stand behind it. It can be hard to choose without trying machines, but the good news is that you can try them risk free. You can conduct your own process of elimination by putting a few of these machines around your house, in rooms where you and the dog(s) spend the most time, and see which one makes a dramatic difference in your allergies.

You have to shop and compare with a "safety net"—meaning buy a machine, try it, and be certain of the company or store's return policy so that if it gives you no relief you can return it for a full refund (*not* a store credit). This is one of the beauties of the American shopping experience: there is the freedom to try a product and get reimbursed for it if you are not satisfied with the results. If you love being close to your dog, but you have miserable allergic reactions doing so, it is worth your while to outfit your rooms with purifiers that will eliminate much of that discomfort.

I don't want to get into the consumer-guide business of shop-and-compare on air purifiers, but I would like to share my own extensive pursuit of dander-free air. For years I had one of those round, pale-gray air cleaners that looked like small air-conditioning units: they were relatively cheap, but I got what I paid for since it made no difference in my symptoms. If you turned it up higher it sounded like a helicopter trying to take off. There was a mesh filter that wrapped around the body of the machine that you rinsed to clean it. Then I got an upright air purifier, which was also an ionizer and was quieter and less cumbersome than the round canister: it was the size of a small radiator and had a replaceable filter plus a mesh filter that could be rinsed. It was some help, but I was still dabbing at my drippy eyes and nose whenever I was in my study (always with one or all of the dogs on beds in the room). I kept on searching and finally hit the jackpot, even though at first I didn't even think it was going to work. Hoover makes an air purifier called SilentAir (the 2000 model for smaller rooms, the 4000 for rooms up to 500 square feet) that is about the size of a portable PC notebook. It works on an entirely different principle: there is no fan, absolutely no noise. I'm no scientist so I don't actually understand the principle of negative ions: particles are magnetized onto a paper-thin filter inside, which then signals when the filter is ready to be changed, usually once a month.

Human allergies to dogs are so widespread that it seemed worth the space it takes to tell you that since I've had that Hoover SilentAir, my allergic reactions have really improved. You should take the time to find a brand of air cleaner that works for you to make you physically more compatible with your dog.

Sleeping Arrangements

HOW MUCH DO DOGS SLEEP?

On average, a dog will sleep fifty percent of the time, rest for thirty percent of the time and be active for only about twenty percent of her day. There is a lot of individual variation, however, so if your dog sleeps more than this amount it should not be cause for alarm.

As the dog gets older there will be changes in the sleep-wake cycle. Some senior dogs get up at night and make noises and pace around, and then they sleep more during the day.

SHOULD A DOG SLEEP IN YOUR BEDROOM?

Most dog trainers will tell you that it really makes a positive difference to have your dog sleeping in the bedroom. Because wolves live in packs and sleep together in dens, your dog expects to sleep with the members of his pack, and especially the "alpha" leader—you. Behaviorists seem to agree that inviting your dog to sleep in your bedroom can make a dog more attached to you and more protective of you.

Professionals usually recommend keeping a puppy crated in your bedroom at night, thereby accustoming him to sharing your sleeping habitat. The same goes—even more so—for an adopted older dog with whom you want to build an attachment. If, for some reason, you are averse to sharing your sleeping quarters with a dog (perhaps you have terrible allergies that would be further aggravated in a smaller space all night), then trainers suggest that you let a puppy (or a newly acquired older dog) spend at least a week in your bedroom at night, for the bonding value. Also, you might change your mind.

SHOULD A DOG SLEEP IN YOUR BED?

What are the ramifications of your dog sleeping with you? If you have a multi-dog home, how does that affect bed-sleeping in terms of harmony among the dogs and enough room for you, with or without a partner? How does it affect your quality of sleep? Or your sex life, if you're in a relationship? What if your dog sleeps with you and you aren't in an intimate relationship with someone, but then you start seeing someone and there are "bed issues"? These are questions you can ask yourself, but keep in mind that they are rhetorical questions with no definitive answers.

The one-bed sleeping issue that behaviorists mention is that you should not allow your dog to sleep on your bed if you have a dog with an aggressive streak or she has been hard to obedience train. In wolf terms, a dog sleeping on your bed has equal status with you—which is only a problem if the dog knows better but has been challenging you and won't follow commands.

DOG BEDS

Dogs usually need to have a bed of their own. Even if they sleep on your bed at night, they can enjoy their own beds the rest of the time. What a bed consists of can be almost anything soft and cozy, from a folded-up old quilt or blanket to the many different kinds of commercially made dog beds. Some dogs are pickier than others about what kind of bed they like. See if there's a way to let the dog try out some beds before you commit to one kind or another.

◆ Kinds of Beds

There are many different kinds of **beanbag-type beds,** but whether your individual dog likes them can depend on what they are filled with. Some have loose cedar shavings inside, others have ground-up foam, while others have a synthetic cotton material.

Another style of bed is the **rectangular piece of solid foam,** one side of which may have a waffle texture.

There are different versions of a high-end, soft **rectangular bed with zip-off covers** in really nice fabrics. The distinguishing characteristic of these beds is that the inside bed is a boxed pillow shape, which has stitching holding the quadrants apart so that all the stuffing doesn't wind up bunched at one end. Superior Pet Bedding, makers of "Wynken Blynken & Fido" make their beds that way (see below for more). My Weimaraners have all loved these beds and they are the pickiest of pooches—often whining and scratching, trying to rearrange other styles of beds.

There are **box-spring beds**—high structures that look like the box spring of a human mattress and are about that big! Dogs love them—they're up high and can survey their kingdom. The only problem is, who has enough space for such a large piece of furniture?

There are also **"cuddler" beds,** which are made of a circle of foam that has a stand-up back attached to the circle with a synthetic lambskin cover. Many different sizes of dogs adore the "cuddler" style because they can curl their backs up against the upright back and it will cuddle them. The elasticized cover can be irritating to try to get back on after washing, but it's worth it when you see how content your dogs are with that style.

There are even **water beds** made just for dogs, believe it or not. There are at least two companies that make them—Woods Waterbeds for Pets and Tasso Doggy Waterbeds—and the companies say that the beds are especially beneficial for dogs recovering from surgery or illness, or those suffering with arthritis. As our grandmothers used to say, "What will they think of next?"

For older dogs (see "Senior Dogs" on page 646) there are a number of **comfort beds,** including some that are heated, and orthopedic beds with mattress foam that qualifies as human-grade.

There are a number of sources for pet beds—especially catalogs and the Internet—where you can look at the products and compare prices and details. L.L. Bean is famous for their durable beds with washable covers, and you can always count on that quality company to stand behind (and replace if necessary) anything that it makes. Drs. Foster & Smith (catalog and www.drsfostersmith.com) have many pet beds (I confess to splurging on two of their high mattress-style beds to entice my dogs off my furniture: those dog mattresses cost more than human ones I've purchased, but they've turned out to be worth every penny because my couches are finally dog-free). Another site worth checking out is www.westpawdesigns.com, as are www.caddis.com and www.kuranda.com for other types of beds.

As mentioned, my personal favorite model of dog bed is from a company called Superior Pet Bedding, which makes a line with a black stitched-on tag that says "Wynken Blynken & Fido." They are rectangular beds, tufted in several places to keep the stuffing from bunching up, with very well-made zip-off covers in gorgeous fabrics. I found mine at T.J. Maxx—various sizes at many different times—and cannot recommend them enough for style and durability. Linens 'n' Things may carry them, too.

◆ About Dog-bed Covers

It's important that whatever kind of bed you get has a removable cover that can be washed. Try taking the cover off before you buy to be sure it's really easy to get on and off. There's no way you're going to throw those covers in the wash every time they get dirty, unless putting the covers back on is no hassle.

Necessities for Canine Care

CLEANING PRODUCTS

So many products we use around the house are unnecessarily harsh and toxic to our dogs. What follows are some ways to make your home safer for your pet while also benefiting you and any children in the household.

Start shopping for "green" and ecologically correct products, which are available at any large supermarket. Others are available at local health-food shops. We all spray and splash vast quantities of overly strong cleaners all over our houses, and our dogs are breathing it in and lying down on it.

Some brands of natural cleaning products include Simple Green, Ecover, Life Tree, Naturally Yours and Seventh Generation.

◆ The Floors of Your House

The floors of your home—what covers them and how best to keep them clean—are the most urgent area to focus on since that's where dogs spend so much of their days.

Carpets If you have wall-to-wall carpeting, you might want to consider taking it up since carpeting collects so much debris—hair, footprints and parasites.

If you can't eliminate the carpet, then you can freshen wall-to-wall or large area rugs by mixing equal parts of baking soda and borax, sprinkling it on the carpet and vacuuming it up.

Wood floors These are best cleaned with warm water mixed with white vinegar. Put the mixture into a spray bottle, squirt a small section of the floor at a time and dry mop it.

Tile or vinyl floors Mix a gallon of hot water with two tablespoons of castile soap. Mop in small sections with a well-squeezed-out mop. You do not have to rinse—and it's not toxic to the dog if she happens to lick the floor.

Bathrooms This is an issue for people whose dogs drink out of the toilet bowl. Certainly stop putting any chemical cleanser in the bowl—because it will wind up in your dog's stomach—and substitute Simple Green, an ecologically friendly product that has instructions for bathrooms. None of my dogs shows any interest in toilet drinking, but maybe that's because I change the water in their bowls several times a day (pretty much every time I walk past the bowls, actually), which seems to satisfy their desire for fresh, cool water.

Dog bedding Wash with the mildest possible soap, like laundry soap for babies. If you have an especially sensitive dog, put the bedding through the rinse cycle once more after the washing process is over.

CANINE CLOTHING

(Dog life jackets for the water: see page 204 of the "Water Safety" section)

◆ Cold-weather Coats (See page 182 in this chapter for more on "Cold Weather Comfort.")

Canine outerwear (for lack of a better identifier) comes in an endless array of materials and styles. Of course, whether or not your dog really needs outerwear depends on a variety of factors, such as whether your climate is very cold, your dog has limited natural insulation and/or she is very small, old or young. Dog boutiques and dog catalogs are full of these coats and sweaters. You're on your own going down that doggie fashion path.

But there are some dog coats that are purely practical, easy to put on, give a good fit and keep your dog comfortable. The Apache River Dog Blanket is one of these: it's a great-fitting coat that is easy on/off and runs between $35 and $70. It is made by a company that makes horse blankets. The manufacturer asks (as all dog-clothing makers do) for the measurement of your dog from her collar to the beginning of her tail. By giving them the girth of her chest, too, you'll get a better fit. Available through Norman Equine Designs, (800) 348-5873 or www.horse-blankets.com.

◆ Visibility Vest

If you hike or jog or walk in the woods with your dog, many safety issues are solved if he can be easily seen—whether by others or you. The Quick Spot reflective vest by Pointer Specialties is a good, straightforward product. The nylon vest is water-resistant, attaches to his collar and forms a blanket on his back, with a comfortable Velcro closing beneath his stomach. There is reflective tape sewn onto each side of the fluorescent orange vest—no one is going to miss your dog. It comes in four sizes and costs about $15. Call (717) 292-4776.

◆ Canine Boots

City dogs who live in climates where it gets cold in the winter have to walk on sidewalks where salt is spread, which burns the pads of their feet. Other ice-melting chemicals like magnesium and calcium chloride can also irritate a dog's feet, as well as cause an upset stomach when he licks his feet afterward.

Dogs in any wintry city would probably benefit from wearing dog boots, but most are so uncomfortable that the dogs can barely navigate in them. Many dog-boot designs are so flawed that the boots fall off before the end of the block. I am including a few honorable mentions, although I am sure there are many more worthy products from good companies, so forgive me for any omissions (and contact me at www.thedogbible.com to make suggestions about other products for future revised editions of this book).

A highly recommended brand of dog boots for comfort and ease is Muttluks from Canada. They are fleece-lined, with leather toe protection and reflective material on the strap. The toughest boots—for rough terrain, hiking, etc.—are highly durable and available through www.muttluks.com or by calling (888) MUTTLUK. You can have custom-made boots in many colors or prints for no more than ready-made costs—from $20 to $45.

Barbara Lamb of Shaggy Lamb Boots in Michigan will cut boots for your dog's paw size and length of leg. Shaggy Lamb boots are good for short walks in any weather but aren't thick enough to stay warm and dry inside on wet or snowy days. She can be reached at www.shaggy-lamb.com or (989) 643-5671.

A warning about booties: be sure that the boots fit snugly, but don't secure them too tightly or you will cut off circulation. If booties are too tight a dog can get frostbitten toes, which require emergency medical intervention.

COLD WEATHER COMFORT

Just because your dog may have a fur coat, don't take it for granted that it's all he needs to keep him warm when the temperature drops. If your dog has a thin coat, especially if it's a breed intended for a warm climate (for example, the delicate Italian Greyhound), you definitely have to provide him with a coat for warm protection and limit him to only short forays outside when it gets really cold. A sweater vest is probably the best protection, since it holds in all the dog's natural body heat and you can layer it with a coat on top.

Don't make the mistake of thinking that just because you have a strong, energetic Labrador he can't suffer from prolonged exposure to extremely cold temperatures. When the temperature outside is low, the longer a dog stays outside the more risk he runs of developing hypothermia, which is a dangerous drop in the dog's core body temperature.

◆ Recognizing the Signs of Hypothermia

If your dog displays any of the symptoms on the warning chart on page 183, you must bring him indoors to a warm environment immediately. A dog whose core temperature has gone down will shiver violently in a rapid attempt to speed up his metabolism to generate warmth: this is what you need to supply for him. Get him into the warmest room you can, raise the temperature and wrap him in warm towels or blankets. You can do this by wrapping him in a fleece or quilted blanket, then throwing some towels and other blankets in the dryer on high, where they will heat up quickly. Then you can wrap him in those.

Stay with the dog until he stops shivering. Once he is rewarmed, encourage him to eat and drink, which will generate more warmth and replenish the energy he expended while shivering.

If he does not improve, or gets worse, get him wrapped up as warmly you can and take him to the vet on an emergency basis, calling ahead to let them know you are coming and why.

WARNING SIGNS OF HYPOTHERMIA

- ❏ Intense and prolonged shivering
- ❏ Weakness or lethargy (especially if the dog is normally active)
- ❏ Disorientation or confusion (not responding to commands, walking in circles)
- ❏ Loss of interest in playing or even walking (may lift paws one at a time)

◆ General Comfort Tips for Cold Weather

Water Make sure your pet is drinking enough water, because dogs can get dehydrated in the cold weather.

Baths If you usually give frequent baths to keep your pet dander-free, don't wash him as much in the winter months. Instead, brush him frequently to increase circulation to the hair follicles and promote hair growth, which is important in the winter. And when you do give a bath, use a dog moisturizing shampoo and/or a dog-coat conditioner to minimize the drying effects that baths can have in the cold, dry winter months.

◆ Foot Comfort in the Cold

Use booties if your dog accepts them. Booties can be great if your dog has really delicate feet, if your weather is cold enough, or if you live in an urban area where salt is used on sidewalks to melt the ice and snow. See the information about booties on page 182 and try to cajole your dog into wearing them.

Remove hair between the foot pads. Some dogs have hair growing between their toes or the pads at the bottom of their feet: this hair can cause trouble if you live where there is ice and snow. Get a small, round-tipped pair of dog-hair scissors from a pet supply company: they resemble the ones men use to snip their nose hairs, but they're tougher, for thick dog hair. Snip the hair growths from between the pads so that ice and snow can't build up in there.

Dogs can get ice balls on their feet when they leave a warm indoor environment and go into very cold temperatures. Since dogs have sweat glands in their toes, the moisture there can form into balls of ice from the abrupt change in temperature. These iceballs can be so uncomfortable that a dog will hop or limp, and they can even bruise or cut the footpad.

Coat the bottom of your dog's feet. If you live in a very cold climate, you can avoid damage to your dog's footpads the way sled-dog trainers do. Apply a layer of protection to the bottom of your dog's feet by spreading a thin layer of petroleum jelly or aloe gel on the dog's footpads before you head out into the bitter cold. You can even spray Pam or one of the generic vegetable-oil cooking sprays underneath his feet right before you go out—it's probably best to do it just outside the door, or your floors might get pretty messy! Even if your dog licks his feet later, these products will cause him no harm. Mushers is a brand of protective foot salve that works very well, too.

Relief for ice-covered feet If ice does form between your dog's toes or pads, you can give him relief with a hair-dryer. Put the dryer on the lowest warm setting and hold the blower at least six inches away from the dog's foot. Dry off the melted ice, rinse the feet in warm water if there is any salt or chemical contamination and gently rub the feet to get the circulation going.

CHAIN (FOR TETHERING OUTDOORS)

Some people who don't have a fenced yard mistakenly think it's okay to put their dog on a chain. A short period outside staked to a chain is all right—but a person has to stay with the dog at all times. Walking your dog or putting him in a dog run for short periods is a kinder choice.

THE DANGERS OF CHAINING A DOG OUTDOORS

- ❑ Dogs left in yards on chains can hang themselves, either by jumping over fences that they couldn't quite clear, or by wrapping themselves around trees or posts.
- ❑ Dogs can suffer or die from not being able to reach their water.
- ❑ Dogs can suffer heatstroke because they can't get out of the sun.
- ❑ Some dogs who are left on chains become extremely aggressive to passersby or anyone trying to enter your property. The chain seems to stimulate antisocial tendencies.

OUTDOOR RUNS

If you want to give your dog some fresh air for a couple of hours but don't have a fenced yard, you can construct an outdoor run. However, dog runs are not a place that any dog should be left for any significant length of time. A dog can perceive being left in a run as banishment, at which point it becomes a punishment.

◆ Construction Tips

A standard-size run is usually about 6' by 10'. The floor of the run should be gravel or grass. If you already have a concrete patio, it is *not* a good idea to convert that to a run, because it is hard on the pads of a dog's feet. The run should be away from weather extremes—heat, cold, wind, etc.

◆ The Best Use of a Run

Since it is not advisable to leave a dog alone in a run for long, the best use of it is if the dog can choose for herself when she wants to go out there. This way, if there's a change in weather—if it gets too hot or cold or it starts to rain—the dog can go back inside for comfort.

If you live in the suburbs and will be at work most of the day, a dog run attached to the house by a dog door is a great solution. Information on dog doors follows.

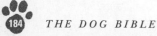

"INVISIBLE FENCES" AND SIMILAR SYSTEMS

My intention throughout the book is to present all the information about any topic and stay neutral myself. Even though there are dogs that do fine with this system, I had a hard time finding any decent justification for going "invisible," since it can be confusing and frightening to dogs.

The concept of being able to contain your dog without actually fencing your property appears to be very popular, although people may not realize the consequences for their dogs. Some of the limitations are foreseen by owners, while others may not become apparent until later. This type of system doesn't make much logical sense, given that it can be more expensive than wire fencing and it creates quite a few problems. This section spells it out for you so that whatever you decide, you are fully informed.

Invisible Fence and other brands of underground electric systems can be installed around the section of your property in which you want your dog contained. An electric cable is buried just below the surface of the ground and an electronic collar is placed on your dog, which she will have to wear whenever she is outside. She receives an electric shock through this collar if she attempts to go past the underground wire boundary.

Although people may think they are saving money compared to the labor and materials of installing an actual fence, the truth is that these electric fences are expensive and can also require maintenance and repairs in the future. Although it's possible to save money by following the instructional video and burying the wire yourself, you have to feel comfortable that you have the time it takes and that you know what you are doing.

When you have the system professionally installed, the company representative will sensitize your dog to the electrified fence and then walk you through the procedure. Introducing your dog to the system begins with placing an "e-collar" (electronic shock collar) on your dog's neck. This collar has a transmitter that picks up signals from electric wires wherever the line has been buried. White flags are placed at intervals in the ground above where the wire is buried (the flags can be removed later). When the dog approaches this "fence line," there is a warning sound or tingling that alerts the dog that she is getting close to the fence. This warning increases if she continues closer to the line. The dog receives an actual electric shock to her neck via the e-collar if she steps on or over the line.

These collars are used in two ways: as part of an electronic boundary system, or as a training device (for the latter see "Collars" on page 266).

◆ Do-it-yourself Invisible Fencing

There are self-install kits that run around $250—quite a savings, since the professional ones start at around $2,000—but don't be fooled into thinking it's easy. Trenching your property to bury the line is the tough part: you should consider renting a power-trenching tool to make it doable. You'll also want a masonry blade or other equipment to cut through any driveway that might be in the way.

◆ Reasons for Invisible Fencing

People presumably choose to install what could be called a "virtual" fence instead of an "actual" fence because they don't like what fencing looks like around a property. Or they may not like what ordinary affordable wire fencing looks like and can't afford the more attractive alternatives.

One solution to the aesthetic problem would be to use the more costly and attractive fencing where it is most visible—say at the entrance to your property—and then switch to the green wire fencing that is sold in rolls. For the most part, this fencing isn't really all that noticeable once it's up—if anything it's the green stakes that can sometimes draw attention to themselves because commercial green colors are so often not shades of green that appear in nature. To make wire fence and stakes blend more into the background, you can just camouflage them. And this is no complicated "Martha" redo—all you have to do is buy a can of flat black spray paint and give a quick once-over to the green stakes once they're in place. You don't have to completely cover the green—an uneven quick coat of black turns them into camouflage color and the fence blends right into the natural background.

Perhaps another reason for choosing invisible fencing is that you have too much property to stake with actual fence. One solution is to contain only part of your land. If you are concerned about seeing "actual" fence cutting through the larger property, you can obviously put the fenced area out of sight of the pretty part of the garden or lawn, and the dog can then run around there without you having to see the fence.

There may be building codes where you live that do not permit a fence around the property, which would be a pretty good incentive for invisible fencing. However, there are now problems in some towns with dogs behind invisible fences running right up to that invisible fence line and barking aggressively at passersby and other dogs, frightening anyone who doesn't believe the electric fence will hold back a dog that aggressive.

◆ Reasons against Invisible Fencing

If you are thinking of doing a virtual fence for your dog's sake, think of it from her point of view before you decide.

You may have heard good things about the invisible fence and not have stopped to realize how powerful a negative experience these collars can be for a dog. Some owners seem delighted and amazed and think their pets are uniquely brilliant because after that first shock the dogs won't venture anywhere near the electric line. Well, why in the world *would they,* folks? They just got zapped.

I'd venture that even the dumbest dog has to view the fence line and beyond as "the demilitarized zone" after being zapped. Yet owners proudly report their dog's reluctance to go anywhere near the fence as proof of his superior intelligence and what a "quick learner" he is.

Shock collars for fences are a punishment tool. Using the fencing risks all the potential negative effects of punishment, a style of teaching that is generally discouraged.

The fences can cause fear and/or aggression. The dog can associate various things in the vicinity with the shock and then freak out about them—if he sees a bicycle or a jogger, he may think that's why he got the shock and then associate that object or person with bad things and become aggressive toward them in the future.

Some dogs become afraid of even going outside at all with the collar.

Evaluating canine personality types The sales representative for a professionally installed system should spend time getting to know your dog and evaluating her before selling you a system. Any electronic-fence salesman should thoroughly evaluate your dog to be certain this system will be appropriate. *Be suspicious if the salesman does not do this.*

You might think twice if you have a highly sensitive dog. For example, if your dog gets rattled by loud noises or is thin-skinned and freaks out if insects land on her or if something unexpected happens to her, such as getting sprayed with water, then she's not going to do well with being zapped electronically.

There is no way to know for sure which dogs will have the hardest time with these invisible fences, but there are some dogs who are so "shocked by the shock" when it hits them that they become terrified of going outside at all.

Others change personality as soon as that electronic collar is placed on their neck and may cower or cringe or look miserable in some other way. Surely this is not the result you want when spending thousands of dollars to give your dog the supposed gift of having the run of your property?

Some dogs may not be upset by being shocked—which would seem to be a reason in favor of using this system. Maybe those less-reactive dogs have thicker skin or more hair covering it, or an easier-going personality. However, if their pain tolerance is so high that a shock means very little to them, that may mean you'll have to raise the shock level down the road to ensure that the dog won't go right through the fence. That stronger shock may wind up having a more intense effect on them.

When not to use the invisible fence It is not advisable to leave a dog outside unsupervised for many hours, especially if your property is large enough for him to go out of sight.

Electronic equipment can malfunction and some collars have accidentally given repeated shocks to a dog, which is bad enough if you're around, but terrible if the dog has been left alone in this situation for hours.

If a dog has any history of being aggressive with visitors, or has ever bitten or tried to bite a delivery person, electric fencing is a bad choice. It may just stimulate more of the same, especially since these "intruders" walk right in unaware of the invisible boundary.

Breaking through the invisible barrier Once that dog has been tempted to cross the shock barrier—and with some dogs' personalities it may take as little as seeing a dog to play with on the other side—she will rarely be willing to withstand the shock again to come back across. She just sees the rabbit or cat or deer and is compelled to follow. Effectively this leaves a dog "locked out," even if she wants to come home.

The system goes down Any break in the underground wire can shut the whole system down. That's why you need to know if there's an alarm or a warning system to let you know if the dog is as good as running around loose because the fence is not activated.

A weak or dead battery in the dog's collar would have the same effect—and it's easy to forget to replace those batteries. You should test the collar frequently by walking toward the fence and listening for the warning sound.

If your dog is a "tester"—and many smart dogs do continually recheck the system, getting close to the fence to see if it responds with a signal or is not on—that will wear the batteries out more quickly.

A power outage that shuts down your lights will disable your electric fence, too.

Endless territorial barking Some dogs can become intensely territorial or bark nonstop inside their electric kingdom.

If you have a dog who is already highly territorial, electric fencing can increase that tendency. The dog is always aware of her boundaries—but the intruder is not. So a person or animal could be attacked or bitten by your dog if he enters the invisible boundaries.

Other dogs come and go freely. One problem is that other dogs and animals are free to go back and forth across the electric boundary while your dog is confined invisibly. This can be mental torture for your dog, or may even be a physical risk if a loose dog were to come on the property and attack your dog or if someone wanted to steal your dog. All they'd have to do is take the collar off and walk the dog away.

And it isn't just the dogs who are rattled—their masters can get jittery about the whole system, too. Many virtual-fence owners do not have peace of mind when their dogs are outside. They look out the windows, check on the dog and keep an eye on him whether there are big temptations such as other dogs going by on a leash or he is on his own.

QUESTIONS TO ASK ABOUT FENCING INSTALLED BY THE COMPANY

❐ Does an alarm tell you if there is a system failure?
❐ What about lightning? Is there a built-in protection against the fence being hit?
❐ Can I get references from recent customers?
❐ Do you evaluate dogs to determine if they are good candidates for the system?
❐ How much training is provided? And what if my dog doesn't get it right away?

◆ Where to Buy Fencing
Invisible Fence: (800) 578-DOGS, www.invisiblefence.com
Radio Fence: (800) 941-4200, www.radiofence.com

DOG DOORS

Dog doors have a flap made of metal or plastic that the dog can push against with his paw or head. These doors are great if you have a fenced yard and want the dog to have the freedom to go inside or out, especially if you are at work all day. The door can be installed between the house and the yard or between the garage and the yard.

◆ There Are Several Kinds of Doors You Can Use.

1. There are doors that insert into a sliding-glass patio door, and these are the easiest kind. You just open the slider, stand the door up beside the open glass, then close the door, applying a rubber weather strip to seal the edge, if needed.

   This door requires no construction and can be taken out at any time. The door consists of a tall panel that blocks off part of the slider. While the dog door is in place this door can no longer be used by people.

2. There are dog doors that require cutting into the bottom portion of a door that people continue to use.

3. There is an in-the-wall model that can be cut right into the exterior wall of your house, thus becoming a permanent part of the structure. Some models come with magnetic "keys" that the dog wears in its collar so that the door opens only when your dog—and no other—comes up to the flap. They have spring hinges and panels made of metal, wood or Plexiglas. This prevents not only strange dogs from entering your house, but also cats, raccoons and similar critters.

There are doors with double flaps for less heat loss in very cold or windy climates. The dead air space between the two flaps helps with insulation. Nevertheless, the loss of energy (heat or cold) is a concern with pet doors.

✦ Adapting Dog Doors for Cold Climates

If you live in an especially cold or windy climate it is possible to use two dog doors and build a "chute" from the door at the house to another dog door at the other end of the chute—sort of like the tunnels you see in airports connecting the plane entrance to the terminal. Using a chute with a dog door in a very cold location prevents the flap of the door from leaking very cold air in winter or even flapping open in high winds.

✦ All Doors Come with a Removable Panel.

There is a panel that slides in and out of the opening of the dog doors. It covers the flap so that the dog cannot use the door, which is necessary for times when you want to keep her inside or out.

✦ Smaller Animals Can Use the Doors, Too.

These doors can also be used by any cats you may have. However, keep in mind that other people's cats and wild animals like raccoons can also use the door and probably will, especially if you have some tasty food out somewhere in the house.

✦ Fear of Burglars

Some people have the mistaken idea that if they have a dog door, burglars will want to enter their homes through it. But they don't stop to wonder why a burglar would want to squeeze through a tiny opening and take the risk of encountering the rightful four-legged user of that door on the other side. Another way to look at it is that a dog door alerts a burglar that there is a resident dog. Burglars steer clear of houses with dogs.

In any case, no normal-sized man can fit through a dog door, even the extra-large ones for dogs like Great Danes (and only in jewel-heist movies does a burglar have a jockey-sized partner or a child along for the purpose).

✦ Installing a Dog Door

Before you do anything else, you need to measure your dog so you can plan on the right size door. A common mistake is to buy a door that's too large. The larger the door, the more expensive it is. There is also a greater loss of heat and air conditioning through the flap as the opening increases in size.

When installing a door, use a level across the top of the pet door to make sure it is parallel to the ground. If the door is installed at a tilted angle, it won't close correctly.

- ❐ The width of the door should be wider by an inch or two than the widest part of your pet (measure him across the shoulder/chest).
- ❐ The height of the door should be measured with a tape measure from the ground up to the height of your dog's shoulders.
- ❐ The rise of the door—the small barrier the dog will need to step over—needs to be included in your calculations. If the rise is too low the dog will need to stoop to get through the flap. If the rise is too high the dog won't be able to leap over it as she gets older and less agile.
- ❐ To calculate the rise, put a board on its side in the doorway and have your dog step over it. You want the minimum height that's comfortable.
- ❐ To estimate the height of the door flap, take the dog's height at the shoulder—say, twenty inches—then take the eight-inch rise he can step over—subtract the height of the rise from the dog's height and you get minimum door flap height of twelve inches.

If you want more than one dog to use the dog door, make sure the opening is big enough to fit the largest dog.

Keep convenience and the future in mind when thinking about where to put the door and what kind to get. Some people recommend choosing the least expensive door and the one that is easiest to "uninstall," because someday you might not want a dog door. (But that would suggest that someday you might not want a dog?! What a preposterous idea!)

DOORBELLS FOR DOGS

Yes, there actually are doggie doorbells. They would be used either instead of a dog door or in addition to it, as a way for your dog to alert you that she wants to go out (or come back inside). You can teach your dog to ring this dog-friendly doorbell instead of scratching or barking to be let in.

This may sound difficult to accomplish until you realize that we have all "taught" our dogs to scratch and bark at the door, either to be let in or let out (depending on whether they are a city dog, a suburban dog or a rural dog), because we have shown up at the door when they do it. The dogs have learned their door communication behaviors from us: the scratching and/or barking behavior would have been "extinguished" (trainer lingo for "they would have stopped doing it") if we had not responded to it.

So you can retrain a dog to use a doorbell instead. You can even have a doorbell on both sides of the door (that is, if you have a suburban or rural dog), so the dog can signal when he needs to go outside or come back in.

The specially shaped doggie doorbell is battery operated; it can be put on the floor or mounted on the wall beside the door. You teach your dog that when she steps on the bell, you'll come running with a treat—she may be ringing your bell more often than you might want!

♦ Using Sleigh Bells as Doorbells.

Get a length of leather that has sleigh bells sewn or riveted onto it. They are available at some hardware stores, Christmas stores or in catalogs. Hang the bells from the doorknob on a strong cord at the dog's nose height.

To teach the dog to use them, close the door and stand with the dog on the inside of the door. Shake the bells and then immediately open the door. Repeat this several times, opening the door each time. The dog should make the connection by observation.

You'll want a second strand of bells on the other side of the door for reentry ringing. The instant you hear your dog ringing those bells, let him in and make a big fuss over him.

DOGHOUSES

♦ Decorative

A doghouse can be a whimsical touch on your property without a truly functional purpose. This sort of doghouse is meant to be decorative and therefore need not follow any practical guidelines.

♦ Functional

There are people who put a useful doghouse in their yard as their dog's main place to sleep and as protection from the elements.

The exterior color of a wooden doghouse will affect the inside comfort. A wooden doghouse should be painted a dark color in winter to absorb heat—and repainted a light color in summer to deflect heat.

There are doghouses in an igloo shape that are made of a synthetic, all-weather material.

The floor of the doghouse should be insulated with some kind of carpet and then lined with cedar shavings, which are good for warmth.

The real issue is not the construction of a doghouse but the philosophy behind it. There used to be more people who believed that dogs should not come into the house. This is no longer considered a fair decision for a domestic dog, unless it is some kind of serious working, shepherd-type dog that must live out with a flock or herd.

Dogs are meant to be with their masters, enjoying life beside them. If you have not taken the time to train your dog to live harmoniously indoors with you, then it is not too harsh to suggest that you buy a barn or farm animal to live outdoors—which is where they belong—and give your dog away to someone who wants the dog inside their house, where pet dogs belong.

RAMPS

♦ Which Dogs Need Ramps?

Older dogs often need the help of a ramp or steps to get into the car; they also may need the help of another style of ramp to get through a dog door or even up onto their favorite chair (or your bed). Very small dogs often can't make the huge leap from the ground into the back of a high vehicle.

A dog with a medical history—such as hip dysplasia, joint problems, spinal problems, recovery from an accident or illness, even pregnancy—can benefit from the extra boost of a ramp.

◆ Kinds of Ramps

There are several kinds of ramps: outdoor ramps for entering or exiting tall vehicles like SUVs and trucks, indoor ramps for furniture and beds, and water ramps. Although I have rarely encountered a product that I felt worthy of singling out for endorsement in this book, where ramps are concerned I have one that is just superb. I use it every day for my dogs, two of whom have had multiple joint surgeries. The Twistep is actually an attached platform that swivels and makes it absolutely easy for my twelve-year-old Weimaraner Billy Blue (even after his fourth joint surgery) to get in and out of the high back of a Ford Explorer. The step attaches underneath the back of the car in about ten seconds and easily swings in and out of place. The toll-free phone number is (888) 284-7742, and they will determine which hitch is correct for the model of SUV you have. The Twistep e-mail address is listed below.

There are ramps that can be placed at the end of a dock or swimming pool—especially pools that only have metal ladder steps—so that a dog can safely get out of the pool.

By the way, the big box of steps that people pull up to their boats can be great for home use for getting your dog up on your bed or a sofa. Contact a marine supply company for prices and availability.

◆ Some Dogs Are Afraid of a Ramp.

Dogs do best in the long run if you give them a chance to deal with the ramp at their own pace. You will get the best results with an encouraging tone of voice and an ample supply of extra-delicious treats to reward brave attempts to use the platform.

Do not force the dog or drag her onto a ramp. This will only frighten her and make her averse to going anywhere near the back of your vehicle.

If you have a smaller dog, don't just pick her up and try to place her on the ramp—this can be too scary for her and doesn't really teach her how to use the ramp, which obviously includes learning how to get up on it first.

◆ Ramp Companies

There are a large number of companies making ramps and steps, with big differences in price. The companies included here all make good-quality ramps. Some are better for bigger dogs, others are best for the smallest. Go on the Web sites listed here and shop and compare. You can always call the companies on the phone and ask for more information.

Pet Steps can be found at C&D Products, (888) 554-7387, www.cdpets.com
Ramps can be found at:
www.petclassics.com, (603) 668-7387
www.bedderbacks.com, (877) 327-5438
www.orvis.com, (888) 235-9763
And my own favorite, www.TWISTEP.com, (888) 284-7742

DOG TOYS

Dogs want to play for most of their lives. Once in a while you'll find one without a playful bone in his body, but most of them keep their minds and spirits tuned up with playful endeavors.

Build up a stash of toys and chewables that you keep in a box out of the way. Once a week introduce a new or once-new toy and take one away to put out of sight and recycle back into the toy bin in the future. The dog(s) will love the novelty.

This also gives you a chance to check on the toys you have out—throw away any of them that are broken or have sharp edges, or are small enough to be swallowed.

• Toys for Chasing or Destroying

Cardboard boxes You know how people with very young children say that at Christmastime the kids seem more interested in the boxes and wrapping paper than the presents? Well, dogs can share that same fascination with the containers that things come in. Dogs love to tear up cardboard boxes of any size—from cereal boxes to packing cartons. You'd be amazed what a big kick they get out of attacking a cardboard container.

If your dog doesn't naturally take to it, wave the box around and say "Get it!" enticingly a few times. Praise them when they begin to rip at it and they'll catch on. Box destruction seems to satisfy their need to destroy something, and even though they may chew off small pieces, it is rare to see a dog who will swallow the wet cardboard, even after gumming it for a while. It can be kind of a nuisance to clean up all the pieces—and it also requires vigilance about the boxes you do *not* want broken down—but it is really satisfying for dogs and saves on costly toys they chew apart in no time!

Frisbee (see "Warnings," page 194) There are Frisbees made especially for dogs from a cloth material with padded edges, so that the dog doesn't get hit by a hard plastic Frisbee or hurt his mouth catching one.

The "Fling Thing" is a good substitute for a hard Frisbee, and it even cleans a dog's teeth while he plays! It is made of a durable, nontoxic material that claims to gently rub a dog's teeth clean when he bites into it. The toy has raised edges that make it easy to grasp. It costs around $10 and can be found at www.westpawdesign.com, or (800) 443-5567.

Homemade "towel burritos" These are my own invention and the favorite toy in our house for chasing, tugging, gnawing and destroying, or just holding as a security blanket. I got the idea for towel burritos when I was reading about working dogs that sniff out bombs and drugs. Their reward for a "find" is to play for a few minutes with a towel rolled up like a burrito. So I figured that if it was enough praise for those hardworking dogs, the towel was probably attractive to all dogs.

To make one, take any old hand towel (or an old bath towel that you've cut into about eight equal-sized squares). Roll the toweling into a sausage and secure it with duct tape (they seem to adore the flavor!), wrapping it a couple of times around about three inches in from the ends of the towel.

Synthetic bones The Nylabone is a very hard, nylon bone that is usually much too hard to appeal to most dogs as a chew toy. The Gumabone is a softer synthetic chew-bone that many dogs prefer, since they can at least put a dent in it or chew bits off.

The Jolly Ball This is a big rubber ball with a rubber handle that a dog or person can use to pick it up. Some dogs go right to work chewing off the handle while other dogs can run around for years holding the handle between their teeth without any attempt to chew it off. You can kick the Jolly Ball like a soccer ball, or you can throw it by the handle for your dog. If you have doubts about whether your dog will chew off the handle, put the Jolly Ball away when you've finished playing, or don't leave your dog alone with it.

Kong toys These are thick rubber toys with a hollow center and ridges on the outside; they come in a number of sizes, from petite to giant.

The Kong was originally promoted as a retrieval toy—one you could throw and make it bounce crazily. Even the toughest chewers cannot destroy this toy—but its value has shifted so that now it is being advertised as the perfect "pacifier" to stuff with tempting goodies and leave with your dog when you go out.

The hollow in a Kong can also be stuffed with something sticky and delicious (cheese, peanut butter) to distract a dog that has a hard time when you leave the house. Once he starts licking that Kong, nothing much else will matter! (See page 594 on "Separation Anxiety" for more on this problem.)

The outside of a Kong can also be used. The Kong Company has developed some ideas and suggestions for melting slices of cheese on the ridged outside of the toy. Bits of meat or chicken or even dry dog food can be put into the cavity and then sealed over with cream cheese or peanut butter.

Rope toys These are just that: lengths of thick rope in colorful nylon or plain cotton with knots in them. Pups love to shake them or play tug-of-war with you or another dog.

Treat Dispensers These are toys that you fill with dog biscuits or the kibble portion of your dog's dinner; the dog then has to move the ball around so that the kibble rolls out. Buster Cube is still the best-known dispenser, but Molecuball is becoming popular.

🦴 Warnings about Toys

- *Tennis balls* are potentially dangerous if you let a dog with strong jaws chew on one—they have been known to pop into a dog's throat and cut off the air supply. So don't leave tennis balls around unless you are with your dog.

- *The Teaser Ball* can be dangerous for a puppy or small dog because they can get their heads stuck inside the outer ball. Teaser balls come in several sizes. The Teaser is a ball within a ball with round holes cut in the outer ball through which the dog can try to extract the smaller, inner ball. A Teaser Ball can be rolled around or a dog can carry it around in his mouth—the problem is that the holes in the outer ball are quite large, and small-breed dogs and puppies can get their heads stuck in there. So never leave a dog unattended with one of these balls.

- *Swallowers of toy bits* are going to wind up in the doctor's office if you allow them to chew up rubber or stuffed toys and then swallow the pieces. Unless you can sit nearby and tell the dog "Leave it" and praise him when he drops it, do not leave toys around him.
- *Flying discs* can be hazardous, even those made of the flexible material deemed safe for dogs' mouths. What has sent some "Frisbee dogs" into surgery is the dramatic leaping and twisting they do to catch the disc. Keep the throws low in front of your dog so that she runs rather than leaps and twists, which can cause serious injury. Use fabric discs, not the plastic ones that can hurt their teeth.
- *No tug-of-war whatsoever* with your dog if she has aggression issues. Tug-of-war is one game that means something entirely different to your dog and you. For dogs, this is a dominance game—and it's fine for them to play tug-of-war with other dogs. But watch how the game plays out and you'll see standoffs, growling and dogs pulling with all their might—a lot of intensity over which of them ultimately walks away with the object. This has significance to them as far as rank within the pack and the entitlements that come with it are concerned. So if you let your dog engage you in tug-of-war and then you stop pulling, you have given your dog a message: she is the winner and she has a higher rank than you.

Your Dog's Daily Schedule

Dogs do best when there is a schedule for their meals, walks, time alone and time with their people. The more structure and dependability you can build into a dog's day, the more you'll eliminate the stress that some dogs experience when they don't know what's going to happen next.

MORNINGS

A dog gets used to you getting up at about the same time every day. He learns how soon after you get up he can expect to eat and be walked. His mind gets used to it and his inner clock gets set accordingly. There are many dogs whose digestive systems seem to run like a Swiss watch once the daily pattern is established: they experience extreme hunger when the meal is expected and then the urge to move their bowels soon thereafter. If you work with it, this predictable regularity can make life easier for you in house-training and planning a schedule for your dog. However, it also requires that you make food and a walk available at pretty much the same time every day.

DURING THE DAY

If you go to a job every day, then you need to work out a way to come home to visit and walk the dog midday—or have someone else do it. Many city dwellers hire dog-walkers to take their dogs out during the day. It depends somewhat on your dog's personality, but you need to make sure that the walker is coming at approximately the same time every day. Some dogs can become anxious if they don't get the anticipated visitor and walk when their inner clock signals it is time.

WORKING OWNERS AND DOG-WALKING SERVICES

If there are dog-walkers in your town or neighborhood, find out what they charge, how many dogs they take at a time and for what length of time they stay out. Someone who limits herself to two or a maximum of three dogs is giving you more for your money and assuring a more personalized, active outing for your pooch. Finding a more private dog-walker is worth the effort. Usually it's just a matter of a few phone calls to dog-owning friends or acquaintances, to your vet or groomer, to the neighborhood pet store or, if you see someone in your neighborhood walking a dog or two, you can ask if they know anyone who walks dogs for other people. It may take only one phone call to sign up with a mass dog-walking service, but what are you actually doing for your dog?

To make a profit, a small business devoted to walking dogs needs to organize groups that have the largest number of dogs possible in each. They determine routes for their employees based on how many dogs can be picked up and returned within one hour. What owners often fail to realize is that if the walk is one hour and there are eight to ten dogs, most of that hour is going to be spent picking up and dropping off other dogs and stopping to pick up after them. Many of the well-known and costly services do exactly that: if you live in a metropolis like New York (or you've caught the numerous movies that depict the mass dog-walkers) you've seen up to a dozen large dogs being walked in a tangle of leashes, proceeding at a snail's pace and stopping constantly at one apartment building or another. Owners are shelling out a substantial daily fee without stopping to consider what the experience is like for their pets. But if you doubt this, you can see for yourself by simply waiting somewhere near your apartment at dog-walking time and discreetly watch the pack of dogs.

What time the walker comes is important, because dogs have an uncanny sense of time and will come to anticipate the walker's arrival within minutes of the usual pick-up time. If the expected visitor does not come at the expected time, it can be stressful for the dog. Some dogs are more sensitive to the actual time on the clock than others, but I've found that dogs who are raised to expect meals, walks and your return home on a dependable schedule seem to develop a louder inner clock. This knowledge of the hour by the clock is not unique to dogs, by the way—you've seen the same thing if you've been around racehorses or show horses. They will all start to pace and whinny in their stalls right around the time of their regularly scheduled morning and evening feedings. If your dog is aware of clock time, explain this to your walker, who may come at varying times because she doesn't know that some dogs have an inner watch ticking. This way the service you are paying for to make the dog's life better doesn't turn out to be a stressor instead.

EVENINGS

If your lifestyle permits you to come home pretty much on schedule—or other residents of your house have a set schedule—your dog will learn that routine and will anticipate it with joy.

However, if you've had a fairly dependable schedule that suddenly changes, that change can throw off a dog who is a creature of habit. It's the flip side of how a schedule can bring security and happiness to such a dog: a disruption to that schedule may make him feel like his world is falling apart.

The more high-strung and anxious your dog is, the more he can benefit from having a daily routine that he can depend on. Knowing what awaits him can help a dog to develop patience and, on some level, to have something to look forward to. For example, you might decide to always give your dog breakfast at the same time you eat it, then take him for a brisk walk, saving the long walk for later in the day. He will soon accept this as the way life is. However, if you come home at the end of the day and do *not* take him for that expected longer walk, you can throw him into a funk.

Your dog needs and must get his exercise regardless of the weather or how you're feeling. For example, let's say your dog expects his second meal at five o'clock—because that's what you've accustomed him to. If you are home before that five o'clock mealtime, your dog will come to you as a reminder that it is his dinnertime. You could set your watch by it!

CAN DOGS TELL TIME?

There is much we don't know about how dogs perceive the passage of time. Many dog owners feel that their dogs get as excited if they return home after an hour as they do after a few days; others say that a dog does know the difference if you go out and leave him for ten minutes or ten days. There shouldn't be a blanket generalization, because individual dogs give the impression that they have very different experiences of time passing.

It's certainly true that many dogs, when they get used to the routine you develop for them, anticipate it, and it helps them deal with the unpredictability in their lives.

QUALITY TIME

This overused phrase is generally applied to families in which the parents both have jobs and are concerned about the amount of time they have available to spend with the children. It is a concept that can be applied to dogs, too: if you are going to commit to sharing your life with a dog, then you have to consider her overall well-being, emotional as well as physical. If you have limited time to spend with the dog, then when you are able to spend time with her, really be there: play, groom, walk, talk, interact. Dogs know the difference between someone who really connects with them, gives them strokes that are from the heart, and those who phone it in, so to speak. So even though you shouldn't drive yourself crazy about the quality of your dog's life, you do need to keep in mind that you and your family, if you have one, are the central figure(s) in that pooch's life. If the dog is going to give you her full devotion—put you on a pedestal and forgive you your trespasses—then don't take her for granted. Try to make your time with the dog quality time, so that you are deserving of her adoration!

GUILTY DOG OWNERS

Forget about guilt! There really is nothing to be gained from feeling guilty about most things, and certainly not about the life you can offer a dog. Don't even wander into negative emotions where your dog is concerned. Do the best you can—it'll be good enough. Believe me: your dog will never blame you or love you less for the time she spends alone in the apartment. In fact, your dog will love you with all her might, because the beauty of it is, that's what dogs are all about. You're wondering how I can be so sure you're a loving owner and not a neglectful, abusive one? Easy. Because you didn't just go out of your way to find this book and then spend your hard-earned money on it—you're actually reading it!

If you're *already* feeling guilty that you don't spend enough time in the apartment with your dog, or worrying whether she gets out enough, then you may be a type-A perfectionist, a be-there-for-other-people kind of person. One of the great things about dog ownership is that you don't have to bring neurotic feelings or unrealistic expectations for yourself (or the dog) into the picture. Both of you are doing the best you can here. If the dog gnaws on a corner of your couch or you're an hour late coming home, it's not the end of the world. Life is complicated enough without giving yourself heartburn over whether your dog is being shortchanged. Dogs exist pretty much to be our companions, to share our lives on our terms. Dogs sleep a great part of the day, as well.

Even if you don't give up being guilty for your sake, you really need to give it a rest for the sake of your dog. If you come home feeling sorry for the dog, feeling sad and apologetic and making a huge fuss over her, it is stressful for the animal. "What is wrong?" the dog might wonder. The dog hears the worry in your voice and may be frightened about why you are upset. She will be confused by a huge outpouring of affection and attention from you when she has done nothing to earn it. If you cater to the dog it can make her feel insecure and shake her confidence in you as the leader—and we know that leaderless dogs try to fill that void by taking the top-dog role themselves, which is just as stressful for them. So if you can't lighten up for your own sake, do it for the pup.

Exercise

Many of the problems people have with their dogs are a direct result of the dog having excess energy because he's not getting enough exercise. Lack of exercise is generally the cause of most destructive behavior—and pent-up energy can also be the reason behind some forms of incessant barking, dog anxiety, depression, hostility, etc.

Like people, dogs need about thirty to forty minutes of aerobic exercise—any activity that gets their hearts pumping for that long. They need it three or more times a week. If your dog doesn't get much regular exercise, you can build up her strength and stamina by following this schedule:

START SLOWLY, BUILD UP SLOWLY

- ❏ A fifteen-minute walk daily for one to two weeks, or two fifteen-minute walks a day if you want to do a morning and afternoon outing.
- ❏ Slowly add a few minutes a day.
- ❏ Assuming that the weather is temperate, your dog should eventually be fit enough to keep up with you on any walk or hike.

HAVE FUN—DO THINGS YOU ENJOY

If you view the walks you go on with your dog as drudgery, your dog is less likely to get the exercise he needs. If you're going to exercise the dog, choose activities you enjoy and you'll be more likely to actually do them regularly. If you like to bicycle, there is a piece of equipment that might suit you: the bicycle Jog-Along, below.

BICYCLE "JOG-ALONGS"

This is a rigid leash that attaches to your handlebar and then to the dog's leash. It allows him to trot alongside your bike so your hands can remain on the handlebars.

The benefit for the dog is the exercise and mental stimulation, as well as the chance to bond to you more deeply, much like hiking together would. But there are a number of safety issues to consider so that a pleasant adventure doesn't go bad.

WARNINGS ABOUT JOG-ALONGS

- ❏ Consider your dog's fitness before asking her to trot alongside your bike for some distance. Build her up to it little by little. The steady running she'll have to do alongside a bike is much different than the stop-and-go dashing around that even the most active dog normally does.
- ❏ Consider the physical conditions, because having to travel any distance in hot weather and on a hot roadway can actually kill a dog.
- ❏ Consider the safety issues of what kind of shoulder the road has for biking, whether there is heavy and/or fast-moving traffic and whether the dog has had a chance to work with you on the bike so that she will know what to do when you are making turns, etc.

HOT WEATHER EXERCISE SAFETY

People love to spend time outdoors with their dogs, but they don't seem to consider the various health risks that their dogs face. A dog's body functions quite differently from ours, particularly in the cooling system: dogs do not have pores in their skin that breathe, sweat and cool them as we do. A dog can only dissipate heat through his tongue by panting and also through the pads of his feet, so you have to keep in mind what it means for him to stand on hot ground or run on boiling asphalt. Keep in mind that something as simple as a cool breeze on a hot day may give you relief that your dog is not experiencing. Please keep a dog's different physiology in mind and keep him happy and safe while you enjoy his company in the heat.

GENERAL SAFE EXERCISE TIPS

❏ Offer water frequently. Small amounts of water given often is safer than letting your dog suck down a whole bowl of water at the end of a strenuous workout.

❏ Dogs need two to three times more water than usual when exercising.

❏ Avoid very hot weather—see "overheating" below.

❏ Dog's footpads need protection from the extremes of hot, cold or rough surfaces that can blister or cut the dog's pads. Consider boots (see the "clothing" section on page 181) or any of the soothing foot creams available for dogs.

❏ No heavy exercise before or after food—some vets recommend avoiding exercise for one hour before and two hours after eating, to help prevent bloat. However, there are no studies to back up this caution. It makes sense, though, so plan ahead and separate your walk and feeding times, or take it very easy if you go out right after eating.

🦴 Caution about Overheating

- The signs of heat stress are glassy eyes and frantic panting— remember them and be on the lookout for them in hot weather.
- Be on the lookout for overheating when exercising.
- Dogs do not have an efficient cooling system—they have no pores in their skin that would allow them to sweat, so the only way heat can transfer from their body is from their paws and tongue.
- Use special care in very hot weather, because dogs lose moisture more rapidly.
- After activity in the hot part of the day, you can cool the dog by wetting him down and encouraging him to rest in the shade.
- In hot weather, exercise very early or very late in the day to avoid heatstroke.
- Keep water with you and offer it frequently during any hot-weather outings.
- If your dog should develop heat stress, get her wet all over to help cool her off and call the vet immediately. This is a true emergency.

GENERAL WARNINGS ABOUT EXERCISE

❏ *Check with your vet before beginning an exercise routine.* The doctor may want to confirm the dog's overall health, musculoskeletal condition and, in particular, his heart and respiratory system.

- *Don't jump right into strenuous activities.* Until you have conditioned the dog (and yourself) with regular exercise and built up her cardiovascular system to have strength and stamina, don't undertake demanding sports such as big hikes or agility training.
- *Exercise consistently.* Sporadic intense exercise carries a much higher risk of serious injuries than regular workouts.
- *Hot weather is dangerous for strenuous exercise.* Dogs overheat quickly, and their system has no quick or efficient way to cool off (see "Caution about Overheating" on the previous page).
- *Avoid midday exercise.* Early morning and early evening are the best exercise times in hot weather. Try to choose times when it's fairly cool.
- *Hit the pool.* Swimming is the only hot weather exercise that carries no danger for dogs. However, swimming is something dogs can overdo, so use caution and know your dog's limits
- *Short-nosed dogs are at higher risk in hot weather.* Pug-nosed breeds do not pant as well, and panting is the dog's cooling system. Take extra water and even a chemical cold-pack if you're going to be outside for any length of time, even with minimal exercise.
- *No exercise for puppies.* Puppies should not jog or do extensive exercise until they are about two years old. Younger dogs should not be putting strain on growing joints and bones by running on hard surfaces. It is not uncommon to see people pulling puppies behind them when they are jogging, so we all need to educate each other about this warning.
- *Jogging can be bad for large, growing dogs.* Up to two years of age, take it easy on the bigger dogs. Larger breeds' skeletal systems mature at a slower pace, so consult with your vet about when your individual puppy may safely begin rigorous running.
- *Overweight dogs are at a higher risk for orthopedic problems.* Slim down your chubby dog with diet before you put him through any paces. In particular, an overweight dog should not do much running that involves quick turns because it puts stress on joints that are already stressed by those extra pounds.

EXERCISE AND DOGS WITH ARTHRITIS

Regular exercise of moderate intensity is recommended. But you should stop the exercise when you see signs of fatigue (see below). You want to keep the dog's muscles fit and limber, but not work her to the point where the arthritic joints are irritated.

◆ Signs of Fatigue

Common signs of a fatigued dog include slowing down, dragging on the leash, stopping or losing enthusiasm for the outing.

Stop the activity immediately if you notice any of the following signs of serious fatigue: limping, heavy panting (more than usual for the weather), breathing in with short, raspy breaths. If you see any of these signs and the dog hasn't recovered within fifteen minutes, call your vet and see if she feels you should bring the dog in to be checked out.

MENTAL EXERCISE

We usually think of exercise as physical exertion, but the mind needs exercise, too. There are a number of activities you can do with your dog that can tire him out as much as or more than physical exertion. Mental exercises may be as simple as having a dog sit before he gets his food or goes out the door—or putting him on a "down" before you toss his ball or toy.

The more your dog works with you—and for you—the better behaved and more pleasantly tuckered out he will be.

If you are away from home a lot, then it is easier on the dog if you've tired him out before you leave. It takes less time to exhaust a dog mentally than it does physically—especially because the more exercise a dog gets, the more fit he becomes and, like a well-conditioned racehorse, the longer and harder he has to go to get tired.

AGILITY TRAINING

Please go to www.thedogbible.com and click on "Inside the Book" for information about agility training and competition.

RALLY-O

This is a competition sport that is a cross between agility and obedience. It is a fairly complicated activity that is gaining popularity. It involves signals and commands between owner and dog over obstacles and courses, much like agility. Many dog trainers offer these classes.

It is recommended that a dog have had at least obedience training before beginning, because paying attention to you is a very important element in the competition. Rally-O requires dogs and handlers to work as partners with plenty of communication—handlers can talk to their dogs on course and give cues using voice, hand signals and body language. It is much less formal than traditional obedience work.

If you are an active person—and have a dog to match—then Rally-O may be for you. However, since you're not racing a clock, Rally-O allows slower-moving dogs and less agile owners a chance to compete on equal footing. To learn more about Rally-O classes in your area and how the sport functions, check these sources:

www.Dogwise.com, (800) 776-2665, carries a number of books devoted to Rally-O, particularly *Rally-O: An Introduction to the Style of Rally Obedience* by Charles Kramer.

For more information on Rally-O obedience, contact the Association of Pet Dog Trainers (APDT), 150 Executive Center Drive, Box 35, Greenville, SC 29615, (800) PET-DOGS (738-3647). Or visit www.apdt.com (and click on "Rally-O").

The American Kennel Club (AKC) also has a Web site pertaining to Rally-O: www.akc.org /rules/rally.cfm.

Water Safety and Emergency First Aid

Many people just assume that all dogs can swim, but not all of them have the instinct to do so—and all dogs have to get used to the feel of being in the water to get comfortable.

KEEP YOUR EYE ON THE DOG THE WHOLE TIME HE'S IN THE WATER.

◆ **Monitor Your Dog's Condition.**
A dog should never be in the water unsupervised. You need to keep an eye on several things to prevent a water-related tragedy.

❑ Check the water temperature and remember that dogs can suffer from hypothermia (see pages 182–183). Even dogs who are used to swimming can get overchilled if they stay too long in frigid water. Call him out to rest or to run around on land to rewarm himself.

❑ Prevent the dog from getting exhausted. Dogs will overdo it, both because they're having a great time and because instinct drives them to please you, or to retrieve for you, until they drop—literally. Make the dog come out and regroup if you see him getting tuckered out.

❑ A dog can get burned in the hot sun. See page 336 for information on sunscreen, keeping in mind that a dog's nose and ears can get burned if you don't put some sunscreen on them.

BREEDS WITH LOW BODY FAT

Dogs like Doberman Pinschers and Boxers don't do well in the water. It may be that the low percentage of body fat in these breeds gives no insulation against the cold; it may also be that dogs with a layer of fat are more buoyant in the water and stay afloat more easily.

Any dog can suffer the same problems in the water that people do, so to keep them safe you need to be aware of the dangers and the ways you can prevent them.

🦴 *Ways Dogs Get in Trouble in the Water*

- Exhaustion
- Muscle cramps
- Panic
- Swallowing water
- Hypothermia

- Inability to find the steps (pool)
- Riptide or undertow (in sea)
- Life jacket caught on something (in sea)

GET A REALLY GOOD RECALL BEFOREHAND

Before you let your dog loose in a natural setting with water, you need a "come" command that he will obey every time. Practice the "come" with excellent treats so that he has it down cold—and do a few extra practices each time before you take him to the water. When you see a problem of any kind, you need to be able to get that dog right out of the water.

✦ Check Out Tide, Current and Wind Conditions.

Generally speaking, if you wouldn't let a school-age child swim in the water, then your dog shouldn't be in there, either. Don't make the mistake of thinking that a dog who is even the most powerful and enthusiastic swimmer is an aquatic animal who can deal with threatening water conditions. Don't make the common mistake of thinking that a dog "knows" when he's had enough, or that the conditions are too tough—he's going on adrenaline and the instinct to retrieve. Generally, a dog has no concept of his personal safety and is not equipped to make decisions that are *yours* to make for him.

- ❏ If there are signal flags on the beach showing riptides, undertow or large waves, do not even think of letting your dog in the water.
- ❏ If a river is moving too fast, debris is swirling or being pulled under, the banks are swollen or there are protruding rocks or other impediments, avoid that area.
- ❏ If a lake or other water looks polluted with floating debris, sewage or surface scum, don't let your dog in there.

✦ Dogs on Boats

Introduce the dog to the boat in small increments of time before you ever go out on the water. Let him get comfortable and acclimate to the feeling of being on the water.

Flotation devices A flotation device is recommended for dogs around any natural water, but especially those on boats because of the chance they can fall overboard. These devices are designed to keep the dog afloat in a horizontal swimming position. When making your purchase, spend some time determining whether the life jacket will help you pull the dog out of the water, if necessary. See whether it will support the dog's weight if you lift him, and whether the straps that attach underneath will hurt his stomach.

These safety products come in many shapes and are really a wise investment for any dog who goes out on a boat with people. One notable product is the MTI Adventurewear dog vest, which is a good all-purpose vest for a remarkably low $20. It does a good job of keeping the dog's neck and body afloat, and is easily adjustable. It is available through MTI Adventurewear, P.O. Box 890178, East Weymouth, MA 02189, (781) 340-5380, www.mtiadventurewear.com.

There are fairly elaborate and often costly versions of canine life jackets for dangerous water sports like white-water rafting or boating in rough waters—but rather than evaluate and recommend these products, it seems a better use of time to question why dogs would have to be put in those situations. Does your dog need to run the risk of being hurled out of an open boat when he has no say in whether he should be there and no way to even hold on? Would your dog not be better off back at base camp or even back at your home? What is the point of bringing a dog along in situations that risk his life? If you stop to reconsider whether to take your dog into dangerous water situations and decide you still want to do so, there are numerous heavy-duty canine flotation devices around. More information can be found at www.nrsweb.com, www.extrasport.com, www.ruffwear.com and www.lotusdesigns.com.

Collar beacon for boaters When boating with a dog, you might want to attach this waterproof beacon to his collar: it will flash a red light 120 times a minute and is visible a half mile away. The beacon costs about $10 and is available from www.ruffwear.com, or (888) RUFF-WEAR.

WATER SAFETY DOG POOL ALARM

What if your dog falls in the pool and can't get out—especially if he is a puppy or older dog who might be confused or weak? (My friend Maidee's elderly dog, Effie Bright, sadly died just that way in the pool at a friend's guest house.)

Now there is a pool alarm for dogs. The people who brought you the Safety Turtle system to alert parents of a child falling in the pool have come out with a canine version. The dog version starts at around $140 with one collar (available in five sizes) and a base unit that sounds an alarm if your dog is submerged for more than a few seconds. You can buy additional collars for $60 each, and for $100 there is also a weatherproof mobile base unit that runs on a battery and allows you to take the alarm to any pool, beach or on boat rides. Contact: eSafetyAlert, P.O. Box 69813, West Hollywood, CA 90068, (800) 892-9551, www.esafetyalert.com.

EMERGENCY FIRST AID

If your dog is struggling in the water or is going under, you obviously need to get him out as quickly as you can. If he is breathing and can move around, let him do so, because it will warm up his body and help him breathe. Shivering is a sign that his body temperature has fallen—which can happen in any temperature water if a dog is in long enough—and shivering will help raise his metabolism. Dry him off and wrap him up as best you can to retain his body heat and get him to the vet right away to be evaluated. Just because your dog seems fine does not mean he didn't get water in his lungs, for example.

If your dog is not breathing or is unresponsive, turn to page 309 in Chapter Eleven for instructions on emergency CPR.

City Dogs

Dogs who live in a city are constantly surrounded by masses of people, other dogs and dozens of things to look at, hear and smell. They have many more opportunities for socializing than country or suburban dogs, whose environments stay pretty much the same without much stimulation. This means that city-dwelling dogs develop skills in dealing with all kinds of people and many other dogs.

While it is common to feel sorry for apartment-dwelling dogs, in many cases they have more interesting, stimulating lives and even get more exercise than dogs who rarely leave a small fenced yard in the suburbs. The reason that city dogs generally receive more exercise than those in a nonurban setting is that a dog in the city *must* be walked.

Although country dogs may have more access to the outdoors and may not even always have to be on a leash, many families in the suburbs just don't have time to take their dogs out for exercise, or may not think they need it. These dogs may not even get as much attention from their owners as city-dwelling dogs, many of whom are owned by people who do feel somewhat guilty about the cooped-up life of an apartment dog and compensate by taking them on long walks or into parks, or by arranging for doggie day care or a dog-walking service.

METROPOLITAN EXERCISE

Time is limited for most people in the city; long leisurely runs with the dog aren't practical. But the dog's need to run and blow off steam is still there. If you can, arrange for ten minutes in a park of throwing a ball or a soft-edged Frisbee to your dog and having her bring it back to you. That kind of intense play and interaction is even better than a walk, because it exercises more of her body and engages her mind. Also see "Working Owners and Dog-Walking Services" on page 196.

◆ Poop Solutions

People who live in cities either have to pick up after their dogs by law, or they simply prefer to live in a cleaner, more civic-minded environment.

Picking up dog poop sounds revolting if you've never done it before, but once you give it a try it's really no big deal. You put your hand inside a plastic bag (making sure it has no holes in it) and then pick up the dog droppings. You then draw the rest of the bag back off over your hand and tie a knot on top.

There are some clever plastic bag holders, which you can hook right onto the leash or onto your pocket, that dispense bags as you require them.

The Internet shopping site called www.containerstore.com has an amusing black plastic dog bone with a big clip for your belt. It's a little extravagant when you could just put some plastic bags in your pocket, but it's convenient. The holder and extra bags cost around $10.

There are several brands of biodegradable poop bags available from purveyors of dog products: Mutt Mitts, Pooch Pick Up Bags, Bags on Board and Dispoz-A-Scoop. They each function somewhat differently, so you should have a look at the descriptions and see which ones might be good for you. There is also The Flushable Bag, which is just that, available through howellkds @yahoo.com.

CITY NOISE POLLUTION

The loud noises that explode from every corner in a city cause more of a problem for dogs than air pollution. When you consider how acute their hearing is—and how loud the honking, sirens, etc. seem to us—you can just imagine the sensory overload that city noise can create for a pup.

◆ Give Some Comforting Body Contact.

If you have a dog who is especially sensitive to noise, or who seems anxious in the city during moments of extreme noise pollution, keep the dog near you on the leash and have some kind of body contact with her. If she's really big you can just put a hand on her head, neck or back; bend down for a middle-sized dog or, if she is small enough to be portable, pick her up.

ELEVATORS

You and your dog might be squeezed into a very crowded elevator at some point in the city. If *you* don't like the feeling, imagine what it's like to be your dog, down at knee level with a sea of legs surrounding you.

Don't put your dog in any trapped situation like a crowded elevator until he has had a chance to get used to the motion of an elevator alone with you. After that, take elevator rides with no more than a few other passengers. If he tolerates this, then you'll know he can probably handle a bigger crowd in the elevator, too.

AGGRESSIVE PERSONALITY

If your dog's reaction to new situations or stressful ones is to be aggressive, then you'll want to avoid crowded sidewalks, entrances to buildings with a lot of foot traffic or anywhere there is a crush of humanity. If those kinds of situations trigger a bad reaction in your dog, do everything you can to avoid putting both of you to the test.

SUGGESTIONS FOR DOGS LEFT ALONE

There are a number of things you can provide for your dog that will improve her environment while you are gone.

✦ A View of the Outside World

Put a chair under a window and you'll encourage the dog to look out the window and enjoy the passing "theater of life."

✦ Give Her Company.

Another dog is the best companion, but if that isn't possible, try a cat (see page 101 for "Dogs and Cats").

✦ Fill the Silence.

Leave the radio on a call-in talk show; the sound of human voices is comforting to most dogs. Or put the TV on a station that has talk shows, soap operas, "judge shows"—anything where people are talking.

✦ Doggie Day Care

If you live in a metropolitan area you should find out about services like this, which take in dogs for the day and arrange activities and groups for them to play in. Ask around about whether there is such a facility near you, and also check the Web site for day-care listings at www.doggiedirectory.com/daycare. If daily care doesn't fit in your budget, see if you can afford a day or two a week. It can give your dog pleasure and mental stimulation while relieving some of the pressure and guilt you may feel about not spending more time with him.

There are often many activities offered, including games, music and snacks. Small dogs are always segregated from large ones, and group playtimes are divided by size. The best facilities have an energetic staff that plays with the dogs and monitors their behavior when they're out together in a playgroup. Some of these facilities have a swimming pool, both for fun and as hydrotherapy for dogs recovering from surgery, for which there is an additional charge.

Is your dog suited to day care? This is a question you need to ask yourself, and a good facility will also make a good effort to screen your dog's personality and attitudes in a group setting. Some "only dogs" fit right in and seem delighted to have canine company, while some dogs unaccustomed to being around other dogs may have difficulty in the "plays well with others" department. A day-care facility should determine this compatibility for every customer in the interest of a safe and pleasant environment for all. For some people it may just be a place to park their dog for the day, but there is the potential for serious fights and physical and emotional trauma to a dog.

Do your homework. Canine day-care centers are opening everywhere to accommodate the growing needs of caring dog owners who have demanding jobs, but you have to consider a lot more than a convenient location and hours. As a loving and responsible owner, you have to do your homework and assure yourself of the all-around safety of a facility you are considering. Use the questionnaire below to tour a facility. You can answer some of these queries through observation, and the rest you can direct to the person showing you around.

Trust your instincts: no matter what information you get, pay attention to your gut reaction to the place—how it's run, what the other dogs are like. If you have qualms, don't leave your dog there. Instead, come back another time on your own and just watch the proceedings for a while to see if your initial doubts are dispelled by what you observe, or if you still don't feel right about it.

QUESTIONS ABOUT A DAY-CARE CENTER

❏ Thorough background check on every dog? (Vaccinations and expirations; parasites)
❏ Is it clean? (odor-free; poop scooped quickly; clean floors; clean water bowls)
❏ Is it large enough? (50 to 100 square feet per medium to large dog)
❏ Is it safe, with nonslip floors, nothing broken?
❏ Sufficient staff? (one handler per ten dogs [maximum], with back-up personnel available)
❏ Well-trained and enthusiastic staff?
❏ Is there an outdoor area? (safely fenced; poop-scooped, clean)
❏ Group dog areas divided by size of dog? How many in each play group?
❏ Play area interesting? (places to climb over and under; toys, balls)
❏ Sufficient play-area time? (how often and for how long does each size group go out?)
❏ How are dog introductions done? (slowly; monitored; small numbers at first?)
❏ How are dogs separated if fights happen?
❏ Where do dogs relieve themselves, if outdoors available? (how many at one time?)
❏ How often are they walked (for indoor facility) and how often? Alone or in groups?
❏ What are the pick-up/drop-off rules and hours? (any penalty for early or late?)

Lost Dogs

There are few things as distressing as losing your dog. One of the greatest risks is the newly adopted dog who takes off or escapes in a panic and doesn't even have a destination or the bearings to find his new home again.

Do not panic, do not despair. Dogs have been found weeks and even months after being lost.

PREVENTION IS THE BEST PROTECTION.

The surest way to avoid losing your dog is to eliminate the ways he can escape. Then you must ensure that there are ways to identify him as your dog.

◆ Inspect Your Fence and Gates.

If you already have fencing around your property, inspect it on foot and make sure there are no areas that are loose, fallen or missing.

Check where the fencing meets the ground and make sure there are no spaces that would encourage a dog to dig out. If there are gaps at the ground line, put rocks, logs or any other blocking material on the *outside* of the fence (if it's on the inside, the dog can shove it aside or dig around it).

Do the latches on the gates function properly? Are they self-closing on a spring? If not, you might want to install spring latches now, especially if a number of people use the gates and might not remember to shut them. Gates left open are a frequent yet easily avoided cause of escaped dogs.

◆ Get ID Tags and/or Collars.

Even if you have to make a temporary tag yourself, *do not let that dog out of the house for an instant without identification*. For many kinds of tags there can be a two-week wait, and if your dog is going to run away, she's not going to wait for a tag.

You have to give Good Samaritans a way to reach you by telephone should your dog cross their path or wind up in someone else's hands. And even once someone gets hold of your dog, it takes a fraction of a second for your dog to take off again. Without a way to contact you, nobody can help reunite you and that rapscallion of a runaway.

◆ Microchip the Dog.

Microchipping has become more accepted as a permanent way to identify your dog. The identifying chip is so small that it fits into a hypodermic needle and is injected under the dog's skin, usually at the shoulder blades, and is virtually painless. It is done at the vet's office for a cost that is usually under $50.

The *theory* behind microchips is that when a dog is lost, a scanner can be passed over the dog by people at the receiving end (known as "end-users" of the product)—be it the pound, shelter or local veterinarians—to pick up the dog's identifying information. But *in practice,* this seldom happens. While some microchip companies have distributed up to 20,000 of their scanners to shelters across the country (free of charge) there are many entries into the microchip market that have distributed *no* compatible scanners at all. This flaw in the concept is serious enough that the Humane Society of the United States (HSUS) issued a press release in 2004 to alert dog owners that there is no centralized system that can read all of the different brands of microchips on the market. This warning was issued when approximately 440 vet clinics housed in one of the nation's largest pet-product retailers were selling and implanting microchips from a company that issued no scanners to anyone.

Over the years, manufacturers claimed they were attempting to make all of their products adhere to one industry standard, but there is still no universal scanner that can detect all microchips, regardless of brand. There is a widespread belief among dog owners that a microchip is their best protection if their dog gets lost—so much so that many people don't worry about whether their dogs are wearing identification tags. But the microchip gives a false sense of security because a dog could be implanted with a microchip that cannot be detected with the available technology. Also, people finding your dog may know nothing about Chips.

If you do choose to have your dog microchipped, find out beforehand what chip scanners are being used at your local animal shelter and veterinary offices in the area. You want your dog chipped with a brand that can be read and interpreted by that locally used brand of scanner. Talk directly to your vet, your local shelter and the chip manufacturer to be certain. And if you travel, do the same thing for the area(s) to which you are headed to find out which is the most frequently used brand of chip.

The AVID FriendChip This system uses PETtrac, a computerized global recovery network. This chip can also be used on cats, horses, birds, reptiles and fish (don't laugh—there are some Koi and other pond fish worth more than many purebred dogs).

The AKC Companion Animal Recovery Service Your dog does not have to be registered with the AKC and doesn't even need to be purebred to participate in this service, which operates in Canada and the U.S. For a nominal fee it can even help with implanted microchips that are different than the ones in its program. Call (800)252-7894 for more information, or visit www.akc-car.org.

⬥ Dognose ID

This is a new process to identify dogs that is similar to fingerprinting humans. The Dognose ID system sends you a kit to make permanent inkless impressions of your dog's unique nose as an identifying feature. The company enters your dog's nose imprint and photo into its database and you receive a pet identity card and a collar tag with an identification number. There is a free Web site and a toll-free search number, which is part of a search network, to help you find your lost dog.

⬥ Confine Your Dog Before Fireworks.

Many dogs are terrorized by the sound of fireworks—or any other loud, explosive noises. Dogs run off and are never found again because in their panic-stricken flight they lose their bearings.

The Fourth of July and New Year's Eve are common times for dogs to wig out when there are fireworks or similar celebratory noises.

If loud sounds startle your dog, there's a chance he may react strongly to fireworks. Your best protection is to put him in a small space like a bathroom or even a walk-in closet (dogs often feel safe in a cave-like den) and close the door until the noise is over.

If there are any noisy events in your neighborhood that you know about ahead of time, you'll be doing your dog a favor by confining him.

WHAT TO DO IF YOUR DOG GETS LOST

Don't waste any time just assuming your dog will find her way home. There are a number of things you can do that will greatly increase your chances of finding her—and just doing something will feel so much better than waiting helplessly.

- ❑ Paste the best photo you have of the dog on a piece of paper. Describe the dog if he's an unusual breed or a crossbred dog who looks like a breed. Offer a reward but don't specify the amount. This will help prevent an unscrupulous person from calculating whether your dog's value is higher than your reward.
- ❑ Large or colorful posters generate more attention. Go to a copy service and spend whatever you can afford to get the most visible announcement.
- ❑ Staple these flyers wherever you can. Grocery stores, pet stores, vet hospitals, animal shelters and schools are good starting points. Blanket the area.
- ❑ At the same time, look around for any "found dog" sign that might be posted.
- ❑ Contact the local newspaper and put a notice in the "lost pets" section.
- ❑ Check the same paper for "found" notices, in case he's been found.
- ❑ Drive around the neighborhood and local shops to see if they'll allow you to put up a flyer, and check if there are any "found" flyers posted.
- ❑ If you have a local radio station that announces lost dogs, ask for their help.
- ❑ Contact local shelters by phone, but also go in every two days to look in person.

◆ Beware of Lost-dog Scams.

If you have put a "lost dog" notice in the newspaper, be on the lookout for scam artists trying to profit from your desperation.

This scam is not a new phenomenon, but it is a frustrating and heartbreaking one, so be on the defensive toward people contacting you if you've run a "lost dog" ad. This attempt to bilk owners of lost dogs began in Chicago, then moved west to Texas, California and Nevada.

Here is what happens: a person loses her dog and places an ad in the local paper about it. She receives a phone call saying the missing pet has been found. The caller often claims to be a truck driver who found the pet while traveling through the owner's city. Then the caller says the pet needed veterinary care so he needs to be reimbursed for the cost before he can put the pet on a plane home. The grateful and relieved owners wire the money. Then they go to the airport or call the airline to confirm that their pet is on the flight the caller told them—and there is no pet on board. This scam was uncovered in part because an airline employee noticed a strange trend of dozens of people expecting their dogs to be on flights—during the winter months when the airline wasn't even accepting pets for transport.

The Nevada attorney general is aggressively investigating complaints about these scams. If you have been the victim of such a trick or are suspicious about someone in Nevada claiming to have your dog, please contact the hotline at their Bureau of Consumer Protection at (800)266-8688 to protect yourself and others from being cruelly duped. Wherever you live, monitor any calls carefully. Tricksters are out there, ready to profit from your vulnerability.

Disaster Preparedness

There are so many kinds of unforeseen emergencies that can happen, and your pets are at your mercy to keep them safe. A natural disaster can strike your community in the form of a flood, blizzard or, depending on where you live, even a hurricane, wildfire, earthquake or tornado. What if there's a fire or a gas leak in your house or apartment building and you're not home? You can also suddenly have a personal emergency that is health-related or requires traveling on short notice. Planning ahead for your dog's safety means one less thing to worry about if disaster does strike.

PLANNING FOR EMERGENCIES

- ❏ Post stickers at every entrance to your home showing how many animals live there.
- ❏ If you have neighbors with pets, discuss with them what you can do to help each other's animals if only one of you is at home when disaster strikes. Exchange house keys and essential information and documents.
- ❏ Talk to relatives and friends outside your immediate area who would be willing to take the dog if absolutely necessary.
- ❏ Red Cross shelters often will not take pets during a crisis and local boarding kennels fill up, so learn where other kennels are within a seventy-five-mile radius.
- ❏ Check with your local animal shelter to find out whether they will take in dogs during an emergency, or whether they know of a community organization that will function as a port in a storm for pets.
- ❏ Locate members of the national hotel/motel chains with pet-friendly policies. Find out any restrictions ahead of time, such as number of pets or size/weight limit. Check out www.petswelcome.com and page 493 of Chapter Fifteen for listings.
- ❏ Ask your vet to give you a refill supply of your dog's medications (antidepressants, anticonvulsants, diuretics, insulin).
- ❏ Keep a record with other disaster supplies of your dog's rabies and other vaccinations (or titer levels), along with other pertinent medical information to ensure that he is allowed into facilities requiring health documents.

YOUR VETERINARIAN'S DISASTER PLAN

Some veterinary hospitals have designated themselves as a resource in case of disaster. The staff has been instructed on how it will operate in such a situation to serve pets who are injured or become homeless. Being available in an emergency means that the facility has things like a generator, emergency supplies and even somewhere that the staff can stay on the premises, if need be. As a disaster resource, a vet clinic has to plan for how to house the pets of clients whose homes may not be habitable. Before an actual emergency situation arises, it would be a good idea to find out if your vet has such a forward-thinking plan and, if so, how you can tap into it.

On the other end of the spectrum, what if your vet has not considered what would happen to the pets in her care at the time of a disaster, or how to be available to dogs whose owners have become homeless? You can encourage your vet to make provisions for these situations, especially if you live in an area prone to natural threats.

TAKE YOUR DOG WITH YOU

All local and federal emergency organizations recommend that people take their pets with them if they must evacuate. Some owners mistakenly think that a dog has self-protective instincts to fend for himself, but just the opposite is true. Dogs will panic and run in a frightening situation, especially if you are gone, and they can get lost, hurt or killed.

Keep in mind that your pet's personality and reactions may change during the stress of an emergency. Keep your dog close to you and keep an eye on him. If he is exhibiting anxious, aggressive behavior, keep him away from people and other dogs.

- **If You Must Leave Your Dog Behind When You Evacuate:**
  - ❑ Never leave a dog tied up outdoors or in a pen. There are too many terrible things that can happen.
  - ❑ Make sure he is confined to a safe indoor space like a bathroom, laundry room or kitchen (these are all areas with fresh water) and put his bed in there. If possible, place a piece of clothing you've recently worn in the room, which might provide comfort.
  - ❑ Either leave a tap dripping into a container (if there's somewhere the overflow can drain) or fill a couple of buckets with water.
  - ❑ Leave enough dry food for a few days (even though for a permanently ravenous dog like Billy Blue it wouldn't last much more than twenty minutes).
  - ❑ If there is a chance of flooding, choose a space with a high counter or somewhere the animal can go to avoid rising water, and turn off electricity to avoid electrocution in high-water emergencies.
  - ❑ Do not leave a slip collar (choke chain) of any kind on a dog left alone. Be certain that his flat collar has an ID tag. If your emergency information is different from that on the tag, tape another phone number to the back of the tag.
  - ❑ Keep cats and dogs in separate areas. Even if they normally get along, there can be problems when the animals are under stress.

PAID DOG-SITTERS IN AN EMERGENCY

In case you are delayed away from home or have a medical emergency, you need someone to stay with your dog(s). Develop a relationship with a paid pet-sitter (or a friend or relative) who can get to know your dog and her habits. As part of the routine, have the person come by occasionally to play with or walk your dog—or just hang out with her. This way she can feel comfortable with the sitter, and you will know that your dog has a backup, just in case.

Make a checklist of everything pertaining to the dog: health issues, medications, the name of her vet, vaccinations, how and what to feed, personality and behavioral issues.

Or contact Pet Sitters International or the National Association of Professional Pet Sitters on their Web sites, www.petsit.com and www.petsitters.org, for referrals.

IDENTIFYING YOUR DOG

There may be chaos and confusion for some time following a natural disaster, and you want to make sure that your dog does not get lost. Many pets survive disasters, but then there is the added tragedy that many cannot be reunited with their families because they have no identification.

Make sure your pet can be identified. She should always have a name tag on her collar. You also should consider an implanted microchip (see page 209 earlier in this chapter). You can get more information on this from your vet.

◆ Tattoos

At one time a tattoo was considered a foolproof way to identify your dog and protect him from being sold for medical research. When I got my first Weimaraners from Friends for Pets in California, they were tattoing dogs to protect their identity and ownership information. But the microchip is a better way to go.

EMERGENCY SUPPLIES, JUST IN CASE

If it gives you peace of mind, you can put together an emergency kit for your dog's needs, should there be a catastrophic event.

DISASTER KIT

- ❑ One-week supply of food, treats and water in an unbreakable plastic bin (replace food and water every six months for freshness)
- ❑ If you use canned food, a can opener
- ❑ Plastic dishes
- ❑ Leash, harness, carrier, whatever you use to contain your dog (he may be very scared and skittish, depending on the disaster, and may need more restraint)
- ❑ Dog bed (if he has one that's not too hard to take)
- ❑ First-aid kit with tweezers, antiseptic spray or hydrogen peroxide
- ❑ Current photos of the dog in case he gets lost
- ❑ Documentation: vaccination records, pet meds, telephone numbers for you and another friend or family member outside your immediate area

Chapter 9

HOUSE-TRAINING

I prefer the phrase "house-training" to "housebreaking," which sounds so harsh. Housebreaking implies that you have to "break" your dog of something; almost as though you and your dog are in a battle of wills. If you understand that emptying her bladder and bowels means more than just a bodily function to a dog, then when you train her *not* to eliminate in the house, what you are actually doing is redirecting her instincts.

This chapter is not about other manners in the house or any obedience training: you will find that in Chapter Ten. This chapter is dedicated solely to teaching a dog not to eliminate in the house. Some of the topics you will find covered in this chapter are:

- ❏ House-training guidelines for puppies, including teaching him to go "on command," using a crate, gating-off an area in the house
- ❏ Charts of how long a puppy can hold it, signs that she needs to go, and the negative consequences of giving freedom in the house
- ❏ Tips for cleaning up pee
- ❏ Working owners and house-training
- ❏ Litter training for little dogs
- ❏ House-training problems and solutions

Wolf Instincts about "Elimination"

MARKING THEIR TERRITORY WITH PEE

Dogs are extremely territorial: they are born with a strong drive to stake their claim and they do so by choosing where they pee and poop (sorry if that sounds like baby talk, but "urinate and defecate" sounds so professorial). Their wolf-pack origins are what cause dogs to mark the boundaries of their area with bodily fluids. Each dog's urine has a distinctive odor that is immediately discernible to other dogs. Once a puppy (or an adult dog) has established several areas where she relieves herself, she will be drawn back to them. This is called "scent-posting" and is a way to mark off territory.

In a wolf pack, the alpha leader, or Top Dog, is usually the one to decide on the boundaries of the pack's territory. There is more about the hereditary wolf origin of dogs starting on page 149. However, for the purposes of house-training, the issue of what comprises a dog's territory is not necessarily relevant—unless you have a multiple-dog household and/or issues of aggression (more on territorial aggression on page 621).

OVER-PEEING OTHER DOGS' URINE

All dogs—starting from the age of eight weeks—look for their own scent or that of another dog to urinate or defecate over. This is called "over-peeing," and it's a way for a dog to impose his presence. When dogs are mature, over-peeing is also a way to stake a higher claim. If you have two or more dogs in your family, you will notice that the ones higher up the ladder cover the lesser dogs' urine with their own; if there is a dog in the pack more senior than they are, that dog will pee on top of the others' markings. You might say, "The last dog to pee wins!"

Keep in mind that nothing about house-training is natural to dogs: in fact it can be counter-instinctive *not* to mark the boundaries of their living area (otherwise known as your living room). So you should cut a puppy some slack while teaching her to live in your house by your rules. One of the secrets of house-training is to recognize that your task is to redirect your dog's instinctual behavior so that she eliminates where and when *you* wish—which can be in direct opposition to her instincts, contrary to her hardwiring.

There is more about dogs' wolf heritage as it pertains to house-training on page 231 in the "House-training Problems" section later in this chapter.

House-training Guidelines for Puppies

(Note about paper-training for city pups: most city dwellers—and some who live in houses but have work schedules with long hours—will probably paper-train or litter-train as a step on the road to complete house-training. Paper-training is covered later in this chapter on page 228.)

THE FIRST TIME YOU BRING THE PUPPY HOME

On his arrival at your house, do not carry the puppy indoors. The first place you should set the pup down is where he will mark, so carrying him inside will guarantee that the first place he will pee at your house is inside it—which is the very place we do not want him to "scent-post." Instead, lead the puppy on a leash outside, giving him the opportunity to mark his new yard—the area in front or back of your house or apartment. Set him down in front of the house, or better yet take him to the backyard (if you have one) and let him "scent-post" there. This area will become his preferred place to do his business.

◆ Teaching a Puppy to "Go on Command"

You can teach your puppy a voice cue to encourage her to eliminate. This is actually simpler to accomplish than you might think. Use any words that suit you—"Hurry up," "Go on" or "Go pee"—as the puppy squats. Quietly praise her as she goes, then make a big fuss with a treat when she's done. Before long, when you say "Hurry up," she'll squat. This can be incredibly useful if the weather is horrible or you're in a rush.

GOING "ON COMMAND"

- ❑ Take your puppy to her "potty spot."
- ❑ Stand and wait as she sniffs around.
- ❑ When she starts to go, do *not* say "good girl"—save the praise for when she's finished.
- ❑ Instead, say the words you'll use hereafter to encourage her to do her business: that phrase—a consistent few words said in a firm yet encouraging voice—that you will continue to use just as the dog starts eliminating.
- ❑ If you consistently say those words whenever your puppy *starts* to pee or poop, as time goes on you'll be able to get her going just by saying that phrase in the same way.
- ❑ As soon as the puppy finishes, give her a big "Yes!" and a treat or a good scratch behind the ears or a tummy rub—whatever is her favorite spot.
- ❑ When teaching her to go on cue, *always* use that phrase the moment she begins and always praise her *right* after she finishes. It should not take long before you can inspire her efforts by using the cue words before she needs to go.

◆ Try Different Surfaces

You want to avoid having a dog that is used to only one type of surface—such as grass—on which to relieve herself. If you don't encourage her to use a variety of surfaces, she may wind up becoming a dog who needs a particular sensation under her feet in order to go.

Once your dog has come to understand your cue words—"hurry up" or "go pee"—you can encourage her to try a variety of surfaces.

Gravel, cement, dirt, etc., are all surfaces that could crop up at some point in her life as the only options for a potty spot—and you don't want her to have to hold it until her eyeballs float just because the ground feels alien under her paws.

Using a Crate

Trainers agree that the most humane, clear and effective way to teach a dog not to relieve himself in the house is to keep the puppy in a crate between the times that he's playing with you, eating or relieving himself. The theory behind the crate is that a dog instinctively does not want to dirty the area where he sleeps and eats.

REASONS YOU NEED A CRATE

◆ House-training a Puppy

This is the number-one reason for having a crate. All the training experts seem to agree that there is no better way to house-train a dog than to confine him in the crate.

◆ Travel

If you need to ship a dog by air, then you need to have a top-quality, high-impact molded-plastic crate like the Vari Kennel, which is FDA-approved for airline travel. Many people also use a crate for car travel, confining their dog in the back of a van or station wagon. If you do travel with your dog in a car and want to stay in hotels or motels—even those that do not welcome pets—they may allow the dog to come inside with you if you bring the crate into the room and promise to keep the dog inside it.

◆ Emergencies

If you live in an area that is prone to natural disasters such as hurricanes, tornadoes, earthquakes or floods, you may need to evacuate. The pet will be secure in her crate and may be accepted in an evacuation center if she is in her crate—or even allowed into a veterinary hospital or animal shelter if she brings her own house (like a turtle).

CHOOSING A CRATE

◆ Crates Can Be Expensive.

If you want to keep the cost down, check local classified ads, penny-savers and garage sales. This is one item (dog doors are another) for which you may not get any real benefit from the great prices of catalogs, the Internet or other wholesale vendors, because the shipping costs can be quite high.

◆ The Collapsible Wire Box with a Metal Tray in the Bottom Is Cheapest.

If you never intend to travel with the dog, then you can get this kind of crate. The mesh allows the pup to see all around her. If you plan to travel with your dog, then you need the molded-plastic kind with a metal mesh door.

◆ Metal Mesh Cages Are Good for Puppy Training.

A crate that is mesh all the way around allows the youngster to see everything going on all around him. He is not isolated or cut off from the sights and sounds of daily life. However, at night or for quiet times you need to throw a big cover over the top and sides of the cage so the puppy has a cozier "den" and less outside stimulation—which would obviously not be necessary with a plastic crate.

WHAT SIZE CRATE?

• **The Crate Should Be Big Enough for the Puppy to Grow Into.**
You don't want a crate that's too big, because then it won't feel secure and den-like. You want it to be big enough for the *grown dog* to stand up and turn around and stretch out in. It should also be snug: just long enough for a dog to lie down comfortably, just wide enough for him to turn around and just high enough for him to stand.

When the puppy is still small, you can place a barrier or panel inside the crate to make it smaller. This way, you won't run into the problem of a crate so much larger than the puppy that he views one part of it as a bedroom and one part as a bathroom.

If you have a friend who can loan you a smaller crate while the puppy is growing, so much the better.

PREPARING THE CRATE FOR A PUPPY

Put the crate somewhere that's part of the household activity, not tucked away. The dog should feel part of things while he's in his "room," not as though he's been banished. It also gets him used to noises and activities without feeling vulnerable or overwhelmed by them.

• **Secure the Crate to the Floor.**
You don't want the crate to slip and slide on the floor, possibly frightening the pup. Put a big towel underneath the crate so it doesn't slip or rattle around when the dog gets in or moves around in it.

• **Make the Crate Inviting and Unthreatening.**
Keep the crate door open when the puppy isn't in it and keep some toys and a chew in there. It should be an inviting place, a safe haven for the pup to come and go to.

• **Do Not Put Any Bedding in the Crate.**
With some puppies, if you put bedding in the crate (shredded newspapers or a towel or blanket) this seems to cancel out the concept of "this is my den to keep clean," and the puppy may feel free to relieve himself on the bedding.

BASIC FACTS ABOUT CRATE TIME

❑ A puppy does not have control over her muscles of elimination before four months of age.
❑ Puppies vary in the development of their self-control—try to judge for yourself.
❑ To estimate the length of time a puppy can stay in the crate, figure an hour for every

month of her age, plus one (a three-month-old puppy, therefore, can be crated for four hours).

☐ Smaller dogs have smaller bladders and have to relieve themselves more frequently.

☐ Adult dogs can stay in a crate for eight hours—and some do—but it's hard on them not to be able to move around for that long or to relieve themselves, and mentally, it's tough not to have anything to do.

LEAVING THE HOUSE

◆ First, Practice Departures.

Before you go out, shut the crate door for a few seconds with the puppy in there, then open it. Shut it for longer amounts of time—a few minutes more each time—while you walk around the room.

◆ Practice Putting Her In and Leaving the Room.

Do this first for a few seconds, then increase the time you're gone to fifteen minutes, then thirty.

If the puppy is whining or crying, DO NOT let him out. That will only teach him to whine and cry when he wants or doesn't want something.

◆ No Departure Drama.

Display no emotion when you put the puppy in or out. Just make it a neutral, routine event.

Comfort Items to Put in the Crate

There are some things you can do to make the crate more welcoming:

- Wrap a hot-water bottle with a big towel. Warmth can feel cozy and like the litter she recently left.
- Put a shirt that you've worn in the crate to keep her company and soothe her.
- Put in a teddy bear or other stuffed toy that you've rubbed all over with your hands.
- Put on some music or the television so she doesn't feel too alone.
- Take a small Kong toy or sterilized bone and stuff it with peanut butter or soft cheese and give it to her right before you close the door and leave (however, keep in mind that this may cause digestive disturbances, since chewing—even on an empty stomach—stimulates defecation).

TIPS ON SUCCESSFUL CRATE USE

◆ **Keep Positive Associations with the Crate.**

Put a treat into the crate and say "In your house" in a high cheery voice. Give the puppy lots of praise for going in there. Never put the pup in the crate as punishment. It doesn't teach him anything, and it turns the crate into something negative.

◆ **Feed the Puppy in the Crate.**

Food gives the crate a positive association. If he won't go all the way in to eat, put the dish inside the crate opening so the puppy has to at least put his head in. Once the puppy will go all the way in to eat, close the door while he's eating but stay right there—he'll need to go out immediately after eating.

◆ **Ignore Crying.**

If the puppy cries or whines, ignore it completely. Most puppies will quit within ten minutes if they don't get some feedback, negative or positive. If a dog or puppy doesn't bark when first put in the crate, give lots of praise.

◆ **Wait until the Puppy Is Tired.**

Put the puppy in after he's tuckered out from playing and ready to crash.

◆ **A Crate Is Not Cruel.**

Do not think of the crate as a punishment, because that's not the point of it. Most puppies, once familiarized with their crates, accept them as safe and cozy places to nap and hang out—sort of like the caves that were lairs for their wolf ancestors. Do not feel sorry for a puppy in a crate—he feels protected in there. And think of the stress that being safely in his crate saves him. The crate will help him to distinguish where and when he can relieve himself. What a crate effectively means to your puppy is: more biscuits, fewer scoldings.

WHERE TO PUT THE CRATE

The crate should be kept in a nice central location—in the kitchen if it fits—since in most homes that's the hub of household activity. The puppy should never be isolated or feel as if he is being shut away—it is important for him to see and hear everything about the daily activity of your home from his crate. He can soak in that homey atmosphere from the safety of his "den." Later on, once the pup has bladder control and understands the concept of house-training, he'll be right there in the center of the household action, accustomed to the sights and sounds.

The puppy should sleep in a crate near your bed, or at least in your bedroom. Sleeping near you helps the pup bond to her human family; the proximity to your bed in the early weeks ensures that you will wake up if she gets restless or whines to be taken out.

If you only want one crate and can manage to move it to your bedroom at nighttime, great. If it's too big and bulky to move, however, consider whether you could borrow one from a friend or buy a cheaper one (that isn't airline-approved quality, for example) just for overnight use in your bedroom.

⬩ Getting the Puppy Outside Quickly

You need to take your puppy to her potty area immediately after opening the door to the crate. If the puppy leaves the crate on her own, the first thing she's going to do is relieve herself, a habit you do not want her to form. When you open the crate door you need to pick up the pup and take her outside. You really should be doing this every time the puppy eats, drinks, plays hard or chews a toy (which stimulates defecation).

Always take her to the same area: she will remember why and it will stimulate her.

Take the puppy out on a regular schedule so her body gets into a rhythm. And do not confuse things by trying to introduce a different schedule on the weekends—the puppy's bladder is going to get used to a certain schedule. Get up and keep the same schedule every single day of the week—it's not as though her bladder knows when it's the weekend!

⬩ How Long Can a Puppy Hold It?

A puppy has a very small stomach, an even smaller bladder and undeveloped muscle control of the sphincter. He needs a lot of help and patience to become house-trained. It should be obvious that no puppy should be expected to spend a whole day in a crate. It will inevitably turn out that he cannot keep control of his bladder. By caging him you put the puppy in an unnatural situation in which he is forced to soil his crate (his den). This interferes with a dog's inborn instinct to keep the den clean—and only because you expected too much time from him in the crate.

HOW OFTEN A PUPPY HAS TO GO OUT

- ❏ Until a baby dog is twelve weeks old, he is going to eliminate every hour or two as long as he is awake.
- ❏ The older a puppy gets, the longer he can wait between walks.
- ❏ A rule of thumb is that a puppy can hold his urine for the number of hours that corresponds to his age in months, plus one. So an eight-week-old puppy (two months) can hold it for three hours—but that is the *most* time he can hold it, so he may feel urgency before that.
- ❏ A smaller breed of dog has a smaller bladder and can thus last a shorter amount of time.
- ❏ Up to three to four months, the time becomes five to six hours at the most.
- ❏ Once a puppy reaches six months he should be able to hold it as long as an adult dog: nine hours, which is a normal workday for many people.

⬩ How to Recognize When a Puppy Needs to Go

If you take the time to notice the signals that can tell you what a puppy is thinking or wanting, it can save you time and trouble.

If a puppy whines or cries at you, this is probably an attempt to communicate the urge to eliminate. Think of this like a little kid being potty-trained who says urgently, "Daddy, I need to go. NOW!" If that parent doesn't respond instantly to the child's plea, the next thing he'll hear is, "It's okay. I don't need to go anymore," followed by a little puddle at the child's feet. If you don't want to wind up like that with your pup, you'd better learn to notice the ways she tries to signal her needs!

A puppy probably needs to go out if she suddenly puts her nose down and starts sniffing the floor, going in circles. Likewise if she starts panting, but she hasn't gotten hot from running around. If a puppy lifts her tail while doing any of this, take note of whether her anus begins to open: this is the main sign that she needs to move her bowels. This may sound as though I'm suggesting you be disgustingly overattentive, but watching body language for signs of impending evacuation really can save you from an even grosser fate: scraping up fresh dog-doo from your floor!

◆ Give a Treat Immediately After Your Dog "Goes" Outside.

As with all positive reinforcement in the learning process, you want to reward the desired behavior *immediately* when it happens. So with house-training, you don't want the dog to wait until you get back in the house for a treat—you want to reward the puppy for eliminating outdoors right after it takes place.

Don't ever assume that the puppy "knows" what you expect of her. By giving a reward instantly after the correct choice by the puppy, you are increasing the chances that she will repeat that behavior.

◆ No Water at Night

Not filling your puppy's bladder makes it a lot easier for her not to pee during the night. If a pup seems really thirsty at night, give her one or two ice cubes, which can be refreshing without filling her bladder.

◆ Getting Up in the Middle of the Night

If the puppy wakes up and fusses or whines, you have no choice but to take her out. She is probably communicating her understanding that she should not empty her bowels or bladder in the house—which means you *must* get up—and pretty darn quickly! You might even want to keep some sweat-clothes or other easily donned clothing beside your bed so you can pull them on, snap on the puppy's leash and carry her out to her "potty spot" (where she has been regularly relieving herself).

Note that a puppy's bladder is smaller and her digestive system works quickly, so when she realizes she has to go out there's only a small window of opportunity between her realization of that need-to-go sensation and that sensation becoming reality.

When you get outside, use your word cue (see the earlier section in this chapter on page 217, "Going on Command") to hurry up the process. Don't make a middle-of-the night outing seem fun: praise the puppy quietly once he goes but then go right back inside. No feeding, playing or cuddling, or you'll teach him the benefits of waking you up. Put him back in the crate and get right back into bed yourself (as if you need encouragement at 3:00 A.M.!).

YOU SHOULD ALWAYS KNOW WHERE YOUR PUPPY IS

There are only three places the puppy should ever be during the house-training period. First, he can be in his crate (resting after playing or waiting for you to take him out). Second, he can be outside with you relieving himself. Third, he might be eating after such a rest stop outside or playing with you.

◆ **Keep the Puppy with You at All Times.**

When the puppy is out of his crate, he cannot be left unattended. Not even for a second. When he's not with you, he's in the crate. Keep the puppy's leash tied to your belt or loop it around your wrist. You go to the bathroom, he goes with you. You sit down to eat or read the paper, he's right there on his leash under or beside your chair—or if you prefer, tethered near his bed (for more on tethers see page 281 in the "Equipment" section).

If he's not attached to you, keep the pup *very* confined in his crate (no extra space to treat as a bathroom). After he goes outside, give him a *great* treat for holding it until you got him outside.

◆ **No Exceptions. None.**

There is a basic, inviolate rule about how to utilize the crate for house-training: the puppy NEVER roams free in the house. He is in that crate unless your full attention is on him, and full attention means just that—a totally focused "quality time" of playing, grooming, feeding and/or taking him for a walk.

In the long run it's cruel to a puppy to be inconsistent, because it sets him up for failure by giving him a freedom he can't yet handle. Anytime he is not under your direct control and he eliminates in the house, he has practiced (and therefore reinforced) that behavior. It's almost like setting your house-training progress back to the beginning, which cannot happen if you have him either in his crate or under close supervision. By keeping him right at your side you remove the opportunity for him to have the freedom to pee anywhere, and you have gone a long way toward getting across the house-training habit.

Take the pup out to his potty area frequently (every hour in the early weeks, plus after every meal and vigorous play session). Give him a really good treat immediately after he has relieved himself, plus generous praise. A puppy's accomplishment in going outdoors should be the cause of the greatest celebration and congratulatory treats he has ever known.

◆ **Restrict Access to the House.**

Dogs are genetically hardwired not to relieve themselves in their den, but the problem is that a puppy isn't going to naturally understand that the huge spaces inside your house are *all* den. Dogs often perceive the less-used room(s) as a good place to eliminate. Most puppies, if left free to roam in a house, will gravitate to the living room or dining room, where in most houses there is less scent of people.

No puppy should EVER have freedom to roam inside the house—not even for a minute. Think of a puppy loose in the house as being equal to letting a toddler wander around a house and a swimming pool. Something bad is bound to happen in both cases (although obviously the toddler is in a more dangerous and serious situation). I use the analogy so you'll realize that by having an unrestricted puppy in the house, you are asking for certain trouble.

FREEDOM IN THE HOUSE MEANS:

❑ The puppy will pee and/or poop somewhere . . .
❑ You might not find it . . .

- ❏ It will be too late to reprimand him *at all* unless you catch him right in the act (although even then it seems unfair to scold him since you allowed him the freedom he could not be expected to handle in the first place) . . .
- ❏ You have to *undo* what you just allowed the puppy to learn: how to use the inside of your house as a toilet . . .
- ❏ You have to clean it up . . .

Think how much easier life will be if you avoid scenarios like that by keeping the pup restricted, for both of your sakes.

GATES

One of the most useful pieces of equipment you can have for raising a dog is a gate that can keep him out of those areas of the house where mischief could occur. By having that area gated off—or, alternately, by having the dog gated into a specified portion of your home—you greatly reduce the amount of monitoring and corrections you will have to do with your dog. The gate takes you out of the role of being the police, freeing your relationship of that burden and putting more fun in life for both parties.

There are baby gates you can use for this purpose, but for a large-breed puppy those are often too low, too flimsy, cannot be opened wide enough or are too easily chewed apart.

◆ Gate Off a Room or Part of a Room.

There are a few different styles of "baby gates," which are often also intended for puppy training. Once a puppy has developed bladder control and can wait until walked to relieve himself, you can increase his freedom but still keep him confined by creating a gated zone for him.

The gates come in plastic, wire or wood—the last choice probably being the worst since the puppy will be able to chew it. There are some gates that form a circle, and these can either hook back on themselves or be left in a semicircle, so that the open side can be placed against a wall.

If your puppy is really small and can fit through the holes in the gate, get a gate that has mesh on the sides, or fit some pieces of cardboard across the outside of the area(s) through which he can escape.

These gates tend to be more expensive at pet stores, so if cost is an issue check your local "have everything" kind of super store to compare baby gates. Think about whether the material can be chewed if used for a canine instead of a human.

◆ Where to Put the Gate

Even though the puppy must be confined, you don't want to isolate him from the natural activity of the household, much as you didn't want to do that with his crate. Getting a puppy used to the sights and sounds of your home is as important to his development as is house-training.

A bathroom is often mentioned as an ideal place to restrict a puppy, but it really isn't: locking the puppy out of sight keeps him out of the social loop—and that's even assuming that you have an extra bathroom to "sacrifice" as a puppy-training den. In fact, closing a puppy into a bathroom can seem almost punitive—sort of like solitary confinement, which is really not conducive to making him part of your family.

If your kitchen is laid out so that it's possible to gate off part of it for the puppy, that is usually the ideal location.

♦ Choosing a Gate

There are two basic kinds of gates: those that stand up inside a doorway or opening between rooms with a pressure mount (if you don't want to screw into the door trim), or those that are installed with hardware and are therefore sturdier.

First consider the size of your dog and therefore the height of the gate: twenty-four to thirty-two inches are standard baby-gate heights. For very tall dogs—or high jumpers and escape artists—there is a forty-eight-inch-high, pressure-mounted gate available in several stores and catalogs, including Care-A-Lot Pet Supply: (800) 343-7680, or www.carealotpets.com.

Evenflo makes an extra-wide soft gate for extra-wide spaces. It is made of tubular steel and a nylon and mesh panel. Visit www.evenflo.com to find this gate and others.

KidCo is one company that makes a quality yet affordable gate in both styles—a pressure-mounted gate in steel for about $70 (unchewable) and a wooden one for $20 more. Many different publications have rated these gates highly. The KidCo gates can be especially easy to install since they are not mounted on the door frame—and you can take them along when you travel or move them to different parts of the house. There is also a walk-through door feature, which is helpful because stepping up and over most dog gates is awkward, annoying and can even cause a fall. This gate fits openings 29½ inches to 37½ inches wide by about 30 inches high. There is an extension kit to fit openings up to 48 inches that costs less than $30.

The KidCo gates are available from catalogs such as J-B Wholesale, (800) 526-0388, or jbpet.com. Two of the lowest prices for KidCo were from www.carealotpets.com, (800) 343-7680, and Ryan's Pet Supplies, (877) 401-7387, or www.ryanspet.com.

Pet Gate is the only steel gate with an optional attachment for height to accommodate any size dog. The gate is also the only one that can mount at an angle for unusual openings. It also features easy-to-use one-hand operation: (800) 318-3380 or www.cardinalgates.com.

ACCIDENTS HAPPEN

If you do happen to find a puddle or a pile in the house, please keep it in perspective: the little critter could not have done the dirty deed unless you had given her the premature freedom to roam the house.

Do not yell or hit or point an accusing finger—you must not threaten the puppy, especially at a vulnerable age when she is just learning what you want.

♦ Catching the Puppy in Mid-pee

Don't worry about cleaning up the accident right that second—you can do that later, after this rare training opportunity. Finding your puppy "in the act" is the best time to make your point about house-training. The moment when you find her squatting is when you want to get her straight outside, so she makes the connection about where to do this next time.

- ❏ *Startle* the puppy by clapping your hands together or slapping an open palm against the wall. This should automatically close down her sphincters and cut off her pee midstream.
- ❏ *Scoop up the pup* if startling her does not stop her in mid-pee. If the puppy is too large to lift quickly, clip on the leash if you can grab one or just lead her by the collar and put her down outside in the potty area.
- ❏ *Stay unemotional* and view this as a great chance to train.
- ❏ Once she finishes *outside*, give her lots of praise.

◆ Feeding During House-training

During the house-training period, feed only a high-quality food (see page 436 for the section on "What to Feed").

Kibble keeps a puppy regular and produces small, neat stools, which are easier for a puppy to hold while learning how, when and where to relieve himself.

Canned foods have a lot of water in them; random foods (table scraps, a changing diet) aren't easy to digest, can upset his stomach, can cause diarrhea—and just generally make it harder for him to control his bowels.

No "free-feeding" (having unlimited access to dry kibble) during house-training—feeding at set mealtimes reinforces your position as the leader and helps to regulate and stimulate the puppy's bowels. If a puppy is constantly eating and drinking, he will be constantly in need of a place to relieve himself. To be blunt, if you control what goes in the mouth, you get control over the other end.

🦴 Cleaning Up Pee

There are many things you can squirt on previously peed areas to discourage re-peeing:

- Binaca or other strong mint breath spray
- Bitter Apple, a chewing deterrent sold in pet stores that you can use only with the windows open, since it can choke people in the room if sprayed around them
- Put ground cinnamon in the clean-up solution (watch out for staining if it's a light-colored solution).
- Water and OxiClean, the miracle cleaner (see below)
- Anti-Icky-Poo is a ridiculous-sounding product that many swear by to completely remove elimination odors. It is available from MisterMax at mistermax.com, or 800-745-1671.
- Do NOT use vinegar—it smells a lot like pee (believe it or not).
- Do NOT use ammonia—it smells *just* like pee (which naturally has ammonia in it).

CLEANUP

You want to get every last vestige of urine. OxiClean, which is one of the newer cleaning products, is made with hydrogen peroxide. Use a strong solution—one scoop of OxiClean to a quart of water. Saturate the spot, a couple of inches past the stain. Let it sit for one hour, then blot with a towel. If it leaves a shadow, shampoo the carpet.

Clean up the area as soon as possible. You don't want it to soak through the carpet and into the padding—it's very hard to get it out if it does. If the urine has soaked through, the only way to be sure you've got the area totally clean is to pull up the carpet and clean the pad first.

Do not use ammonia-based cleaners—ammonia is a component of urine and smells like urine to a dog. Ammonia products attract a dog to the area you're trying to neutralize and actually encourage a dog to pee there.

Pet stain–removal products are formulated to handle pet mess (urine, feces, vomit, blood) by neutralizing the odor—enzymes break down the waste until the smell is gone.

◆ Cleaning Old Stains

Old stains may still have enough odor to attract a puppy. Pet supply stores sell black lights, which you can shine on carpets and other suspicious areas to see if the remains of old messes are still there. These are best treated with enzymatic cleaners and may need a couple of treatments.

ADJUSTING HOUSE-TRAINING FOR THE WORKING OWNER

Owners who have full-time jobs may feel guilty that they can't give the puppy more time and exercise. Paper-training is one way to go.

A crate is too confining for a puppy if you'll be away all day, so set up a baby gate in part of the kitchen so that the puppy has a play area and a paper area.

Give the puppy a good play session in the morning before you go to work, and then take her out for a quick potty stop.

Someone will have to come home at lunchtime and feed the puppy, walk her and spend some time with her. If you can't afford or can't find a good dog-walking service, then you'll have to dash home yourself, unless there's a friend or family member who can fill in.

Stay low-key with the puppy when and if you do come home—if you get her all worked up and smothered with love, she'll have a harder time coping with you leaving again right away.

◆ Paper-training vs. House-training

You cannot house-train and paper-train at the same time: house-training means that the dog learns to go only outdoors, while paper-trained dogs go only on the paper. These are two different concepts for a dog. There are times in apartments in the dead of winter that paper-training might be an intermediary step.

If you have quick access to the outside, then straight house-training is probably your best bet. But if you live in an apartment, especially in a city, then it will probably make it easier on you and the puppy to have the intermediary step of paper-training.

Just realize that although house-training may seem like a huge job, every puppy in the world (well, almost—there are always exceptions) does eventually get house-trained, just as all children become potty-trained. Every parent who struggles through "potty-training" a child just has to remember that it is rare to ever hear of an adult who still wears Pull-Ups. Almost every dog graduates to being unmonitored, too.

◆ Paper-training in the City

In most cases, the paper is a first step for house-training, since puppies shouldn't go outside before sixteen weeks and the completion of their puppy shots.

Carry the puppy around outside as much as possible to get her used to outdoor sights and sounds.

When you're using paper-training as a step toward full house-training (which some say is not a good idea), give only quiet praise for going on the paper. Keep your big enthusiasm for going outside later.

Put plastic underneath the newspaper so it doesn't leak through to the floor.

Change papers each time the dog goes on them—you can put a slightly soiled sheet of the paper underneath the clean ones so that the scent encourages the pup. Use odor-neutralizer around the papers so the puppy doesn't sniff the edge of the paper and go from there.

Good candidates for paper-training are small males and small to medium females. Any larger dog will create too much urine and needs the outdoor exercise anyway.

LITTER-TRAINING FOR LITTLE DOGS

Dog litter is a good option for those with small dogs (under thirty-five pounds) or puppies when the owner is older or physically slower or handicapped, lives in an apartment or without direct access to the outdoors, or has long, unpredictable hours and cannot get home to walk the dog on a predictable, humane schedule.

The litter is made of grassy-smelling, nontoxic pellets. The product, developed by Purina, is called Second Nature; there is a starter kit that comes with a litter pan and training guide. The litter is more sanitary and less smelly than newspaper because it is antibacterial, and it's easier to clean up since you just use a scoop as you would with kitty litter.

The key is to get your dog used to the pellets, which can feel unusual under his feet. In the case of Purina, the company recommends putting newspaper in the litter pan at first and then gradually adding litter as the dog gets used to the pan itself.

Paper-training and litter-training are intended for situations in which a puppy or a small dog with a small bladder cannot physically hold her pee for very long. However, litter-training is not supposed to take the place of exercising your dog and giving her fresh air and a look at the outside world. You still want to get your dog outside, although a little dog doesn't need half a dozen walks a day, even if she does need that many opportunities to empty her tiny bladder.

HOUSE-TRAINING PROBLEMS

◆ Puppies Pee Even After House-training.

If the puppy is peeing in the house even though you are following house-training guidelines, there may be something amiss.

Puppies often get UTIs (urinary tract infections). If the puppy has a UTI, he won't be able to hold or control his urine. Telltale signs include small, frequent amounts of pee and a bad/strong smell. Have the urine tested by the vet.

Another reason for frequent peeing is too much water intake. Offer one cup of water about five times a day. If he always finishes it and looks around for more, offer him half a cup more each time. Always take him immediately afterward to his potty area.

Remember that a puppy has to go out the very first thing in the morning and the very last thing at night—and at least two times during the day, too.

The puppy "makes" in her crate. It is a dog's natural instinct to keep a sleeping and eating area clean. House-training works because dogs have a built-in desire to be clean.

Puppies will do this if they were raised in a dirty kennel, came through the puppy-mill pipeline or were crated too early and too long, which forced them to dirty themselves because they lived in their own filth. Sadly, the barbaric conditions of puppy mills can short-circuit this inbred tendency to cleanliness. Some of these puppies will walk through, sleep in or play in their own feces.

There are occasionally puppies who don't even start out with the natural desire to be clean, but even they can be trained.

Several other reasons why a puppy may be soiling the crate:

1. The crate is so large that there is an area separate from the sleeping part where he can go.

2. There is bedding in it, which encourages elimination.

3. The puppy has been in there so long that his little bladder can't hold it anymore.

◆ This Problem Can Be Solved by Changing the Picture.

Stop crating for the moment.

Create a small area in a bathroom or hallway for the puppy. Put down newspapers in the back and a crate with the door propped open in the front. This gives him the chance to be clean: he can sleep in the crate and do his business on the papers.

After two weeks of this arrangement you can start reintroducing him to the crate, but only for short periods. Start with a maximum of two hours at a time, and only when you are home to keep an eye on him.

Do not put any bedding in the crate.

After a couple of weeks, the puppy should be staying in the crate for at least four hours at a time without soiling it. At that point you can continue increasing the amount of time he spends in there.

If crate-soiling problems come up again, go back to the small area with papers and hope your puppy is just a late bloomer. As with all dog training, never go forward to a greater degree of difficulty until you have the basic foundation well-established.

◆ The Puppy Won't Go Outdoors.

This happens often with city puppies.

If there's a park anywhere nearby, you might head for a patch of grass and dirt there to teach him the "hurry up" command, so he knows exactly what you want when you go out.

The simplest fix is to head out for a big walk first thing in the morning. Go for as long a walk as you can, which can often get the puppy's system working. If you have time before you go out, make a laxative concoction of warm water mixed with some canned food, which stimulates urination. Let him drink as much as he wants and then head off on your long walk. He will relieve himself somewhere along the way.

If the puppy won't have a bowel movement outside, you can buy glycerin suppositories for infants. You can slip one up her bottom first thing in the morning and then head off on a walk. This isn't recommended more than once a day for three days in a row, but it has a high success rate.

◆ **Puppy Comes Back After a Walk and Soils in the House.**
Probably a problem in basic house-training. You need to get back to square one and emphasize the basics.

- ❒ Give the puppy no chance at all to relieve himself indoors.
- ❒ Know when he has to go—after sleeping, after eating—and take him out right away.
- ❒ Teach him—or reinforce—the "hurry up" command (or other verbal cue) if you have not done so already. When you take him out, go to the same area every time.
- ❒ Notice what sort of location or surface he has preferred in the past and either take him to that place every time or, if you have your own property, increase the amount of that surface in the yard—whether it's dirt, sand, grass, etc.
- ❒ No fooling around or playing until he has done his business.

● *Why does a dog get un-house-trained?* If a dog is house-trained but starts soiling in the house again, it's probably a sign of stress. This is generally less true of a puppy who soils inside, which is probably a case of incomplete house-training or a need to tighten up the puppy's ship a little.

What can cause a dog's stress? The greatest burden that many dogs feel is that no alpha leader has been clearly established in the home—in the pack. This means the dog becomes overwhelmed with feelings of inadequacy and the (imagined) pressure of protecting the property and doing the decision-making instead of a true alpha, who is equipped for it.

If you have not actively assumed alpha positioning in your household, then you have done your dogs a disservice and placed unkind burdens on them to "cover" for you when you fail to assume command of the pack. At times like this it's important to put things in perspective and remember that your dog's natural instincts come from her wolf heritage. People so often ascribe human motives like revenge onto dogs, which does not help to understand the behavior or to keep it from happening in the future.

For a detailed discussion of the alpha's role in a dog pack, and your place in the canine aspect of your home, refer to page 152 in Chapter Seven.

◆ A Male Dog Is Lifting His Leg Indoors

This is a tough one to solve because it's often about dominance issues. The gesture is not about house-training, it is a power play: the dog is putting *his* mark on *his* territory.

If the dog isn't neutered, do so now: his peeing is primarily about marking territory, which is practically a moral imperative common to unrestricted un-neutered males.

Clean thoroughly everywhere there's ever been a pet accident (see page 228, "Cleanup").

The dog cannot be loose in the house until this phase is over. Have him with you on a loose lead.

As with secretive peeing, take the dog to where he has lifted his leg and feed him there. Dogs don't want to eat and eliminate in the same area.

If nothing improves, you need a professional trainer to address the dominance issues between you and the dog.

◆ Dog Urinates or Defecates on Your Bed.

Your bed is the most potent scent-posted area of your house—you haven't actually relieved yourself there (one hopes), but because you've slept there the sheets and pillows are saturated with your smell, at least from the dog's perspective.

An anxiety-ridden dog will go to the pack leader's most definable area to relieve herself—and that would be your "private den."

Keep in mind that while a dog may be house-trained, those imposed rules benefit humans but do not correspond to a dog's natural instinct.

◆ A Female Dog Pees in Her Sleep.

This is a medical problem, not a house-training one. Some dogs leak urine, especially spayed females after about six years of age. Take your dog to the vet for a checkup. There is a medication available for this situation that a dog takes for life to stop the leaking.

◆ Old Age and Peeing in the House

As dogs become seniors, some of them begin to make mistakes in the house. Do not scold the dog, who may already be confused and even mortified. Just clean up and start confining the dog during the periods of the day or night in which his mistakes seem to happen.

Talk to your vet about changing the dog's diet, which can sometimes help.

◆ The Dog Is Secretly Peeing Somewhere in the House.

If there's a part of your house without family scent, some dogs may not view that as the house or as being indoors. Some of these favorite places for secret peeing can be a formal dining room, a formal living room (especially under a piano), a guest room or the youngest child's room (lowest on the family power ladder).

The first thing you'll need to do is to neutralize the pee smell (see page 228).

Next, go sit in the place the dog has been peeing. You want to spend time there doing some reading or paperwork so you can infuse it with your smell and presence. This way, the dog comes to recognize that space as a legitimate part of the family "den." It is preferable if you can even get down on the carpet a couple of times so your scent is established in the room. Once your smell is in there, the dog will view it as "the house."

Give the dog his meals in this area for a while. Do some light training— "sit"/"down"—in this area, too.

Make sure the dog is getting enough chances to walk outside. Three walks a day should be minimum, but four is really ideal. If the dog doesn't have enough chances to relieve himself outside, you may have initiated the secret peeing because you were overly harsh in your reaction to an "accident" he may have had. What he learned from that was to not pee around you. You can fix this aspect of the problem by not giving him the opportunity to be off alone—either he's in the crate or he's in the house and tied to your belt or wrist by a leash. When he does his stuff outside, make a big happy deal of it.

✦ The Dog Can't Make it through the Night.
Small dogs have small bladders—and even smaller bladders when they're growing. Until the smaller breeds reach six months or so, you can expect to get up a lot more often to take that puppy out than you might have bargained for!

Some dogs need to go poop in the middle of the night, but that is often a function of eating dinner too early. Either feed dinner very late—before his last walk of the night, which might stimulate his bowels—or, if you have a flexible schedule, you can feed the second meal mid-afternoon, which gives his system time to digest and eliminate by the time of his last walk.

✦ The Dog Won't Go Out in the Rain.
Few dogs really like going out in the rain, but they can learn to accept it and even enjoy it. A lot has to do with your attitude, and if you have comfortable rain gear that keeps you dry, then walking in the rain can actually be pleasant. If you sound upbeat and encouraging to the dog, she'll pick up on your attitude and go along with it.

A hard, cold rain is toughest on those dogs who have the least protective covering—short-haired hunting dogs, Dobermans, etc.—although even they get used to it. The first couple of minutes are uncomfortable, but once a dog is drenched she seems to accept being wet right through—you can't be wetter than soaked! Just remember: if you're willing to brave the elements, so should your dog be, regardless of which of you is able to carry an umbrella!

✦ "Hello Peeing" (Also Called "Submissive Peeing")
This usually happens when you or visitors come in the door. This is not really a house-training problem—it can be inherited (especially with American Cocker Spaniels). It is very much an *emotional* issue—a relationship issue between you and the dog.

Submissive peeing can also come from being corrected too harshly in the past—some dogs are more sensitive to this than others, especially if someone has been really loud, angry or hit the dog before. This harshness may be what is causing him to urinate when he sees you.

This dog lacks confidence and needs a lot of encouragement in general.

Solutions to submissive peeing

- ❏ Stop raising your voice or yelling at the dog for any reason; obviously, don't strike the dog, either.
- ❏ Homecomings: ignore the dog *completely* for about ten minutes when you come home. That means literally: Do not look at him. Do not touch him. Do not bend down or reach out toward the dog. Let the dog approach you and then try to crouch down so you're not in a dominant position—and even once there do not turn to look and make eye contact with the dog (this is also a dominating/threatening thing to do in dog circles).
- ❏ After ten minutes reach out to pat the dog by scratching his chest—don't reach over his head, which can also be perceived as a threat. Keep the greeting calm and very low-key.
- ☑ Keep some treats in your pocket or near the entrance, and toss one or two to the dog as you come in, without any other contact.
- ❏ Do not scold the dog for submissive peeing. Ignore the bad, praise the good.
- ❏ Build his confidence with positive reinforcement—make things fun.

THINGS *NOT* TO DO WHEN YOU FIND A HOUSE-TRAINING ERROR

A harsh, loud reaction is the worst possible response.

Never hit, yell or rub his nose in it.

If you go ballistic over a puppy (or any dog) peeing in the house, you're telling her *not to pee when you're around*. What happens in the dog's mind is that you and urinating are linked as a bad or scary combination—which means the dog may not pee when you take her outside, either. (See page 232 under "The Dog's Secretly Peeing . . ." for what could be the ultimate result of being too harsh.)

ELIMINATE MEDICAL PROBLEMS AS THE CAUSE OF HOUSE-TRAINING PROBLEMS.

Bladder infections or other medical problems are not uncommon—in fact, they're a real possibility, particularly if you've just adopted a grown dog.

◆ Diarrhea

A pup with diarrhea cannot comply with house-training, but he may also be ill. A puppy with bad diarrhea can dehydrate to a life-threatening degree very quickly. Be sure to contact your vet if a puppy has diarrhea and let the doctor decide whether you need do anything except give him a neutral diet (see "Diarrhea" in the "Medical" section).

◆ Prednisone

Drugs like Prednisone (which veterinarians give for a variety of skin and other ailments) can cause increased water intake, which in turn causes increased urination. The dog needs more chances to go outside.

◆ Polydipsia/polyuria

These simply mean drinking too much and peeing too much, and they're conditions that can result from vigorous exercise or extreme hot weather, both of which cause increased water intake and therefore increased urination.

Chapter 10

TEACHING MANNERS

You may well wonder how there can be entire books written about training—whole *shelves* of books, actually, each purporting to have the magic key to a well-behaved dog—and yet *The Dog Bible* has only one chapter devoted to the subject. How can that be possible when this book claims to thoroughly cover every aspect of dog ownership? The reason is that training a dog is really pretty simple, once you grasp a few concepts and are consistent in applying them. It's sort of like all those diet books that claim to have secret formulas for you to lose weight—when all weight loss really boils down to is fewer calories going in and more calories being burned up. You just have to stick with the program. Like dieting, teaching manners to your dog takes commitment and discipline (on *your* part), and while you may get faster results with some dogs than others, the results will always require some effort to maintain.

This chapter is not focused on the typical training commands, the obedience commands tested in dog shows or taught by many traditional trainers. There is much more to manners than drilling a prescribed, strict way for a dog to heel or come; here we are talking about manners more than anything, about a dog understanding what you want and being responsive to it. It's about "civilizing" your dog so that living together is a pleasant experience on both sides and you're able to develop a way of communicating.

There is really no mystery about getting a dog to behave in ways that please you. Dog trainers have evolved into teaching two simple fundamentals: reward the behavior that you want and ignore behavior that you don't. There's no secret to success other than an owner's commitment to sticking consistently with this simple plan.

Some of the topics you'll find in this chapter are:

□ Training classes—group or private
□ The latest philosophy about training
□ Ways to reward desirable behavior
□ Ways to correct a dog effectively while avoiding punishment
□ Using language and tone to your advantage when communicating with the dog
□ Mistakes in communication and avoiding them
□ Training commands: tips for success
□ Training equipment: collars, harnesses

The Learning Process

Dogs will repeat a response that brings them a reward—and they'll be less likely to repeat anything that does not bring a reward.

Don't yawn and think, "Wow—tell me something I *don't* know," or feel irritated that you're being patronized. Embrace the Zen simplicity of those two linked ideas and you'll have everything you need. No need to buy books devoted entirely to training (and then give up halfway through because the theory bogs you down). No need to feel there's something amiss with you or your dog because you can't execute commands with military precision. Follow along with the ideas in this chapter and discover your own communication style with your dog.

TRAINING HAS TO BECOME PART OF YOUR LIFE.

Shaping your dog's behavior isn't something you do once and it's over. Training is part of an ongoing "conversation" between you and your dog. Every day you reinforce what he already knows.

◆ Training Is Not A Chore.

Training doesn't need to be a boring obligation that both of you look for ways to avoid. It should be fun, a way to bring you together and develop communication pathways.

◆ Training Can Make You Feel Awkward.

Don't be discouraged if in the beginning training is frustrating or makes you feel foolish. It's natural for both you and the dog to be somewhat ill at ease until you get the hang of each other.

Think of training exercises as two people learning how to ballroom dance together: you expect some toes to get stepped on before you glide smoothly across the floor.

◆ Don't Change Your Personality.

A strange thing that happens to many dog owners is that their personality changes when they embark on training their dog. Instead of viewing it as a fun project that they'll do together with their pup—a mutual discovery of ways to communicate—people often view dog training as a serious work assignment, a challenge to transform their dog into a super-obedient foot soldier who follows orders. Because of this, a person who is warm and cozy with her dog may suddenly adopt a military bearing and tone of voice in teaching and correcting her dog. His mistress' attitude is alien to the dog—especially a sensitive dog, who may think his owner's harsh tone means he's already done something wrong before he begins.

DOG-TRAINING CLASSES

Everyone's recommendation is to take a class if you want to have a well-behaved dog. But it's important to evaluate those classes to be sure you'll both be comfortable.

The considerations that follow apply to any dog training you are evaluating—from puppy kindergarten to advanced agility training.

✦ What Is the Space Like?

Is it safe? If it is indoors, are there dangers to dogs like electrical cords or furniture in the way? If it's held outside, is the area level and free of debris? Is there a designated "toilet area" for the dogs (with a trash can where people can deposit what they pick up from their dog)? Is the place clean? Cool in summer, warm in winter? Is the space large enough? Crowding can create stress between dogs and lead to fights.

✦ Picking a Teacher

If possible, go watch the trainer you are considering before you sign up and bring your dog. That way, you can see whether you think it'll be a good fit for you and your dog. The trainer's method should feel comfortable and logical to you, even if there are ideas that are new to you. You should feel at ease with the trainer's personal style of explanation, of handling the dogs and dealing with the owners. Get references for a trainer from your vet or the local shelter—someone who used the trainer and had a great experience and result. You be the judge of whether that person's dog has good behavior.

✦ How Are Students Screened?

Based on questions asked of you, it will be clear whether all the practical aspects are considered. Are the size and age of dogs matched up so that they are basically compatible? What about the vaccination policy? Even though some facilities require that your puppy have had two sets of shots, that rule should really not be cut-and-dried, because vets do not all keep to the same schedule of what vaccines they give at what intervals. Simply requiring a statement from clients that their puppy is under a vet's care for overall health is a reasonable basis for inclusion.

✦ How Big Is the Class?

Classes in cities tend to be larger. That is fine as long the space accommodates the number of dogs and the teacher has an assistant(s) so that all the participants get enough attention. A class generally shouldn't be larger than fifteen students.

✦ Is the Class Well-organized?

Are all the "rules and regs" spelled out clearly so everyone knows what the classes will cost, what the cancellation policy is and whether there is a refund or makeup policy for missed classes?

Can other family members attend to learn what the puppy is learning? This is a good policy if they have it.

WHAT KIND OF CLASSES ARE BEST FOR YOU?

Are group or private classes best for you, or should you consider sending your dog away for intensive training?

GROUP IS BEST IF:

❑ You have the time to fit into the group schedule and also practice on your own.

❑ You know you can make all the classes over a two- to three-month period—missing even one class can put your dog behind the others.

❑ Your dog has no special behavior problems except being out of control.

❑ The class should have no more than ten. Closer to five is even better.

❑ There should be a sense that all the participants are having a good time.

❑ Your dog doesn't have many other chances to interact with other dogs.

❑ Some dogs with problems do best if they are trained away from their home environment.

PRIVATE IS BEST IF:

❑ You can afford it.

❑ Your schedule doesn't permit a weekly class time.

❑ Your dog has home-related issues: aggression, house-training, barking.

❑ You want lots of personal attention.

❑ You don't have patience for other participants in a class who might try to make it all about them.

SENDING THE DOG AWAY TO TRAIN IS BEST IF:

❑ Money is no object—$1,000 a week is not an uncommon price, and most trainers need three or four times that amount to "shape" a dog.

❑ You have no time to practice the training.

❑ Your dog has serious problems you can't tackle alone.

❑ You are committed to upholding the good manners, responsiveness and respectfulness that the trainer will have instilled. A trainer can get things off to a good start but you still have to follow up.

❑ You are ready to earn your dog's respect by working with her when she returns, since she'll come back responding to the trainer.

THE DOG'S AGE AND TRAINING

◆ Older Dogs

There's no such thing as a dog being too old to learn new tricks. It may take longer for an older dog to learn something than it does a puppy, but if the dog is motivated, he will soon catch on.

◆ Young Puppies

There's no such thing as "too young" to start learning. Ideas have changed about this. It ~~used to~~ be thought that you could not start a puppy before six months old (some trainers still think so), but for many puppies, sooner is better.

There is now KPT—Kindergarten Puppy Training—because studies have shown that even a puppy as young as three *weeks* old can have adult brain waves and can learn. KPT trainers will work with you and a puppy as young as two to three months old.

◆ Training Small Dogs

See Chapter Sixteen, which covers small-dog issues, but suffice it to say that people generally let their little dogs get away with murder. Small dogs do not think of themselves as small, so treat them as full canine citizens. You may be surprised that they can live up to that expectation.

Whenever your small dog does something obnoxious, imagine if he were a Rottweiler doing the same thing. How would you react? Would you allow it?

Just because your dog is petite and adorable, you aren't doing him a favor by being too lenient. If you allow your dog to be unruly, he will become unpleasant for others to be around and you won't be able to take him places with you—which should be one of the bonuses of having a wee pooch.

PHILOSOPHICAL ISSUES ABOUT TRAINING

◆ Don't Judge Yourself or Your Dog.

Think of yourself as a beginner: don't expect fast or perfect results.

Expect and accept mistakes on both your parts as part of the learning process.

Ignore the mistakes. Praise the accomplishments.

◆ Be Patient.

Be realistic and kindhearted in your expectations.

If the dog isn't learning as quickly as you'd like, picture her as though she were a child learning to walk or ride a bike. Would you be impatient and critical with that child?

You'd be kind to anyone else who was just learning something, so extend the same generosity to a dog, who is adapting her natural instincts and habits to human ways.

◆ When the Dog Obeys You MUST Reward.

Drop any grudge you may have about how long it took your dog to follow a command. No matter how long it takes, you have to be gracious and pleased. Put any impatience or frustration behind you. Anger has no place in the learning process.

Never grab at the dog or yank on her neck when she seems slow or stubborn. You may want to strangle her but you have to park your frustration. Most dogs do their best to gain their master's approval: give your pup the benefit of the doubt and praise all attempts to please.

If you're in a public setting and your dog won't come back to you, for example, don't allow yourself to feel humiliated that you're not being obeyed. She still deserves rewards for effort.

...ve Complete Control/Obedience.

...leash with absolute certainty, then don't even be tempted to let ... You will be reinforcing the idea that he can take off and be out of

...e leash but not yet being a model host when guests arrive, the last thing ...ow him to be off-leash when visitors come. You will be frustrated and annoyed ... dog behaves—and your guests may not be too thrilled, either.

...re, removing the leash before you have control sets you back in the communica-...edience you have been building in your training.

✦ Have the Dog Drag the Leash in the House.

ONLY when you are at home should your dog wear a leash: this allows you to enforce verbal commands calmly—having physical command before verbal command makes it much easier. The leash lets you avoid yelling, lunging, grabbing, etc.

If the dog chews the leash, spray it with Bitter Apple. Right before you go on a walk say "leave it" right as he tries to put the (now-bitter) leash in his mouth.

Give him *big praise* the moment he stops himself and lets go of the leash—or does not chew it at all. Shorten the leash so there isn't a big loose dangle in the lead to tempt him.

Never ever leave a leash or any similar dragging/hanging equipment on an unsupervised dog. If the leash gets caught on something, you could have a tragedy.

✦ What If Your Dog Threatens You?

A growl or glare is a serious threat, and a threatening dog is neither normal nor acceptable. Sharing your life with a dog is not supposed to be a contest—training is not about proving who is the boss.

Do not ignore or try to justify a threatening attitude or behavior, but do not try to resolve it right then and there, either. Confrontation is dangerous, and you could get hurt.

If you feel scared of your dog, trust your gut instincts and back off. Stop what you're doing and get a professional to help.

Training Rewards: Positive Reinforcement

"Reward" does not just mean hearing the words "good dog" with a pat on the head: that gets old pretty quick. A dog will get bored or annoyed being asked to do the same thing over and over without *meaningful* positive reinforcement. Forget about lip service: to a dog a reward should also include treats or playtime with a favorite toy.

Food and physical contact are "primary reinforcers." Both are more powerful for the dog than verbal praise, which could be called a "secondary reinforcer." The best way to promote learning is to use the primary reinforcer first, followed by the secondary.

HOW POSITIVE REINFORCEMENT WORKS

- ❏ Reward the behavior you want.
- ❏ Ignore the behavior you don't want.

✦ Food Treats

Some trainers believe that food treats should not be an ongoing part of training. They think it's "wrong" for a dog to work for food, and that if food is expected, then the dog won't continue to respond.

Trainers who are generally opposed to the continued use of food for training work still think that food rewards are a great tool to improve a dog's attitude or temperament or to get an adult dog or puppy started in his training. This is especially true for adult dogs who may have had bad previous experiences and are shy, afraid or so full of energy that they have trouble focusing.

Unpredictable treats are best. Studies of a wide range of animals have shown that intermittent (or sporadic) treat-giving is a stronger training reinforcement than giving even the greatest treat every single time the animal performs. Once the dog is responding consistently, become inconsistent: dole out the goodies only after two or three good responses in a row.

Phasing out treats These trainers also say, however, that as soon as your dog is responding well with treats, you need to phase them out.

Whenever you start teaching a new behavior, you can begin with treats but prepare to phase them out. If you give generous verbal or physical praise, the dog will not mind the treats being phased out. Using a towel burrito (see page 193) or other favorite toy is a great reward, too.

Reward only the best responses to the command—the quickest reaction or the most complete or precise response. This way you not only keep the dog coming back for more (not knowing when the next treat will be forthcoming) but you also keep the quality of your dog's learning at a high level.

✦ Affection Rewards

There are trainers who believe that the owner's approval and acceptance are the most powerful things in a dog's life. In order for affection from you to work most powerfully as a positive reinforcement, the *kind* of affection you deliver has to be suited to the individual dog.

Affection favorites Most dogs love to be scratched behind the ears, under the chin and on the butt above the tail.

Stroking the ear flap between your thumb and finger or gently grasping the entire ear where it joins her head and running the ear flap through your fingers in a stroking motion can be especially soothing and pleasurable for many dogs.

Run your hand down her back in a massaging motion. Rub her chest. Some dogs will lie down and offer their stomachs for rubbing.

Does your dog like what you're doing? To discover what your dog loves most, watch her expression— some dogs smile, others just look more relaxed. Whenever you're showing affection to your dog you know she loves it when she wags her tail, comes close to you or nudges you with her paw or nose to continue when you pause.

Pay attention to your own praising style: does it suit your dog, or do you need to modify your behavior?

When and How to Praise

Well-timed praise from you is fundamental to the dog's learning process. Since the foundation of training is so simple and universal, what makes the difference in an effective dog trainer—or a happy dog owner—is *how* and *when* the praise (or lack of the same) is doled out. When teaching a command, the word has to be quickly linked to the action you want through immediate praise.

Don't be a tightwad with praise. You won't "spoil" your dog by lavishing him with enthusiastic words and affection.

Praise for trying, not just for succeeding. Learning is hard for a dog, and can be stressful, too. Praise at every opportunity.

Training Corrections

PUNISHMENT

Avoid Physical Pain and Intimidation.

Earlier dog-training techniques relied on a punitive philosophy as the way to respond to mistakes (punish the dog for not doing something or for doing it incorrectly). However, those beliefs about learning have now been discarded. Current thinking is that we should ignore the bad behavior or unwanted responses. With no reinforcement, the poor behavior will stop. Keep in mind that anything a dog does is just *behavior*—at least until you've taught him and he *understands* what you consider to be *misbehavior*.

Aversion Therapy

This type of therapy is still used by some trainers—you create an unpleasant sound with a shake-can or a high-frequency whistle that startles and frightens the dog, who will then associate that sound with his behavior and avoid doing it in the future. This is a training technique requiring split-second timing and should be administered by a professional to get the desired result.

Time Out

This is a powerful tool against dogs, who are pack animals. A dog who is ostracized for even a few minutes experiences that as a much harsher negative response than it might seem to you. This is different than ignoring your dog—it means actually putting him by himself, whether in a crate or closed room, for just a short time.

If the dog "knows better" and does something you have forbidden—like jumping up on furniture or on you—don't get mad, get even. In a neutral tone of voice say "Too bad. Time out" and put the dog on the tether for a few minutes. If he lies quietly on the tether, tell him "Good boy" and give him a treat. If he continues lying quietly give him another treat or two and then release him from the tether.

You need to react quickly to a problem so that it's clear to the dog what behavior you did not like. The correction must come *right as* the behavior is happening (otherwise, don't bother correcting at all). Your precision in responding is critical. The correction has to be one that doesn't make the dog fear or distrust you and leaves no doubt about what displeases you.

IGNORE THE DOG WHEN SHE'S DOING SOMETHING WRONG.

If the dog is staring at you at the table, bringing a forbidden item in her mouth or whining at the door, try to become deaf and blind to her. If you deny what a dog wants—attention and praise—and *give no reaction at all,* the dog may correct herself.

SOME DOGS WOULD PREFER NEGATIVE ATTENTION OVER NO ATTENTION AT ALL.

You can use this information to make a plan about how to handle situations that need correcting. Not getting attention—or being purposely ignored—makes most dogs miserable and could be considered their punishment.

VERBAL CORRECTIONS CAN MEAN NOTHING.

Verbal "explanations" are probably experienced as "blah blah blah" nagging by a dog. Don't think like a human when it comes to registering a negative reaction to your dog's behavior. Think like a dog. Dogs crave our attention—it means the world to them. Withhold it to make your point.

REMOTE PUNISHMENT

One way of correcting unwanted behavior is to administer an unpleasant punishment without the dog realizing that it's coming from you. This could be a spray of water or a shake-can crashing to the floor.

The punishment (the spray of water or can of pennies crashing to the floor) has to be timed in such a way that it seems to the dog to have just come like a thunderbolt from above—and most importantly seems to be a direct result of whatever she was doing at the time.

Since remote punishment has to be given *immediately* after the behavior and you need to be forearmed, you may have to pull a "sting operation" on the dog: you may have to set her up for some of the activities you don't like (stealing food off the counter, chewing household items, etc.) so that you can be ready to administer the surprise retaliation.

◆ Spraying Water Is a Useful Correction.

Water spraying is valuable because it is shocking to the dog, yet causes no harm.

Using a garden hose If the problem happens outdoors, it is tempting to use your garden hose with a large dog, but for a small dog it may be too strong. However, it might be best to avoid using the hose to correct your dog, because when she understands where the water came from it can give her a lifelong terror of garden hoses. This can make it misery for all concerned if you ever want to rinse or cool her down with a hose.

Squirt bottles A squirt bottle of water can work with a small dog. A "sport bottle" (with a twist-open nozzle) can work well with a large or small dog indoors. However, it requires practice and some adeptness to squirt the dog without being obvious. Standing around a corner or behind a door, counter or piece of furniture can work to hide your involvement in the watery correction.

The spray attachment on your kitchen sink You can use your sink hose to good effect in an emergency. I've used it to break up food-related fights in the kitchen by just aiming it at the heads of both dogs. At that point, who cares whether the dog(s) develops a lifelong fear of kitchen faucets? You really only need to soak your kitchen with spray that first time, because if there's ever another problem you only have to threaten with the sink hose. Say "Ah!" to catch the dog's attention while you grab the spray attachment—and when it is pointing at him he'll probably slink away at the memory of being soaked—without even a drop of water spilled!

Sequence of Events in an Effective Correction

- Say "No" in a low and quiet voice.
- Startle him right away with a loud noise to make him stop what he's doing—make a big noise with a slap on a hard object with your hand, or drop a book or a shake-can on the floor.
- When he looks up, startled (thinking his action caused the noise, not you), immediately say "Good boy!" Always praise him for stopping whatever he was doing, so he associates you only with good feelings but the scary noise with what he was doing when the noisemaker "fell out of the sky."
- Instantly redirect his attention to a substitute activity that you want him to do instead.
- If the dog is too excited to hear you, put a yummy treat right under his nose and make a kiss-kiss noise or a clucking noise—this way, you can keep his attention until you can hand him a fun toy to play with. This is like when little kids are messing with the wrong thing and you stop them by instantly replacing it with something permissible.

Communication between People and Dogs

HOW TO USE YOUR VOICE IN TRAINING

◆ **Use Consistent Commands.**

Once your dog has learned a command, do not vary it. Use it the same way—same tone of voice, same phrase—every time you give the command. Don't confuse the dog by saying "Come," "Come over here," "Come on boy," "Come on, Come on," etc. Pay attention to what you're saying and discipline yourself to use the same phrase every time—and only one at a time. For example, "Come on . . . sit down . . . stay . . . okay?" has *four* requests in it, but not one command that a dog can understand clearly and follow.

Develop a personal vocabulary. Make a vocabulary that works for you, one that you can consistently use for exactly what you need/mean to say.

"Ooops" is a great word. "Ooops" is such a wonderful training word because it expresses a gentle reprimand. It's a word that by its very nature cannot sound angry—it implies "Nope, try again," rather than the harsh way that "No!" can sound. You can use "ooops" when a dog has not done what you wanted, ignored you or offered some behavior other than the one you requested (like lying down instead of sitting). "Ooops" sounds cautionary but forgiving, especially because when you use the word, you are generally going to give the dog another chance to do your bidding. It's a great word to train yourself to use instead of others because it will make you a more forgiving "boss," which means a better learning environment.

◆ Tone of Voice in a Command

How you say a word—the tone, the inflection at the end of the word—must be the same each time in order to get a reliable response from your dog. Change the tone and you alter the whole meaning for him. If you pay attention to your voice, you will gain control of it just by focusing on it.

Be aware of how you use a word, especially the word "down." If "down" means "lie down," then it *cannot* be interchangeably used to tell a dog not to jump up on people. ("Off" might work, but only if you don't use it to signal a dog to get off a piece of furniture or get out of a car, which is different.)

◆ Some Pointers about Using Your Voice

Use short, repeated, energetic sounds to encourage activity such as coming to you. Use a sound/word in a way that helps get the point across.

Use one long sound to discourage activity ("noooo") when the dog is starting to do something or is even in the process of it. Or to be soothing at the vet: "Gooood girl."

Develop the habit of saying the word "Goood" all drawn out at the very moment that your dog complies with a command. It is a vocal reward that you can attach to a physical reinforcement.

◆ The Pitch of Your Voice

A low-pitched voice means authority. If you give a command in a low voice, you will get a better response. Using a low register shows your dog that you are confident and serious; this is partly because the mother dog growls low and slow to control her pups. A dog will be more likely to listen when you use a lower pitch.

Lower does *not* mean louder—just drop your voice a decibel or two. A voice teacher would tell you that the sound needs to come from your chest, not your throat (which has a piercing, higher pitch).

Women with high-pitched voices can practice sending their voice up from their chest instead of speaking from the upper-throat/nasal area. It may sound affected to you at first, but try it on your own at home and get comfortable with a softer pitch. Your voice will sound more pleasant.

If the dog ignores your command to come, remain unemotional about it and say "Nooo" in a low, growly voice. Then say "Come" again in a nice, cheery tone. See what difference the pitch of your voice can make to the dog—and remember this for everyday life.

Use a higher pitch for praise. Men (or women with deep voices) should practice using a higher voice to encourage their dog, even if they feel silly. When you want to encourage your dog to continue what he is doing, you have to think like a cheerleader: use a high-pitched "Come on! That's a good boy! You can do it!"

Really effective trainers make their dogs enthusiastic by using a happy, energetic voice and by using the dog's name with high-pitched enthusiasm.

HOW TO AVOID COMMON MISCOMMUNICATIONS IN TRAINING

Dogs don't speak English. Well, that's not entirely true. It's more like they're ESL (English as a Second Language) students, because they can *understand* a large vocabulary of our language if we take the time to talk to them. This is not meant to be sarcastic—some of our dogs really can pick up the sense of what we mean a lot of the time. But don't confuse this with a dog really understanding human language the way other humans do.

Some people chat a lot to their dogs and get the impression they're being understood. They assume that, when it's something important they're trying to get across, that their dog should know what they mean. In fact, the dog may not respond to what you're asking for because he is confused about what you want. Dogs can get the gist of things we do with them routinely and the sound of our words and the inflection in our voices, but that does not mean they actually understand our language, especially in unfamiliar situations.

◆ **Your Dog's Name Is Not a Command.**

Remember that dumb phrase that people used in grade school when someone called their name? "That's my name, don't wear it out"? Every time you find yourself trying to communicate with your dog by saying nothing more than his name in a variety of inflections ("Oscar?" "Oscar!"), just remember that annoying kid at recess who kept saying your name over and over.

Our dogs get can tune us out if we say their names many times a day in a wide variety of tones of voice. We're all guilty of this at times. But we're wasting our breath because a dog can't read our minds (even though there are times when it seems she can). When all you say is the dog's name and you're convinced she still knows just what you mean, it's probably because she's picking up and responding to visual clues that you don't even realize you are sending out.

Pay attention to your habits and you'll probably notice that you often just call out the dog's name with an up-inflection, an annoyed tone, a sharp voice, etc., without a command like "come" or "wait" after it. This lack of clarity can increase a nervous or high-strung dog's natural anxiety. Another downside to a dog hearing his name over and over for no apparent reason is that it can desensitize him to his own name. After a while, he may not even react when he hears it. If you persist in saying his name without any meaningful command attached, you are "using up" your dog's attentiveness. The dog will assume you don't know what you want and will ignore you.

◆ **"No" is Not a Command.**

"No" doesn't mean anything—yet we growl and scream and order it at our dogs.

Are you saying "No" over and over? Constantly nagging, getting on the dog's case? Is he doing something wrong (everything is what it will begin to feel like to the dog, as it would to you if you were relentlessly told "No!" about everything you did)?

Remember to praise the good. Praise the dog when he stops a misbehavior.

You know the saying about how you catch more flies with honey? Well, dogs have feelings of self-worth or confidence that can be enhanced or diminished by how you communicate with them. It's in your hands.

◆ Illogical Negative Commands

"No bark" or "No pull" are quite ludicrous things to say to dogs. First of all, they don't speak English—much less understand the concept of "not" doing something—especially when that something is a word they haven't been taught to respond to in the first place.

"Good sit," said after a dog sits also means nothing. If "sit" means "sit down," then repeating the word "sit" with a meaningless noise before it ("good") would be confusing at best . . . the dog already is sitting. *That* is what's good. Any further comment with the word sit is a pointless repetition, even with a nice tone of voice.

REPEATING COMMANDS—THE BIG NO-NO

Every training book says to not repeat a command over and over, because you'll numb the dog to the word(s).

We repeat ourselves because we don't have the count-to-three patience to wait for the dog to respond to what we've asked for. It's like clicking the mouse multiple times (and freezing up the computer) because you can't just wait for the icon to open up.

This patience concept is a good one to keep in mind not only around dogs, but also children, coworkers and people in the outside world in general.

Don't worry if you do repeat commands. Paying attention to what you're doing is half the battle. Repeating yourself is a habit you can break by slowing yourself down mentally—your dog will benefit as much from this as you will.

With a dog who already has training but is accustomed to your repeating your commands, try the following exercise to retrain yourself:

Retraining yourself to say things only once

1. Give a tiny treat so he knows what you are holding. Then give a command.

2. WAIT. Don't move.

3. Count to thirty—that's thirty *seconds* (although it will feel like thirty minutes).

4. Say nothing more, and don't move. Just wait and watch your dog.

5. If he does it, give the treat immediately. If he ignores the command, turn away and ignore him. He'll be shocked (after all, he's waiting for you to repeat the command over and over rapidly).

6. Try the above sequence again. Your dog will get with the program eventually—if not sooner.

◆ **Getting Louder**

If your dog isn't responding, don't get frustrated. Raising your voice to get a reaction does nothing—except raise your own frustration level while rattling the dog.

Dog/Human Dominance Issues

"Getting dominance over your dog" is a dangerously misunderstood concept. What you want is to establish yourself as the pack leader, but that has to be done in dog terms. You want to establish the right dominance/submission level between you and your dog in order for him to accept your training requests and social expectations. The chart below is a reminder of the dominance issues between people and dogs, but to really understand this subject, see Chapter Six. In fact, it's not a great idea to start training your dog until you have spent some time with the information in that chapter.

Dog to Human Dominant Behaviors

- Pushing his ball into your lap/hand to be thrown (high-ranking dogs initiate play).
- Pushing his head into your hand/lap to be patted.
- Leaning against you (the canine way of showing strength).
- Barking back at you when you give a command.
- Growling even slightly when touched during chewing/eating/sleeping.
- Refusing to release a toy or bone.
- Mouthing your hand when you brush/toenail clip/leash/bathe him.
- Pulling at your clothing.
- Pushing past you in a doorway (higher rank goes first).
- Lying across a doorway (controlling it).
- Lying in a hallway watching human activities (guarding territory).

Training Commands

This section covers the basic manners that every dog should know. It is not intended to replace training with a private dog trainer or taking a training class, because just reading a book is not going to be enough. Most dogs need to go to classes for socialization purposes, and to deal with other dogs while trying to learn commands. Only in a real-life situation can you get the skills you need—while seeing other owners struggling with their dogs. It can give you patience to get the perspective on your own pooch's progress when you see other dogs being less-than-stellar students.

Manners are less complicated than you might think. You can incorporate training into your daily life with your dog, and before long, you'll have a companion who understands commands (and may actually anticipate them, depending on her personality and also on how consistent *you* are).

The commands that follow are: "come," "sit," "down," "enough," "go to your bed," "off," "stay" and "wait."

This is just the basic list of manners. If you have any problems with your dog's behavior, that is covered in Chapter Sixteen: "Problems Great and Small."

Teaching "Come"

"Come" is probably the single most important command you'll ever teach your dog. A well-learned "come"—on leash and off—can make your dog a pleasure to be around. Having a reliable "come" means the dog will not be a bother to people and she will not be in jeopardy because you can always call her out of a potentially dangerous situation.

The other side of that coin is that an *unreliable* "come" command is a source of frustration, embarrassment and possible tragedy. There are few emotions as intensely unpleasant as calling for a dog who does not come when you are in a rush to go out . . . or she is running over to people on a beach blanket . . . or she is about to walk onto a road.

GET THE BALL ROLLING

The "come" command can be taught in segments. If you can commit to taking the time to lay a good solid base, it will make all the training that comes afterward so much easier.

1. Prepare a baggie of small tasty treats like bits of meat or cheese.

2. Stand a few feet away from the dog and say her name in a cheerful, up-inflected voice. As soon as the dog begins to move, encourage her to continue toward you by moving away from her.

3. You will need to do this walking backward, however, because you want to be squarely facing the dog during training. You'll want to practice moving backward as quickly as possible, which will trigger the "chase instinct" in your dog. It also makes "come" much more fun than if you were just standing still.

4. Stop moving as the dog gets close to you.

5. Now use verbal reinforcement: "What a Goood Girl!" or "That's my good dog" or any personal words of praise and encouragement that you want.

6. Give her that tasty tidbit as soon as she reaches you.

7. As soon as she begins to move toward you, reward the effort immediately. Say "Yes!" enthusiastically and get that treat in her mouth as fast as you possibly can. In trainer-

speak, saying "Yes!" is called a "reward marker," a way to identify the exact behavior you are glad the dog gave you and that you'll pair with a food treat any second. You are using an edible treat to entice your dog so you can "mark" the first part of "come"—the first steps coming toward you. What you are reinforcing at this point is just the beginning of "come." You want the dog to know that moving toward you will bring her great benefits. Eventually when she hears the word "Come!" she'll automatically start moving in your direction.

There are two schools of thought about the "come" and whether it should include sitting upon arrival. Some trainers believe that a dog should sit as soon as she comes to you. I've always felt that just coming back from wherever they've been and getting close enough that I can pat them is as good a response as I need. However, many trainers say that every command has to have an "end" from the animal's perspective. That may be why many dogs are taught to sit squarely in front of the person who has called them. You can alter this command to suit your own lifestyle and your dog's individual personality.

◆ Best Tone of Voice for "Come"

The tone of voice you use to call your pooch must be at least some of the following: upbeat, cheery, enthusiastic, eager, happy, encouraging, hopeful.

You cannot have a voice that sounds angry, frustrated or punitive. The dog will avoid you—especially if your whiny, irritated, fed-up tone has often been backed up with an even more negative reaction from you when the dog finally gets there (or you've gone after him).

By calling "Come!" you should realize that you are asking a dog to leave something enjoyable to obey you. You have to make "come" such a pleasurable-sounding experience that she thinks it might be even better than what she's engaged in.

Just remember that every positive experience of "come" is a building block for a lifetime of obedience. So every pleasant-sounding "Come!" that is followed by pats or treats or praise will increase the likelihood of more obedience.

BEST PHYSICAL POSITION FOR YOU IN THE "COME"

Standing upright is not enticing to any dog—it's intimidating, as is leaning forward toward him.

Bend down from the waist like a dog's "play bow." If your dog is shy or timid, you can try lowering your profile by going down on one knee so you don't look too intimidating. This makes you look more inviting.

Turn away from the dog as you call him and clap your hands.

◆ Don't Move toward the Dog.

If you're calling "Come" and going toward the dog, your physical movement is signaling him to stay where he is. By going toward your dog, you are actually preventing him from coming forward to you. From the dog's perspective, it's as if your forward motion blocks his forward motion toward you.

Our instinct is to chase a dog who isn't coming to us, but in most cases you can't move fast enough to catch a dog. Also, in situations where the dog is headed for danger, you are driving him *into* the danger if you are chasing him.

So the best way to get a dog to come to you is to turn sideways (which is less threatening than head-on), call his name in the most upbeat, enthusiastic voice you can muster and move in the opposite direction. The dog's instinct is to chase. From his point of view, he will be going toward you.

INCREASING YOUR ODDS OF SUCCESS

Only lots of practice will assure you of a dog who comes every time you call, but there are things that will increase the odds of success. You can try some or all of these at various times in your dog's development. Some are fundamental rules about "come," while others are pointers that work for some dogs.

SUCCESS WITH "COME"

- ❏ In the beginning, never call your dog to come unless you have control with a collar and leash so that you can reinforce the command with the leash if necessary.
- ❏ Never call a dog unless you are sure the dog will definitely come (because otherwise—if he is distracted or doesn't understand the command yet—you will be teaching him NOT to come when you call).
- ❏ Start when the dog is not distracted by something else.
- ❏ Use a clear consistent signal: "(your dog's name), COME!" always with a bright tone of voice and an up-inflection.
- ❏ Do not repeat the command. Be patient with the dog so that he can process the request and decide whether to comply.
- ❏ Try clapping your hands together briskly as added encouragement. Turn slightly sideways.
- ❏ Bend forward from the waist in a "play bow."
- ❏ The moment the dog starts to respond, use an encouraging, soothing tone: "Gooooood boy."
- ❏ Move away, looking back at him over your shoulder to lure him to follow.
- ❏ If you want to run and make it into a chase game, so much the better. But if that's too exciting for your dog and he gets jumpy/bitey, then you should stop as he gets to you. Stop, play bow and give him a treat.
- ❏ Success comes in stages: First make sure that the "come" has been well learned on a leash before trying it off-leash. Then have it well learned indoors before trying it outside, and finally have it well learned at a close distance before trying it from afar. If you don't have a solid foundation, the whole thing will crumble before long.
- ❏ Have an edible treat or one of the dog's favorite toys to offer when she comes to you—but remember that tests have shown that giving random treats works even better than giving something on *every* recall. It has been proven that after the foundation has been laid for a response, "intermittent" rewarding gives the greatest results when training any kind of animal.

- If the dog does not respond, go over and get as close as a few feet—or even inches—away from him. Have a really delicious treat in your hand—some food item that your dog cannot resist. Give him a sniff of your hand if necessary. Once he has seen and smelled the delicious morsel, say his name but not the word "come." As soon as he takes a step toward your closed hand, say "Come" in an enthusiastic voice (but not a loud, jarring tone). This pairs the word "come" with the motion of coming toward you. The treat reinforces the action.
- Give the treat and lots of praise and pats.
- Remember to always turn away from your dog when you call him.
- Reward with play—treats are good, but play can often be better, depending on the dog's personality.
- Return to whatever else you were doing, or invent something to do so that you can ignore your dog for a while—no interaction at all, just ignore him. A minute is even enough.
- Don't give the dog any attention until you are ready to practice "come" again a minute or two later.
- Make an effort to always sound like someone you would want to come to: cheerful and enthusiastic, not cranky and annoyed.

PUPPIES AND "COME"

Up to six months of age, puppies don't want to be left behind. So until then, "come" is something they instinctively want to do. After that, independence sets in and some dogs stop wanting to come or actually start to take a hike without a thought about you.

◆ If the Puppy Does Not Come, Do Not Get Mad.

Don't jump to the conclusion that he knew what you wanted and was being stubborn or rude.

Go over to him, get closer, bend down and call him invitingly. Do this calmly, encouragingly. Don't let your anger/frustration seep through. This teaches him that he has to come, but assures him that you're not mad. "Come" always needs to be an upbeat, positive command. No exceptions.

◆ The Puppy Can Stop Being Interested in Coming.

Make a game of it or have a tasty treat to entice him. Let him see or smell the treat, then back away, telling him "Come!" (say it *once*—do not repeat it over and over). Praise him as he continues toward you.

Crouch down. Let the dog come right up to you for the treat. Pet and praise him as he eats it from your hand.

◆ Play Hide-and-Seek to Make "Come!" More Fun.

Call the puppy from different rooms in the house. Go outside and hide behind a tree, calling out, "Come!"

◆ Use Praise-filled Encouragement.

Go on the assumption that your dog is in the process of coming to you, that he's trying to find you if you can't see him. If he's in plain view and chasing squirrels but not responding to you, give him the benefit of the doubt and hope that he's weighing his options. Call out, "What a good boy!" or "Good dog"—whatever you want to say in an encouraging tone after you've called, "Digby, Come!"

Be enthusiastic the second you see him head your way and as you see him getting close. Keep on praising right until he reaches you. Clap your hands and use a word or phrase that's comfortable for you to reinforce his progress back to you.

I say the word "Yippee!" because it sounds really celebratory to me. I say that and the dog's name as he is getting closer. The more impressive the show of obedience—for example, if he was in the middle of playing or hunting or has come from far away—the bigger fuss I make over the dog when he comes.

Have a fun version of "come" practiced by as many people in your household as are involved in the dog's life.

Think about it: if the payoff isn't pleasurable for the dog, why would he do it?

MISTAKES WHEN TEACHING "COME"

◆ Doing Nothing If the Dog Doesn't Respond

If you say "Come" and nothing happens, DO something! Back up, clap your hands, squat down, sound happy—make it happen!

◆ Repeating the Command

People often shout Come!" in a variety of tones of voice—with increasing annoyance or loudness—until finally they get fed up and sound really firm and convincing. But going through a whole drama around the word "Come!" only teaches the dog to wait until that many calls before coming. If you don't get the job done on one assertive, cheerful "come," then you are teaching your dog to wait for the umpteenth call before responding.

◆ Assuming the Dog Knows "Come" and Never Practicing

Since "come" is one of your most valuable and vital tools of communication, keep it shiny. If you don't use it and praise rapid response times, the dog won't remember what it means. Use it every chance you get, and reward it with words, strokes and treats.

◆ Scolding the Dog When He Does Get There

This is probably the worst and most common mistake people make: their dog doesn't come at first, or doesn't come swiftly, so they give him a tongue-lashing and sometimes worse when he does finally roll in. You can see that there's no way that kind of reception is going to reinforce the "come" or make the dog want to do it again anytime soon.

◆ Calling the Dog for Unpleasant Tasks

If you need your dog to come for some reason that won't be appealing to her—like having her nails clipped or having a bath or being put in a crate—then do not use the "come" command. You don't want the dog's "reward" for coming quickly and obediently to be something she dislikes. So instead, leave the word "come" out of it entirely. Go to the dog—find her or get her—and take her by the collar or clip on a leash and just do what you need to do.

◆ Assuming That All Situations Are the Same

At home your dog may come to you most of the time. That's because there aren't many distractions at home, so he can focus on you. Also, when you call it's usually for something pleasurable—a walk, a meal, getting brushed, a drive in the car, etc. So he comes willingly. But when you take a dog outdoors and let him off the leash, he is often less likely to obey for several good reasons. See the chart below.

Why Dogs Don't Come When Called

- All of the distracting sights and sounds and smells outside.
- When you call him it's usually to end the fun and make him leave: as soon as he gets to you, you put on the leash and take him home. (To solve this, call the dog a few times, make a big show of delight that he came, give him a scratch or pat wherever he likes it best and then release him with an "okay." If you do this every so often, he won't always associate "Come" with leaving, just with getting affection. Other times, you can give a small tasty treat for a "Come" and then release him. The next time you call "Come," give a few pats and then slip the leash on and he'll still associate "Come" with something positive.)
- If he doesn't come right away, you may get anxious or frustrated and call him in a harsh or annoyed tone—which makes him anxious.
- Not coming is positively reinforced by the fun of running around. In other words, by not coming the dog is assured of a better time than by going to you.

SOLUTIONS TO COMMON PROBLEMS WITH "COME"

◆ Dog Stops Halfway to You.

You probably gave the dog an unfriendly greeting at some point when he didn't come in a way you found satisfactory. Some dogs are so sensitive to rebuke that the next time they are asked to follow a command, they become apprehensive. A super-sensitive dog with a previous unpleasant experience of being called may stop partway to you. He stops to get a sense of what kind of mood you're in. But the problem only worsens if you get annoyed with the dog for stopping halfway and then you repeat "Come" harshly—this only reminds him of why he's unsure of returning to you in the first place. So try to be as gentle and forgiving as you can with your dog during the learning process—and in the case of a sensitive dog, even more so.

The fix for this problem is to put the fun back into "come." First squat down (which is a nonthreatening position), clap your hands and verbally praise and encourage the dog to come to you. Have a food treat ready and lots of pats and praise. Practice "come" as much as you can stand it in the house, trying always to make it fun with your tone of voice, hide-and-seek games and occasional food and toy rewards. The more times "come" is a great experience, the stronger the obedient response will be.

◆ Dog Comes but Avoids the Leash.

If a dog is grabbed and immediately put on a leash the minute he comes, he learns to avoid "the grab." By grabbing the dog and leashing him to end his freedom, you are punishing his obedience.

The fix for this problem is to not grab. Don't shoot your hand out to grab that collar. Instead, squat or bend down in a nonthreatening position, reach beneath the dog's neck to gently take hold of the collar (so that he can't try to dash for freedom) and make a big fuss over him, patting him.

The other fix is classic "counterconditioning." If the dog does not like the feeling of his collar being held, then you want to "countercondition" his response (this is trainer-speak for "change his reaction"). You want to give him treats and affection when your hand is on his collar. You want to make him eager to come and to have his collar held. So with a dog who is touchy about his collar, you want to praise him verbally, give a treat, touch his collar and give another food treat. Next you'll touch his collar and give the food at the same time. After several repetitions of that, the food will become the reward after he has let you touch his collar.

If this fix doesn't work, turn to a food treat. Don't just give a treat outright. Hold the treat in your fingers, let him sniff and lick it, and while he's doing this scratch and stroke his chest and take hold of his collar without making a big issue of it. Once you have hold, let go of the treat and give it to him.

◆ Dog Runs Away When You Call.

Your dog may have been chased in the past when she ran away and she may think it's a great game.

The fix for this problem is to turn the tables on the dog. You run away from her! Make it seem like too much fun—clap your hands and call her again but in a very cheery voice. She will want to join you if you seem to be having a good time.

The other fix is not allowing the dog off the leash in the first place. If you don't have a solid recall, then your dog should not have complete leash-free freedom. You should still be working on a long line until you have that recall down cold. By letting your dog run free you are giving her numerous chances to "practice" *not* coming.

Teaching "Sit"

"Sit" is probably the first thing you'll learn in the training class, and it will probably be the most useful command you'll have other than "come."

There's no big secret to training "sit," other than an awareness of your own body and tone of voice. How you stand and how you speak to the dog are both especially important in this command.

Think of the Golden Rule with "sit" (or any dog training). Try to touch and talk to your dog in a way that you would like to be treated—especially if you were learning something new. People can get particularly frustrated when their dog doesn't understand "sit" and execute it immediately—so they wind up pushing and yanking their dog with angry frustration in their voice. If you find this happening to you, cool it. Give the poor pooch a fair chance to understand and then give you the right response.

TWO EASY WAYS TO GET A DOG OR PUPPY INTO THE SIT POSITION

One is the food method. The second way to get a *puppy* to sit is the scoop-under-her-butt method (both described below). For grown dogs, the second method would be to lift gently on the leash and press gently with your non-leash hand on top of her hip bones, guiding her into a sitting position.

◆ The Food Method

Food is the clearest way to demonstrate to the dog or puppy what you mean when you say "Sit."

1. Hold a tasty morsel in your fingertips.

2. Get down to the puppy's level (crouch beside him) and say "Sit" as you hold the morsel just above his nose.

3. He will reach up for the morsel: keep it right above his nose while moving it backward, above his head.

4. Hold it there—as he lifts his head to eat the food, his other end will automatically be on the ground, sitting.

5. Praise him warmly.

If you have another morsel handy, do it again right away: say "Sit," hold the treat above and behind his nose (as though you wanted to tease him), then move it slowly back as he reaches up for the treat until his nether region sits down. The minute his butt touches the floor, give him the morsel and say as many enthusiastic words of praise as you can without feeling too stupid.

It does not matter how long his bottom stays on the ground. It's okay if he gets up instantly, since this command is not about "stay."

This exercise is about making "sit" a positive and rewarding experience.

⬥ The Scoop-under-him Method of Training "Sit"

This method works for small dogs or younger puppies. It requires you to crouch down beside the puppy. Place your right arm (if you're right-handed) behind the puppy beneath her tail, with your forearm directly behind her knees. This will allow you to scoop her off her paws and fold her back legs under her from behind. Your other hand goes on her chest. As you say "Sit," press lightly with the one hand on her chest and press against the back of her knees with your other arm, scooping the pup down into the sitting position.

REWARDING THE "SIT"

The best reward for "sit" is a chest rub or scratch. It encourages the dog to stay in the sitting position to receive this pleasurable touch. People often think patting on the head is good, but the head pat can make a dog duck down, almost to escape it, especially if the person has a heavy touch. Scratching or massaging the chest area is rewarding and also maintains the sitting position naturally.

TONE OF VOICE

⬥ Do Not Say "Sit" with an Up-inflection.

You don't want to say any command as though it is a question. With "sit," many people seem to naturally put a question mark in their voice after the word "sit." But you're not asking whether he is willing to sit—you are just giving him a quiet command to do so.

⬥ Remember to Use a Happy, Warm Voice.

That is how the dog knows he has pleased you: the tone of your voice, not what you are saying. People say a bunch of words on the false assumption that their dog understands English. You can be certain that a dog's primary reaction is not to a string of words but to your tone of voice, your facial expression and the praising touch from you. So you need to be sure that all those things register as positive.

⬥ Smile When You Praise Your Dog.

You may not be sure if your voice is friendly enough. It might sound silly to you, but if you're smiling, your tone of voice is almost certainly upbeat. Smiling will affect your tone and make it warmer.

RESISTANCE TO "SIT"

If your dog resists you, it's because he doesn't understand what you want.

Don't get impatient without giving him a fair chance to comprehend your desires. If you have a breed that's known for being independent or headstrong, don't assume the worst of your dog before you've given him a chance. Every dog is an individual and deserves your full support. Give every dog the benefit of the doubt in this and all training.

Show your dog what you want and he'll give it to you, provided you haven't made it into a battle.

Do not make sitting into a shoving match. It isn't a test of wills. Or muscle strength.

If the dog sits but gets right up, *that is fine:* do not become angry or annoyed or react negatively. You are not teaching "stay," just "sit." So if he stands up, view it as another chance to practice the "sit:" tell him "Sit" in a nice voice, guide him into it and praise him warmly.

Teaching "Down"

A Note about Leashes: As with all training in the early stages, it is helpful to have the dog dragging a leash so you have something to get hold of other than the dog's collar. This is especially true of teaching "down," because if you need an additional tool with a dog who is less than cooperative, you can hold the leash right down on the ground in front of him—with mild tension on the leash—so that when he submits and begins to lie down, that pressure is automatically relieved.

The "down" is considered a yardstick to judge your dog's inborn personality, as well as how he's feeling at the time that you ask for the "down." When a dog goes down he is showing submissiveness, which some dogs are reluctant to do.

THE DOG DOESN'T HAVE TO SIT FIRST.

People mistakenly think you have to ask the dog to "sit" before you teach him "down," but the two behaviors really do not have to be linked. If the dog is resistant to lying down, it can sometimes help to get him to sit down first.

Using the same concept as for "sit," you can demonstrate "down" to your dog with or without food.

"DOWN" #1: THE FOOD-BAIT METHOD

This is the most effective of the three best-known ways to teach a dog to lie down. It requires stillness and patience from you.

1. Put a delicious treat in your hand with a closed fist, with the back of your hand facing up.

2. When you say the word "down," use a deep, slow voice and try to make the word sound sort of like what you want—with a drawn out "owww" as the middle sound. Do not use a quick, high-pitched tone of voice. And do not say it in a quick, staccato voice that sounds like a reprimand. Avoid the common mistake of putting a question mark, or up-inflection, after the word "down," which sounds as though you doubt what you're asking.

3. Bring your fist slowly down onto the ground in front of the dog. Don't move your hand, and don't open your fist and show the contents. Don't distract the dog by moving around, saying anything or taunting him with your fist with the treat in it.

4. WAIT HIM OUT. Your instinct will be to wave your fist or to repeat "Doowwn." Doing nothing is often the hardest assignment of all.

5. As long as the dog's attention is still on your hand or your face, give him time to work it out. He's thinking about it. If his mind is elsewhere, then you have to get his attention back on you and start over.

6. As soon as the dog begins to slide down, praise him verbally and withdraw your fist slightly, holding it close to the ground, As soon as he's down on the ground, give him the treat.

"DOWN" #2: THE THROUGH-YOUR-KNEES METHOD

This is a simple technique and involves no manipulation or force on your part. Sit on the floor with your knees drawn up and your feet on the ground, making a teepee shape with your legs. Your goal is to entice your dog to lie down by luring her to go under your "leg teepee" from the side.

Sit your dog on one side of you, more or less looking at the side of your legs, so that if she crouched down she could look right through the teepee beneath your knees. Take a treat in your hand opposite the dog and drag it very slowly on the floor through the teepee to the side of your knees. Your dog will have to drop down on her belly to go after it. The moment that the dog's stomach touches the ground, reinforce the action immediately with your voice saying, "Dowwwn. Good Sally!" And then give her some more treats.

Get her back in a sitting position and try it again. Say the word "Dowwwn" and slide another treat through your leg teepee from the far side, teasing the dog to go down on her stomach to get the treat.

◆ Very Small Dogs

If you have a small dog, raise your knees only a little way off the floor, just high enough to allow the dog to get underneath if she is down on her stomach.

◆ Very Large Dogs

Some bigger dogs will resist any physical attempt to get them into a "down." Try the food-bait method or the through-the-knees method above. If you have one of the giant breeds, such as a Saint Bernard, Mastiff, Deerhound, Wolfhound, etc., then you'll need to sit on a chair and make a "bridge" of your thighs for the dog to go underneath.

"DOWN" #3: THE PUSH-HIM-DOWN-PHYSICALLY METHOD

Kneel down beside your dog. Have him in a sitting position. Put one hand on his spine between the shoulder blades—on top of his back just behind his collar. Position your other hand beneath one of his front paws. Lift up and out on one front paw as you apply pressure to the shoulder blades. You are manually collapsing the dog, so don't do it quickly or roughly in a way that could frighten him or cause resistance. Be firm but gentle, and move slowly. Praise him when he goes down onto the floor.

NOTE: *This method is not advisable with very long-backed dogs like Dachshunds. Long, low breeds are hard to shift onto one shoulder for the enforced "down." Try one of the other methods instead.*

This method is just the "sit" in reverse. Once the dog is sitting, take a tasty morsel in your fingers and, with the other hand, place your open palm on the dog's shoulder and back. Hold the food tidbit in front of her nose. Instead of raising it above and behind her head as with the "sit," you want to hold it very close to her nose but in front of her, then lower the treat to the ground while saying "Doowwn."

Teaching "Enough"

"Enough" is an important response to teach because it has so many applications. You can use "enough" to tell a dog to stop barking. You can also use it to send the dog away from you at the dinner table or to stop him from sniffing a visitor. You can use it to tell two dogs who are playing too rough to chill out.

SAY "ENOUGH" IN A LOW, QUIET VOICE

Take the shake-can (see page 280) and punch the air with it in her direction—one short jab straight out in front of you, toward the dog.

If she doesn't stop what she's doing or move away after the first time you say "Enough," then stand up and "push" the dog away by standing up in front of her and walking her backward, pressing her away by body-blocking her.

Sit back down, cross your arms and look away.

The most important part of this is to turn your face away. Break off all visual contact with the dog. If you keep eye contact the dog will stick around, trying to read your face.

If you have body-blocked the dog away from you, then looked away and given no visual encouragement, but she still comes right back to where you're sitting, then you're going to have to repeat it all over again. "Air punch" the shake-can and say "Enough" in a low voice.

If you get no reaction and she continues to hover, body-block her backward again. Do not make eye contact (because the dog will be looking for it, for validation).

When it finally sinks in—when the dog gets the message and backs off (or stops barking) when you say "Enough," it's time to reward her. Give her verbal praise the moment she changes what she's doing. You also want to give her a food treat, but you don't want her to come back toward you. So you have to go to her, or call her to you for the food treat that accompanies her compliance with "enough."

Teaching "Go to Your Bed"

This is one of the handiest and most underused commands. It's great to be able to send the dog to her bed (or anyplace that you've designated as her "place") if she's in the way or when there is a visitor at the door.

This is a command that lets you get the dog out from underfoot—in this case, away from the front door—and then release her to do as she wishes.

Use a firm tone of voice and say "Go to your bed," as you point to that place with a straight arm. Do not repeat the command—just stand there, with your arm out pointing at the bed, looking right at it. You can toss a treat onto the bed. Most dogs will catch on pretty quickly, and as soon as their paws touch that bed you can heap praise all over them. In fact, you *have to* give the dog buckets of praise, but she can't come to you for it because that would defeat the purpose of the "Go to your bed" command. So you have to toss treats to her or take the treats over to her bed and make a fuss over her there.

Once you've given this command, it requires releasing the dog fairly quickly from your control. Part of what will make a dog pick this up quickly is that it generally requires compliance for no more than a few minutes before the dog is released.

"Okay" is my release word, but we use it in many other situations, too. So if you choose "okay" be aware of the other times that you may use the word: you can mistakenly release your dog if you're leaving the house, you say "Okay" to someone and the dog thinks you're speaking to her.

Teaching "Off"

(See page 582 in the section on Problems—"Jumping.")

Dogs jump up for two reasons: to get attention and to show how happy they are to see you. To a dog, it's a naturally happy action.

People are the ones who need to be disciplined about dogs jumping up: if you ignore a dog who jumps up, he will stop doing it.

Never pat a dog who only has his two back feet on the ground. This goes for everyone in your household—and it has to be totally consistent. If everyone does not join the effort, you can forget about correcting the habit. If anyone ever praises a dog for jumping up, he will be encouraged to keep on doing it.

Do not expect your dog to figure out when or with whom it's okay to jump up. The answer has to be nowhere, no one, no time. If you want your dog not to jump, you can NEVER pat him after he jumps, or do anything pleasurable—speak or laugh in a friendly way, give a treat, throw a toy, etc.

You have to correct or ignore anything the dog does without all four of his feet on the ground—including draping himself on your lap when you're sitting down.

Have a leash on the dog, but without any pressure or tension on the leash. Then set up whatever situation usually makes him jump, such as you coming in the door. As soon as the dog goes to jump up, either step on the leash with your foot, or step hard into the dog with a raised knee and hope you catch her with it and knock her off you.

Another training method that works for some people (depending on the relative height of the person and the dog standing on her hind legs) is for you to catch the dog's two front feet and pull them slightly apart—just enough to make her feel uncomfortable and off-balance. When she starts to struggle, just let go and ignore her completely, unless or until she sits down. Then you can make a big fuss over her for having four feet on the ground.

After a correction, be warm and pet her, but be unemotional, because if you are too enthusiastic it will rev her up and she'll want to jump again. And make sure to show no lingering annoyance for her having jumped in the first place.

The easiest thing to do, which requires much less setup, timing and physical effort from you, is a cold shoulder. Just fold your arms, look away from the dog and maybe turn your body, so instead of facing her you're ignoring her completely. Most dogs are baffled by this and will stop jumping. You have to praise immediately when she gets down: generous praise with words and food treats the *precise second* that she has all four feet on the ground. These exercises are the most effective when you reinforce them at the very moment that the dog executes your wishes.

Teaching "Stay"

WHAT "STAY" ACTUALLY MEANS

Stay means remain right where you are, in the position requested—either "sit, stay" or "down, stay." So when you ask for "stay," you have to be clear that that's precisely what you want—it's not the command to use if you want the dog not to rush out the door in front of you, or to remain in the house when you go out.

If you use "stay," then you have to release the stay command with "okay" or whatever word you've chosen as your release word. Think of the word "stay" as being like the word "freeze" in that childhood game in which no one could move a muscle until the person in charge said they could. Technically speaking, that is true of "stay" with a dog. If you said "stay" to a perfectly trained dog and left the house, theoretically he should still be in that same position when you return.

HOW "STAY" IS USED

"Stay" is used for short periods, such as when you open a door. Or get out of the car. Or wait for a traffic light to turn green. "Wait" or "Go to your bed" are used for longer periods, in which the dog can be in any position as long as she is not moving around.

"Stay" is taught in all training classes. It is usually done with the dog on a "down, stay," and then the owners walk around their dogs without the dog breaking from that position. The goal in the class is to move farther and farther away from the dog (including out of sight in more advanced training work) without the dog changing position.

We're thinking here of the short, sweet, functional use of stay.

START SMALL.

The best chance for success with "stay" is to start short and work your way up to more time, making the stays longer as the puppy or dog "gets with the program."

As with any training or learning program, if compliance with a longer "stay" seems to disintegrate, just go back to the previous successful point. Refresh "stay" at the length of time at which you had success, and then take a break. If you try to go too fast or too far, all the good you've accomplished together will unravel.

Do not increase the length of the "stay" and your distance away from the dog at the same time—it's too much pressure on her. Increase either one, but make sure your dog has mastered the first command before you add the other one.

Don't push it for the dog or yourself. Each dog has her own learning curve and each owner has her own patience level—those two dynamics have to mesh for learning to be successful and pleasurable.

THIS IS NOT THE ARMY.

Don't make the mistake of thinking that you have to behave like a drill sergeant when teaching your puppy to "stay."

Be aware of your body language and demeanor. To teach "stay" you have to give the dog your undivided attention, with total eye contact and attention to the dog's own attention span. Make sure she sees what you want and that she is still interested—otherwise, you'll go backward in your progress.

Your voice should be as kind and neutral as in any other learning process. Being harsh and commanding does not build trust or communication or inspire the desire to do more for you. In fact, that drill-sergeant voice can a frighten a "soft" dog and can give the impression to any dog that she is in trouble or has done something wrong—just because of the way you have given a simple command.

Think of yourselves as a team and you won't feel that you have to put on a military attitude. If the dog succeeds, you succeed. It takes two to do these dance steps, and the point is not to trip your partner or step on her toes, so to speak. It's to be in sync as much as possible.

PRAISE GENEROUSLY.

You have to thank your dog for doing what you want—especially in a command like "stay" in which she is doing "nothing." Not moving around or bolting off can often take more effort for a young dog than actively doing something.

The moment the puppy complies with your "stay," *give praise.* "Thank you, Jackie" or "Good girl, Jackie" are always appreciated by a puppy trying her best to please you. Since dogs don't start out having a clue or natural inclination to do the odd things we ask of them, how will they begin to catch on if we don't cheerlead them to our finish line?

Continue quietly praising during the early learning-curve period—as long as the puppy is staying, say her name and praise her until you release her. "Good Jackie, good stay. Good girl. Okay!" and then let her play a little and take a break.

GIVE TREATS DURING THE "STAY."

In the early days of teaching "Stay," you can give small treats to the dog as she sits or lies there without getting up. This makes it really clear that this "doing nothing" is a really good thing.

Eventually you can give treats every so often when you ask for a "stay," or when you ask for a longer "stay." Think of treats as an insurance policy: to pay off the good behavior as an unexpected jackpot, which will keep the dog hanging in there with the hope of another one.

IF THE DOG BREAKS THE "STAY"

If you can *prevent* your dog from breaking the "stay," it will go a long way to giving you lasting success with this command.

Don't get all over the puppy for moving. Don't jerk the leash or raise your voice or act menacing. All that kind of attitude inspires in a dog is discomfort, anxiety, fear and confusion, because if the dog was staying and then stopped staying, she was being compliant until that second.

The only thing you want to correct is that moment of getting up or moving off. This is where your alert watchfulness comes in—as you see the puppy begin to get up, you say "Siiit, staay" and repeat the stay hand command—hand down by your side, with the palm facing the dog's face. Praise the moment that she sits back down. "Good Jackie, good stay." Keep your voice as quiet and calm as you'd like the dog to be.

BE KIND IF PROBLEMS OCCUR.

Gently return the dog to the previous position and repeat "Stay," giving the hand signal of palm facing the dog's face. Don't move away and try to prove anything. Make it easier for her, not harder, to be successful. Both of you should stay still. Quietly praise the dog. Give her a little treat. Say the word "Stay" again and move aside a little. Then release her as a reward.

Go back to shorter periods of staying, and decrease the distance between you and the dog to build her confidence and ensure your eventual success with a good "stay" command.

Teaching "Wait"

This is a good command to use before you exit the house, cross a street or get out of the car.

If your door leads to an unfenced area, put a leash on your dog before starting. Otherwise, that isn't necessary.

STAND WITH YOUR BACK TO THE DOOR.

Move in front of your dog so she's facing you. If she crowds in on you, walk gently and slowly directly at her, herding her and pushing her backward with your forward motion. Move her about three feet back, away from you and the door.

◆ She May Try to Slip Around You to Get Closer to the Door.
Block her by moving quickly in front of her in every direction she tries.

◆ Say "Wait" in a Quiet, Low Firm Voice.

Then open the door a little bit. *Do not repeat "Wait"*—even though it's hard not to repeat yourself, or to say *something,* when you want to control the dog with your voice and you don't have that control yet.

◆ Most Dogs Try to Make a Break for It.

All you can do is block the dog's forward motion with your body. Or you can close the door quickly, as long as you're really careful not to shut it on the dog (no kidding—it happens). That's why it's good to open the door just a little way, so you don't have so far to go to close it.

Note: Do not say "Stay" instead of "Wait." Wait means "halt forward movement until released." Stay is about "staying still in one position until released." "Stay" is more control than we need here. All we're asking the dog for is self-control. Momentarily stopping the dash for freedom is all it's about.

Closing the door or blocking with your body shows her that the door will shut if she doesn't wait. Barging ahead will shut the door. Waiting patiently will open it.

SUCCESS DEPENDS ON AN IMMEDIATE REWARD.

You have to be ready to open the door immediately if the dog hesitates even a little when you say "Wait." If she stops her forward motion for a moment, you have to reinforce her *the second* that she stops pressing forward. You can expect her to be more patient later.

◆ No Leash Tugging—No Restraining

"Wait" has to be the dog making the choice for herself. The instant that the dog shows a hesitation in her natural forward motion after you've said "Wait," you're on your way.

Then use the release word you've developed—such as "okay!" or "go!"—and allow her the freedom to run around. The release and freedom are her rewards.

🦴 *Tips for Success with "Wait"*

- Do not repeat "Wait." Say it once—your body and/or the shutting door works after that.
- Do not use a leash to hold back the dog: it's about her self-control.
- Do not use the body-block any longer than necessary—as soon as the dog stops coming forward, tip back and stand up straight.

Training Equipment

There is a variety of equipment that can be used to teach and control your dog. You may be surprised by all the negative points in this section about training paraphernalia but when it comes to this equipment, the only side I'm on is the dog's, since he can't defend himself against the often harsh and cruel devices that people will buy. There are even warnings about the Gentle Leader head collar. I do believe your dog would want someone to point out how these collars and other contraptions might feel on him. This section gives you the information you need to make decisions for yourself.

Training Collars

"CHOKE CHAIN" (OR "SLIP") COLLARS

This is the kind of training collar that most people and many trainers use for obedience training and leash-walking.

♦ **To Be Politically Correct, They Are Now Called "Training Collars."**
"Slip collar" is another new name for a choke chain but whether the name sounds more or less harsh, the fact of the matter is that these collars *are* designed to apply a choking pressure on a dog's neck. Some are made of chain, others of nylon. But while the nylon may look and sound less harsh, the issues remain the same (see "Warnings," page 267).

The collar is designed to slide over the dog's head. When a leash is attached and pressure is applied, the collar slips against itself and tightens on the dog's neck, choking him or pinching his neck. The effect on the dog lasts until that pressure is completely released.

♦ **These Collars Are Intended as a Tool for Training.**
Chain collars should be on the dog only for teaching purposes and then removed. In theory, once your dog has learned to walk properly on a leash, *the chain collar is not intended to be used anymore.* Unless a dog temporarily loses his good manners on the leash and his memory needs jogging, the choke chain should be put away.

♦ **The Chain Should Not Be Used Instead of a Fixed Collar with ID Tags.**
Chain collars are used in addition to the leather or nylon collar that has the dog's identification tags on it. Many people keep a chain collar on their dogs permanently and even affix the dog's license to it, especially people who live in cities and have to walk their dogs often. However, this is unwise for the reasons listed below.

♦ **Problems with Choke Chains**
The collars are often put on the dog incorrectly because users have not grasped the simple dynamic of a chain that slips back "against itself" to apply pressure to the dog's neck—but that releases when pressure is released on the leash.

Correct placement Have a trainer or a pet store employee show you the correct way to thread the two rings and chain together before putting the collar on the dog. Owners often do not know the correct way to use the collar, so they keep it in the incorrect position, which constantly chokes the dog.

Correct usage These collars are often not fully understood by people who use them. Sometimes even a professional trainer will not instruct his students in the timing and angle of the leash-jerk or the instant release.

Slip collars are one of the most difficult tools to use during dog training, and yet everyone puts them on dogs thinking it is the right thing to do. Most people who use the slip collar do so almost uselessly—it takes a high skill level to use one of these effectively . . . and to be able to *stop* using one of them.

Correct reinforcement When used by a trainer, a slip collar is used to *reinforce* a command—an often subtle reinforcement, not a punishing sharp yank of the leash. As with all training tools, these are just the means to an end. As soon as the dog makes the connection to what you want of him, the collar should be phased out.

WARNINGS ABOUT CHOKE CHAINS

- ❑ Neck, spine and throat injuries can occur. The collars even come with a warning to that effect.
- ❑ A chain collar used on a growing puppy puts a herky-jerky pressure on his windpipe and on the developing spine and neck.
- ❑ People have gotten complacent about the danger. They are so accustomed to seeing slip collars on dogs that they may not have stopped to consider the serious discomfort and potential damage that these tools can cause, especially in rough hands.
- ❑ People keep using choke collars on their dogs. The collar should be phased out over time.
- ❑ Choke chains can choke a dog. If a dog wears a chain collar without a person at the other end of a leash attached to the ring on the collar, the collar can get hooked on anything the dog brushes against—and when it tightens, he will pull against it, tightening it even more. Dogs have gotten hooked up when playing with another dog, catching the choke chain on the other dog's collar or on a tooth.
- ❑ A choking dog can die right in front of you. You may not be able to rescue a dog from his own panicked reaction if he has too much pressure pulling on his own neck if the collar gets hooked on something. Some dogs just pull back against the strangling sensation, and with all their weight on the collar it tightens even more, panicking them more and making it nearly impossible for you to get the collar off.

PARTIAL-SLIP (OR "GREYHOUND") COLLARS

These collars are also called "limited-slip" collars or "martingales," and they provide more control than a conventional collar.

Dogs with relatively narrow heads (like the Greyhound) often discover that by backing up and ducking their head they can slip out of their normal collars. The limited-slip collar prevents this by tightening enough to prevent the collar from slipping off, without tightening enough to choke the dog.

This kind of collar can be used for training when you want to limit the choking action of a traditional chain slip-collar (as described above). This collar is a cross-breed of a flat collar and a slip-style chain collar, although there is no chain involved. This collar is all flat nylon with two rings that hold a smaller circle of nylon material. When pressure is applied it gently tightens the whole collar.

"PRONG" COLLARS

Also known as "pinch" collars, these have wide, rigid rectangular links; each link has four metal prongs on the underside that dig into the dog's neck when you apply pressure on the leash. On a smooth-coated dog like a Boxer or a Beagle, these collars can be cruel or even barbaric. The collar clearly causes pain on delicate-skinned dogs; the prongs are so long that they inflict pain when the metal digs into the dog's skin, even on a heavy-coated breed like a Rottweiler or a German Shepherd.

Some professional trainers use these collars with powerful dogs for early leash-training, but when a dog is properly trained to walk beside you, there should never be any pressure on the leash—and there should be no excuse for an owner to be able to dig metal prongs into her dog's neck.

Maybe people who put prong collars on their dogs haven't taken the time for training classes because their dogs are often pulling on the leash while they walk, despite the digging prongs. And because the owners constantly apply pressure, the dogs are not even being taught how to release that pressure by heeling more closely. Other people use the collars to make their dogs look more tough and impressive. There are those who believe that these owners should wear one of these collars for an afternoon to experience what it is like.

ELECTRONIC COLLARS ("E-COLLARS")

This is a collar with a transmitter in it that allows you to deliver a mild shock to the dog from a remote device. The advocates and manufacturers of these collars are lobbying to remove the word "shock"—they like the more obtuse phrase "remote trainers." They also don't want the word "shock" used to describe the voltage that the collar delivers to a dog's neck: they want it referred to as "stimulation" or "static correction." But a rose by any other name is still a rose.

♦ How Do Dogs React to Shock Collars?
Dogs have a range of reactions to the "electric stimulation" that the collar delivers—from cringing to yelping. The amount of shock delivered is adjustable, but even on the lowest setting, a sensitive dog can fall apart when that shock hits his neck—and it can take a long time to rebuild the dog's confidence level and to reestablish his trust in you.

+ **The Use of Electronic Shock Collars as a Training Aid Is Controversial.**
Many people believe these collars should not be available directly to owners because of the possible misuse and abuse of the tool—which is more likely to be used in a humane way under the control of a dog behaviorist.

In the hands of an unsophisticated, untrained owner, an E-collar could very nearly be a weapon. At the least, the collar will be ineffective if the user does not understand the precise timing required to get a message across to the dog without freaking him out. The intended use of the E-collar is to get a message across to the dog and then stop using the tool, but people often buy it thinking it will be their dog's everyday collar.

+ **An Electric Shock Is Obviously an Aversive Stimulus.**
Using an E-collar is the opposite of the "positive reinforcement only" theories of training that have become standard thinking in current dog training. So if there *is* a place for the E-collar, it is probably only in the hands of a serious dog professional who needs to work out a life-or-death situation with a problem dog, or is competing at a very high level of performance and utilizes the collar for split-second communication with a highly motivated and dynamic dog who does not experience such a collar as a punishment.

One theoretical defense of the E-collar is that it allows the handler to identify the exact instant that the dog does something undesirable—and presumably teaches him self-control. Detractors say that a dog zapped this way does not learn to modify her behavior to please people, all she learns is that when the collar isn't on she can behave as she pleases. However, emphasizing a negative behavior goes against the grain of most current training theory, which is to ignore behavior you don't like and reinforce that which you do want. The theory of positive teaching is to put an immediate *positive* marker on behavior—with a clicker or the word "Yes!" and a treat.

Halters (Also Known as Head Collars)

There has been a general evolution in training attitudes and methods that has led the way toward a kinder, affirmative style of teaching dogs. The head collar, or halter, is a tool that has been favored by many trainers who espouse gentle methods. They have found that the halter can make training more effective, especially for dogs who are wound up or are strong pullers, since the halter can eliminate a battle of wills between a person and his dog. The general consensus has been that by reducing pulling and resistance, a halter can reduce frustration and friction on either end of the leash. However, some controversy has emerged that questions the positive value and possible negative effect of the halters, depending on when, where and how they are used—a debate that you'll learn more about below.

THE THEORY BEHIND HEAD HALTERS
Traditional flat collars put pressure at the front of the throat, beneath the dog's jaw, which causes an instinctive pulling forward and away from you (the opposite of what you want). Halters are de-

signed to put pressure at the back of the neck behind the dog's ears and then on his muzzle, causing the dog to drop back toward you in reaction.

✦ Pressure on the Back of a Dog's Neck Can Calm Him.

The design of the halter takes advantage of responses that are built into dogs from puppyhood by their mothers. Mother dogs pick up their puppies by the back of the neck—and the youngsters instinctively go limp and submit to this motherly manipulation. Lifting a puppy by the scruff is the mother's way of controlling him—and the Gentle Leader can have the same effect for you. Pressure by the halter on the back of a dog's neck can touch off the kind of neurochemical response that used to make the puppy relax and stop resisting when his mother picked him up by the scruff.

✦ Pressure Across the Bridge of the Dog's Nose Tells the Dog to Chill Out.

The nose pressure from the muzzle strap on the head collar signals to the dog that he should defer to the person holding the leash because muzzle pressure is one way that dominant dogs control other dogs. A mother dog will put a misbehaving puppy's muzzle (or even his whole head) gently in her mouth to get him back in line. The halter encourages submission to the person holding the leash because it taps into a dog's wolf heritage: a dominant wolf conveys that he is in charge when he takes an annoying young dog's muzzle lightly in his mouth (without biting down).

The training halter can teach even the hardest-pulling dog not to strain at her leash. Similar to horse training, if you can painlessly control forward motion at the head, especially the nose, then everything else will follow. And that is how a halter is intended to work on a dog: the lightest pressure on the leash and the dog corrects herself. When the halter is used correctly, you have more control without using force; the dog stops yanking or pulling, there's no sore arm for you and no sore neck or windpipe for the pooch.

WHEN TO USE THE HALTER

Some trainers consider the halter a fine piece of equipment for walking a dog every day, once they have demonstrated its use; others view the halter as a tool to be used only whenever particular issues arise, in order to diffuse the situation and eventually solve the behavior issue. For example, the halter can be effective if you put it on *before* problems occur in situations when you feel it's likely your dog might misbehave or be out of your control.

You may get the best results if you already have the halter on in a situation when you anticipate problematic reactions. For example, in my house with Scooby Doo, I know that he gets so excited about visitors that he goes out of his tiny mind, crying and wanting to mouth them (he does the same thing to me every time I come in the door, but the difference is that I know how to handle it). So, when I know that company is coming, I put the head collar on Scooby, patting him and using a gentle tone. In your case it might be that your dog is a strong puller who freaks out with joy when you get ready to walk him. Once the guests are settled down I take the halter off Scooby because it has done the job of easing him through his initial burst of adrenaline.

HOW TO USE THE HALTER

The halter can be used for simple dog-walking and can prevent leash-pulling, lunging, barking and jumping on people. It can also be used for many behavior problems inside the house and for training puppies, too.

The brochure that comes with the Gentle Leader suggests leaving it on all the time except for a six- to eight-hour break at some point—but I would add, never without supervision. Use it only when you are at home once the dog accepts the halter without any rebellion. If a dog is resisting the halter, trying to rub it off or roll away from it, she runs the risk of hurting herself while trying to claw her way out of the halter, or hooking the halter onto something in the house with disastrous results. In any case, it seems logical to me that any dog who would wear the halter on her own without any rebellion is not a dog who needs to be wearing it around the house or all day—except for on-leash walking.

The illustrated brochure has some good tips in it, and although it's possible to figure out the various uses of the halter on your own, you're probably better off working with a trainer in the beginning so you can see what a gentle touch is needed to use the halter correctly and humanely.

◆ Special Home Use of the Head Halter

The halter can actually have an effect on the way a dog thinks and perceives his surroundings. It sort of takes him down a notch—if he was trying to gain an edge or was just anxious about not being clear that you were the leader of your home (see page 154, "Dominance Issues," to understand more about what makes your dog tick and see how the head halter has particular value in clearly establishing your leadership). In some cases, it can have the effect of bringing calm and clarity that can make high-strung dogs more cooperative in daily life and can also relax particularly tense ones.

Some dogs who are fearful or shy can benefit in a different way from the reassurance they get while wearing the head collar. Feeling more secure can make a dog more confident, which can make him more open to learning.

◆ Puppy Training with the Halter and Drag Line

When you are home and the puppy is loose with you, the drag line can help with house-training and chewing issues. You can tie the long line to your belt and when you see or feel the puppy starting to chew something you can stop the behavior by *gently* pulling on the line—yanking or jerking is not necessary and can even hurt a dog's neck. Then give the dog an acceptable toy instead. Another use is that if you see or feel the puppy sniffing or circling to indicate he's about to eliminate in the house, you can stop the action with a simple upward pressure on the halter, then carry him outside to relieve himself outdoors where you will shower him with praise, of course.

STOPPING UNWANTED BEHAVIOR WITH A HALTER

The drag line allows you to make contact with your dog when she's doing something you don't want—without reinforcing her unwanted behavior with your "negative attention" like getting up or calling out to her. Just as some children misbehave to get their parents' attention (even if it means being yelled at or being punished) there are some dogs who will do things they know will make you stop what you're doing and pay attention to them. Unpleasant attention is better than no attention for some individuals.

If the dog is **barking** and won't stop when asked to be "Quiet" (see page 548 on barking problems), all you have to do is pick up the end of the drag line from across the room and *gently* pull on it to stop her behavior. She stops barking because the nose loop closes her mouth, raises her head so that she may even sit, and now that she's calm and quiet the attention you give her can be positive—affection, a treat, a little "conversation" to reward her quietness. This is the essence of "positive reinforcement" (see page 240).

For a dog who usually **jumps on people,** be prepared for times when you know he may try it and give him a "sit" command instead, which you can reinforce by gently lifting the drag line. *You want to prevent the jumping in the first place.* As soon as he sits, then tell him "Stay" and reward him as long as he retains the "stay" instead of jumping. Do not turn your back on the good behavior just because it came easily with the head collar—continue reinforcing it. ALWAYS ask for a "sit, stay" when you know that previously he would have jumped. Reward his effort, he will eventually choose to sit when he wants attention or something else from you.

POPULAR BRANDS AND WHERE TO FIND THEM

The most popular and best-designed brand is the "Gentle Leader," which is sold in pet stores and some veterinarians' offices. "Halti" is one of the other brands, but my experience and testing done by several independent dog-product specialists have found the fit and function of Gentle Leader to be superior to other brands. If you are unfamiliar with the Gentle Leader (which is the leading product in this category) and/or other halters, do yourself and your dog a favor and try one.

Gentle Leader is a trademarked product of Premier Pet Products, in Richmond, Virginia. They can be reached at (888) 640-8840 or www.gentleleader.com for information on where you can buy one from a store in your area.

ADDITIONAL EQUIPMENT WITH THE GENTLE LEADER

◆ You Can Buy a Small Tab That Hangs Down off the Head Halter.

The tab is where the leash would normally clip. It's like a very short leash for indoor use (or even outdoor off-leash). This tab is sold by the Gentle Leader company, but it's really just a metal clip such as that found on a nylon leash with a short (four to six inches, depending on your dog's height) piece of webbed nylon leash material hanging from it.

You can save a few bucks and even do some recycling if you happen to have an old nylon leash that got a knot stuck in it or was chewed by a puppy. You can make your own tab by cutting the nylon webbing below the metal clip on the old leash. Test its length so that it will be long enough for your fist to close around it (if you wanted to catch hold of it hanging from the halter) and then leave enough so that you can form it into a knot below that holding zone. You can use an old horsemen's trick to clean up the frayed, cut edge by lighting a match and holding the flame just below (not on) the nylon. The heat that rises from the flame will melt the frayed edges just enough to give a smooth, finished edge.

With or without the tab you can put the halter on when company is coming or for any other event that generally makes your dog hopped up. Just having the halter on often has a calming effect even without a leash attached. Having the tab means you don't need to attach a leash.

FITTING THE HALTER

A Gentle Leader has two loops of nylon webbing, one of which goes around the dog's muzzle and the other behind her ears, with a ring under the chin where the leash hooks. The strap behind the ears fastens tightly and then a strap runs loosely across the muzzle. When the dog pulls she feels pressure at the back of her neck and the strap across her nose tightens temporarily. As far as sizing goes, "petite" would be for a dog under five pounds, "small" would be up to twenty-five pounds, "medium" is twenty-five to sixty pounds, "large" ranges from sixty to one hundred and thirty pounds and "X-large" is for giant dogs over 130 pounds.

Special Warning: *Exercise caution when trying to use a halter with Bulldogs, Pekingese or any of the breeds with flattened faces and airways that are limited because of their anatomy. These dogs can have difficulty breathing when they are exerting themselves or feeling stressed. Experiment with your dog, and if his usual breathing difficulties get worse while wearing the halter, take it off immediately, contact your vet and tell her what happened.*

◆ Converting to a Regular Collar

The Gentle Leader can be used as a normal flat collar at any time by following the instructions that come with it. This is great if your dog graduates from needing the extra control of the halter, or has only a few issues that require that special touch, in which case you can convert it back into a halter when you anticipate that those situations might arise.

WHAT STRANGERS THINK ABOUT HALTERS

Halters are not widely used yet in America—but the time may come, since in England more than half the dogs wear them. The limited use of halters in the United States can mean that when you walk your dog with a halter, people may mistake it for a muzzle. This misunderstanding may lead strangers to think that your dog is aggressive, and they may react defensively, by dragging their own dog away or even trying to avoid your dog entirely if they are not dog-walking themselves.

As the halter gains popularity, people will learn that it is not a muzzle. They will see that a dog wearing a halter can open her mouth naturally and drink or eat or play ball. Firsthand proof that a dog's inner child is free while wearing the halter is that my dog Scooby Doo (who was wearing his halter to improve his over-the-top greeting style) was able to fit his mouth around a soccer ball and bring it as a peace offering to the man who comes with the "monster" lawn-mower.

DRAWBACKS TO HALTERS

There are detractors to halters who feel that they suppress a dog's natural exuberance and that they can damage the dog's spine if the person uses too much pressure on the leash. These critics also feel strongly that the halter should only be used in isolated cases as a corrective tool, which will then be phased out.

One downside I've found with putting the halter on with guests around is that if the dog is bothered by it, he may try to rub his face all over the guests because his face feels itchy. Some dogs seem more uncomfortable than others and may get a martyred expression when the halter is on. If it subdues your dog—which will make training easier for both of you—the halter sure beats the alternative, which is that your *guests* will be the ones with martyred expressions about the dog's overenthusiastic greeting at the door!

However, there are dogs who resist the halter so violently that they can hurt themselves physically, and it is just too devastating emotionally to be of any use as a training device.

The other problem is that some people with limited mobility find it really difficult to get the halter on, especially if the dog is very active. The irony is that those dog owners are the very ones who most need a humane, energy-controlling restraint.

SOME DOGS *DETEST* HALTERS.

There are some dogs who flip out when you fit a head halter on them, but most will calm down within a few minutes and before long will accept it as they do their everyday collar.

Regardless of the high praise for halters, there are a few dogs who simply cannot stand them. These dogs just freak out, no matter how gently and slowly you try to accustom them to the halter. We're not talking about the common first reactions, such as a dog pawing at her face or trying to rub off the halter on people or furniture, or even dogs who get down on the ground and try to get the halter off. Dogs with these reactions tend to settle down in minutes when they don't get anywhere with their shenanigans. The dogs who really HATE the halter have a total meltdown—and you don't want to push them over the edge.

◆ What to Do If Your Dog Freaks Out

If your dog loses her mind when you put the head halter on her, there is another option—an alternative training device called the "Sense-ation Harness." This is an anti-pull harness that works on a theory similar to the Gentle Leader in that it turns the dog back toward the handler. A section about harnesses begins on page 275.

◆ Difficult Dogs May Be Made Worse by Wearing a Halter.

When the word "difficult" is used, it generally applies to dogs who are candidates for special classes for dogs who are deemed "overly reactive," the ones who can become easily aroused and may have a hard time regrouping.

It takes *all* dogs a bit of time to accept the halter, so you shouldn't give up on the contraption at the beginning just because your dog is having a hissy fit. Encourage her to walk with you, using a breezy upbeat tone, trying to focus her attention outside of herself. However, if after several attempts it's just too hard on one or both of you, you might want to consider the Sense-ation Harness.

THE SENSE-ATION HARNESS

This is a restraining device that does not inspire resistance in most dogs when you put it on. There doesn't seem to be an adjustment period: the harness goes on, and off you go.

A major difference between the two products is that because the Gentle Leader controls the dog's head and the Sense-ation Harness does not, the halter is better for modification of aggressive behavior. So if you have a very dominant dog looking for confrontation with other dogs, the halter might give you better security.

The harness is tricky to get to fit correctly, but it's easy to put on: it goes over the head and buckles under the chest. The leash attaches to a ring that is at the *front* of the dog's chest—which serves to reorient him to you when he pulls.

If you have a delicate-skinned dog, you may wish there was comfort padding under the armpits, but otherwise there should not be a problem.

◆ Controlling Harnesses

This style of harness is intended for walking small dogs, such as the smaller poodles. These tiny dogs are prone to having collapsing tracheas (a condition in which the cartilage in the neck collapses temporarily when the dog is excited), so clearly a collar of any kind should be avoided for walking. For these dogs, you want to relieve the pressure on the neck, and a halter would achieve the same goal.

For other dogs, harnesses don't give more control than a halter—in fact, they give less control because the dog can resist you with her whole body.

◆ No-pull Harnesses with Chest Pressure

This kind of harness works on the principle of negative reinforcement: the bad feeling (a pinching or tightening around the dog's chest and/or behind the front legs) stops when the dog stops pulling. If you reward the moment when he stops pulling, you will mark and reinforce the desired behavior: a loose leash. If you continue to reward the loose leash, then you will be using this harness correctly—which is as a training tool, not a lifelong walking device. For more on positive reinforcement, see page 240.

Most brands of harness that have a line that tightens are so tricky to put on that you may be too worn out to go for a walk by the time you've hooked it all up properly.

◆ The J.S. Sporn Halter

This product is considered by many to be the best-designed, highest-quality no-pull harness made. It is also considered by many to be the easiest to put on: the nylon collar goes on like a regular collar and the two lines go around the legs and hook back onto the collar. This gives more control than other no-pull harnesses and eliminates the possibility of the dog pulling backward out of the harness (which can happen with some of the other brands). The J.S. Sporn Halter can be found through

Yuppie Puppy Pet Care, New York, NY, (800) 223-1140. The manufacturer will not sell directly to owners, but you can go to www.sporn.com for information on stores and catalogs that carry the harness.

◆ **Therapeutic Harnesses for Arthritic Older Dogs**
There are a few styles of harnesses to balance and lift the hind end of older arthritic dogs. Some veterinary hospitals have them for dogs who are discharged after orthopedic surgery. The Bottom's Up Leash was developed by someone whose Lab had become old and wobbly. The $34.95 harness cradles the hind end with gentle support. (800) 805-2001.

Different Kinds of Leashes

There are practical aspects to consider when purchasing a leash, many of which you won't think about until after you've bought one that has some annoying qualities. So this section is your chance to make decisions about a leash that will be safe for your dog and pleasing to you.

CHOOSING THE BEST LEASH FOR YOU
You want a leash that is strong and flexible with smooth edges. If you pull it through your hand it shouldn't feel slippery.

◆ **Metal Snaps. The Metal Snap Should Be the Smallest Size That Will Safely Hold Your Dog.**
A heavy snap can be uncomfortable for a dog to lug around. A heavy snap that hangs underneath the chin can pull on the choke chain and tighten it. A large snap can hit a dog in the face, especially if the dog is a small one.

◆ **What Length Is Best?**
Leashes come in four different widths. The widths most commonly used for comfort and control are the ½ inch and ⅝ inch.

A six-foot leash is considered the standard length for training as well as for walking. But leashes are available in lengths from four to fifty feet.

◆ **Different Leash Materials**
  ❏ A leather leash can be elegant and beautifully made, although a leather leash is prone to decay. The leather can get dry and crack if not cared for with leather conditioners, and the stitching can give out, especially on the buckle end. If you keep such a leash for many years, it can break when you least expect it.
  ❏ A nylon leash is probably your best bet for a functional leash that can be washed in the washing machine as needed. Also, because they are relatively inexpensive, you generally have a choice of colors to suit your fancy.
  ❏ A chain leash can be hard on your hands if you try to hold it or grab it by the chain itself (they usually have a synthetic or leather loop handle). Also, the cheaper ones can rust when wet.

A short chain leash can help house-train a puppy at night and prevent having to crate her, since she won't soil where she sleeps.

THE LONG LINE

A *long line* is a thin, clothesline-type rope that can be anywhere from thirty to fifty feet long. There are a couple of different long lines: the first one is a very thin, round cotton line like a clothesline that skitters behind the dog. You cannot safely pick it up because it will burn your hands.

There is another, slightly different kind of long line called the SoftWeb Long Line, from White Pine Outfitters, which is designed to drag along easily behind a dog. This line is thicker and wider than the skinny rope, and runs from $12 to $42. It can be ordered from the company at www.whitepineoutfitters.com.

A long line usually has no handle, so that if your dog is off-leash you can let her drag the line behind her and there will be no handle to catch on anything in her path. The long line just whips along behind a running dog, even through underbrush.

The long line allows you to let a dog play off-leash outdoors and reduces the chance of losing control of her. Having the line attached to her collar, which creates some tension as she runs, is a reminder to the dog wearing it that she has to answer to a higher power: you.

Another benefit of the long line is that you can step on the end of it if you can't get control of the dog, and she won't be able to continue. (Suggestion: Before going on such a walk, make sure that the soles of your shoes will give you the full contact with the long line and not just allow it to slither along underneath your foot. This is especially important if you're going to an area where you haven't been before and there may be more attractions to distract your dog from respecting you.)

REEL-TYPE RETRACTABLE LEASH

A plastic handle and casing holds fifteen to thirty feet of retractable leash in the form of a thin, strong nylon line. This spring-loaded line uncoils from the casing, which also serves as the handle. The button that allows the line to move in and out or stops it from reeling is also part of the handle. The leash reels freely in and out unless you activate the lock button with your thumb, which stops and locks the leash. Although it can be great in a park or for walks out in the country, the following is a long list of reasons not to use one.

◆ Potential Problems with Retractable Leashes

At first glance it seems like a great idea to have a leash whose length the dog determines, but in real life the possible dangers seem to outweigh the benefits.

You can burn or cut your hand if you reach for the line. A thin rope is not meant to be held in your hand because there is pressure pulling against it, but it is a natural instinct to reach for the leash to pull back an unruly dog.

A retractable leash will not retract when it is under tension. This means you can't shorten it when your dog is pulling against it. So in an emergency situation—say he's trying to cross the street to chase a squirrel or run down the block to get at another dog—you are helpless with too much leash and no way to shorten it and control him.

The leash can break if the button pops out when the leash extends. The break can occur when the dog bolts and the leash goes out to its maximum length. If you walk a strong, unpredictable dog—even if you buy the heavy-duty size—you do not have one hundred percent assurance that the leash will not jam or break.

These leashes can be a risk to animal safety. You need to have perfect timing and be vigilant every moment the dog is on one of these leashes, because in a second he can take off and the leash will extend with him. He can dart out into the street and be hit by a car. Or you can encounter another dog, the abundance of leash can wrap around the two of them and chaos will ensue.

The dog could wind up getting hurt if the leash hits him hard in the neck. It is best to use this style of leash on a flat buckle collar, because it could really choke him with a slip-collar (choke chain) if the tension does not release because he's pulling against it.

Other people are endangered because you have less control as your dog approaches others. This leash is not really safe to use on a city street or anywhere there are other people walking because the line can trip people or get wrapped around their legs, cutting or bruising them. When he's farther away from you, he'll be able to frighten people, jump on them, etc.

If you aren't adept with the release button, you can mistakenly loosen the line at a critical moment. The release/lock button on the plastic handle is worked by your thumb: be sure you are familiar with this control, have practiced with it and can use it with confidence before you venture out in a public area.

This leash is not a good tool for obedience training because it encourages a dog to pull. Using the reel-out leash with a choke collar could also encourage a dog to develop poor habits, because he'll get used to feeling pressure on the choke chain collar as he pulls on the leash to extend it—when the point of most training collars is that the dog should learn to avoid any tension on the leash.

Miscellaneous Training Equipment

"GET OFF THE FURNITURE" DEVICES

There are a variety of devices made to keep dogs off furniture. These devices are triggered either by the detection of motion and vibration or by physical contact with the device.

They use either a noise or a mild electrical shock to stop the dog's unwanted behavior. If you would rather use a device that makes a noise, there are two cases in which you'll have the greatest chance of success: with an easily startled dog, or with a dog who has just begun to go up on the furniture. These devices are battery-powered and produce a high-pitched tone when there is movement or vibration from your dog on the furniture. However, most dogs get used to the sound and ignore it.

There is a third type of device that you activate yourself with a manual switch, but this is generally discouraged because it's all about timing the shock. Everyone will be inconsistent with administering the shock and the dog will become confused and upset.

◆ Choosing a Device

There are several things to consider when choosing one of these contraptions: it has to function whether you're home or not, it has to work reliably, and if it works by making a noise, that sound cannot be similar to any normal household sound, such as the sound of the microwave or a fax machine.

Battery-powered high-pitched tones

❑ Scraminal (www.uniquedistributors.com/scraminal.html, (800) 333-4793)

❑ Tattle Tale (www.kiienterprises.com/tattletale/index.html, (315) 468-3596)

Mild shock devices

Many people don't like the idea of using a shock device, but experts say they tend to be more effective because unlike a high-pitched noise, a dog does not get used to them. However, "mild" is relative: trainers suggest that you try the device on your own skin. The shock level should be no more than a hit of static electricity (like when you walk on a nylon carpet and get a sting when touching someone else).

❑ Scat Mat (www.scatmat.com, [800] 767-8658) gives a shock when the dog touches the device, which you've placed on the out-of-bounds funiture.

❑ RadioRepel (www.safepets.com/radiorepel.html, [888] 734-7650) works something like an invisible fence: the dog wears a collar and the transmitter that activates it is put under or near the forbidden furniture. When the dog gets nears the forbidden furniture while wearing the collar, the transmitter emits a warning beep. If the dog continues closer to the furniture, he gets a shock through the collar.

MUZZLES

Muzzles are a "behavior management tool," a temporary way of protecting people or other dogs when a dog has to be handled in a situation that is too stressful for him. There are really only a few situations in which people muzzle their dogs.

Aside from dogs with serious aggression/terror issues, a short-term reason for a muzzle is a medical emergency. When even the sweetest dog is in pain from an injury, she might bite. And there are also dogs with such fear of the vet that even the simplest visit requires muzzling. A muzzle can make it temporarily safe for a dog to be around people in certain situations, but needing a muzzle at all is a warning sign. If your dog is enough of a danger that she needs to be muzzled, you definitely need a trainer with experience in this area.

🦴 A Muzzle Will Not:

- Stop biting
- Stop chewing
- Make strangers acceptable

- Make children likable
- Make the vet bearable
- Manage a visit to the groomer

◆ The Groomer

Some dogs are terrified of the grooming process. Sometimes this is because of previous bad experiences, while other times the fear has no discernible cause. If you have a dog that is otherwise sweet-natured but trembles and becomes aggressive when it's time to go to the groomer—*don't make him go there.* Give him a bath or a shower yourself at home. Forget about a sleek clip job—you could learn to do it yourself (or a modified version, if it's a difficult job). Otherwise, just brush him and call it a day!

I realized this when my friend Maria's chocolate standard poodle, Luna, went from happy-go-lucky to cringing and shaking just by being driven to the groomer's. That turned out to be her last visit there. Never one to hold my tongue, I jumped to Luna's defense. While Maria may be silently cursing me as she struggles with *two* foamy standard poodles in her tub, you can bet that Luna is happy.

◆ What Kind of Muzzle?

Safety for the dog is the most important consideration, yet people may not know that wearing a muzzle puts the dog at risk. Any muzzle not used correctly can be dangerous for the dog.

Soft muzzles made of fabric are better for a dog's comfort than the old-fashioned basket style. The soft muzzle allows a dog to eat and drink to a small extent. Because the muzzle allows a dog to open his mouth enough to get a treat, a soft muzzle could be useful in a behavior modification program (the intention being to get the dog out of a muzzle, of course!).

There are two muzzle brands that have good reports from the dog consumer guides. These are the Mikki muzzle (from Jeffers Pet Catalog, [800] 533-3377) and the Cozy Quick muzzle (from Four Flags Over Aspen, [800] 222-9263).

◆ The Danger of Muzzles

Soft muzzles restrict a dog's respiration because they restrict his ability to pant. Since panting is a dog's only way of cooling off, a muzzle left in place for any length of time could cause a dog to overheat.

The soft muzzle should not be left in place for more than ten to fifteen minutes—and even less time than that if it is hot and humid.

Muzzles should be avoided by all short-faced breeds such as Pugs and Bulldogs, who have enough trouble breathing as it is.

SHAKE-CAN

A shake-can is a training aid used by many dog trainers. It seems to crop up in so many training manuals that you might wonder how people ever trained dogs before they had a noisy metal can to shake at them.

There is no mystery about where to get one—just put about ten pennies in a can, preferably a heavier metal can like one that held fruit or vegetables. Pennies are used because apparently, when they bang against each other, they create a high-frequency sound that can be shocking or even painful to some dog's ears. Put duct tape over the top of the can to close it completely. Even though a soda or beer can is easier to seal because it only has a hole on top, the aluminum doesn't make as good a jingling sound as the heavier metal of a can that had food in it.

◆ Using the Shake-can

There is a pretty widespread misunderstanding and misuse of the shake-can. The whole point is to startle or distract a dog. It is not intended to terrify or hurt him. The can is not to be shaken like a martini shaker or a tambourine. It is intended to make a quick, sudden sound—the motion should be a short quick jab in the air with the can.

That sound is supposed to stop a dog's activity. If he stops and looks at you, that is when you praise—because you are praising him for stopping. That is the basic function of the can: to interrupt what the dog is doing long enough to change the dynamic.

You can use the shake-can when the dog does not respond to a verbal command—this is especially useful in the car or at the door if you want to stop the dog from barking in an aggressively territorial way. Then you can praise and give a treat, and you can both take a deep breath.

TETHERS (INDOOR)

A tether is a training tool—a four-foot-long, nylon-coated cable (like the cable used to lock up bicycles) with a strong snap at both ends. The purpose of a tether is to restrain your dog for short periods of time—always with you there in the same room. You always have to be present when the dog is hooked up.

A tether is not a punishment, and it should never be used for long periods of time.

USES FOR THE TETHER

- ❏ It can be used as a tool to teach a dog to be in a room with you and/or guests or other family members without demanding anything from you.
- ❏ You can use it as a "time-out" to settle down an unruly dog.
- ❏ You can use it during mealtimes to teach a dog to lie on her bed while you eat.
- ❏ A tether can be used to supervise a puppy when she is outside of her crate, so you can keep an eye on her for house-training.
- ❏ You can use a tether outside to desensitize and eventually calm down a dog who flips out when people are in the pool or playing some kind of ball game.

◆ How to Set Up the Tether

To use the tether, you'll need to have something to clip it onto, and the best thing to use is an eye-bolt. For the hardware-store challenged, that's the eye half of a hook and eye—the bolt is the "eye" that a hook hooks into. If you (or your landlord) don't mind the hole it makes, you can screw the eye-bolt right into the wall, probably into the baseboard. You can put an eye-bolt in the room(s) where you spend the most time.

The other option is to make a portable tether-holder, which is relatively easy to do, even for the not-handy types. This allows you to have a tether anywhere you might take the dog and need to be able to restrain him. Screw an eyebolt into a small piece of wood about four inches square and one to two inches thick. Slip the tether cable under any door, put the wood block on the other side and clip it on. Close the door, which will hold the tether in place. Then clip the other end onto your dog's collar.

NOTE: *You cannot use a portable tether in a house with a lot of "people traffic," because someone might open the door you're using as your tether bolt and smash into the dog. However, if you can lock the door on your side while the dog is attached to it, that would solve the problem.*

Wherever you attach the tether, put a dog bed or comfortable bedding such as a thick quilt beside the tether hook, along with a chew toy that your dog likes. This way, when you restrain him it is a pleasant experience.

◆ Getting Started with the Tether

The first mission is to make a positive association with the tether for the dog. He shouldn't be scared. Being clipped to the tether can be a shock to some dogs, who may panic at being tied so short, so you want to accustom him to the feeling on his collar before actually using it.

First attach the tether to his collar without anchoring the other end and say, "Yes!" or "Good Boy!" and feed him a treat. This begins the process of making the tether a totally positive experience.

Now attach the tether to the hook you've put in the baseboard of whatever room you hang out in most. Tell the dog to "Stay" or "Wait," back up a little and then return to give him a treat.

Vary the distance so that the puppy or dog will lie there without trying to follow you or panic about the tether and have a meltdown trying to get away.

Chapter 11

YOUR DOG'S HEALTH

NOTE: *These pages cover nearly every aspect of your pet's physical well-being,* **but this chapter is not intended to take the place of a veterinarian.** *Please do not use this material to try to diagnose medical conditions in your dog. Do not ignore this as a routine legal disclaimer: it's serious stuff. Be humble and prudent in dealing with your dog's physical problems. You are not equipped to make decisions about what is ailing your dog. If you delay treatment or make a wrong guess and try to treat a dog without getting professional advice, it could cause your dog to suffer unnecessarily, or even cost her life.*

This chapter covers most of the medical issues that can arise in your dog's life, from warnings about a variety of dangers, to emergencies and how to handle them, to choosing a veterinarian (either traditional or alternative) and building a good working relationship with her. You will find an overview of preventive health care and a discussion of controversial issues, such as routine vaccinations.

The chapter begins with Section 1, which is all about choosing and interacting with a vet; Section 2 covers vaccinations and the diseases they prevent; Section 3 discusses warnings and emergencies; Section 4 features a big chart of "everyday dangers" to dogs; Section 5 offers a more in-depth, alphabetical look at the diseases and medical conditions that affect dogs; and finally Section 6 is a brief discussion of alternative medicine.

You will find that I was a little more personal in this chapter and have shared some me periences that I've had with my dogs. I hope they are interesting or can help you with your own situation, but of course, every dog is unique and it would be imprudent for you to make any decisions for your dog based on my experience.

Reading what follows will make you a better-informed health-care consumer: you'll be able to go to the vet prepared with observations, questions and a better grasp of many routine health issues. However, bear in mind that attempting to judge your dog's physical health is one of those situations that proves the saying: "A little information is a dangerous thing." Some topics you'll read about here may put your mind at rest, while others may give you new worries. The rule of thumb about any health issue is, "If in doubt, contact your vet."

In this chapter you will find:

- ❏ Different Kinds of Veterinarians
- ❏ Curing or Preventing "Vet Fear"
- ❏ Pet Health Insurance
- ❏ The Controversy about Vaccinations
- ❏ An Inoculation Schedule for Puppies
- ❏ 911—Medical Emergencies
- ❏ CPR and the Heimlich Maneuver on Dogs
- ❏ Household and Environmental Dangers to Dogs
- ❏ Alphabetical Listing of Medical Conditions
- ❏ Options in Confronting Cancer
- ❏ Parasites and Pesticides
- ❏ Alternative Medicine

Veterinarians

Various abbreviations follow the names of veterinarians and other animal experts. Here is a list of the most common:

WHAT THE LETTERS AFTER THE NAME MEAN

- ❏ DVM: Doctor of Veterinary Medicine (four-year program at college of veterinary medicine, usually preceded by an undergraduate degree)
- ❏ VMD: Veterinary Medical Doctorate, given by the University of Pennsylvania (same training as DVM)
- ❏ BVMS: Bachelor of Veterinary Medicine and Surgery (five-year degree offered by universities in the United Kingdom and other countries)
- ❏ MRCVS: Member of the Royal College of Veterinary Surgeons (may join RCVS, the organization that regulates and licenses practitioners in the U.K.)
- ❏ BVSc, MVSc, DVSc: Bachelor, Master or Doctor of Veterinary Science (trained for research rather than for clinical practice)

- DACVB or Dipl.ACVB: Diplomate of the American College of Veterinary Behaviorists (one of many specialty boards certifying veterinarians who receive that specialized education and pass an exam and other requirements)
- ACVS: American College of Veterinary Surgeons, or AVDC, American Veterinary Dental College
- CVT, RVT, LVT: Certified, Registered or Licensed Veterinary Technician (passed a state or federal exam after graduation from an accredited veterinary technician program)

TWO PHILOSOPHIES OF VETERINARY CARE

Just as with human medicine, there are different philosophies on how to approach wellness care (preventive care) and interventions when problems arise. In American veterinary care, there are basically two schools of thought. The one that the majority of vets belong to is called the American Veterinary Medical Association (AVMA), which follows the standard Western ideas about medicine and health. The second and smaller group, which opposes this status quo, is called the American Holistic Veterinary Medical Association (AHVMA), which teaches natural or holistic medicine based on homeopathic remedies and the avoidance of chemical medicines for prevention or cure.

The members of AHVMA hold different views about virtually every aspect of dog care, from questioning the desirability of giving routine vaccinations and the frequent use of antibiotics and other drugs, to avoiding commercial dog foods. Some homeopathic vets claim that commercial dog food is killing dogs. Others are opposed to any vaccinations on the grounds that they contain chemical agents that cause severe allergic reactions, compromise an animal's immune system and cause emotional imbalance.

The philosophy of health care that you follow for yourself will influence the choices you make for your dog. If you visit a mainstream, Western-trained doctor and have no interest in what are called "alternative" health care modalities (health foods, herbal remedies, chiropractic, acupuncture, osteopathy, etc.) then you will probably follow the same course for your dog. If you gravitate toward organic foods and embrace homeopathic remedies for yourself, then you may be more comfortable with a veterinary practitioner whose training and outlook mirror your own belief.

I tend to follow a traditional approach to medical care (with some chiropractic, acupuncture and Chinese herbs thrown in for good measure—for me *and* my dogs). The majority of pet owners go in the mainstream direction, too, so this chapter is focused in that direction. However, you will find information about alternative veterinary practice at the end of this chapter, beginning on page 401.

However, choosing a vet from one philosophy does not rule out using one from the other philosophy. It is possible to take advantage of theory and practice from both perspectives, if you have the time and flexibility to pursue differing diagnoses and treatments for your dog. Vets of both "persuasions" can be open-minded about "bridging," or making use of other kinds of veterinary care when appropriate. Only you will know whether a combination of the two philosophies is best for you and your dog.

A THIRD KIND OF VET

Vets who make house calls are another category of vet, not in philosophy or training, but in where they do their work. There is even an organization that represents them called the American Association of Housecall Veterinarians (AAHV), which lists their members online at www.athomevet.org but does not have a phone number or address.

◆ The Advantages of a Vet Visit at Home

Convenience The convenience factor is a big selling point for people with multiple pets, children or other factors that make getting out of the house a burden. If the vet comes to your house, it can save you from having to juggle your schedule to make an appointment at a vet clinic, the hassle of getting there and the amount of time lost when you have to endure a long wait. If you work from home or have other obligations there, you lose none of that travel and wait time. Instead, a house-call vet usually gives you an appointment that is within a thirty- to sixty-minute range (allowing for traffic, weather and other calls going overtime) and you can carry on with what you are doing at home until he arrives.

Avoiding trips to the vet If your dog is traumatized by going to the vet, you can eliminate or reduce her visits there. Some dogs have been so frightened in the past—or are so terrified by the odor that other stressed or fearful pets give off in a vet's waiting area—that it is very difficult to help them overcome that terror (see page 288). So although you may still need visits to a vet's office or an animal hospital—as explained below—you are making life easier on yourself and your pet by having routine vet visits at home.

Avoiding sickness You are not exposed to sick pets if you don't go where the sick pets are: the vet's office. No matter how well a vet's offices are cleaned, there is still a chance of contagious dogs passing on their illnesses to others. Avoiding this is especially appealing for dogs whose immune systems are compromised (by illness or age) and those (whom I call the "vaccination rebels," see page 300) who are raising their dogs without immunizing them against diseases or are significantly limiting their use of vaccinations.

◆ Home Vets Can Provide Different Levels of Service.

Not all veterinary issues can be solved in your home, and blood work or other diagnostic services usually need to be done in a medical office, as do many urgent situations. Some home vets work out of their trucks or vans, while others have mobile clinics in which they can even do surgery requiring anesthesia. The chart on page 287 has questions you should ask beforehand so that you have a sense of how much protection and service you can expect.

Questions for a House-call Vet

1. What percentage of your practice is house calls?
2. What days and hours are you available?
3. Do you also practice in a clinic, or are you affiliated with one?
4. What services do you provide at home, and which do you not?
5. How do your clients handle emergency situations?
6. Do you draw blood and handle other diagnostics or lab work?
7. Do you need to see the dog's previous medical records at the visit, or beforehand?
8. Is there anything I need to do before you come?
9. What is your policy on follow-up calls after your visit— do you charge for that time?
10. What are your fees and how do you accept payment?

CHANGES IN VETERINARY EDUCATION

Dog behavior has become an area of expertise for many vets. Animal behavior and misbehavior has become part of the curriculum at many veterinary colleges, and continuing courses for vets also include it. There are specialists in animal behavior to whom other vets refer their difficult cases. We tend to think of vets only as dispensers of medical advice and intervention, but more and more they are being trained in the areas of human-dog interaction. If your dog is behaving badly or you have problems dealing with his behavior, do not bypass your vet as a source of support, advice and referrals.

CHOOSING A VET

A veterinarian always has at least two customers for every patient: the dog and the owner or owners. So when choosing a vet, we need to keep in mind that there are two distinct versions of "bedside manner" to evaluate and two different kinds of communication skills that a vet needs to possess. Do you pick a vet because you feel comfortable, or because *your* dog seems to be at ease? Or should it be a combination of both?

◆ Communication

You need to feel comfortable asking the doctor questions. If you ask a question—perhaps one that is simple or even neurotic—you shouldn't feel that you have annoyed the vet. It's not all that different from choosing a doctor for yourself, or a pediatrician for your children. Do you like the way you interact with them, and do they show their expertise and compassion in a way that is appealing to you?

◆ Convenience

Does the clinic have a location and office hours that generally accommodate your schedule? Will your vet or one of her colleagues ever meet you at the clinic after-hours for an emergency?

◆ **Emergency-care Facilities**

Many small animal hospitals utilize specialized emergency facilities for the needs of their clients outside of normal hours. Although this does not seem as comforting in an emergency as being able to go to a doctor and a staff that know you and your dog, it probably makes the most sense to have a location that is staffed and prepared for whatever may happen to your pet at odd hours. Realistically, there's no way that even a substantial private vet practice could maintain high-quality care during office hours and also provide emergency intervention around the clock. There just wouldn't be enough qualified staff and doctors to do both well. So the question is whether your vet's emergency facility is accessible to where you live. For example, if it is more than an hour from your house, that sounds like a long way to go in the dark with a very sick animal. If there is a closer emergency veterinary hospital, you can get your vet's opinion on whether he thinks it's okay to use it instead.

The First Vet Visit

MAKE AN APPOINTMENT IMMEDIATELY WHEN YOU GET A NEW DOG.

You need to see your vet whether you're adopting a grown dog or getting a new puppy. The doctor should meet your pet without any particular medical agenda. It's important for the vet simply to meet the pooch. You want that first visit to take place when there is no emergency, no serious health issue, not even a routine vaccination. Just a low-key checkup that allows the vet to get a sense of the dog's personality and condition and gives the dog a chance to have a positive experience with the doctor.

◆ **The Vet's Office Should Be a Pleasant Destination for the Dog.**

Your goal is to have a dog who goes to the vet with enthusiasm rather than fear. She should be excited about the interesting smells, new dogs and that tasty biscuit at the end.

YOUR ATTITUDE AT THE VET'S

How you react to the vet's office will influence your dog's experience. Make a point to be upbeat and unconcerned from the moment you go into the office until after you leave. Your relaxed attitude will have a positive effect on your dog and set the tone for future vet visits. This is true whether you have a small puppy who doesn't know enough to be nervous, or you've inherited a dog who becomes frantic and salivates at the first whiff of the vet's office.

◆ **People in the Waiting Room May Be Nervous.**

Dog owners may be afraid of getting bad medical news about their pet—or uncomfortable about what other dogs (or their own) may do while waiting to go in. You may be more anxious than you realize. Be aware that how you interact with your dog will communicate to her not just how you are feeling, but how she should react.

◆ How You Touch and Talk to Your Dog Influences Her Attitude.

Your hands and voice have a lot to do with what your dog's first veterinary experience will be like, and they will influence all the other visits to follow. Your frame of mind translates to the dog in the way you touch her, how you hold the leash, and your voice.

◆ Any Apparent Tension That You May Have Will Confirm a Dog's Anxiety.

Even if you don't really feel it, talk to the pup in a cheery "Isn't this fun?" kind of voice at the vet's office. Make sure that when you pat her, it isn't brisk nervous little pats, but slow soothing ones. You want to give her the impression that everything is fine; treat this as a nice social visit with a treat for her at the end.

◆ Speak in a Low, Calm Pitch, Slow and Steady.

Beware of using a clipped or choppy voice. Think of the way a carriage driver helps to stop his horse by saying "Whoooaaa there." You need to say "Gooood dog," with a similar calming effect. Making this effort can slow you down and make you more mellow, too.

WHAT IF YOUR DOG FREAKS OUT AT THE VET'S?

If your dog has a meltdown the minute you open the door to the vet's office, don't react. Just carry on as if it weren't happening. Dismiss this terrified behavior with a chipper, pleasant response such as, "Oh come on, let's go on in."

◆ Do Not Try to Be Comforting and Reassuring to the Dog.

Don't croon, "Oh no, poor doggy is upset, what can I do?" to a whining, cringing dog. Although it may sound backward to you, showing sympathetic concern to a dog who is panting and trembling gives her the impression that you are worried, too. If your dog is anxious or downright terrified, you will help her by ignoring her. Be affectionate with long, massaging strokes, not the pat-pat-pat kind of touching that can actually arouse a dog rather than calm her.

PUPPIES AND THE VET

◆ Protecting a Puppy's Health at the Vet's

Hospitals for humans are dangerous places for the very young, old and those with compromised immune systems. Hospitals are where sick people go, and their illnesses can spread, no matter how clean or well-run a hospital may be.

As with human hospitals, veterinarians' waiting rooms are notorious places for disease to spread, certainly really contagious ones like kennel cough (for more on this illness, also known as Bordatella, see page 301 in "Vaccinations").

◆ NEVER Let a Small Puppy Down on the Floor at the Vet's.

Don't let him sniff or play with any other dog in there. Puppies are physically vulnerable because their immune systems are not fully up and running yet. It doesn't matter whether people tell you their dog has had vaccinations or is in good health—an adult dog can carry an infectious disease that doesn't affect his strong constitution but could sicken a puppy.

Keep your puppy in your arms in the vet's waiting room. Even if you see another cute puppy, do not put your young dog on the ground. Some of the dogs visiting a vet are obviously sick, and your little baby still doesn't have the immunization to protect him against common dog illnesses.

Once you get into the examining room, put her down on the metal examining table only after it has been disinfected and massage her or play a little, using all aspects of this first visit to give her the feeling that being here is lots of fun.

◆ Inoculations

Puppies must have a series of inoculations and vaccinations to protect their health. They get the first set at age six to seven weeks, and then return every month to get another shot (for a full explanation go to page 297 later in this chapter).

◆ Intestinal Worms in Puppies

Worms in the intestinal tract are normal for dogs, especially puppies. In fact, puppies are normally born with roundworms, which they get from the placenta or directly from their mother's milk. Intestinal parasites are impossible to avoid completely, so the puppy's stool should be checked every time you have an appointment for inoculations. Before each vet visit for puppy shots, prepare a baggie with a stool sample, preferably from that day.

MULTIPLE DOGS AND THE VET VISIT

I always take all my dogs to the vet regardless of which one has the appointment (sometimes to the consternation of other patients). Depending on your canine crew, you may need a saintly vet and attendants, since it does get a little crowded in the examining room and requires extra concentration from the humans. However, I think it makes the sick dog feel a little better because the other dogs keep him company and he doesn't feel so alone. Three lively, large dogs does make the waiting room something of a daunting dash for the other animals and owners who don't quite expect a pack welcome, but it's a good learning experience for everyone and, if nothing else, it takes their mind off why they came in the first place. There is not a significant health risk for adult dogs at the vet's—the danger of getting ill there applies to young puppies who have not been vaccinated (or any very ill dog who has a compromised immune system).

If your dog is vet-frightened, then going as a tagalong can also be a sure way to desensitize him. This was true of my dog Jazzy, who had been in the shelter for more than six months (with who knows what vet experiences) when she came to us. She was reduced to a puddle just by being outside the vet's building. But now she goes in with only minor anxiety after having come away from those tagalong visits with nothing worse than a pat from the vet and a biscuit just for having shown up. The reason this matters is because when she needs veterinary care, she won't have to deal with her own panic on top of whatever medical problem she has.

Going to the vet as a tagalong gives the fearful dog a chance to have a stress-free experience at the vet's office: interesting sights, sounds and smells, plus a crunchy snack on the way out, without so much as a look in their ear from anyone in a white jacket. If you have only one dog and he has this problem, either go along on a friend's vet appointment or just stop in at the vet at random times for a treat.

✦ A Word of Caution about Returning Home from the Vet's

In a multiple-dog household, there can be an odd reentry issue back at home if only one dog has been to the vet's office. This can happen if one dog has stayed at the vet for a procedure like X-rays or surgery and been picked up later. The vetted dog smells different to his buddies back home, whether it's from office smells or chemical odors following procedures. Perhaps this makes the dog's own smell suddenly unfamiliar to his housemates, but be prepared for them to treat each other like strangers. I have been through a few episodes of my dogs circling each other, hackles raised, even some growling, as the "medically tainted" dog returns to the den.

I've found that if the reintroduction takes place outside or in a larger area, there's a better chance of a quick resolution. Try to let the homecoming dog out of the car to reorient herself for a minute so she's on the ground and ready to deal with the possibly tense greeting from her brothers or sisters who seem not to know her.

Getting a Second Opinion from Another Vet

As with human medicine, there are times when another doctor's advice is helpful in determining what course of action to take—and just as with human doctors, it can feel awkward to look for another professional's advice. But in both canine and human medicine, the secure and intelligent doctor will always welcome a colleague's input, because two brains may really be better than one when making a complex diagnosis.

YOUR VET MAY ENCOURAGE A SECOND OPINION.

It may be your vet who suggests that you seek out another opinion. If your vet stays "in the loop" he can run interference, consult with the specialist and be involved in the ongoing decisions. This is the best scenario, because it saves you from awkwardness when broaching the subject with your vet and initiating that second opinion.

Many primary vets believe it is their obligation to notify an owner of the availability of a board-certified specialist, especially if their own diagnosis and treatment have been unsuccessful.

A number of specialized veterinary facilities actually require a referral from a family vet in order for you to make an appointment. This may be good professional politics because the specialized facilities don't want to be perceived as "stealing" or "poaching" from family vets, on whom they depend for referrals. But this referral system is also used because the specialized facilities rarely do routine wellness care or smaller medical matters.

REASONS TO GET A SECOND OPINION

There are several reasons—some of them listed on page 292—that you might seek out a second opinion from another vet about your dog's medical problem.

- ❏ Your dog has a rare condition.
- ❏ You'd like to explore the choice of medical treatments for an illness or injury.
- ❏ The illness/injury requires special expertise or equipment.
- ❏ Diagnosing the dog's condition presents a challenge or is confusing.
- ❏ You'd like to get further information about tests, surgical procedures or the newest medications.
- ❏ You want another opinion about a treatment plan and the expected outcome.

◆ You May Have Lost Confidence in Your Vet.

You may be uncomfortable with how your vet is handling your dog's current medical problem. She may have personal problems or be overwhelmed by her schedule or other problems at work, but whatever the case, your confidence in her may have suffered. It may be that this is the first time you have faced a large medical problem, and now you see your vet in a different light. Perhaps your vet didn't give you choices about how to deal with your pet's illness—yet you feel there must be options. Or the choices your vet suggests don't seem right to you. Your vet may not encourage a dialogue and/or does not seem to listen to your comments or questions about test results and treatments.

◆ Your Vet's Treatment Did Not Work.

If your dog is not getting better you may want to get a second medical viewpoint. If your dog has been sick and his regular vet's plan of action has not been successful, the doctor should be glad for a chance to consult with another doctor to consider alternative treatments.

◆ You May Want to Go to a University Clinic for Specialized Treatment.

All veterinary colleges have clinics and specialists affiliated with the hospital. Your dog's condition may require technologically advanced tests that are available only in a teaching hospital. You may want a doctor with a specialty practice to give an opinion and perhaps perform surgery or other treatments.

KEEPING THE SECOND OPINION SECRET

People often think their vet will be angry that they're seeking another opinion. They don't want to hurt his feelings by saying they want a second look from another vet. But, as noted above, many specialty veterinary facilities will only give appointments based on referrals from regular vets. Your vet will eventually have to know that you're getting a second opinion anyway, because in many cases it is necessary for any consulting vet to get copies of X-rays or other tests or procedures that your vet has already performed on the dog. Not having the dog's records does your dog and the second vet a disservice. The doctor won't have the full medical picture that he needs to form an opinion, and repeating tests is often miserable for the dog, as well as impractical and costly. This is why you should level with your primary vet.

WHERE TO FIND THAT SECOND OPINION

Depending on the severity and rarity of your dog's medical condition, there are several resources for another point of view. You can ask whether your vet has a colleague at his own clinic who might take a look at your dog. You may want to see a different general-practice vet. Or you might need a veterinary specialist, which can mean one in private practice, one who is part of a specialty vet group or a doctor affiliated with one of the veterinary colleges.

You can also use the Internet to get referral names from professional organizations such as the American Veterinary Medical Association (AVMA) (www.avma.org). There is also the American Animal Hospital Association (AAHA) (www.aahanet.org), the American College of Veterinary Internal Medicine (ACVIM) (www.acvim.org) and the American College of Veterinary Surgeons (ACVS) (www.acvs.org).

Pet Health Insurance

I recommend that all dog owners buy pet insurance before they do another thing for their dogs. When you get a new dog, signing her up for insurance is vitally important —and if you don't do it, the day may come when you need serious medical care for her and you'll kick yourself for procrastinating about having insurance to help you. If you already have a dog and don't have him insured, don't wait another minute. Accidents and illnesses happen when we least expect or are least prepared for them, so why tempt fate when having health insurance would make any problem more bearable?

There is a ten-day waiting period after enrolling a dog (so that people can't enroll at the moment they need urgent medical care) and please believe me that you need to live cautiously until those ten days have passed. When I adopted Jazzy, I was feeling secure about her physically because she was a two-year-old picture of health. After a lifetime of purebred dogs with their inherited disorders and weaknesses, I had finally opted for a mixed-breed (she seems to be a cross between a Smooth Collie and some kind of sled dog) and I imagined trouble-free health without the inbreeding problems. However, I am cautious by nature and immediately signed her up for health insurance (I learned my lesson after finding Yogi Bear, the eight-week-old Rottweiler left on the side of the road in a cardboard box, only to discover six months later that he had no hip sockets). So when Jazzy took off after a deer and ruptured her cruciate ligament (which holds the knee together), as bad as I felt for her joint replacement surgery and recuperation, I would have felt a whole lot worse if insurance hadn't picked up most of the $3,500 bill.

◆ **Veterinary Care Is More Expensive than Ever.**
Big health decisions for your dog often ride on the cost of sophisticated medical diagnostic tools. Complicated surgeries that can be performed on dogs have evolved to equal many of the procedures available for people. In fact, the first MRI and CAT scan machines that vets used were the recently outdated models from human hospitals. Until vets had this technology, they could neither diagnose nor treat many animal infirmities without exploratory surgery, as was once true in human medicine.

Both the above tests, as well as ultrasounds and X-rays, are often used to help veterinarians find answers to whatever is ailing your pet. But those are just the *tests*. After those diagnostic tests are done, an operation or medications might be recommended. So the big question is, would having pet insurance make a difference to you if the doctor were to tell you that she wanted to do an MRI on your sick dog—and the charge was going to be $1,000?

If an MRI or CAT scan were suggested to diagnose your child, it's fair to say that your health insurance would cover it—or, if you didn't have the coverage, you would find a way to pay for that test. But how would you feel if the patient was your dog? Would you not do the testing because of the cost? Would you feel frustrated or guilty about that? Or would you pay the bill and kick yourself for not having gotten the insurance? Signing up *today* seems like it might be the best choice.

✦ Are You a Person Who Generally Believes in Carrying Insurance?

You may have insurance for your car, home, belongings, death, disability, etc. Pet insurance may be another important investment you might want to make. Whatever it costs to insure a pet is much less than the amount you will get back if your pet has any kind of significant medical problems or procedures. As with any insurance, if you go through a year with no claims, then consider the premium a good investment in your peace of mind.

✦ Pet Insurance Doesn't Cover Preexisting Conditions.

If your dog has a complicated or expensive medical condition, the insurance company will request all of the dog's prior veterinary records when you make a claim, especially a large one. For example, when Jazzy had her knee surgery so soon after I had added her to my policy, the insurance company understandably wanted to see all of her prior veterinary records. They paid the claim when it was clear that I had just adopted her and that her shelter medical records showed no sign of the leg injury.

✦ There Is a Deductible and an Annual Limit on Claims.

Insurance may not pay one hundred percent of the bill, but it sure beats the alternative. When you are beside yourself with worry because your pet is ailing and you have a huge medical bill on top of it, you will be so grateful for any of the burden that the insurance relieves.

✦ You Pay the Vet, the Reimbursement Comes to You.

One difference between pet and human insurance is that the vet does not have to "belong" to an insurance plan or company, and he does not do any billing on your behalf. The insurers ask you to get their form signed by the vet, with his diagnosis and treatment noted, and attach the doctor's bill (already paid by you). The insurance companies require that you return paperwork to them within a certain number of weeks or months for them to consider the claim, so if you're reasonably organized it shouldn't be a problem.

The other highly positive difference between animal and human doctors is that for now, pet insurers have no impact on the vet's medical decision-making process. Each vet does what he believes is best for every animal without having to worry about an insurance company dictating his choices (as is now often the case in human medicine). There are already forward-thinking vets who are wondering what might happen when the pet insurers get more powerful.

• There is Often a Multiple-pet Discount.

If you have more than one dog and/or cat, you will probably pay a reduced fee for covering all of them. The fee per animal is based on age, with older dogs costing substantially more to insure than younger ones. This is based on an actuarial table that shows more need for medical care as dogs age. I would recommend that you not drop coverage on your older animals just because the premium goes up—maybe you figure that a senior citizen leads a safer, more sedentary life. All it takes is one bout of gastrointestinal upset—with the lab tests, possible X-rays and medication—to pay you back for the premium you paid.

And don't forget the high percentage of older dogs that get cancer (half of those over age ten), which—though some forms can be successfully treated—is hardly cheap. When my dogs have problems beyond the capacity of our regular vet, he refers us to a specialty veterinary hospital that is staffed entirely by subspecialists: vets who have been trained and received further degrees in ophthalmology (eyes), oncology (cancer), etc. I have met pet owners in these waiting rooms who have spent $5,000 to $10,000 on their dog's care because they didn't have insurance. These are regular, working people who can ill afford such enormous bills, but they view their dogs as family members and will pay anything to make them well or keep them alive.

• There is an Additional Premium for Cancer Care.

It is understandable that there is what the insurance companies call a "cancer endorsement," given the terribly high percentage of dogs who get some kind of cancer and the high cost of treating it. You pay this additional premium, and if your pet does get cancer, you get more coverage for diagnosis and treatment.

• Caveat Emptor: Beware a Few Loopholes.

As grateful as I am for the existence of pet insurance companies, they are still insurance companies, and paying reimbursements is not the thing they like to do most. So, at least in the case of VPI, the company that I use, your claim has to be submitted within sixty days or is not valid. They can be very hard to reach by phone, and when they refuse payment on a bill they require a written appeal from you. I have found that if they still refuse reimbursement after an appeal, it's frustrating because you don't get a satisfactory explanation and you really can't reach anyone. But since that's only happened to me once in a dozen claims, I am not complaining so much as pointing out the downside of pet insurance.

• Choices in Insurance Companies

It is prudent to pick a company that has been in business a long time. For names of other companies go to www.thedogbible.com, "Inside the Book."

FINANCIAL AID FOR MEDICAL CARE

What happens if your dog needs costly medical care that you can't afford? Even routine medical bills can be a nightmare for people who have lost their jobs, had serious medical problems of their own or simply don't have the necessary resources.

Well, believe it or not, there are foundations and funds that exist solely to provide financial assistance for pet health-care costs. You may be asked to show proof of income by some of these organizations, and some help only specific breeds.

In addition to the foundations listed below, you can ask your vet if he knows of any such foundations in your area. If you have a purebred dog, you can contact the breed's national club to find out whether it is aware of any funds that can help.

- ☐ Help-a-Pet, P.O. Box 244, Hinsdale IL 60521; (630) 986-9504; www.help-a-pet.org. This organization provides financial assistance to dog owners who cannot afford medical expenses.
- ☐ IMOM (In Memory of Magic), Inc., P.O. Box 282, Cheltenham, MD 20623; (866) 230-2162. This group offers funding for dogs who face death or euthanasia if they don't get immediate care.
- ☐ Labrador for Life, 24507 S. Skagit Hwy., Sedro Woolley, WA 98284; www.labradorlifeline.org. This group helps Labrador Retriever owners or rescuers who need assistance with health-care costs.
- ☐ The Travis Fund, Tufts University School of Medicine, 200 Westboro Rd., North Grafton, MA 05136; (508) 839-7907; www.tufts.edu/vet/gift/p&p.html. This fund aids owners who cannot afford the full cost of the care they receive at Tuft's Foster Hospital.

Vaccinations and the Diseases They Prevent

◆ How Immunity Works

The theory of immunization is the same for dogs as it is for people: a small amount of the disease you want to protect against is injected into a dog, stimulating her body to produce disease fighters called antibodies. Then, if the dog should be exposed to that disease, she will already have the antibodies to fight it off.

Puppies receive antibodies through their mothers' milk. The protection against disease that puppies receive usually lasts for several weeks and gradually fades, although the rate differs greatly from dog to dog. It's important to understand that as long as the mother's antibodies are still working in the puppy's system, it doesn't matter what vaccinations he receives—his own immune system won't produce antibodies. Anything he's exposed to will basically be neutralized.

However, people have misconceptions about their dogs' risk of disease and the importance of puppy shots. For years we have been told that a puppy is at risk of life-threatening diseases if she doesn't receive the full smorgasbord of shots. Now these traditional beliefs are being questioned.

IMPORTANT BULLETIN: In 2003, the American Veterinary Medical Association (AVMA) issued new guidelines to reduce or eliminate some yearly vaccinations. Now it says that unnecessary stimulation of the immune system does not result in enhanced resistance and may be harmful. Their new recommendation is to vaccinate adult dogs no more than every three years. This is a significant departure from the yearly vaccination theory that prevailed for decades. It is particularly interesting because proponents of "alternative" veterinary medicine have been giving this warning for decades. Unfortunately, the only owners who listened to this warning were those who were already proponents of nontraditional medicine.

(On a personal note, when I first adopted from Friends for Pets [the California rescue for Weimaraners], Diane Monahan, who runs it, warned me against giving the dog all her vaccinations simultaneously. I was skeptical of her claim that Weimaraners had become very ill or died from over-vaccination. How could all those vets be wrong? I didn't fully believe her contention that some breeds were more sensitive to vaccines than others until years later, when my third Weim, Scooby Doo, developed swelling and hair loss around the inoculation site. I was lucky that that was the extent of his adverse reaction.)

The AVMA recently divided vaccines into three different categories, based on how frequently they should be administered—if at all. The "core" group (distemper, parvovirus, adenovirus and rabies) are all highly recommended vaccines, but only every three years. Studies show that the vaccines for parvo, distemper and adenovirus last seven years. Rabies, the only one required by law, lasts three years. Other vaccines are divided into "non-core"—those that are optional depending on your dog's individual circumstances—and finally those that are "not recommended."

AVMA Vaccine Recommendations

- Core diseases: Rabies, Parvo, Distemper, Adenovirus-2
- Non-core (optional) vaccinations: Leptospirosis, Bordatella, Parainfluenza and Lyme Disease
- Not recommended: Coronavirus, Giardia, Adenovirus-1
- Not recommended: Bordatella is not effective against "kennel cough" and can also cause the illness.

GENERAL TIMETABLE FOR PUPPY VACCINATIONS

Because there are several infectious diseases that barely even exist anymore, there are vets who give only two vaccines: distemper and parvovirus.

Good spacing of the shots is at eight weeks, the second at eleven or twelve weeks and the third booster at fifteen or sixteen weeks of age. Your vet will guide you in scheduling these immunizations, which is why there can be some differences in when the boosters are given.

Once a puppy has her full set of shots, there are those who say you no longer need an annual booster. However, most progressive vets will give a puppy her first set of shots, then her booster one year later, and after that go to once every three years.

◆ **Why Give Shots Every Few Weeks?**

In most puppies, the maternal immunity fades somewhere between six and sixteen weeks. If you give a vaccine during that time, there's a good chance it will be erased by maternal antibodies while they are still strong in the puppy's system.

The puppy shots are spaced out at four-week intervals so that the puppy will not be unprotected for very long between the time that the maternal immunity fades and the puppy's own antibody protection begins, triggered by those vaccinations. After the puppy has had his shots, it is possible for your vet to do a blood test to check that the puppy's immune system has produced antibodies in response to the vaccines and find out whether he is protected (see "Titer Testing" below).

VACCINE TITER TESTING

◆ **What Is a Titer Test?**

A "titer test" is a blood test that shows the presence and strength (or concentration) of your dog's immunological response to a viral disease such as distemper or parvovirus. The test will also determine how strong your dog's immune system is. If your dog has satisfactory levels of vaccine titers, then he does not need further vaccination against the disease.

The cost of titer testing has been going down as more people recognize the benefits. Laboratory testing ranges from about $50 to $100 for CDV (canine distemper virus) and CPV (canine parvovirus) testing.

Vets who subscribe to the less-is-more theory of shots say that if vaccines are necessary, they must be given separately. If you agree with this thinking, then ask your vet to order "single-valent" vaccines (vaccines that contain only one virus and therefore can confer immunity to only that disease) so he can give your dog one that contains only parvo, for example, and then two weeks later a single-valent dose of distemper.

◆ **There Are Two Kinds of Titers.**

It's important that your vet order vaccine titer testing, not disease titer testing. This is the difference between the two from the laboratory's point of view: if a dog were very sick from an active viral disease when the blood was drawn, then the titer levels in his blood would be very high as his body fought off the disease. The lab would be looking for those high levels and a positive test result. But if they were testing a normal healthy dog for vaccine titer levels, the lab would be looking for the titer levels in the dog's blood at lower levels—which would indicate that the dog's system has a healthy "immune memory" of having been vaccinated in the past and therefore would be able to fight off that illness should he be exposed to it.

Which titers to test? Even though there are dozens of vaccines available, measuring the titers for just two vaccines is considered to provide a reliable picture of your dog's immune system. A test that shows good immunity to CPV and CDV indicates that the dog's immune system is "competent," meaning that it is strong and able to withstand exposure to the disease.

✦ Are Titer Tests Trustworthy?

Blood-titer-level testing has been criticized for being unreliable, but if the blood is tested at an excellent facility the only problem could be a false negative. It used to be that to get a reliable result, the titers had to be processed at the laboratory of a veterinary school with properly validated results, such as Cornell, Michigan State or the University of Colorado. However, there is now a good in-house titer test for the vet's office that is considered reliable: the "TiterCHEK" test kit. A veterinarian has to buy it, but then can get results without waiting for labs. Your vet can draw blood from your dog when you first arrive for the annual checkup and she will have the results in fifteen minutes. If those results show a low titer level, it will indicate that the dog needs a booster vaccination.

✦ What to Do about Low Titer Levels

If your dog's titer levels are low or borderline, your vet may suggest revaccinating and then testing the titers again. Your dog may need that booster shot to stimulate a stronger immune response. However, other doctors believe that if the dog's titer is low it is *not* a sign that you need to vaccinate, that the titer tests only measure the antibodies circulating at the time blood is drawn. These doctors believe that if your dog were exposed to the disease in question, the memory response in the cells would go into high gear and protect him from illness. Scientists are in universal agreement that "memory cells" often hold the bulk of immunity in the body and will often make titer testing totally unreliable. In fact, challenging the animal with the actual disease is the only true way to test whether he has immunity, but this can be a risky proposition, because what if his immunity is not sufficient to ward off the illness? This is why it is probably safest to revaccinate every three years (instead of the previous yearly standard) and why this makes more sense than relying on titer testing.

THE CONTROVERSY ABOUT VACCINATIONS

Although it is now known that vaccinations have historically been overdone, they have nonetheless contributed to an enormous reduction in infectious diseases such as distemper, hepatitis and parvo that used to kill countless dogs. These diseases are now very rare in many locations. It is generally believed that the movement to reduce vaccines to the least possible amount is a positive one, but experts also caution that we must not forget the good that vaccinations can do and the danger of advocating a population of totally unvaccinated dogs.

✦ Over-vaccination Is Generally Believed to Be Unhealthy.

The radical change in medical thinking about vaccinations is that there can be too much of a good thing, and that vaccinating too frequently can cause numerous long-term health problems. This warning is not a news bulletin to those who follow nontraditional health practices. However, questioning routine vaccinations is a big shock to the Western veterinary system, because yearly vaccinations have been considered the standard of care for so long. Cynics will say that yearly vaccinations may not have been necessary, but that there was an obvious financial benefit to the manufacturers of vaccines—with the boon to veterinarians being that they could depend on the revenue of every well-tended dog in their practice getting the full array of shots every year. In fairness, the vets believed they were protecting those dogs from life-threatening diseases—up until their own regulatory body changed its position on vaccinations.

◆ The "Vaccination Rebels"

Many dog owners, breeders, rescue workers and other caretakers in the alternative animal-medical-care movement have always believed that vaccinations do more harm than good in dogs who cannot tolerate the shots. The flaw in this thinking is that there is no way to know which dogs will react poorly until after the vaccine is given. The "vaccination rebels" have taken a stand against all vaccines by citing this problem as well as various other health problems that seem to result from constant vaccinations throughout a dog's life.

Shedding vaccination antigens This is a rather radical theory put forth by vaccination rebels, who are opposed to any puppies being vaccinated but at the same time want the benefits of those vaccines. This group's solution to protecting their unvaccinated puppies is to have them "hang around" with vaccinated pups. They claim that vaccinated puppies shed antigens, and that their unvaccinated puppies can pick up those antigens. Although, scientifically, there is a possibility that vaccinated dogs can confer immunity on other dogs, the problem is that there is no way of knowing which of the unprotected puppies is getting what immunity—or if they are getting any at all.

Protecting unvaccinated puppies The question of how to protect unvaccinated puppies is debated among the vaccine rebels, who support totally isolating the unprotected puppy. Dr. Pitcairn, a holistic vet/author who is opposed to vaccination, suggests that the way to protect these puppies is to keep them safe from contact with the outside world until they are seven months old. Most owners will not have the opportunity to come into contact with a vet who is this much of a rebel, since most vets fall into the traditional or more progressive categories.

A competing holistic viewpoint is that keeping a dog in an isolated environment weakens her entire immune system. These practitioners of unconventional dog care recommend taking your puppy around with you on a limited basis, using your judgment about what seems like a safe, clean environment.

Do not ignore social development. Social development should not be ignored to conform to some unrealistic theory about totally isolating dogs to protect them from disease. Most progressive vets agree that pups should be isolated from the general population until their last vaccinations at sixteen weeks. However, this is an important growth period for young dogs, and they absolutely need as much socialization as possible. A commonsense compromise might be to take the dog out on car rides and to arrange "play dates" with dogs who you know are current on their vaccinations.

◆ Talk to Your Vet in Person about Vaccinations.

Vaccinating is an important enough subject to warrant scheduling an appointment for a discussion about whether your dog would be better off with fewer vaccinations or even none at all. (One exception would be rabies, which is governed by individual state laws.) You and the doctor may want to consider not vaccinating a sick, injured or elderly dog, or one with a chronic health problem, or one with a family history of drug or vaccine sensitivity, or one from a breed known to be at risk for immunological reactions (see chart below). Talk about whether you can vaccinate only for "clinically important" diseases—those that could be a serious threat to your dog, such as parvo and distemper.

If your dog is more than one year old, you can measure his serum antibody titers (see page 298) to determine whether he really needs further vaccinations at any given time. A new trend will probably be to have an annual titer test—rather than annual vaccinations—so that a dog is only immunized against diseases his own body cannot fight.

Dogs Predisposed to Autoimmune Diseases

NOTE: *In addition to the breeds listed, other at-risk dogs are individuals and breeds of white or mostly white dogs—American Eskimo Dogs, Samoyeds, Maltese—and dogs with "coat-color dilution" such as white Shepherds, blue and fawn Dobermans, merle Collies and harlequin Great Danes.*

Akita	Old English Sheepdog
American Cocker Spaniel	Poodles (especially standard)
Dachshund (especially long-haired)	Scottish Terrier
German Shepherd	Shetland Sheepdog
Great Dane	Shih Tzu
Irish Setter	Vizsla
Kerry Blue Terrier	Weimaraner

QUESTIONABLE VACCINES

◆ Bordatella (Kennel Cough) Vaccine

Kennel cough is a highly communicable upper-respiratory disease that is a problem in boarding kennels, training classes, dog runs, veterinarians' offices and especially pet stores. Bordatella is really just a doggie cold, but it is so contagious that it can be spread by an infected dog coughing, sniffing or even breathing near another dog. Bordatella is an airborne infection, the most difficult kind to prevent because a dog can be infectious before he shows symptoms. This illness can go from being an unremarkable "dog cold" to a lower-respiratory disease such as pneumonia, and can even be fatal.

A common symptom of bordatella is that the dog sounds as though something is stuck in her throat. You will know when a dog has kennel cough because she has a deep cough that sounds raspy and painful, like a croupy cough in a child.

Bordatella vaccination is required if your dog gets boarded or plays in dog parks or runs or participates in obedience classes or competitions. However, you might reconsider whether you really need your dog to participate in situations in which they mandate this controversial vaccine, because the irony is that the vaccine does not actually protect against bordatella—and may even harm your dog. So as crazy as it sounds, there are a lot of venues that require this vaccine, even though it is widely acknowledged to be a waste of time and money, besides being another stress on your dog's immune system and something that can put him at risk of getting the illness.

The vaccine is basically useless because kennel cough is caused by a host of bacterial invaders that no single bordatella vaccine would be able to stop. It is a misconception that the vaccination has any protective qualities, because there is no safe way to protect a dog from getting any of the various strains of the illness. Some doctors feel there is a chance that the vaccine can reduce the severity of the illness and possibly limit its spread.

There are two types of vaccine, the injectable and the intranasal, a spray that is put into the dog's nostril. The nasal spray is often blamed by those who believe that the vaccine itself can cause the disease.

Whenever possible, the vaccine that is supposed to protect against kennel cough should be avoided. The first problem is that the vaccine does not work on all viral strains. And the second, more worrisome reason to avoid it is that in some cases the vaccine actually causes the illness. There have been outbreaks of kennel cough in a multi-dog setting (private or commercial) in which only the dogs who had been vaccinated came down with the illness. The likelihood of getting kennel cough from a vaccine is so high that there are even training classes and boarding facilities that will refuse a dog for several weeks *after* a bordatella vaccination, for fear the dog will come down with the virus and pass it on to the other dogs.

Warning: *If you have a vet who gives routine bordatella vaccinations—which used to be done before the bad outcomes became clear—not only should you refuse such vaccinations for your puppy, but you might want to reconsider the vet you have chosen. There are so many good veterinarians out there who stay abreast of changes and developments in their field. Why stay with a doctor who practices outdated medicine that could harm your pet?*

Long-term harmful effects include permanent damage to the dog's immune system, which increases the dog's susceptibility to chronic, debilitating diseases affecting the blood, endocrine organs, joints, skin, central nervous system, liver, kidneys and bowel.

✦ The Lyme Disease Vaccine

Originally developed to protect against the tick-borne Lyme disease, this vaccine has been discredited. The original vaccine actually *gave* some dogs the disease, which has the unfortunate quality of recurring for life, and caused kidney failure in others. This was a "whole-cell" vaccine that, astoundingly, some vets still use.

There is a newer vaccine made with recombinant DNA technology, which is similar to the Lyme vaccine for humans that was taken off the market (because the unfortunate people who were first given the vaccine then developed not just Lyme disease, but arthritis and other serious ailments).

Dogs can still get Lyme disease after vaccination, since it is only seventy-five percent effective—and yet many vets in the Northeast apparently still give Lyme disease vaccine, despite the proven danger.

The risks are substantial, and the gain is questionable, but there are vets giving Lyme vaccine even to little puppies, whose immune systems are even more vulnerable. Any vet who suggests giving the Lyme vaccine to a dog of any age, without explaining all of these risks, may be placing that dog in jeopardy.

High-risk dogs are considered candidates for the vaccine—hunting or tracking dogs, dogs who run free in tick-infested areas like woods or tall grasses—but in my opinion, why risk a fine working dog's health?

Chemical prevention is still the best medicine for Lyme disease—either a Preventic collar or one of the monthly applications.

Your eyes and fingers are the most efficient tick prevention you can get. Hang a firm bristled brush by your back door—or keep it in the car if that's how you take your dogs walking—and give her a brisk brushing from head to tail when you get back to remove any superficial ticks. For the next fifteen or twenty minutes keep an eye on the dog's head and back to see whether any ticks emerge from her coat. Sometime before the end of the day, run your fingers through her hair or over her coat to feel for any ticks that might have survived your earlier investigation.

ADVERSE REACTIONS TO VACCINES

The vaccines that are conventionally given to dogs can cause the same bad reactions as any chemicals, drugs or infectious agents. Reactions can happen immediately or up to forty-eight hours later. Delayed reactions can occur from three to forty-five days after receiving the vaccines. The peak time for an adverse reaction is ten to twenty days.

Symptoms include fever, stiffness, sore joints, polyarthritis (lameness moving from leg to leg), abdominal tenderness, nervous system disorders, susceptibility to infections, blood problems like hemorrhages or bruising, and high fevers.

◆ If Your Dogs Has Had Bad Reactions in the Past

Dogs who have had allergic (anaphylactic) reactions in the past need special care. In fact, the AVMA recommends avoiding revaccination for such dogs because the risk of an anaphylactic reaction is greater than the risk of infection.

◆ Bad Reaction to Rabies Vaccine

Some dogs get a lesion (sore) from a rabies vaccination, usually at the site of the vaccination. This lesion usually appears three to six months after the rabies vaccination. The skin can remain like that for months or even years.

Localized loss of hair at the site of the vaccination has been seen in Poodles, Yorkshire Terriers and Silky Terriers. They may have circular areas of hair loss with the newly exposed skin turning darker. The skin may become thickened and scaly.

Since the rabies vaccine is required by law, you have no choice but to vaccinate your dog. The first thing you can do is to change manufacturers. Find out which company made the vaccine that your dog reacted to and be sure to request that your vet use a different manufacturer next time around. Please go to www.thedogbible.com for information about "Diseases Dogs Can Pass to People."

Warning and Emergency Charts

The following charts cover urgent emergencies and life-threatening situations that require contacting your veterinarian immediately; there is also a chart of warning signs that might help you avoid a bigger medical problem. In a true emergency, a vet will probably recommend that you come in immediately if his facility is open. If it is closed, a doctor may be willing to meet you there. Otherwise, you should go directly to the nearest twenty-four-hour veterinary critical-care facility.

Know where an emergency facility is located and make sure you have good directions (or better yet, do a dry run). You don't need the extra pressure of trying to find the place when you're in the midst of a canine emergency. Make sure that the telephone numbers for the vet and the emergency facility are posted near a phone somewhere in your house and that everyone in the household knows where they are.

The following charts are divided into categories by the kind of medical problem. The "warning" charts indicate symptoms to watch; the "emergency" charts list urgent emergencies that require immediate attention.

If any of the conditions on the warning charts befall your pet, don't hesitate to call your vet during office hours or within a day of noticing the symptoms. These are signs that suggest your pet may have something wrong. Keep an eye on him and follow whatever advice the doctor gives you on the phone. If you have any doubt about whether waiting to call or see the doctor is a good idea, *do not wait*. You're better safe than sorry. However, if you are an overly anxious owner and "cry wolf" too often, you're less likely to get the kind of quick response you need in a real emergency. Therefore, study the charts that follow and make a cool-headed evaluation of the situation before reacting.

SUDDEN CHANGES IN YOUR DOG'S BEHAVIOR ARE THE ONES TO NOTICE.

Report to the vet so he can better evaluate the situation. No one knows your dog the way you do, so it falls on your shoulders to pay attention at all times to any changes in her usual energy, attitude and behavior. If the change is really out of the ordinary for your dog—or is something that makes you frightened or anxious—you might as well skip waiting for the vet to call back, since in a busy veterinary practice that return call might not come until the end of the day. Instead, call and tell the vet's office that you're really concerned, and ask whether they could fit you in as soon as possible so the doctor can see your dog himself and talk to you in person.

The warning signs below mean something *may* be wrong and that you should keep a close watch for further developments. The emergency charts are conditions that require immediate medical attention.

NOTE TO PUPPY OWNERS: *Any of the conditions on the warning list become urgent emergencies if they involve a young puppy, who (like a human baby) has fewer reserves and can go downhill more quickly than an adult or older dog.*

WARNING SIGNS OF PAIN

- Heavy panting
- Labored breathing
- Increased body temperature (see page 315 for normal)
- Loss of appetite
- Lethargy or restlessness

TRAUMA EMERGENCIES

- Hit by vehicle, bicycle, etc. (even if dog seems fine)
- Fight with another animal, especially if wild or unvaccinated
- Any eye injury (no matter how small)
- Head trauma
- Puncture wounds to torso
- Bleeding that cannot be controlled with pressure
- Deep laceration (cut) with bone showing or skin gaping
- Fall from window (car or building)
- Broken tooth or loss of a healthy tooth (put tooth in a jar of milk)
- Porcupine quills embedded anywhere
- Hit by a weapon (bullet, arrow, etc.)
- Shock or burn from chewing on an electrical cord

DIGESTIVE WARNING SIGNS

- No intake of food or water for twenty-four hours
- Diarrhea or vomiting for more than twenty-four hours
- Excessive water intake (without increased activity)
- Dejected/depressed attitude
- Some vomiting (two or three times) without pain or blood
- Sudden weight gain or loss
- Drooling, bad breath
- Loose stool but without blood, bad odor or dark color

DIGESTIVE EMERGENCIES

- Vomiting blood *or*
- Vomiting more than two to three times in one hour *or*
- Attempts to vomit with nothing coming up *or*
- Nonstop choking/coughing/gagging
- Swallowing a toy or other foreign object
- Diarrhea that is foul-smelling or bloody *or*

- Diarrhea more than two to three times in one hour *or*
- Stool that is black or tarry
- Rectal bleeding or protruded rectum
- Unable to have bowel movement despite straining
- Bloat—a distended stomach
- Swollen or painful abdomen
- Ingesting poison or medication overdose

RESPIRATORY EMERGENCIES

- No breathing or severely labored breathing
- Difficulty breathing: blue tongue, gasping, noisy breathing
- No pulse or heartbeat
- Near drowning
- Gums or tongue white or bluish

SKIN-EXPOSURE WARNING SIGNS

- Bumps that are painful, red, oozing or hot to the touch
- Rash/heavy shedding/scratching/chewing at spots
- Nonstop head shaking
- Sudden bruising, red dots on skin
- Nosebleed without trauma
- Scratching at irritated, foul-smelling ears

TOXIC/SKIN EMERGENCIES

- Snake, scorpion or spider bite (or dog bites a toad)
- Multiple bee or wasp stings
- Swelling or hives on face (from stings or other)
- Ingestion of rodent poison or snail bait (bring container or name of product)
- Ingestion of antifreeze
- Ingestion of human medication
- Direct contact with insect poison or spray
- Nonstop violent sneezing

EXPOSURE WARNING SIGNS

- Overheated from jogging/playing in hot weather
- Overheated from too much time in car in sun/heat
- Cold from extended low temperatures in snow/ice/wind

- Moderate itching/odor from body
- Discharge from eye, ear—any orifice

EXPOSURE EMERGENCIES

- Shock or burn from chewed electric cord
- Fire: smoke inhalation or burns
- Heatstroke: heavy panting, extreme weakness, body temp. over 104°F
- Fever over 105°F (normal temperature = 101.5°F)
- Frostbite/hypothermia

NERVOUS SYSTEM/MUSCULAR WARNING SIGNS

- Sudden change in behavior—refuses to play or walk
- Unusual frequency of sleep, lethargy
- Changes to eye(s) or vision
- Crying when touched or picked up
- Sudden limping or lameness for more than twenty-four hours
- Shallow breathing, rapid breathing without exertion

NERVOUS SYSTEM/MUSCULAR EMERGENCIES

- Seizures
- Tremors
- Sudden blindness
- Eyes moving rapidly from side to side
- Ambulatory problems (staggering, tilted head, going in circles)
- Dragging hind end, unable to use back legs
- Extreme lethargy or depression
- Collapse, loss of consciousness
- Severe pain that causes whimpering or crying
- Sudden inability to use one or more limbs
- Biting at imaginary objects
- Prolonged, repeated tail chasing (symptom of serious seizure disorder)

URINARY/REPRODUCTIVE EMERGENCIES

- Crying while trying to urinate
- Slight or no urine output
- Bleeding from genital area
- Swollen testicles or scrotum

911 Dog Emergencies

Just thinking about what you'd do for your dog in a life-threatening emergency is enough to make most people hyperventilate! With a bit of luck, you'll never have to practice any of these techniques, but it's not a bad idea to read about them and plant the information in the back of your brain. Simply dealing with *the idea* of a life-threatening emergency for your pet can be stressful, but practicing a few maneuvers in your head will make it so much easier if you should ever face any of these situations.

GENERAL TIPS ABOUT EMERGENCIES

◆ Keep Your Wits about You.

In an emergency situation, remember to keep breathing so that your brain has good fuel to think clearly and make good decisions. Whatever happens is not going to be a test of your competence. Anything you're able to do will be much better than that done by someone who panics in a crisis. For anyone in any kind of emergency, it isn't about executing procedures in textbook fashion, it's about keeping your cool, having enough information to evaluate a situation and doing your best until you can get professional help.

◆ Call Your Veterinarian After Any Emergency.

No matter what the outcome, it's important to get in touch with your vet, because any serious medical event, especially one requiring emergency first aid, may have further repercussions that a trained medical professional should evaluate. The emergency may have done more harm than you are able to determine, or it may have been a symptom of an underlying medical problem that needs addressing. It's great to be able to be there in your dog's hour of need, but don't underestimate what the dog's doctor may determine afterward.

◆ Do Not Medicate a Dog Internally or Externally.

Do not make any medical decisions or take action without speaking to or seeing your vet first. For example, do not even put hydrogen peroxide or ointment on a wound—it can make matters worse, depending on circumstances.

◆ Nothing Can Take the Place of Professional Veterinary Care.

This section is intended to walk you through stabilizing the dog sufficiently to be able to safely transport him to the vet. I'm not saying this because of legal concerns. I'm saying it because if you care about your dog as a family member, then you owe it to him to have a professional give him a clean bill of health after a serious medical event.

PET FIRST AID

Pet CPR and other first-aid courses may be offered by your local American Red Cross—look up the numbers for your area. The pet courses are modeled after Red Cross programs for people, and teach the basics of pet emergency with remedies for poisoning, fights and choking, using dog and cat mannequins.

The first two sections that follow deal with handling life-threatening emergencies where the dog's breathing or heartbeat are in jeopardy. The third section is an alphabetical list of common emergencies and what to do until the pet is seen by a vet.

THE ABCS OF EMERGENCY CARE

"A" equals Airway. "B" equals Breathing. "C" equals Circulation. Just as in human medical emergencies, you have to stay focused on the victim's ability to breathe before you deal with anything else. If your dog has been hit by a car and you are focused on splinting his smashed leg—but you don't give your first attention to "A," opening and protecting his airway—he could die from lack of oxygen.

If you have learned CPR for people, you will recognize many of the steps in animal CPR. The truth is that CPR for dogs is rarely effective when done at home, but if you're far from medical help, it's all you've got.

So here's a run-through of what to do in a canine emergency:

◆ Scene Safety

1. Despite the desire to dive right in to help, you *must* make sure that whatever traumatic event happened to your dog does not still pose a threat to you.

2. That means to look before you leap: a vicious dog, fast traffic, deep water, electric power lines down—whatever the case may be.

3. If necessary, get additional help before going forward, or there may be two victims instead of one.

◆ Airway

The question of whether the dog's airway is open has to be asked if the dog is unconscious. The ways to find out are the same with dogs and people:

1. *Look*—Can you see her chest rise, or breath going in or out of her nose or lips?

2. *Listen*—Can you hear any air going in and out of her nose or mouth?

3. *Feel*—Get near her mouth and nose to feel if there's any breathing going on, or put your hand on her chest to see whether you can feel anything that way.

4. If she is panting, crying, barking, making any sort of noise or you can hear her breathing, then the answer is "Yes!" to that vital question of whether her airway is open.

5. If there is no air exchange going on, that means the dog's airway is blocked and you have to clear it.

A Very Important Warning: *Even the nicest dog can bite without warning if she has been hit by a car or is otherwise in pain or shock. If a dog is conscious but panicked or is having a seizure, do not put your fingers in or near her mouth, or you might get bitten. Remember that dogs in pain or fear or having seizures may bite defensively.*

Clearing a Blocked Airway

1. Lay the dog on his side.

2. Gently tilt his head back slightly, extending it so that his throat is in a straight line. Try to catch hold of his tongue and pull it out between his front teeth so that it can't block his throat.

3. Using a sweep of your finger, try to remove any vomit or objects in his mouth that could be blocking the airway.

◆ Breathing

If you can't tell whether he's breathing or not, hold a tissue or cotton ball near his nostrils and see if it moves. Or, if you have a mirror, hold that under his nose and see if it fogs up.

If he is breathing Let him stay in whatever position is comfortable for him. Notice if there are any unusual gasping, gurgling or rattling breathing sounds, and make sure to tell the vet later.

If he is not breathing: begin CPR.
Warning: *Do not attempt CPR on a conscious dog.*

1. Reposition the neck in a straight line to open the airway.

2. Begin rescue breathing (this is like CPR for humans).

3. Seal the mouth by gently holding the lips and mouth together and put your mouth over the dog's nose.

4. Exhale as though you were blowing up a balloon.

5. If air will not go in, recheck the airway by straightening the head and neck and try again.

6. If air does go in this time, give the dog four or five breaths, then watch a moment and see if he breathes on his own.

7. Check circulation (see page 311) to be sure the dog's heart is beating. There's no point in blowing oxygen in if his heart isn't beating to circulate it.

If he does not start breathing: continue CPR. If the dog does not start breathing or only takes shallow breaths after you began rescue breathing, continue rescue breathing.

Continue to breathe for him until he starts breathing on his own, a vet comes to your aid or you have given twenty minutes of artificial respiration.

- ◆ **Circulation**
  1. You need the dog's heart to be beating to circulate oxygen in the bloodstream.

  2. Check the dog's heartbeat and pulse by putting your hand (or stethoscope, if you have one) on the dog's chest wall where his left elbow touches his chest.

  3. Feel for a pulse with a light touch of your middle and first fingers high up on the inner thigh where it meets the body. If you cannot feel it there, try the underside of the ankle (front or rear paw) just above the heel pad.

  4. If you can't find a heartbeat or pulse, you need to begin CPR.

  5. Turn the dog over if necessary so he's lying on his right side, with the left side of the chest facing up.

CPR FOR DOGS UNDER THIRTY POUNDS

- ❏ Kneel facing the dog's chest.
- ❏ Place one hand on top of the dog's ribs behind his elbow.
- ❏ Place the other hand underneath the ribs, behind the elbow.
- ❏ Press the two hands together, compressing the chest one-half to one inch.
- ❏ Combine with rescue breathing—five compressions for each breath, and try to keep going at as fast a pace as you can tolerate.

CPR FOR DOGS THIRTY TO NINETY POUNDS

- ❏ Kneel facing the dog's back.
- ❏ Extend your arms straight with one hand resting on top of the other (as in human CPR), and lock your elbows straight.
- ❏ Now place your joined hands, with the palm down, where the dog's left elbow would touch his ribs if he were standing.
- ❏ Compress the chest about one to three inches in, depending on the dog's size.
- ❏ Combine compressions with rescue breathing. Do five compressions for each breath, then recheck the pulse to see if it has returned.

CPR FOR DOGS OVER NINETY POUNDS

- ❏ Follow the same rules as for the previous weight with one exception: do ten compressions for each breath, then recheck the pulse.

CPR FOR A DROWNING VICTIM

1. If there is any chance of spinal injury (from trauma or a fall associated with the drowning), try to keep the dog's back and neck in a straight line, using a surfboard or other flat board, if possible, to move him.

2. If the dog is limp, unconscious and unresponsive, wrap him in a towel or blanket to preserve his body temperature.

3. If the dog is breathing, transport him immediately to an emergency veterinary facility.

4. If the dog is NOT BREATHING, you must initiate CPR, first attempting to remove water from his lungs. Lay the dog flat on his right side (so that you'll be able to feel for a heartbeat on the left side) and compress the side of his chest several times with your palms flat, one on top of the other. If any water comes out, that's good—if he starts breathing, that's even better. Transport immediately as above.

5. Feel for a heartbeat just behind his left elbow. If there is a heartbeat but he is still not breathing, check the back of his throat for obstruction (follow directions in " Clearing a Blocked Airway," page 310).

6. If there is no obstruction, you will breathe for the dog: Close his muzzle by placing your hand firmly around it (put his tongue inside his mouth so he doesn't bite it) and blow into the dog's nose. The larger the dog, the more forceful the blow. Watch to see if his chest rises (or ask someone else to watch) when you blow. Give him fifteen breaths, then two quick chest compressions, then check again just behind his left elbow for his heartbeat to return. Continue until his heartbeat returns, he regains consciousness and he begins breathing again. If someone else can drive and you can continue CPR in the back of a closed truck or station wagon (without any jeopardy to yourself), you can get to professional assistance that much sooner.

Choking

If the dog is conscious and you can open her mouth, look for what may be blocking her airway. If the obstruction is not visible, proceed with the Heimlich. If you can see the object and there is someone available to help you, one person should hold her mouth open (preferably the person the dog knows best) while the other person removes the object.

It would probably be a good idea to practice these maneuvers with your dog so that you feel comfortable and confident about how to line yourself up and where to put your fist in the dog's sternum area. What could be worse than having a dog struggling for breath as you realize the instructions make no sense to you? Figure it out ahead of time, and hope you'll never need to do it. However, be sure you practice *without* doing the actual in-and-up thrust with your fist, which can make a dog vomit.

NOTE: *These instructions sound easier than I imagine they would be in real life. Who knows if a choking (panicky) dog would submit to your initial efforts to lay her down? Having never done a Heimlich on a dog myself, I have no way to know for sure.*

THE HEIMLICH MANEUVER

◆ The Heimlich for a Small Dog

1. Lay the dog on her side on a flat, hard surface. If at all possible, have her head lower than her butt, which you could do by putting her on any kind of board and slanting it.

2. Place one hand in a fist underneath the middle of the dog, just below the sternum (breastbone). Feel for where the ribs come together at the breastbone—just as you would for a person—and nestle your fist in there. If your dog is really tiny, use your knuckles.

3. Place your other hand against her back. Think of this as sort of sandwiching the dog's midsection between your hands.

4. Press in and up toward her face with the lower hand. As with a person, you are basically trying to force air back up the esophagus to eject the stuck object.

5. If the object pops out, great. If not, be prepared for the dog to drop down unconscious. Do not think your dog is dead. Blacking out is the body's natural response to choking on a foreign object that cuts off the air supply. The same thing happens to people who are choking.

◆ The Heimlich for a Large Dog

1. Kneel beside the dog, facing his flank. Depending on your dog's height, you might want to bend over him and wrap your arms around him instead of kneeling. If he's really tall, you won't have good leverage from the ground.

2. Feel underneath him in the center of his abdomen for his breastbone—the hollow place where the rib cage comes together in the middle. Place one hand in a fist in that hollow and wrap your other hand around it to give you the power to thrust in and up toward the dog's head.

3. Keep thrusting short, strong jabs inward until the dog coughs out the obstruction or becomes unconscious. As above, unconsciousness is the body's natural reaction to the air supply being cut off. This does not mean that your dog has died—but it does mean you must keep on vigorously trying to clear his airway.

Once the dog is down and unconscious The next steps are the same for any size dog—and almost identical to the Heimlich and CPR for people:

1. Lay the dog on his side.

2. Open his airway by positioning his head so that his windpipe is open—there should be a straight line up the underside of his throat to his mouth.

3. Do two Heimlich thrusts with your fist pressed up into the sternum.

4. Use your fingers to check his mouth for any object that may have been expelled.

5. Give two rescue breaths (see CPR, page 310). If the breaths do not go in, continue the Heimlich.

6. Reposition the head to be sure the airway remains in a straight line and is open.

7. Do two more thrusts. Repeat checking the mouth, giving two rescue breaths, giving two thrusts, checking the mouth.

8. Check the pulse (see CPR page 311) every few sequences.

9. Continue until object is expelled and dog breathes on his own.

Checklist for Medical Emergencies

If you telephone the vet about an emergency, she may ask for information about your dog's condition. Before you place that call, try to have answers to the questions on the checklist below:

HEART (PULSE) RATE
☐ Normal for a puppy up to one year is 120 to 160 beats per minute (bpm).
☐ Normal for an adult thirty pounds or less is 100 to 160 bpm.
☐ Normal for an adult more than thirty pounds is 60 to 100 bpm.

To get the pulse rate, feel with a light touch of your middle and first fingers high up on the inner thigh, where it meets the body. If you cannot feel it there, try the underside of the ankle (front or rear paw) just above the heel pad. Watch a second hand and count the beats for fifteen seconds. Then multiply by four (sixty seconds) and that is your dog's heart rate.

RESPIRATION RATE
Normal for adults is ten to thirty breaths per minute.

Use the second hand on a watch to count how often the dog's ribs rise and fall for fifteen seconds, then multiply by four for the respiration rate. This can be hard to get if the dog is panting hard from heatstroke, anxiety, overexertion, thirst, etc.

TEMPERATURE

A dog's normal temperature is 101.5°F. The normal range is 100.2°F to 102.8°F.

Anything above 104°F is a fever; anything below ninety-nine degrees is also a sign of illness.

◆ Taking Your Dog's Temperature

One of the first steps in finding out whether your dog is sick is to take her temperature, because this is often the first sign of illness. If you call your vet about your dog's condition, it is also usually one of the first questions she will ask you: "Is the dog running a temperature?" You'll need a rectal thermometer to take the dog's temperature—buy one and keep it with the dog's equipment. You'll also need a small jar or tube of Vaseline-type lubricating jelly.

How to take her temperature Have someone else hold the dog's head and scratch her neck or ears quite hard to distract her from the other end of her body. Shake down the rectal thermometer to ninety-six degrees or below. Dip the end of the thermometer into the lubricating jelly and then insert the end of the thermometer into her rectum about an inch. Hold her lightly under the stomach to keep her from scooting away, and have the person at her head scratch her neck to distract her. Leave it in for three minutes (which will seem like an eternity to all of you!). When you remove the thermometer wipe the bulb end gently by running it through a paper towel or tissue—avoid contact with your fingers, since their heat might influence the thermometer. Once you've wiped it, hold it up until you can see the temperature reading.

COLOR OF THE GUMS

Pink is normal and shows good circulation. Abnormal colors of the mucous membrane are blue, brown, yellow, dark red, very pale or nearly white.

◆ Capillary Refill Time (CRT, or "Cap Refill")

What you want to check is your dog's circulation, which you can do by pressing a forefinger on the gums above your dog's upper teeth. The speed at which the blood returns to an area that you've pressed gives an indication of the dog's circulation and how well his body is *perfusing* (circulating oxygen). Press the gums, which will normally go pale where you press. When you release your finger, the color should return within two seconds. If cap refill takes longer than two seconds, be sure to tell the vet.

◆ Does a Dry Nose Mean Illness?

It is nothing more than an old wive's tale that a dog with a dry nose is not well. A dry nose actually means the dog is quiet, doing nothing. Of course, it's possible that the dog is inactive because she's not well, or she could just be tired and sleeping. Feel your dog's nose while she's sleeping or right after she wakes up—it should be dry. If your dog's nose is always dry, there might be a problem—which could be any condition that makes her inactive or dehydrated. Take her to the vet to be evaluated.

A CANINE FIRST-AID KIT

The first-aid kits sold for canine emergencies are not a good investment. The couple of necessary ingredients they contain are items you should have anyway. And some of the kits contain items that you should not even be using on your dog without the advice of a medical professional—things such as hydrocortisone cream and antibiotic ointment. Many of these kits are filled with items that seem absurd—who would put on sterile gloves to treat his own dog?—and a full bottle of iodine, which you should never put on a dog's wound.

✦ Contents of the First-aid Kit

There are a few basic emergency supplies for medical situations that you should keep in a plastic bin or a big zippered plastic bag. These items are not designed to replace a visit to your vet, nor should you attempt any medical intervention without your veterinarian's advice or approval, other than taking your dog's temperature (to report to the vet when you call her about whatever is worrying you).

One item that may not be familiar to you or your vet is Diarsanyl, an excellent stomach-soothing paste made from French clay that has been used for years in Europe for dogs, horses and cows. It is now available without prescription, but only from vets (who can get it from the medical supplier Phoenix Pharmaceuticals). It is excellent to have on hand for a dog going through cancer treatments that are affecting her stomach, to restore the natural balance of the gut after antibiotics or for dogs with delicate stomachs or who have thrown up because of intestinal irritation.

🦴 *Fido's Medicine Cabinet*

- Rectal thermometer
- Petroleum jelly (for lubricating the thermometer)
- Hydrogen peroxide (to wash out wounds)
- Scissors for animal hair (with rounded tips to cut hair from hot spots/wounds)
- Gauze pads (for wounds) and tape (to hold the gauze in place until you get to the vet)
- Ecotrin (or generic) coated aspirin (for pain or fever)
- Benadryl (or generic) antihistamine (for insect bites, allergic reactions, itching)
- Aloe gel (to soothe irritated skin)
- Kwik Stop powder (or cornstarch) (for bleeding nail/faulty pedicure by owner!)
- Pepcid AC (for upset stomach, rumbling)
- Pepto-Bismol tablets (for diarrhea or upset stomach; some vets don't like this)
- Diarsanyl (for stomach soothing and rebalancing)

The reason you need to have these items at home is because there are times when an immediate remedy for a situation (such as a bug bite that is causing swelling or hives or itching) can avert a potentially serious medical problem. However, this does not mean you should bypass the vet and self-prescribe in a medical situation. Some vets will talk to you on the phone and work with you to resolve a problem without coming into the clinic, but in many situations the vet needs to see the dog himself.

◆ Hiking/Traveling First-aid Kit

For hikers, campers and hunters who might be far from facilities when their dogs get hurt, there is more reason for a canine first-aid kit. The Hiker First-Aid Kit, which costs less than $40, can be worn on your belt. To order, call (888) RUFF-WEAR or visit their Web site, www.ruffwear.com.

Emergencies

The six emergencies listed below require immediate attention from you before you can even transport the dog to professional help.

- ❐ BLEEDING: Put direct pressure on blood vessels near the wound. Elevate the wounded area if possible. Wrap the area with a clean towel and tape around it, but not so tightly as to cut off circulation. Avoid tourniquets—they are too dangerous, since cutting off the blood supply often leads to amputation.
- ❐ BACK INJURY: In cases of trauma, protect the spinal column to avoid paralysis and other possibly devastating consequences. Always check the ABCs first. If the dog is not breathing or his pulse is weak, deal with that first, remembering to protect the spinal column by shifting the dog with the spine always in alignment. Move the dog minimally by sliding him onto a board (if the dog is small, a cutting board or tray from the kitchen can be used; if medium, a boogie board or snowboard will work; if large, plywood or anything board-shaped around your home, such as an ironing board, a surfboard or a shelf from bookshelves will do). Secure him on the board by covering him with a towel or sheet and then taping around it onto the board to keep his spinal column secure during transport.
- ❐ BROKEN BONES (FRACTURES): Don't try to do anything fancy yourself—just get to the vet, keeping the dog as calm and warm as possible. Put the dog in a carrier or move him with blankets into the car.
- ❐ DROWNING: Hold the dog upside down with your arms around his lower abdomen and gently sway him for thirty seconds to force the water out. Perform CPR if necessary.
- ❐ FROSTBITE: Do not rub. Apply warm but NOT HOT water (105°F to 108°F) for fifteen minutes. Cover loosely and transport to vet.
- ❐ BEE STING: In some dogs, as with people, a bee sting or spider bite can cause a life-threatening allergic reaction. If you can see the stinger, scrape it off with the edge of a credit card or some other thin edge (do not use tweezers, which can release more toxin). If your dog has broken out in hives from the sting and/or his face, tongue or lips are

swollen, you need to get right to the vet, who can give an injection of epinephrine if the reaction is serious. Most vets want you to administer Benadryl before coming in, but check with your doctor.

HOW TO GIVE A PILL

Because there are several emergency situations that require giving your dog a pill, here's the easiest way: take the most delicious food you have available (cheese, meat, peanut butter) and use it to make a ball all around the pill. Your dog will pop it right down the hatch! No need for prying open jaws or sticking your finger down the dog's throat—only to have him spit the pill out anyway.

Everyday Dangers to Dogs

ACETAMINOPHEN (TYLENOL)

The active ingredient in Tylenol is acetaminophen, which can be a deadly poison for dogs if over-ingested. Large doses of acetaminophen can lead to liver damage, including liver failure. People are often told that this drug can be fatal to cats in very small doses but that dogs can tolerate small doses. However, this does not take into account dogs who get into bottles of Tylenol that are not properly stored or get into Tylenol that is in the trash. Make sure there is no way your dog has access to Tylenol in your house.

ALCOHOLIC DRINKS

Believe it or not, dogs do manage to drink liquor—usually because glasses with liquor still in them have been left on coffee tables. If the drinks are especially sweet or creamy (like Baileys or eggnog) it makes them more attractive to a dog. Alcohol itself isn't really toxic (unless ingested in large quantities), but it takes relatively little to get a dog drunk, and this can cause problems for very young or old dogs.

ANTIFREEZE

Antifreeze can leak out of a car or truck at your home onto a hard surface, or it can be found on city streets under cars and in the gutter. It is a bright green liquid that is sweet and attractive to dogs—and it can also kill them. If you suspect that your dog has licked antifreeze, get to a vet immediately.

APPLE, APRICOT AND CHERRY STEMS, LEAVES, SEEDS AND PITS

The stems, leaves and seeds (or pits) of apples, apricots and cherries can cause vomiting and are potentially lethal if ingested in sufficient quantities.

BLOAT

Bloat is a condition brought on by eating quickly—especially a large amount—combined with exercise, excitement and/or excessive water drinking. Other causes of bloat that cannot be controlled are an abnormal spleen, poor stomach motility and just bad luck. The risk is greatest for deep-chested dogs such as German Shepherds, Poodles and especially Great Danes (there are even owners who opt for a precautionary operation to surgically affix the internal abdominal wall and the stomach of young Great Danes). Bloat worsens very quickly and requires immediate action—a dog needs emergency surgery to save her life.

◆ **Symptoms of Bloat**

Distended abdomen (swollen so tight that it sounds like an air-filled drum if you tap it with your finger); *abdominal pain* (a worried expression on the dog's face; he may look at his sides); *retching or vomiting without bringing anything up; or sudden, severe weakness (and signs of shock).*

BONES

Chewing bones can kill a dog, or sometimes "just" cause them great pain and require emergency surgery if the esophagus or intestine is punctured. All bones except marrow bones can splinter into knife-like pieces that can get stuck in the intestinal tract, cut it or even perforate it, causing life-threatening peritonitis. (See Chapter Thirteen, "Nutrition").

CANDY, NUTS

Don't leave a dish of candy or nuts out on a low table. Although human treats are not life-threatening, if a small dog ingests a whole bunch he may get an upset stomach, which is misery for him and a mess for you to clean up.

CAR/SUV

Jumping in and out of the high back of an SUV or truck can damage a large dog's spine or legs over time. The larger the dog, the heavier the landing, and there is substantial concussion on the bones and joints of the front end. Either devise a way for a softer landing—perhaps by teaching your dog to wait and then partially lifting him to the ground to soften his landing—or get a Twistep (see page 192) or a similar ramp or step and teach the dog to use it to get both in and out of the vehicle.

CHASE/PREY INSTINCT

Dogs who chase have to be protected from themselves. A dog with a strong drive to catch prey will do so without regard for his own safety. You need to have a leash on such a dog in any situation where there is something that the dog can potentially chase. Dogs who are generally cautious about streets and cars will chase a squirrel right into traffic; they will run right off the edge of a cliff, off a balcony and into raging water when they are running after prey, or even a ball. Ledges, embankments, rough seas, high decks and patios are all places that pose danger.

CHEWING TREATS: RAWHIDE, COW'S HOOVES, PIG'S EARS

(For more on all these, see "Treats" in Chapter Thirteen, "Nutrition").

Warning #1: There have been reports of salmonella found on imported beef and pork-derived products such as rawhide chews and smoked pig hooves, skins and ears. Although it is often not such a danger to dogs, the salmonella bug is a common cause of serious gastrointestinal infection in people. Younger children might be at most risk for infection because they are frequently on the floor and in closer contact with the dog and the chews. Until recently there was no known link among people, dog chews and salmonella. However, in tests done in England, salmonella was found to have survived the processing of rawhide chews from China and Thailand. You should keep these treats out of children's hands and wash your own hands thoroughly in hot water after handling any of these products.

Warning #2: You should only give chews when you will be around. It's important to keep an eye on the dog's demolition progress to make sure it goes smoothly.

✦ Rawhide

Most dog owners purchase tons of rawhide in various forms because it seems like the best treat to keep a dog happily chewing. But the risks are that rawhide can get stuck in the dog's throat and cause choking, or can irritate the throat on the way down. If your dog swallows a large piece, the rawhide can cause an obstruction once it hits the stomach or intestinal tract. (For more information, see page 460 in Chapter Thirteen, "Nutrition.")

✦ Cow's Hooves

Hooves are more dangerous than rawhide; they are hard enough to break a dog's tooth. Like bones, hooves can break off into sharp splinters and cause partial intestinal blockage. These obstructions are difficult to diagnose—until the sharp edges of a hoof fragment press against the bowel wall and threaten to puncture it. If the bowel is perforated, there is always the risk that the infection that follows—from the leaking intestinal contents—can be fatal.

✦ Pig's Ears

If a dog eats too much of these rich, fatty treats, they can upset his stomach. I avoid them for my dogs since the ear has no long-lasting chewing value: a dog can crunch down a pig's ear in a flash. (Also, for selfish reasons, I'm a little squeamish about the hairs that are often still on the ears—it's hard not to think of Wilbur in *Charlotte's Web*.)

CHOCOLATE

Most people have heard that chocolate can kill dogs. You've probably heard that if your dog accidentally ingests some, you should speed her to an emergency hospital and/or stand watch over her for signs of shock. This is probably a more dramatic scenario than the average household chocolate product would require.

The danger of chocolate depends on what kind of chocolate is consumed and how much. The most toxic kind of chocolate is baker's, which is pure unsweetened chocolate or cocoa powder. High-quality gourmet baked goods and chocolate candies may be higher-risk because they may be made of dark chocolate or baker's chocolate. However, when milk or other ingredients are added to chocolate, it becomes less dangerous. The toxic ingredient in chocolate is called *theobromine,* a substance that is similar to caffeine.

◆ Toxic Amounts for Dogs

For milk chocolate, one ounce per pound of body weight is toxic. For pure dark chocolate like baker's chocolate, it only takes a tenth of an ounce per pound of an animal's body weight to cause a health hazard.

◆ Serious Symptoms

If your dog has ingested a toxic amount of chocolate, you can expect the reactions to be vomiting, rapid and/or irregular heartbeat, agitation, heavy panting and muscle tremors. Death is possible in rare cases.

If you have a small dog who accidentally eats a large quantity of chocolate (versus a large dog who eats a small amount), you should contact your vet to ask his opinion. Even if you know what kind of chocolate it was and can estimate that your dog did not eat much, you still might want to place a call to your vet's office. Let your doctor or the doctor on duty decide whether an in-person visit or, if it is after hours, a trip to an animal emergency facility is necessary. Otherwise, he may tell you to keep a close eye on the dog for signs of an adverse reaction—particularly convulsions.

While there actually isn't much real cocoa in many chocolate products—milk chocolate and "chocolate-flavored" products pose little threat—chocolate is still not good for dogs because food containing chocolate is usually high in fat, which is dangerous for dogs (see "Fatty Foods," page 323).

CHRISTMAS TREES

Everything about Christmas trees holds potential danger for dogs, although the ones most at risk are generally puppies, whose curiosity drives them to try to put everything in their mouths. The ornaments on the bottom branches are within their reach, as are the branches themselves. There is really no way to remove all the lower branches—it would ruin the look of the tree, and the puppy could probably still reach the ornaments from the next level of branches. Puppies grab for glass ornaments, which break in their mouths or on the ground, where they can step on the sharp pieces. They will definitely help themselves to candy canes or any other edible decorations. They can bite down on a light cord and get shocked or cause a fire. If there is tinsel on the branches, they can swallow it and have it tangle up in their mouths or throats.

The biggest problem is that the tree itself could come crashing down on the puppy or dog if she tries to pull something off a branch. If she gets a grip on an ornament that does *not* come loose, she'll pull the whole branch with it—and the tree will follow.

Spraying the tree with one of the bitter-tasting products is only a halfway measure, since the pup will grab hold and bite down or pull before he tastes the bitterness.

There are only two sure ways to make the tree safe: put it behind a baby/puppy gate, or put it in a room that is off-limits to the dog.

CIGARETTES

If you smoke, or allow others to smoke around your dog, you are endangering the dog's health. Secondhand smoke contains more than 4,000 substances, of which forty are known to cause cancer in people and animals. Pets can develop respiratory infections, lung inflammation and asthma from breathing in the smoke around them. Puppies, older dogs and dogs with illnesses or other physical weaknesses have an even higher risk of developing certain kinds of cancer.

◆ **Cigarette "Replacement" Products**
Be especially careful with nicotine patches and gum. They need to be kept out of reach of dogs both before and after use, because they are attractive to dogs and can lead to poisoning.

CLEANING PRODUCTS

(See "Indoor Air Quality" on page 325.)
There are household products that can be dangerous for your dog, especially any that are used on the floor, right at a dog's nose level. Closely follow directions on the use of any such product. Some examples you might not consider are fabric softeners, room deodorizers, spray propellants and dry-cleaned fabrics.

The levels of possible hazard are listed on every household product from most to least toxic: "Danger," "Warning," "Caution" or no signal word at all. Try to find non-pesticide household products that are marked with the warning word "caution," which signifies the lowest level of toxicity.

COCOA MULCH

This is a peat moss/shavings type product that is sold at many nurseries and used by many landscapers to cover planting beds or around planted shrubs and trees. It is lethal to dogs (and cats). Because it smells like chocolate, especially when damp, it attracts dogs, who eat it. Theobromine—the same ingredient used to make all chocolate, but especially dark or baker's chocolate—is what kills them.

COLD

Dogs with thin coats who were bred for warm climates cannot tolerate the cold (see page 182 in Chapter Eight, "Everyday Life with Your Dog"). Many dogs should be protected from the discomfort of being cold, and in some cases from actual hypothermia.

COLLARS

A dog with a loose nylon collar can get caught and strangle, while a choke chain can hurt the dog wearing it, as well as the one playing with him. (See page 266 for more on collars).

DAIRY PRODUCTS

Dairy products (milk, cream, cheese) are not really dangerous to most dogs, but are hard for them to digest because they lack the enzyme necessary to digest the lactose in the milk. Just as with lactose-intolerant people, dairy products can cause intestinal gas and diarrhea in some dogs. (Because my dogs adore milk so much, once in a while I'll give them a quarter of a cup of milk, diluted with an equal amount of water.)

DISULFOTON

Dogs have a potentially fatal attraction to this extremely toxic insecticide, which is the chemical treatment against aphids and other plant-sucking insects. Some of the trade names for the insecticide are Disultex, Di-Syston, Dimaz and Solvirex.

Disulfoton is also used as a fertilizer; rose-plant treatments generally contain it. Dogs can ingest enough while digging in the earth around treated plants to be poisoned. A single teaspoon of a pesticide that contains one percent disulfoton can reportedly kill a fifty pound dog.

ELECTRIC WIRES

If a dog chews on an electric wire (and puppies especially seem as drawn to them as toddlers can be) it can start a fire or electrocute the dog. Tuck all the cords you can beneath carpets, or tape them up behind furniture. Coat them with an anti-chew product sold at pet stores (or you can make your own by mixing rubbing alcohol together with Angostura Bitters and Tabasco).

FATTY FOODS

Many people give their dogs snacks of such high-fat foods as chocolate, turkey skin, bacon, sausages, hot dogs and fried foods. If a dog eats foods that are high in fat, it can cause pancreatitis, an inflammation of the pancreas. As in people, the pancreas produces digestive enzymes and contains the cells that produce insulin.

Signs of pancreatitis are generally an acute onset of vomiting, sometimes with diarrhea—even water is often immediately vomited. Abdominal pain can result in a hunched posture and a pain reaction when you feel the dog's belly. The dog needs to get into the hospital, because he can become very sick very quickly and need IV antibiotics and fluid to bring down the inflammation of the pancreas. Although treatable, it can be deadly in some cases. Once a dog has recovered from pancreatitis, her system is weakened and she is prone to getting it again; she must always stay on a strict prescription diet.

Some breeds are more susceptible to pancreatitis than others. According to some reports, the smaller, more energetic breeds seem especially prone: Toy Poodles, Cocker Spaniels, Miniature Schnauzers and other small, terrier-type dogs.

FLOOR COVERINGS

◆ Synthetic Flooring

Allergies and irritations in dogs can result from a variety of floorings. Sheet vinyl flooring is one example. There are high-tech chemicals used in manufacturing, and flooring is known to be a primary source of household contamination through a process called "outgassing": the release of odorous and possibly toxic fumes. Flooring manufacturers are working to limit the amount of harmful chemicals in floor materials, but in any case, these chemicals are outgassed for only a few weeks, after which there are no more measurable toxins. You can reduce the toxic levels even further by allowing flooring materials to air out before bringing them into the house for installation.

♦ Carpeting

Carpets can worsen allergies for some dogs, causing weeping eyes and hot spots. If you have a dog with serious allergies—and you, too, suffer from them—removing any wall-to-wall carpeting and replacing it with hardwood or ceramic flooring is the best present you can give to your red-eyed pooch.

FLY STRIPS

Plastic fly strips, which are impregnated with the chemical methomyl, are potentially lethal to dogs and other small animals. Don't hang them in your house or closets.

FOXTAILS

Foxtails are tail-like clusters of seeds on certain types of grasses. They have sharp points to penetrate the ground when they fall, and there are barbs on the seed cluster that don't allow them to come back out of the soil or whatever they've pierced. The problem for dogs is that these plant pieces can work their way into the body—particularly the feet, but also the nasal passages, eyes or ears—as the dog sniffs, head down. Foxtails are not an issue when green, but in the dry season avoid areas with these grasses, or groom your dog thoroughly afterward (especially the undersides of paws, stomach, armpits and inside the ears). Once foxtails embed in your dog's flesh or orifices, they must be removed by a vet, and immediately. Foxtails can cause serious, sometimes fatal infections if you delay treatment.

♦ Symptoms

Nose symptoms include sudden violent sneezing, bleeding from either nostril and pawing at nose (get to a vet immediately, because a foxtail can weave deep into the nasal canal and must be surgically removed before it can reach the brain). Ear symptoms are a tilted head, pawing at ear, shaking his head, whimpering and walking stiffly (you need the vet because you may not even be able to see the barbs in there). Throat symptoms include gagging, retching, coughing, eating grass, stretching his neck and swallowing continuously. Eye symptoms are redness, swelling, tearing, discharge and squinting.

GRAPES AND RAISINS

This fruit can be toxic to dogs when ingested in *very* large quantities: there is a potential for severe reactions, including death. Some dogs who have been sickened ate grapes right off the vine, ingesting between nine ounces and two pounds (which worked out to be between one half ounce to one ounce per kilo of body weight), while small dogs can be sickened by four or five grapes.

Although there have been reports of dogs who have suffered kidney failure after ingesting large amounts of grapes or raisins, this has not been clinically proven to be the case, and no one yet knows what the possible cause of the physical problems might be and exactly what role the grapes or raisins have played.

In any case, because of the severity of the signs and the potential for death for any dog who eats excessive amounts of grapes or raisins, the ASPCA Animal Poison Control Center suggests aggressive medical treatment. A veterinarian may induce vomiting, administer activated charcoal to absorb liquid in the dog's stomach or pump the stomach. This is usually followed by IV fluid therapy for at least forty-eight hours or more, depending on the result of blood tests for kidney damage.

A few grapes or raisins now and again won't cause any problems, but people are urged to limit a dog's access to and intake of these two foods. Stay alert to any raisins or grapes your dog might have found. If a whole bunch is missing, you can watch for signs of a toxic reaction or, to be on the safe side, go right to a vet for emergency treatment.

HALLOWEEN

Although Halloween seems like a fun holiday, it poses special dangers to dogs. Don't leave your dog outside, where pranksters could harm him. Indoors, keep him away from candy (swallowed wrappers are as bad as the sugar and chocolate) and away from pumpkins with candles, which can tip over. Consider keeping the dog in another room during trick-or-treating, since the parade of strangers in scary costumes can frighten him, even to the point where he tries to run away. And don't put a costume on your dog unless he seems to enjoy it and cannot chew off and swallow any small pieces.

HEATSTROKE

Dogs can experience heatstroke more easily than most people realize, and owners often place their dogs in mortal danger without realizing it. Physical conditions that might not even be uncomfortable to you can be life-threatening to your dog.

ILLEGAL DRUGS

Marijuana, LSD and other illicit drugs can have the same effect on dogs that they have on humans, except that dogs are much smaller and the drugs may be even more dangerous. Call the vet immediately. Don't worry about your own discomfort or fear about having to admit that you had the stuff around: it's more important to be honest about what your pet ingested and get him medical assistance.

INDOOR AIR QUALITY

Household cleaning products pose a substantial health risk to dogs, who are more vulnerable to indoor air pollution than people are. Pets spend up to twenty-four hours a day indoors, they spend all their time near the floor, where the higher molecular weight of chemical solvents makes those substances settle, and they breathe substantially more air for their body size than children or adults, which exposes them to greater quantities of toxins in the same air space. The chemical-based products can cause allergic symptoms in some dogs (sneezing, skin irritation, depression, asthma), while others have stronger immune systems or less reaction to low levels of airborne pollutants. When choosing cleaning products, the natural (Simple Green) or "old-fashioned" (vinegar and water) are less toxic.

INSECT STING, BITE

If you saw where the bee stung, scrape the stinger off (do not use tweezers, which can release more toxin) using the edge of a credit card or something similar. Make a paste of baking soda and water and apply it to the area. You can also apply cold to bring down swelling and discomfort. Call the vet's office to ask about giving an antihistamine like Benadryl, since many vets will prescribe it over the phone for a mild allergic reaction (for emergency bee stings, see page 317). Generally speaking, the dosage is one milligram per pound of oral Benadryl. If your dog is outside where bees are prevalent, you should always have Benadryl on hand.

MACADAMIA NUTS

The ASPCA's Animal Poison Control Center has shown that these nuts are poisonous to dogs.

ONIONS

Consuming a lot of onions (in onion soup or onion tart, for example) can be toxic to a dog, causing a condition known as Heinz body anemia. In large quantities, onions can cause changes in the dog's red blood cells so that they can't function normally. Small amounts of onion generally aren't a problem, but this condition is a gradual toxicity that can build up over time, so you should take care that your dog avoids human food that has onions in it. (Billy Blue must have a cast-iron stomach, because he once pilfered an entire large onion tart intended for a dinner party and seemed to suffer no ill from it—although we were nearly all gassed out of the house.)

OVEREATING

Especially at holiday times, some people feel that if the people are going to stuff themselves, their dogs should keep them company. Wrong! You would be doing your dog a disservice to give him lots of rich, fatty foods that his body isn't accustomed to. You also need to guard against the dog "counter surfing" in the kitchen during holiday food preparations, or helping himself to food left unprotected on low tables—or high ones, if he's a big dog.

Gorging on rich food can cause pancreatitis in some dogs (see page 323 under "Fatty Foods"). But it can also cause bloat, which is every bit as serious and potentially life-threatening (see page 319 in this section).

PLANTS

◆ Houseplants

It is not good for your plants to have a dog digging in the roots and chewing the leaves. Some plants are also toxic to dogs, and can cause diarrhea, vomiting or worse (see "Dangerous Plants," page 327). You can spray the plants with an anti-chew product like Bitter Apple or a homemade concoction. If the dog likes to dig up the dirt, you can sprinkle cayenne pepper or ground black pepper on top of the soil to dissuade him.

◆ **Dangerous Plants**

- ❏ *Azalea*—vomiting/diarrhea; excitement or depression.
- ❏ *Amaryllis and bulb*—can be fatal in very young or old; vomiting/collapse.
- ❏ *Japanese yew (especially the berries)*—can be fatal; loss of coordination, diarrhea, collapse, heart problems.
- ❏ *English ivy*—leaves and stems can cause mild stomach upset; fruits/berries are potentially fatal in large quantities.
- ❏ *English lily or day lily*—potentially lethal (more so to cats)
- ❏ *Mistletoe*—mild reaction, increased blood pressure, only problematic for dogs with kidney or cardiac problems.
- ❏ *Eucalyptus, holly and poinsettia*—mild intestinal reaction.

◆ **Potentially Poisonous Plants**

Lily of the valley; oleander; rhododendron; azalea; rosebay; yew of all kinds; foxglove; laurel; lambkill; calico bush; dog hobble; dog laurel; fetter-bush; male berry; stagger-bush; rhubarb Rheum species (leaves only); autumn crocus; castor bean; sorghum leaves; elephant's ear; mushrooms; daffodil bulbs; nicotiana leaves, tomato plants.

For the most complete list, go to the Web site of the ASPCA at www.aspca.org, or the Humane Society of the United States, at www.hsus.org.

POISON

If you have any doubt about whether your dog was exposed to or swallowed a poison, you have to watch him carefully and act quickly on anything you see.

1. Contact your vet, an emergency vet facility or the ASPCA Animal Poison Control Center (see page 328) immediately for advice on how to stop any poison from being absorbed into your dog's system.

2. Wait until your vet or the poison control center in your state gives you instructions on what to do next. Do not take any action on your own.

3. The medical provider will want to know what chemical has poisoned your dog and how much she was exposed to—it helps to have the original container available.

🦴 *Symptoms of Chemical Poisoning*

- Unexplained vomiting
- Unusual drooling
- Unusual behavior
- Difficulty breathing
- Convulsions or unconsciousness
- Burns around or inside the mouth

4. Have a bottle of hydrogen peroxide available at home, but never administer it without a medical directive.

The ASPCA Animal Poison Control Center, (888) 426-4435, is a 24/7 telephone assistance line for veterinarians and dog owners. The flat fee of $50 for a phone consultation includes as many follow-up calls on that event as necessary. Any doubts or questions that you may have can be directed to the APCC for advice on the next step to take.

PRESCRIBED MEDICATIONS

Just about any of the drugs prescribed for dogs can cause problems, so if you think your dog is having a bad response, contact your vet right away. Many dogs can have various reactions to antibiotics, and all pain relievers of the NSAID variety (see page 375) can potentially be toxic to the liver, kidney and stomach.

Drug interactions can cause problems, so always ask your vet, "Are these drugs okay given together?" and "What are the possible side effects of combining them?"

Also, see individual medications like Rimadyl, below and on page 377.

PSORIASIS CREAM

The creams that people use for the skin condition psoriasis are potentially lethal to dogs, in whom they cause renal failure.

RIMADYL

This drug is a popular NSAID (non-steroidal anti-inflammatory drug) that is often prescribed for arthritic and other joint-pain problems, especially in older dogs. Rimadyl has sickened some dogs, while helping others enormously.

Labrador Retrievers seem to be particularly at risk from this drug, although this has not been proven. Some have died, perhaps from liver damage caused by the drug. These adverse reactions have not been clinically proven, but be alert to your dog's reaction to this medication. See the "Warnings" section of "Medications" on pages 375–377 later in this chapter.

SLUG BAIT

Metaldehyde, the active ingredient in the pellets sold to attract and kill slugs in your garden, is potentially lethal to dogs.

SMOKING

Secondhand smoke has been associated with lung and nasal cancer in dogs.

If you cannot stop for the sake of your own health, then maybe you will be able to stop if you know that you are jeopardizing your pet's health by smoking around her (especially a small lap dog who spends a lot of time up near your face).

SNOW GLOBES

Many people have snow-globe collections, but it would probably never occur to anyone that these globes can kill their pets. The liquid inside is a form of antifreeze—just as sweetly attractive to dogs as antifreeze is, and just as deadly. Once again, it is the smaller dogs that are most at risk—they can die tragically from licking up the spilled liquid from a broken snow globe.

STINGS, BEE

Bee stings generally happen around a dog's face, because his nose is what he uses to explore the world around him. Scrape down against the sting site with the flat edge of a credit card (trying to use your fingers or a pair of tweezers often just pushes the stinger farther in and releases more toxin). To soothe a sting (anywhere but the mouth) make a paste of baking soda and water or milk of magnesia and dab it on the site. A cold compress can also help.

Facial swelling is the usual symptom. Minor swelling will go away once the stinger is removed, but if the dog has been stung inside the mouth it can inhibit breathing. Any major swelling—or the chance that the dog was stung inside the mouth—requires a get-right-to-the-vet trip (see "Emergencies" on page 317).

STRING, ROPE

Dogs like to chew on rope or string or even panty hose (once it's worn it smells deliciously like you). If you know your dog has eaten string or yarn or anything long that could get tangled inside her, contact your vet. The strings can wrap around her intestines and are potentially fatal. *If you see any piece of stringy material sticking out of your dog's anus, do not pull on it: you could cause intestinal damage.* Only a veterinarian should deal with it.

SUN AND CARS

Never leave a dog in a hot car or in the sun—not even for five minutes. Even if your car is in the shade when you leave it, the sun will often shift and shine right through the windshield. It doesn't matter if your windows are down on a boiling hot day: the inside of the car becomes an oven anyway.

Never leave a dog in the car with the windows shut. Never leave a dog in the car for an extended period without checking on him. (For more see page 362).

SUN AND SKIN

The sun can burn a dog's skin, especially around the muzzle; a light-colored, short-haired dog is vulnerable to sunburn pretty much anywhere. For dogs like this, who are going to spend time in the sun even just going for a walk, use sunblock lotion on their most exposed parts: the head and back. Use any form of sunblock intended for children, since those are usually more gentle, and use an SPF number of 15 or higher. The easiest way to apply it is with a "sports spray" that makes a fine mist and is waterproof: cover the dog's eyes with your hand before spraying his head. If the dog does not like being sprayed, spray it on your palm and rub it on him. (see pages 336–338 for more on sun protection and signs of pre-cancer).

SWIMMING POOLS

Pools are dangerous, because even if a dog knows how to swim, if she doesn't know how to get out of the pool she can panic and try to claw her way out on the wall—and potentially drown due to exhaustion. Dogs should NEVER have access to any pool that only has a metal step ladder to get in and out on. Few dogs are able to use them: most will drown trying unsuccessfully to exit the pool. Grown dogs need to be shown where the steps are in any new pool, since even a veteran swimmer may go to where she is accustomed to finding steps and panic if there is no exit where she expects it.

Puppies need to be taught where the steps are in a pool. You need to get into the water with the puppy the first few times and encourage her, directing her with your hands toward the steps. You can even go to the steps yourself once the puppy is swimming and call her to you—when she gets near the step area the first couple of times, guide her so that she understands that the steps are under the water. Young dogs should not have access to a swimming pool unless you are at home and outside with the dog, or able to see and get to the pool if anything happens to the pup.

WATER SAFETY

Dogs can swim naturally, but there are still situations that can be dangerous for them. A dog needs to wear a life jacket on a boat in case he falls overboard, or if he's going to be in cold water and/or fast currents long enough to get fatigued.

Pools, hot tubs, ponds and even fountains can be drowning hazards for your dog, so please have these areas fenced. If he does fall into cold water and seems to show signs of hypothermia (a body temperature below normal), wrap him in towels and keep him as warm as possible while transporting him immediately to your vet.

WATER IN THE WILD

Leptospirosis is a potentially fatal bacteria that dogs can get by drinking or going into contaminated water. The disease is passed via the urine of an infected wild animal, which stays contagious in ponds, soil and on grass for up to six months. This disease can cause kidney or liver failure and even death, and it can also be passed from animals to humans—without the dog showing any sign of illness. Leptospirosis had virtually disappeared, but it may be emerging again—since the end of the 1990s it has been found on Long Island and in upstate New York, and in Pennsylvania.

The vaccination for this disease is widely used and is often combined with the distemper/parvo shot. BE CAREFUL: this vaccine is often blamed for causing bad reactions. Also, the virus occurring in the wild is often not included in the vaccine.

Try to keep your dog away from puddles, ponds or muddy, stagnant water in the woods. Watch for flu-like symptoms, which are an early-warning sign, and for loss of appetite, fever, vomiting, listlessness and increased thirst and urination. Treatment usually includes up to two weeks of antibiotics and intravenous fluids.

WOODEN STICKS

There are a number of human food items that use wooden sticks—often in outdoor settings—which if not properly disposed of can entice dogs who come upon them. The flavorful sticks can be found at backyard barbeques, fancy cocktail parties or weddings, or at the beach. Wooden skewers for kabobs or satays, Popsicle sticks or sharp toothpicks can all be dangerous once they go down a dog's hatch. These sharp sticks can perforate the GI tract and spread infection throughout the dog's body. Even wooden ice cream sticks or coffee stirrers are potentially harmful, because if a dog chews them, the wood will splinter and enter into the intestinal tract like a dagger.

XYLITOL

Xylitol is a sweetener found in certain sugar-free chewing gum and candy. It can cause serious, even life-threatening problems for pets.

Dogs who have eaten significant amounts of gum or candy sweetened mostly with xylitol may have a sudden drop in blood sugar resulting in depression, loss of coordination and seizures. The symptoms develop quite rapidly—sometimes less than thirty minutes after ingestion—which means you need to seek veterinary treatment immediately.

Diseases and Medical Conditions

ADDISON'S DISEASE

This is an endocrine disease that occurs when the adrenal glands do not function properly. Symptoms are loss of appetite, weakness and vomiting, and the dog just generally becomes very ill. The illness can be diagnosed with a blood test and is easily treated by replacing the deficient hormones in pill form. The outcome is generally fine. No breeds are at a special risk for this disease, but it is most prevalent in young female dogs; most victims are around five years old.

ANAL PROBLEMS

Long-haired dogs need frequent grooming, which includes the hair around their bottoms. When you groom, check the anal area, since you don't usually see it under the long coat. Be on the lookout for signs of possible problems, and don't hesitate to have your vet check out anything that seems to be bothering the dog "back there." In some cases, early detection can prevent serious health problems later. If you ignore anal sac problems, your dog could develop an abscess that might rupture, cause infection and be a painful mess.

Problems include scooting (dragging his hind end on the floor), straining to have a bowel movement, pain or reluctance to be touched near the tail and/or chronic licking of the anal

🦴 *Symptoms of Anal Problems*

- Scooting, dragging his butt on the floor
- Frequent licking of the anal area

- Swelling on either side of the anal area
- Dog suddenly jumps up to check his butt, as if bitten

area. With scooting, there's a ninety percent chance that the anal sacs are not emptying properly, while ten percent of the time your dog has tapeworms (see page 333).

◆ Scooting

A dog dragging his bottom on the grass or carpet—which is called "scooting"—can be a sign of problems in that area, the most common reason being that the dog is trying to empty his anal sacs. These sacs, which are about the size of grapes, are on either side of the anal opening. They produce a very sharp, foul odor—much like a skunk's scent glands. The anal sacs—and the liquid they expel on feces—are a throwback to the ancestral wolf background, in which animals in the wild identified each other, maintained ties to the pack and staked out territory with this odor-identifier on their droppings. The scent from the anal sacs is what makes dogs sniff each other's butts and each other's feces. Each dog's odor on the stool is a personalized scent.

Dogs cannot empty the sacs voluntarily—the sacs empty during vigorous exercise, or the secretion is released with a normal firm stool if a dog is extremely nervous. Anal sacs become impacted—infected, or filled with the fluid that normally is expressed along with feces—in some dogs.

◆ Which Dogs Are Usually Affected?

Anal-sac problems occur more frequently in male dogs (often unneutered dogs that do not breed), although the reasons are not clear. Anal-sac problems also occur often in house dogs who live a sheltered life, perhaps because they don't get frightened, which is one of the causes for the anal gland substance to be expelled. Smaller-breed dogs and older dogs tend to have the problem. Dogs that have soft stools for long periods of time are also at higher risk.

◆ Treatments for Anal-sac Problems

1. Manual expression of the glands: If you want to save on the expense and hassle of going to the vet every time your dog needs his anal sacs expressed, you can ask the vet or veterinarian's assistant to teach you how to do it yourself. Basically you hold a tissue at the anus and squeeze the two glands together toward the center, although the angle at which you apply pressure can be difficult to gauge without some experience.

2. Metamucil: Many dogs have been helped by having one teaspoon of Metamucil mixed with a little water into a high-fiber dog food. A low-calorie or senior dry dog food formula usually has a high fiber content, too.

3. High-fiber breakfast cereal: Add a cereal like Fiber One or All-Bran to the dog's dish. Use one teaspoon for every ten pounds of the dog's weight.

4. Surgical removal of the anal glands: If a dog's glands get constantly blocked or infected, a common procedure in veterinary medicine is to remove the glands surgically. However, these glands play an important role in dog-to-dog communication,

giving other dogs sex and social information. Surgery is not a step that should be taken lightly. This is something you should discuss with your vet only if your dog has this problem chronically and suffers from repeated infections.

5. Antiseptic or antibiotic flushing of the glands: This is a less invasive measure to try before any permanent removal is considered. Again, discuss with your vet.

✦ Tapeworms

Only a small percentage of dogs suffer anal-area discomfort due to tapeworms. A dog with tapeworms will pass white, rice-sized bits on his stool. If you see this, bring the stool sample to your vet for verification. If it is tapeworm, your dog will need medication to kill the worms and better flea control to prevent reinfection, since fleas are the crucial link in the tapeworm's life cycle.

✦ Anal Ulcers (Perianal Fistula)

A serious problem underlying scooting can be an anal disease that causes swollen, painful ulcers near the anus. German Shepherds are the breed primarily afflicted, but a mixed breed with German Shepherd in the mix could also be at risk for it. You will be able to see these lesions (sores) around the anus, and they will get worse. Early treatment is the most successful, especially if using the newer steroid treatment.

Treatment for anal ulcers often consists of surgically removing the lesions with freezing or dissection, but the downside is that some dogs are left with fecal incontinence (leaking stool) and the lesions come back again. Sometimes the tail is amputated. Another alternative that was developed by a professor at Kansas State's veterinary college consists of using cyclosporin (a strong immunosuppressant) in place of the high cost and pain (and, often, failure) of the previous surgical treatment. Early detection and administration of cyclosporin is effective nearly seventy percent of the time.

✦ Other Anal Problems

There are a number of other possible reasons for your dog's anal discomfort. Your vet will be able to examine her and run tests to see whether she has any disease of the large bowel that could cause diarrhea, food allergies or rectal cancer (which can be deadly).

✦ Something's Stuck in There!

On a medically insignificant note, if you have a country dog who often eats grass, some of the grass may not get expelled when he has a bowel movement. The long strands of plant material can remain in the anus and not fully exit when the dog passes stool. Sometimes a dog can ingest something else long and stringy that may protrude after a bowel movement, too. Wearing rubber gloves and/or putting your hand inside a plastic baggie, you will need to grasp the protruding piece of grass and *very, very gently* try to pull it out of the anus. You can put your other hand under the dog's stomach to keep him from trying to scoot away. Your dog may look startled or embarrassed, but he will be grateful to you for doing something for him that he could not do for himself.

NOTE: *If there is any resistance to the gentle pressure you apply when pulling out the offending protrusion, STOP! Take the dog to the vet immediately. The grass or "stringy whatever" may be somehow wrapped around something inside the dog, and you can do harm by pulling hard.*

BLOAT

See "Intestinal," page 363.

CANCER

You may wonder how frequently cancer is found in dogs, since it seems that so many of them get it in some form. The statistics say that cancer will affect half of all dogs and cats over ten years old. It is the most common cause of death in dogs (and cats) over the age of ten. Cancer kills fully half of all senior pets. But it is also true that fifty percent of all dogs diagnosed with cancer may be cured, and there are some cancers that dogs can live with as a chronic illness, just as others live with diabetes.

◆ Why So Much Cancer?

Twenty or thirty years ago, there was rarely any cancer in dogs—but there were also few dogs living to as ripe an old age as ours do today. Advances in veterinary care and preventive medicine have allowed our pets to live to the ages when cancer develops—and we have more sophisticated equipment to diagnose the disease. There are certainly environmental factors at work, but there hasn't been funding for much research into what factors most affect dogs.

◆ Which Dogs Are Most at Risk?

Just as there are people who are genetically at a higher risk to develop certain cancers, so are there breeds of dogs with a much higher incidence than others. The first eight breeds mentioned on page 335 have more of a certain kind of tumor than other breeds and develop cancer at an earlier age. Boxers get skin cancer more than any other breed. Rottweilers have the highest incidence of cancer of the long bones (the leg bones, which is how I lost my beautiful Yogi Bear at a mere six years of age). There are also breeds that are the least at risk—see chart on page 335—which is good news for owners of these breeds.

Dogs are more prone to cancer than people are.

- Dogs are thirty-five times more likely to get skin cancer.
- Dog are four times as likely to develop a breast tumor.
- Dog are eight times as likely to suffer bone cancer.
- Dog are twice as likely to develop leukemia.

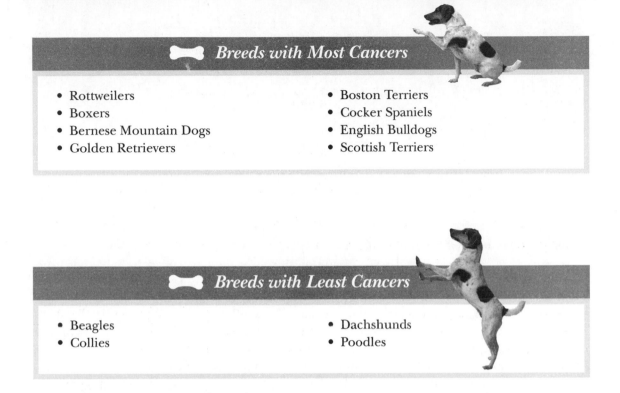

Breeds with Most Cancers

- Rottweilers
- Boxers
- Bernese Mountain Dogs
- Golden Retrievers

- Boston Terriers
- Cocker Spaniels
- English Bulldogs
- Scottish Terriers

Breeds with Least Cancers

- Beagles
- Collies

- Dachshunds
- Poodles

◆ Preventing or Reducing the Chance of Cancer

Secondhand cigarette smoke and cancer in household pets is being considered in scientific studies, and these leave little doubt that if you smoke it should not be done around your pets in closed spaces. Smokers often do not want to believe that their smoking can harm their dogs, but the facts show otherwise: secondhand smoke can harm pets as well as people.

Lung cancer is rare in dogs—perhaps one dog in 25,000 gets it—but dogs that live in smoking households have a sixty percent greater risk of lung cancer than other dogs. Some studies show that the risk of lung cancer is the highest for dogs with short noses, such as Pugs, or even dogs with medium-sized noses, such as Poodles. Other studies show that long-nosed dogs such as Collies and Wolfhounds are *twice as likely to get nasal cancer*. The speculation is that carcinogens (cancer-causing substances) are trapped in the nasal passages of those dogs.

Ways to Prevent Sunburn

1. Keep at-risk dogs completely out of the sun from 10:00 A.M. to 2:00 P.M.
2. Put a T-shirt on the dog when outdoors.
3. Provide shade outside over the dog's favorite area.
4. For indoor sunbathers, pull drapes or block off sunny rooms from 10:00 A.M. to 2:00 P.M.
5. Spray children's sunblock with an SPF of 15 or higher on sensitive areas.

Protect dogs against harmful rays of the sun.

To use a T-shirt as protective clothing, pull the shirt over the dog's head and ease her front legs through the armholes. The body of the T-shirt should now cover most of the dog's torso. An infant-size shirt works for toy dogs, children's sizes fit most small and some medium dogs, and larger dogs generally require adult sizes.

The same types of sunscreen products made for people will work on dogs, but remember that no product is one hundred percent effective, and even the waterproof ones have to be reapplied after time and exposure to water. Use one with an SPF of at least 15 and apply it at least fifteen minutes before exposure. A spray-on product will probably be easier to use than a rub-on lotion. Sunblocks to avoid are those with zinc-oxide in them and those that contain PABA, since they can be dangerous if swallowed and dogs tend to lick off anything you put on them. Distract your dog right after applying sunblock (or any skin product) by feeding her, playing with her or taking her for a walk, so that she has no opportunity to lick it right off—and may even forget about it later.

Dogs most at risk for sun damage and skin cancer are light-colored, thin-coated and hairless breeds, which have less natural protection from the sun's dangerous ultraviolet rays. Long-haired and dark-skinned dogs have fewer problems because their hair covering and pigment give them natural protection.

Breeds Sensitive to Sun Exposure

- Australian Shepherd
- Bull Terrier (white)
- American Staffordshire Terrier
- Beagle
- Boxer (highest skin-cancer rate of all)
- Bulldog
- Chinese Crested
- Collie
- Dalmatian
- Great Dane
- Greyhound
- Italian Greyhound
- Shetland Sheepdog
- Whippet

Nasal solar dermatitis (sunburned nose) can affect any dog with a pink or white nose who gets sunburned there. Because they have no hair to protect the area, if the burn is severe, the top layers of skin are lost and there can be skin erosion and deeper ulcerations. It is often referred to as "Collie nose," because it particularly affects Collies, Shelties and Australian Shepherds.

Dogs in Australia and the southwest United States—especially those in Arizona, Southern California, Nevada, New Mexico and Texas—are more at risk for solar dermatitis (sunburn) because the sunlight is so intense. Any dog that spends a lot of time outdoors in the sun in these geographical areas must be protected.

Snow reflection at higher altitudes is a problem for white-coated dogs who spend a lot of time outdoors in snowy areas, such as the Rocky Mountains. The reflection of constant ultraviolet light on a dog's sensitive areas is cumulative, and skin cancers are often not discovered until the more chronic effects of long-term exposure suddenly appear. These dogs especially need daily protection from those harmful rays.

Signs of sun damage progress to increasingly serious, and repeated sun exposure can cause an often deadly condition in a dog. Ultraviolet light can cause the same dangerous damage in dogs that it does in people.

STAGES AND COMPLICATIONS OF ULTRAVIOLET DAMAGE

- ❏ Reddened skin in thin areas such as the scrotum, belly, inner thigh and nose
- ❏ Faded skin color
- ❏ Hair loss
- ❏ Thick, red, scaly blotches
- ❏ Rough patches
- ❏ Appearance of "blackheads"
- ❏ Secondary infection
- ❏ Blisters with fluid
- ❏ Formation of scabs
- ❏ Lesion or depression beneath scabs
- ❏ Nodules, skin tumors and plaques associated with cancer

Feeding a high-quality dog food that has no chemical preservatives and contains amino acids and antioxidants such as vitamins E and C improves your dog's overall health. However, not much is known about how such food may help reduce the incidence of cancer. There hasn't been much scientific research into this area, and while a fair amount is known about people and cancer, it isn't known if this information would apply to dogs.

Herbicides on grass are known to cause lymphoma, a kind of cancer.

Eliminate any risk of a female getting mammary tumors by spaying her before she comes into season (for more on this, see page 391 under "Spaying").

As your dog reaches "senior status" (generally considered to start at seven years of age), schedule checkups at the doctor *twice* a year instead of once a year. That way you can point out any lumps or bumps or other issues that might be an early warning.

Watch for small physical changes in your dog—even small symptoms such as a nosebleed, lethargy, a new mole or a strange odor can be early warning signs of cancer. Many people don't want to seem neurotic and take their dog to the vet, but your sharp eye or hands are your dog's best protection. Don't hesitate: if it's nothing important, so much the better. But if it does turn out to be a cancer, then you've gotten a jump on it. Most cases of cancer have a better outcome if they are discovered early.

Possible Warning Signs of Cancer

- Abnormal swelling that persists or continues to grow
- Swollen glands
- Unusual lumps or masses anywhere on the body
- Sores that do not heal
- Unexplained weight loss
- Loss of appetite
- Bleeding or discharge from the nose or mouth
- Bad odor, especially from the mouth
- Difficulty eating or swallowing
- Reluctance to exercise or play
- Loss of stamina
- Persistent lameness or stiffness
- Difficulty breathing, urinating or defecating
- Change in behavior and/or attitude

COMMON CANCERS IN DOGS

◆ Bone Cancer (Osteosarcoma)

Osteosarcoma is the most common form of bone cancer: it accounts for eighty percent of all bone tumors in dogs. The tumors are usually found in large and giant breeds such as Great Danes, Saint Bernards and Greyhounds (although why this is so is not clear), and often in the long bone of the front legs.

There are few early warning signs of bone cancer, so it's rare to find it in the early stages. Lameness is a common symptom, but until limping, lameness or swelling become chronic problems, people don't usually go to the vet with them. Osteosarcoma is an aggressive cancer that metastasizes (spreads) quickly; by the time osteosarcoma is diagnosed, the cancer has often already spread to the lungs or other bones.

Standard treatment for bone cancer is amputation followed by chemotherapy, since most of the time the cancer is already in the lungs in microscopic amounts. Amputation removes the origin of the cancer, while chemo slows the growth of cells in the lungs. The dog may get IV treatment every two or three weeks, usually for a total of three to six times.

The prognosis when a dog is given chemotherapy following amputation is that fifty percent of the animals will live longer than one year and twenty-five percent will live for two years. Most owners are happy with their decision to amputate, because three-legged dogs manage very well physically and it buys them precious time with their dogs.

Affordability is a reality of life, and not everyone can afford cancer treatment. It is hard not to feel guilty about this, but your love for your dog has to be weighed against practicality and other demands on your resources. The amputation is expensive: in the low thousands for the surgery itself. Chemotherapy can be double that number. If you already have cancer coverage through veterinary pet insurance, it may change the decision you make for your dog's care.

◆ Mast-cell Tumors

Mast-cell tumors are the most common skin cancer tumors in dogs—ten to twenty percent of all canine skin cancers are mast cell, and twenty-five percent of the malignant skin cancers are mast cell (which are all potentially malignant). These growths are dangerous because they are so common, can occur anywhere on a dog's body and are hard to recognize. Growths appear most frequently on the dog's trunk or limbs but sometimes on the head or neck. A tumor can look like a swelling under the skin, a fatty cyst, a pimple, a wart or even a rash. The classic tumor is a new bump on top of the skin that is often red, irritated and itchy—but it can also be under the skin and soft. In fact, it can look like almost anything, as I found out.

Doctors advise medical investigation of any lump that your dog develops, and I can't agree enough, especially because mast-cell tumors are treatable—but deadly if not treated. They are also easy to miss. In the case of my old gentleman, Billy Blue, he had an unremarkable lump on his skin—sort of a mole—for months, but I just didn't like how it was changing. The vet didn't feel it looked suspicious but took a needle biopsy anyway (see page 340 under "Diagnosis"). It came back as Grade 2 (see page 340) and required a really large incision site around it—but that prevented what otherwise might have been the untimely end of poor Mr. Blue!

Are some dogs more at risk for mast-cell cancer? Most mast-cell tumors occur in older, mixed-breed dogs, but some breeds have a higher statistical risk. Flat-nosed (brachycephalic) dogs like the Boxers, with their broad heads and short snouts, are especially prone. The problem with the dogs at risk is that they will always have a greater chance of developing mast-cell tumors in other places (however, with mast-cell cancer, this is not an indication that the first cancer has spread).

🦴 *Breeds at Risk for Mast-cell Cancer*

Beagles	Bulldogs	Rhodesian
Bernese Mountain	Labrador	Ridgebacks
Dogs	Retrievers	Schnauzers
Boxers	Pugs	Terriers

Diagnosis of mast-cell cancer Mast-cell cancer is diagnosed initially by "fine-needle aspiration" (FNA), which in most cases can be done right in the vet's office. With a local anesthetic, a fine needle is used to withdraw a few cells for microscopic examination. If there is anything suspicious, the doctor needs to perform a biopsy (the removal of a small amount of the tissue) to be able to classify the tumor (see "Classifications" below) and know if it is malignant. The biopsy is also an outpatient procedure, involving only light sedation and a stitch or two to close up the small site from which the tissue is sampled. A biopsy result will take a few days and will show the grade of the tumor, which is ranked 1, 2 or 3 from less malignant to very malignant. A doctor can also determine the stage of the disease (the size of the tumor and whether it has spread) by needle aspiration, biopsy or ultrasound of the lymph nodes.

CLASSIFICATIONS OF MAST-CELL TUMORS

- ❒ TYPE 1 (localized): Usually cured with removal.
- ❒ TYPE 2 (variable growth): Curable when thoroughly removed but can grow back. Followed by radiation if cancer cells extend to the margins of the surgical site. Chemotherapy recommended if tumors have spread.
- ❒ TYPE 3 (malignant, ill-defined borders, difficult to remove): Usual treatment: surgery, radiation and chemotherapy, or only chemotherapy if tumor has spread. Long-term prognosis is poor: average of six to twelve months.

Your dog's future with a mast-cell tumor depends on many variables. Immediate treatment and a smaller tumor are both factors with better outcomes, but heredity plays a part, too. Even though flat-nosed breeds have a greater chance of getting mast-cell tumors, studies of Boxers show that they are easily cured because the tumors are easily removed and well-differentiated. The location of the tumor counts, too. Tumors along the extremities have the best outcome, while those in the groin area or oral cavity seem to spread early. Areas around the testicles and scrotum can have very malignant tumors, although only about ten percent of mast-cell cancer develops there and not all those tumors are even malignant. It is conventional to remove a mast-cell growth with any classification because of their rapid growth and tendency to be malignant.

✦ Melanocytoma Skin Cancers

Canine melanoma—called melanocytoma—can occur in the skin, and these tumors are usually benign. Melanocytomas are prevalent among Schnauzers (Standard and Miniature), Doberman Pinschers, Scottish Terriers, Irish and Gordon Setters, Vizslas, German Shepherds and Golden Retrievers. Scotties and dark-skinned dogs have the greatest chance of developing malignant melanoma. The most common and problematic tumors occur in the mouth. Other locations include the pads of the feet, the nail beds, the lips and behind and inside the eye.

Symptoms of oral melanomas include very bad breath, trouble chewing or food falling from the mouth while eating, bleeding or swelling on one side of the face and/or weight loss.

How the cancer is managed depends in part on where the tumor is located in the mouth. The most common treatment is surgery and radiation, which is intended only to reduce suffering and eliminate the smell associated with oral melanoma. There is no cure for this form of the disease. The average survival following diagnosis can range from six to eighteen months. If the disease has advanced, the dog will probably not live more than three to six months.

◆ **Lymphoma**

This cancer affects the lymph system and is one of the most common malignant cancers in dogs. If caught early, it responds well to chemotherapy. More than seventy-five percent of dogs whose lymphoma is found early will have complete remission, although this kind of cancer is likely to recur. Note that "remission" is different from "response." The remission rate is usually around seventy to eighty percent for most protocols for a five- to twelve-month period. Twenty-five to fifty percent of dogs may be alive after one year after receiving what is called a second "rescue" round of chemo.

Lymphoma is the most responsive cancer to chemotherapy, with an average survival rate of twelve to fourteen months. The chemo is not used to cure the disease with toxic levels of the medication, but to maintain quality of life. Although some doctors say that dogs do not have the kind of side effects from chemotherapy that humans do, this is not true. Unpleasant side effects are common, just as in human chemotherapy (see more on "Chemotherapy," page 344).

Breeds at risk for this form of the disease are Airedales, Bernese Mountain Dogs, Boxers, Bulldogs, Golden Retrievers and Rottweilers.

◆ **Mammary Cancer (Breast Cancer)**

This cancer is common in female dogs. Fifty percent of the tumors are benign, while the other half are malignant. Of those malignant tumors, fifty percent have the tendency to spread. The best prevention is early spaying, before the first heat cycle.

◆ **Hemangiosarcoma**

This is an aggressive and quite common cancer of the blood vessels. Tumors usually appear on the liver, heart muscle and skin, but most often on the spleen. German Shepherds and Golden Retrievers are especially susceptible to this form of the disease. The prognosis is usually poor because of this cancer's tendency to spread.

◆ **Brain Tumors in Dogs**

This is a very rare cancer in dogs. The signs of a brain tumor can be subtle—for example, the dog may suddenly urinate in the house—or the symptoms can be overt, such as seizures. Treatment can give a dog three or more years of quality life, depending on the individual case. But if the tumor is inoperable due to its position and is highly malignant and growing quickly, most vets will not recommend prolonging the dog's life.

Advanced radiation therapy technique This is a treatment for brain (and other head) tumors that until recently was only available to humans. It's called stereotactic radiosurgery, and it is a targeted radiation that doesn't harm surrounding tissue. It delivers a high dose of precisely targeted radiation right at a brain tumor. In people, it is the treatment of choice for certain types of brain tumors.

At the University of Florida, they have been experimenting on dogs and cats with this treatment and have had great results. The animals have had few side effects. Depending on the individual situation, the single-dose treatment can last for anywhere from fifteen minutes to two hours. This is a big improvement over traditional radiation treatments for brain tumors, which have to be repeated three to four times a week—with general anesthesia (and its complications and dangers) each time. The University of Florida may be the only veterinary hospital in the United States that offers this treatment to dogs, but a trip to Gainesville may be worth it for many people whose pets have this problem. The single-dose treatment makes it much easier on you and your dog, which can offset the trouble and expense of a trip to Florida. The cost in 2002 was about $2,200, which was less than most traditional treatments that take place over weeks. Some animals are eligible for a $700 subsidy because the treatment is part of the university's research. For more information, call the University of Florida's Small Animal Clinical Sciences Department at (352) 392-4700.

GENERAL CANCER TREATMENTS

So how do you treat a disease that millions of people will face every year with their dogs? There are many factors to consider when deciding how to deal with a dog's cancer. The kind of cancer your dog has—intestinal, external tumor, etc.—as well as your dog's age and general health make a big difference in the prognosis for successful treatment. Some cancers are easier to attack and offer a greater chance for recovery; with others, it may be a matter of buying a limited period of good quality of life that you can share with your dog.

✦ The Costs

The costs of cancer treatment in animals can rival that of humans: look into pet insurance with a "cancer endorsement" well before your dog reaches eight years of age (a cutoff for initiating insurance coverage with many companies). Learn everything you can about the insurance company's list of coverage exclusions and the maximum benefits that are allowed. The costs depend on where you live in the country, whether you use the services of a specialized veterinary facility with an oncology (cancer) department and what treatments are available and appropriate. A course of chemotherapy can cost well over a thousand dollars; other treatments can be many times more than that.

✦ Choices in Cancer Care

Which route you choose has many components. There is the difficulty for you—financially but also in frequency of medical visits and complications of aftercare—that cannot be ignored. This is especially true if your dog is already really old and infirm and/or the prognosis for survival or for a good quality of life is not good. However, there are owners who will pay any amount and put their animals through significant discomfort (from surgery to chemotherapy or radiation therapy) if they can gain as little as six months or a year of extended life with their dog. Those opposed to this way of viewing a sick animal would say that the dog's quality of life needs to be considered at least as much as—if not much more than—the emotional needs of the people attached to him. Clearly these are emotionally loaded and highly subjective issues that are too personal and individual to be decided anywhere except in private.

✦ Philosophical Concerns about Cancer Treatment

Leaving aside the cost, there are some owners who may not feel that high-tech medical care is the best choice for their dog, or for them. Is your dog the sensitive type, so that it would be another kind of torture to put him through multiple procedures, hospitalizations and anesthesia? Keep in mind that there are *people* with cancer who choose not to put themselves through an aggressive treatment when they believe that the extra time it will give them will come at the cost of a diminished quality of life. So you have to do this kind of thinking for your dog. It helps a great deal if your primary vet shares the viewpoint that the dog's quality of life is the first consideration, because it allows you to have someone caring and knowledgeable share in the decision-making process.

Your dog's physical and emotional state This is one of the practical matters to consider when he is diagnosed. How old is your dog and what is his health like, aside from the cancer? In the case of bone cancer, does he have the strength to come through the operation, rehabilitation and chemo? Will he have the energy and desire to enjoy whatever life will be left to him afterward? Or is he so emotionally fragile, old and/or infirm that it would be kinder to let him live out whatever time is left to him without surgical intervention, using pain medication as needed?

Oncologists will almost always recommend doing everything possible. That makes sense from their perspective, since their specialty training is geared toward aggressively treating cancer. But we must keep in mind where these doctors are coming from, because it is not easy to make a decision for your dog if it contradicts what these good doctors recommend.

No matter what any vet tells you, chemotherapy is unpleasant for dogs. Oncologists (cancer specialists) may downplay the side effects like nausea, fever, loss of appetite, vomiting and weight loss because they genuinely believe that dogs do not suffer the way people do from chemotherapy—although that may be a result of their understandable bias in favor of the work they have been trained for and are dedicated to. The vets *believe* that cancer treatment is not that bad for a dog, but that does not mean that a dog does not suffer—in some cases significantly—from being put through it. You have to be your dog's advocate.

✦ Surgery

The most straightforward approach to cancer is to cut it out—or, in the case of bone cancer, to amputate the entire limb that has the disease so that it cannot spread. But there is often the concern that some cancerous cells may have been left behind or that the cancer has already spread. In that case, surgery is followed by another therapy, such as radiation or chemotherapy.

✦ Radiation

This is a localized treatment that is often used when cancer has not spread, or after surgery as "insurance" that no stray cancer cells survived. Radiation—which is not painful when administered but can be very painful afterward—kills normal cells along with the cancerous ones, so the treatments have to be given in a number of smaller doses. Treatment can vary from once a day for three weeks to every other day for four to six weeks. A mold is made of the dog's body in the position he will have to be in when receiving radiation to be sure that the exact location is radiated each time. The dog has to be anesthetized every time so that he will be perfectly still and the radiation can be directed to the exact site of the cancer. Treatments last from ten to thirty minutes.

There are essentially two different types of radiation therapies. The most common type is teletherapy, in which the radiation emanates from an external source. Brachytherapy is a less common form of radiation therapy in which tiny radioactive beads are inserted into the tumor. This is an option for human prostate cancer treatment, and can be used in dogs for deep-seated tumors such as those in the prostate or solid tumors that cannot be removed surgically. An advantage to treating dogs with brachytherapy is that a precise dose can be delivered to the tumor with one treatment; once the correct level has been reached, the beads are removed and the treatment is completed.

The side effects of radiation can include tissue death, organ dysfunction and blindness.

◆ Chemotherapy

Chemotherapy is the use of medication to kill rapidly dividing cells in cancers that are in multiple sites or where surgery or radiation are not appropriate. There are fifteen to twenty drugs that have been carefully studied and are used routinely in dogs with cancer. Many of the drugs used are the same ones used for people, but unlike humans, most dogs do not lose their hair or get oral ulcers (however, it is *not* true, as some oncologists would have you believe, that dogs do not suffer other terrible side effects).

Before each treatment the dog's blood is tested to monitor the red and white blood cells and the liver and kidney functions, and then treatment is given either once a week or once every three weeks. Each treatment lasts from fifteen to sixty minutes. Most drugs are given intravenously, at doses a dog can tolerate over a longer period of time.

There are many different chemotherapy protocols, and, put simply, the less complicated treatments create fewer side effects—but are also less effective (there is a successful response to treatment in only sixty percent of dogs). The more complicated chemo protocols cause more side effects, yet are also more effective, with up to a ninety percent response.

Side effects from chemotherapy are often grossly underestimated. Many oncologists tell people that dogs usually tolerate anticancer drugs quite well and that the effect of these drugs is generally mild—but in reality that is rarely true. It is rare for a dog not to have some type of side effect, ranging from nausea to death. Some dogs have hair loss, based on their breed: generally only dogs with continually growing hair (such as Poodles and some Terriers) will lose hair. Most dogs experience gastrointestinal symptoms such as nausea, vomiting and diarrhea, which normally occur within a few days after chemotherapy begins; a vet can prescribe an antinausea medication to relieve those symptoms. However, many more, often severe, symptoms may develop, and it is crucial for loving, generous owners to consider this before putting an already sick dog through what can be a grueling treatment.

CANCER CACHEXIA (WEAKNESS, WEIGHT LOSS)

Cancer affects the entire body, not just the site where the tumor is developing, and it often changes the metabolism of the dog's body so that she becomes weak and dehydrated and loses weight. These changes are referred to as "cachexia" and can occur even when the dog is still eating and acting normally. Research has shown that these symptoms can begin very early in the course of the cancer and can continue after a cancer has been successfully removed or treated—in fact, cachexia can be fatal to a dog whose cancer is in remission.

It's important to do everything possible to prevent the wasting effects of cachexia, but it's not just a case of feeding more food to counteract the weight loss. It's the composition of the dog's diet that is central to preventing and treating cachexia. Researchers have learned that cancer cells crave sugar (carbohydrates) but cannot break them down efficiently, and so they deplete the body. Cancerous conditions in the dog's body also affect protein metabolism, fat and amino acids in unusual and potentially life-threatening ways.

There is only one commercial diet formulated to counteract the effects of cachexia. Hill's Pet Nutrition has a food sold only through vets called Prescription Diet N/D, which specifically meets the needs of the canine body as it copes with cancer and cancer treatments. Many vets believe it is a good and useful food, while others disagree. Real-world results with this product have been mixed. You can also try any of the suggestions in the list below—which is based on suggestions from the veterinary oncologists at the University of Pennsylvania vet school—on how to make eating more appealing to a dog suffering from cancer. Check first with your vet or oncologist before trying anything on your dog, because every situation is unique. If your dog's cancer hasn't required any dietary restrictions, then be willing to try as many of these suggestions as it takes to encourage your dog to eat.

PERKING UP YOUR DOG'S INTEREST IN FOOD

- ❏ Conventional wisdom has been to warm meals to increase aroma and palatability. New evidence shows that a dog might be hungry, but will associate certain flavors or smells with feeling sick. Some dogs with food aversion do better with room temperature or chilled food.
- ❏ Don't try to coax a dog to eat if she's showing overt signs of nausea: gulping or drooling at the sight or smell of food, turning her head away from food, spitting out food placed in her mouth or burying food under bedding.
- ❏ Try novel food items once your dog shows interest in eating again. However, the dog must be feeling fully well or the eating aversion will just transfer to the new food.
- ❏ Adding chicken broth or garlic powder can make food more appealing to some dogs.
- ❏ Offer food in a new place, or have a new person give the food, in case the dog associates her previous feeding routine with the unpleasantness of nausea or vomiting.
- ❏ Give your dog company—dogs are social animals, and eating with other dogs or being coaxed to eat at the same time that you do might have a positive effect.
- ❏ Appetite stimulants can revive your dog's interest in food, but are best used to help overcome food aversions *after* she no longer feels sick.
- ❏ If nausea and vomiting are the problem, discuss antiemetic drugs with your vet.
- ❏ Don't schedule any treatments (such as taking pills) around mealtimes—you want food to have only positive associations and not further irritate her stomach.

- Divide food into many small meals and increase desirability with canned food instead of dry, or warm water on dry food.
- For advice on special diets for cancer patients please go to www.thedogbible.com and click on "Inside the Book."
- Always check any dietary changes with your vet first: for example, high protein intake can be a problem with kidney or liver dysfunction.

◆ Cancer from the Dog's Perspective

Discomfort for the animal needs to be assessed with your doctor ahead of time. Many owners do not want to pursue cancer treatments with debilitating effects, since there is no way the dog can understand the side effects—on top of the discomfort the animal is already suffering from the cancer itself. The advantage that you gain in time (an alien concept to a dog) really needs to be weighed against what the dog has to go through, without the benefit of being able to decide for himself.

◆ Sources for Detailed and Timely Cancer Information

The following Web sites give up-to-date information on cancer. They may also be a link to clinical trials that are under way at various veterinary institutions which might be helpful to your dog.

- The American Veterinary Medical Association (www.avma.org) features news on canine cancer, information about care options and news on other topics.
- The Cornell University College of Veterinary Medicine Web site is located at www.vet.cornell.edu/cancer.
- The University of Pennsylvania site is www.oncolink.upenn.edu/specialty/vet_onc/.
- The Tufts University School of Veterinary Medicine (www.vet.tufts.edu) gives updates on cancer and other illnesses, along with contact names at the school.
- The Veterinary Cancer Society (www.vetcancersociety.org) lists specialists by location and links to information about university-run clinical trials, oncology specialists nationwide and cancer-information Web sites. The Society is based in Schaumburg, Illinois, and can be reached at (619) 460-2002. They may be able to steer your dog to some of the clinical trials that offer free cancer treatment if you take part in their study. This gives you the chance to receive promising new therapies, often together with traditional care regimens, without the financial burden.
- A veterinary cancer awareness program called "Biting-Back" is hosted online at www.bitingback.com.

COUGHING

There are a number of conditions that can cause coughing. Any time your dog coughs enough to make you aware of it—or coughs with a sound in her throat—it's an indication that you should take her to the vet as soon as possible. A healthy dog does not cough.

Do not ignore coughing. It may not sound or seem like a serious problem to you, but coughing can actually be a sign of significant disease: there are so many possible reasons for canine coughing that you need to put the problem in your vet's hands, then have confidence and patience as he sorts it out.

Do not try to treat a cough or decide to handle things yourself. Don't guess at what's causing the cough. As you can see from the list of possibilities, it is beyond your ability to make a diagnosis. Do not give human cough medicine to a dog (this sounds obvious, but you'd be surprised how many people try it). The ingredients need to be appropriate to a dog, but more importantly, you need a vet to find out *why* the dog is coughing in the first place.

✦ Conditions That Cause Coughing

The first two reasons for coughing are the most common in dogs—all the others are fairly rare.

- ☐ Bordatella (kennel cough) is a contagious cold with cough (see page 301) and the most frequent reason for a dog to cough.
- ☐ Chronic bronchitis is the persistent inflammation of the bronchi, the tubes that pass air to the lungs. Smaller breeds are susceptible as they get older.
- ☐ Heart disease affects dogs older than eight and functions just as it does in humans. As heart valves deteriorate, the heart enlarges. This puts pressure on the bronchi and can lead to fluid in the lungs—both of which cause coughing.
- ☐ A collapsed trachea affects smaller breeds and means that the cartilage rings in the trachea have lost their shape. The collapse can happen during exercise or even during mild excitement or normal breathing.
- ☐ Pneumonia is inflammation of the lungs, which can be caused as it is in people: through viral, fungal or bacterial infection, inhaling harmful gases or inhaling vomit or food into the lungs.
- ☐ Heartworm is an internal parasite that lives in the pulmonary arteries, but it has to be in an advanced stage to bring on coughing (see page 382–383 for more).
- ☐ Cancer of the lungs as a primary site is rare in dogs, although secondary spreading to the lungs is quite common (as with osteosarcoma). But lymphoma can cause enlarged lymph-nodes, which can put pressure on the trachea and make a dog cough.
- ☐ Congestive heart failure (CHF) can result in coughing. Small- to medium-sized dogs who are coughing are at a higher risk of this being the reason.
- ☐ Tracheal collapse, or narrowing, produces a dry, harsh or honking cough. The classic sound is a "goose honking" cough. Toy and miniature dogs are at risk for this.
- ☐ Laryngeal paralysis is damage to a nerve in the dog's voice box, which may cause the dog to lose his bark or to have noisy, raspy breathing. It can also cause a dog to breathe like a child having an asthma attack, or cause a gagging cough during or right after eating or drinking. If your dog is diagnosed with laryngeal paralysis, put him on a diet, since even a few pounds can worsen the condition. A dog with this problem is at risk for overheating, so avoid exercise on hot days, since dogs often cannot handle exercise well in the heat and may collapse. Keep him cool and calm and generally limit his exercise, using your own judgment about how he responds to getting worked up.

Consult with your vet as needed. Surgery is a possibility if you and the vet feel that the benefits outweigh the risks. The dogs most likely to get laryngeal paralysis are large-breed dogs as they grow older, including Golden Retrievers, Saint Bernards, Newfoundlands, Irish Setters and Siberian Huskies. Older Labradors and Rottweilers are also at a significantly higher risk. Dog breeds that risk inheriting this disorder are Bouvier de Flandres, Bull Terriers (in the United Kingdom), Dalmatians, Siberian Huskies and Husky mixes.

◆ Information to Diagnose the Cough

The more information you can bring to your vet, the better her chances of finding out what is causing your dog's cough.

- ❑ Tape-record the cough if at all possible. If the vet can hear the cough herself, it can help her figure out the cause.
- ❑ The time of day is relevant: nighttime coughs are associated with fluid retention in the lungs, which occurs with congestive heart failure.
- ❑ A soft, nocturnal cough is also often a cardiac-related cough. It is a cough that may become productive as the condition progresses.
- ❑ Dry, non-productive coughing can be the sign of an environmental allergy.
- ❑ A persistent cough in middle-aged to older dogs is most likely a sign of chronic bronchitis. This generally refers to an otherwise healthy dog who has been coughing for up to two months without an apparent reason. Because of the persistent cough, the airways have been continually inflamed, leading eventually to the plugging of the small airways. The resulting cough sounds dry or harsh, but is frequently associated with gagging or retching after the cough because of fluids in the airway. The cause is unknown and treatments generally just lessen the symptoms.

◆ What Makes a Cough Worse?

- ❑ Tugging on a leash can worsen a cough for a dog that already has underlying problems. If you have a dog with an underlying problem that results in coughing, you should not use a collar to attach the leash to: try either a head collar like the Gentle Leader or a harness (see page 269).
- ❑ Irritants in the air such as cosmetic perfumes, powders or cleaning agents can all worsen a cough.
- ❑ Living with a human who smokes increases a dog's chance of developing chronic small-airway disease.
- ❑ Obesity can make breathing harder, but looking for weight loss through increased exercise can be difficult since any exertion can be hard for a pooch who has CHF, chronic bronchitis or some of the other cough-inducing conditions. A reduced calorie intake is probably the way to go, but certainly discuss the weight issue with your vet.

CUSHING'S DISEASE

Cushing's Disease is one of the most common hormonal diseases in dogs older than ten and is found more often in female dogs. It occurs when the adrenal glands produce too much cortisone.

◆ Breeds Most at Risk for Cushing's

The dogs most often affected by this disease are Beagles, Boston Terriers, Boxers, Dachshunds, German Shepherds, Golden Retrievers, Miniature and Toy Poodles, and Yorkshire Terriers.

◆ Symptoms of Cushing's

The "Symptoms Indicative of Cushing's" list below seems crazily long, but it is so important not to mistake normal aging for this illness. Identifying and treating the disease early can make all the difference in an older dog's quality of life. Those with the disease tend to have quite a few of the symptoms below.

SYMPTOMS INDICATIVE OF CUSHING'S DISEASE

- ❏ Metabolism: constant panting; shortness of breath; seeking cool surfaces to lie on; increased water intake; increased urination; diarrhea; day sleeping/night restlessness; increased appetite/obesity; vomiting; insulin-resistant diabetes
- ❏ Skin/hair: thin; wrinkled; slow to heal; thinning hair; decreased hair on body; darkening skin on abdomen; blackheads; chronic/frequent infections
- ❏ Neurological: seizures
- ❏ Psychological: depression or bizarre behavior; decreased interest in owners; general lethargy
- ❏ Motor: muscle weakness in back legs; extreme muscle stiffness; skull-like appearance to head

◆ Diagnosing Cushing's

Unfortunately, the signs of this illness are confusingly similar to many of the symptoms of aging, so it often goes undiagnosed. A vet must order a complex series of lab tests—urine, blood and a hormone-stimulation test—to diagnose this disease. If your dog does have one type of the disease, your vet may prescribe the time-tested medication Lysodren (also called mitotane) or a newer drug, Anipryl (also known as L-Deprenyl).

When Cushing's is found and treated early enough, a dog can regain her normal activities.

DEPRESSION

Many symptoms of emotional depression are similar to the signs of a dog being physically sick or in some kind of physical rather than psychological pain.

Talk to your vet about using human-grade treatments for depression, but understand that many veterinarians and behaviorists do not believe that dogs can suffer from depressed feelings. However, a vet who is more open-minded about the possibility may be willing to try a medication on your dog that is tailored for anxiety or depression.

SIGNS OF A DEPRESSED DOG

- ❑ Ignoring food
- ❑ Lying with head down for hours
- ❑ Lethargy, listlessness
- ❑ No interest in activities around them
- ❑ Doesn't care about going out, have to be cajoled
- ❑ Not interested in favorite games or toys

NOTE: *The above symptoms also often accompany hypothyroidism (low thyroid gland activity); these signs may also accompany other medical conditions, so you need to rule out all physical possibilities with your vet before addressing a possible emotional component to your dog's state of mind.*

DIABETES

Diabetes is a common and serious problem in pets. It is a disorder of the pancreas gland, which produces a hormone called insulin. Insulin's purpose is to drive nutrients, specifically glucose or blood sugar, into the cells. It is the body's most important fuel cell. When the body doesn't have enough insulin, glucose builds up in the bloodstream, a condition known as hyperglycemia (high blood sugar). With nowhere else to go, the glucose spills over into the urine, resulting in excessive urination.

Because they are losing so much water, diabetic dogs compensate by drinking a lot, which in turn leads to more frequent urination.

Even when diabetic dogs eat more, they aren't getting the nutrients they need to function, so they lose weight and become weak.

SIGNS OF DIABETES

- ❑ Enormous appetite
- ❑ Excessive thirst
- ❑ Frequent urination
- ❑ Weight loss
- ❑ Weakness

◆ What Causes Diabetes?

The cause of the onset of diabetes is not known, but there are contributory factors: genetic predisposition, infection, insulin-antagonistic diseases and drugs, immune-mediated disease and pancreatic inflammation. Long-term treatment with corticosteroids for other conditions can also predispose a dog to become diabetic.

◆ What Breeds Are at Risk?

Any breed or mix of breeds can develop the disease, but the two most common breeds that develop diabetes are Poodles and Miniature Schnauzers. The disease is seen more commonly in females and usually develops between six and nine years of age. Obese dogs and dogs that have had recurrent bouts of pancreatitis seem most prone to the disease. Long-term treatment with corticosteroids for other conditions can also predispose a dog to becoming diabetic.

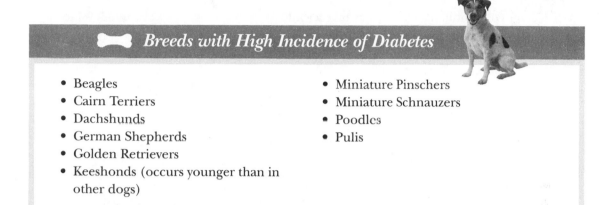

Breeds with High Incidence of Diabetes

- Beagles
- Cairn Terriers
- Dachshunds
- German Shepherds
- Golden Retrievers
- Keeshonds (occurs younger than in other dogs)

- Miniature Pinschers
- Miniature Schnauzers
- Poodles
- Pulis

◆ Homeopathic Vets Have Their Own Theories.
Holistic veterinarians have theories of their own about the onset of diabetes in dogs, although their conclusions are still controversial. Those who advocate home-prepared, meat-based foods blame processed, high-carbohydrate foods as a cause of diabetes. Others say that the commercial foods leave dogs malnourished, and that their bodies are therefore stressed and at risk. Yet others point a finger at vaccines as a physiological stress for dogs that leads to chronic disease, including diabetes.

◆ Treating Diabetes
Diabetes is often thought of as a disease without a cure, but it can be managed successfully. If it is detected early enough, the disease can even be reversed. Diabetes is conventionally managed with once- or twice-daily injections of insulin, a high-fiber diet and regulation of the dog's mealtimes. Exercise is important because it leads to weight loss, which can improve a diabetic animal's condition. One of the most important aspects of managing the disease is keeping the dog on a regular schedule of feeding, exercise and insulin injections. If you cannot be home for a dependable dinnertime, there are timed-release feeders that can be set to open at the right hour. For dogs on raw diets, or being fed canned food, these time-release feeders are also available with refrigerated compartments to keep food fresh.
Wow-Bow ([800]-326-0230) makes a hand-cut kibble formulated for diabetic dogs. See page 441 in "Nutrition" for more on Wow-Bow.

◆ Ongoing Testing
Testing is easy with urine dipsticks available from your vet. The homemade cup holder to catch urine that is generally recommended sounds primitive, but it works. Take a thin wire clothes

hanger, open it up and bend the end. Stick a paper cup on the bottom and as the dog urinates place the cup beneath the stream (your dog may give you a "What's up with you?!" look that gives new meaning to the phrase "No more wire hangers").

Keeping close tabs on the glucose level and proper insulin level is especially important during the first stages of treatment, when it may take a while to determine the right insulin level for your dog. Regular checks of these levels are also important, since changes in dosage and/or type of insulin are often necessary to bring the disease under control. The test for blood-sugar levels is called the blood glucose curve, and it involves the dog spending a day at the veterinary clinic. Over a period of twelve to twenty-four hours, blood is drawn at specified intervals to see when the blood sugar peaks and decreases. This way your vet can calculate—or recalculate—the amount of insulin to give and the timing of injections.

Regular blood tests are advised at least every six months to check for other conditions that could aggravate the diabetes, and other more sophisticated tests are also available. Cushing's, liver disease, hypothyroidism and infections are common complications of canine diabetes that can be identified with blood tests.

Regular urine cultures are important, too. Diabetic dogs are prone to bladder infections, so urine cultures should be done to check for this. Dogs may not show any signs of bladder infection and a urinalysis may look normal. Some vets will recommend cranberry supplements to help control bladder infections.

◆ Diabetic Emergencies

Dogs can get too much insulin if they get their regular dose but haven't eaten enough food or if you've changed the type of insulin. The result is a drastic drop in blood-sugar levels, a condition known as hypoglycemia (low blood sugar).

◆ Symptoms of Low Blood Sugar

Signs of hypoglycemia are confusion, sleepiness, shivering, staggering, collapse or seizures. If you suspect your dog is having a diabetic emergency of this kind, you need to get sugar into her bloodstream very quickly. You can do this by rubbing corn syrup, such as Karo, or honey onto her gums. You should see an improvement in her behavior within thirty minutes. If you do not see any change, or if you find your dog at the stage of collapse or having seizures, get to the vet immediately.

Another condition that can affect diabetic dogs is ketoacidosis, or severe hyperglycemia, which results when acids called ketones build up in the blood. This is a toxic condition that is an immediate life threat. Signs of ketoacidosis are weakness, vomiting, rapid breathing and breath that smells like nail polish remover (acetone). Take your dog to the vet immediately if you see these signs.

If your dog has diabetes, make sure everyone in the household is familiar with the symptoms on the chart on page 353 and understands the importance of getting emergency medical attention for the dog.

DISTEMPER

The canine distemper virus exists wherever there are dogs. It is the number one disease threat to the species, and it is highly contagious.

✦ Symptoms of Distemper

There are many signs of distemper, but because they aren't typical, people may delay going to a vet and seeking treatment. The symptoms are something like a bad cold: fever, congested head, bronchitis, pneumonia, intestinal inflammation, listlessness and poor appetite are all common in the early stages. As the disease progresses, there can be squinting and/or infection of the eyes, weight loss, vomiting, nasal discharge, coughing and diarrhea. In later stages, the virus can attack the central nervous system with paralysis or twitching. Because of the variety of symptoms, any young dog who seems sick should go right to the vet.

✦ Which Dogs Are at Risk?

Puppies are most susceptible to infection, although distemper strikes older dogs infrequently. If a puppy gets distemper, the death rate can be as high as eighty percent. Even if a young dog does not die from the disease, she may be permanently impaired. Possible infirmities include damage to the central nervous system, including paralysis, and a compromised sense of smell, hearing or sight. There can also be an increased risk of pneumonia. Distemper can resurface in older dogs, creating problems with the central nervous system.

   (A personal anecdote: One of my childhood Bedlington Terrier puppies, Falstaff, got distemper despite having come from a reputable breeder who had immunized the litter against the illness. Apparently, some vaccines fail. I was told there was little chance of a small puppy's survival because of the effect on the upper respiratory tract, but I spent hours with Falstaff in a hot steamy bathroom, helping to clear his lungs. He did survive, but his puppy coat never matured into the white fluffy Bedlington coat, and his personality remained anxious and clingy throughout his life. And he certainly never lived up to his namesake's girth, because my Falstaff remained as skinny as a Whippet, perhaps partly because of his early infirmity.)

EAR CROPPING

The only thing to say about the regrettable custom of ear cropping is that it is cruel and barbaric. The practice is a terrible indictment of how humans have been willing to turn a blind eye to the needless physical torture of dogs they buy (or even pass on a street and admire). A few unfortunate breeds—primarily Great Danes, Doberman Pinschers and Boxers—have been subjected for decades to having the back halves of their ears surgically removed and the remainder then splinted to stand upright. It is hard to fathom how, just for a look that seemed more fearsome, people could sanction putting dogs through the pain of the procedure and the weeks of misery afterward as their young ears are pinned together and swathed in tape on top of their heads to force them to stand upright.

It is a relief to know that times are changing. In Great Britain, they have gone a long way to banning the practice; it is now deemed "unethical but not illegal"—but this is a fine line for obscure reasons, the thrust being to end the practice. In the United States, no veterinarian who is even slightly progressive will agree to cut a dog's ears.

Probably the most disturbing thing about the future of ear cropping is that the AKC has used its lobbying power to *protect* the practice. There was a law being drafted in California that would have made it a crime in that state to crop a dog's ears, but the AKC successfully lobbied to defeat the bill. Once again (the support of puppy mills being the primary black mark against the organization), we have to remember that the American Kennel Club does not exist as an advocate of health, safety or humane treatment of dogs. They are an organization that charges a fee to register puppies from litters from registered breeding pairs, and sponsors dog shows (the "breed standards" like ear cropping being descriptions that apply principally to dogs competing in shows). Never confuse the AKC with the HSUS (Humane Society of the United States) or the ASPCA (American Society for the Prevention of Cruelty to Animals).

EAR PROBLEMS

Ear problems are the most frequent kind that vets see—ears that are itchy, smelly, bloody and/or crusty from infection, ear mites or something getting lodged in the ear like water, plant matter or an insect. The dog's ear anatomy has evolved as the perfect petri dish for bacteria and parasites to thrive. Certain purebred dogs like Cocker Spaniels, with long ears that hang down, are prime candidates for big ear problems. My Cocker Amalfi was at the vet every other week with ears stinky from infections I could not seem to conquer with any medicines.

If your dog is shaking her head and seems bothered by her ear(s), it can be a sign of infection/irritation inside the ear. It could also be a foreign object like an insect, plant matter or water that went into the ear canal. Anything going on in a dog's ears could be a sign of infection that only a veterinarian can cure. The longer you wait, the worse it gets and the harder it is to treat.

EAR SYMPTOMS REQUIRING THE VET

- ☐ Nasty smell
- ☐ Discharge coming out of the ear canal

- Bloodiness or crustiness around ear opening
- Frequent head shaking, ear scratching
- Pain in the head/ear area

◆ Treatment for Ear Problems

Don't try putting any cleaning tool like a cotton swab into your dog's ear canal. And don't even think of putting any over-the-counter ear medications for people into your dog's ears. A dog's ear has a different structure than the human ear, and furthermore, you have no way of knowing what is actually bothering the dog's ear.

The vet may need to sedate your dog and address whatever is going on in the ear with flushing and cleaning. If you don't go right to the vet, you miss the chance to clear up what may be a minor problem before it becomes a more serious one.

Surgery to eliminate the ear canal ("ablation") may sound radical, but it's often the kindest solution in the case of a dog that has persistent ear infections. In Cocker Spaniels and other breeds with long ear flaps, the inner part of the ear canal may have to be surgically altered in order to give full relief. The dog usually heals within a couple of weeks and is trouble-free after that—and may be a much happier, more active participant in your life without the constant discomfort in his ears. I did the ablation with Amalfi, my Cocker who was at the vet constantly with ear problems, and I was only sorry for his sake that I hadn't done it sooner. I could just imagine what an improvement it was for him over the suffering of pain and swelling he had been living with, and the loss or diminishment of hearing that resulted from chronically swollen tissues.

EQUILIBRIUM (BALANCE) PROBLEMS

"Vestibular Syndrome" is a broad collection of symptoms that basically have to do with a dog's equilibrium—or the loss of it.

◆ Signs of Inner-ear Problems

The symptoms of equilibrium problems can be frightening to watch and live with. Your dog will suddenly start going in circles, or turn and tilt her head up to the ceiling. You may worry that

🦴 Signs of Vestibular Syndrome

- Falling
- Rolling
- Head tilting and turning
- Vomiting
- Salivating

- Stumbling
- Staggering
- Abnormal eye movements
- Loss of appetite
- Walking in circles

your dog has suffered a stroke or seizure, but most of these symptoms have to do with the inner ear (the vestibular apparatus), which regulates balance and equilibrium, as it does in people.

◆ Diagnosing Vestibular Syndrome
This malady is difficult to diagnose. Ear infection is often to blame, but when that is ruled out, a vet may consider whether the problem is a brain disorder called central vestibular syndrome. MRIs and CAT scans are used to determine what may be going on, especially to rule out brain tumors. There is a long list of serious illnesses and diseases that can cause these equilibrium problems, so dogs of all ages and breeds can be affected. It's important that if your dog has any of these neurological/balance issues you seek out veterinary attention as soon as possible. There is no treatment for idiopathic central vestibular syndrome—most cases just get better on their own, although it sometimes leaves a permanent head tilt.

EYE PROBLEMS
Information about eye problems is on www.thedogbible.com, "Inside the Book."

FOOT PROBLEMS
The thick, tough skin on the bottom of your dog's feet can become cracked and painful. Some dogs lick their paws to ease the soreness, and that makes the situation worse.

◆ Causes of Footpad Problems
A dog's footpad can crack from constant exposure to chemicals such as rug shampoo and floor-cleaning agents, running on hot asphalt roads and walking on icy sidewalks where salt has been sprinkled. If all four feet are involved, then you know that the problem has to be something in the dog's environment.

Zinc deficiency is another reason for cracked footpads. Growing puppies can have this problem if their diet is deficient in zinc (or sometimes, ironically, when the diet is not balanced and has *too much* vitamin and mineral supplementation).

◆ Avoid Salt-containing Ice-melting Products.
If you live in a snowy or icy climate, choose salt-free melting products such as Safe Paw. Most packages will note whether the product is "pet friendly."

◆ Breeds at Risk for Cracked Footpads
Siberian Huskies and Alaskan Malamutes are the breeds most often affected by what is actually not a zinc deficiency, but the fact that their bodies can't absorb or utilize zinc properly.

Fast-growing puppies or teenagers of larger breeds are also at risk: Great Danes, Dobermans, German Shepherds, German Short-haired Pointers, Rhodesian Ridgebacks, Labrador Retrievers, Standard Poodles and even Beagles.

Bull Terriers can have a zinc deficiency that results in acrodermatitis, an inflammation of the skin in the paws or feet.

• Treatment for Zinc Deficiency

Vets usually adjust the diet and supplement with various forms of zinc, where necessary. If the dog does not respond to oral supplementation, a doctor can give a zinc IV, or low-dose cortico-steroids to help a dog absorb the medicine from the intestinal tract.

Soaking the dog's feet in water and applying petroleum jelly or other ointment to help hold moisture in the pads is the treatment of choice for other vets.

Sporting and sled dog owners use footpad-protection products such as Musher's Secret (www.jbpet.com) or just plain petroleum jelly on their dogs' feet.

Other products used to soothe or protect footpads include Bag Balm, Blue Foot, Protecta-Pad cream and Tuf-Foot. These were developed to prevent drying and cracking on working or field dog's footpads.

FROSTBITE

Frostbite is the condition that happens when exposure to severely cold temperatures damages skin tissues. Healthy animals can withstand subzero temperatures if they are dry and out of the wind. Frostbite is most likely to happen if an animal is injured or has no shelter. Frostbite can be minor or severe: in the first case only the tips of the ears are affected, while more extensive freezing causes the loss of toes, tails and, most seriously, limbs. The ears are the most likely part to be affected, followed by the tail and the feet.

If a dog's limbs are affected he may die, because the bacteria in his dying tissue can result in severe infection.

• Symptoms of Frostbite

At first, the damaged tissue looks normal, but within forty-eight hours the damaged tissue will swell and become painful. Within a week—while the blood flow and nerve supply have been cut off—the affected tissue dries up and turns black. Twenty to thirty days later, it falls off.

• What to Do

If you suspect your dog has been frostbitten, contact your vet immediately. The vet will want to assess the dog's condition, perhaps daily for several days, while removing dead tissue. She will usually prescribe medicine for pain and antibiotics to fight infection.

The best treatment is to rapidly thaw the frozen tissues with warm (not hot—103°F to 105°F) water. Do not rub the area.

HAIR LOSS (ALOPECIA)

There are two reasons for a dog to lose hair: either it's falling out, or it's being pulled or scratched out.

• Reasons That a Dog's Hair Falls Out

Hair usually falls out because of an endocrine disorder such as hypothyroidism (treated with thyroid hormone) or Cushing's disease (treated with Lysodren or Anipryl—see page 349), a sex hormone imbalance or a dermatosis related to growth hormone.

Infections can cause hair loss and are treated with the antibiotic that the vet deems appropriate, often combined with an antibacterial shampoo.

Hair can enter a "falling out" stage—usually from a stress such as surgery or other hospitalization, or from whelping (giving birth)—in which the hair just falls out. No treatment is necessary, because the hair does grow back.

Parasites can cause bald spots on a dog. The vet can do a skin scraping and see if the dog has a skin parasite such as mites or fleas, which can then be treated with topical or oral medications.

✦ Scratching, Chewing or Licking Hair Out

Poor diet is another cause for hair loss, so have a quick look at Chapter Thirteen, "Nutrition," to make sure that your dog is getting a balanced diet (especially people with small dogs, who may think they are pampering their pets with bits of chicken or steak, without realizing that that is not all a little dog needs).

Allergies are the main reason that a dog will scratch until her hair falls out, usually because something is irritating her skin. Treatments range from antihistamines, allergy shots, anti-itch shampoos and conditioners, to steroids in severe cases.

Canine baldness can also be age-related, but that is seen mostly in Dachshunds, who tend to lose hair in front of their ears, and on their chest and stomach.

HEART

Heart disease in dogs, as in people, usually develops in middle age and affects many older dogs. More than three million dogs develop heart (cardiac) problems each year; many of them may be in heart failure. This statistic is only related to dogs who get a yearly examination from their veterinarian (which unfortunately is not the majority of pets) so you can infer that millions of other elderly dogs are actually suffering from cardiac disease.

Heart failure is a threat to an older dog's health. As with humans, it means that the heart is unable to pump sufficient blood to meet the body's needs. The heart muscle has to work harder to pump blood, and it can be further damaged by this effort.

There are two common kinds of heart disease in dogs, both of which can lead to heart failure over time. Chronic valve disease (CVD) occurs when a dog's heart valves lose their ability to close properly, which causes abnormal blood flow; the other kind is when the muscle walls of the heart become thin and weak.

✦ Signs of Heart Disease

Unfortunately, many owners don't bring their dog to the vet until there are severe signs of heart failure, at which point it may be too late to do anything about it. This is a compelling reason to get a yearly checkup for your senior canine citizen, because your vet can identify early signs of cardiac problems. The early stages of the disease have no visible symptoms, but by the time the dog has moderate heart failure he'll have an enlarged heart with coughing, lethargy and difficulty breathing. When a dog has severe heart failure he'll have difficulty breathing even when resting, will be unwilling to do any exercise, may faint, lose his appetite and lose weight.

A heart murmur is often the first sign of chronic valve disease. A routine checkup can uncover a murmur, which indicates that there is a leaky valve in the heart.

Cavalier King Charles Spaniels are a particularly susceptible breed; they can get lesions in their hearts even before they're a year old.

✦ Chronic Valve Disease (CVD)

CVD is a slowly progressive disease in which the heart valves degenerate. It is by far the most common cardiac disease in dogs and the most frequent cause of congestive heart failure. Doctors don't know what causes it (although it does seem to be genetic) and there is no treatment to prevent it.

A dog can live for years with CVD with proper treatment, which can include a low-sodium diet and medications. Other dogs can develop congestive heart failure within months of a murmur being discovered, so it all depends on the underlying cause of the murmur. A murmur does not mean that a dog has heart disease, and as long as the heart is not enlarged, and there are no other symptoms, life goes on as normal.

A cough is the most obvious sign of heart trouble, particularly a hacking or deep cough. These are all things to discuss with your vet.

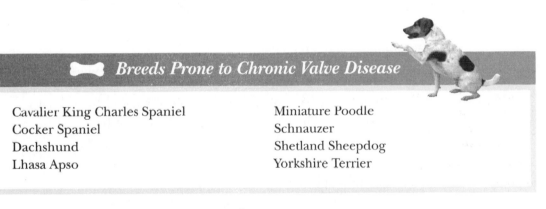

Breeds Prone to Chronic Valve Disease

Cavalier King Charles Spaniel	Miniature Poodle
Cocker Spaniel	Schnauzer
Dachshund	Shetland Sheepdog
Lhasa Apso	Yorkshire Terrier

✦ Treatment for Cardiac Disease

There is no cure for heart disease in dogs, but more treatments are becoming available all the time. Early detection is always the key to the best outcome—which is true of any disease and for people as well—but the success of treatment depends on individual circumstances. There are veterinarians who specialize just in cardiac care, and if your dog's situation warrants it and your situation permits it, your family vet may refer you to one of these animal heart specialists. Medication is usually prescribed to manage the condition, and this includes diuretics, ACE inhibitors and many of the other cardiac medications for people.

A pacemaker, which has a pulse generator with a power supply and a tiny computer that monitors and controls the heart's rhythm, corrects the same abnormalities in a dog's heart performance. The wires for the pacemaker are threaded through a neck vein, and the pacemaker itself goes under the skin at the back of the dog's neck—once the hair grows back after the surgical procedure, you can barely feel the device through the skin.

A canine cardiologist will consider a dog of any age for a pacemaker, unless the dog has other serious health issues such as cancer, which would shorten his life and pose a risk for surgery. The success rate for pacemaker implants in dogs is about ninety-five percent.

The cost is generally somewhere around $2,000. The pacemakers come from manufacturers who donate the ones that are at the end of their shelf life for human use, but these are still suitable for canine use because dogs live much shorter lives than people do. Many of the donated pacemakers go to a clearinghouse at the Ohio State University College of Veterinary Medicine in Columbus, where they are sterilized, packaged and sold to other schools. Ohio State sends about eighty-five refurbished pacemakers a year to surgeons around the country, while some schools and cardiologists get pacemakers directly from the manufacturer.

HEATSTROKE (SEE ALSO PAGE 336 FOR "SUNBURN")

The normal temperature for dogs is considered to be 101.5°F; the normal range is 99.5°F to 102.5°F. Above and below those temperatures, a dog's body begins to malfunction. Heatstroke occurs when the body has more heat than it can dissipate. There are two ways this can happen: exercise or environmental heat. Heatstroke can always be prevented, but once it happens it can easily be fatal.

✦ What Heatstroke Is and the Damage It Can Do

Signs of heatstroke include loud excessive panting, profuse salivation, high fever, vomiting and restless pacing. This is followed by the inside of the mouth becoming dry and red or purple. The eyes glaze over and the dog has trouble standing or walking. Eventually, the dog collapses.

Heatstroke has officially occurred when a dog's body temperature reaches 109°F or higher: at this temperature, body cells begin to die. When the body temperature reaches 109°F, a dog will begin to vomit. He will soon go into shock as his body sends all available blood to his vital internal organs. His blood may also begin to clot, which soon causes uncontrollable internal bleeding.

Damage takes place within minutes: seizures and unconsciousness from swelling in the brain, gastric ulcers from reduced blood supply to the digestive tract, permanent kidney damage from dehydration.

At this point, the dog's death is imminent.

DOGS MOST AT RISK FOR HEATSTROKE

- ❑ Small-headed, short-nosed breeds (Boxer, Pekingese, Pug, Mastiff) are not "well-designed" for cooling through panting
- ❑ Puppies
- ❑ Older dogs
- ❑ Sick dogs (with conditions such as hypothyroidism and heart or kidney disease)
- ❑ Dogs with heavy coats
- ❑ A high-energy dog that doesn't stop playing/running in the heat
- ❑ Dogs that live outside most of the time (these are in danger on very hot days)

❑ Black-coated dogs (such as Dobermans and Rottweilers) that can easily get overheated in warm temperatures

◆ What Causes Heatstroke in Dogs?

Dogs can suffer from heatstroke easily: conditions that may not even be uncomfortable for you may be life-threatening to your pooch. Jogging with an owner on a hot day is definitely dangerous: even going for a *walk* with him when it's very hot can cause heatstroke. There are times when exposing a dog to direct sun through the window of a moving car—even an air-conditioned one—can be risky. There have been cases of small dogs actually dying in a car being driven by their owners in very hot, sunny conditions.

Dogs are susceptible to the effects of heat because their skin works differently than ours. We have many sweat glands and tiny capillaries in our skin, and the sweat we produce when we get overheated evaporates, which cools the blood in those capillaries. Dog skin has neither sweat glands nor blood-cooling capillaries.

Dogs cool themselves by panting, which allows cooler air into their lungs to dissipate their body heat. Blood vessels in the tongue and mouth are cooled as the saliva evaporates. Panting is not an efficient cooling system, and a dog can easily enter the danger zone: the point at which he cannot cool himself down.

WAYS TO KEEP YOUR DOG COOL IN THE HEAT

❑ If your dog is outside during the day, make sure there is lots of shade for him.

❑ Walk the dog in the cool of the day, preferably early in the morning. By the end of the day, even though the sun has gone down, the ground and pavement are still really hot.

❑ Stand on grass or shaded surfaces when outdoors with your dog; asphalt and concrete absorb heat and can burn footpads.

❑ Always take along water and a bowl anytime you're out and about with your dog, but especially in hot weather.

❑ Don't shave off all the dog's hair. You may think that fur is hotter, but a pet's fur actually helps insulate him from the heat (and can help prevent sunburn). Try a "puppy cut" instead.

❑ Fill a hard-sided plastic kiddie-pool with water: your dog(s) can use it to drink from and to walk or lie down in to cool off, especially after a walk or playing.

❑ Leave your dog at home when you run errands—your car turns into an oven in minutes, even parked in the shade.

❑ Do not leave your dog in a car—not even for a minute—if you must take him along. If you doubt this is serious, do the following: put on a heavy coat and hat and sit in that car yourself for five minutes. See?

◆ What to Do if Heatstroke Occurs

1. Get him out of the heat and into a cool shady area. If it is just the early effects of heat exposure, it may be enough to put him in a cooler setting with frequent sips of small amounts of water, or ice cubes to lick.

2. Take his temperature with a rectal thermometer. Glass is preferable to digital, because the latter doesn't always register high temperature from heatstroke.

3. If his temperature is below 104°F, keep him in a cool place and allow him to drink only sips of water (a lot of water can make him vomit, further dehydrating him).

4. With a temperature above 104°F, the dog may already be unresponsive to you, unable to stand or having seizures. You need to lower the dog's temperature before you do anything else, but someone should contact the vet so they will be expecting you.

5. Begin cooling him with water-soaked towels or a spray hose with cool (not cold) water. Concentrate on the head, neck and underneath the front and back legs. Rinse and cool the tongue, but don't let water run down his throat (it can get into his lungs).

6. Take his temperature again: once it reaches 104°F, stop the cooling process. More complications can occur, since his body cannot regulate his thermal system now.

7. Take him to a veterinary hospital to be checked out, even if he seems to have recovered.

◆ What to Do When You See a Dog in a Hot Car

A car can be deadly on a hot day—when the sun hits a car on an eighty-degree day, it takes fifteen minutes for the temperature inside to reach 130°F to 170°F. And that is even with the windows slightly open.

The temperature can rise even faster with any of the following: a dark car color, poor ventilation, the heat created by a panting dog (even greater with multiple dogs), high humidity and direct sunlight.

It is a criminal offense in several states to leave an animal in a hot car. You can go into nearby stores and ask them to page the owner of a dog left in a car, but be prepared for the owner to react poorly and be defensive or volatile because she is humiliated or ashamed of what she's done. Defensiveness is the usual reaction of owners who are confronted with having baked their dog in a car.

Common excuses from such owners are: "It's a cloudy day"; "I'm parked in the shade"; "I left the windows open a little"; "I haven't been gone long"; "I've always done this with no problems."

Don't get into a big debate with the dog's owner if she is angry about being corrected. However, if you have the stomach for a confrontation, suggest that if she wants to know what her car feels like to her dog, she should get into her car wearing a wool coat and hat and see how many minutes *she* can stand it!

Do not try to liberate a dog in a locked vehicle, even if the dog is suffering heatstroke. It's a criminal offense to touch someone else's property (which means the car and/or the dog), and the owner may go after you legally.

Call the local police or animal control or ask someone else to call while you stay near the dog.

INTESTINAL PROBLEMS

✦ Bloat (Gastric Dilatation-volvulus, or GDV)

This potentially fatal condition happens when the stomach overextends after eating, rapidly filling with gas, secretions and food. Air accumulates rapidly in the stomach (dilatation), the stomach fills to the point where it twists back on itself, rotating on its axis (volvulus) from 180 to a full 360 degrees, causing pressure, severe pain and compression of other organs.

There are theories about what causes bloat, but it is a condition not clearly understood. Bloat generally happens when a dog with a tendency to gulp his food eats a large meal, takes in excessive air along with it and then drinks excessively and exercises vigorously. However, bloat can also occur mysteriously, for unknown reasons.

The most susceptible dogs are large ones with deep, narrow chests (see chart below), but studies have shown other factors that can increase the chance of bloat. There is also a link between bloat and dogs who are high-strung and experience stress around changes in their routine (such as hospitalization, being boarded or big changes in the home environment).

RISK FACTORS FOR BLOAT

- ❏ Increased age (six to seven is the average)
- ❏ Large or giant breed (especially Great Danes)
- ❏ Deep, narrow chest
- ❏ Overweight
- ❏ Immediate relative (parent, sibling or offspring) who suffered bloat
- ❏ Increased speed of eating
- ❏ Only gets one meal per day
- ❏ Stress around mealtimes, or generally

Experts say that breeding larger and larger dogs may be a factor in bloat, because the tendency toward bigger dogs has created biochemical imbalances. While breeders have constantly leaned toward bigger dogs over hundreds of years (except for toys, of course), the dogs' internal organs have not increased in size in proportion to their bodies, which has compromised their ability to function and increased the likelihood of certain diseases. Bloat is one of them (along with cardiomyopathy and hip dysplasia).

Until a recent five-year study was completed (at the Purdue University School of Veterinary Medicine), most of the preventive recommendations about bloat had little or no scientific basis. Perhaps the most surprising contradiction of earlier beliefs that came out of the study was that you should *not* raise the food bowl to spare a large dog from stretching down to eat. The recommendation used to be the opposite, but the new study actually showed that raising a food bowl increases the chances of bloat. Another earlier unproven supposition was that you should moisten dry food or avoid dry food completely, but this did not seem to be relevant.

Preventing bloat can be as low-key as giving a dog who has already had an episode of bloat or is a member of a breed at risk for bloat several smaller meals a day rather than one large meal. This is generally considered better for all dogs' health, anyway.

◆ Diet and Bloat

Factors that increase the risk of bloat:

Higher fat in the diet increases the risk of bloat by almost double. If a dog is fed dry food that lists fat as one of the first four ingredients, the risk of bloat goes way up.

Dry foods containing citric acid that were moistened with liquid before feeding were also to blame for a higher incidence of bloat—three times higher.

Older dogs are more at risk every year, with a reported twenty percent increase with every year of a dog's age.

A close relative who experienced bloat gives a dog a more than sixty percent chance of developing it too—this means siblings, parents and/or offspring.

Fearful, stressed dogs are at a hugely increased risk for bloat—almost three times more than a happy, relaxed dog.

Dogs who eat quickly and get only one meal a day are more likely to bloat.

Factors that decreases the risk of bloat:

Meat meal in dry food listing "bone" in the top four ingredients decreased the chance of bloat by half.

Including canned meat in the diet lowered the chance of a dog getting bloat.

Home-prepared foods seemed to lower the risk enormously, too.

◆ Myths about Causes of Bloat

Limiting water or exercise before or after feeding is no longer believed to increase the chances of a dog developing bloat.

Raising the food bowls of tall, large dogs has been standard practice for years, on the theory that a raised bowl discouraged a dog from gulping air into his stomach while eating. The Purdue study was surprising because it showed that an elevated food bowl actually increased the chances of bloat developing. I used to feed my huge Rottweiler Yogi Bear from a bowl on a stand, and Scooby Doo, the very tall Weimeraner, was eating out of a bowl up on an antique child's chair—until I learned about the Purdue results.

Gastropexy is a preventive surgery that may sound radical but can be safe and effective in drastically reducing the chance that a high-risk dog will get bloat. This procedure has to be done under anesthesia, so it makes sense to do it when your dog is having anesthesia for another procedure, such as spaying, neutering or teeth cleaning. It involves suturing (stitching) the dog's stomach directly to the abdominal wall: if the stomach is anchored, it cannot twist.

PRECAUTIONS TO REDUCE CHANCE OF BLOAT

- ❏ Feed in a stress-free environment.
- ❏ Give two to three feedings throughout the day, not one large meal.
- ❏ Slow down the speed of eating by placing a clean rock or other object in the bowl that the dog has to eat around.

❑ Someone should be around following feedings to look for signs of gastric disturbance (discomfort, excess gas, belching, vomiting).

❑ No strenuous exercise or gulping water for one to two hours after eating.

❑ Keep your dog from becoming overweight.

❑ Do not breed a dog with a first-degree relative who had bloat.

❑ Consider gastropexy in a high-risk breed.

Dogs with comparatively elongated stomachs such as Basset Hounds, Dachshunds and Cocker Spaniels are at risk. Overweight dogs also have a tendency to bloat, so you clearly would not want to have a dog from an at-risk breed become fat, increasing his danger of bloat.

🦴 Breeds Susceptible to Bloat

- Airedale Terrier
- Akita
- Basset Hound
- Bloodhound
- Borzoi
- Boxer
- Collie
- German Shepherd
- Gordon Setter
- Great Dane

- Greyhound
- Irish Setter
- Irish Wolfhound
- Newfoundland
- Old English Sheepdog
- Rottweiler
- Saint Bernard
- Standard Poodle
- Weimaraner

You must know the warning signs of bloat and respond very quickly, or your dog may not survive. It is not always easy to see stomach distension in some dogs, so you want to watch for some of the earlier symptoms: general anxiety and restlessness, pacing and whimpering, drooling heavily, panting, retching and trying to vomit without success.

Get your dog to a vet for an evaluation. If the dog is experiencing bloat, then her life depends on being properly diagnosed and getting immediate emergency surgery. Be sure that whatever medical facility you choose is prepared to do that.

Have an emergency medical plan in place so that if your dog develops a medical emergency—such as bloat, a serious accident or any after-hours medical problem—you'll know how to get to the nearest twenty-four-hour critical-care center.

WARNING SIGNS OF BLOAT, IN ORDER OF INCREASING IMPORTANCE

❑ Anxiety and restlessness

❑ Pacing, whining or whimpering

- ❏ Panting or labored breathing
- ❏ Heavy drooling
- ❏ Retching with attempts to vomit (nothing comes up)
- ❏ Visibly distended stomach, sounds hollow when tapped
- ❏ Increased stomach enlargement, tender when touched
- ❏ Shock: weakness, pale gums, shallow breathing, rapid heartbeat, collapse

The outlook for a dog depends greatly on how quickly the signs of bloat are noticed and how soon afterward she is in the hands of a surgeon. A dog who does not receive immediate medical care for bloat will die, so you can see that these warnings are not overstated. Of the dogs suffering bloat who *do* get into emergency surgery, ten percent will die in surgery, nearly twenty percent will die from complications in the post-operative week, and seventy percent will go home in good shape. The differences have to do with how severe the bloat was and how soon the dog got to a hospital. It is major surgery—usually with sixty to ninety minutes on the operating table—and a dog's survival is questionable if he was really sick when he arrived.

Gastropexy is usually done at the end of the surgery. The stomach is secured to the abdominal wall, because without this procedure, the disease almost always recurs within a year.

✦ Constipation

Constipation is defined as "infrequent or difficult defecation." A constipated dog may strain to defecate. He may seem to be in pain when defecating, or pass small or no feces.

The normal frequency of bowel movements in dogs ranges from three times a day to once every day or two. Just as people vary in their elimination habits, so too do individual dogs. Be observant and learn what is normal for your dog; depending on the individual, a dog can go up to two days without defecating without any bad effect.

✦ Causes of Constipation

- ❏ Obstruction is the most common cause: eating bones, or ingesting foreign bodies such as stones, hair or sticks that can't be digested and cause blockages along the digestive tract.
- ❏ There can also be a tumor in the rectal area, or a perineal hernia, in which pouches develop out of the rectum so stool gets stuck.
- ❏ Lack of exercise and movement can also cause constipation, because moving around enhances the colon's movement and activity.
- ❏ Medications for other conditions can slow down the digestive process.
- ❏ Neurological diseases can affect elimination.

✦ What to Do for Constipation

Increase exercise. Increase dietary fiber. Increase the dog's fluid intake—this is not easy to do, except that you can encourage drinking by having multiple water bowls around the house and changing the water frequently to make it more enticing. Dogs often like running water or newly poured water, so consider leaving the toilet seats up if that will encourage your dog to drink. There are dog water bowls designed with running water that recirculates, if you prefer that option (my dogs wouldn't give it a lick, but others swear by it). If things don't get better in a day or two, see your vet to determine if there is an obstruction of some kind. Do not attempt any kind of medication or stimulant yourself.

◆ Diarrhea

Dogs get diarrhea for a number of reasons, but generally it's because they've eaten something that does not agree with them. The treatment for diarrhea is food that is soothing and binding. Boil up three to four cups of rice and mix it with some chicken or even a can of high-quality chicken dog food. Feed small amounts of this mixture for a day or two. If you don't see definite improvement in his bowel movements—if they're not getting firmer and less frequent—then take him in to the vet to see what else might be irritating his stomach.

You can also give Pepto-Bismol tablets to a dog to coat his stomach lining and calm the diarrhea, although some vets do not like to use this product with animals.

Diarsanyl is a paste that soothes an animal's stomach, absorbing toxins. It is a time-tested product made from a natural French clay that you can only get from your vet (she can order it from Phoenix Pharmaceuticals if she doesn't know about it) which is widely used in England and Europe.

◆ Gas (Flatulence, Farting)

It seems as though there is nothing quite as dreadfully pungent as the gas that some dogs emit—either SBD (Silent but Deadly) or with an audible warning.

Even though gas can make a dog's belly swell up, this kind of intestinal gas is not related to bloat (see page 363).

◆ What Causes Gaseous Emissions?

Intestinal gas is basically caused by intestinal fermentation. Dogs that eat with too much gusto often gulp large amounts of air with their food. This usually causes belching, as it does in people who "hoover" down their food. However, even though some air may be burped up, there can still be pockets of swallowed air that continue down the digestive tract and have to exit at the other end.

◆ What Can You Do about Gas?

Some dogs are just gassy, and some breeds even tend toward digestive gassiness, so you may not be able to "cure" them entirely. If you're giving table scraps or any variety of snacks or human food, stop putting that extra strain on her digestive system. Try a diet that is high-quality and low-residue (not a whole lot of what is called "insoluble fiber" on the ingredients label).

You can start by changing the brand of food the dog eats or switching to one with different primary ingredients. Try feeding mostly high-quality canned food instead of an all-kibble diet.

Activated charcoal can absorb some of the gas in the intestines, so it doesn't have a chance of exiting as smelly gas. Some over-the-counter products to aid human digestion and reduce gassiness contain activated charcoal as the main ingredient. Ask your vet if she thinks that giving your dog treats with activated charcoal in them might help your dog's digestive process.

• Change Your Dog's Eating Habits.

Slow down the speed at which your dog gobbles. Try putting a few smooth, clean medium-size rocks in your dog's dish. She'll have to eat around them, which will slow her down. This is something they do with horses who eat too quickly (which can cause a life-threatening disorder in horses called colic).

Feed more frequent, smaller meals. If your dog isn't ravenous waiting for that one meal of the day, he may not be as likely to inhale it.

Separate dogs. In a multiple-dog household, try separating dogs at mealtimes so that food is not being gulped to keep a "sibling" from "elbowing in on the bowl."

• Inflammatory Bowel Disorder (IBD)

Various causes are suspected in cases where a dog has chronic recurring diarrhea (ranging from soft stools to bloody or mucous liquid), which may be accompanied by vomiting.

To diagnose IBD, the symptoms have to continue for at least one week and then a series of blood and fecal tests are done to eliminate other possible reasons for intestinal inflammation. It may not be necessary to go to any sort of specialist—your own vet may have an endoscope to make the diagnosis. He sends the samples to the same lab as a specialist does. If an intestinal irritability is diagnosed promptly, there is a high rate of success in dealing with the disorder.

• Symptoms of IBD
- ❐ Diarrhea
- ❐ Discomfort after eating
- ❐ Intestinal rumbling from gas
- ❐ Vomiting
- ❐ Poor appetite
- ❐ Weight loss

• Change in Diet

A dog with IBD can have some or all of these signs. After lab tests are done, it is customary for vets to try a new diet temporarily, because it's necessary to rule out food allergies as the cause of the bowel symptoms. A diet is usually prescribed that uses a protein source that the dog is not likely to have previously consumed. Fish, duck, venison, even kangaroo are all available in commercially prepared canned food for just this reason: many dogs become allergic to the same protein source over a lifetime. Using a different protein source has helped many dogs.

• Medications

Some vets treat with medication, in particular antibiotics, to bring the overall bacterial load of the intestinal tract back to normal. An immunosuppressive drug like a steroid may be given to lower the inflammation in the bowel.

◆ Vomiting

It is often not a cause for alarm if your dog throws up. It is quite natural for dogs to vomit if anything is bothering their stomachs. Sometimes the whole contents of their stomach will come up, other times if their stomach is empty their vomit can be a foamy yellow-greenish liquid (stomach bile).

◆ Reasons for Vomiting

The dog may have swallowed something indigestible—for example, small pieces that break off the chew treats you've given her. There could be chips of bone in the vomit, pieces of rawhide, chips of chew hooves, all of which would explain what triggered the vomiting. Other times there may be plant matter in the vomit or strands of undigested grass, which the dog has eaten to settle a "funny tummy," and that may bring on the throwing up.

Generally speaking, a dog who throws up an irritant that she has eaten will appear to feel fine within minutes. She'll show no ill effect from throwing up or from the cause of the irritation. This kind of vomiting is not a cause for alarm, because the body has expelled the offending matter and solved the problem.

But if your dog retches several times and seems lethargic or withdrawn afterward, that is reason to get to the vet's office. You want to diagnose the cause of the vomiting and get treatment for it as soon as possible. A dog that vomits repeatedly and brings up only frothy liquid may have a serious underlying medical problem such as pancreatitis (a life-threatening illness that is covered on page 323), stones or other kidney problems, ulcers, cancer, etc.

◆ Eating the Vomit

Among the most revolting canine habits is a dog eating his own vomit (if you live in a multi-dog household, there can even be a sort of mad dash to see who gets there first. Back in the days when dogs were wolves, the mother wolf regurgitated food for her pups. Wolf pups beg food from their mother by pawing and biting at her lips when she returns to the den, trying to get her to vomit. This ancestral wolf habit has been bred out of domestic dogs (perhaps because people find it disgusting) but it explains why dogs will instinctively re-eat their vomited food. This is also the instinctive reason that dogs lick your mouth and face: to stimulate you to regurgitate for them, Nice, eh?

KIDNEY DISEASE

Inflammation of the kidney (one or both) is usually caused by a bacterial infection (leptospirosis), ingesting antifreeze, or Addison's disease. It is quite common and begins with fever and pain in the kidney area. A stiff-legged gait and hunched-back posture are characteristic symptoms of the disease, as is a change in your dog's normal pattern of urinating. Antibiotics are the usual treatment.

Kidney disease is diagnosed with blood work and managed with a fluid replacement (IV or subcutaneous), antinausea medication and a specialized diet such as Hill's K/D diet (Hill's was the first commercial company to focus on diets for dogs with illness. Wow-Bow in Deerpark,

New York ([800]-326-0230) makes a special kibble for dogs with kidney problems and it can be customized for your dog. See page 441 in "Nutrition" for more about this special dog food company.

Plenty of fresh water should always be available—dogs with kidney disease get very thirsty—and their exercise should be moderate, not strenuous.

◆ Kidney Transplant

This will not apply to many people, but there are people who are willing to do anything possible for their dog with kidney failure—and they may not know that kidney transplants are available. If your dog has kidney failure and meets certain criteria, transplants are available at the UC Davis School of Veterinary Medicine in California. The operation is considered only for dogs in the early stages of renal failure. A dog can be accepted as a transplant candidate if she is still active, not anemic and her weight has not changed (she is not a good transplant candidate if she has already lost fifteen to twenty percent of her body weight). Success is not guaranteed.

The best possible donor is a related or same-breed dog. If you can't get that, the next best donor would be a dog under six years old, healthy and of the similar size and weight. An animal shelter near UC Davis provides donor dogs if the recipient's owners will adopt them afterward.

LAMENESS, LIMPING

If your dog is lame or limps, it could just be a strained or sprained muscle, especially if you notice it after she has exerted herself physically. Because soft-tissue damage is hard to diagnose in dogs, veterinary medicine doesn't use the terms "sprain" or "strain," but instead calls it "overuse syndrome" or "sore dog syndrome." If you have an older dog, arthritis may be the underlying cause of the lameness (see more below on arthritis). But of course your dog may also have fractured or broken a bone or done damage to tendons or ligaments, all of which must be professionally determined.

SIGNS OF MUSCLE STRAIN/SPRAIN

❏ Limping
❏ Crying/yelping when placing weight on the limb
❏ Unable or reluctant to go up/down stairs
❏ Refusal to get up

☐ Unable to extend a limb
☐ Unable to flex a limb
☐ Unable to support any weight on a limb
☐ Limb dangling, no muscle tension

On the one hand, it doesn't make sense to rush off to the vet when your dog starts limping, since there is nothing much that she can do except prescribe rest. On the other hand, limping could also be an indicator of something serious, which should not be ignored.

When to See the Vet about Lameness

- When the dog is lethargic (rule out Lyme and other tick-borne diseases)
- When signs have no apparent cause
- When the dog has been unusually active
- When the dog has not been physically stressed
- When rest does not help for a couple of days
- When you have nagging doubts

◆ Determine the Cause

The way to decide what to do about lameness is to consider what the dog was doing before the symptoms appeared. Sporadic and strenuous exercise can cause lameness if the dog is not in shape. If your dog is usually sedentary and you take him on a long hike, he's going to be sore afterward, as you would be if you weren't conditioned. If the dog found canine companions who inspired him to leap and chase, he may be muscle-sore.

Arthritis is a common cause of lameness. Older dogs get arthritis, which is the inflammation of whatever joint in the body is affected. Two types of arthritis affect dogs: there is degenerative joint disease, which progresses slowly, causing destruction of the cartilage protecting the bones in the joint. This kind of arthritis is age- or trauma-related and affects the load-bearing joints (the legs) in particular. The other type of arthritis involves the immune system and is known as inflammatory arthritis, which includes infectious and rheumatoid arthritis.

OCD (osteochondrosis) is a joint disease that affects the cartilage of the shoulder, elbow, hock or knee joints of growing pups from large, fast-growing breeds. It presents as lameness when they reach six to nine months and can go on for weeks or months, causing the puppy significant pain. It happens more often to males. It can even affect a Labrador Retriever that has been carefully bred to avoid hip dysplasia.

The exact cause of this infirmity is not known, but it begins as abnormal development of the deep layers of joint cartilage. As the condition progresses, a small piece of cartilage may become detached. There is a hereditary predisposition toward OCD, and excess dietary protein during puppyhood may also be to blame. Some breed clubs screen for OCD by X-ray—just as they do for hip dysplasia—before breeding so that the condition is not passed on. In any case, owners of large-breed puppies should take care not to overfeed with high protein.

Some dogs respond to severely restricted exercise (although confining a large, rambunctious youngster is a lot harder than many vets seem to think). This is followed by X-rays to determine if healing has taken place. The condition often results in arthritis when dogs are middle-aged. Surgery is recommended for some dogs to remove the diseased fragments of cartilage, and the normal prognosis is for complete recovery.

Knee ("stifle") problems A torn cruciate ligament in the center of the knee is one of the most common knee problems in dogs. The ligament can be thought of as a twisted rope that begins to unravel. The problem is usually a tear (also called a rupture if it is torn all the way through) in the two ligaments that form an "X" in the knee joint, making the joint unstable.

Surgery is the only solution to the problem: the doctor replaces the torn ligament with a synthetic material much like fishing line, which threads over the knee joint in the "X" pattern. Another option is a fairly new surgery called tibial plateau leveling osteotomy (TPLO), which means cutting the bone (osteotomy) and securing its new position with a plate and screws. There are also total joint replacements, but these are more theoretical, since they are very rarely done. The first option of the standard ligament replacement will probably have the best outcome with an older, more sedentary dog, whereas a young, highly active dog may often get more stability and strength in the joint from the TPLO.

◆ Which Dogs Are at Risk?

Apparently, the statistics show that older dogs and Labrador Retrievers and Rottweilers are most likely to tear the cruciate ligament—although my own experience contradicts that, since Yogi Bear the Rottie was one of the few dogs I've had whose knees were fine! My other dogs seem to have had very bad luck with their knees—and you can imagine just how grateful I was to have pet insurance. Roma, a Golden Retriever from a very nice breeder, ruptured her back knee running up a hill when she was only four years old. Then Billy Blue, the slowest moving of my dogs, tore *his* knee when he was eight and had the "fishing line" repair. My vet sent us to an orthopedic specialist who did a $1,000 MRI and discovered that Billy Blue had a torn meniscus (see page 373). Then, to my consternation, only one month after I adopted one-year-old Jazzy (a small, smooth-coated Collie mix who was quicker and more agile than any dog I'd ever had—and presumably free of the inbred problems of purebred dogs), she blew the cruciate ligament in her back knee. The orthopedic specialist said that the only way to get long-term stability for a dog as young and athletic as she would be the more invasive but ultimately more stabilizing TPLO.

The recuperation can be as torturous as the surgery. They tell you to keep your dog completely confined, except for brief leash walks for bathroom purposes, for six weeks (I thought *I* would need to be tranquilized by the end of what felt like six months!).

Doctors will tell you there is a high statistical chance—fifty percent—that a dog that has had one cruciate ligament injury will rupture the opposite knee ligament within one to two years. Sure enough, Jazzy was right on schedule and ruptured her other back knee. This time I opted for the "fishing line" surgery.

Torn Meniscus The menisci (the plural of miniscus) are fibrous pads that sit on top of the tibia. They can tear or rupture just like the cruciate ligament. A vet can sometimes identify with manual manipulation whether it is the kneecap or the joint, but it is most often diagnosed at the time of a ligament injury just by looking at the pads in the joint. An MRI would rarely be used for this.

◆ Remedies for Strains and Sprains
Don't do anything at all until you have taken your dog to the vet or have at least had a phone consultation—the worst thing you can do is self-diagnose or just use any remedy that sounds good without finding out the underlying cause. Once you have your vet's approval, these are some of the remedies she may suggest:

1. *Apply cold:* Cold reduces pain and swelling in the first twenty-four hours after injury. Apply a bag of frozen vegetables or a gel freezer-pack wrapped in a dishcloth or paper towel. Use for fifteen minutes, wait an hour, then repeat.

2. *Restrict activity:* When the dog starts feeling better, he probably still needs more time to heal, so leash-walk him only for a few more days.

3. *Apply heat:* Once twenty-four hours have passed since the injury, a heat pack will increase the healing of circulation and reduce stiffness. Make a heat pack by wetting paper towels, putting them inside a baggie and warming them in the microwave for twenty seconds (more or less; check to make sure it is not hot, just pleasantly warm). Apply to the area.

◆ Remedies for Pain
Glucosamine is widely used for dogs with arthritis, postoperative, and other joint pain. As with formulations for people, there can be significant differences in the quality of the source and type of glucosamine, the amount formulated in each dosage and whether it is balanced with another compound like chondroitin. One of the reasons that many vets and owners use the well-known brand Cosequin over less-expensive or well-known formulations is that they are assured of the quality and strength of that brand. If you have a large dog, be sure to get the "DS" or "double strength," because otherwise your dog won't be getting enough to be therapeutic.

There are dry dog foods that include and advertise that they contain glucosamine, but you cannot rely on that since they cannot possibly include a therapeutic dose in a day's food—and the quantity your dog will get becomes negligible if you also feed canned or fresh meat. Another way to give glucosamine to your dog is to put a supplement containing it into your dog's food (see page 453 for a description of one such product, Platinum Plus). However you decide to give glucosamine to your dog, the amount your dog needs is what will make the difference. Talk to your vet about the dosage, but trust your own eyes to determine whether your dog seems to move better after a few days. If you don't see improvement, ask your vet's opinion about increasing the amount of glucosamine until you do get results.

MEDICATIONS

◆ Pain Medication

Years ago, there was much less attention given to the issue of pain in dogs—in fact, even after surgery no pain medication was given. Thankfully, that has changed. Now, enlightened doctors consider pain medication essential for all surgeries, even routine ones—neuters and spays are now followed by pain relief, too. Be sure you discuss this with your vet ahead of time to be sure she is supportive of this philosophy. For more on pain relief see pages 397–98.

More attention is being given to the aches and pains of old age—mostly arthritic in nature—that affect millions of dogs as the elderly canine population grows. Improvements in veterinary care allow dogs to live longer and become old enough to develop all those pains! Pain medication is also needed for dogs with various kinds of cancer, since half of all dogs over ten years old are going to get cancer of some kind.

Signs of Pain

- Acting aggressively or crying out when area is touched
- Constant barking or whining
- Pacing, restlessness
- Trembling
- Panting, rapid breathing (tachypnea)
- Licking, chewing or scratching at the affected area
- Increased heart rate and temperature
- Lying abnormally, frequent position changes
- Sleeplessness
- Wide-eyed, dilated pupils

❒ Good old-fashioned aspirin is the choice of some doctors for a dog's pain. Enteric-coated aspirin such as Ecotrin is the best choice for pain or fever. The coating keeps the aspirin from dissolving in the esophagus or even in the stomach, protecting a dog's highly sensitive gut. However, these products cannot be used postsurgically due to the potential for bleeding.

- NSAIDs (nonsteroidal anti-inflammatory drugs) are Advil-like drugs that are generally effective at reducing inflammation and relieving pain, just as they are in people. The medications are widely used to give pain relief and protect the cartilage. There are relatively few reported side effects with long-term use. Although Rimadyl (a newer NSAID that is often used to treat arthritis in older dogs) has come under attack—there have been serious problems reported with this particular drug—the truth is that all NSAIDs are potentially dangerous. Nevertheless, most vets believe that the benefits of NSAIDs usually outweigh the risks.
- Etogesic was from the "first generation" of NSAIDs used on animals. Although doctors do not prescribe it as frequently anymore, it is still an effective medication for many dogs. It is also much less costly, which is a consideration if you have more than one dog who needs it, or if you have to give it for a long time. For what it's worth, two of my dogs responded better to this drug than the newer, more popular ones.
- Deramaxx is one of the newest anti-inflammatory nonsteroidals. Many dogs get good relief from this chewable tablet.
- A liquid NSAID called Metacam, which has been in use in Europe for a decade, was only introduced into the States in 2004. My own experience has been a "Hallelujah!" with this drug: Billy Blue had two small fractures in his foot, got no relief from any of the "Big Three" NSAID pills and had an orthopedic surgeon suggest surgery that would have effectively eliminated his ankle joint. On the second day of Metacam, a dog who would not even stand up to go out to pee was joining us on walks in the woods—Mr. Blue was still gimpy, but he came along without complaint. Metacam seems pricey, but the larger bottle is a better value and lasts a long time. I consider it a godsend to an older gent (Mr. Blue) who was becoming a sedentary shut-in until he got Metacam

◆ Warnings on NSAIDs

The Advil-like drugs known as NSAIDs (nonsteroidal anti-inflammatory drugs) are a class of medications that work well to control pain but can be rough on the stomach—and sometimes the liver and kidneys. Because canine gastrointestinal tracts are sensitive, there can be G.I. and liver problems (characterized by appetite loss, vomiting, diarrhea and eventually weakness and apathy). If a dog on any NSAID shows any of these symptoms, he should be taken off the pill immediately. Check with your doctor, since there have been canine deaths associated with these drugs.

There are several drugs being used to relieve the pain associated with arthritis, and more are on the way. No drug works all the time for all dogs, but most of these medications are effective in controlling pain. Etogesic was a member of the earlier generation of prescription NSAID drugs; it is not as frequently prescribed now.

Talk to your vet about which NSAID he thinks you should try first, and if your dog does not get relief, you can try another (but only under your vet's supervision and always allowing a couple of days for your dog's stomach to settle down before trying the next medication; I was not patient enough with Billy Blue and switched him right from one drug to another, and I felt terrible because on top of his foot pain, his guts were a wreck for a week).

Dogs are sensitive to gastrointestinal upset. These medications must be taken with a full meal, which is the same recommendation for humans who take Advil and stronger versions of it.

Never mix two NSAIDs. It can wreak havoc on your dog's system, especially her digestive system, if you mix two kinds of NSAIDs or even give one and then switch too quickly to another. You need to wait—usually a couple of days—for one medication to leave her body before starting the other.

◆ Adequan by Injection

Adequan offers pain relief by blocking the enzymes that cause inflammation and injure joint cartilage. The shot is intramuscular and is injected twice a week for a month and then once monthly. It takes only a moment. Once your vet has decided it is appropriate for your dog, you may not even need an appointment—you can bring your dog in and just "pass her back" without accompanying her for the injection. Jazzy, my two-year-old Collie mix, was limping/lame months after her second knee surgery. None of the NSAIDs made a difference, nor had glucosamine. But Adequan had her running and turning at high speed (her only gear) within days.

◆ Fentanyl Skin Patches for Pain

These patches were designed for serious pain relief in people suffering from cancer pain, and they can be used to ease pain for dogs with cancer or the aftereffects of major surgery (such as fractures and amputation). Because it is delivered into the bloodstream through the skin, there is no involvement with the digestive system or potential gastrointestinal side effects. Fentanyl (pronounced FEN-ta-nill) is a controlled substance in the same group of drugs as morphine and opium. It is a human drug that can be used for animals (like so many of the sophisticated medications), and the sealed patches come in varying sizes related to the body weight of the patient. The vet has to shave the area for placement out of the dog's reach—on the back, neck or side of the dog's chest. If the patch does not adhere, the vet may place a couple of skin staples (the ones used in surgery instead of stitches). The patch is sometimes covered with a dressing to ensure that it remains attached and that no child or other animal can get at it. Alternately, the dog may have to wear an Elizabethan collar to avoid licking the patch.

Advantages of the patch Fentanyl is also available in a lozenge form or as an injection, but studies have shown that the transdermal patch provides consistent relief for a dog over a four- to five-day period. Scientific studies have also shown that the patch is more efficient in dogs than morphine administered directly into the spinal canal for chronic pain and after orthopedic surgery. Many vets have found that the patch needs to be applied *before* the surgery in order to be fully effective during the recovery period; otherwise, additional analgesics have to be used for the dog's comfort until the patch becomes effective. Duragesic is the brand name of the patch made by the Janssen company in Belgium for use by people with terminal pain—mostly cancer.

Cautions about fentanyl You have to watch the dog for signs of excess dosage such as suppressed respiration and dramatically reduced activity and appetite. Overdoses cause sleep and potential respiratory arrest, although no deaths seem to have been reported. If a dog swallows a patch there is less chance it will create a problem than if she licks or chews it and gets spacey or sleepy.

The patch is pretty expensive. A single patch for a medium-sized dog costs about $60 and you often cannot buy just one. Another problem is that a person with addiction or drug-abuse issues may try to get hold of these patches for personal use.

I tried fentanyl patches for Yogi Bear, when he got bone cancer, but for the price, I was not that impressed with the results. He seemed uncomfortable with the patch—which needed staples to remain stuck on his skin—and it did not seem to dramatically alter his pain or mobility. A number of vets prescribe the patch in particular situations, but studies of its efficacy in dogs have been inconclusive.

◆ Warnings about Prescribed Medications

Many pills are chewable and taste good. This can make them easier to administer, but it raises the danger of overdose if a dog gets into the supply. Be really careful where you store these pills.

Cortisone (prednisone) This is used to relieve itchy skin, among many other uses. Common side effects are increased thirst and panting and more frequent urination. In rare instances it can cause aggressive behavior, so monitor your dog, especially around other dogs. There are many valuable uses for this drug, but it is often overprescribed as a long-term treatment for skin conditions, and there are significant negative side effects when it is used long-term.

Antibiotics are used for infection. Some can cause irritability, lethargy, and/or indigestion. The normal, healthy flora that lives in a dog's gut can also be knocked out along with the targeted bacteria. It should help to give a big spoonful of yogurt with every dose of antibiotics. You can also use the stomach-soothing paste Diarsanyl, available only from your vet, either two hours before or after giving the antibiotic so it does not interfere with the antibiotic's absorption. The Diarsanyl will restore balance to the stomach.

The danger is in the misuse of antibiotics, much like the issues surrounding antibiotics in human medicine: antibiotics are being prescribed too often and being used too casually (creating a loss of natural immunity in pets), and courses of antibiotics are not being completed, creating drug-resistant bacteria and illnesses that are resistant to cure. Veterinarians and owners need to carefully evaluate the options in every medical situation. Save antibiotics for the rare occasions when not using an antibiotic might literally cost a dog his life. If antibiotics are prescribed for your dog, for heaven's sake use them EXACTLY as prescribed. And give your dog the entire dose and for the entire amount of time recommended by your vet, right down to the last pill.

In rare cases, a dog can have an allergy to penicillin, so if it is prescribed, ask your vet what signs to be on the lookout for.

Rimadyl This is used for osteoarthritis and other inflammatory pain, and like all NSAIDs it puts extra stress on the dog's liver. When a dog uses Rimadyl or any of this class of drugs over a long period of time, the dog *must* have routine blood tests to assess liver and kidney function. Although the drug company claims that side effects are rare, other reports show that problems happen, especially in Labrador Retrievers, which is especially worrisome because Labs are the most common breed in the U.S. and many of them suffer from joint problems and pain (although that may be why the statistics are tilted that way). This may mean that many Labs are taking Rimadyl without their owners being aware of the dangers. People need to be educated about the symptoms of liver problems: loss of appetite, vomiting and diarrhea. When there are problems with liver function, the dog will become weak, apathetic and very ill. Many vets stand behind this drug and frequently prescribe this medication—perhaps without knowing that it has been implicated in bad reactions such as vomiting, diarrhea and lethargy in thousands of dogs. So even if your vet does not tell you about the dangers, please know that if your dog exhibits any of those signs, you must stop the Rimadyl immediately. The reaction can be serious, but the dog should recover quickly if the problem is caught in a timely fashion.

B.A.R.K.S. (Be Aware of Rimadyl's Known Side-effects) This Internet-based consumer group was created to share stories of problems with the drug and the harm that came to their pets. According to the group's reports, Pfizer, the manufacturer of Rimadyl, has contacted members of the group and offered to pay their medical and diagnostic bills.

NEVER Give These Drugs to a Dog

Aleve: can cause kidney failure, stomach injury
Advil (ibuprofen): can cause liver failure
Tylenol (acetaminophen): toxic to dogs

✦ Giving Pills

Disguise the pill inside a ball of meat or cheese. This is the easiest method. Favorites are hot dogs, canned meat, peanut butter, soft cream cheese or any cheese you can mold around a pill or capsule. The trick is to first give some of the goodie, without any medicine hidden in it. Then give a ball that has the pill or capsule in it—most dogs will just wolf it down, not even pausing to chew and discover the secret center. Coating a sticky capsule with butter or margarine is also a good trick.

The "Pill Pal" This is a small feeding cube made from New Zealand beef with a slit in the middle, into which you can shove a pill or capsule. It's available from www.oceaniaproducts.com.

✦ Liquid Medicine

Your vet can give you some large syringes with the needles removed. They are marked on the sides so you can be sure of the quantity you're giving.

   Raise your dog's head by the muzzle with one hand and lift the lip on one side.

   Ease the syringe into his mouth and—keeping his muzzle elevated so the liquid goes "downhill"—press the plunger slowly and gently so the liquid goes down his gullet.

✦ Applying Eye Medication

Eye medicine for dogs is usually an antibiotic ointment for conjunctivitis or other eye conditions. These ophthalmic ointments come in tiny tubes that are difficult to use, because you have to press out just a tiny little bit from the small tube while holding your dog's eye open. This is harder than it sounds. Eye drops are also difficult, because the dog's natural reaction in both cases is to close his eyes.

Sit down and place your dog between your legs with her back to you. Take the cap off the tube but set it down where it can't be squashed.

Hold her muzzle up from behind and squeeze a length of ointment across the length of the eye. Try not to touch the surface of the tube to the eye. Don't release the dog for a moment until the ointment has been distributed across the whole eyeball.

Eyedrops Have the dog sit in front of you with her back to your front. Place one leg on either side of her flanks from behind. Bring your legs close to her flanks in a confining but reassuring way. Reach around and lift her head from under the chin, bracing her back and neck against your legs. Open her eyelid a little, hold the eyedropper or bottle near the outside of her eye and brace your fingers around her eye so you have aim and steadiness. Squeeze the drop right in her eye.

◆ Giving Ear Medicine

Make sure you apply the cream or liquid deep into the ear canal, holding the dog's head to the side so you can massage just where the ear joins the head to encourage the medication to get deep inside. If you have been given antibiotics for an ear infection, it is especially important to finish the whole course.

PARASITES AND PESTICIDES

Dogs can be infected by many different kinds of parasites, many of which cause diseases. Worms, for example, may sound disgusting or dirty, but they are a natural part of a dog's life and can be easily treated by your vet. Various insects can create problems in your dog's life; each functions quite differently, and they therefore have to be dealt with in different ways.

◆ Some Thoughts about Chemicals on Our Dogs

The conundrum about pesticides is that they are a health risk to humans and animals. We use chemicals to deny parasites the "free lunch" they take off our pets while transferring diseases, yet we pay a price in exposure to the toxic chemicals that we put on our dogs to protect them. Keep in mind that chemicals move through the intestinal tract, go through the internal organs of filtration—the liver and kidneys—and are eliminated in urine and feces.

Eventually, most pesticides we use in America on plants and animals cause enough damage that they are banned—and then another chemical replaces them until the ill-effects of *that* product are documented. Those in charge of testing and regulating consider some level of damage to be "acceptable," but what amount of risk are you willing to take? These products that are designed to protect our dogs against parasites will make some of them sick, so give some thought to weighing the risks and benefits of pesticides on your pet, depending on her state of health and lifestyle.

Proponents of alternative health care make a passionate case against pesticides, but I don't see how most of us can avoid them until there is another way to eliminate fleas, ticks and the misery they bring. Certainly we'd all prefer not to expose our pets or ourselves to chemicals, but realistically many of us have parasites in our surroundings and have to objectively weigh the risks and benefits.

⬩ **What Is in These products?**
The active ingredients in these spot-on preparations—imidacloprid, fipronil, permethrin, methoprene, pyriproxyfen—have all been linked to serious side effects in laboratory animals.

Several of these products warn on the label that cats that have close physical contact with treated dogs are at special risk of toxic exposure themselves. How potent can a product be if a cat can get sick just from rubbing up against her dog?

"Inert ingredients" cause further damage. These can be as toxic and damaging as the active ones, sometimes even more so. The difference is that the current regulations do not require the inert ingredients to be rigorously tested, or even listed on the products. This means that there are undisclosed toxic ingredients in these products, in addition to the ones we know have caused adverse effects on mice, rats and dogs in laboratory tests.

TOXIC INGREDIENTS IN PARASITE PRODUCTS FOR DOGS

❑ Fipronil: neurotoxin (nervous system damage), carcinogen (cancer-causing) in people, teratogen (damage to the fetus), organ damage
❑ Imidacloprid: neurotoxin, carcinogen, teratogen, organ damage
❑ Methoprene: neurotoxin, organ damage
❑ Permethrin: neurotoxin, carcinogen, teratogen, autoimmune, organ damage

Permethrin This is the effective ingredient in tick repellents like Defend EXspot, Hartz Control, Advantix and BioSPOT. Packaging says to use once a month, but its maximum effectiveness diminishes after two or three weeks. Defend EXspot is one product that does allow a reapplication every two weeks.

Fipronil (Frontline) This controls ticks for slightly less than thirty days. Some people use Frontline once a month and a permethrin-based product two weeks later, giving a rotating schedule of medications that gives good coverage throughout the month. Some owners and vets have noticed subtle neurological reactions from Frontline, including emotional clinginess, under- or overactivity, convulsions, lethargy, tremors, stiff limbs and lameness. However, you have to weigh this small possibility against the devastating effects of the tick-borne disease that the product guards against.

Preventic collars These contain amitraz, which is an effective tick killer and repellent. They work better than collars used to, but any household with children or other pets must avoid them. Even though they are toxic, the collars apparently have an appealing taste. After you put the collar on and whenever you touch it, you must wash your hands thoroughly. Children cannot touch these collars at any time, so keep that in mind if your dog does not live with children but might come into contact with them.

Other products that target fleas but get a poor response for tick control are Revolution-Rx (selamectin) and Program Rx (which is very good at flea egg control). If you live around ticks, you could apply a topical product for tick control. Advantage Rx (imidocloprid with permethrin added) and Advantix also kill ticks.

◆ Fleas and What to Do about Them

These horrible little insects can live in your house while feeding periodically on your dog's blood. It isn't really the flea bite that causes the problem, it's the flea's saliva that causes skin irritations on dogs. For a dog that is particularly allergic to the flea bites, it can become a major problem. The dog will lick and bite at his irritated skin, causing what is called a "hot spot," which in turn can become infected—and this can mean multiple vet visits with a variety of medications.

Fleas spend only a small part of their time feeding on your dog (or even on the human members of the household). The rest of the time, they are laying eggs in your house and yard that will hatch into more fleas who are just waiting to procreate. Fleas reproduce year-round in many parts of the United States, and can thrive indoors even when the weather is cold outside. Therefore, in order to control fleas, you have to attack them not just on your dog but also in your yard and your house. You have to kill the adult fleas (which are the ones that bite) and you have to kill developing fleas before they reach adulthood.

You cannot safely "bomb" your house or yard, because the sprays and foggers are highly toxic to the environment and to us. They contain ingredients with a "quick kill" component to destroy adult fleas, along with an IGR (insect growth regulator) that keeps the immature eggs from developing. However, it is much more responsible and environmentally friendly to focus your attention directly on your dog and to clean your house as rigorously as possible until the life cycle of the fleas has been ended by the on-dog products. The sure way to eliminate fleas is to keep to a set regimen: vacuum the house daily (put a flea collar in the vacuum bag to kill any fleas or their larvae), wash the pet's bedding frequently, and keep using the flea products on the dog every month (see below).

You can use a topical product that you apply monthly. Revolution is available only through your vet and has numerous benefits: it controls fleas by causing a sort of neuromuscular paralysis in the insects, and it also prevents heartworm, ear mites, scabies and ticks. It kills adult fleas and also prevents eggs from hatching. BioSPOT is a topical anti-flea product that is available in pet stores. It also prevents flea eggs from developing and protects against ticks and mosquitoes.

Anti-flea pills work by releasing a chemical that keeps the flea eggs that are on the dog from developing to maturity—although they have no effect on adult fleas. Sentinel is a flavored pill that protects against fleas, heartworm and intestinal parasites (worms) by preventing flea eggs from hatching. Because Sentinel does not kill adult fleas, its effectiveness won't be seen for several weeks if you have a flea infestation. If that is the case, you'll need a spray to kill the fleas that are already populating your dog.

Interceptor also takes care of heartworm and intestinal parasites, and Program kills flea eggs.

Capstar is a daily pill that can be used as part of a total flea prevention program to kill off even severe flea infestations in a few hours. It can even be given to puppies from four weeks of age.

However, note that it is a pill that must be given every day to retain effectiveness, unlike the much easier once-a-month products.

Never use multiple flea products at one time. Read the manufacturer's warnings very carefully—for example, giving your dog a flea bath and putting a new flea collar on him is a dangerous combination.

Avoid high-traffic dog zones in hot months. Dog "play parks," dog runs, hiking paths, beaches or any venues where dogs convene are likely locations for a big flea infestation, especially in the hot months when fleas do their multiplying.

WHAT DOES NOT WORK AGAINST FLEAS

- ❑ Flea baths used to be a common treatment for dogs but are now considered fairly useless, since the fleas often still infest the dog's bedding and household carpeting. The fleas get washed out of your dog's hair, but their cousins will jump right back on as soon as the dog shakes dry.
- ❑ Make sure you treat all animals in the home, because dog and cat fleas are interchangeable—and if there is one flea, all animals are affected (even though some may not scratch).
- ❑ Chemical flea collars have gone out of favor, both because there were health questions about putting the anti-flea toxin right against your pet's skin and because more effective, less toxic and longer-lasting products were developed.
- ❑ Electronic flea collars have never been proven to do anything.
- ❑ Vitamins and supplements such as garlic, brewer's yeast and vitamin B provide no protection against fleas.

◆ Mosquitoes and the Diseases They Spread

Heartworm is a potentially fatal disease that can get to any dog—even one that stays mostly indoors—in a geographic area where mosquitoes breed. The disease begins when an infected dog—with tiny immature heartworm larvae circulating in his blood—is bitten by a mosquito that takes in the larvae. The larvae then develop within the mosquito over two to three weeks until they reach the infectious stage. At that point the mosquito feeds again on a healthy dog and transmits the infectious larvae, which take months to migrate through various organs in the body and reach the dog's heart. Once inside the heart, the worms grow up to fourteen inches long and cause significant damage to the heart, lungs and other organs.

RULES FOR MOSQUITO CONTROL

- ❑ Consult with your vet before applying any repellent to your dog.
- ❑ Use only repellents approved for use on dogs (it can be a horse product, but the label must say "safe for use on dogs").
- ❑ Do not use mosquito products intended for people.
- ❑ Don't use any product containing DEET, which research has shown to cause serious adverse effects in dogs.

❑ Avoid citrus oil extracts (citronella) and essential oils: some animals are sensitive to these products.

Preventing heartworm starts with keeping mosquitoes off your dog to lessen the chance of her being bitten. The safest method to repel mosquitoes may be to apply a pyrethrin-based flea spray in accordance with directions for dogs.

Some insect repellents are safe for use on dogs—many of them are horse products approved for canine use. Some approved products (with the manufacturer in parentheses) include: Flysect Super 7 (Equicare), Pet-Guard Gel (Virbac), VIP Fly Repellent Ointment (VPL), Flea and Tick Mist (Davis), Adams Flea and Tick Mist (VPL), Happy Jack Flea-Tick Spray (Happy Jack).

Heartworm pills Your vet can prescribe a monthly heartworm pill (chewable or not). Heartgard, Interceptor and Sentinel are the best-known brands. NOTE: *Prior to taking this medication for the first time, a dog must get a quick blood test in the vet's office to be sure she has not already been exposed to the heartworm. If that were the case, not only would the heartworm medication not work, it could cause irreparable harm to the heart.*

An annual heartworm test should be done, even on a dog that has been taking medication throughout the year, to be certain that there are no mosquito larvae in his blood.

Warning: *Do not even consider using the once-every-six-month, time-released heartworm medication called ProHeart 6. It has been recalled from the market by the Food and Drug Administration after more than 5,000 dogs were reported to have adverse reactions to it. About 500 dogs actually died; the FDA said the deaths were not all directly attributable to the medication, but clearly this is a product to be given a wide berth.*

✦ Increased Risk of Heartworm When Traveling

Because so many people choose to travel with their dogs, the incidence of heartworm has traveled with those dogs and can now be found across most of the United States. Many dogs have immature larvae in their blood, unbeknownst to anyone. All it takes is for a mosquito to bite them and contaminate a local dog, who in turn can then pass on the heartworm to another dog.

When you get back from traveling with a dog, a visit to the vet is the best protection you have to find out whether your dog picked up any internal parasites such as heartworm, roundworm or hookworm, or external parasites such as fleas, ticks, mange, etc.

Texas has dramatically more reported heartworm cases than any other state in the United States. A 2001 study conducted by the American Heartworm Society (funded by Merial, the manufacturer of Heartgard) identified the states with the greatest incidence of the disease. Texas had close to 40,000 cases, followed by Florida with just under 30,000, Louisiana with nearly 19,000, North Carolina with 17,000, Georgia with 14,000, Mississippi with 11,000, Tennessee with 10,000, South Carolina and Alabama with 9,000 each, Indiana, Arkansas and Missouri with 8,000 each and Illinois and Michigan with 7,000 apiece.

◆ West Nile Virus

The West Nile virus is transmitted by feeding insects such as mosquitoes, which have fed on infected birds that are carrying the virus. Those mosquitoes can then pass the disease to humans and other animals. The virus cannot be transmitted directly between animals, or from animals to people. The disease has spread across the U.S., although it is still a rare virus.

Dogs are not at risk for West Nile, even though owners are concerned: the virus has only been identified in wild birds and horses. The risk to pets is very low: dogs are fairly resistant to developing any illness if they are exposed to West Nile virus, although cats can become ill.

Elderly dogs, very young ones and those with illnesses that compromise their immune systems could be at higher risk. However, few of the pets that have been exposed have gotten sick. Cases of infection causing disease are very rare, having happened only to pets with compromised immune systems.

Preventing West Nile is best accomplished by reducing the chance of your pet being bitten by mosquitoes.

PREVENTING MOSQUITO BITES

- ❏ Keep pets indoors during early morning and evening hours.
- ❏ Prevent contact with dead birds or squirrels that might be infected by the virus.
- ❏ Only use mosquito repellent approved for use in pets to prevent bites. Check the product label to see whether it is safe for pets, or ask your veterinarian for a recommendation. Many insect repellents designed for human use contain a chemical that can cause serious illness in pets.
- ❏ If pesticides are sprayed in your area, keep pets indoors during spraying and for a few hours afterward.

Symptoms of West Nile are similar to those of Lyme disease (see page 386) so if your dog displays several of the symptoms on page 385, first eliminate the possibility that she is suffering from Lyme disease (especially if there are ticks anywhere nearby) since it is highly unlikely for a dog to come down with West Nile. If your dog shows some combination of these symptoms, it is very important to contact your veterinarian.

◆ Mange

Mange is a general term indicating an infestation of mites, of which there are two common kinds: sarcoptic and demodex (or "puppy mange"). Mites are microscopic, eight-legged insects that cause skin irritation that can become very itchy, with patchy hair loss if infection results. These mites burrow under the dog's skin and reproduce there, causing an intense itching that dogs scratch so fiercely that they can get secondary bacterial infections, which then have to be treated with antibiotics.

Revolution usually treats this mite problem, and is an important safeguard for Collies and Collie-crosses (see "Warning" on page 385).

Decreased appetite   Abnormal head posture
Depression   Circling
Difficulty walking   Convulsions
Tremors

You cannot tell by yourself that your dog has mange, because it mimics flea allergies and other skin irritations. The vet will examine a skin scraping under a microscope, although mange is hard even for him to identify this way. Mange is usually treated with two or three weekly injections of ivermectin. Some vets use a sulfur dip.

Warning: *Ivermectin must never be used on Collies, Shetland Sheepdogs, Collie-crosses and other herding breeds, because it is toxic to them.*

Dogs catch sarcoptic mange (which is also called scabies) from other dogs—it is very easily spread and can be caught from foxes and foxholes, too. This means you may have some pretty angry friends if your dog is the one doing the "giving." Unfortunately, a dog who has been cured of mange can get it again. Generally, people won't catch the other kinds of mange from their dogs, but it can cause temporary rashes in people. In the case of dog-scabies mites, they can spread to people about a third of the time.

Demodex is the second kind of mange—it is also known as puppy mange. It is quite common in pups and much less contagious than sarcoptic mange, because it is spread from mother to offspring and generally not dog-to-dog. It is much easier to find on a skin scrape, and while not as itchy, it does cause hair to fall out. It is usually self-limiting and will resolve on its own.

However, this kind of mange can be extremely serious in older dogs, in whom it usually develops when the immune system is challenged by illness. There used to be a treatment bath in which these older dogs were dipped, but it was very toxic and is no longer available. A vet will usually prescribe ivermectin by mouth, except for Collie-type dogs, who will get Interceptor instead.

◆ Parvovirus (CPV)

This highly contagious virus attacks the intestinal tract, white blood cells and sometimes the heart. CPV is spread dog-to-dog, which means anywhere dogs congregate there is a risk: dog parks, dog shows, boarding kennels, pet shops, etc.

Symptoms The first signs of CPV infection are depression, loss of appetite, vomiting and severe diarrhea, which will appear five to seven days after exposure. Some dogs dehydrate and even die after projectile vomiting and bloody diarrhea. Other dogs can recover without complications.

Treatment The main thing to do for a dog with CPV is to start an IV immediately to counteract the dehydration. Antibiotics may be given to prevent secondary infections.

Prevention Dogs of any age should be vaccinated against CPV, with few exceptions. Keeping kennel areas clean is also important. Do not allow your dog to come into contact with any dog feces on the street, especially before the dog reaches six months of age.

◆ Tick-Borne Diseases

There are a number of different kinds of ticks crawling around across the country—many of them in the same geographic areas—and spreading a number of worrisome illnesses. Medical knowledge is constantly evolving about which kind of tick carries which kind of disease. For some years people were told that the only ones posing a serious risk to dogs were the tiniest ones, deer ticks. There were big charts on the walls of vets' offices depicting different breeds of ticks: dog owners could study these religiously, learning that they only had to worry about ticks that were often too small to see, even when engorged. But it turns out we should worry about other ticks, even the ones we *can* see.

The medical wisdom for a long time was that no disease transmission took place from "dog ticks" (small and brown) or the "Lone Star ticks" (presumably named after the state of Texas). "Wood ticks," the bigger kind that swell into plump gray balloons filled with your dog's blood and then fall off, are revolting but harmless. Diseases are transmitted by quite a few different kinds of ticks. In addition to the dreaded Lyme disease, there is another, more deadly tick-borne disease, known as ehrlichiosis, and also Rocky Mountain Spotted Fever.

Rocky Mountain Spotted Fever (RMSF) Despite its name, this disease exists in two-thirds of America. There are two types of tick species—American dog ticks in the East and Lone Star ticks in the West—that carry the bacteria that causes RMSF. There are human cases of RMSF, the majority of which occur in the southeastern and south central U.S., with most occurring in Oklahoma and the Piedmont region of Virginia and North Carolina.

The Lyme Vaccine This has been seriously discredited as a treatment to protect a dog from getting a tick-borne disease. Dogs have contracted full-blown Lyme disease from the vaccine, which means they will suffer from the disorder periodically throughout their lifetimes, since it is a recurring illness. The vaccine was apparently released before being properly tested—it was also given to many unfortunate people, who were seriously sickened by it.

Shockingly, it appears that there are vets who are still giving Lyme vaccine shots. The problems with this vaccine have been widely documented, so administering it would be an example of a very poor practice of medicine based on ignorance of current research.

Symptoms of all the tick-borne diseases are similar. The dog is lethargic, runs a fever and in the case of Lyme, will often have a sudden onset of very severe lameness and may vomit. A vet has to do blood tests for antibody levels, but the tests are not always definitive. In all cases the dogs are put on a three-week course of antibiotics. The diagnosis of "chronic Lyme"—that is, of the disease recurring—is rare and probably overdiagnosed, and means an additional but unnecessary three weeks of antibiotics.

✦ Worms and Other Intestinal Parasites

Worms that can infect a dog include tapeworms, roundworms, whipworms and hookworms. Then there are the intestinal diseases caused by single-cell forms such as protozoa, *coccidia* and *giardia*. All of these can be eliminated with the right medication.

The vet will find out whether your puppy or adult dog has worms by examining a fresh stool sample. Some worms are visible to the naked eye—you might actually be able to see tapeworms and roundworms yourself, right on your dog's stool. The doctor's office will still run fecal tests on the stool to confirm the type of worm(s), because there are different medications intended for each of them.

Puppies have intestinal worms; it's normal. Most puppies are born with roundworms. The usual way in which puppies are infected with roundworm is from their mother, before birth. Puppies can also get them from nursing, since the mother's colostrum (which comes in before the milk) can carry them, and they are also spread by the placenta. There are also some kinds of worms—hookworms and whipworms—that puppies can get from their environment. Because there are so many ways to get a variety of worms when they are young, all puppies are treated routinely and repeatedly with wormer medication to eliminate these parasites. Puppies need to be wormed as early as two weeks, and then every two weeks until the puppy reaches sixteen weeks.

This means that if you are buying a puppy, do not be alarmed that something is wrong with the pup or think the breeder is dirty if the puppy is on worming medicine or has worms. However, these worms can be passed to children, so it is important to thoroughly eliminate them.

SEIZURES

Seizures (also known as convulsions or epilepsy) are uncontrolled bursts of neurological activity in the brain, which can last from a few seconds to several minutes. They can be frightening to witness, especially if you have children in the house. Even though the reason for seizures is usually not identified, there are a variety of reasons that dogs have seizures, and your vet may want to do tests to get more information. Epilepsy accounts for about five percent of all diseases seen in dogs.

✦ Treatment of Seizures

People with epilepsy do better over the long term when the epilepsy is treated *before* the seizures become frequent. It is thought that the brain "gets used to" having seizures, even though most seizures don't seem to cause brain damage (unless they are very long or happen in clusters).

In dogs, phenobarbital is the most commonly used drug to control seizures. Some vets recommend medication when the dog is having more than one seizure a month, other doctors medicate when the dog has only three or four a year. In other cases, the medication is given for the rest of the dog's life.

✦ Diet and Seizures

Research has shown that diet can affect the effectiveness and toxicity of phenobarbital. The effects of the drug differ if the dog is fed a "maintenance" diet, a low-protein diet or a low-fat, low-protein diet. Although the full implications of the nutritional study are not yet known, if you have an epileptic dog, talk to your vet before changing your dog's diet.

Breeds at Risk for Epilepsy

Beagle	Golden Retriever	
Belgian Tervuren	Irish Setter	Saint Bernard
Boxer	Irish Wolfhound	Schnauzer (all sizes)
Cocker Spaniel	Keeshond	Siberian Husky
Collie	Labrador Retriever	Vizsla
Dachshund	Pointer	Welsh Springer Spaniel
German Shepherd	Poodle (all sizes)	Wire Fox Terrier

WHAT TO DO ABOUT A DOG HAVING A SEIZURE

- ❏ Stay calm. There is no danger to your dog.
- ❏ Move furniture aside so he doesn't hurt himself.
- ❏ Put a pillow underneath his head, if possible.
- ❏ Move cautiously, since a seizing dog gets disoriented and could turn on you when coming out of it.
- ❏ Do not attempt to put anything in his mouth—it's probably clenched shut anyway, but dogs do not swallow their tongues.
- ❏ Stroke the dog gently—always with extreme caution, because a disoriented dog can turn on you.
- ❏ Try to time how long the seizure lasts—and what was happening before, during and afterward—so you can tell the vet.

◆ **Emergency Care for Seizures Is Needed If:**
- ❏ The seizure lasts more than ten minutes.
- ❏ A second seizure begins before the dog has recovered from the first one.
- ❏ There is more than one seizure in any twenty-four-hour period.

Although only the three conditions above warrant an emergency visit, have your dog checked out by the vet any time there is seizure activity. In a nonemergency seizure, still call the vet afterward and be sure to tell the receptionist why you want your dog checked out. With any luck, she will give you an appointment for as soon as the vet can fit you in.

✦ Itchy skin (Pruritus)

This is primarily a warm-weather problem that comes from flea-bite sensitivity (actually, it is the flea's saliva that irritates a dog's skin). For half the dogs who suffer from itchiness, fleas are the root cause of the problem (see the section on controlling fleas on page 381 in this chapter). If flea-bite sensitivity is not a possibility or has been eliminated by flea-control products, a vet can consider other possible causes of itchiness, such as food or environmental allergies, bacterial skin infection, ringworm or parasitic mites.

Corticosteroids (cortisone products such as prednisone) are inexpensive and effective for itchiness but have to be used in the smallest dosage and for the shortest time. They are frequently dispensed no matter what the underlying cause, but this medication only deals with the symptoms, not the underlying reason for the itching. Your vet may suggest over-the-counter antihistamines to control itching. In order to tell whether it will help your dog, vets suggest you give the medication for at least two to three weeks. Successful over-the-counter antihistamines include Benadryl, Chlortrimeton, Temeril and Tavist, but as with any other medication issue, don't even consider trying anything on your dog without your vet's full involvement. If your vet does prescribe antihistamines, she will tell you they can make some dogs drowsy (as they can some people) and cause vomiting, and that you should call her in the case of more serious side effects such as tremors, loss of balance or weakness. Prescribed drugs such as Elavil, Sinequan, and Atarax have also been shown to be effective for severe itchiness.

✦ Lick Dermatitis

This is a medical condition in which a dog licks repetitively at one spot, usually on a front leg, although the spot may change. The dog often licks the skin until it is raw. If an infection occurs where the dog licks (which is often the case), be sure to see the vet, who may prescribe antibiotics.

Large breeds are often the ones affected—Golden Retrievers, German Shepherds, Great Danes and Dobermans frequently suffer from this disorder.

There can be several reasons for excessive licking, and many vets think dogs do this because they are bored and/or neurotic. If that turns out to be the case, then the best treatment is to get the dog's mind off the obsessive licking with lots of exercise and diversions for his mind. This can mean taking the dog with you in the car or on foot as much as possible to stimulate his mind.

Ideas about this licking have been changing, and it seems that in some dogs the obsessive licking may be a peripheral sensory nerve disorder.

If you cannot stop the dog from licking, your vet may suggest an anti-obsessional drug such as Prozac or Anafranil (generic name, clomipramine).

✦ Hot Spots

Hot spots are raw areas that develop on the skin, and they often become red and ooze pus. The area is painful and itchy for the dog, who scratches it, making it worse. Some people seek out "veterinary dermatologists," although for the most part, a good general vet can apply the same simple principles to relieve discomfort, control infection and promote healing. Save your time and money and let your dog's primary doctor treat the problem.

The usual treatment for hot spots is for the vet to clip the spot first so that all hair is removed from the affected area. Then she'll clean the area with an antibacterial product and prescribe medication, sometimes injected, followed by oral medication. Corticosteroids such as prednisone are usually given to stop the itch/scratch cycle. Sometimes a drying solution is applied to dry the wounded area out and speed the healing process.

Susceptible breeds are those with a dense coat, such as Golden Retrievers, Labs, Collies, German Shepherds and Saint Bernards.

You can buy a protective covering to put on your dog to keep her from licking herself. Surgi-Sox leggings is a shirt/bodysuit that is made of Corium, a four-way stretch fabric that is washable and can be worn around the clock. It covers the front legs, chest and torso to keep a dog from licking hot spots or abrasions. It is available in four sizes, for dogs from fifteen to ninety pounds. Information can be found at www.surgi-sox.com or toll-free at (877) 787-4479.

◆ Mange (Scabies)

Mange (technically sarcoptic mange) is a skin condition caused by tiny mites that burrow just beneath the surface of the skin. It infests dogs of any age, breed or size, and is very contagious to other dogs and to people. (For more on mange, see pages 384 of this chapter.) This kind of mange is extremely contagious, so you must contact the owner of any dogs that your dog has been in contact with recently, and keep the dog isolated until this problem is resolved.

The symptoms are intense: itching, hair loss and, if untreated, crusty sores all over the dog. But diagnosis is difficult, since the vet has only a small chance of finding one of these mites at work when she looks at a skin scraping under a microscope.

Treatment for mange, until recently, required multiple insecticidal dips. However, these dips were highly toxic and are virtually unavailable anymore. Newer products are safer and more effective, such as ivermectin (although NEVER for Collies, Shetland Sheepdogs, Australian Shepherds and other herding breeds, which have severe allergic reactions to the medication).

Be sure to treat all dogs and cats in the household even if they aren't scratching, because if you see the signs of any parasite you can be sure all pets are affected, even if they are not displaying signs of discomfort. There is no need to treat the actual house, because once the mites are separated from the dogs (or human hosts) they die off in one to two days.

Demodectic mange mainly afflicts puppies and is not contagious to other dogs. Many puppies pick it up from their mothers while nursing. It is a microscopic mite with eight legs that causes puppies to lose hair around their eyes, muzzle and other areas on the head. There is no need to treat bedding or the house, it will die off on its own.

◆ Small Skin Wounds

Deep cuts If your dog has a wound of any serious nature—that is, if the cut is too deep or wide for the edges to fall right back together, do not hesitate to go to the vet. Avoiding a vet visit to save time and/or money could prove to be a false economy if the wound does not heal properly or gets infected.

Superficial wounds If your dog has only a superficial wound—perhaps one that you didn't even see initially and now has dried blood on it—then all you want to do is get it clean by flushing the area with warm water—do NOT use hydrogen peroxide, iodine or soap. Just flush the area— maybe in the bathtub or shower if you have a spray attachment. Gently dry the area and apply some antibiotic ointment, the kind you'd use for yourself. Wrap some gauze bandaging loosely around the wound—if you wrap too tightly you'll cut off circulation to the area, which would bring another set of problems.

If you have any doubts about whether you are doing the right thing, don't hesitate to let your vet do a better job of it.

SPAYING AND NEUTERING

Six months is traditionally the age at which both male and female puppies are altered. Between four and six months is considered the optimal time. Neutering your dog can minimize potential physical problems and can often reduce both a dog's tendency to wander and any dog-to-dog aggression. The list of benefits is below.

◆ Spaying

"Spaying" is the term for sterilizing a female—although the terms "altering" or "neutering" are also used. The operation involves removing the female's entire reproductive organs—the uterus, fallopian tubes and ovaries—rendering her incapable of carrying babies. It is the equivalent of a total hysterectomy for a human female.

Most dogs recover from the surgery in a day or two, with a normal appetite and energy. You will be told to keep her relatively quiet for about a week and only walk her on a leash so that she cannot run and do herself any internal damage while she's healing. The vet may use stitches that the body just absorbs over time, or she may ask you to return in about ten days to have the stitches removed.

◆ When to Spay a Female

A female reaches sexual maturity anywhere from six to twenty-four months of age, although most females come into heat the first time before their first birthday. Don't worry if your female dog reaches her first birthday and hasn't come into season yet. It may just be that she came into heat and you didn't realize it. Some dogs bleed very little or lick themselves clean before it is evident.

If you don't plan to breed your female, many American vets encourage spaying before she comes into season. It seems to be a human projection of feelings to claim that there is any emotional value for a female dog to go through a first heat or have a litter. In Europe it is commonly believed that early spaying increases the risk of some forms of urinary incontinence (see "Urinary Issues," page 399). However, this has to be weighed against the important benefit of lowering the risk of mammary tumors, which wins out for most doctors.

Females do not come under a sex-hormone influence until they reach puberty, when there is a short, sharp burst of estrogen, then a prolonged, two-month surge of progesterone if they have not been spayed. The dog's behavior is profoundly affected until the two hormones pass out of her body. One unpleasant habit triggered by the hormones is called "object guarding" or possessiveness. This can become a learned behavior, often for life. It develops most often in terriers, and although it can be reduced with training, it's preferable not to allow it to develop in the first place.

If you haven't already spayed your female before her first season, then avoid spaying for two months after she comes into season. There can be a serious drop in progesterone levels during that time, with the emotional disturbances, irritability, depression and aggression that can go with it. Also, the increased blood supply to the uterus creates a slight increase in surgical risk.

Early spaying helps eliminate mammary and reproductive-tract cancer. Spaying before the first season reduces your dog's risk of getting mammary tumors (the equivalent of breast cancer in people) to virtually zero. Removing the reproductive organs also removes the possibility that *those* organs could develop cancer. The incidence of mammary tumors in unspayed female dogs is high. Spaying before the second, third or fourth heat can also reduce the risk of mammary tumors, but after a dog has come into season four times, there is ever less protection against the risk of mammary tumors forming.

◆ MALES—What Is the Best Age at Which to Neuter?

"Neutering" and "castration" are two words for the same procedure. It involves general anesthesia but is a simple procedure in which the male dog's testicles are removed from the scrotum through an incision just in front. The pouch of skin that holds the testicles may look the same for a while after neutering, because it can be somewhat swollen right after the procedure. However, without the testicles inside to hold its shape, the loose skin will eventually shrink up and disappear.

Despite what some people believe, a male dog does not need to experience copulation. This is a human projection of a human desire. Dogs are driven by instinctual and physical needs. A dog's needs actually change if we alter the drive to reproduce by neutering or spaying—just as we alter many other of the dog's inborn drives. Do not view this as "cruel or unusual," any more than it is cruel or unusual not to let a dog roam free in the road, eat out of a garbage can or chase the neighbor's cat.

Castration before or after puberty does not make a significant difference in whether neutering is effective in altering the dog's behavior. However, the later you wait after puberty, the more ingrained the dog's behavior will be.

There has been a small trend toward neutering very young—as early as eight weeks of age. This is an idea that doesn't seem to have caught on widely, although some vets, veterinary organizations and shelters have given approval to the idea of spaying a female or neutering a male at eight weeks. Ask your vet (or the breeder) what she thinks the advantages or disadvantages of early neutering might be.

Some vets aren't comfortable with the young age for surgery, which is understandable. Most vets are accustomed to doing the procedure on an older—and therefore larger—puppy, so they may not be comfortable operating on a smaller animal with smaller organs.

There is also a more recent trend toward *later* neutering of male dogs—at about one year of age—on the theory that it allows the male hormones to masculinize the dog's physical aspect. This is a decision to be made in concert with your vet, accepting her experience in helping shape your decision.

Regardless of the dog's age, castration almost always improves behavior, especially in dogs with behavioral problems. Sometimes dogs are castrated late in life: research done on dogs up to twelve years old at castration showed an improvement in their behavior.

◆ Neutering by Injection

The newest idea in population control for male dogs is an injection, which takes the place of castration. It is the first nonsurgical technique to be approved by the Food and Drug Administration. This chemical sterilant (Neutersol Injectable Solution) is injected directly into the scrotum. The smallest needle available is used: in studies done on hundreds of dogs, the vast majority experienced no pain with the injection.

There are differences between injectable sterilization and traditional surgery: the latter reduces testosterone production, the former does not. Also, Neutersol may not eliminate some of the behavior problems common to intact dogs, such as roaming, marking and aggression.

◆ Mounting

Dogs reach sexual maturity at six to nine months. They may become more attentive to smells, increase marking, roam, fight and mount. Mounting is usually about social signaling—specifically showing dominance—and is not about sexual gratification. Dominant dogs of either sex can mount others of the same sex to show seniority in the pack. Testosterone, the hormone flowing in a puppy's bloodstream, is what makes him mount, clasp and thrust his pelvis on another dog.

◆ Changes Caused by Castration

Neutering is important for any dog with aggression or other behavioral problems. It's not a "cure" for difficulties in the dog's personality, but in about half of the dogs castrated, it does bring about advantageous changes. If there is any need for proof that neutering can mellow a male dog, just look at the breeding, raising and/or training of other domesticated animals (horses, cattle) and how frequently castration is used to make the animals more manageable.

Castration before puberty is said by some doctors to prevent a male dog from fully developing his adult physique. The effect of the male hormone testosterone probably begins before birth. There is a large surge of testosterone just before or at the time of birth, which "masculinizes" the male dog (there is no equivalent for females).

Dogs generally need ten percent less food after neutering.

- Sexual experience does not make a dog more emotionally stable.
- Castration does not make a dog more or less "frustrated."
- Puberty doesn't mean a dog reaches emotional maturity (they're still teenagers whether neutered or not).
- There *is* a tendency to gain weight afterward, but it's controllable with quality food and daily exercise.
- Neutering does not affect watchdog behavior.
- Neutered dogs hunt the same way they always did.

CHANGES IN MALES AFTER NEUTERING

- ☐ Less aggression toward other male dogs.
- ☐ Less aggression from other dogs toward yours (your dog's odor changes).
- ☐ Less resistance to your authority: your dog will make less of an effort to be dominant.
- ☐ Less likelihood of mounting other dogs or people.
- ☐ Makes the dog generally easier to train and be around.
- ☐ Less urine marking in the house (if there was any before).
- ☐ Less tendency to take off and roam.
- ☐ Cannot get testicular cancer, much less likely to get prostate diseases.

CHANGES IN FEMALES AFTER SPAYING

- ☐ Cannot get cancers of the reproductive system.
- ☐ Will not get potentially dangerous uterine infections.
- ☐ Very unlikely to get breast cancer if spayed before first birthday.
- ☐ May become more mellow, more responsive and retain commands better.
- ☐ Dominant females may become *more* aggressive (loss of progesterone).
- ☐ Can stimulate appetite and change her metabolic rate, causing weight gain.

◆ Misconceptions about Spaying and Neutering

It is a myth that a female dog will be "happier" if she comes into season or has a litter—these are human ideas. Living among humans alters so many of a dog's "natural" instincts that removing the drive to be impregnated and have babies is only one of many. People project their own feelings and romanticize what pregnancy and motherhood "mean" to a dog. In animals, the drive to procreate has no emotional significance—it is just another basic instinct like hunger or thirst or staying warm and dry.

Dogs do not necessarily get fat once they have been neutered. As with people, what makes a dog fat is more food than his activity level can burn—which is to say, too much food, too little exercise. However, it is true that some males do become less active after castration, which would lower metabolism. And many females do get hungrier after spaying, so they will need food with lower fat, along with plentiful exercise to maintain their previous weight.

Also, as puppies near six months (and maturity, for the smaller breeds) it is a good idea to cut back on the quantity of food they eat or even switch to food with lower fat content (or higher protein) if you see them starting to put on weight.

◆ Men Who Identify with Male Dogs

Some male dog owners cannot deal with having their dog castrated because they "empathize" too much with their male dogs. These men should really not need to be told that their dogs' testicles are not as central to the dog's enjoyment of life as a man's are to him. There are other ways for a man to bond with a dog and feel close to him. Neutering is too important for the dog's well-being for the owner's emotional issues to get in the way of a good decision.

But wait! Having said that, lo and behold, there is actually a solution to this problem: it is called "renticles." Yes, there are synthetic prosthetic testicles that can be put into a dog's scrotum after the real ones are removed for neutering. So, for those men who cannot stand the idea of having a dog without balls, their dogs can have artificial testicles (but only your vet knows for sure) without the problems the real ones bring.

SPINAL-DISK PROBLEMS

Ruptured disks are the usual reason that dogs are not able to get up, which happens suddenly or slowly in different cases. Ruptured spinal disks (the technical term is "intervertebral disk disease" or "degenerative disk disease") are the most common neurologic syndromes in dogs. These dogs may exhibit signs of problems before the disks rupture, but it is often just an out-of-the-blue inability to move.

Most of the disk problems in dogs, about eighty percent, occur in the lower back (the "thoracolumbar spine") and this means only the hind legs are affected. However, this is the kind of disk disease that is more likely to strike suddenly, when the dog has done a low-impact jump off something, or even without any unusual movement.

◆ Which dogs are at risk?

Certain breeds with legs that are disproportionately short for their body length (technically known as "chondrodystrophoid" breeds, meaning those with faulty cartilage development) are the ones whose spinal disks change abnormally at an early age. Dachshunds are by far the most afflicted of any breed, with Pekingese second (the last two breeds on the list on page 396 do not look chondrodystrophoid, but their disks are).

Dogs that get this are usually older than three, although the degeneration can start as the dog is maturing in the first year. And there are some breeds, such as German Shepherds and Labradors, who get disk disease even without disproportionate legs.

Breeds at Risk for Disk Rupture

Dachshunds	Basset Hounds	Beagles
Pekingese	Lhasa Apsos	Miniature Poodles

◆ Symptoms of Disk Disease

The terrible thing about this condition is that your dog may wind up permanently paralyzed and there will have been no warning signs. You will know that your dog has this problem in one of two ways. Either she will have painfully tight neck muscles, will not be able to lower her head enough to eat or drink, may walk or stand with an arched back to relieve the pressure on the spine or may show other signs of discomfort, such as trembling, crying or whining, or trying to hide. If the disk damage is severe, she may lose coordination in her front or rear legs.

The second form of this infirmity is shocking because, without warning, the dog will let out a yelp or scream and just collapse: often her hind legs do not function but she will drag herself with her front legs. Other dogs cannot move at all.

◆ Can You Do Anything to Prevent a Ruptured Disk?

Although this affliction can occur without warning or direct relationship to anything the dog has done, you still should be cautious with the at-risk breeds and the kinds of activities they are allowed to do. For example, Dachshunds and Pekes, at the very least, should never go up and down staircases—it puts extra pressure on their spine. Jumping on and off furniture or into cars is probably not a good idea, either. Ask your vet—and the breeder, too—if they have any suggestions for safety measures you can take in your dog's everyday life.

◆ How Can You Manage Disk Disease?

If your dog is showing signs of pain or impaired movement—especially if she is a member of one of the at-risk breeds—get to a vet for evaluation as soon as possible. Many vets will prescribe rest and medication, while others will want to operate before the disk(s) rupture.

◆ What Should You Do If the Disk(s) Rupture?

This is as drastic an emergency as you're likely to find: the sooner your dog is seen by a veterinary surgeon, the greater the chance of restoring the use of her back legs. Some disk ruptures do tremendous damage to the spine, which can cause permanent paralysis within minutes. In other cases, fast intervention restores the use of the back legs. Every hour counts. Researchers have found that immediate surgery (within twenty-four hours in most cases) helps dogs recover from the most serious cases.

The outcome of the surgery depends on whether the dog still has sensation and can feel pain in the back legs. Doctors have found that a dog that's able to feel pain will likely walk again.

Time is of the essence: when dogs lose the ability to feel deep pain for thirty-six hours or less before surgery, only fifty percent of them walk again.

Disk surgery is very expensive—anywhere from $2,000 to $5,000, and there is no guarantee that your dog will be in the fortunate fifty percent. Also, talk to your vet ahead of time about what care a paralyzed dog will need if she remains paralyzed even with surgery. Fifty fifty odds are not great, so you should try to get support for making a decision that suits your way of life.

SURGERY

◆ Warnings on Certain Breeds and Anesthesia

There are only two groups of dogs that present certain challenges to the anesthesiologist—even though various other breeds claim special vulnerabilities. If you do have a dog in either of the following categories, talk to your vet about whether she is comfortable doing the procedure, or if she would prefer that you go to a specialized hospital setting with an anesthesiologist present.

Brachycephalic breeds The dogs with flat faces and pushed-in noses—which includes Pugs, Boxers and English Bulldogs—tend to make noise when they breathe. The noisier the dog, the more severe the problem, so during the surgery an anesthesiologist needs to use a medication that will knock them out swiftly in order to secure an airway. After waking up from anesthesia and once the tube is removed, the medication has to wear off quickly and completely so that the dog is able to compensate for his own malformed airways.

Sighthounds These dogs present their own challenge in receiving anesthesia, so talk to your vet about this. Sighthounds don't have enough body fat to hold a large amount of anesthetic drug; they also metabolize anesthetics more slowly, so they sometimes can have a prolonged recovery from anesthesia. Although vets rarely use barbiturates nowadays (which would pose the problem), it is still worth it to raise this topic beforehand with the doctor who will be doing the surgery.

◆ Analgesia (Pain Medication) Before and After Surgery

You want your pet to have the least possible pain before, during and after a surgical procedure. This is especially important for orthopedic procedures, since bone surgery entails significant pain during the recovery and recuperation periods. People generally don't realize that these two aspects of surgery—the anesthesia used to put the dog out and the analgesia used to relieve the pain—are actually connected when it comes to what choices the surgeon or anesthesiologist makes in how to medicate your dog.

How much pain do dogs feel? This is a fairly new question in veterinary training. Vets used to be taught that dogs perceive pain differently than humans do, and that no analgesia was necessary after surgery. Surgeons were trained to believe that an animal's pain after surgery was not their concern—in fact, that the dogs would stay still and rest better if their pain was not relieved at all. Forward-thinking veterinary schools and practices now embrace the generous application of analgesics before, during and after surgery. In fact, AAHA (American Animal Hospital Association) standards now support pain management. The association encourages vets to make a conscious assessment of pain and use analgesics accordingly.

Pain relief BEFORE surgery helps your dog the most. A knowledgeable vet will tell you that having pain medication in the dog *before* surgery makes a difference in how much your dog will suffer when recovering. Under general anesthesia, a dog's brain is sleeping—so it doesn't receive any information—but pain messages still get to the spinal cord, and the dog will wake up in less discomfort if analgesics have been administered while he was under anesthesia.

Be your dog's pain-relief advocate. Ask questions before the surgery, not afterward. Just by asking questions you show that you want to be on top of what is going to happen. Pain management after surgery should not be an "option"—pain relief is central to your dog's quick and humane recovery. A doctor who doesn't support analgesia after surgery is behind the times, holding on to an old-fashioned and cruel outlook. You cannot change his mind, but you can sure change vets and go to a more sophisticated, modern-thinking vet practice where there is ample pain prevention and attention.

Ask the vet how analgesia will be handled postoperatively. By asking this question—and thus showing your concern for your dog's comfort—you may influence the kind of anesthesia your dog will receive during the operation and which painkillers he'll get afterward.

A lot of vets still don't offer pain relief for neutering and spaying. This is unnecessary cruelty. Analgesics before, during and after any surgery not only make the process easier for your dog, they improve the outcome of the operation. For more, go to www.thedogbible.com, "Inside the Book."

PAIN RELIEF FOR SURGERY

❑ **BEFORE**:   Morphine or a related drug (as a premedication)
               NSAID: injectable Rimadyl or Deramaxx
❑ **DURING**:   Correct level of anesthesia
               Local anesthetic as needed (tooth extractions)
               Morphine or derivative as needed
❑ **AFTER**:   Morphine or transdermal fentanyl patch (serious orthopedic surgery)
               NSAIDs for three to four days afterward (Rimadyl, Deramaxx)

♦ **Equipment to Prevent Wound-Licking**

After surgery (or when your dog has skin problems that might prompt him to lick himself) the vet may give you a huge, hard-plastic cone to wrap around your dog's neck. This contraption—which fans out around his face and makes licking himself impossible—is known as an Elizabethan collar, undoubtedly because it is reminiscent of those wide pleated collars worn in those days. But the hard-plastic collar (much wider than a dog's head, and sometimes bigger than his shoulders) also makes it impossible to go through doorways or even walk into a room without crashing into the walls. It can make lying down painful and/or awkward. (I would have loved to try something else for my Cocker Spaniel, Amalfi, who was so stunned by how the blinders-effect of the Elizabethan collar caused him to knock into furniture as he walked past that he refused to budge when the collar was on. He just stood stock-still in the middle of the room with a pained but patient expression until we took pity and liberated him.)

There is now a transparent version of the Elizabethan, which solves the problem of the dog being unable to see around him but still makes navigation treacherous. However, there is a new option, which may be a "better mousetrap." A company called Bite Not Products has come up with an alternative: their collar is just a very wide, thick band that fits around the dog's neck with an elastic chest band that holds it in place. The collar is flexible, machine-washable plastic that comes in seven sizes. You can reach them at (800) 424-8366, or by visiting www.bitenot.com. If you need your dog not to lick and the Elizabethan is hell for him, give one of these a try.

Also, see the listing for the bodysuit for dogs on page 390 of this section, under "Skin."

TAIL DOCKING

A dog's tail is a necessary part of his anatomy for everyday tasks like jumping, turning, waving away insects, and general balance. It is also an essential part of a dog's equipment for communication through his body language.

In 1986, at a conference for the World Society for the Protection of Animals in Luxembourg, it was decreed that there should be no more docking of dogs' tails. Obviously, tail docking has continued since that time; but, countries like Great Britain are leading the way toward ending this pointless mutilation.

If you are getting a breed of dog in which tail docking is the norm, consider asking the breeder to leave your dog intact. Even if it is too late, and they have already docked the whole litter, at least by asking you are raising the consciousness level of dog breeders, with whom change must initiate.

TEETH

Please go to page 424 in Chapter 12, "Grooming Your Dog" for everything related to dental health.

URINARY ISSUES

◆ Excessive Urination and Thirst

These two symptoms are classic signs of several serious ailments in dogs. If you notice either or both of these behaviors in your dog, take her to the vet to determine whether she may be suffering from kidney disease, diabetes or Cushing's disease.

◆ Incontinence

Urinary incontinence is the involuntary leaking of urine. The dog has no control over it. Incontinence can become a huge nuisance if it is not treated and resolved. Leaking urine is unhealthy for the dog, because it predisposes him to a severe urinary-tract infection. In a convoluted way, urinary problems can become "life-threatening" if the dog's people get fed up living with the mess and take their dog to the pound, where he may be put to sleep. There are many possible causes of incontinence; it may take some sleuthing for your vet to figure this one out, with your help.

◆ Cystitis as a Cause of Incontinence

Cystitis is a urinary-tract infection that can cause a dog to need to go out frequently to urinate, have accidents in the house, strain to urinate or have blood in her urine. The first thing the vet will do is a urine test to rule out an infection. With an infection, the dog may have an abnormal urge to empty the bladder but can do so only in small amounts. The dog may whimper during urination. Antibiotics treat these infections, and urination returns to normal in a few days.

◆ Urinary Problems from Bladder Stones

Urinary-tract stones have the same symptoms as cystitis, and the stones may be accompanied by bacterial infection. There are several types of stones in dogs, and the treatment varies depending on their composition. Treatment often begins with increasing water intake to increase urine output, but surgical removal is generally recommended so that the stone(s) can be analyzed. There are two different kinds of urinary stones which can form in the bladder or the kidneys, and different ways to manage them. Please go to www.thedogbible.com and click on the "Inside the Book" tab to better understand and handle this dangerous condition.

◆ Sphincter Incompetence

The most frequent reason for urinary leakage is that the ring of muscle that usually controls the flow of urine out of the bladder loses the ability to contract fully. Sphincter incompetence usually happens when the dog is lying down, often when sleeping and completely unaware of what is happening. It happens most often in spayed, middle-aged females.

Treatment usually involves restoring the muscle strength and tone of the sphincter with a prescription drug called PPA (phenylpropanolmomine), which is sometimes used together with a synthetic estrogen (DES).

Information about Incontinence for Your Vet

- Does it happen when the dog is asleep and unconscious, or awake and aware?
- Is it a large or small amount each time?
- Does it happen in one puddle in the same location, or is it a constant dribble?
- Does the urination seem uncomfortable—does the dog whimper?
- Are there problems getting up or moving around?
- Does he drag his hind legs or sometimes lose control of his bowels?
- How much water does your dog drink, and how often?
- Does your dog have other medical problems such as diabetes or kidney disease?

◆ **Underlying Disease**

Medical problems such as diabetes (see page 350) or chronic kidney disease (page 370) are also causes of urinary incontinence.

◆ **Questions from the Vet**

The vet needs a lot of information to make a thorough diagnosis. Much of this information will come from questions she needs to ask you, but you'll be better able to give the correct answer if you anticipate the questions.

Alternative Medicine

Many vets are now adding holistic methods such as acupuncture, nutrition, herbs and chiropractic adjustments to the traditional methods they use to treat pets. The American Veterinary Association has been urging members to learn more about alternative medicine for conditions such as lupus (an autoimmune disease), arthritis, kidney disease, Lyme disease, ruptured disks, diabetes, skin problems, anxiety and stress. And there are veterinarians who practice only these alternative methods (see page 403 at the end of this section for contact information).

There is no way to do justice to the complexity of alternative veterinary care in a limited amount of space. In researching alternative medicine for this book, I found that to really understand and take advantage of nontraditional ways of preventing and healing medical problems, you need to immerse yourself in the subject. The advice, ingredients and techniques of herbal and homeopathic medicine can be confusing and often seem contradictory to a "virgin" eye.

When determining whether to include specific topics from alternative medicine in *The Dog Bible*, another problem for me was that the field lends itself to self-medication—"recipes" of herbal ingredients, "remedies" for various ailments—which encourages people to mix them up and take care of their own dog. In theory, I like the idea of people taking responsibility for their own health care (and that of their animals), regardless of which philosophy of medicine they follow. But in reality, I think it is inherently dangerous for anyone to look at her dog's symptoms, draw a conclusion and then proceed to give or do something to an ailing animal. Since many of the elements of holistic healing are readily available in health-food stores (unlike antibiotics and injections that a Western veterinarian might use), I would hate to think that if I included holistic veterinary health specifics here that I would be encouraging anyone to make decisions about her dog's health. (I confess having done that very thing myself and was way off the mark: I made a fool of myself and jeopardized my dog's welfare.) What our vets have that we don't—besides a decade of training—is the experience and power of observation from which their advice flows. Never underestimate its value, no matter where you seek veterinary care. I have explained all of this in painful detail because I do not want to appear biased against alternative medicine—you need to know why I have given it less space.

There are several really good holistic veterinary books if you want to immerse yourself: *Dr. Pitcairn's Complete Guide to Natural Health for Dogs & Cats* is the granddaddy of holistic dog care, but Celeste Yarnall's *Natural Dog Care: A Complete Guide to Holistic Health Care for Dogs* (Castle Books, 2000) is a good book, too. And one of the most charming-looking and highly useful books around is a little gem called *Natural Healing for Dogs and Cats A-Z* by Cheryl Schwartz, DVM (Hay House, Inc., 2000).

What follows are some aspects of alternative medicine that may be interesting and useful no matter what veterinary road you follow.

MASSAGE

Holistic vets, acupuncturists and other providers of alternative medicine believe in the benefits of massage for dogs. They say that dogs who get massaged benefit the same way people do, and it is also a special bonding time for people with their dogs.

BENEFITS OF MASSAGE

- ❏ Improves general health by increasing blood circulation and enhancing all the body systems (lymph, circulatory, respiratory, nervous, digestive and immune).
- ❏ Relieves stress, tension and anxiety and improves sleep patterns, which helps with behavioral problems in dogs.
- ❏ Helps the body eliminate wastes and improves skin and coat.
- ❏ Relieves muscle spasms, improves muscle tone, increases flexibility and decreases inflammation or pain in joints
- ❏ Improves athletic performance in speed, strength and stamina.
- ❏ Speeds rehabilitation after surgery, illness or emotional or physical trauma.
- ❏ Improves the human-canine bond by providing quiet "down time," increasing communication between you and establishing a greater mutual awareness.

◆ How to Massage Your Dog

Massage is not something you pay someone to do, it's something you do yourself for your dog. Besides the closeness this fosters, there is the bonus that massage costs nothing after the relatively minor cost of an instructional book and/or video.

There are different styles and philosophies of dog massage, many of them described and demonstrated in books and on videotapes. If you are interested in learning more about these products and perhaps buying one of them, the *Whole Dog Journal* put together in the November 2002 issue a consumer guide to the massage books and videocassettes that are available, complete with thorough descriptions. You can back-order that issue by calling (800) 424-7887. (While you're at it, do yourself and your pooch a favor and get a subscription—you'll learn something fascinating and new about training and nutrition every month.)

The conditions in the list that follows are situations in which massage is not advisable. Call your vet if you have any doubts.

CONDITIONS FOR WHICH DOG MASSAGE SHOULD BE AVOIDED

- ❏ Cancer (avoid direct contact with tumors)
- ❏ Serious illness
- ❏ Open wounds
- ❏ Unusual rashes

☐ Fractures
☐ Jaundice
☐ Fever
☐ Nausea and vomiting
☐ Immediately after meals

NOTE: *Miniature/toy breeds and puppies require a light, soft touch.*

VETERINARY CHIROPRACTORS

This is actually another subspecialty of canine doctors—since these practitioners get chiropractic training above and beyond their veterinary degrees; they then have to take written and practical examinations before they can become members of the American Veterinary Chiropractic Association (AVCA). Practitioners believe that there are three groups of dogs who can particularly benefit from chiropractic manipulation: older dogs, those with previous injuries and dogs whose lives include highly athletic duty.

If you believe in the benefits of chiropractic adjustments for people, then you should consider having your pet checked out, too. For more information about chiropractic for animals, see the AVCA's Web site: www.animalchiropractic.org. For a listing of the vets who are certified chiropractors in your area, go online to www.avcadoctors.com. The organization can also be reached by phone at (918) 784-2231.

The American Veterinary Medical Association (AVMA) represents 65,000 vets, but it can still be difficult to find one in your own area. There are fewer holistic vets. To find one, check the AHVMA's Web site: www.ahvma.org. Or write or call American Holistic Veterinary Medical Association (AHVMA) at 2214 Old Emmorton Road, Bel Air, MD 21015, (410) 569-0795. For a listing of alternative providers, go to www.thedogbible.com, "Inside the Book."

VETERINARY ACUPUNCTURE

The positive results of acupuncture on dogs and horses is so dramatic that it removes any doubt that people might have about the dramatic benefits of this practice—especially in situations where Western medicine has nothing to offer or has not helped—since there's no way a horse or dog can know the effect you are trying to achieve with acupuncture needles.

I was one such skeptic until I watched an acupuncturist rebalance my horse's endocrine system: he hadn't been able to sweat for days because his glands were not functioning. Limo had been dangerously overheating in 100°F weather, yet with three acupuncture needles he began to pour with sweat. Next I was amazed by how with one acupuncture treatment my lethargic, sore-backed Cocker Spaniel turned into a ball-chasing fool. I lay down in the horse's stall to get a treatment myself (the acupuncturist had treated people before horses, and had been a prodigy concert pianist before that—it was California, after all).

Veterinary acupuncturists have to undergo rigorous training and testing, and if you're lucky enough to have one in your area, give her a try just for the experience. To find one you can contact the AHVMA, the alternative veterinary medicine Web site at www.altvetmed.org, or most directly, the International Veterinary Acupuncture Society, P.O. Box 271395, Fort Collins, CO 80527-1395, (303) 449-7936, www.ivas.org.

Chapter 12

GROOMING YOUR DOG

 Brushing and washing your dog can be a pleasurable experience for both of you, although either of you can dread it if the dog is fighting you because she's miserable or frightened. If your dog is started early in her life being touched by grooming equipment and human hands, she'll be comfortable with the experience (see "Puppies," page 408). If not, you'll also find suggestions on how to make bath-time a good experience no matter what your dog's age or past experience.

WHAT YOU'LL FIND IN THIS CHAPTER:

- ❏ Brushes and combs
- ❏ Electric clippers
- ❏ Types of coats and frequency of grooming
- ❏ Starting grooming in puppyhood
- ❏ Difficulties grooming
- ❏ Professional grooming
- ❏ Skin in winter months
- ❏ Grooming emergencies (skunk, tar, paint, etc.)
- ❏ Baths, including shampoos and advance preparations
- ❏ Ears, teeth, nails
- ❏ Wrinkles and folds

BRUSHES AND COMBS

Although you'll see different breeds mentioned below after every type of brush, keep in mind that your dog's coat may be unusual for her breed. For example, there are Labs and Rottweilers with unusually thick, rough coats, and Golden Retrievers with feathers (long hair on the legs) that are so thick and long that they require the same grooming needs as an Afghan Hound's coat. So experiment with different brushes to see what gives you the best result with your dog's coat.

How often you should brush your dog is covered on page 407 in this section, but try to brush at least once a week, working against the direction of hair growth, then with it.

◆ Grooming Glove

There are a few different styles and constructions, but the main idea is a cloth glove with a rubber palm area covered with bumps that grab and collect dead hair. It seems to please dogs: they can feel your hand right through the glove and get a scratchy massage. This is good for smooth-coated, short-haired dogs such as Weimaraners, Labs, Pugs, Greyhounds and Dobermans.

◆ Natural Bristle Brush

This can have the kind of densely packed bristles that are soft yet sturdy—similar to some of the nicer finishing brushes for horses or even the kind of wood-handled, high-end English hairbrushes used for people (if you have such a hairbrush and it's getting on in years, there's no reason you can't demote it to a dog brush if your dog's coat is compatible). When you use this kind of brush, it's helpful to also get a slicker brush (see below) so you can clean the bristle brush. Hold a brush in either hand and brush the two together, rubbing the bristle brush against the metal teeth of the slicker to rub off the dead hairs. This is good for medium-coated and long-haired, silky-coated dogs such as Golden Retrievers, Rottweilers, Afghans, Lhasa Apsos and Yorkshire Terriers.

◆ Slicker Brush

This has a long handle at right angles to a rectangular metal brush-head (of various sizes) that is loaded with thin wire bristles—sort of like a grooming version of a wire barbecue-cleaning brush. The slicker is really good for long flowing tails and leg feathers, but it's harsh when used against the dog's skin, even if you are gentle. Try brushing it against your own skin to get a sense of how intense it can be with any pressure applied, and let your dog's reaction guide you. Good for many of the dogs listed above and also for Salukis, Borzois, Maltese (and all small, silky-haired breeds) and Wire-haired Terriers.

◆ Steel Combs

Many dogs have long silky hair that can be groomed using a steel comb, which is available with different-sized teeth—some spaced closely together for the finer, softer hair, while other combs feature thicker teeth further apart. Combs can also be used alongside bristle brushes to comb the dead hair out of the brush as you are working. A "Collie comb" is one such wide-toothed comb: it is intended to get at the downy undercoat, which is what keeps these breeds warm in extremely cold weather.

Dogs with luxurious coats generally shed a lot and need a dedicated grooming schedule—a good, deep brushing at least twice a week, especially against the grain and all the way down to the tender skin on their stomachs. During shedding seasons, especially in the spring, you may want to learn from a groomer or your dog's breeder how to use a shedding blade to shorten the otherwise long process of a dog losing her winter coat. Good for double-coated breeds like Collies, Siberian Huskies, Akitas, Malamutes, Shetland Sheepdogs, Chows, Samoyeds and Keeshonds.

• Static Electricity

The little shock that can tingle when you touch or brush your dog. This usually happens in dry weather. There are two ways to avoid shocking your dog when you brush her: You can dampen the brush while using it and pay attention to where you are standing. Avoid standing on synthetic fiber carpet. Stand on a hard floor, on a wool or cotton rug, or put a towel down on top of synthetic carpeting before you begin grooming.

ELECTRIC CLIPPERS

If you have any of the breeds that need to be shaped or "cleaned up," you might want to consider getting a good clipper. Not only does clipping your own dog save you considerable money (the cost of a professional grooming session or two immediately amortizes your clipper purchase), but it saves you time that you don't have to schedule picking up and dropping off the dog. It also gives you some nice "bonding time" with your dog.

• Which Kind of Clipper Is Best?

Oster dominates the market and, while there are other professional-quality clippers, Oster is available everywhere at a reasonable price, is easy to use and comes with a good instructional video to send you on your way.

Clipper motors come in a variety of power levels, which generate different numbers of strokes per minute (more is better), levels of noise and vibration (less is better) and speed and amount of heat buildup (less is better). For most home use, the Oster Professional Clipper Kit (with video) (model 78096-109) will give you the best value for all of the above elements.

• Learning How to Use Clippers

You might want to either ask a professional groomer if you can watch him work or, if you have a nice relationship with your dog's breeder, ask her if she could demonstrate her technique with the clippers. Some breeds need their ears shaved close, while others need top knots shaped, bodies trimmed, etc. Personally, I can barely brush my own hair, but I managed to give Pango, Pandora and my other Bedlington Terriers a show clip when I was a child, and as an adult learned a different technique for Amalfi, who had the enormous leg feathers and long, hairy ears of a show-quality Cocker Spaniel. It may sound daunting, but give yourself time and permission to botch a few trimmings and it can be kind of fun—sort of like having a living doll to play with.

An instructional video is a great way to learn—or relearn—and the Oster video is considered one of the most useful, covering several different hair types.

Electric clipping is not done on the Terrier breeds that go to shows; they need to have the dead hair plucked out of their coat in a time-consuming process called "stripping."

- Put a rubber mat on a counter or washer/dryer.
- Lubricate the blade with oil before, during and after use.
- Keep oiled blades in a zipped bag.
- Blades heat up during use: test one on yourself so you don't burn the dog.
- Turn the clipper off (except when actually clipping) to keep the blades cooler.
- Snap on the blades only when the motor is running (except with the Wahl brand).
- Blades get dull after extended use: replace or send them to the manufacturer for sharpening.
- Clip with hair growth, or for a shorter, closer shave, clip against it (from tail to neck).
- Don't clip a dirty or wet dog—this wears out blades and can hurt the dog's skin.

Clippers are good for curly-coated and wire-haired breeds, such as Bedlingtons and other soft-coated Terriers, Poodles, Schnauzers, wire-haired hunting dogs, Cockers and other Spaniels.

TYPES OF COATS AND FREQUENCY OF GROOMING

Shedding occurs all the time for dogs with heavy coats, but the main shedding seasons are in the spring and fall, when a new coat comes in. For the heavy-coated dogs, this means daily brushing with a slicker brush to keep their hair off your clothes and furniture. Ask a breeder or groomer to show you how to use a shedding blade, which pulls out a lot of the dead hair painlessly.

• Double-coated Dogs

Dogs with a thick undercoat beneath the fur need a lot of brushing. These breeds have a downy undercoat that can mat down painfully against the dog's skin if you don't groom it. Imagine having braids that are put in too tightly: that's how a matted undercoat must be like to a dog. To keep the undercoat from matting, you can divide the soft hair into small sections and brush it backward. Collies, Siberian Huskies, Akitas, Malamutes, Shetland Sheepdogs, Chows and Keeshonds are examples of dogs with double coats.

• Long-coated Dogs

It can be a daily job to keep these dogs feeling and looking good. Grooming requirements should be a serious consideration in your choice of breed, because these dogs demand a lot of your time. Even if you elect to turn over the serious grooming work to a professional, you still need to maintain some degree of control over these dogs' coats, and you may have neither the time nor the desire to do this.

Soft, cottony hair tangles easily and requires at least a quick daily brushing to keep tangles from forming. Tangles can become uncomfortable or painful for the dog, and once they have formed, or if matting takes place, it can require total shaving of the dog—sometimes under anesthesia, because otherwise it would be too painful.

Work with small sections at a time, similar to double-coated breeds. Afghan Hounds, Shih Tzus, Lhasa Apsos, Maltese, Pekingese and Cocker Spaniels are examples of breeds with soft cottony hair.

Do not shave long-haired dogs Why make a beautiful dog ugly? In hot weather it does not make a long-haired dog any more comfortable to take off her coat. Contrary to popular belief, shaving a long-haired dog may actually make her more uncomfortable in warm weather. The coat gives her insulation against the heat, as it does against the cold in winter. Long-haired breeds have less coat in the summer anyway, having dropped their undercoat in the spring. Many groomers say that you should pick one coat length and stay with it throughout the year: the process of going from short to long and back to short can be a shock to a dog's system.

START GROOMING IN PUPPYHOOD

◆ Let the Puppy Lie Down or Stand
Whatever seems most comfortable for her and for you is fine. Some dogs seem to feel less vulnerable if they are standing instead of lying on the ground, while others choose to lie down and seem more relaxed that way.

You can set the pup on a towel on top of your dryer or on a counter, so you don't have to bend or crouch. This is easier on your back.

◆ Hold the Puppy While You Brush
He won't have much of an attention span and will probably squirm and resist, but don't stop when he does that. Just carry on, brushing gently, not for a long time but enough to brush, say, half of him—then end the experience with something really pleasurable, such as a soft brush on his belly or a firm brush behind his ears and around his neck, where all dogs get itchy.

◆ Preparing for a Professional Groomer
If she's a breed that requires professional grooming (Poodles, Cockers, Terriers, etc.) you can make that upcoming experience easier on her by getting her used to the sound and feel of an electric trimmer. If you have an electric razor or any household tool that might hum or give a buzzing sensation, that should give a sense of the vibration she will feel when an electric trimmer is used on her eventually. (See section on p. 411 on "Professional Grooming.")

◆ Grooming Small-dog Puppies
Groom any small dog (young or old) right on top of a table or counter. Choose a countertop that you can cover with a towel, or a rubber bathtub mat if it is slippery and the puppy seems scared.

◆ Large-breed Puppies

When a large-breed dog is a puppy, she can be put on any raised surface to be groomed. Once she's an adult, you may find it easier for your medium or large dog to lie down for grooming. If you haven't taught her this from puppyhood, you will need to give her encouragement at a later age to lie down to be brushed. For most people, it is easier to sit down on the floor beside the dog than to bend over her. The dog will eventually relax if you are stroking her with your other hand while brushing and talking to her.

◆ Flipping Your Dog to the Other Side

See if your dog will accept you flipping her over gently by taking hold of the bottom of her front and back legs at the same time and slowly pushing them upward while she's lying down.

The dog may panic the first time you try to flip her, but just use a soothing voice, put your hands under the bottom legs a little closer to her body and try it again, so that you are moving her torso at the same time as her legs. You can teach a dog to accept being flipped over if you move slowly and reassure her with your voice. It can really be a useful move to have in the future if at any time a vet has to see both sides of your dog when she's lying down.

Trust your own judgment about whether your dog is going to trust you on this one, but even if she gently puts her mouth on your wrist to warn you to stop, you can gently say "Nooo" in response to her mouth and accomplish the move while praising her enthusiastically for her trust and acceptance. If your dog is particularly scared or resistant to this move, consider a little food treat as added reward for going along.

◆ Positive Desensitization

By handling the dog all over when you're grooming her, you are desensitizing her in a positive way. She will be more accepting of being handled by people in ways that might be unpleasant or surprising for her, whether it's by children or even adults who are quick or a little rough.

Touch the puppy all over her body as often as possible: lift her ear flaps and rub your fingers around the opening (for future ear cleaning), feel between her paws, especially between her toes (for later toenail cutting), touch her tail, which she needs to become accustomed to for later ministrations such as temperature-taking. The more the dog accepts your hands and brush on her body, the more she will enjoy it.

While grooming, pull gently on the dog's skin (it's usually a bit loose at the back of the neck), stroke her ears right down to the tips (a very relaxing motion for a dog), lift up her tail and feet. All these things go into making her into a model canine citizen.

Start brushing your puppy even when she has very little hair to brush. Use a very soft brush (test it against your own skin) so you know it is a pleasurable experience for her.

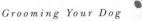

◆ Dealing with a Struggling Dog

If the dog struggles and pulls away, *do not let her go,* or you will be teaching her that struggling and squirming is the route to freedom. Instead, grasp her collar and give it a little shake (not angry or impatient) with a firm "No" in a low, no-nonsense tone.

As soon as the dog stops struggling and calms down, make a big fuss congratulating her and then *do* let her go. If she takes off, wait it out. After a minute or two you can go get her and resume the grooming session. If she struggles again, be firm without being angry—praise her and even give her a treat when she settles down—then continue with your grooming.

❑ Do not let the dog get away, or you'll be teaching her that struggling gains freedom.

❑ Do not take pity and sound sympathetic or apologetic—the dog will take advantage of your perceived weakness.

❑ Do not make brushing a test of wills if you meet resistance. Go back to lying her down on her side and being stroked.

❑ Do not keep on brushing. Just get the dog comfortable with being on her side and being touched. Praise her for giving you no resistance.

◆ A Dog Who Hates to Be Brushed

❑ You want to teach the dog to associate the brush with good things.

❑ Get some very tasty treats in a little bowl.

❑ Sit on a comfortable carpeted floor with her—it's fun and relaxing for the dog to have you down there with her. Stroke her, put her at her ease.

❑ Let her sniff the brush and say "Yes!" and give her a treat as she smells it.

❑ Touch her gently with the brush (don't brush yet) and say "Yes!" then give a treat again.

❑ Continue touching her slowly and gently on different parts of her body with the brush—without any brushing motion—for as long as she stays comfortable.

❑ Stop while she is still relaxed and calm for as long as you can, until you see she is getting anxious or fed up.

❑ A few short sessions are better than one longer session, which may tax her patience.

❑ If she gets wound up and wants to play with the brush, hold a treat in your fingertips and let her lick at it while you touch her a few more times with the brush. You want to desensitize her to the feeling of being brushed.

❑ End the session on a positive note with a "yes" and a treat, with you still on top of the situation, not with the dog all wound up.

◆ A Dog Who's Really Frightened of Grooming

If the dog's fear of being brushed is deeply rooted, you need to change her association with the brush itself. Good things must happen when that brush appears. This means you need to have a couple of brushes around the house (or carry one with you when you're going to be home for a while) and have some great little tidbits in your pocket at the same time. Pick up the brush, stroke the dog with your other hand and give a treat. Pick up her ball or favorite toy and show her the brush—even touch her lightly with it if she can stand it—before you throw the ball (which is the positive association—no edible treat required). Show her the brush before setting down her meal.

Once she's relaxed about the brush you can begin actually brushing her—but do it slowly and gently, with lots of those yummy treats for now. She will eventually come to enjoy being brushed, as long as you choose a brush that does not hurt her and you move slowly to diminish her previous anxiety.

◆ "Touchy Dogs"

Some dogs hate to be touched on certain areas of their bodies. For many it's the feet, others their rear end or tail, but if you try to make it a pleasurable experience they'll eventually accept your touch and even come to enjoy it.

Make touching that dog's sensitive area a low-key pleasure. Give a treat as you touch that part of her body. Speak in a relaxed, cheerful voice. Only touch gently, then do another part of her body, then return gently to the first location.

Many dogs hate being groomed because it hurts. Be gentle and use a brush that does not cause pain on your dog's type of coat or sensitive skin. Try the brush against your own skin to see whether it is needle-like, or whether you just have to adjust the amount of pressure you use with each stroke.

PROFESSIONAL GROOMING

There are several breeds—Cockers, Poodles, Spaniels and Terriers, among others—that need to be groomed by a professional unless you want to teach yourself to become a semiprofessional. The trimming involved can be time-consuming and is often beyond the scope of most people (except perhaps a hairdresser for humans—and he's probably sick of grooming when he gets home).

Double-coated breeds (Collies and Shelties, Malamutes, Huskies, Chows, etc.) can occasionally benefit from a groomer, because it will make your grooming job easier and may also shorten the length of time a dog sheds each season.

◆ Finding a Groomer

Dogs don't generally like going to the groomer so it will make the whole experience less traumatic if you find a knowledgeable, caring individual and leave the dog there for as brief a visit as possible. Start by asking friends, coworkers and neighbors with dogs if they have any recommendations.

Veterinary bathing services Some vets offer a bathing service (but usually not clipping), which you might want to consider if you don't have the time, space or desire to wash your dog yourself. If you have a long-haired dog whose brushing you have neglected, his coat can become seriously matted, which a vet's staff would probably be able to handle. However, if you have a breed that needs extensive clipping, you'll need a full service groomer, and your vet may be able to make some suggestions of local professionals.

Ask your breeder. To find a good groomer, you can also ask the breeder, if you got a purebred dog directly from someone in your geographic area. The breeder might help you find a groomer—or let you watch her groom her own dogs, if you want to try to figure it out for yourself.

• Make Regular Grooming Appointments

If you have a long-coated or double-coated dog, you can keep her from becoming painfully matted by taking her to the groomer on a regular basis. Matted hair takes a while to build up, but once a mat begins it can be virtually impossible to pull out: the dog will need to be shaved, and even that can be unpleasant when hair is tightly matted to the skin.

• Communicate with the Groomer

Make it clear to the groomer what you want your dog to look like: for example, if you have a poodle you want kept "natural looking," make sure that is clear. If you have an English Sheepdog whose face you want trimmed, make sure you are both in agreement on how much to take off. If you have a toy breed but do not want any of the frilly bows and nail polish, make sure you let them know that.

• Plan Ahead

If you know you want your dog spiffed-up for any holiday, it helps to make an appointment months in advance. Thanksgiving and Christmas are very busy times for dog groomers, because so many people want their pets looking their best for company—so get your appointment way ahead of time.

• A Very Anxious Dog

If you have a nervous, skittish, frightened dog, going to the groomer can really be hellish for her—even if the groomer is kind and/or fast.

You have three options when grooming an especially high-strung or anxious dog: learn to do the trimming yourself, forgo all fancy clipping and just wash and dry the dog yourself or have the grooming done at the vet's, so that if tranquilizers make the most sense, they can be administered by a medical staff with doctors available should something go wrong.

• Cautions about Professional Groomers

Tranquilizers Some groomers tranquilize dogs before working on them to make their job easier. Some of these groomers don't even let owners know they use tranquilizers, while others may mention medicating the dog but downplay the importance—suggesting it's done everywhere, or there's no risk, or it's for the dog's own good. The only problem is that they may be grooming a dog for its coffin: there are health risks in administering tranquilizers, and dogs do die from being given too much or having an adverse reaction.

Ask a groomer ahead of time whether he sedates dogs. If he says he does, you can request that your dog *not* be drugged. Or maybe you should just keep a dirty dog and not gamble? Because there would be no way to know for sure that your dog had *not* been medicated, even if the groomer agrees not to.

Keep the appointment short You do not want a groomer who keeps your dog for longer than is absolutely necessary. That means that the groomer should schedule appointments so that a dog stays for approximately the amount of time it takes to groom him—which, depending on the breed, can be anywhere from two to four hours for a wash, dry and trim.

If your dog is badly matted or tangled, more time will be necessary, but barring that, a half day is the most a groomer should require.

A groomer should schedule her dogs with the correct amount of time between them, and not expect your dog to sit in a cage for hours until she gets around to him. If a groomer wants your dog dropped off in the morning but won't give you a pick-up time, then you probably should not leave your dog with that person. It's not fair to the animal to be kept in a confinement cage next to other anxious dogs, listening to blow-dryers all day.

YOUR DOG'S SKIN IN THE WINTER

Most dogs shed their coats in preparation for winter, and your dog will probably grow a new coat, too. Even in warmer climates, a dog's body reacts to the number of daylight hours and grows a winter coat even if it isn't necessary for the climate. Long-haired and medium-haired dogs will grow a substantial undercoat that traps insulating air to retain warmth. If you live in an area that gets cold in the winter, your dog's coat and skin may react to the dry indoor heating and fluctuations in temperature.

◆ Dogs Can Get Sunburns in the Winter Just as Skiers Can.
Sunlight reflects off snow and can cause a burn. Light-colored dogs need to be watched for the telltale sign of "solar dermatitis": reddened skin.

◆ Brush Your Dog Frequently.
This will help remove dead hair and spread oils from the skin, which help make the coat shinier. Although you should bathe the dog in the winter only as necessary to keep her coat clean, a clean coat insulates better against the cold than a dirty one.

◆ Use a Moisturizing Shampoo and Conditioner.
This will help keep the skin from getting dry and flaky. Use only those made especially for dogs.

◆ Make Sure the Dog Is Entirely Dry Before Going Outside After a Bath.
If you don't, she may get a chill, especially if she is very young or a senior citizen. If you're concerned that she's still damp, you can use a blow-dryer, but always on a very low, "air-only" setting, since hot air not only hurts and can burn a dog, it can actually set a dog's hair on fire.

◆ Fat Supplements for Dry Skin?
Fatty-acid supplements to a dog's food are sometimes recommended by a vet, but if your dog is eating a high-quality food with a good proportion of fat, then adding fat supplements will probably only cause her to gain weight. However, a dog may not be digesting or absorbing the fat or

other nutrients in her food, even in cases where the food is top-quality. In this case, your vet should examine the dog and do some lab tests to find out more.

If you do add an oral fat supplement to your dog's food—many oil additives make promises galore—and dandruff or other skin dryness problems do improve, then you need to reconsider what you are feeding your dog. This dramatic improvement with a fat supplement should be a warning that you need to upgrade the quality of food you've been offering.

GROOMING EMERGENCIES

It's fine to read about these remedies, but on the other hand, horrible emergencies present themselves with no clear solution. I don't know which of the rules below you would have followed if you had been in my situation: two Weimaraners and a short-haired Collie running through fresh tar on a new driveway? Their legs and bellies were covered in thick, sticky tar with pebbles attached, and they were totally freaked out. On Weimaraners, there's no hair to clip and their skin is as delicate and soft as silk. Nothing worked, not olive oil, not even a product called Goo Gone. The dogs were crazed by having this sticky goo stuck with pebbles all over them, and I didn't know what to do except use the forbidden: turpentine. When that hit the delicate Weim skin, it gave "freaked-out dog" a new meaning. I followed that with many shampooings, rinsings, and applications of aloe gel to reduce the redness and sting. You wouldn't wish such a fate on a dog, as they say.

Here are some solutions to common grooming emergencies:

◆ Chewing Gum, Tar or Other Sticky Ingredients
Try to roll a fingerful of peanut butter around the substance to loosen it. If that doesn't work, clip it out.

◆ Paint
There's nothing to do but clip it out. NEVER use turpentine or other chemical solvents on a dog (despite the anecdote above). They are toxic if she licks the area, they are flammable and they irritate the skin. If it is more than a very small amount of paint, you might want a groomer to give the dog a total haircut and let it all grow back.

◆ De-skunking Your Dog
For years, people believed that the best way to remove skunk odor was to give their dog a tomato-juice bath, but it is no longer considered an effective or user-friendly solution. No matter what preparation you use, with a long-haired dog the important thing is to get the solution worked right down to the skin with your fingers.

- ❏ Peppermint mouthwash is one of the quicker, easier solutions for de-skunking: wet a cloth with the mouthwash and wipe it on your dog's coat. Then bathe the dog or rinse him thoroughly.
- ❏ A gallon jug of white vinegar can be used in the same way.

❐ There are commercial "de-skunking" solutions sold in pet stores that are purported to work well, or you can mix up your own concoction following the recipes in the chart below.

Two scientists came up with solutions you can make at home to clean the odor from skunk spray. The recipes that follow first appeared in a publication of the American Chemical Society called *Chemical & Engineering News.*

Warning: *Do not prepare these mixes ahead of time. They produce oxygen and will explode in a closed container!*

🦴 *Skunk Shampoo*

Formula #1
- One quart 3% hydrogen peroxide
- ¼ cup baking soda (sodium bicarbonate)
- One teaspoon liquid dish soap

Dilute with an equal amount of water.

Rub into the coat, rinse many times with ample fresh water.

Formula #2
- One gallon warm water
- One cup Snowy bleach (sodium perborate)
- Three tablespoons liquid detergent

Rub into the hair, rinse thoroughly with lots of water.

✦ Porcupine Quills
Go right to the vet's office or an emergency veterinary facility if this happens after office hours. Do NOT try to pull out the quills yourself—they have little hooks on the end that really hurt if you try to remove them. This requires the vet's help.

✦ Tearstains
White (and other light-colored) dogs often get reddish-brown tearstains below their eyes. "Tearstaining syndrome" is seen most frequently in the miniature and toy Poodles and in Maltese Terriers and is caused by an overflow of tears: the protein in tears called lactoferrin binds to iron and causes the stain. But the underlying problem is the excess tears. This can be caused by abnormalities in the ducts, which could be a defect from birth, or caused by infection or trauma later.

You should get a thorough ophthalmic exam for your dog to determine the cause of the tearduct problem and what medical or surgical options you may have now to correct it.

Bathing Your Dog

HOW OFTEN TO GIVE A BATH

Frequent bathing hasn't yet been embraced by most dog owners as a concept, but people are coming around. For years people were told that it was a bad idea to wash a dog too often—that it stripped their coats' natural oils or something—so they should only be bathed a couple of times a year. This meant a lot of greasy, smelly dogs who were unpleasant to touch. What puts the shine in a dog's coat is high-quality food, more than bathing or the lack of it. Also, male hormones can give an animal a shinier coat: in horses, a stallion always has an extra-shiny coat, and the same is often true for intact dogs (although this is obviously no reason to forgo neutering a dog).

A newly bathed dog is a pleasure to touch, smell and look at: smooth to the touch, odor-free and shiny or fluffy-looking, depending on the type of coat.

◆ You Can Bathe Your Dog as Often as Once a Week.

Depending on what kind of life your dog has, if you use a good-quality dog shampoo you can even bathe her weekly. All dogs get dirty pretty quickly—country dogs roll in nasty things and splash through mud and puddles and lie down in dusty places. City dogs walk on streets and in gutters covered in unspeakable grime—and even if it's only their paws, stomachs and muzzles that touch it, that doesn't make it any less filthy.

◆ Frequent Bathing Is Good for Human Allergy Sufferers.

Washing away the dander on a dog's skin removes what most people are allergic to: the dead skin cells. Weekly baths can make living with a dog possible for people with dog allergies.

◆ At Least Once a Month Is a Good Plan.

If your dog does not look, feel or smell dirty to you, then mark your calendar and give him a bath once a month anyway. If other people spend time around your dog, just for the heck of it ask their opinion of his cleanliness, to make sure it isn't your blind adoration of your dog that is keeping you from the tub.

BEFORE THE BATH

◆ What if Your Dog Is Terrified?

Most dogs don't really love getting a bath—which is a huge understatement for those who absolutely *detest* getting bathed. Many of my dogs have run into another room at just the sight of me carrying a stack of their bath towels and a bottle of shampoo—although they submit with a shrug when I go get them for their bath. If your dog is bath-phobic, you'll know because he will do some version of cowering, slinking and trembling as he gets nearer to the bathroom. For some dogs, a bath is so traumatic that their personality can even change during the bathing process.
Attitude is everything You can positively affect the process and bring about a change in your dog's reaction just by how you handle it. Be calm and pleasant about the upcoming bath—speak soothingly in a cheerful voice from the moment you gather the towels. Keep that demeanor right

through the washing and drying, never getting rough or cross. This is the way to slowly but surely change a freaked-out, toenails-digging-into-the-floor, trembling dog into one who walks calmly into the shower or tub and lets you do what you have to do, resigned to his fate. Both Jazzy and Scooby Doo were so terrified the first time when I led them into the shower (from previous horrible experiences, I have to assume) that Scooby threw up and Jazzy lay down outside the shower and would not stand up to enter under her own steam.

Take the dog to the shower on a leash. Do not try to call the dog to you or into the bathroom. There is no way that a frightened dog should be expected to overcome his emotions and follow obedience commands into the face of the very thing that terrifies him. Bring along some treats if you think some sugar will make the medicine go down more easily. If you simply clip on a nylon leash and walk purposefully into the bathroom using a friendly, encouraging voice, the dog will have little choice but to follow. You need to have a leash on the dog during the bath anyway, so you might as well put it on early. You don't want to drag the dog, but don't stop to coax or sweet-talk him, either. It's a no-choice situation for him.

Do the bathing yourself. Do everything you can to avoid taking a fearful dog to a grooming establishment.

BRUSH THE DOG WELL FIRST

Brushing a dog beforehand leaves less hair to wash and dry, if some of it is only going to fall out anyway. Pre-brushing also puts less dog hair in your drain.

If there are tangles, they will only get worse once wet. If the dog is really badly tangled, you may have to take him to a professional groomer, or you'll just wind up with a problem that you can't solve without scissors.

◆ Mats Pose a Problem.

Matting generally occurs in the armpits, between the toes and behind the ears. Mats can get tight to the skin and are risky to cut out, since you could cut skin. However, a mat can't be left there, either. Mats will eventually become sores—and sores can become infected. Depending on the severity of your dog's matting, you may want a professional groomer or the vet to remove the matted hair.

If you have a dog with long, silky hair, or one who already has mats, you can use a detangler like Johnson's No More Tangles for kids (or a similar dog product) beforehand. Try spraying it on the bad areas, work it in with your fingers and then continue with the bathing process.

PREPARE A "BATH BUCKET" BEFOREHAND

◆ Get All the Cleaning Supplies Together Before You Give the Bath.

For example, you can get one of those cheap plastic buckets from a paint store that are small but wide enough to hold everything you'll need. If you have a place to store your bath bucket, then whenever it's bath time all you have to do is grab the bucket and go. In the bucket you can keep a rubber scrubber (if you have a short-haired dog) or a Zoom Groom, which also works to get the loose hair from a medium-haired (Golden Retriever–type) dog. I've had good luck with the

Zoom Groom, a patented grooming tool that has hard-rubber protrusions that gently grab dead hair. Any rubber grooming brush with lots of rubber bristles is also a great way to distribute shampoo evenly.

◆ **What You'll Need**

- ❏ At least three towels per medium-size dog. Collect a pile of your old bath towels or beach towels, but keep in mind that although large towels sound appealing, they aren't as manageable to work with. You'll get water off with the first towel, which you can then put down on the bathroom floor to collect the excess water and keep the dog from slipping in it. Or you may want to use a bath mat or large towel alongside the tub or outside the stall shower for spills and "after-shake."

- ❏ Artificial chamois towels can also work well and leave you with less to clean up, because there are no towels to wash and dry. These super-absorbent dog towels are like the synthetic chamois you use to dry your car. They soak up a significant amount of water, and after they're wrung cut, they dry quickly. These towels usually cost under $5 and are available from pet stores, pet catalogs like Drs. Foster and Smith, (800) 381-7179 or KV Vet Supply, (800) 423-8211 or from The Dog's Outfitter, (800) 367-3647, or Jeffers Pet Products, (800) 533-3377.

- ❏ You may want a rubber bath mat to put inside the tub if you think your dog may slip and slide. A tub mat is a good idea even if your tub has those (usually slippery) non-slip treads. If a dog gets spooked by sliding around, it's going to make giving the next bath a lot harder. If you don't have a mat, put a bath towel on the bottom of the tub.

- ❏ A restraint system for the bathtub is a great way to keep the dog where you want so you can just concentrate on giving the bath, not on keeping him inside the tub. They consist of one or more rubber suction cups that attach to the tub with a cushioned, lasso-style built-in collar, or a clip that attaches to the dog's own collar. EzyBathe and Hold 'Em Bathing Restraint (both available from Jeffers Pet Products), got the highest ratings when the *Whole Dog Journal* rated bath products.

- ❏ Use a nylon collar for baths, since leather will get ruined in the process. If your dog usually wears a fancier collar, get a cheap nylon one just for the bath. If his normal one is nylon, think of the bath as a free collar cleaning.

- ❏ A pet showerhead is the most important item you'll need if you are giving a tub bath, since thorough removal of bathing products is necessary to avoid skin irritation. A contraption like this is invaluable for wetting down but especially for rinsing off a dog—otherwise you waste time dumping bowls of water on the dog, which rarely gets a longer-haired dog completely rinsed. You can probably find a hose and spray head with a diverter at a home-improvement or hardware store, and they can be installed with a wrench in place of your usual showerhead. Otherwise, there is a "pet shower" made expressly for this purpose (for around $20 from The Dog's Outfitter). It will also be useful for you or for children whose hair you want to rinse in the tub, or just to use to spray-clean the bath.

    There is another style of rubber hose that fits over your tub faucet and has a sprayer on the other end, but this kind can often pop off when there is a lot of water pressure.

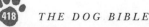

◆ What Shampoo to Use?

Any mild dog shampoo will be fine. There are so many on the market. Just read the labels and look for nice ingredients such as aloe, tea-tree oil and oatmeal, all of which are soothing. If your dog has any kind of skin condition, get your vet's advice before trying any kind of bath product on her. Vets often carry medicated shampoos that treat specific irritations.

If the skin problems are mild, buy shampoos especially for sensitive skin and see which ones give you the best result.

What to Avoid in Dog Shampoos

❏ You cannot use a human shampoo, even the best quality. The PH of a dog's skin and hair is different from ours, and most are too harsh for dogs—even baby shampoo. If you are in an emergency situation and *have to* use human shampoo, dilute it by half with water.

❏ Do not use a flea/tick shampoo if you already use a product such as Frontline or have a flea collar on your dog. You are not supposed to mix or double-up on these products, which can be toxic for your pet if more than one is used at a time. So-called flea shampoo doesn't actually control fleas much better than regular shampoo does: they both wash away the insects, but there's no real lasting effect. The control of fleas has more to do with eliminating them from the immediate environment, anyway. (See page 381 in the section on "Fleas.")

❏ Citrus oils, citronella or d-Limonene in shampoos may deter fleas for a while, but these ingredients can irritate the skin and remove natural oils, especially if used often.

❏ Itchy skin/dandruff shampoos advertise that they are medicated or skin-soothing, but they may contain unsafe ingredients. Dandruff shampoos with coal tar (a possible carcinogen) should only be used for dogs with heavy scaling (dandruff). Otherwise coal tar can cause more dryness and itching. Aloe vera, coconut oil, avocado oil, wheat germ oil and oatmeal are gentler ingredients that may relieve itchiness.

❏ Sulfur-based ingredients such as sodium laurel sulfate and other similar ingredients can be effective in calming itchiness—unless you use them too much, in which case they can actually make the itch worse. You can substitute—or even alternate with—the alternative anti-itch shampoo ingredients mentioned above.

❏ Products should not have fragrances that are pleasant to humans because dogs are not comfortable if they have an unnatural smell on them. A fragranced shampoo will likely have a reverse effect from what you wanted: the dog may want to roll in the nearest nasty thing if this shampoo leaves him smelling the way *you* do stepping out of the shower.

❏ Silicone derivatives and other "coat-glossing" ingredients in shampoos can make a dog's coat shiny and soft, but they can also build up on the hair and skin, interfering with their natural balance.

◆ Safety Tip for People with Cats

Some shampoos are labeled for use on both cats and dogs, while some are labeled just for dogs. A product labeled only for dogs should never be used on a cat. The ASPCA Animal Poison Control

Center gets calls about this all the time. A cat's toxicological response is different than a dog's—a product that is safe for dogs can cause severe problems for cats.

WHERE TO GIVE THE BATH

◆ Small to Medium Dogs

If you have a small to medium dog, you can just lift the dog into the bathtub and either bend over or crouch down beside her. If she's small enough, you may want to use the kitchen sink, especially if you have a sprayer attachment, which will be useful for rinsing (and rinsing out the sink afterward, too!).

◆ Medium to Large Dogs

If you have a medium to large dog, you may want to use a stall shower, if you have one, or get into the tub with the dog and use the shower attachment (see page 418) while you're standing. Since you can't usually lift a larger dog, it is sometimes easier to lift up both her front feet and put them in the tub. Then lift her hind legs and swing them over the side and into the tub.

◆ "Do-it-yourself" Dog-grooming Locations

These are available in some communities, where you can use their tub and water and leave the mess behind.

GENERAL BATHING TIPS

❒ Bring the dog into the bathroom yourself. Don't try to call or coax your dog into the bathroom, because after the first time she gets a bath she's going to know exactly what you're up to with that armful of equipment. She may even enjoy the bath once she's in, but dogs aren't generally going to be gung-ho about coming into the bathing area. So why make it a test of wills? Just clip on her leash and have her follow you in without making a big deal about it.

❒ Shut the bathroom door behind you. Close off all escape routes beforehand.

❒ Use warm water, never hot. With a dog who is itchy, try cool water only.

❒ Cotton balls in the ears aren't necessary, although some people feel better putting them in there. If you are rinsing from above and saving the head until last, there's really not much chance of water getting into the ears.

❒ Use only a dab of shampoo. It is helpful to squeeze the shampoo into a rubber brush or onto a clean sponge and scrub it around on the dog that way, rather than putting a handful of shampoo directly on his back and then trying to spread it around. It does not take a large quantity of shampoo to clean a dog, nor does it have to foam up into a big lather.

❒ Putting oil in the eyes or ointment around them is something that groomers will sometimes do, but you can just hold your hand above the dog's eyes as you rinse above them. Dogs will instinctively shut their eyes if water is coming from above, so the chance of shampoo getting in their eyes is pretty slim.

- Wash the head last and without soap or much water. Dogs really don't like water on their faces. They shake themselves the most when their heads are wet, so you want to save the head until last. But you don't have to drench the face, either. Use an old washcloth or disposal cloth, wring it out to dampness, and wipe firmly around the face and muzzle without any soap, so that you don't have to put her through misery with a ton of rinsing.
- Don't forget the underside of the dog—the armpits, belly, chest and feet all need to be soaped, rubbed and fully rinsed.
- Rinsing is very important. Shampoo or conditioner left in the dog's coat can be a real irritant to the skin.

◆ Drying the Dog

Dry thoroughly If the dog isn't fully dry (and sometimes even if he is) his first inclination will be to find a pile of something to roll in that will return him to his pre-bath condition! Keep him inside or on his leash until he is fully dry. Drying off is an important part of the bath.

Let the dog shake. A dog can get a lot more water off than you can. Put a towel draped loosely over the dog when he first shakes, before you begin to dry him off.

A hair-dryer is unpleasant for many dogs. However, you can accustom yours to it by any of the desensitization methods recommended in the book (see the methods on page 410 for dogs who hate being brushed). A dryer does keep a silky dog's long hair from tangling and makes brushing easier. However, a dryer can aggravate a dog's skin if it is itchy, flaky or dry. **Warning:** *Never use a dryer on a hot setting. Dog hair is flammable. This is not an idle threat: besides causing pain with the heat, you could actually set the dog on fire.*

White dogs have special needs. A white coat is hard to keep white, especially on a long-haired dog whose coat touches the ground and whose beard is always in food and water. However, there are shampoos especially for this. The shampoos will say they have "optical enhancers," which is fine. You just don't want any product containing bleach or peroxide.

Ear Care

All dogs' ears need to be looked at and wiped out, but long-eared breeds (Spaniels of any kind, Beagles, Basset Hounds, etc.) have ears that require frequent attention to keep them clean and healthy.

EXCESSIVE HAIR IN THE EARS

Some breeds have hair that grows inside the outer ear canal and traps wax and other dirt. A groomer will need to remove this excess hair periodically. It is not a good idea to use tweezers to try to pluck out this hair yourself, because plucking hurts and you could damage the delicate ear tissue with the pointed tips of the tweezer. But you do want that hair removed, because it reduces airflow into the ear, which is needed to prevent infections.

Groomers use a drying powder that stiffens the hairs, then clamp and twist the hair out with a surgical clamping instrument called a hemostat. If your dog has excessive hair at his ear openings, leave it to the professionals unless you are willing to learn how to do it yourself. If you do want to try doing it yourself, ask your breeder or a groomer to show you how to do this safely and comfortably.

EAR CLEANING

◆ Breeds with Long, Heavy Ears

Floppy-eared dogs can have chronic ear infections. Dogs such as Cocker Spaniels, English and Irish Setters, and Basset Hounds and Bloodhounds are prone to have ear infections and other ear problems. Dogs with erect ears rarely have such issues, except for German Shepherds, who despite their short, tall ears tend to have similar problems. Infections with both yeast and bacteria are not uncommon for dogs who are affected, and they can also have mites.

◆ Ways to Clean the Ears

For a dog without any ear problems, you just want to keep the opening to the ear clean. It's most comfortable for the dog and effective in getting the ear clean if you use a moistened cotton pad to wipe inside the opening of your dog's ears. Alternately, you can use a tissue that you double over and wrap around your index finger to wipe around in the exterior ear crevices.

Ear-cleaning solutions There are a couple of different solutions to clean the ears: the ones sold by pet stores are good if you have a dog with ears that need cleaning deep down. Otherwise, you can make your own solution and store it in any plastic cosmetic bottle: ⅔ water, ⅓ white vinegar (the same organic method you can use to clean out your refrigerator). It's nontoxic, nonirritating and has a good antibacterial effect. However, it does not have any deep-cleaning activity.

Cleaning the outside of the ears One good way to clean the ears externally is to dampen a cotton pad (the round or square flat ones, not a cotton ball) with the vinegar solution. Hold up the flap of the dog's ear with one hand and with your more adept hand rub away any dirt or dark waxiness that is beneath the flap or at the ear opening. You'll see there are lots of nooks and crannies to a dog's outer ear, so you need to gently rub the cotton inside all of the crevices to get it really clean. You can go into the ear canal as far as the tip of your finger wrapped around the cotton pad—or even as far as your fingertip wrapped around a thick tissue. Just keep using new cotton and/or tissue until there is no more dirt on them.

Cleaning the inside of the ears Another way to clean the inside of the ears is to use one of the commercial ear-cleaning solutions. Holding your dog's head at an advantageous angle, squirt some of this solution directly into the ear canal—don't put the tip in too deep or squeeze with too much force, because the eardrum is delicate. Then massage the fluid throughout the canal from the outside, rubbing your fingers right below where the ear attaches to the head. Try to massage the fluid into the ear canal quickly before the dog shakes his head and shakes it all out.

The ear wash brings to the outside whatever debris or wax is deeper in the ear, so that you can wipe if off at the opening.

Warning: *Do not use cotton swabs (Q-Tips, etc.) under any circumstances—all they do is encourage you* *to go too deeply into the ear canal, where you can hurt the dog by packing in wax further or even rupturing the eardrum.*

SCRATCHING AT THE EARS

If you have a dog who fusses a lot with his ears, scratching them with his back paw nails, lessen the chance that he'll hurt himself with his nails by cleaning his ears frequently. Scooby Doo is like that—his ears get superficially dirty because he's always digging in the woods, and they are red and irritated after he scratches. Dogs use their hind feet to scratch their ears: if you hold his back leg when he's trying to scratch with that foot you can see how much force is behind it. There may only be a minor itchiness to the ear, but a dog can do some damage to the ear with sharp toenails and substantial muscle-strength behind them.

EAR SOOTHING

To soothe his ears afterward, I rub some aloe gel on the underside of his ear flap—you can find one hundred percent aloe gel in any drugstore (with the tanning products or body lotions). Put a dab of the clear gel on your fingertips and rub it gently around the clean underside of the dog's ear. Aloe is a natural substance (from a cactus-type plant) that has healing, soothing properties and is often used to soothe skin after sunburn and other minor burns. It absorbs immediately into the skin.

SIGNS OF EAR INFECTION OR OTHER PROBLEMS

If you have any doubts about whether your dog's ears require professional attention, then there's a good chance that they do. There are not always outward signs of the ear infection, but dogs will scratch at an ear with a back paw or rub their head against things in discomfort. Other times a dog may tilt his head or be off-balance because of an inner-ear infection. There is often a nasty odor from the ear(s) and a discharge that ranges from dark brown to black.

Don't hesitate to make an appointment with your vet—as with any infection, the longer you wait the worse it may become. (See Chapter Eleven, page 354, for more information).

RADICAL SURGERY FOR CHRONIC EAR INFECTIONS

If you have a dog who gets numerous ear infections, you may at some point want to consider surgery. Every severe ear infection that a dog suffers through causes scarring, which eventually can nearly close the ear canal. For dogs with chronic ear infections that will not resolve, there is a surgical option: "ablation" is the removal of the entire ear canal, which eliminates the environment in which the infections have thrived. Ideally, this surgery should be done by a veterinarian who specializes in the procedure. It sounds drastic, but for dogs who suffer with the irritation, pain and worsening hearing of constant infections—along with massive amounts of antibiotics—this surgery is often an act of kindness. I opted for it with Amalfi, my Cocker whose ears always reeked and drove both of us crazy—he was comfortable for the first time in years within days of the operation.

Dental Care

About eight out of ten dogs older than three will wind up with dental problems, specifically gum disease. As with people, if you treat dental disease in the early stages, it won't get worse. But if a dog's teeth accumulate tartar, then the gums become inflamed, "doggie breath" follows, and the bacterial infections that result can enter your dog's bloodstream and become a danger to your dog's overall health, affecting vital organs.

You can find a canine dental specialist by contacting the American Veterinary Dental Society (AVDS) at (800) 332-AVDS. According to their statistics, dental disease is the most common problem dogs face, affecting eighty-five percent of dogs older than three.

AWARENESS OF CANINE DENTAL HEALTH IS A FAIRLY NEW PHENOMENON.

Just as there is a wide range of human dental conditions—some of them genetic—so are there differences among dogs. In some dogs more than others, plaque builds up on the teeth, which allows tartar to develop, on top of which more plaque builds up.

◆ Every Dog's Teeth Are Different.

The tendency to build up tartar and plaque may be an inherited trait, or the chemistry in some dogs' saliva may encourage tartar formation. You can have a three-year-old purebred dog who has enjoyed superb nutrition but still has brown teeth and inflamed gums, while an eight-year-old mixed breed with questionable eating habits may have "pearly whites."

◆ Check Out Your Dog's Teeth Before Doing Anything Else.

If you look inside your dog's mouth and there is a buildup of crusty stuff on the teeth—check the side and back teeth, too, if her gums look red or inflamed—make an appointment with your vet. In a case like this, a dog's teeth need professional cleaning. Home brushing won't make much difference until that plaque is scraped off with dental tools. But once your vet gets your dog's teeth on the right track, you can take over from there in maintaining clean teeth and perhaps reducing the need for future professional cleaning.

SYMPTOMS OF DENTAL PROBLEMS

Check your dog's mouth every week and look for broken, discolored or missing teeth, and for pale or bleeding gums. Dogs don't have an easily recognizable way to communicate dental pain, but if they have a dental problem they may exhibit some of the behavior listed in the chart below. I humbly admit that I did not take my own advice and only after noticing Billy Blue being "under the weather" did I take him to the vet—who found three broken teeth, two of them infected. Talk about feeling guilty. . .

Signs of Dental Disease

- Foul breath
- Bleeding gums
- Chewing only on one side
- Dropping food from mouth when eating
- Licking lips and teeth excessively
- Pawing at the mouth
- Rubbing face on the ground
- Drooling
- Bad reaction (snapping, snarling) when patted on head
- Pain in the mouth (broken tooth, abscess, tumor, swelling)
- Refusing chew toys previously enjoyed
- Dropping toys
- Change in eating or chewing habits
- Decreased appetite
- Slow weight loss

TEETH-BRUSHING

Times have changed where dogs' tooth care is concerned. I never had a vet clean my dog's teeth or tell me to do it myself at home—and I was never aware of dental problems even in Pango, my "first sibling," who lived to the ripe old age of sixteen. But so much has been learned about canine health and wellness over the last few decades, and canine dentistry is one area that has come a long way. Veterinarians now stress dental care from the first puppy visit at eight to twelve weeks of age, encouraging people to accustom their young puppies to having their gums and teeth brushed. More is now known about the serious danger of a bacterial infection and inflammation in a dog's gums getting into his bloodstream and entering his heart, lungs, kidney or liver.

So if you've been cohabiting with dogs for a long time without ever getting involved with their teeth—as I have—then it looks like it's time for us to get with the program and learn some new dental hygiene habits for our pooches.

◆ How Often to Brush or Check Your Dog's Teeth

Your dog's dental-care routine depends on your own motivation and the condition of his teeth. If he's one of the unfortunate ones who builds up tartar quickly, then your brushing will really make a difference. It's going to be easier to keep those teeth clean if you can give them a rubdown or brushing every day, or at least every other day. Some veterinary dentists recommend brushing a dog's teeth daily, while others say several times a week, but it really depends mostly on your individual situation. If you have a dog with shiny white teeth, then I don't see why once a week wouldn't be sufficient.

◆ Products for Home Dental Care
- ❏ Use canine toothpaste, because human toothpaste is too sudsy and has too much fluoride for dogs.
- ❏ You can make toothpaste of half salt and half baking soda, slightly moistened.

- ❏ Start out by using a gauze square wrapped around your finger or a washcloth with your index finger behind it. Once the dog accepts that in his mouth, you can graduate to a brush.
- ❏ Use a soft- to medium-bristle child's toothbrush—once the dog has gotten used to the feeling of bristles on his teeth and gums, you can try a dog toothbrush, if you want, or just stay with the kid's brush.
- ❏ There are dental wipes you can use instead of brushing, if that seems easier for you and your dog. One brand is DentAcetic—you wrap the wipe around your finger and rub the dog's gums and teeth.
- ❏ Using an oral gel is the next best option if brushing won't work for you. Rub a drop or two of a product like Maxiguard gel on your dog's gums and teeth every day.

♦ **Accustom a Dog to Having His Teeth Touched.**

Get your dog used to having his mouth messed around with by dipping your finger into soup and then rubbing your finger gently over his teeth and gums. Then wrap gauze around your finger and gently rub the teeth in a circular motion. Finally, introduce a soft dog toothbrush and use a canine-friendly toothpaste to begin gently, but firmly, brushing his teeth, similar to the way you brush your own teeth.

PROFESSIONAL TEETH-CLEANING

People are reluctant to have their dog's teeth cleaned—perhaps they are fearful of anesthesia, or they can't see the problem. Owners try to put off a dental exam and cleaning (as some of them do with their own teeth), probably not fully understanding that regular teeth-cleaning is an investment in your dog's comfort and long-term health. Your dog may seem fine—he's eating and playing the way he always does—but that doesn't mean that tartar and plaque aren't building up on his teeth, or that he doesn't have gingivitis (inflammation or infection) in his gums.

All dogs can benefit from teeth-cleaning, but small-breed dogs are more at risk for dental disease. Little dogs' teeth are closer together, and they often don't chew big bones or gnaw on exercise toys the way larger dogs do, which can help reduce plaque.

♦ **A Vet Has to Be Sure Your Dog Is a Candidate for Cleaning.**

A dog in poor health, or one with a compromised immune system or other problems, may not qualify for a routine teeth-cleaning. Unless there is an urgent dental matter, a good vet will avoid or postpone any dental work in these situations.

♦ **Anesthesia-free Teeth-cleaning Outside a Vet's Office**

People seem intrigued by the idea of someone cleaning their dog's teeth without anesthesia, mistakenly thinking it is safer and that they are doing their dogs a favor. They have probably never stopped to realize that for a dog, having a stranger's hands in his mouth with tools can be terrifying and miserable. Also, these service providers are often taking a big risk with your dog's health—they won't be able to do a thorough job, and you'll have no recourse if anything goes wrong. The risk of going outside a vet clinic for dental care is much greater than a dog having professionally administered anesthesia for his teeth-cleaning.

A service provider who advertises "anesthesia-free" teeth-cleaning and is doing it without the supervision of a vet is *doing so illegally*: they are "providing veterinary services without a license." These "dental hygienists" are in the back of pet shops or may even have some human dental training, but you are risking your pet's life by not having a vet check out the dog's overall health ahead of time to see whether he is a candidate for teeth-cleaning.

Not using anesthesia is unfair. It can be painful and traumatic for a dog to be awake when someone is prying his jaw open and prodding around. The inside of a dog's teeth need to be scraped—just as yours are at the dentist—but trying to do this on a fully conscious dog is unfair to him. And vets and veterinary dentists say that they can give a more thorough examination and a better cleaning when the dog is unconscious.

Anesthesia is easier. Anesthesia makes teeth cleaning easier on everyone. There are tools like the ultrasonic scaler that vibrate or make other noise that is too frightening for a dog who is awake. If there is a lot of plaque on the teeth, it takes some serious scraping to remove it. Cleaning a dog's teeth under anesthesia is kinder and safer, it's as simple as that.

◆ Teeth-Cleaning without Anesthesia at the Vet's

There are situations in which a veterinarian may think that a dog needs dental care but, after giving him a physical exam, decides the dog has a medical condition that would rule out the use of anesthesia. In situations like this, especially when a dog's teeth are seriously encrusted with tartar, a doctor may elect to do the work without anesthesia and do the best job he can.

SITUATIONS IN WHICH ANESTHESIA SHOULD NOT BE USED FOR DENTAL CLEANING

- ❏ Congenital heart defects (including murmurs)
- ❏ Congestive heart failure
- ❏ Arrhythmia (irregular heartbeat)
- ❏ History of seizures
- ❏ Recent injury or infection of any kind
- ❏ Compromised kidney or liver function

DISCOLORED TEETH

If a tooth turns a pink-purplish color, it means it has been damaged. Discoloration is usually from blunt trauma, a blow to the tooth that causes the inner core—the pulp—to become inflamed. Other causes of a tooth that has turned a pink-purplish color are infection of the pulp from a blood-borne disease, excessive chewing on hard objects or improper use of dental cleaning equipment. Canine dentists recommend that all discolored teeth should be treated, especially in older dogs where the tooth pulp is probably not going to heal on its own. Treatment consists of either repair or removal of the tooth.

Toenails

Toenail-clipping is unpleasant for most dogs. For some dogs their toenails are a big issue: they are extra sensitive, or they simply cannot tolerate having their feet messed with.

Each canine nail has a blood vessel inside, but every dog's feet are different. In pale-colored nails, you can see the darker vein that comes down toward the tip, which makes it easier to snip off the tip of nail before the vein ends. However, it is also easy to nick the end of the vein, especially if the dog keeps pulling his paw away and you get rattled or your hand gets jerked.

If you have never cut a dog's nails, get a lesson from your vet, vet's assistant or a groomer, and practice on a calm, experienced dog. If you just wing it and experiment on your own dog, you run a risk of making a mistake on at least one nail, scaring yourself and your dog about nail-cutting in the future.

REASONS FOR KEEPING NAILS TRIMMED

You have to keep your dog's toenails short. If nails get long they can start to curl under and cause complications. Walking on too-long nails can be painful and even cause lameness. If the nails get too long, they may break off in a jagged way that can be painful to the dog, cause bleeding or increase the risk of infection.

✦ The Correct Length for a Dog's Nails

You want a dog's nails to be just off the ground when she is standing. Some dogs don't need their toenails trimmed. A dog's nail length depends on how much exercise the dog gets, the kinds of surfaces she runs on, the angle of her particular feet and whether the nails touch the ground when walking or running. Too-long nails can force a dog's foot out of position.

✦ Only the Dewclaws Need Cutting on Some Dogs.

Dewclaws are the useless toe (a vestigial, evolutionary throwback above the foot on the inside of the leg. If that nail gets too long, it can snag on things and rip off. Some purebred dogs have the dewclaw removed entirely as small puppies.

✦ You Can Tell Nails That Do Need to Be Cut.

If a dog has pale nails, you can see when it's time to cut because you can see the nail growing well beyond the quick—either that, or the nails are long enough to click on the floor when the dog walks, or they touch the ground when the dog is standing and are long enough to be pushed aside by the floor. If a dog spends a lot of time running outside, especially on hard ground, her toenails usually get worn down during play. However, some dogs walk in such a way that their daily walks don't result in any such natural trimming. Some dogs have naturally long claws, especially on the front feet, even if they do a lot of running around.

GETTING A PUPPY USED TO NAIL-TRIMMING

As with any other process to which you introduce a dog of any age, you want to make nail-trimming a positive experience. Many dogs become terrified of nail care because people get forceful and rough with them when they first resist their paws being held and the nails cut. There is no reason for this adversarial situation to exist.

The steps outlined below are technically called "desensitization" in training-world lingo. You may need many days to get your dog to accept nail-trimming, especially if he has had a traumatic experience with it in the past.

◆ Start Slowly and Gently.

Go slowly and don't move to the next step until you have attained a certain comfort level with the previous step. First, take the puppy's paw in your palm and present a delicious treat with your other hand. Don't put any pressure on the paw, just praise her. When she removes her paw, take it back with an open palm and wait to give the treat until she's had her paw there for a little longer.

◆ When She Removes Her Paw, Don't React Negatively.

Keep your goal in mind and remember that you are going to have a lifetime with this dog, so what matters is laying a good groundwork. Just lift her paw again and repeat the exercise until she successfully leaves her paw in your palm. You can call it a day and come back tomorrow to continue building confidence.

If she resists, don't turn it into a contest of wills or a physical battle for control of her feet. It has to be a willing joint effort—even if there's reluctance on her part. You have to elicit the dog's cooperation despite her fear. If you see signs of tension in her body or facial expression, back off to a point on her body where you can touch without resistance. Do not push the limits of her patience—end the session on a positive note.

◆ Positively "food reward" the dog when he leaves his foot in your hand. Say "Yes!" (but quietly since you don't want to stir him up). If he accepts your touch on his foot, then gently hold his other paws one at a time and say "Yes!" and give a treat on each one. If he resists your hold—or starts to panic and struggle—relax your hold and just touch his paws instead of holding them. If he resists *any* pressure on his foot, say "Nooo" in a gentle voice and touch him further away from his foot—on the knee, elbow, shoulder or wherever he will accept your touch. Food-reward the acceptance and work your way back down to the feet. When he accepts your hand pressure, say "Yes!" and food-reward him.

◆ Add Pressure and Restraint Little by Little.

Don't lose your temper or rush this process. Every time the dog allows you to keep her paw a little longer with your fingers wrapped around it, you are making great progress. Now you can add the nail clippers, touching them against the pup's nail. Let her sniff the clippers, give her a treat, then you're ready to cut.

✦ The First Little Snip

The first cut you make should be just a smidge off the pointy nail tip. Give an improved treat immediately—something more delicious than you've used before. Do the same thing with each nail, stopping on a positive note so you can return at a later time. There's no need to finish all the nails in one day—not now and not ever. Some dogs get mentally overloaded before you can finish all four feet, and that's not a problem because there are lots of other days in every week.

✦ The Clipper Itself May Be Causing the Tension.

Spend some time associating the clipper with positive rewards—show the clipper, feed her a treat. If she isn't too nervous about it, then show her the clipper and bring it along when you do pleasurable things such as going for a walk or driving in the car. Or put the clipper beside her food dish, unless it makes her too nervous to eat.

Touch her with the nail clippers on places other than the paws—the shoulders, legs, neck, back or anywhere she'll accept it—and then work your way down to her paws. Feed a treat and say "Yes!" every time she trusts you to touch her with the tool. Every so often, squeeze the clipper so she gets used to the sound and motion of it.

✦ Find a Helper to Make It Easier on Everyone.

A helper would be good at this point, if you have anyone who can sit with you for five minutes. Have the helper sit on the floor with you and the dog and let her speak soothingly to the dog and feed him soft, small bits of tasty treats right at the moment that you have the clipper positioned on his nails. Take very small nips off the tip.

After the first time or two you can work alone, using small bits of cheese, hot dog, etc., and giving him a piece *immediately* after he has allowed you to clip each nail. Whenever the dog is especially compliant or relaxed, say "Yes!" with calm enthusiasm and give several treats right in a row to reinforce the good behavior. This is a well-known training practice based on the idea that when a dog "hits the jackpot" unexpectedly it makes him eager to continue a behavior in the hope of "jackpotting" again.

Try to move swiftly and decisively. This isn't always easy, but if you don't hesitate and worry over how much you're taking off each nail, it can be less stressful for you and the dog. You won't cut the quick as long as you only clip a small piece off the tip each time.

As soon as you sense stress in the dog—he starts trying to jerk his paw away, puts his mouth near your hand, etc.—stop clipping and stroke him, get him relaxed, give a treat if he lets you pick up his paw again, and try one more clipping with an immediate "Yes!" and a treat, and end the session.

NAIL-TRIMMING EQUIPMENT

Nail clippers for dogs come in two basic styles. There is the scissors type, which is designed along the lines of a hedge trimmer and is usually the "better" kind of nail clipper. It has quick, sharp blades that fit around the nail (similar to a good gardening pruner, with two inwardly curved blades). There is also the guillotine style of clipper: the nail fits into an opening and you squeeze the blade down onto it. Avoid this design because it can pull the nail and make the dog jumpier.

Make sure the blades are sharp. A dull blade puts more pressure on the nail and can be uncomfortable for the dog.

Never use human fingernail or toenail clippers on a grown dog's nails. They compress the nail flat—causing pain—and leave the dog with a poorly angled cut.

The angle you cut at makes a difference as far as the risk of hitting a vein is concerned. If you look at the curve of a dog's toenail, cut it on a diagonal going away from the toe itself, the kind of angle you'd use to cut the stem of a flower. If you try to cut straight up and down on a nail, there's a greater chance that you could cut the quick.

WHAT TO DO IF YOU HIT A VEIN

The dog may yelp, which can startle you and make you feel terrible, and the sight of the blood dripping off her nail doesn't help. It can be a traumatic event for both of you—but maybe even more so for you. Do not let the dog get up and run around—he needs to stay still.

Have Kwik-Stop powder handy. You can also keep a small container of plain cornstarch available if you do hit the quick on a nail. At the first sign of blood, all you have to do is take a pinch of either powder and press it against the cut tip for a few seconds. Both of these products save the day by stopping the bleeding before the dog can track it all around the house.

Weekly nail-trimming keeps the nails from growing too long, according to some experts. Taking just a pinch off the tip every week eliminates the risk of hitting the quick and keeps the nails at a constant length. On the other hand, some people believe that cutting a dog's toenails makes them grow faster; it probably depends on the individual dog. The quick recedes into the nail every time it is cut—so, just by frequently nipping off the tip, you are keeping the toenails under control.

◆ Black Toenails Are Difficult.

This is because you cannot check where the quick ends to avoid nicking it and drawing blood—with pale nails you can see the pink core of the quick. When in doubt, just clip the absolute tip of the nail.

TIPS FOR NAIL-CUTTING

Some of the following steps can be skipped if you have a dog who is naturally mellow about nail-cutting. Alternately, if you have one who is especially freaked out about it, you can slow things down to his tolerance level.

- ❐ Choose a time when the dog is really tuckered out from a walk or playing. You don't want to attempt nail-cutting first thing in the morning when he wakes up raring to go. You want him wiped out, in a quiet environment, with nothing going on in the house to stimulate him or distract you.
- ❐ Try different positions with the dog—some dogs are comfortable lying on their sides on their beds or a rug, while others seem to feel less vulnerable sitting up or even standing. With a larger dog, this means you sit down on the floor next to him. Smaller dogs can be on a tabletop or even on their backs in your lap.

- ❏ If your dog has hairy feet, trim the hair away from the nails at a separate grooming session. This way you can see what you're doing.
- ❏ Sit on the floor with the dog, pat him and relax him with your voice, then gently grasp his foot in your hand. Do this without a nail clipper at first. Most dogs will reflexively pull their feet away, some of them in a slightly panicky fashion.
- ❏ Once he'll let you hold his paw, touch the toenails with the clippers just to acclimate him—praise with food and voice when he stops struggling.

Chewing their own toenails can be a normal part of self-care for some dogs, who do it as part of their grooming ritual. However, it can also be a reason to go to the vet, who can tell you if there is an underlying problem.

Wrinkles and Folds in the Skin

Dogs with lots of loose skin around their mouths and necks are a special challenge to keep clean and healthy. These folds are a moist, warm environment in which germs can grow, so these areas need to be thoroughly cleaned and dried.

Bassett Hounds and Bloodhounds, Bulldogs, Coonhounds, Chow Chows, Pekingese, Mastiffs and Shar-Peis are some of the breeds with wrinkles around the face. Here are some tips on keeping these dogs clean and infection free, along with ways to correct minor redness before it becomes more irritated and potentially infected.

CLEANING WRINKLES AND FOLDS

- ❏ Lift folds of skin to check for redness, sores, rashes or a funky smell.
- ❏ Sprinkle unscented talcum powder directly into any folds that are reddened.
- ❏ Use a disposable, unscented baby wipe to thoroughly clean inside all the crevices.
- ❏ Use the gentlest possible canine shampoo and make sure you rinse and dry completely.
- ❏ To clean facial crevices, use a cotton ball or swab dipped in hydrogen peroxide.

Chapter 13

NUTRITION

A Wake-Up Call about Your Dog's Food

In this chapter you'll learn some of the startling facts about dog food that convinced me to look at my dogs' nutrition in a whole new light. It radically affected my attitude about commercial dog food and completely changed what my dogs get to eat. I'm ashamed to say that until I researched this book, I trusted dog food companies without really reading labels or understanding what the words meant. I hope you'll learn from my mistake, take responsibility for your dog's nutritional welfare and consider making some changes in your dog's dinner bowl, too.

Every time we buy dog food we're making a statement with our money about how much our dog's physical well-being and longevity matter to us—but we haven't been using that financial power wisely if we just keep buying from the big manufacturers without holding them accountable for the sometimes horrible stuff they put in those enticing bags. Now that you'll have the sorry truth about what many of the bigger food companies put in their food, you can explore some of the fine smaller dog-food makers who deserve our support.

Some of the topics you'll find in this chapter are:

- ❏ Is the incidence of cancer in dogs related to food ingredients?
- ❏ The truth about ingredients in supermarket and "pet superstore" dog food
- ❏ Is the dramatic incidence of cancer in dogs related to food ingredients?
- ❏ The true meaning of all the words on pet food packaging
- ❏ Natural vs. preservatives: what does that really mean?
- ❏ How dry food is made and its ingredients
- ❏ The debate between dry and canned food

- Adding supplements to food
- Puppy feeding, with new facts about whether puppy food is good
- Dogs with food sensitivities and other allergies
- Feeding a raw diet: what's that all about?
- Vegetarian dogs: how to have one, the pros and cons
- The diet/bad behavior connection: is it affecting your "difficult" dog?
- Nutritional problems, like loss of appetite, finicky eaters, obesity, bloat

The health and welfare of our dogs is greatly influenced by what we feed them. As consumers become more educated about dog-food ingredients, the companies eventually have to respond; there seems to be a movement toward improving the quality of ingredients in general dog foods, and there is an increasing number of smaller companies dedicated to making dog food of excellent ingredients. A list of some of those companies appears on page 441.

DOES DOG FOOD CONTRIBUTE TO CANCER?

Although there is no conclusive proof, personally I have come to wonder whether the epidemic of cancer riddling our dogs has been caused by the dreadful ingredients (and the extreme treatment of them) that make up kibble? This is only my own theory, but I can't think how else to explain the following statistics: half of all dogs over ten years old are expected to get some form of cancer; the disease kills half of all canine senior citizens. Am I the only person noticing that this was not true of dogs only a few decades ago? I wonder why the dogs our parents grew up with lived to a ripe old age and died of natural causes? How can it be that the dogs many of us had as children also lived to fifteen years old and died of old age—*not* the ravages of cancer?

At first I thought it was like cancer-detection in people—often there only *seems* to be more cancer because modern tests have made it possible to detect the disease sooner. But sophisticated testing is generally not the way that cancer is discovered in dogs. Most canine cancer is found because of visible symptoms of the disease—tumors, lameness, etc.—which are outward symptoms of the disease after it has already taken hold.

My personal inclination is to think that the danger to our dogs resides inside the bags of dog food: they are full of mysterious and possibly dangerous ingredients, often the bottom of the barrel from processing the discards of a food industry that is filled with carcinogens and chemicals. Our dogs live alongside us, breathing the same air as we do, drinking the same water. The only environmental difference is in what they eat. Think about it: where in his environment is your dog bombarded with obvious cancer-causing chemicals? If he isn't swimming in a lake full of PCB's, if he isn't drinking polluted water from manufacturing run-off, if he isn't breathing air full of asbestos or radiation, then what he is ingesting must explain the alarming cancer rate in dogs.

Economically successful mass production of animals for consumption in the United States involves chemicals in their feed and environment. The agri-business slaughterhouse refuse that goes into dog foods is alarming enough, but we can't forget that even the best parts of those slaughtered animals were pumped full of growth hormones and antibiotics when they were raised. The animals we all eat may be having a devastating effect on both our species and the canines who share our lives. I worry for all of us, particularly our children, but our dogs may be at even greater risk because their life spans are so much shorter than ours. It is urgent that we make healthy choices in what we feed our pets.

FEED FOR PIGS, COWS, CHICKENS—OH, AND DOGS, TOO

If you're like most people who use commercial dog food, you believe you're doing the right thing for your dog. You buy a decent brand, one recommended by "a breeder of champion dogs." Or maybe you go to the extra expense and trouble of going all the way to your vet's to buy Science Diet, thinking that is an expression of love and concern for your dog's well-being. You probably assume that a decent company is putting good stuff in there—the vet believes that, too. And yet all you have to do is look at the actual ingredients in regular Science Diet to see they are no better than the lowest quality food sold at the supermarket.

We are all suckers for good advertising, I just as much as the next person. Here's an example of how cautious you have to be in responding to clever marketing: while researching this book I saw full-page ads in magazines announcing the arrival of a new Iams food made of "New Zealand lamb" and other wholesome ingredients. The picture on the ad was just like the front of the bag: a bucolic vision of rolling green hills dotted with free-range sheep, and a beautiful English Springer Spaniel in the foreground. I was relieved that I'd have something positive to report in this book about one of the big dog food companies (I had already learned, to my dismay, that regular Iams dog food was one of the lower quality foods on the market). I figured this new food showed the company was responding to the demands of informed customers. But when I called them to learn more about their new food—expressing my enthusiasm for what I assumed was organic lamb, since sheep in New Zealand are raised naturally—the pleasant man on the phone had no answers to my questions about that lamb, or in what form or quantity it was in the food. So I asked for their official list of what was in the food. I was stunned to find, when it arrived, that there was no mention whatsoever about the actual presence of lamb in the product—although the glossy pamphlet showed the same pretty sheep on Kiwi hills.

I guess we can't really afford to extend the benefit of the doubt where dog food is concerned. We need to look out for ourselves and our beloved dogs, not naively assume that companies making food for our four-legged family members share our point of view. Big multinational corporations doing agri-business are guided in making and distributing dog food the same as any large profit-oriented business makes its proverbial widgets: keep costs down, keep productivity up, increase revenue by any means necessary and smile at your healthy bottom line at the end of each fiscal quarter. Meanwhile, *we* are smiling at our adored dogs, not realizing that that we may be jeopardizing their health and welfare.

The same regulatory agency, the Association of American Feed Control Officials (AAFCO), that defines what goes into commercial pig feed and deals with Mad Cow Disease, is presumably looking out for the physical welfare of your little Cavalier King Charles Spaniel in setting standards and defining the ingredients in the tiny kibble you so caringly feed him. But I doubt that sawdust and ground beaks and feathers was what you had in mind to put in his delicate tummy. I had never taken the time to find out the true ingredients of commercial dog food either, but the everyday word for "powdered cellulose" is "sawdust," and the definition of "crude protein" is "ground beaks, hair and feathers."

Many of the big pet-food companies originally made feed for farm animals and industrially raised animals (and still do). That food needed to efficiently and quickly put weight on animals destined for the market; it had to be inexpensive to manufacture; it had to survive long periods without spoiling, all so it could be sold at an attractively low price to farmers and "mega-farmers." No one was too worried about exactly what went into pig, cow and chicken feed as long as it met some basic criteria and accomplished these goals. So when these big companies—Purina is one of them—operated in the pet food end of the business, they had a production plan and philosophy already in place.

Dogs used to have a very different place in the American family. They used to be viewed more or less as a "thing" every family should have for the kids to run around with or for protection. People enjoyed the animals or ignored them, but there was very little consciousness about the *dog's* experience of his life. Dogs often lived out in the yard, slept in a dog house, were brushed or bathed once a year (if they "really needed it") and ate whatever was put in their bowls. It goes without saying that a dog's life has changed dramatically from the "Cinderella" of yore to the princess of today—normal treatment of a dog twenty years ago would practically be considered animal abuse now.

Except there's just one scary thing: we all may be sharing our lives very differently with our pampered dogs today, but many of us are still filling them with pretty much the same kibble they used to give that poor all-American backyard dog.

Until the end of 2003, the official nutritional guidelines for dog foods were twenty years old. A great deal had been learned in the medical field about canine health and wellness during that period, but their foods were being made the same old way. Then in 2004, the results of a national study came out that warned about the growing obesity among dogs and cats. The conclusion, based on this report, was clearly that our companion animals have to eat less food. Pet food companies had to be pretty unhappy about that since, obviously, the more food your dog eats, the more product they sell (which may be why instructions on the bag recommend such ridiculously large quantities of food—certainly enough to make a dog too fat). The official report also indicated that pet foods need to be reformulated, but it's unlikely there will be a change anytime soon.

WHAT TO LOOK FOR IN FOODS

❏ *Good quality animal proteins at the top of the ingredients list.* You're looking for whole, fresh meats or meat meal from a specific source—for example chicken meal, not "poultry" meal. The first ingredient in canned food should be whole meat, fish or poultry.

❏ *Whole, unprocessed grains* (like rice or brown rice, whole ground barley and oatmeal) are a more expensive but nutritious way of providing roughage. The less processing that is done, the greater food value is retained.

❏ *Whole vegetables like potatoes, tomatoes, peas and carrots.* Once again, as little processing as possible.

- *Fat or protein should be identified by species.* "Chicken fat" or "beef protein" is better than a mystery mixture of unknown origin.
- *Organic ingredients are great, but be careful.* Organic foods are wonderful for us and our dogs because they limit exposure to chemical pesticides and fertilizers, but the word "organic" can be used a variety of ways in dog food (anyone can use the word, since there is no one to police "organic" in animal food).
- *"Human grade ingredients"* Manufacturers who use this phrase on their products—even if a dog food company uses the same meat and rice that go into human foods—are technically breaking the law. Regulatory laws don't allow "human grade" on dog food, but some premium food makers do it anyway—because they are telling the truth (at some risk, at least theoretically, to themselves).

WHAT TO AVOID IN FOODS

- *By-Products (Meat or Poultry)* indicate a lower-quality dry dog food. They have nutritional value but less than meat or meat meal, which are more expensive and handled more carefully.
- *Fats or proteins from unknown sources.* "Animal fat" is a catch phrase that can include low-quality, inexpensive fats from source, even including old restaurant grease.
- *"Dedicated fiber sources"* are less desirable because they are by-products of other food manufacturing processes.
- *Crude protein* is not an ingredient that a dog's body can utilize. It is not what most people would even think of as protein, since it refers to beaks, hair, hooves, feathers and tendons.
- *"Powdered cellulose"* is the fiber source with the lowest value of all. It is defined by the AAFCO as "purified, mechanically disintegrated cellulose prepared by processing alpha cellulose obtained as pulp from fibrous plant materials." A less fancy description is "sawdust."
- *Artificial colors or flavors* are unhealthy chemicals which can have long-term health consequences and should not be necessary to entice a dog when the food has good quality ingredients. Colors are meaningless to a dog but are used to attract the human buyer.
- *Sugar or other sweeteners.* Cheap dog foods use sweeteners (corn syrup, sucrose and ammoniated glycyrrhizin) because dogs have a sweet tooth. Sugar in the diet can aggravate health problems like diabetes in dogs.
- *"Food fragments"* are lower-cost by-products that come from processing another food, for example wheat bran, which is what's left after the nutritious wheat kernel is removed. Many products have some food fragments, but look out for multiple fragments from one food—which is a way to hide a large amount of a low-value ingredient. For example, a food that lists corn in various forms has a lot more corn that it does meat protein, which may therefore deceptively appear first on the ingredient list.
- *Flavor and texture enhancers.* If food is made of good ingredients, it shouldn't be necessary to boost it with any additives.

SOURCES FOR MEAT IN DOG FOOD

Animals that are raised for human consumption are controlled by certain regulations and are inspected at the slaughter facilities. The meat in pet food comes from two sources: slaughterhouses and renderers. Not all parts of a slaughtered animal are fit for human consumption; the leftovers can be used in livestock feed, pet food and other products. "Renderer" is another way of saying "recycler" of many kinds of dead animals: the leftovers of slaughtered animals, livestock from farms, and animals euthanized by veterinarians or animal shelters (a creepy thought). The whole carcass of various kinds of animals or just certain parts will be ground up to form a "rendered" product. Examples of rendered products are "meat and bone meal," "chicken meal" and "chicken liver meal."

ALPHABETICAL FOOD INGREDIENTS

The AAFCO (Association of Animal Feed Control Officials) I mentioned previously is the regulatory body that also sets the definitions for ingredients in animal feed. I am including a sampling of ingredients that appear frequently in foods or may be confusing—like all the different ways the word "meat" can occur.

- ❏ *Animal digest* (from beef, chicken or lamb)—material resulting from chemical and/or enzymatic hydrolysis of clean and undecomposed animal tissue, excluding hair, horns, hooves, feathers and teeth. (See Digest of Meat.)
- ❏ *Animal fat*—obtained from the tissues of mammals and/or poultry in the commercial processes of rendering or extracting. It is higher quality when identified as being from one source like lamb, beef or poultry.
- ❏ *Barley*—consisting of eighty percent sound barley and must not contain more than three percent heat-damaged kernels, six percent foreign material, twenty percent other grains.
- ❏ *Beef (meat)*—the clean flesh derived from slaughtered cattle and is limited to that part of the striate muscle which is skeletal or from the tongue, diaphragm, heart or esophagus, with or without the accompanying fat and the portions of skin, sinew, nerve and blood vessels which normally accompany the flesh.
- ❏ *Beet pulp* ("dried, plain" or "dried molasses")—the dried residue from sugar beets. It is used as a source of fiber and, despite misinformation, it contains no sugar and it does not swell in a dog's stomach and cause bloat.
- ❏ *Brewer's rice*—the dried extracted residue of rice resulting from the manufacture of beer or wort (the liquid portion of malted grain); what is left over after it has been used in a distillery for brewing alcoholic beverages.
- ❏ *Brown rice*—the unpolished rice left over after the kernels have been removed.
- ❏ *Chicken*—the clean combination of flesh and skin with or without bone, from parts or whole carcasses of chicken (excluding feathers, feet, heads, entrails).
- ❏ *Chicken by-product meal*—the clean, ground, rendered parts of the chicken carcass, such as necks, feet, undeveloped eggs and intestines (exclusive of feathers).
- ❏ *Chicken meal*—chicken which has been ground or otherwise reduced in particle size.
- ❏ *Corn/ground yellow corn*—This is the whole corn kernel, ground or chopped. Adds flavor,

bulk and texture but should not be high on the ingredient list (meaning it was used as an inexpensive protein source).

- *Corn gluten meal*—the dried residue from corn after removal of the larger part of the germ and starch—what's left after the manufacture of corn syrup or cornstarch. Inexpensive dog foods use this to provide a large proportion of the total protein in the food instead of higher quality, more digestible sources of protein like meat.

- *Digest of meat (beef, chicken or lamb) by-products*—material resulting from chemical and/or enzymatic hydrolysis of clean, undecomposed tissue from non-rendered clean parts *other than meat*—including but not limited to bone, blood, brain, kidneys, intestines freed of their contents, lungs, spleen (does not include hair, hooks, horns and tissue).

- *Dried kelp*—dried seaweed.

- *Fiber* roughage from plants only (dog food ingredients like hair, hooves, bones, fish scales or feathers do not contain fiber). These complex carbohydrates aid digestion and basically normalize the digestive tract. As with so many things in life, a moderate amount of fiber is necessary and beneficial while too much upsets the natural balance.

- *Fish Meal*—the clean ground tissue of undecomposed whole fish or fish cuttings, with or without the oil extracted.

- *Glucosamine and chondroitin*—components of cartilage used by humans for antiarthritis; small amounts in dog food were unlikely to have an effect but most dog food companies stopped using these ingredients when several states banned them as not approved ingredients for dogs.

- *Meat*—the clean flesh of slaughtered animals like chicken, cattle, lamb and turkey. "Flesh" can include striated skeletal muscle, tongue, heart, esophagus, overlying fat and skin and the nerves and blood vessels usually found with that flesh.

- *Meat by-products*—the clean, unrendered parts of slaughtered animals, *not including the meat*—a clue that inferior meat sources are used, since by-products are what is left after the good quality meat has been removed. By-products include lungs, spleen, kidneys, brain, liver, blood, bone and stomach and intestines cleaned of their contents.

- *Meat meal (beef, lamb)*—a rendered product from mammal tissues excluding blood, hair, hoof, horn trimmings, manure and stomach contents.

- *Meat and poultry by-products*—non-rendered clean parts, *other than meat*, including bone, blood, lungs, spleen, kidneys, brain, liver.

- *Oil (canola, sunflower)*—beneficial because they are lower in saturated fat than other plant oils and higher in monounsaturated fat than any oil except olive; canola oil is high in Omega-3 fatty acids.

- *Poultry by-products*—these are the clean parts of slaughtered poultry like heads, feet and internal organs (heart, liver, spleen, stomach, intestines), excluding feathers.

- *Soybeans*—usefulness of this plant protein to the dog's digestive system is unknown: dogs are reported to lack an enzyme in their digestive system that is needed to break down the bean. Some dogs (like some people) do not digest soybeans well and become gassy.

- *Soybean meal*—a by-product of the production of soybean oil.

❑ *Wheat*—contains gluten, which causes allergies. Few dogs ever develop actual food allergies. They may have an intolerance to one ingredient, although wheat is no more likely to cause this than any other ingredient.

If you doubt whether I am overstating any nutritional facts—or you want to learn more—order the disturbing book by Ann Martin, *Food Pets Die For.*

CANNED FOOD OR DRY?

Dry and canned foods generally have the same vitamin, mineral and amino acid ingredients, however the nutritional values are quite different. Personally, what I learned about how dry foods are made is what inspired me to switch my dogs to predominantly canned food. But what goes into the food in the can also influenced me. What follows are descriptions of how the two kinds of dog food are made and some of the advantages and disadvantages of each.

Some of the clear advantages of canned food are that it contains more whole foods (poultry & meat) and higher quality protein. It has fewer chemicals and preservatives. Artificial colors and flavors are much less common. Surprisingly, canned foods have fewer calories and are more filling.

HOW DRY FOOD IS MADE

The first thing that has to be done to make kibble is to create a dough that will work in the machinery that shapes the nuggets. The dough is made from one of the grains and then blended with a meat-product meal such as poultry by-product meal and whatever additives are in that company's recipe. Then the dough is put through an extruder, a machine that pushes the dough through a long tube. There are different kinds of extruders (which are used to make sausages and many other foods and products) but this kind often uses high heat while pushing the dough through. At the end of the extruder, there are small openings—like cake decorating tips or those on a pasta machine—so that the dough exits in the chosen shape and then is cut and dried in a variety of ways. Because extruders cannot handle wet or greasy materials, dry dog foods have a large proportion of starch or grains like potato, wheat or corn. Once the bits of dough are dried, most products are sprayed with fats or other flavorings.

ADVANTAGES OF DRY FOOD

❑ *Convenience*—You can travel with it, store it in automatic feeders, it doesn't have to be refrigerated once opened, and is less messy to prepare.

❑ *Economics*—Dry food is less expensive. If you have multiple dogs or one large dog, food that is economical would seem to make sense. Having three large dogs myself, I debated whether to follow the clear conclusion that canned is better, but then questioned why my dogs should be penalized with a lower quality meal. I took responsibility for dogs with larger nutritional needs, so I have to step up. Suppose it costs me an extra dollar, even two dollars a day to feed canned food: that's less than one Starbucks drink. Good quality food (dry or canned) costs us more because it costs the companies more to make it: chicken feet, feathers and beaks cannot cost a manufacturer as much as beef muscle meat.

SOME OF THE HIGH QUALITY BRANDS

There is no one "best" dog food—in fact there are more excellent ones all the time. Here are just a few of the names of manufacturers of high-end dog foods—most make canned and dry foods:

Active Life, Artemis, Avo-Derm, Azmira, Boulder Creek Farms, California Natural, Canidae, Drs. Foster & Smith, Evolve, Excel, Flint River Ranch, Innova, Lamaderm, Lick Your Chops, Merrick Pet Foods, Natural Balance, Natural Life, Neura, Newman's Own Organics, Nutro Natural Choice, Pet-Guard, Pinnacle, Prairie, Sensible Choice, Solid Gold, Spot's Stew, Triumph, Wellness, Wysong.

Now that you know what the ingredients mean, try any of the foods to find one your dog likes. Try a food for a few weeks, and if you have a dog who is healthy but just isn't looking terrific, try your second choice for a while.

Even with all the excellent dog foods listed, people still ask what *I* feed *my* dogs? But that's not the point! Any of the foods utilizing safe, nutritious ingredients is a great choice. And remember: patronize your local independent pet store that gives you the freedom of choice.

HOMEMADE FOOD

I didn't think people would take their dogs' nutritional health seriously enough to cook for them—but I underestimated you, folks! For those who have the time and desire, information and recipes are at www.thedogbible.com, "Inside the Book."

CHANGING DOG FOOD BRANDS—DOES VARIETY MATTER?

You may be sick of giving your dog the same food day after day, but dogs do not get bored by their "cuisine." Dogs do not need variety in their food: this is a projection of what a person would feel about having the same food every day. In fact, for some dogs it can be hard on their digestive systems to switch brands, and may cause gas and/or diarrhea, at least at first. Some nutritionists say to find one the dog seems to enjoy and stick with it. There is no "best" food for all dogs. They are individuals. Be ready to change if your dog doesn't do well on a food. You can usually tell by how he looks.

When you start a new food, watch your dog for about a week to see how it affects his coat, eyes, ears, energy level, mood and bowel movements. If he seems to be having digestive problems, or after a couple of weeks does not seem to be thriving, then you should probably move on to another food. If you have to change foods, do it gradually over a few days, adding more of the new food to the existing brand in his bowl. Once you find a brand that works for your dog—meaning that he has no gas, has firm stools and his coat is shiny—many experts say to stick with it.

However, other pet nutritional experts believe that changing brands a couple times a year can do the dog good because it assures that he is getting the broadest possible spectrum of nutrients. If there are any excesses or insufficiencies for his needs in a particular food, then changing to another, equally-high-quality food should balance things out. There is also a possibility that if a dog eats the same food for years, food allergies and intolerances can develop. Some recommend, if you've been feeding only a chicken-based food, that you switch off with a beef, lamb or fish-based one to prevent food reactions. Yet others say that food allergies can only be dealt with by offering protein ingredients that the dog has never had before, so by introducing him to every protein you lose the ability to have a remedy if he ever does become intolerant to one.

Changing foods can upset a dog digestively and even trainers, when called to work with a "problem dog," always check the nutritional situation first. Many of them claim that dogs with behavior issues should get lower protein with a dry food, preferably one of the brands without preservatives.

◆ Taste Buds Can Get Spoiled Early On.

Exposure to certain flavors and textures of food early in life can shape the dog's preferences later on. The temperature of a dog's meal, the odor, texture and taste from early days can leave a dog with a strong desire for those qualities in his food. When you are switching the dog to any new food, keep in mind the importance of this familiarity and gradually mix the new food in with the old.

KEEPING DRY DOG FOOD FRESH

Dry dog food can become rancid, moldy or otherwise compromised. If the food does not look right—a different color than usual, moldy—it has probably gone bad. If a food does not smell right and the dog is reluctant to dig in, it's possible that the antioxidant agents that preserve the food are not doing their job.

The higher-quality dog food manufacturers are using natural preservatives, which are less effective than the BHA, BHT or ethoxyquin found in lower-end products. No matter what type of preservatives are in your dog's food, it can turn rancid quickly if it is exposed to hot temperatures and oxygen. Dry dog food is supposed to be stored in a cool, dry location which people often do not do.

◆ Safety Storing Dog Food

❏ The original bag is considered the best storage location by almost every manufacturer. Most recommend keeping that bag inside a bin that can be sealed with a lid. The bag was designed to keep moisture out and vitamins in.

❏ Many people like to pour the food into a plastic tub of some kind. If you want to empty the bag, be sure the plastic container you pick is FDA-approved food-grade plastic, not just any garbage can.

❏ Wash and dry any container when empty, *before* you put in a new bag of food to eliminate any remnants of the previous bag that may have gotten old.

❏ Watch out for a dog hesitating or refusing to eat: the food may be rancid.

HOW AND WHEN TO FEED ADULT DOGS

Eating once a day is no longer considered the best thing for a dog. It was not long ago that it was generally believed that by the time a puppy was a young adult, one meal a day was sufficient. The thinking now is that older puppies need to eat twice a day, throughout their lives. There seems to be a general consensus that while one daily feeding may be more convenient for the owner, it is not in the dog's best interest.

◆ Eating at Set Times

When your dog becomes accustomed to eating at certain hours—let's say soon after you get up in the morning and then again sometime in the late afternoon or early evening—his body pretty much sets his clock by that schedule. His brain and stomach tell him it is mealtime and he will expect to be served pretty close to that time. If you are home around regular feeding times, you may find that your dog will come to remind you that his "tummy alarm clock" is ringing.

♦ Free Feeding
Keeping a supply of kibble in a bowl so a dog can eat at will tends to work only in a single-dog family where there is no competition for the food (which would encourage some dogs to overeat).

♦ Table Scraps
If you make a habit of putting your leftovers into your dog's bowl, you may be teaching her to prefer human food to her own food. Fatty scraps can also upset your pet's stomach. Just because a dog *will* eat anything, does not mean that she *should* eat it—and it certainly does not mean that you should facilitate it. People think they're doing a dog a favor, giving her the old leftovers from the back of the refrigerator shelf. Your dog is not a living garbage can: the garbage disposal in your sink is a better place for the nasty fat you cut off a steak. And if you feed a good canned dog food with that boring kibble, you'll see a big change in your dog's eagerness for his meals.

♦ A Feeding Danger: Bloat
Bloat or gastric torsion is caused by gas building up very quickly in the stomach after the dog eats (eating very quickly increases the risk). This gas can cause the intestines to twist. It requires immediate surgical intervention to save the dog's life. On the outside, the stomach looks extremely distended, as though it could burst. In fact the intestines can burst internally, which is what makes this event life-threatening (for more on bloat, see page 363).

Larger breeds are more prone to bloat and therefore benefit even more by having twice-daily mealtimes. Once-daily feeding may increase your dog's risk since some people believe that keeping some food in the stomach and intestines is beneficial as a preventive measure against bloat.

TIPS FOR SAFE FEEDING

- ❏ Feed smaller meals twice a day.
- ❏ Wet dry food right before feeding.
- ❏ Do not allow heavy exercise right before or right after eating.
- ❏ If your dog has gas, it's a sign his food isn't agreeing with him.

FOOD & WATER BOWLS
You can use any heavy dish made for dog feeding—preferably one that won't slide around the floor as the dog eats. Some people prefer a rubber-bottomed stainless bowl; others like ceramic. Generally it's good to pick a material you can put in the dishwasher occasionally for a more thorough cleaning.

♦ Raised Bowls for Tall and Older Dogs
There is some controversy about whether it benefits or harms tall dogs to have their food bowls raised up. As dogs get older and get arthritis in their shoulders, neck and back, leaning down to eat and drink can be painful. Raised feeders have become more popular and there are many choices in the design because it is awkward and difficult for some of the taller dogs

to bend all the way down to the floor to drink or eat. You can make or buy a raised box about twelve or eighteen inches high that holds both dishes but there are "doggy diners" in many sizes and materials.

However, a study from Purdue University that came out in 2005 showed that raising food bowls in large breeds could actually increase the incidence of bloat, which is a life-threatening emergency. Talk to your vet, see if she has an opinion about this for your individual pooch.

◆ Fluid Replacement Drinks for Dogs

Rebound Sports drink for dogs. No kidding. Doggie Gatorade, if you will, but formulated for a dog's needs to prevent dehydration and replenish lost electrolytes due to heavy exercise or illness. I guess if you use it for a young dog, you could also call it "Puppy Pedialtye"! Rebound has less salt and sugar than the human version of a sports drink and contains the amino acids and vitamin E that dogs' bodies need.

It may do a world of good for dogs engaged in heavy physical exertion, whether it's athletic activity like agility or Rally-O competition, rescue work, hunting, coursing or even a big run on the beach on a hot day. The reason I say that sports drinks make sense is that I spent many years in the horse world, competing and breeding jumpers. It was routine to put electrolytes into the horses' water buckets whenever it was very hot or they had sweated heavily, to encourage them to drink and also to replace what their bodies had lost. For more information about the product, or to find a retailer, call (888) 645-9501 or visit their Web site www.rebound4dogs.com.

HOW AND WHEN TO FEED PUPPIES

◆ Is Adult Dog Food Good for Puppies?

There is a new school of thought that puppies have historically been fed food that was too rich, a practice that led to problems later in life. Many vets now recommend feeding adult food to pups, because there is less chance of overnourishment, obesity and the bone problems that can result from feeding nutrient-rich puppy food. Talk to your doctor about this.

When should you switch to adult food? There used to be a belief that you feed puppy food for a year, based on the fact that almost all dogs, whether large or small, have reached skeletal maturity at one year. Large-breed dogs continue to grow for up to another year, but much more slowly. However, with the newest thinking that puppy food may not even have a place in your growing dog's life, you can see that nutritional theories are changing all the time.

If your vet or breeder has encouraged you to feed puppy food to your pup, at what point should you switch to adult formula? There is some disagreement in this area, with some breeders saying three months should be the cutoff and others saying to keep a growing dog on puppy food until four months. Another school of thought says that if you stop feeding puppy food when the dog is neutered—at about six months—the puppy has gotten the nutritional value but now won't run as much risk of gaining weight if you change to adult food at that point. The reasoning is that after neutering, a dog's energy requirements are generally lower and you wouldn't need to worry about the dog's weight when eating the lower-calorie adult food.

After learning about dog foods in this section, you may make a feeding decision yourself, or you may want to share the decision with your vet or yur dog's breeder. However, as noted earlier, most veterinary educational programs pay little attention to the subject of nutrition. Most breeders have done things one way throughout their careers and if their puppies and dogs have always done fine it's not easy to change people's habits or ideologies, so you may be on your own to make this decision.

◆ Feeding Toy Breed Puppies

Tiny dogs have even tinier stomachs, which can hold very little food at a time. Up until they are at least four months old they may need four to six meals a day just to get enough fuel into them. Pound for pound, toy breed puppies can need as much as fifty percent more calories than larger breeds, therefore most of the advice that follows in this section does not apply to their very special requirements. See Chapter Seventeen for more on small dogs.

FEEDING LARGE-BREED PUPPIES

Many pet nutritionists recommend feeding large-breed puppies the food developed for them—but contrary to what you might think, these foods do not pack a "bigger punch" just because the dog is going to be bigger: quite the opposite. Regular puppy food has the same amount of protein and calcium as large-breed food, it's the calorie content that is different. And it may further surprise you to know that the *large-breed puppy should be getting fewer calories*. Specialists suggest feeding the lowest calorie-dense food of the large-breed products and measuring out the quantity carefully.

◆ Is Extra Calcium Needed for a Large-breed Puppy's Bones?

There was a misconception for many years that a large-breed dog needed more calcium when he was growing because he was going to have big bones. Whether in humans or animals, calcium does not work alone in the body—it requires phosphorus to build bones. So adding calcium upsets the balance between the two. In fact, too much calcium during growth leads to large but weak bones that lack the density needed for strength. The result could be bone and joint disorders and susceptibility to fractures.

A FAT BALL OF FUR

We all like to think of puppies as round and plump, but being fat is not good for a dog at any point in her development. And if we are overfeeding fat (which is found in high proportions in all puppy foods) and calories, it will cause a fast growth rate on a weak skeleton. A puppy does need double the calories of an adult dog, but most of us are giving way too many calories to the growing pooches. Just as with adult dogs, the way to determine if your puppy is fat is by standing next to her, facing her tail and running your hands along her sides from her shoulders back to her hips. Believe it or not, you should be able to feel the puppy's ribs without digging in your fingers. When you look down at the puppy's back from above, you should see an hourglass figure, with a waist, not a sausage shape.

If your puppy turns pudgy or round-sided, take ten percent off each meal. Ignore any pleading, hungry-looking eyes afterward: you're doing her a favor in the long run.

It can take one to two weeks for a puppy to lose that extra weight. Reassess by the "feel method" and keep the puppy on the reduced amount of food until she gets a waistline. At that point, you can adjust the amount of food little by little so that you can achieve a lifetime goal for her: that she always has a waist.

ARE TABLE SCRAPS OKAY FOR PUPPIES?
Putting some tasty morsels of human food into your dog's dish as a treat from time to time is not really a problem, as long as the quantity you put in is *very* little. Table scraps in moderation should not be a problem, but a puppy's diet certainly should not have more than ten percent of people-food in it. Please control yourself. No matter how crazy you are about that adorable pup, just remember that food does not equal love. Please read the difference between dry and canned foods and consider giving your puppy a generous amount of high-quality canned food, which will be just as big a treat as anything you have to offer from your plate.

If you make it a daily habit to put tasty tidbits of your own or any special flavorings in puppy food, you may be creating a picky eater. Obviously, if your puppy gets an upset stomach, you should either stop giving people-food or notice what it was you gave her and avoid that ingredient in the future.

THE PUPPY'S FIRST MEAL OF THE DAY
The very first thing that should always happen in the morning is that you bound out of bed to get up and walk the little one—*immediately*. Then, when you give her breakfast, you'll need to instantly walk her again (because what you put in one end comes out the other—sometimes frighteningly fast when they're little). Only *after* her needs are met can you think about your own, like brushing your teeth and having a cup of coffee.

IF YOU'LL BE GONE DURING THE DAY
The nicest arrangement for a young puppy is to have a human around all day to hang out with—and serve him several nutritious meals. However, in our society, most people generally go out to work, which can mean that no one will be home for the entire day. If your lifestyle does not permit you to be home a lot when the puppy is little, wherever there is reference to times and interaction with the puppy, think of ways to amend it to fit your particular schedule.

◆ Somebody Needs to Walk and Feed the Puppy.
A young puppy needs to go out at least once, if not twice, during the day. If you can't do it yourself, you'll have to ask favors of family or neighbors, or pay someone to do it. Just remember that as soon as that person walks in your door, the puppy needs to come out of her crate and go *immediately* outside (perhaps being carried) to avoid an accident indoors. Then the person can play

with the puppy and feed her and walk her once more. As soon as you come home after work, you need to do the immediate walk/feed/walk routine once again.

◆ **Get the Puppy on the Schedule That Suits You.**
You want to teach a puppy when she's young that when meals are served, she'd better get right down to the business of eating them. If you let her dillydally about eating, she'll wind up taking charge of the mealtimes. Put food down for fifteen minutes—if the puppy hasn't paid attention and eaten in that time, then take it away. She'll learn to eat when it's offered (remembering, as always, that puppies of very small breeds need food left down all the time).

HOW MANY MEALS A DAY?
There is differing advice about the schedule to follow when raising a puppy. Some say that you should feed three meals a day until five months, while others advise to feed four times a day until three months, then three times a day to six months of age.

When a puppy reaches six months, most agree that you can reduce feedings to two daily—one early when you get up, and the other sometime in the afternoon. However, depending on your work schedule, that second meal may have to be at night, which can have some effect on housebreaking and the time at which you give the puppy her last walk of the night.

◆ **Skipping a Meal**
It's fine if the pup does not want to eat occasionally, as long as there is no sign of any problem, and she has normal stool, her normal water intake and good energy. Once again, this is not true of toy-breed puppies, who are prone to hypoglycemia and serious health consequences if they do not eat frequently and consistently throughout their puppyhood.

FEEDING DURING HOUSE-TRAINING
Until your dog is completely house-trained, she needs to have a very predictable regimen. This will "teach" her digestive system to work on a schedule. Feed at least three times day, always at the same time. Feed the same amount each time and give her regular food—no additions of anything that could disturb her digestion. Free-feeding is not a good idea during house-training.

PUPPY NUTRITION PROBLEMS
The most frequent feeding-related problems for puppies are vomiting, diarrhea and intestinal gas—all of which are generally passing problems. In order to correct whatever is keeping your puppy from eating, you need to know what some of the possible causes might be so that you can address the problem (see list on page 448).

◆ **The Puppy Won't Eat.**
In the same way that human babies and children can easily weaken without sustenance and quickly dehydrate from illness, so can a puppy. This means that a puppy who won't eat is a puppy at risk. It's important for young dogs to have a fairly constant supply of food and water. The Raising a Great Puppy Chapter, page 106, goes into these issues as well, but basically what you need

to know is that a growing pup does not have the fat stores or fluid balance of a grown dog. Therefore, if your puppy is not taking in enough to sustain her, you have to do something.

◆ A "Dining Area"
One basic piece of wisdom is to create a "dining room" for the puppy, where her water bowl is always ready for her and where you place her food dish. Having a predictable place to eat—and eventually learning when meals will be served—goes a long way toward putting most puppies at ease about filling their little bellies.

POSSIBLE REASONS FOR PUPPIES REFUSING FOOD

- ❑ Medical: diarrhea, vomiting, lethargy, worms in stool. A thin pup with a protruding belly might have parasites. Call the vet and make an appointment.
- ❑ Stress: adjusting to a new home or too much stimulation from other pets or kids. Give the puppy a space of her own, limit the amount of touching and interaction.
- ❑ The weather: Some puppies are affected by certain weather patterns. For example, if the weather is hot and muggy you may find that when it changes, the pup's appetite improves. Try to keep her environment comfortable.
- ❑ Brand of food: Feed her usual brand, slowly introduce a new brand.
- ❑ Eating location: Overstimulation from too much activity in the "dining area" can be distracting to some pups. Make a quiet puppy dining area.
- ❑ Loneliness: She either needs someone to keep her company while dining, or the presence of another dog for "competition," which she had with her littermates. Keep her company while she eats; other dog(s) hanging around can stimulate instinctive competition over food.

◆ Vomiting and Diarrhea
These are generally symptoms of a puppy having gotten into some people-food that was somehow left at her eye level or that she got out of the garbage. Dogs throw up quite readily if something does not agree with them—vomiting is a good natural defense in an animal that will put almost anything in its mouth. Digestive upsets are usually temporary with puppies.

◆ When to Call the Doctor
It is not necessary to contact or visit the vet unless the puppy throws up repeatedly, or acts lethargic and ill. Once dogs throw up, that will usually be the end of it. Gastrointestinal disturbances usually take a day to work their way out of the digestive tract. Wait about twenty-four hours and the upset stomach will probably have cleared up on its own.

◆ Intestinal Gas
Some commercial dog foods cause gas in some dogs. "Some" is the operative word, because the ingredient that may irritate one puppy and create intestinal gas may not have that effect on others. If your puppy emits gas a few hours after she eats, there's a good chance that the food doesn't

agree with her. Try a different brand (get only small bags until you settle on one food) until you find one that does not aggravate her stomach.

Gas can also be caused by the way the puppy is eating—gobbling down the food without chewing it and taking in air. If your puppy seems to eat too quickly, wolfing down air with the food, add some warm water to the kibble before feeding it. This should slow the puppy's gulping down and lessen the problem.

◆ Bloat

Bloat is a life-threatening problem in which the stomach fills with gas or fluids, then swells, and the intestines twist. Large, deep-chested breeds are most often affected. The cause of bloat is usually that a dog will eat a big meal, consume a lot of water and exercise vigorously soon afterward.

If you should see your puppy's stomach blow up like a hard balloon—not the cute little after-meal puppy belly—rush her immediately to a vet. A dog can die if not taken immediately for emergency surgery. See page 363 for information on bloat.

Prevention of bloat is to feed more frequent, smaller meals, and to make sure that your pup doesn't gulp large quantities of water right after eating and/or exercise heavily on a full belly.

Special Dietary Needs

MEALS FOR MEDICAL CONDITIONS

Dogs with a variety of medical conditions—including kidney disease, cardiac problems, diabetes, pancreatic disease and intestinal disturbances—can benefit from foods formulated to help manage their illnesses. These specialty foods are sold through vets, who prescribe them based on a diagnosis of the dog and then monitor his progress. The first company to study, test and market these specialized foods was Hill's with their Prescription Diet line of foods (although the same company's Science Diet regular dry food is no match for any of the premium products).

No dog food can actually prevent or treat disease, but it can help you to manage your dog's condition. Your vet should be able to explain how a special diet will affect your dog's individual medical situation.

CONDITIONS HELPED BY SPECIAL DIETS

- ❐ Bladder stones: There are two kinds of bladder stones—*struvite* and *urate*—which specialty diets can help prevent. For the newest information, please go to www.thedogbible.com and click on the tab "Inside the Book."
- ❐ Cancer: "Cachexia" is a common syndrome with cancer in which the dog loses his appetite and his metabolism and energy needs change. Food for a cancer patient should be rich in nutrients, easily digested, high in fat, low in carbohydrates and aimed at lessening cachexia.
- ❐ Cardiac disease: Generally there is fluid retention, because this disease causes the heart to enlarge and become less efficient. A low-sodium diet helps reduce fluid buildup, allowing the heart to function more easily.

❐ Diabetes: As in people, this endocrine disorder is caused by a deficiency in the hormone insulin, which metabolizes glucose from the bloodstream into the tissues. Food for diabetic dogs has moderate fat and fiber levels, complex carbohydrates account for nearly half of the calories and the food contains starches that are digested and absorbed more slowly.

❐ Food allergies: When a dog's immune system becomes overactive to a specific food ingredient, the result is coat and skin problems. There can also be gastrointestinal reactions. These diets usually contain an unusual protein source (such as fish or kangaroo) that won't trigger an allergic reaction.

❐ Gastrointestinal problems: Problems with the digestive tract usually result in chronic diarrhea and sometimes vomiting and loss of appetite. Specialized diets help soothe the intestinal lining and restore normal digestive functioning. The diet must be highly digestible, contain a single-source, high-quality protein, a single-source, gluten-free carbohydrate, reduced fat and moderate fiber content.

❐ Kidney disease: Progressive loss of kidney function means that the dog's body cannot filter and excrete waste products efficiently. An adjusted diet minimizes the accumulation of these waste products and, if possible, slows the progression of the disease by normalizing the blood chemistry.

❐ Liver disorders: Dietary changes can significantly impact the liver's ability to function and regenerate. Limiting protein and adding easily digested carbohydrates and high-quality fats will help control ongoing liver damage and improve liver function.

❐ Obesity: Reducing fat and calories is the key to helping a dog lose weight. Increasing fiber lessens caloric density and provides the bulk needed to satisfy hunger.

DOGS WITH FOOD ALLERGIES

◆ What Causes a Reaction to a Food?

It can take up to two years for an allergy to develop, which explains why a dog can eat the same food for a long time and then seem to "suddenly" have an allergic reaction to it. Usually, the problem is the protein source in the food—either meat or grain. This was the reason that, years ago, pet-food manufacturers developed a lamb and rice food, which was originally considered hypoallergenic. At that point in time, most dogs had never eaten lamb. Now that lamb has become a popular ingredient, its intended purpose as a novel source of protein no longer has value. So innovative pet-food makers have had to be imaginative in coming up with new protein sources, such as fish and kangaroo. The grain portion of food that dogs are usually allergic to is the corn or wheat, so the new antiallergy foods have an alternative grain, such as oats, or a starch, such as potatoes.

◆ Symptoms of Food Allergies

You may learn that your dog has food allergies if she is constantly itching no matter what the season and has chronic ear infections or digestive problems such as diarrhea or vomiting. You must go to your vet to rule out other possible causes for her symptoms; then it's up to the doctor to evaluate whether the problem is food allergies. There's no easy medical test or reliable blood test to find out what is triggering your dog's allergy. The remedy is generally to follow one of the suggestions below.

◆ Solutions to Food Allergies

There are two ways to deal with what may be irritating your dog. You can conduct an "elimination diet," in which you switch to a food made of ingredients your dog has not been exposed to and then, one by one, you add the ingredients you were originally feeding. When you feed a food that brings on the reaction again, you will have found the offending product. The second—and perhaps more efficient—solution to the problem is to just permanently switch to a food with a new protein source. The new protein sources are foods like fish, rabbit, venison and even kangaroo, which are totally foreign to most dogs.

You may have to feed an elimination diet removing the previous food for at least eight weeks before you see an improvement in your dog's symptoms.

◆ Fish-based Is Best.

Some veterinary specialists prefer fish diets for pets with food allergies. Fish is considered an excellent protein source, and the omega-3 fatty acids can help reduce the inflammation that may bother an allergic dog. If your dog has already been exposed to one type of fish, that doesn't mean she won't be sensitive to another. Some of the foods are made with herring and catfish, two types of fish that most dogs have not previously encountered.

◆ Don't Change Foods to Avoid Allergies.

Since allergies take a long time to develop, some doctors who treat them feel it is not a good idea to vary your dog's food as a preventive measure against food allergies. They feel that the more protein sources you introduce to your dog, the greater the chance that you'll expose her to one she's allergic to, which will trigger the food sensitivity. They say if the dog is feeling and looking good, leave well enough alone and don't just change her diet for the sake of change.

◆ Sources For Antiallergy Foods.

Companies that make canned and dry foods especially for allergic dogs, include the pioneer in the specialty nutrition field, Hill's, with its Prescription Diet D/D (fish and rice); Iams, with its Response KO/Canine (kangaroo and oat) and Response FP (fish and potato); Innovative Veterinary Diets (IVD) (rabbit, duck, venison or whitefish, all with potato); Nature's Recipe Allergy (with venison meal and rice or vegetarian); Old Mother Hubbard (fish and sweet potato wellness); and Waltham (catfish).

Supplements to Dog Food

There is really no need to add anything to a high-quality natural food. Excessive amounts of certain nutrients are actually toxic for dogs and can interfere with their body's ability to absorb other nutrients. However, some people seem determined to fiddle with their dog's dinner bowl—they can't just leave well enough alone. So this section is for them, so they'll know something about what they are giving their dogs—and for you, in case you've been considering some supplements. Before you give your dog anything out of the ordinary, please discuss it with your vet, since you may be doing something harmful without realizing it.

ANTIOXIDANTS

This has become a trendy word in dog food, so some products list antioxidants individually as beta-carotene, vitamin C, vitamin E, etc.. Alpha-tocopherol is the only kind of tocopherol that the body can actually use as an antioxidant—the others are often used to preserve the food *when it is in the bag,* not when it is in the dog's body. There is no harm in these ingredients, although whether there is enough in the food to make a difference is another question.

CALCIUM

NEVER add minerals like calcium to your dog's diet unless your vet has specifically instructed you to. This goes for phosphorus and magnesium, as well. The ratio of calcium to phosphorus in the diet is essential to developing healthy bones and joints. Excessive calcium can interfere with the absorption of copper, zinc (see page 453) and other minerals. It can also cause bone deformities. Fast-growing, large-breed dogs do NOT need extra anything, certainly not excessive calcium, which can negatively affect joint formation and maturing cartilage, especially in growing, large-breed pups.

BREWER'S YEAST AND GARLIC

There is no proof that brewer's yeast or garlic does anything to deter fleas or any parasites. People think it does—or their grandmother told them it does—although they are healthy ingredients as B vitamins found in some of the quality foods.

OIL

If your dog has dry, flaky skin or her coat isn't shiny, just adding oil to her food may make no difference. Most ingested oil just goes right through the dog, adding a few calories along the way. First your vet will want to see what underlying medical conditions might be causing the skin problems (thyroid, intestinal parasites, skin infections, fleas, allergies or hormonal problems are a few of the possibilities). If treating any medical condition does not alleviate the problem, the vet may have a particular oil that might address the skin issue.

VITAMIN/MINERAL SUPPLEMENTS

Only if the vet recommends a general-purpose, multivitamin/mineral supplement should you consider it. Another possibility is to give a balanced canine multivitamin (from natural sources, if possible), but only twice or three times a week. Added nutrients will be available to the dog's body but you won't be suppressing or overwhelming his body's natural functioning.

Do not give human vitamins and supplements to dogs. This may sound logical to you, but you'd be surprised how often people do it, often with a dog who is sick and not getting better with traditional veterinary care. What people don't seem to consider is that the human body is much larger than the dog's (unless you're a little old lady from Pasadena with a Saint Bernard) and what is an acceptable amount of vitamins and minerals for us would be an overdose for a dog.

✦ Zinc

Too little zinc can cause hair and skin problems as well as problems with the immune and reproductive systems. Siberian Huskies and other northern breeds have a hereditary tendency to be deficient in zinc. Because this is a specific and known deficiency, keep an eye on your dog if she is this type of breed. If she seems to have poor general health and the quality of her coat is questionable, talk to your vet about zinc supplements. Bedlington Terriers require a diet high in zinc as nutritional therapy for a genetic disorder. Excessive amounts of zinc may be toxic and can interfere with the absorption of other minerals. As with any supplementation, it has to be done in consultation with your vet.

PLATINUM PERFORMANCE PLUS: A VERY SPECIAL SUPPLEMENT

I've only encountered a few products in researching this book—and in my years with dogs and other animals—that I really want to share with other dog lovers. Platinum Performance Canine Plus is a dietary supplement, a vitamin/mineral/glucosamine powder that you put on the dog's food. It is formulated and made by an equine veterinary group in northern California, where I learned about Platinum Performance years ago because it helped my horse enormously.

When I began having lameness problems with my dogs—especially Yogi Bear, the foundling Rottweiler (who was thrown away in a box in the road because he was born without functional hip sockets), I wondered about the horse supplement for him. Cosequin (which is probably the best-known brand of glucosamine supplement for animals) had not made a noticeable difference in Mr. Bear's pain. That's how I found out there was a canine version in Platinum Performance (the "Plus" is their formula with 500 milligrams of glucosamine per tablespoon, versus 200 milligrams in the regular formula—Yogi weighed 120 pounds, so he needed the big boy's dose). The product made such a miraculous difference in Yogi's ability to get up and around without pain that I have been giving it twice a day to all my dogs, young or old, whether they have physical problems or not.

Several friends whose dogs had joint problems (and had also tried Cosequin with minimal improvement) are now converts to Platinum Plus, too. My friend Eileen's two six-month-old Lab brothers (from a supposedly good breeder) would be so crippled after running on the beach that they would *drag* their hindquarters around, whimpering. Since going on Platinum Plus they have never had another "paraplegic moment." At eight years old, my friend Sharon's Labrador, Becca, got a little brother. Even though she was fit, her joints were so achy that she couldn't play with him. Now on Platinum Plus she can outrun Toby in the woods (well, not quite, but she can keep up). I feel sort of evangelical—as if I'm telling stories about people throwing away their crutches at Lourdes—but there are so many supplements out there, how can you know which ones work best? So this is a personal endorsement, but don't doubt my motives: I pay the same as anybody else for the tub of Platinum Performance that FedEx brings to my door.

- Fresh bioactive long- and short-chain omega-3 essential fatty acids
- 2:1 ratio of omega-3 to omega-6 acids to correct fatty acid imbalances
- Twenty trace minerals (cellular division, function and tissue structure)
- Nineteen amino acids (enzyme and cell function)
- Multiple free-radical scavenging antioxidants
- Water- and fat-soluble vitamins
- Carnitine, taurine, arginine, glutamine
- 200 milligrams glucosamine sulfate per tablespoon (for joint health)
- OR 500 milligrams glucosamine sulfate per tablespoon for the "Plus" formula

Platinum Plus is fairly expensive, but then Cosequin is really pricey, too (and it doesn't have all the other health benefits of Platinum Plus, either). Give the folks in California a toll-free call at (800) 553-2400 and they'll tell you anything else you'd like to know. And I'd really like to know what experiences you have—please contact me at www.thedogbible.com with your results. I sure hope it helps you as it has me, because we all know the nagging frustration and worry you feel about having a lame dog whose pain you want to relieve.

FEEDING A RAW DIET

There is a somewhat new trend of feeding dogs a diet of raw meat. A small but fervent movement of pet owners adhere to a theory that the best diet for dogs consists of raw meat, poultry and their bones. There are a few slightly different schools of thought about the raw diet, but the best-known one is called BARF ("Biologically Appropriate Raw Food" or "Bones and Raw Food"). You can take the middle ground, which is to feed raw food that has been dehydrated, killing bacteria but preserving nutrients. Innova Evo is one such food; the Honest Kitchen is made in a human food factory (and does happen to be one of the foods I feed my dogs (www.thehonestkitchen.com).

✦ Dangers of Raw-feeding

With all that raw-feeding requires (buying, safely storing and serving raw meats), very few people have the time or resources to feed their dogs this way. Raw meat, and especially raw poultry, are carriers of salmonella and other food-borne illnesses that present health risks to dogs and people. Many vets and veterinary nutritionists do not support raw-feeding, because the meat supply that reaches the grocery stores in America is often contaminated with microbes, viruses and parasites: salmonella, *E.coli* and yersinia are but a few of the common contaminants of raw food. Another danger is in consuming raw bones. Even the bones in chicken wings and necks (which are what BARF encourages) can lodge in a dog's esophagus and intestines.

Even if some dogs can eat contaminated foods without getting sick, those raw foods are still going to be in daily contact with your hands, refrigerator, cutting boards and countertops. You and others in your household, especially the very young and old, could become seriously ill from exposure to these foods. This throw-the-raw-chicken-on-the-floor feeding style is controversial. Those promoting raw feeding believe it is more "natural" for dogs to eat as their wolf ancestors did many generations ago, except that the raw chicken or beef at the butcher's counter has little in common with what would be consumed by a wild dog after a kill. Just as the domestic dog's coat, skin and ability to withstand weather conditions have changed considerably since those ancestral days, so has the dog's digestive system.

◆ Consider Rare, Not Raw

Cooking most foods increases their digestibility. This is true for humans and canines. There is a small, celebrity-studded fad for all-raw diets for people. The proponents of raw feeding who claim that cooking destroys nutrients, or that heat harms food, are being somewhat fanatical. It's one thing to stock up on raw almonds, quite another to do so with chicken carcasses.

When a diet becomes hotly contested and passionately believed in, it inspires semireligious devotion. There are testimonials from people that their dogs' coats are shinier and the animals seem altogether healthier on a raw diet—but the question is, what were they feeding before? Was it inferior product? Was it dry food only? As I mentioned, I found my own dogs' health improved considerably when I switched to predominantly canned food when I'd previously had them on a top-of-the-line dry food, as advocated by almost everyone. Who knows if it was the *rawness* of that diet that benefited their dogs, or just the greater amount of meat protein?

VEGETARIAN DIETS

Vegetarians and vegans sometimes want their dogs to be vegetarians, if they are opposed to the killing of animals for any reason. Yes, dogs can live on vegetables alone, just as people can; a vegetarian diet just needs enough protein and nutrients. Basically, dogs are omnivorous and most of their energy comes from carbohydrates. Dry commercial foods derive carbohydrates from cereals, legumes and plant foodstuffs. Vegetarian dogs have become common enough now that some of the major dog-food companies have come out with meat-free foods.

Some dogs are on vegetarian diets to help control allergies, but that is a separate issue and something to be determined by a veterinarian who is a board-certified specialist (see page 284).

Dr. Pitcairn's Complete Guide to Natural Health for Dogs & Cats is a well-regarded book that focuses on "alternative medicine" and devotes substantial space to a canine vegetarian diet. Among other rather unusual advice, he advocates raw zucchini, carrots and parsley in the dog's food. You may be interested in giving it a try if, ideologically, what Pitcairn proposes appeals to you. It may be a question of whether you have the time necessary to prepare well-balanced vegetarian meals for your dog. It might be workable to prepare a week's food at once for a small dog or two (putting portions aside in freezer bags), but in a household like mine, with three large dogs, it would be impossible to cook a big vat of vegetarian food every other day. (Besides, it would be mutiny if I changed their beloved, recently adopted meat-based diet. So I'll say on behalf of my dogs—and on behalf of dogs anywhere subsisting on oatmeal and zucchini in meatless households—that no self-respecting dog would ever willingly CHOOSE to be without meat in her diet.)

◆ Vegetables as "Fibrous Filler"

There are actually specialists in dog diets—there are veterinary nutritionists in mainstream veterinary care with medical degrees beyond DVM: they can also put the letters DACVN beside their names. Research has been allocated to discover the best food for dogs—and vegetables are nowhere near the top of that list. Veterinary nutritionists generally think of vegetables as a "fibrous filler" to accompany a good protein-rich (i.e., meat) diet for dogs. It would be unusual for a veterinary practitioner to give high marks to vegetables as a staple of canine nutrition. Vegetables are not as nutritious as some dog owners would like to believe and not really desirable as the primary ingredient for sustaining good energy and health in a dog. Vegetables have a large amount of indigestible fiber and water—not the stuff from which strong canine bones, muscles and nerves are made.

This is not just an ideological position of mainstream medicine versus the nutritional counterculture—if, in fact, that would be the phrase that applies to Dr. Pitcairn and other nontraditional care providers. It is a free world, after all, and people who take a nontraditional path are often ahead of their time. However, while there is always room for other opinions and points of view, it is imperative that people not project their own ideologies and nutritional issues onto their pets ("I'm a vegetarian and it's a way of life for me, so my dog must be one, too.").

The often-cited reasoning by vegetarians who want to make their dogs vegetarian, too, is that when dogs were wild they ate a little of everything. But carnivores who eat grasses and berries and nuts often do so to sustain themselves until they can latch onto what they see as a proper meal—preferably, something with two wings or four legs.

MISCELLANEOUS EDIBLE INGREDIENTS

◆ Eggs

I can't seem to find any official information about feeding eggs to dogs, but since eggs are a perfect protein source, and since so many dog foods include eggs, they certainly can do no harm. I give all my dogs a raw egg as a treat periodically. They adore it, and slurp it right up. (I was once told that raw egg white makes dogs throw up, but I've never seen a dog have this reaction, even my poor Lulu when she had stomach cancer.) I give it separately from their food because it would otherwise just go down the hatch barely noticed in the frenzy of mealtime. The only problem I've had with feeding raw eggs is that any time I crack an egg in my kitchen to cook, there is the clatter of a dozen paws and I find three pairs of hopeful eyes staring up at me.

◆ Grass

It is sometimes said that dogs eat grass because they feel sick to their stomachs and the grass makes them throw up—or that it serves as an internal cleansing. There doesn't seem to be much truth to this, given that it's very easy for dogs to throw up without grass when they have an upset stomach (ask any dog owner who installs new wall-to-wall carpeting). That said, I have had dogs who swallowed a large piece of chew-hoof that they couldn't digest and, when they threw it up, there was also a clump of grass.

There is another idea that dogs eat grass because their diet has too much meat compared to what their wolf ancestors ate. This point of view holds that the modern canine diet is unbalanced in some way. That doesn't make much sense, since most of us feed primarily kibble and proportionately little meat. High-quality kibble contains vegetable matter along with beneficial vitamins and minerals

It may be that dogs just enjoy eating grass. Almost every dog I've ever had has eaten grass with gusto whenever he encountered it. While no one knows why they like it, there is no reason for them not to eat fresh, clean grass. In fact several natural-dog-care books suggest growing rye or barley grass for dogs from sprouts, the way that people grow "cat grass" indoors from ready-to-grow kits.

◆ Milk
Milk is a controversial food for dogs. Some nutritionists say that milk and dairy products are great for dogs, and others say that pasteurized milk is indigestible for them. The experts seem to agree that raw milk, fresh from a cow or goat, is a great food, but since raw milk was banned long ago from supermarkets in America, you'd need to live on a dairy farm to have access to it. My feeling is, everything in moderation: an occasional small bowl of milk, even diluted by half with water, is such ambrosia for my dogs that I am delighted to offer it and have seen no ill effects.

◆ Water
Water is really important to a dog's health—it helps regulate all the body's systems. But a dog will only drink water plentifully if she has bowls of really fresh, clean water that are frequently emptied and refilled. Strange as it may seem, dogs tend to be really picky about drinking "used" water in a dirty bowl and want fresh cold water at home, even though many dogs will drink sour milk or muddy puddle water (which, by the way, you shouldn't let them do—see page 330—for warnings on health dangers in stagnant water).

At least once a day (even more if multiple dogs drink from the bowl), pour out the water in your dog's bowl and refill it—after sponging it out.

Look at the surface of the dog's water before you pour it out and you'll see why it needs frequent changing: a layer of dust or oiliness from the room or previous sips by the dog. And you'll probably see debris that has dropped to the bottom. The emptied bowl may not seem dirty to you, but water that sits out often has a slimy layer at the bottom that can signal the beginning of algae formation.

◆ How to Make Baked-liver Treats
At dog shows, handlers keep little bits of baked liver in their pockets as bait to entice their dogs and get them to pay attention. You, too, can have your dog eating out of your hand.

Simple recipe: Cut beef liver into long thin strips and place on an oiled piece of aluminum foil on a cookie sheet. Bake at a low temperature (200°F) until the meat is cooked through—or even longer until it dries into a kind of homemade jerky. You can do the same thing with beef kidneys, slicing the kidneys to bake until dry.

You can make these and use them as flavor enhancers for your dog's dinner if she is a finicky eater, or you can use the baked goodies as special training treats. After you have cooked and cooled them, break them into chips and put the treats into a plastic container in the refrigerator.

DIETETIC TREATS

If weight gain is an issue for your dog, avoid high-calorie snacks. While fresh fruits and vegetables make great snacks, dogs sometimes can't relate gastronomically to round-shaped foods such as cherry tomatoes or strawberries. They often will lick at it and then wind up eating it later. They may roll the fruit around on the floor but not eat it until you break it open for them.

🦴 Snacks

Fattening Snacks to Avoid
Peanut butter in a Kong toy
Chunks of cheese
Chips or any other human snack foods
Pig's ears
Bread or other human carbohydrates

Slimming Snacks to Embrace
Raw carrot sticks: a raw carrot makes a great chew toy
Any raw vegetable your dog will eat: tomatoes can be popular
Cooked vegetables: Carrot sticks and green beans can be steamed
Whole fruits: strawberries, plums, cubed apples, papaya or banana [Warning: *grapes can be a problem, see p. 324*]
Mini rice cakes: low fat and filling (avoid salted or flavored)
Popcorn: air-popped or popped with any vegetable oil—but no butter or salt (and not microwaved with fats and salt)

SPECIAL "STRICT DIET" TREATS

If your dog is on a restricted diet for a condition such as kidney disease, and he can only eat canned foods carried by veterinarians, you can make high protein snacks out of his specialty canned food. Open both ends of the dog food can and push it through in one piece. Put foil on a cookie sheet and spray lightly with cooking spray. Using a cheese slicer or a sharp knife, cut very thin slices of the wet food and lay them flat on the cookie sheet. Sometimes, if the can is chilled first, the food will be easier to slice thin.

Put slices in a hot oven (500°F) and bake until they resemble crisp crackers. The amount of time will depend on your oven, but keep an eye on these treats because anything this thin can burn easily.

CHEWABLE TREATS

Chewing is a physical and emotional need for most dogs, though some seem to need it more than others. There are dogs who can happily spend half their waking hours chewing vigorously on whatever is offered to them.

◆ Hard Chew Toys

Many veterinary dentists are opposed to giving hard nylon bones and cow hooves to dogs. They say that a toy should be resilient—you should be able to depress it with your thumbnail or bend it gently. These doctors see a lot of dogs with cracked teeth and say that dogs who gnaw on hard unyielding objects risk such fractures. Based on the opinions of a number of dentists, I've compiled a list of chew items to avoid which usually includes cow hooves, animal (as in beef) bones, hard nylon toys, rocks and ice cubes.

◆ Rawhide Chews

There are two descriptions of where rawhide comes from, even though the most logical definition is that it is the *hide* of the animal. There is very little processing involved—it's basically leather. The uncooked skin, or hide, of cattle is stripped of hair, then washed, shaped and dried. The Tufts University Veterinary School publication, *Your Dog*, contradicts this definition of rawhide, stating that it is not made from animal skin but rather from connective tissue, which is the internal connective tissue between organs and between muscles and bones. Pressed rawhide is different—it is processed, similar to pressed wood, and made of a variety of parts. It breaks apart more easily and is generally more digestible.

There are a number of things that people need to know about rawhide treats so that they can safely give their dog the pleasure of chewing them. The information below is not intended to alarm you and rob your dog of the pleasure of rawhide mastication, but there are some things you will want to know in order to make good decisions for your pet.

Where Rawhide Comes From Matters. Make every effort to buy rawhide products that have been made in the U.S. (not just packaged here). American hides are the best because there are stricter regulations on the cattle industry in the United States than there are in other countries, higher standards of cleanliness in the slaughterhouses and only hydrogen peroxide is used to bleach the hides. Some tanneries in the Far East and South America remove hair from the hides using arsenic, lime or acid—all of which remain in the leather, even if it is washed afterward. Obviously, these chemicals are bad for your dog.

No seal of approval There is no health regulation of rawhides because they are not technically a food. This means you have to pay attention and make decisions for yourself without any official "seal of approval" about the relative safety of the product. The "all-natural" claim on many labels means virtually nothing, since it does not reflect how the cattle are handled before slaughter or what happens to the hides during processing.

The danger of salmonella to pets and people Pet chews can be contaminated with bacteria such as salmonella, which can cause serious illness in dogs and the people around them. Young puppies and critically ill dogs can get very sick if exposed to salmonella, and even healthy dogs can suffer from intestinal symptoms. There is also the worrisome possibility of cross-species contamination; even a healthy person can be affected by salmonella poisoning. Symptoms are diarrhea, abdominal cramps, vomiting and nausea, with effects lasting up to a week. Infants, elderly people and those with impaired immune systems are at the greatest risk.

As with many bacterial illnesses, hand-washing is the key to health. If you handle a rawhide chew, wash your hands. If you have toddlers or other small children who might pick up a rawhide chew and put it in their mouths, then avoid the risk and don't let your dog have rawhide around a young child. There's also some risk of the child getting bitten if he plays around a dog who has a prized chewie and wants to guard it. Consider giving rawhide to your dog only during the little person's nap time or nursery-school hours.

The good news is that salmonella is only a threat in theory, because there have been no recalls of any rawhide product in the U.S. due to salmonella. Of course it could happen anytime, just as there were recalls of pig's ears in 1999 because of salmonella contamination.

Other dangers of rawhide Intestinal obstruction, stomach upset and dental problems are complications that can arise from rawhides. If the dog tries to swallow a big wedge-shaped piece of rawhide, it can stick in the throat or lodge in the bowel. There can also be intestinal blockage and upper-airway obstruction when a dog chews off a large piece of rawhide. Most of these problems are not emergencies—they just cause vomiting and/or diarrhea.

Rawhide comes in many forms. There are big rawhide "bones" with a knot at either end, thin "pencils" of rawhide and a "pencil" made of chopped rawhide that crumbles and is easier to chew but doesn't last as long. By experimenting with your dog, you can discover what form of rawhide chews are best-suited to his chewing style and appetite. See the descriptions below to determine what kind of rawhide will give your dog the most pleasure without jeopardizing his health.

POINTERS ON RAWHIDE USE

❑ Medium to light chewers do the best with rawhide because they can gnaw off small pieces at a time.

❑ Light chewers won't make much progress and heavy chewers may try to bite off and swallow large pieces.

❑ Avoid rawhide bones with added components. If the knots at the ends are separate pieces, the dog can chew them off, then try to ingest them all at once.

❑ Avoid very white rawhides that seem too lightweight for their size, an indication that they contain formaldehyde, which is a bleaching agent.

❑ When in doubt, bigger is always better (less chance of choking).

❑ Always supervise the chewing.

❑ If you have a large dog with an aggressive chewing style, rawhide may not be the best idea for her. If your dog chews off big chunks of rawhide—rather than chewing small bits off the edges—it can result in internal problems. Hard-core strong chewers, or dogs who gulp their food, may be better off with another type of chew, such as a Kong.

Rawhide for passive chewers Some dogs have tender mouths or sensitive teeth and seem to approach rawhide not as a greatly appreciated treat but as an uncomfortable obligation. As many dogs as I've had who spend some of their happiest evenings working away at a rawhide chip, I've had others who just ignore the chew. And then there's Scooby Doo, my 100-pound, World's-Tallest-Weimaraner, who will walk around with the rawhide piece in his mouth, crying until you take it back and give him a pressed rawhide in its place (it's easier on his delicate mouth, apparently).

Pressed rawhide, which is made of (sometimes brightly colored) tiny pieces smashed into a shape, can be good for gentle chewers. This rawhide crumbles when the dog chews it so it doesn't become a big, dangerously gluey chunk. However, in some dogs, rawhide in this form can cause loose stool.

"Dental cleaning" rawhide It is not true that rawhide can clean tartar off your dog's gums or teeth—tartar is at the gum line, where even aggressive chewers can't reach with a rawhide. There are "dental chews," which are often sold in vet's offices, that claim to clean the dog's teeth as she chews, and they must have some cleansing action to justify their name and the claim on the package. However, actual teeth cleaning is best done by the vet, or by you, under the vet's supervision

🦴 Other Animal-product Chews

Pig ears	Beef ears
Lamb ears	Dried beef neck muscles

(see page 426 in the "Grooming" section).

FRESH BONES

◆ "The Good Old Days"
Do you want to play Russian roulette with your dog? If not, then disregard those things people like to say in defense of bone-giving, such as "My grandaddy's dogs ate chicken bones all their lives on the farm." Just because *they* did it and no harm came to their dogs (as far as they know)

doesn't mean it is a practice to be continued today when so much more is known about canine health (it would be like someone insisting that smoking is not a problem because his grandfather lived into his eighties and smoked two packs a day).

Chicken, turkey, beef rib, steak and pork bones are the worst kinds. Dogs' jaws can generate several hundred pounds of pressure in a bite, which can cause a bone to shatter into small splinters that can lodge in or puncture the intestines later.

BONES TO AVOID

☐ No bones from your plate: Avoid real bones, except beef shinbones such as the marrow bones in osso buco, the Italian veal-shank dish (see below).

☐ Bones from lamb chops and steaks: These look perfect for a dog, with delicious bits of meat and fat attached, but these bones can be deadly inside your dog's intestinal tract.

☐ Chicken bones can splinter and pierce the dog's intestines or stomach. Cooked chicken bones are the most dangerous, but raw bones can also splinter into needle-sharp points.

☐ No sharply angled cut bones, or bones cut into small pieces.

☐ No cooked bones from baked, broiled or barbecued meat (too dry and brittle, likely to splinter).

CHOOSING THE RIGHT BONES

◆ Raw Marrow Bones

You can get beef marrow bones at the butcher or supermarket—cut two or more inches long, they are full of marrow and the bones don't splinter (unless cut too short).

If you give raw bones to your dog, keep them outdoors or in an uncarpeted area, otherwise the fatty marrow may stain your carpet or the dog's bed.

Some dogs don't like the bones raw.

◆ Cooked Marrow Bones

If you decide to cook bones, there are two ways to do it: boiling and baking. You can put them in just enough boiling water to cover and let them simmer; some marrow will be lost in the water. There are nutritionists who say that bones should be boiled precisely so that the marrow *does* dissolve, since it is too rich for dogs to eat without getting an upset stomach. Every owner has to make a decision about this. Boiling is considered preferable to baking bones, which makes them dry and brittle and more likely to splinter.

If you buy a lot of bones at once, the rest of them should be frozen, not refrigerated. Bones can go bad within a few days; they can also get soft enough for the dog to be able to chew through the normally too-hard bones.

◆ Dangers to Others from Bones

You might not want to introduce real bones into some household situations.

Pregnancy Pregnant women who handle raw meat and bones risk being exposed to toxoplasmosis, an infection that can cause miscarriage. Raw bones can harbor salmonella and *E. coli* bacteria.

Multi-dog households If you have a multi-dog household, there is the possibility of fights where real bones are concerned. The higher the prize, the greater the stakes, where dog rivalry is concerned.

Children If you have children in the house, keep in mind there is a chance that your dog, with a real bone, may be transformed from great-with-kids to snapping or even biting.

Dietary Problems

LOWERED MEAT/PROTEIN FOR BEHAVIOR PROBLEMS

There is a trend toward attributing the behavior problems of difficult dogs to their diet. This sounds a bit like the "Twinkie Defense" (which was an unsuccessful attempt to exonerate a defendant on the grounds that his high intake of sugary junk food was responsible for his crimes). But who knows for sure—maybe there *is* something to the idea of diet being connected to behavior in dogs. There is no consensus about what kind of diet causes problems in some dogs. One theory is that feeding more protein and fewer carbohydrates reduces hyperactivity and makes dogs more receptive to training and less likely to be distracted. Some say that a hallmark of a high-quality food is that it has meat listed as the first *and* second ingredients, since any substance in a food is listed in order of its percentage. However, there is a growing contingent of dog trainers who believe that for a dog with behavior problems, especially those related to aggression, a low-protein food is the first step in solving the problems. Some believe that a dog food that's free of chemical preservatives is the answer for dogs with behavior problems. "Human-grade ingredients" are also often mentioned as being positively correlated with good behavior, except that this claim on dog food is meaningless and not monitored.

◆ Overfeeding

A young dog will gobble up everything in sight during the first year of life, its greatest period of growth. If you are a new dog owner, you may think that this voracious eating style is going to be normal for your dog throughout his life—and you may even try to encourage and maintain this amount of food.

Obesity will follow if owners treat their dogs as people with food disorders: ingesting food as a reward and as a way to express love, happiness and acceptance. Eating becomes a habit, an addiction. Dogs need to be fed an amount that keeps them somewhat lean.

FINICKY EATERS

◆ When You First Bring Your Dog or Puppy Home

In her first days with you, your new pup may not want to eat. She may be having a hard time getting used to her new environment (even if it might be nicer than where she was, in the case of a dog that has been "rescued" or is from an animal shelter). If the new dog is a puppy, you need to go out of your way to entice the little one to eat, because puppies (like human babies) have fewer fat stores and can become dehydrated more easily than adult dogs.

♦ **Toy-breed Puppies Are a Special Case**

These little babies are prone to low blood sugar (hypoglycemia), and the puppy's life may depend on you getting her to eat. Toy babies need three to four meals a day, and even two missed meals can put them in critical condition. (See the section on Small Dogs in Chapter Seventeen, page 618, for more information.)

♦ **Psychological Reasons for Not Eating**

A dog that insists on one kind of food instead of another is usually manipulating the humans. This is a game that the people initiate and then encourage, as though their dog being finicky is somehow positive. As soon as a person caters to a dog's reluctance to eat by offering something better and tastier, the person is teaching the dog to hold out until the really good stuff gets served. If the person establishes a complex ritual of what goes in the dog's dish and how it is presented, the dog will come to expect that—and will refuse anything else. These feeding games are unnatural to dogs and totally unnecessary for their well-being.

♦ **Medical Reasons for No Appetite**

If the puppy or dog does not want to eat and has other symptoms of illness—such as lethargy, vomiting or diarrhea—you should take her in to the vet for an evaluation. Take note of any behavior that is unusual for the dog—or any new circumstances in the environment that might be affecting her. This information is important for the vet to be able to figure out why the dog does not want to eat.

♦ **Ongoing Lack of Appetite**

A dog's lack of appetite is usually a passing thing—don't turn it into something more by hand-feeding the dog or offering ever-more delicious treats instead of nutritionally balanced dog food. If you make a big fuss over a dog not eating, you are creating a problem that really isn't there: dogs are individuals, and like people, each has his own metabolism, hunger levels and attitude toward food. Some pooches are "chowhounds" who will "hoover" down anything edible at any time, while others have small appetites—or some days none at all.

♦ **Suggestions on Dealing with Picky Eaters**

Take the dish away. It is widely suggested that if your dog doesn't eat his food within fifteen minutes of putting it out, then pick it up until the next usual mealtime. This helps your dog develop a routine whereby his digestive system alerts him that a mealtime is coming and his bowels also get accustomed to when they will be stimulated by food.

Boost the flavor and smell. Increasing the smell of the food can stimulate appetite in a dog who just isn't interested in eating. Your dog may be one of those rare creatures who can take it or leave it as far as food is concerned. You'll know this because the dog may get enthusiastic about cheese pizza but her own dinner never seems to put a smile on her face, so to speak—in fact she may leave it uneaten much of the time.

There's no harm in putting a tablespoon of a flavor enhancer in the dog's dish along with the kibble: a little garlic for some, liver or kidneys, pan drippings or gravy, a raw or cooked egg, cottage cheese, a spoonful of canned dog food, the water or oil from canned tuna, even a small spoonful of canned cat food, which is intensely smelly and flavored and appealing to dogs. This is a contradiction of the advice above about *not* improving what's in a picky dog's dish—but if your goal is to get her to eat, you have to experiment.

An easy food enticement that I discovered inadvertently is a heaping forkful of spaghetti—I don't know why it is so appealing to dogs, but they seem to gobble up pasta. If you want to try pasta for your picky eater, boil up a box of spaghetti and, after draining it, mix it with some oil and/or pasta sauce. It will keep for about five days in the fridge, and you can take out a forkful a day to put in the dog's dish.

Keep the dog company. Some dogs do much better if they have your companionship while they are eating: they don't like being left alone. They may hate to be left out of the action, and if you aren't there they wonder where you are and what they are missing. If your company makes the difference, it should only take a few minutes, and if it works, it's worth it.

Reduce the dog's stress level. This may sound a little new-agey, but some dogs really do seem to experience general anxiety or stress. If you can determine what in his environment is making him feel that way, then you can remedy the situation and he may relax enough to eat confidently.

OBESITY

One quarter to one half of all dogs in the Western world are fat. The heaviest dogs are the middle-aged ones, four to seven years old. That is the age group that can either stay fit and youthful, or get fat and sedentary and lose years off their lives. We Americans are getting fat as a nation, too, and it's thought that as people overfeed themselves and their children, so do they overfeed their pets.

Do not judge what a dog's perfect weight should be by watching dog shows, because those dogs need to have fat to win. A Golden Retriever or Labrador that has winning conformation in the shown ring today is probably between eight and fifteen pounds heavier than he should be. This is what the trend has been, even though the breed standard states that these dogs should be shown "in hard-working condition." What wins in the show ring may only be a trend—but it trains the eyes of spectators to accept fat (and think it is muscle) in a show dog.

THE DANGERS OF OBESITY

The National Academy of Sciences' National Research Council recently issued a report that dogs suffer the same consequences from obesity as people: increased risks of cancer, a mild form of diabetes, liver disease, arthritis and other ailments that put them at risk for premature death. One of the most important areas in which extra weight affects any dog is in the joints—hips and knees hold up much better if they don't have all that weight to support. What is interesting and worrisome is that these risks begin with only a moderate weight gain, and from an early age.

Labrador Retrievers are the most popular dog in the United States—and they're also a breed that tends toward fat. This means that half the dogs in America are overweight—and probably half the dogs in the country are Labradors or Labrador mixes. A fourteen-year nutritional study of forty-eight Labradors showed that feeding the dogs twenty-five percent less than the standard amount meant *they lived two years longer than those fed the larger portion.*

WHAT DOES "OBESE" LOOK LIKE?

The obese dog has a rectangular shape—he's boxy. He does not curve in at the waist, in front of the hips. His belly hangs down. When you feel the dog's sides, they are mushy, covered in fat. Don't kid yourself that "it's just a lot of hair" or that your dog "is really big-boned" (an excuse made about overweight people, too).

◆ Three Areas of the Dog's Body to Test for Fat

1. *The neck*: Press your thumb and finger deep into the side of the dog's neck in front of the shoulder, then pinch the fingers together. If you have pinched more than a half inch of neck, the dog is overweight. Older dogs carry most of their excess fat in their necks and may actually look thin in other areas.

2. *The ribs*: Stand next to your dog, facing toward his tail. Put your thumb on the middle of his spine halfway down his back and spread out your fingers over his last ribs. Now run your fingers up and down that rib cage: you should be able to feel the bump of actual rib bones when running your hands down his flanks. The belly is tucked up—no flab hangs down behind the rib cage.

3. *The hips*: Running your hand over your dog's rump, the area above his tail—you should be able to feel the two bumps of his pelvic bones without pressing in.

Seen from above, the dog's waist should nip in noticeably—there should be a curve behind the rib cage. The bird's-eye view should not be of a rectangular shape, or one that bows out at the sides—it should be a curvy flank that has a waist.

WAYS TO FEED WITHOUT FATTENING

◆ Do Not Follow Feeding Charts on Food Bags.

These charts almost always indicate that you should feed your dog much more food than would be good for her—sometimes four to five times more. Obviously, the food company wants her to eat as much as possible so you'll buy more dog food. But these charts do not take into consideration the variables in a dog's life that influence how much exercise she gets, her energy level and how efficiently her metabolism works.

◆ Get a Measuring Cup for Portion Control.

Don't just use any old cup or a plastic scoop. Get a one-cup measure and go by that to determine the portion you want to feed. If you've been measuring "by eye," you'll discover the old rule of thumb that "*your* eyes are bigger than *his* stomach." If properly measured, the amount of food may look like too little to you—if so, get a smaller bowl.

◆ Offer Less-appealing Food.

If the food is less delicious, most dogs will eat less of it. Do not apply your attitudes about food to your dog: it is not unfair or unkind to make a dog's mealtimes less interesting when it will make the rest of his life *more* interesting—because he'll be around to enjoy his old age in better health.

♦ Add Fiber to the Diet.
Roughage can help control weight because boosting fiber can make a dog feel fuller sooner. Adding ten percent of corn, barley or wheat-bran products can satisfy a dog's hunger sooner and do it with less calories. This is not one of those "if some is good, more must be better" kind of things. Too much fiber can prevent dogs from absorbing nutrients, so you want just a small fraction of your dog's dinner bowl to be fiber.

♦ Try the Pumpkin Diet.
This is a system that some nutritionists swear by. Reduce your dog's normal food by a third and replace it with an equal amount of canned pumpkin (not for pie—it should be minus the spices and sweeteners). Dogs seem to love pumpkin, which has the texture of canned dog food and provides vitamins and roughage with less calories. It also makes most dogs feel more full so they don't beg and scavenge as much.

🦴 *Anti-obesity Advice*

- Adult dogs need fewer calories than they did when they were growing up.
- The metabolism slows down, so the older dog needs fewer calories.
- Feed what maintains the weight—go by what your dog looks like. This is an ongoing experiment by you to determine how much and how often.
- If the dog slows down, cut back. If your dog's daily exercise decreases—if he gets hurt or you do (and can't walk him as far or as frequently)—then he needs fewer calories.
- The change in seasons can cause a change in exercise levels. Some dogs get out less in bitter winter weather; other dogs can't take the heat and loll around in the air-conditioning during the summer months.
- Don't blame your vet if she tells you the truth. Some people actually leave good vets because they did not want to hear the truth: that their pets were fat. Maybe it's that people identify so strongly with their dogs that when the dog is criticized, the owner's feelings are hurt.

Chapter 14

DOGS AND CHILDREN

 NOTE: Dogs and kids seem like the most natural mix imaginable, but the vast majority of dog bites every year are directed at children. These terrible events often happen because children are not taught how to behave around dogs, dogs are not introduced properly to children and they simply do not understand each other's language. At the end of this chapter there is a section to share with your child, no matter what his age. "Scooby's Twenty-Five Rules for Kids" is probably the most valuable asset in this book. Please take advantage of it to avoid accidents.

Some of the topics covered in this chapter are:

❑ Some natural incompatibilities between children and dogs
❑ Introducing your dog to children
❑ Ways to protect children and dogs
❑ Dog care responsibilities at different ages
❑ Dogs and new babies
❑ Toddlers and dogs
❑ Chart of childhood stages and interactions with dogs
❑ Special section for children: "Scooby's Twenty-Five Rules for Kids"

A dog's behavior is usually a reflection of the children in a family. A dog raised in a household with more than one noisy, active kid will frequently behave the same way the children do. A child who is considered hyperactive will often get a dog wound up enough to also be labeled as difficult or hyper. A child who throws tantrums and shows little self-control can influence a dog to spin out of control, too. People whose children are thoughtful, mannerly, easygoing and able to exhibit self-control will usually have a dog who is a great companion animal, with moments in which she is the model of decorum.

Some Natural Incompatibilities between Dogs and Kids

A child's view of the world is usually about Self, not focused on the needs or reactions of Others. This is true of all kids when they are toddlers, nursery-school age, and many kindergartners who are entirely self-centered. This is not a value judgment, it's a reality—and only parents can change their child's viewpoint where the family dog is concerned. For your child's safety, you need her to see things from her pup's point of view so that she can understand how her behavior affects the dog and learn her dog's "sign language."

Dogs are not four-legged humans; methods of communication are entirely different in the two species. There are some similarities between dogs and people, but the "language" of dogs has to be taught to children like any foreign language—otherwise, signals from dogs can be misinterpreted. It is utterly essential that the child be taught from an early age how a dog thinks, what makes him tick and how to avoid provoking him. Children need to have canine communication methods spelled out—sometimes over and over again, depending on how wound up a child gets playing with a dog. The danger in a dog-loving and canine-sensitive environment is that if the adults treat the dogs as creatures with feelings and needs—if dogs are spoken to and spoken about in a conversational way—a child can forget even more readily that a dog who loves her can also harm her.

DOGS HAVE SHARP TEETH

One of the hardest lessons for some children is to realize that *the dog will never be a child's equal playmate.* The danger of biting is always there, fundamentally because a dog has a mouthful of teeth with which to express a range of emotions. Every family must realize that even in the most innocent and simple interaction between dogs and children, there is one deadly serious fact: most dogs have jaws strong enough to inflict severe injury on a child. All it takes is for the dog or child to make an error in judgment or communication. Even the most wonderful dog can bite a child who surprises or hurts him.

◆ Pre-biting Behavior

To determine whether your dog is a good candidate for living with children, you need to learn some things about his behavior. The best way to find out is just to watch him in some areas. If your dog is uncomfortable in any of the following situations there is a chance that he would bite.

- ❑ *Food guarding.* Does the dog growl or lunge if anyone gets close to his bowl when he's eating?
- ❑ *Toy guarding.* Can you take a toy or chewie away from him safely?
- ❑ *New people.* Does your dog have a big reaction to visitors or people at the door? Are arrivals—and, to a lesser degree, departures—events that put your dog over the edge?

❑ *Anxiety around children.* Does your dog seem anxious around kids? Does he pant or pace or behave in ways you haven't seen before? Do you feel you have to keep an eye on him around children?

PACK POSITIONING, DOMINANCE ISSUES WITH CHILDREN
(See the section on "Dominance Issues," pages 98, 130 for more on this topic.)

Dogs place children below them on the pack ladder. In order to have a safe and harmonious child/dog household, you have to move a child up that ladder. But since "pack position" is the dog's compass in life, if you're going to correct the pecking order in your home, you will have to make the shift gradually.

❑ A small child must not try to seize a commanding position with a dog, because if the dog has already determined by instinct that she is above the child, her instincts may inspire her to defend that spot if the child tries to "take it away" from her.

❑ Have the child give a couple of simple commands to the dog (for more on this, see page 485).

❑ Depending on the child's age, he should be given every opportunity to feed the dog and hold the leash (always monitored by an adult who understands dogs and pack hierarchy). Both of these tasks place the child above the dog.

❑ Never let a child play rough games with a dog—no wrestling, no toy pulling, no chase games. The dog cannot play games with a child that the dog can win because they will remind the dog that he is stronger than the child—information that does not need to be reinforced.

SOME DOGS JUST DON'T LIKE KIDS.

Some dogs just do not like children. Dogs are individuals with their own personalities, and there are some dogs who may be better off in a household without children.

For most dogs, children really take some getting used to—while other pooches just naturally gravitate to kids. (Kind of like some grown-up people!)

❑ Some breeds are naturally good with kids. Other breeds are not at ease around children but can do well with children that they have been raised with. Other breeds just can't take the loud squeaky voices, the quick motions and dramatic emotional displays.

❑ Sensitive or timid dogs may feel intimidated or overwhelmed by the intensity of small children. Children are louder and move much more quickly than adults. Children's voices and crying can be startling in their suddenness and fervor: some dogs can get "caught up" in the drama.

❑ Tough and feisty dogs may view children's behavior as requiring them to put the small human in his place—especially if the child is a rough-and-tumble type. So a child who plays roughly—shouts or gets physical with others—may stimulate a dog to follow suit.

❑ Small dogs are in jeopardy with children—a toy breed can easily be hurt or killed by a child's innocent play. This is not just hyperbole—small dogs are truly fragile. In the case of some children, a tiny dog is not all that easy to differentiate from a stuffed animal.

AN OLDER DOG IS OFTEN A BETTER CHOICE.

If you don't yet have a dog but are expecting a baby or already have a little one, you consider getting an adult dog over a young one. Regardless of an individual dog's ten, a more mature dog will be safer and make fewer demands on your time, energy and pat. mature dog has a known temperament, and her reactions to the baby will be predictable. 1. is too much risk of harm to any youngster with the playful puppy's mouthful of razor teeth. puppy, even from the best breeder, can also be a carrier of parasites (see page 379).

Although it can be tempting to get a puppy, or to see a baby together with a puppy, the cards are stacked against you. Consider the strain of trying to train the pup while coping with a small child.

INTRODUCE YOUR DOG TO SOME CHILDREN.

Your dog may know nothing about children. If you have a dog who hasn't been exposed to children, then she has a big shock coming! If your dog is already grown up, then it may be even harder to adjust to the different ways that children move and speak.

Pick a child or two whom you know to be fairly calm and reasonable. Obviously, you'll want to talk to the parents first, and then to the children. Tell them you'd like to use them to help you make your dog friendlier to kids.

Bring your dog to a meeting place away from home, so you don't have any territorial issues. With your dog on a leash, stand with the dog near the children and talk to them, explaining why they are meeting the dog and that you need their help. If you are at ease with the children, that should usually put your dog at ease.

Watch your dog around a child or two and see whether she is eager to be part of their play, or cowers and cringes at the sound and touch of a child. Does the dog flatten her ears, tuck her tail, look worried or not behave as her usual self in other ways? If that is the case, then you need to respect that and give that dog some distance from children.

◆ Give the Children Some Rules to Guide Their Encounter.

Do not have the kids approach the dog. Explain to them that your dog is shy about kids, maybe a little nervous, so she needs to be able to come over and check them out in her own good time. Tell the children not to make fast movements or loud, screechy kinds of sounds. These movements can frighten the dog, who might even think she's being attacked.

Very important: the kids need to be told that they must not stare at her. Explain that direct eye contact is really rude in the dog world. And it can make some dogs want to fight.

If the dog seems uncomfortable or tense, tell the kids to ignore her—to really pretend she isn't there, to not even look at her. Give the children some biscuits or other treats that they can toss toward the dog.

DOGS WITH A HISTORY OF BEHAVIOR PROBLEMS

These dogs are a particular risk with children. You have to give special consideration to whether such dogs should be allowed to mingle with children.

Aggressive dogs can harm a child without much warning. Even if their aggression problems have been previously resolved, it may only take something that raises the stress level—a new situation, with unfamiliar children—to provoke a dog who had problems before.

CHILDREN WITH A HISTORY OF BEHAVIOR PROBLEMS

These kids are at special risk: ensuring that their interactions are safe and healthy demands a great deal of time and energy from parents (who may already be maxed-out on being vigilant and "hands-on" in various other areas of child-rearing and dog-tending).

Consider what a dog's quality of life is going to be like in a situation in which he may be constantly monitored, corrected, shut away, etc. There are some conditions that can predispose children to have difficulties with dogs.

CHILDREN AT RISK WITH DOGS

❑ Children with attention deficit disorder, oppositional defiance disorder or conduct disorder.
❑ Children who are physically or mentally challenged.
❑ Children who have been abused or are abusers.

Ways You Can Protect Children with Dogs

Children will copy the way adults behave toward a dog, just as they mimic everything around them. So make sure that the children who might be in your dog's life do not raise their voices or their hands to a dog . . . which means making sure that no adults are ever seen showing overt anger or aggression to any animal.

❑ Children who already own a dog can be a problem, because their familiarity can make them so comfortable around dogs that they are casual around unknown dogs. These children may not know anything about the warning signs and signals that dogs send to other dogs and to people. A dog's natural tendency is to give himself some room rather than having to go on the offensive, but you have to teach children "canine body language."
❑ Kids often aren't taught—or forget to remember—the way to approach and handle a dog. They may provoke a dog by petting him while he is eating. They may startle a dog that is sleeping. It's rare for a young child to be able to see things from another point of view—especially that of a pet. They have to be taught to do this.
❑ An older dog may have little patience. As a dog ages, he may feel lousy part of the time. A senior citizen can have the pain of arthritic joints, eyesight and hearing that are failing, and slower responses. A child can't understand the discomforts of aging—so he doesn't perceive that a dog wants to be left alone.

- Some children may tease and taunt a dog for fun. Any teasing is ultimately no fun for a dog, even if he seems to go along with it at first. Excessive teasing can cause a dog to lash out in frustration. Nine- to twelve-year-old children may experiment with the limits of a dog's tolerance—by restraining the dog and then calling him, by playing monkey-in-the-middle or by getting the dog to bark or growl by holding a toy or treat just out of his reach. Children need to be taught that these games are cruel: one way to do this would be to ask how they would feel if someone did the same thing to them.

- Identify potentially dangerous situations. An adult needs to continually assess possible risks for injury or inappropriate behavior between the dog and the child—situations that change as a child gets older. By anticipating problems, you can minimize the risks. This may mean that dogs and children should be separated at high-risk times such as birthday parties, when you might want to consider restricting the dog to a locked bedroom—locked so that no child can inadvertently open the door.

- If a new child is involved or if the child(ren) or the dog are tired, sick or upset, monitor the children's interactions with the dogs.

- Take your child to obedience training classes with you and the dog. Depending on how young (and short) the child is, you might want to hold the leash at the same time so that when the child gives a command—"sit," "down" and "come" are the ones he can try—you also have hold of the leash to reinforce the dog's compliance. However, at the end of the day, the dog has to pay attention to the child, not to you (even though *you* are the one with treats). Once the dog does accept and obey commands from the child, the child will automatically be in a higher position than the dog.

- Desensitize your dog to childish interruptions. Without children actually around, you should do a practice every few days of teaching your dog to accept surprises. When he's eating, put your hand near the bowl and put some treats in with his food and pat him; when he's sleeping, gently wake him up and give him a little rubbing, then leave him alone again; when he's chewing on a toy, slowly take it away from him, give him praise and a treat, then give him back the toy. Don't do any of this too frequently or you'll wear out your welcome, but teaching your dog to happily accept anything a human does around him or to him will prepare him for the random behavior of a child. (It's a good habit to practice even without children in the picture.)

- Grown-ups have to pay attention to any situation that creates stress for the child *or* the dog. Some examples are a car ride for the dog and the child, strangers visiting, holiday events and parties, the arrival of a strange dog. Change can raise anxiety levels—death, birth or an illness in the family, moving or environmental catastrophy. Parents who have difficulty setting safe boundaries for their children's behavior toward the family dog may wind up with a pet who has become fearful and anxious—and so "on edge" that he may be easily provoked to bite any child.

- Do not expect a child under six to be responsible for a pet or to have a full understanding of the risks involved in handling a dog.

SALMONELLA RISK TO YOUNG CHILDREN AROUND DOG'S RAWHIDE

There have been reports of salmonella found on imported beef-derived rawhide dog chew toys. Generally, this link between people and dog chews has not been considered as a potential source of salmonella. However, in tests done in England, salmonella was found to have survived the processing of rawhide chews from China and Thailand.

Although it is not a danger to dogs, salmonella is a common cause of gastrointestinal infection in people. Younger children might be at the most risk of being exposed, because they are frequently on the floor and can be in closer contact with the dog and the rawhide chews. Keep these treats out of children's hands, and wash your own hands thoroughly in hot water after handling rawhide.

Kids and Dog-Care Responsibilities

NOTE: *For a more detailed discussion of these issues, please see the special chart on "Stages of Childhood Development and Interactions with Dogs" on page 482 later in this chapter.*

There are trainers who believe that it is a poor idea to push children to take responsibility for the family dog; they propose that dogs should be completely the responsibility of the adults until the children become teenagers. These trainers believe that children do not have the self-control or maturity to have full responsibility for another being's welfare. They say that children should have no more than a secondary role in dog care. More likely this should be determined on an individual basis, depending on your child's age and personality and what the demands of dog care are in your location and lifestyle.

GROOMING

From age seven you can allow a child to do some light grooming, such as brushing the dog— although you should be there the whole time to make sure the brushing is done gently and in the direction the hair grows.

Toenail clipping is still way out of a child's league. However, a child can assist you by patting and soothing the dog while you cut the nails.

A child can help you give the dog a bath or shower (for how to do this yourself, see page 416 in Chapter Twelve, "Grooming Your Dog").

WALKING THE DOG

From age eight to ten, some kids are strong and mature enough to walk a dog alone—although obviously that depends on the size, strength and obedience training of the dog and how many potential problems there are in your neighborhood. Picking up after the dog and making sure he doesn't relieve himself on people's property is something you can explain to your child, and he can also learn by watching you pick up after the dog.

MEALTIMES

Feeding the dog can become something the child does when asked by the time she is nine or ten, as long as you have a dog who has already accepted his young mistress as "above" him in the family hierarchy. If you "free-feed" (see "Nutrition" feeding options on page 443), then your child can replenish the kibble in the bowl as needed and wash the bowl out. As with almost anything at this age, you still need to ask whether it was done and then check to make sure it really was. If you customarily give your dog two meals a day, then you may need to assist the child if anything needs to be added to the bowl, or any part of the chore requires more height.

Warning Signs of Dog Distress Around: Kids

- Acute change in normal behavior: withdrawal, circling, patrolling.
- Changes in vocalization: barking, whining or abnormal sounds.
- Change in appetite, especially food-guarding or refusal to eat with child present.
- Changes in how much the dog is sleeping or resting, and new locations.
- Increased reactivity: barking/growling/patrolling/lunging in new situations (or with less provocation).
- Gastrointestinal signs associated with stress: vomiting, diarrhea.
- Separation anxiety exhibited only when left with children: vocalization, destructiveness, elimination, salivation, increase or decrease in activity.
- Outright aggression in the presence of children.

New Babies and Dogs

If your dog is good with children, this is no indication of how he might be with an infant. Infants are different than children. Children are perceived as humans by dogs, whereas a baby might not be, as strange as that may seem. The way infants move, smell and sound is so different from adults and even small children that some dogs don't easily make the connection.

A CARDINAL RULE: Never leave a baby or a small child unattended with a dog for any amount of time. Think of a dog as a swimming pool with no fence. A dog is an "attractive nuisance" from the point of view of a child; the combination of the two of them is an accident waiting to happen.

- ❏ Dogs are curious about babies, especially if they've had little exposure to them. Most dogs adapt quickly. However, for safety's sake, assume that your dog's reaction will be negative.
- ❏ Even if your dog has been friendly to children in the past, *assume nothing*. You will have a sense of your dog's attitude by how he has acted toward babies he has seen on the street or wherever he might have encountered strollers or baby carriers.

 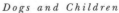

- A diaper pail that locks is essential—female dogs are prone to raid diaper buckets because it is a natural female instinct to lick up the feces and urine of puppies to keep the sleeping area clean. If a dog ingests any part of a diaper she can choke or develop bowel obstructions from the made-to-expand-with-liquid diaper material. The smell of a dirty diaper can invite a dog to investigate the stroller or crib—and maybe tip it over, resulting in a screaming baby, scared dog, or worse.
- If the baby is screaming, crying or waving her arms and legs, these are all behaviors that can elicit an investigative, predatory or play-leap reaction in a dog. A struggling, crying infant can seem like wounded prey (more in the following section on the "prey reaction to babies").

Special Warning: Baby Swings have triggered serious attacks. The motion has activated the instinct to chase prey with tragic results.

A DOG WITH "PREY RESPONSE" TO BABIES

A frightening warning: most of the newborns attacked by dogs are under a week old. Never, ever leave any dog unattended with any baby at any time—and that includes not leaving a dog free in the house unless the baby is behind a firmly closed door.

The biggest problem with infants and dogs is that the dog may fail to recognize the baby as a human being. A baby doesn't sound, look or smell like you. A dog may perceive a baby as prey—as something to chase or hunt. Dogs who are predatory often have problems with babies, but dogs with a variety of other personalities can cause problems, too. You have to view a dog as a potential danger to an infant until the dog has proven himself to be consistently neutral, gentle or friendly.

◆ Dogs with a History of Aggression Need Special Caution.

Does your dog react negatively to mailmen, delivery people, visitors and/or other dogs? Even a dog who is totally gentle and protective of a child might accidentally hurt the child if the little one comes between the dog and whatever makes the dog behave aggressively. The consequences of a negative reaction are very serious.

Easily startled dogs Dogs who startle or seem alarmed when they are awakened need close supervision in the presence of children. These dogs are highly sensitive to interruptions or surprises—and those go hand-in-hand with children.

Prey response is the most dangerous—and potentially deadly—reaction that a dog can have to a baby. If your dog has been bred to chase and kill small game—or you have seen this kind of behavior from your dog—you are especially at risk for your dog perceiving your baby as such. This is especially important if your dog has had little or no exposure to infants.

◆ Remedies for Prey Response

Significant daily exercise to tire out such a dog is the first step. Generally speaking, a tired dog is always a happier, more relaxed, less reactive dog.

There are medications that have measurable antipredatory effects. These medications are the antidepressant amitriptyline and the anxiety-reducing drug buspirone. These medications have to be used at the same time you work with a trainer to modify the dog's behavior, for example, long "down, stays" in the baby's room (always supervised), etc. Some dogs must stay on the medication for longer to get the desired effect—it will wear off once discontinued. A professional trainer will help you evaluate if your dog needs to stay on it indefinitely, which you should also discuss with your vet.

CLEANING UP BEFORE THE BABY ARRIVES

Both your dog and the environment in your house and yard should be spick-and-span before the baby comes home. Your dog should have a thorough checkup, including tests of his stool for worms of any kind. There are some parasites that can be passed from a dog to a child: ask your vet. Make sure there are no fleas in the house before the baby comes home. Any treatment of the house or carpets needs to be done well in advance and then fully aired out before a newborn can safely come into the environment.

◆ Make Sure the Yard Is Kept as Sanitary as Possible.

This means that if there are dog droppings on your property, they should be picked up on a daily basis so that parasites cannot breed.

◆ Do You Have a Large Amount of Dog Feces to Deal With?

If you have a large dog, or more than one dog, you may want to get a "Doggie Dooley" or some version thereof. This is an above-ground or slightly sunken septic system for animal waste. It eliminates any need to handle the feces because, with a long-handled scoop, the stool can be picked up and deposited right into the disposal system. There are several different models, none of them expensive, all available through the KV Vet Supply catalog (800)423-8211 or wherever you get pet supplies.

PRACTICING AHEAD OF TIME FOR THE BABY'S ARRIVAL

Begin acclimating your dog to the changes ahead by preparing months before the baby arrives. Major changes to the routine of the household or the environment itself take time to adjust to, and some dogs finds it more difficult than others. By introducing the changes in advance, you allow your dog to adjust without directly connecting the baby to the upheaval and the stress of adjusting.

To keep the "baby preparedness exercises" positive and non-aversive, think of them as games, so they're fun for you and the dog. Remember to reward your dog with enthusiastic praise *immediately* after she gives you a good response.

◆ Basic Obedience

Good canine manners makes it better for everyone in the household. "Sit," "stay," "down" and "come" are all commands that the dog needs to know and obey reliably. Pretty good is not good enough. It is a false sense of control and safety.

- ❑ Be realistic and honest about your dog's obedience reliability. When excited by your coming home with the baby, will he give you a good "sit" or "sit, stay"? Does he do that when there are other kinds of exciting stimuli?
- ❑ Take an obedience class or obedience refresher. Doing this can only serve you well. Even if you feel that your dog's responses to commands are already snappy, classes will provide

more outside distractions and more chances to be wound up and still listen to your commands. The class has to be fun, pleasant and based on the positive-reward concept. The dog must feel good about himself, and you, because you want him to have positive feelings and responses to the baby. The goal of sharpening his obedience is for the dog to like and respect you and the baby—not to comply out of fear. Reliable obedience should lessen confusion for the dog and reduce any negative, frightened emotions for you.

◆ Expose Your Dog to Other Babies

If you have friends with babies, try to spend time with them (with your dog on a leash, light muzzle or whatever control you feel you might need if you have any qualms). If there aren't any babies in your life, go to sitting areas in parks, shopping areas or wherever you think there might be babies around. Babies babbling—and especially crying—can take some getting used to. The more practice a dog has, the better she'll be at dealing with those sounds in her own house.

◆ Put the Dog on a Long "Down, Stay" in the Nursery.

Some trainers feel that practicing this in the month or two before the baby arrives can give you some control over a dog whose exuberance worries you. You can practice the same long (even up to half an hour, let's say) "down, stays" when you are feeding the baby later. Start when you are months away from your baby's arrival with rules such as not allowing the dog to hang out in the nursery alone.

◆ Practice Baby Activities While Dog Is on a Sit or Down and Stay.

Have a doll that you pick up wrapped in a blanket, so it is visually realistic for the dog. Cradle the doll in your arms, walk around, sing to it and especially *talk to the doll* the way so many of us do to babies: high pitched, sing-song . . . because that is often the same voice people use with dogs.

Play recordings of a baby fussing and crying ahead of time—many dogs have trouble adapting to those sounds. Playing a tape should help desensitize the dog.

Reward the dog with praise and goodies for staying in a "sit" or "down" while you're doing baby stuff.

THE BABY'S HOMECOMING

Unless you have a home birth, the baby's homecoming is usually when he is a day or two old. If so, before the baby gets home, have someone take clothing that the baby has worn or even blankets that have been around him back to your house. This allows the dog to get accustomed to the smell before the baby is actually presented to her—and with a dog's sense of smell being as acute as it is, this preparation should make the actual meeting less intense for the dog.

◆ The Baby's Mother Should Greet the Dog without the Baby Present.

Another family member should carry the little one, or, ideally, the baby should optimally be put down in his room first, before the dog is brought in to be with the family. Let some time pass before the baby and dog meet so that all the bustle of arriving home and the sights, sounds and smells of the infant being in the house have had a chance to sink in.

- ❑ Keep the dog in a separate room or outside. Bring baby items to the dog in the first few hours so he gets used to the odor of the little one.
- ❑ The first introduction can take place when both the baby and dog are calm and quiet.
- ❑ One parent should focus on the baby, the other on the dog.
- ❑ The dog should be on a leash and on a "sit, stay" or "down, stay."
- ❑ If you doubt the dog will hold a "stay" or think he may leap at the baby, use a muzzle or halter-style collar (that the dog is already used to) so that you have complete, calm control over the dog.
- ❑ Start with a ten-foot separation. Either the parent holding the dog or the one holding the baby should come forward a step at a time, calm and collected, unemotional.
- ❑ If the dog remains calm, he can sniff the baby—but not up close. He should gather sensory information from a safe distance.
- ❑ If the dog seems agitated, or too excited, don't go that far forward. If the dog hesitates or balks, call it a day. Remove the dog from the nursery—always pleasant, never harsh. No bad feelings from you: keep it relaxed and simple.
- ❑ It may take a number of at-a-distance introductions before they can come closer together if your dog has prey drive, aggression or fear issues.
- ❑ The dog should eventually be allowed to sniff the baby up close, but only after as many slow introductions as are necessary to reduce the dog's excitement to practically nothing.
- ❑ She can be allowed off-leash around the baby once you feel the dog's interest level isn't too high—but when in doubt, WAIT. Everything to do with the dog and the baby should be super-cautious and unrushed.
- ❑ The ultimate goal is to reach a point when the dog shows no interest in the baby's various odors and noises—when the dog no longer stares fixedly at the baby and instead goes about her own business in the baby's presence. Almost every dog will eventually get to this point—for some dogs it can take weeks, even months, while others will get there in hours or days. Don't get frustrated if your dog takes longer—your negative emotions can get in the way of your relationship with the dog and the dog's perception of your baby.
- ❑ Until that neutral plateau is reached, keep a secure door between the baby and the dog when you are not right there, including at night.
- ❑ If you want to leave baby's door open but are fearful about your dog having access to the room, put a baby gate there so the dog can't get in, but you can hear if the baby cries. Another option is to get a baby monitor so you can hear what is going on all the time no matter where you are in the house, even with the baby's door shut.
- ❑ When changing the baby or in any other situation in which the baby might move around or vocalize in a tantalizing way, put your dog in a "down, stay" or "sit, stay" at some distance and reward with praise and tidbits, so she associates positive feelings with being around the baby at a distance.

✦ Do Not Isolate the Dog.

If you are feeding, bathing or changing the baby, do not shut out the dog.

Include the dog verbally, especially if you normally say silly little things to the dog and "explain" things to her.

Give the dog a special rawhide or other treat only at certain times—the times when you're with the baby. This way, the dog will associate a yummy treat with being in the baby's presence. Remember to wash your hands with hot water after handling rawhide.

VISITING SOMEWHERE WHERE THERE IS A DOG

If you're taking your baby to a home with a dog(s), be aware (because the dog's owner might not be) that these dogs may have any or all of these reactions, especially if they aren't used to infants. So either do not go to those homes, or request that the resident dogs be kept away from where you are, without offending the owner. You'll be doing everyone a favor.

CHOICES IN HOW TO EXPRESS AFFECTION TO THE BABY OR DOG

✦ Give the Dog Positive Attention Only Around the Baby.

One theory about how to encourage your dog to love the baby is to give him affection and treats only in the presence of the baby, so that he associates the child with good things. It may be that for some canine individuals this is what helps them over the hump to accept and love the baby down the road. You might want to consider it.

✦ Separate Dog and Baby Times Entirely.

Sometimes people do the opposite of the above theory and think of "dog time" and "baby time" as mutually exclusive. This point of view comes from the idea that lavishing the dog with affection and treats will satisfy him, reassure him and keep him from being possessive of you or competitive with the baby. Only you know if this is the best solution for your dog.

"SIBLING RIVALRY"

You may wonder whether giving the dog special time alone will keep him from feeling jealous about being excluded from the time with the baby. This theory may have some value, except that so much of your time is probably baby time, it seems to make more sense to integrate the two and just make it all part of normal life. You have enough to worry about with a new baby without adding the guilt/obligation to the dog.

Keep your perspective on all this: the baby is part of your family and the focus of your attention at least in the early period, and for many couples this was also true of the dog when they first got him. But if you don't view this as a "sibling-rivalry situation"—in which the dog and baby are in some kind of competition for your time and love—then it won't be that way.

✦ You Will Make the Family Structure You Want.

Try to realize that you are in control of the new family structure that will evolve with your pets and your baby—it will become whatever you make it. Dogs are part of our families, they have adapted to us as their "pack." However, we can never forget that down deep, a dog's hardwiring is as a member of a *wolf* pack, and there is no sibling rivalry among wolves. The basic issues for dogs (and the wolves they are descended from) are about pecking order within the pack. On top is the alpha pair (you, or you and your partner), and everyone else is in descending order.

You should be able to shape your newly enlarged family to suit yourself—unless you have a dog with a really difficult personality, or one who has been so hopelessly indulged (by you!) that he cannot tolerate having to wait or not being the center of things.

Nugget of Wisdom: In any situation with your canine family member, try to keep in mind that you are not the tail being wagged by the dog.

Toddlers and Dogs

PROBLEMS ARISE WHEN THE BABY REACHES THE WALKING/CRAWLING STAGE.
Most of the problems that come up between dogs and toddlers happen when the babies reach around a year old. The just-crawling, learning-to-walk stage in babies is probably the toughest for the dogs who are sharing a house with them. The ages from eighteen months to about four years old are the most challenging time to integrate a child with a dog.

Toddlers move and gesticulate and propel themselves in unpredictable, sometimes bizarre ways. These little people make an ever-changing array of noises as they totter and stagger around, trying to explore everything in their path. Like sleeping dogs. Or the eyes and noses of wakeful ones. Or the tails and toes.

You can almost imagine one dog telling another, "Be scared . . . be *very* scared" where toddlers are concerned.

Some terrible accidents between dogs and toddlers occur, and they are all avoidable—most are provoked by normal toddler behavior that causes a dog to bite the child's face. These tragedies are often followed by the discarding or putting to sleep of a perfectly nice dog that was doing what came naturally to her when pushed and provoked by a small human. Parents call the incidents "unprovoked," but if they were watching closely, and knew even the basics of what matters to dogs, it should have been obvious that a day of reckoning would have to come.

HOW TODDLERS PROVOKE DOGS

- ❑ *Competition over valued items:* The child interferes with the dog's toys, bed, crate, usual resting area or the water or food bowls.
- ❑ *Physical challenges:* The child pats the dog on his head, holds his muzzle, hugs him around the torso or neck, gets hold of the feet, leans on the dog's back, tries to pull the dog by his collar or otherwise force him to do something he doesn't want to do.
- ❑ *No escape for the dog:* If a dog becomes cornered or otherwise cannot escape the unwanted advances of a toddler, the dog may snap, lashing out with his teeth.

No toddler is safe around any dog if neither of them is under control. The child has to be behind a baby gate, or the dog has to be in a crate or on a leash held by an adult who is monitoring the child's every move.

Toddlers and young children make advances to dogs that may seem cute to onlookers but to a dog can seem threatening and unacceptable: a toddler careens over to a dog, wants to grab it around the neck in an unbalanced hug or comes right down at the dog's face with her lips ready to plant a kiss.

These actions aimed right at the dog's head, a most vulnerable area, can elicit a spontaneous defensive snap or bite. Often the dog has been left with no other choice but to use her teeth, because the signals she has been giving about backing off have been ignored.

◆ The Crate as Sanctuary

If you can teach a small child that the dog's crate is off-limits, then you have protected that crate as a true den and "bolt hole" for the dog. Make that crate as cozy and inviting to the dog as possible—put a nice folded quilt in there along with a favorite toy.

If the crate becomes someplace that the dog can retreat to in the spirit of prevention and avoidance, then your toddler and pet can cohabit more safely.

Below you will find a chart of warning signals that a dog will give to a child that he finds to be menacing. At each step, as the dog perceives more incoming behavior from the toddler—or as the dog's prior warnings have been ignored—the danger of a biting incident increases.

DOG WARNINGS TO TODDLERS

- ❐ The dog tries to move away.
- ❐ He tries to move again, maybe with a menacing stare.
- ❐ He gives a low growl.
- ❐ He snaps at the air near the child.
- ❐ He bites at the incoming toddler's hand or face.

Special Section:
Stages of Childhood Development and Interactions with Dogs

(NOTE: *"She" refers to the baby, "he" refers to the dog.*)

Newborn to Six Months

An infant's arrival into a family changes the routines of every member. The dog often becomes low man on the totem pole, and the meals, attention and exercise to which he is accustomed may be altered or temporarily suspended.

The baby brings new sounds—crying, babbling, cooing—that initially can be disturbing for some dogs. There will also be new sounds from the adults responding to the infant—who will often use a happy, high-pitched voice for the baby that is similar to the tone they had previously used for the dog. This can confuse or disorient him at first.

As the baby's motor skills develop, she may reach out and grab the dog. This can be startling or painful to him. By six months, the baby will be starting to sit up by herself. She will perhaps be pulling herself along the floor, preparing to crawl. There is potential for interchange between the dog and the baby that can lead to biting. Most dog bites to infants are in the head, face and neck, and it is fair to assume that the vast majority could have been avoided altogether if adults understood the danger of the baby propelling herself into the dog's space.

Dogs who are anxious, or have shown uncertainty in new social situations, will need special monitoring and assistance in adapting to a new baby.

Six to Twenty-four Months

A baby's motor skills are developing rapidly—she is crawling, then cruising (using objects for support) and eventually walking. A child's curiosity and mobility can cause problems for a dog. A child learning to walk is unsteady and can be knocked down by a dog or his wagging tail. A toddler will motor right over anything in her path—including a sleeping dog of any size or temperament.

A dog often becomes the object of a toddler's curiosity: the pet's most vulnerable and tender parts are often prime targets for poking, prodding, pinching or mouthing. A dog has to contend with this new behavior, which occurs at unpredictable times and with varying intensity.

Dogs that do best in a predictable household may handle these changes poorly. Dogs who have controlled their fear or pain around a pre-toddler may feel provoked now, threatened by the same child's evolving behaviors. He may signal discomfort by growling or snapping at the baby for grabbing or fondling him. Unless parents are observant and vigilant in picking up the dog's reactions and removing the baby, the dog may be forced into action because his warnings have been ignored. The dog bite may seem unprovoked but it rarely is: an adult has to pick up early signaling of the dog's discomfort.

Two to Three Years Old

The toddler moves into the preschool years with growing curiosity and motor skills. Dogs' toys may be taken . . . their food messed with . . . their dog beds appropriated . . . their sleep rudely interrupted. Children of these ages do not consider the consequences of their actions or generalize from one incident to another. They don't necessarily learn from their mistakes, so a dog's signaling may become more pronounced.

◆ Small Dog Care Responsibilities Can Begin at This Age

The child can help you wash the dog's water or food bowls, and can help carry dog food into the house. The child can help tidy up the dog's toys and sleeping area(s). Children love to imitate their parents: you cannot start too young to connect some work and responsibility with having a dog in the family.

◆ Caution: Do Not EVER Allow a Toddler NEAR a Dog's Food.

This has been mentioned elsewhere but cannot be stressed strongly enough. Do not make the perilous mistake of being cavalier about the dangerous mix of small children around a dog and his food. No matter how much you may trust your dog, you cannot trust a child to do what you expect or to follow your rules precisely—toddlers are exploring the world around them and often have no real understanding of the safety rules you make. Some dogs can misinterpret the presence of a child near their food and become aggressive. This can even happen with a dog that has previously accepted the child near his food dish. Children are quick and unpredictable: the child could suddenly squat down near the bowl or put her hand in it. And on the other side of the dish you've got a dog whose natural instinct is to growl menacingly and then snap and finally bite to protect his meal.

Even handing treats to a dog is hazardous for a young child, unless you want to cup your hand around the child's and control how that tempting item is offered. For example, you can tell a two-year-old to give Trixie a cookie, but the child may offer the biscuit and then retract it (as if teasing, but really just not understanding what the food means to the dog). Or the child may put the cookie to her own mouth, which is eye level with the dog's teeth. Or she may give the biscuit and then drop it. If the child tries to pick it back up, the dog's teeth and the child's hand could arrive on that biscuit at the same moment.

Three to Five Years Old

As the baby's new playmates begin to enter the picture, they bring with them smells, noises and activity that are alien to the dog. For a dog that is already suffering from fear or uncertainty, new children only intensify those feelings. Such dogs need somewhere safe they can go. If there isn't an area set aside in the house where a dog can't be bothered, he may respond aggressively.

At this age, most children stand above the eye level of a medium-sized dog. This means that for the first time in the child's life (and what has been a large part of the dog's life) they are at a turning point: the child who has been lower-ranked in the family (the dog's "pack") will no longer be subordinate to the dog.

This is the period of your child's growth when you can take preventive measures to ensure that your dog accepts your child's increasing authority. The dog should not be cornered into a defensive-aggressive posture, which might cause him to bite. Depending on how this transition is handled, a dog can gracefully accept this change in his rank (a fluctuation that would happen naturally in a wolf pack), or he can feel threatened by this major change in the child's size and conduct.

This is the time in your child's life when you want to encourage her to begin taking a leadership position with the dog. How the child makes that change is crucial to her success in continuing a positive relationship with the dog throughout their life together. To be sure that the change happens in a positive way, you need to be present in even the most routine interactions between your child and the dog. The change in the balance of power between them will be reflected in even the smallest interchanges, and your intercession may be needed.

Your child will follow your lead in how she relates to the dog: she will mimic your body language and tone of voice when dealing with the dog. For this reason it's extremely important that you realize that you are a role model and always being watched. Your child will be watching everything you do: dealing with your dog in a firm, gentle, calm manner will promote that same behavior from your child.

Promote any behavior that puts the child in a dominant position above the dog, but always with a knowledgeable adult present to monitor the exchange. Simple activities like putting on the dog's leash to go for a walk are a good beginning—but be right there to make sure everything is done in a gentle, calm way so that the child's actions don't cause resistance from the dog. The child can go with you on the walk—which she may already have been doing—and you can let her hold the leash for a short while when you are in an area where there's nothing that could entice the dog to bolt.

If your dog is already obedience-trained (which he certainly should be if the child is older than three), you can help the child to practice making the dog do the simplest things, such as "come" and "sit." However, don't expect excellent compliance from the dog, since a child is too small in stature and personality to truly dominate. But if you teach a child to stand still and tall and hold up a forefinger while saying "Sit" in a firm, pleasant voice, the dog actually may sit!

Teaching the child to immediately give sincere praise to a dog for any attempt to please her is as important as any obedience the child could get out of the dog. "Good boy" is probably the most important thing a child can learn: that warm praise from his little buddy can make all the difference to a dog who is still amazed that the baby is turning into a boss of him!

Another obedience command that comes in handy for smaller children is one that gives them the ability to stop a dog from being too rambunctious around them. Practice with your child standing tall and still. She should hold up a hand, palm outward and facing the dog, while saying "Off." The instant the dog stops the offensive behavior (barking, pushing or mouthing the child) is when the child needs to put "Gooood boy" to use. If a child learns the sequence of *request* (said only once, followed by a patient wait for a response) and *praise* when the dog responds, right there you'll have more than some people ever learn about communicating successfully with their dogs in a lifetime.

Go slowly. Don't expect too much from either the dog or the child. They both may pleasantly surprise you.

Six to Eight Years Old

At this developmental stage, a child has high energy and needs to feel control over her environment. Age six is quite particular and can sometimes be an especially difficult developmental age. A child can ride an emotional roller coaster as she outgrows babyhood and begins more serious schooling. Parents often try to give the child more autonomy and less supervision as the child experiments with being less dependent on them. At this age, a child can be unpredictable; it is best not to burden the child with absolute expectations about dog care. Let your child take on as many responsibilities as she wants.

During this period, kids often begin to make up games with the dog, often with a teasing element: monkey-in-the-middle (tossing a ball between two kids); putting a leash on the dog, who is then pulled into various fantasy games; teasing the dog with a high-pitched voice; dangling a toy over the dog's head; or playing tug-of-war with a toy. These are common behaviors of children this age, who actually love their dogs—they view what they're doing as "only playing." The highest rate of dog-bite injury can be found among five- to nine-year-old boys. The above-mentioned "games" may be responsible for that statistic. This kind of play has to be stopped, with an explanation of why, and other games substituted that don't tease the dog.

The dog should no longer be threatened by the child being near his food—but if he is still being protective of his territory, see page 538 in the "Problems Great and Small" chapter for suggestions on how to desensitize your dog to your hands being near his food bowl.

SIX TO EIGHT YEARS OLD—DOG-CARE RESPONSIBILITIES

From age seven you can allow a child to brush the dog. Although toenail clipping is still way out of a child's league, she can assist you in giving a bath or doing more elaborate grooming—after you have taught her the best method to use for your breed, of course.

Nine to Twelve Years Old

This preadolescent phase may be the first time that some children really are thinking about how others feel—realizing how their actions affect others.

At this stage, kids can take on more responsibility for the dog, including feeding, exercising and grooming. However, it is also a time when children indulge in provocative teasing, if they weren't taught not to when they were younger. Holding a toy or treat out of reach, restraining the dog then calling him to come, or "faking" a throw with a ball and then laughing are all ways they can incite the dog to bark or growl. These children—and perhaps their parents—may assume that what they are doing is as fun for the dog as it is for them. That is, until the dog snaps, the child gets bitten and the dog is possibly banished from the family (without anyone having fully understood how they arrived at this sorry moment).

NINE TO TWELVE YEARS OLD—DOG-CARE RESPONSIBILITIES

By age nine or ten, most kids are strong and mature enough to walk the dog alone—unless, of course, the dog is some huge powerhouse without great leash manners. Picking up after the dog and making sure he doesn't relieve himself on others' property is something you can explain to your child at a younger age and practice with her now.

Feeding the dog can become the child's responsibility at nine or ten, as long as you have a dog who has already accepted his mistress as "above" him in the family hierarchy. If you "free-feed" (see for feeding options on page 452), then your child can replenish the kibble in the bowl as needed and the bowl can be washed as needed. As with most anything at this age, you still need to ask whether it was done and then check to make sure it really was. If you customarily give your dog two meals a day, you may need to assist the child if there is anything added to the bowl or if any part of the chore requires more height.

"Scooby's Twenty-five Rules for Kids"

NOTE TO PARENTS: *An encounter between a dog and adult which causes frustration due to a communications breakdown can result in a bite when a child is involved.*

The Humane Society of the United States recommends playacting and practicing dog-related situations with your child as if there were a dog present. Act out situations together with your child. They may save your child's life—or her face. This isn't just about your family dog, since a child will probably encounter many dogs in her life.

The Following Is for Children

This section is just for kids. I call it "Scooby's Rules" because my dog Scooby Doo needed help being nice with children. He is a really, really big, tall dog—some little kids say he's so big he could almost be a small horse. One little girl asked if I had a saddle so she could go for a ride! (I hope you know to never sit on any dog—even a nice big one—because a dog's back isn't as strong as a pony's. Even if you're just trying to have fun, a friendly dog can turn nasty if you try to get on him, because it could hurt or frighten him.)

The reason for "Scooby's Twenty-five Rules for Kids" is that the one thing that used to really frighten Scooby—and this is going to sound crazy—was *children. He was scared of children.* That's kind of weird, huh? Scooby is twice as big as most little kids, so if he was scared of you, it's kind of like the elephant being afraid of the mouse. I guess Scooby is one of those dogs who just doesn't understand smaller people. Since I know other dogs who have this same scaredy-cat problem with kids, I thought I'd better tell kids so they don't get hurt accidentally.

Scooby's trouble feeling comfortable around kids probably happened because he didn't meet any children when he was a little puppy himself. He didn't get a chance to get used to kids because he wasn't around them, so you smaller people were kind of scary to him. People who raise litters are supposed to introduce young puppies to children so they can feel comfortable around people who are young, too. But whoever owned Scooby's mother didn't do it for him when he was a little pup. I couldn't do it because I didn't even get Scooby until he was five months old. I got him at the animal shelter, so I'm not sure what kind of life he had before. The truth is, Scooby is a little bit of a nut. Even though he's such a big guy, he's scared of almost everything: little things like spiders, bigger things like umbrellas, and once a bag of apples rolled across the floor and he hid under the bed! There are probably lots of dogs like my Scooby Doo: they think kids are interesting and cool and fun . . . but a little scary. So it's up to *the children* (that's you) to help dogs be comfortable and happy around them.

You can read Scooby's Rules with your parents, or you can read them by yourself, but it's really important that you tell other people what you read. Even *parents* need your help, because they might know *some* of these things, but not all of them. Also, your brothers and sisters need to know Scooby's Rules, too, especially if this is your first family dog. Maybe you could bring the "Twenty-five Rules for Kids" into your class at school and see if the teacher would like to share them with everyone.

1. **Talk to the owner before you go near a dog.** Ask if the dog is friendly. Ask if the dog is used to children (now you know—but some dog owners might *not* know—that kids are something special for dogs to get used to). You can make friends with dogs in your neighborhood, as long as the owners agree and are there for the first meeting.

2. **Do not pat a dog on top of the head.** A dog may not like that. Your hand coming over the top of his head can be scary. He can't see your hand above him—so he might think you're going to hit him. Touch a dog on his shoulder instead.

3. **Do not look right in the dog's eyes.** Dogs think it is really rude to stare. Your mom probably tells you not to stare at people, too, right? Except the difference with dogs is that staring right at their face makes them think you want to fight with them. So don't stare into a dog's face—if he thinks you want to fight him, who's going to win that fight? The one with the most big, shiny, sharp teeth.

4. **Your own dog is not *all* dogs.** You probably understand a lot about dogs because you are growing up with one. But every dog is different. Don't ever think that "dogs are dogs," and what works with your dog at home will be the same for all dogs.

5. **Hand signals can be dangerous.** Don't try to give a strange dog any commands or use a hand signal you know from your own dog. Most dogs have learned hand signals that tell them what to do—but maybe not the same hand signals that you know for "sit" and "shake." The dog may not like signals he doesn't know; you can never tell how a dog will react to something strange to him.

6. **Do not reach over a fence to pat a dog**—or reach into a crate or into a car window to pat a dog. When a dog is on his own property he wants to protect it, so don't put your hand anywhere near a dog in a car, a kennel or his fenced yard.

7. **If a dog lifts his lip and shows you his teeth,** it means he wants you to go away. Right away. So if any dog ever shows you his teeth, DO what he wants and back off.

8. **A dog who lies down and shows his tummy to you** is showing that he wants to be friends. It means he trusts you. He wants you to rub his tummy, so go right ahead.

9. **Respect a dog's "personal space."** Don't touch or bother a dog when he is eating, sleeping or even peeing!

10. **Don't surprise a dog.** Even the nicest dog can turn mean if he is surprised. If a dog is resting, don't just come up behind him and pat him. A dog can be shocked by something touching him when he doesn't expect it. It could make him scared or angry enough to bite. So let a dog know you're there by saying something before you touch him and make sure he heard you.

11. **An older dog may not feel well,** so just leave him alone. An old dog can feel pain in his body; maybe he doesn't see or hear so well, either. An older dog is like your grandpa or grandma: when people and dogs get older they have some problems and sometimes they just want to be left alone.

12. **Don't bother a mother dog with her puppies.** She does not want to be disturbed. She does not feel safe letting strangers touch her babies or even come near them.

13. **Running right toward** the dog can frighten him. Walk slowly toward a dog; say a few friendly words so he knows you are a nice person.

14. **Not all tail-wagging is happy.** People probably told you that a wagging tail means a dog is happy—but there are times when a wagging tail means something else. If the dog's tail is low and sweeps from side to side, that is a happy wag. But there can be danger if the dog holds his tail high and stiff and it wags only at the tip. If there is another dog around, the dog with the high tail might try to start a fight.

15. **Screaming or yelling loudly can upset a dog.** It's natural for kids to be loud when they're having a good time, but dogs have such good hearing that they can hear a leaf fall off a tree. So loud kid-voices can hurt their ears and put them in a bad mood.

16. **Jumping up and down** can frighten a dog. He can get worried and think you're going to do something bad to him.

17. **Pulling a dog's ears or tail is NEVER a game to a dog.** It's like someone pulling your hair. It hurts: it can make a dog angry.

18. **If you see a dog by himself, he may be lost.** He may be scared or confused, so he could hurt you. Don't try to make friends with him or rescue him. He might be so upset that he tries to chase or bite you. Tell an adult and they'll figure out what to do safely.

19. **Stay away if a dog looks hurt or sick.** When dogs are in pain or don't feel well, they can be mean to people. If a dog has been hit by a car, he could be in a lot of pain, or be in shock. There is a good chance he will bite. Tell an adult, so they can call the owner or get help for the dog.

20. **Stay away from dogs who are fighting or growling.** You could get badly hurt if you get in the middle of two dogs having an argument. Even if it's your own dog, do not put your hand anywhere near them, and do not try to grab a collar. Call an adult for help.

21. **Be a tree when a dog you don't know comes up to you.** Stand straight with your feet together. Hold your hands up under your chin, and hug your elbows in close to your body. Don't let any part of you stick out. Make yourself into one solid pole, like a tree trunk. If no part of you is moving, there's nothing for a dog to bite.

22. **Stand still until the strange dog walks away.** Many dogs will just sniff you and leave. Once the dog walks away, you can walk away. But don't run: move slowly. And don't turn and run—walk backward, slowly. If you run, it makes the dog want to chase you.

23. **Don't run away from a dog.** Running really fast can frighten a dog. It can also make the dog want to chase you or hunt you like a rabbit. And if it's a race between you and a dog, who do you think would win? The one with four legs!

24. **If you are walking, running, skateboarding or riding your bicycle** and a dog growls, barks or runs at you, push something at him to bite instead of you. Push your bike, your backpack or your skateboard at the dog so he bites one of those and not you.

25. **If a dog knocks you down or you fall, be a big solid rock.** Stay very still. If you don't move around, the dog will be less interested in you. Think of yourself as a rock or a boulder. Scrunch up on your knees with your head down, facing the ground. Curl up into a ball with your fists covering the back of your neck and your wrists over your ears. In this position you are less interesting to a dog. If you cover your head and face with your arms, it can protect you from being really hurt.

Things Kids Do That Annoy Dogs

NOTE: *This list is designed to teach parents and other adults about children and dogs so that they can then handle situations their own way. The important thing to know is that it is natural for your dog to react*

poorly. There is nothing wrong with your dog—a dog can react negatively to these activities of normal children.

❏ A child's display of affection can be loud, shrill and spontaneously physical. To a dog, a child's behavior can seem threatening. You need to explain this to the child.

❏ Roughhousing is never a good idea. A child pushing a dog down to the ground, wrestling with a dog, taking a ball out of a dog's mouth—any of these games are likely to wind up with a dog being rough the one way he can: with his teeth.

❏ Children's movements can be rapid and unpredictable. This tendency is similar to the behavior of certain prey—which can confuse a dog or make her more reactive in a situation. Children's food, clothing and body parts are moving targets for dogs, and easier to grab than an adult's.

❏ Whistling or blowing in a dog's face is unpleasant for him. It can provoke aggressive behavior in a dog.

❏ Some children may tease and taunt a dog for fun. Excessive teasing can cause a dog to lash out in frustration. Preteenage kids may experiment with the limits of a dog's tolerance by restraining the dog and then calling him, or getting the dog to bark or growl or whine by holding a toy or a treat just out of his reach.

❏ Some dogs don't like to be patted on the head. A hand coming over a dog's head may be threatening. The best place to touch a dog—once you get the owner's permission—is on the dog's chest or shoulder.

Chapter 15

TRAVELING WITH
A DOG

 Indulge me in a little personal theory about dogs traveling with their people. It's not strictly scientific, but bear with me: it's one perspective on the changing nature of people's alliance with dogs. At the same time, it might shed some light on the kind of reception you can expect when traveling with a dog today.

In the earlier part of the twentieth century, travelers, for the most part, were wealthy aristocrats: stories, photos and paintings often depict them in the company of their canine companions. Then in the second half of the twentieth century, people's dogs were often more a part of the household than the family, so when the people traveled, the dog stayed home, which was technically her place. But as the century wore on, dogs became more enmeshed in the emotional lives of their owners. As we've entered the twenty-first century, dogs have become as important to many of us as any of the *people* in our lives, and many owners do not want to go away without their pooches (for their own sake, more than for the dog's).

More and more people want to take their dogs with them when they travel, but many of the establishments that serve them have not yet caught up with this trend among their clients. It is getting easier to travel in America with a dog because it is good business: as more people want to do this, more hotels are accommodating them. So every time you bring your dog on the road with you, remember that you are paving the way and setting an example for those who will follow. Each of our dogs is an ambassador, so be on your best behavior "on the road."

SOME OF THE TOPICS THAT ARE COVERED IN THIS CHAPTER INCLUDE:

❐ Finding dog-friendly establishments
❐ The practical aspects of staying in a hotel

- ❏ Supplies needed for a traveling dog
- ❏ Dealing with travel problems in a car, including nervousness and carsickness
- ❏ General car safety
- ❏ Options when leaving your dog behind when you travel
- ❏ Outdoor adventure travel with your dog
- ❏ Airplane travel

Finding Dog-friendly Establishments

Turn to the Internet for reliable, timely information. Since more establishments are becoming dog-friendly, the best way to get up-to-date information on what's out there is to turn to the ever-amazing Internet and ask the search engine anything you want: "travel with dogs," "dog-friendly hotels" or whatever comes to mind. Below are some sites to start with.

SOME GOOD TRAVEL WEB SITES

www.petswelcome.com is a Web site that claims 25,000 dog-friendly listings of hotels, ski resorts and campgrounds; www.takeyourpet.com, www.petsonthego.com and www.orbitz.com also have many listings; www.traveldog.com has a variety of information, from camping and back-packing to dog-friendly destinations and lodgings, but there is a fee of $4.95 per month, with longer memberships available.

www.healthypet.com is a list of American Animal Hospital Association–accredited hospitals in the U.S. and Canada.

DOG TRAVEL BOOKS

There are books devoted just to traveling with dogs. California is a leading state in offering dog-friendly travel (just as they are trendsetters in many other areas of American life!). Several travel books focus solely on that state—*The Dog Lover's Companion to California* is a good one, and is actually one of a series that includes Chicago, Colorado, Oregon, New England and New York City.

AAA has a national edition of a pet travel guide in its seventh edition, called *Traveling with Your Pet—the AAA Petbook*. Contact the AAA chapter in your area to get a copy.

There is a series of guidebooks called *On the Road Again with Man's Best Friend* for different regions of the United States. They are now out-of-print (and some information may be out of date) but used copies might still have some value for canine travelers.

SOME DOG-FRIENDLY HOTELS

It's good to know that more American hotels are opening their doors to dogs. They run the gamut from quirky bed-and-breakfast inns that welcome dogs and even have a "paw-print guest register," to high-end hotel chains like the Four Seasons, Loews and Peninsula, where canine guests are as pampered as the human ones. What follows is a sampling of some individuals hotels.

- ❏ **The Peninsula Hotel** in Beverly Hills (310) 551-2888 and other locations, is so pro-dog their resident canine columnist, Billy Bean the Beagle, will give a personal welcome.
- ❏ **The Four Seasons** in New York (212) 758-5700 and various other locations, gives dogs the royal welcome with dog-walking services, a dog bed, a ceramic water bowl, biscuits and a room service pet menu waiting in the room.
- ❏ **The Metropolitan Hotel** (formerly Loews New York) on Lexington Avenue at 51st Street in New York City has a "Privileged Paws" frequent-stay program. After five nights a dog earns a free meal from the pet room-service menu and a complimentary bowl of fluoride-enriched distilled water (the container top doubles as a flying disc toy). After staying ten nights in the hotel, they will upgrade your pet (and you, as well) to a suite. Following fifteen nights, you don't just get the suite but also an hour with a professional walker. (866) 638-7669
- ❏ **Loews Hotels** offer a "Loews Loves Pets" program at the chain's nineteen hotels across the U.S. and Canada that features extensive amenities. The Jefferson, in Washington, D.C., provides local dog-walking routes, a personalized food and water bowl on a puppy place mat, toys, treats and even items you might have forgotten, such as beds, leashes, collars and pooper-scoopers. There is no pet deposit or limit on canine weight. The Jefferson, 1200 16th Street N.W., Washington, D.C. 20036; (800) 235-6397 or www.loewshotels.com/hotels/Washington_Jefferson. Also, The Regency (below) is a premiere Loews Hotel.
- ❏ **The Regency Hotel** (212) 759-4100 on Park Avenue and 60th Street is as fancy as its address suggests. If you travel to hotels that charge around $500 a night, then this is the place for you. They provide a "Puppy pager" to contact you if there's a problem with your dog in the room.
- ❏ **The Hotel Monaco** chain (in San Francisco, Seattle, Denver and New Orleans, among other locations) offers a dog-friendly package that includes gourmet dog cookies, bottled water and a bowl, dog tags and dog beds. (877) 536-0508, or www.kimptonhotels.com
- ❏ **The Ritz-Carlton Hotel** in Chicago (312) 266-1000 is an elegant, expensive hotel that does not charge for dogs and offers them gourmet pet room service and grooming at the Ritz Kennel Salon.
- ❏ **New York City hotels** downtown like *The Soho, TriBeCa grand* and the *W Hotel* gives dogs an enthusiastic welcome.
- ❏ **Starwood Hotels and Resorts** (including Westin, Sheraton and St. Regis) have a PAWS program with every possible amenity.
- ❏ **The Woof Cottages at the Boat Basin** (866) 838-9253 on the island of Nantucket were introduced in 2004 and are specially designed one- and two-bedroom cottages with a pet-friendly environment for dogs and cats. They offer a welcome basket of treats and play toys, a "Nantucket" bandanna, a "Blissful Bed" (which they say is the "ultimate in pet comfort"), food and water bowls, dog-walking services and lists of pet-friendly attractions, vets, dog runs and pet-supply stores on the island.
- ❏ **Motel 6** is a pet-friendly, low-priced lodging chain that offers no enticements to dog owners other than welcoming dogs at no charge which is sometimes all a weary traveler is seeking.

Outdoor Adventure Travel with Your Dog

Call me crazy, but I have never understood people who want to go on hiking trips *without* a dog—it seems like such a waste to me to be in some beautiful mountainous trail and not have a dog leading the way, enjoying herself twice as much as you are!

If you want to get really serious about equipping and training your dog to be a mountaineer, there are little books like *A Guide to Backpacking with Your Dog* by Charlene LaBelle.

SERIOUS HIKING/CAMPING

There are actually well-designed backpacks for dogs that allow them to carry their own supplies. The rule of thumb is that a well-conditioned adult dog can carry as much as a quarter of his weight, as long as it is in a pack that fits well and the weight is distributed evenly. To get your dog accustomed to the pack, practice with it at home before the trip: take her for modest walks with the pack on her back, and increase the distance as she gets accustomed to the feel and physical demands of it.

Other hikers might be skeptical about dogs coming along—one of their issues may be their desire not to step in dog poop—so take a light gardening spade to dig holes and bury your dog's waste if it's anywhere near the path.

♦ **Beware of Strict Rules When Camping with Your Dog in National Parks.**
In a location like Yosemite, where most trails are off-limits to dogs, park rangers will not only give you a summons for having a dog off-leash or on a leash longer than six feet, but they will also impound your dog (and charge you for it) until you leave the park. Rules vary from park to park, so check on each one separately before you go, but take these leash laws seriously—there is a significant fine and threatened jail time if dogs are left off their leash.

For more relaxed rules, try national forests: they are less insistent on leash laws and have more wide-open areas and fewer fellow human visitors.

- ❑ **Tenaya Lodge at Yosemite** (888) 514-2167 is near the south entrance to Yosemite National Park, where dogs are allowed but only on a leash and on paved trails. There are no limits on the size of your dog, but there are some restrictions on where dogs are permitted. All "dog visitors" are housed on the ground floor with sliding glass doors that open onto a grassy area. There is a midweek "Bowser Package" that includes two nights, in-room pet amenities and food and water dishes, and complimentary dry food for around $400 and a $50 nonrefundable pet deposit.
- ❑ **The White Mountain National Forest** in New England encompasses 770,000 acres in northern New Hampshire and Maine and has dog-accessible trails. For information, contact the White Mountain National Forest Supervisor's Office, 719 Main St., Laconia, NH 03246, or call (603) 528-8721. Also visit www.fs.fed.us/r9/white, or contact the Mount Washington Valley Chamber of Commerce, P.O. Box 2300, North Conway, NH 03860, (800) 367-3364, or www.mtwashingtonvalley.org.
- ❑ **The Inyo National Forest** in California is located between Yosemite National Park to the north and Sequoia and Kings Canyon National Parks to the south. This forest is 1.8 million

acres in size, with 400 lakes, 1,200 miles of trails and hundreds of waterfalls. Many trails are considered particularly good for dogs. Dog-friendly lodging is plentiful in the charming ski resort town of Mammoth Lakes. Contact the Inyo National Forest Ranger Station at (760) 873-2400, or visit www.fs.fed.us/r5/inyo; the Mammoth Lakes visitor bureau can be reached toll-free at (888) 466-2666, or at www.visitmammoth.com.

❑ **Uncompahgre National Forest** in Colorado is 100,000 acres where the Rockies meet the San Juan Mountains, a rugged park with roaring rivers, waterfalls and mining towns. Dave's Mountain Tours takes people, with or without dogs, on Jeep excursions through the back country. Contact Uncompahgre National Forest, USDA Forest Service, 2250 Highway 50, Delta, CO 81416, (970) 874-6600, or www.fs.fed.us/r2/gmug; Ouray Visitors Bureau, P.O. Box 145, Ouray, CO 81427, (800) 228-1876, www.ouraycolorado.com or Telluride Chamber of Commerce, P.O. Box 2113, Telluride, CO 81435, (970) 728-9006.

❑ **Superior National Forest** in Minnesota covers 3.9 million acres and contains 4,000 lakes between Lake Superior and the Canadian border. Lots of dog-friendly lodging, camping and restaurants can be found in lakeside Grand Marais. Contact Superior National Forest Supervisor's Office, 8901 Grand Avenue, Duluth, MN 55808, (218) 626-4300, NF@fs.fed.us, www.fs.fed.us/r9/superior or Grand Marais Chamber of Commerce, 13 N. Broadway, Grand Marais, MN 55604, (218) 387-9112, www.grandmaraismn.com.

❑ **European Hiking Tours** are available through the Europaws division of California-based vacation packager Europeds, www.europeds.com.

◆ Some Other Dog-friendly, Outdoors-oriented Locations

❑ **The Tamworth Inn** (15 Cleveland Hill Road, Tamworth Village, NH 03886, (800) 642-7352, e-mail: inn@tamworth.com, Web site: www.tamworth.com) lies between the White Mountains and the Lakes Region of New Hampshire. The town park in the New England village of Tamworth allows dogs, and there are miles of free, groomed cross-country ski trails for snowshoeing and dogsledding (and hiking when the snow melts) that are open to dogs, too.

❑ **The Three Buck Inn** in Tahoe City, California (135 Alpine Meadows Rd. # 34, Tahoe City, CA 96145, (530) 550-8600, e-mail: threebuckinn@juno.com) doesn't just allow dogs, they consider them important guests. There are fancy dog beds, toys, a canine spring-water feeder, an on-site dog-sitter and a fully stocked dog bath in the garage. Near the Alpine Meadows and Squaw Valley ski resorts, as well as Lake Tahoe, which offers swimming in the lake, cross-country skiing, and mountain biking on the river bike path.

❑ **The Ritz-Carlton Bachelor Gulch** at the base of the posh Beaver Creek Mountain in Avon, Colorado (P.O. Box 9190, Avon, CO 81620, (970) 748-6200 or (800) 576-5582, www.ritz carlton.com) has everything for dogs that it does for people, including a fancy spa for both species; treats, a dog bed and bowls in the room for your dog; and all kinds of mountain sports and activities. There is a $40 nightly charge for dogs, but no weight limit.

◆ **Not Quite Camping and Hiking**
Here's a destination that allows you to walk around town with your dog and eat and sleep with her by your side, but doesn't require packing hiking boots for either of you.

❏ **Key West,** in the Florida Keys, has many dog-friendly lodgings, outdoor restaurants that welcome dogs and many popular tourist destinations that welcome them, too. Louie's Afterdeck bar is on Waddell Avenue, right next to Dog Beach, which is just what it sounds like. Key West Chamber of Commerce, 402 Wall Street, Key West, FL 33040, (350) 294-2587, or www.keywestchamber.org.

"SUMMER CAMPS" FOR DOGS AND PEOPLE

There are specialty dogs-with-their-people camping experiences that give new meaning to the phrase "togetherness." I have seen advertisements for a couple of camps that sound great. Camp Gone to the Dogs in Brattleboro, Vermont, has summer and fall sessions that you can check out at www.campgonetothedogs.com, to see if you're made of the sort of stuff that can take all that organized togetherness. There is also www.glenhighlandfarm.com, which is Camp Border Collie & Furry Friends (all breeds welcome), located seventy-five miles southwest of Albany, New York. The camp takes only twenty attendees per week, there is luxury camping or nearby hotels, and the camp fees support the on-site sanctuary for 150 abandoned Border Collies and Border Collie mixes.

Once again, the Internet is probably the most comprehensive source for this, but perhaps even better is another great compilation from the *Whole Dog Journal* of sleepover and day camps in their January 2003 issue. You can request it at (800) 829-9165, but first inquire if they have done a more recent survey since then.

◆ **Things to Consider about Camps**
There are a number of questions you should ask yourself (and then a camp director) when deciding whether a camp is suited to you or even whether camping is the right choice for you and your dog. A camp can be an intense experience, so give some thought to your personality and your dog's and how you both handle a busy planned schedule, close quarters with other dogs and people, and whether you have personal goals that fit with that camp. Some camps specialize, but most include some agility, herding, fly ball, obedience training, hiking, swimming and training for different sports. So if you want to relax and hang out with your dog in an unstructured way, you'll want to choose a camp accordingly, since all those planned activities might overwhelm you.
Accommodations These can range from cabins to motel rooms, tents and dorm rooms. Day camps provide lists of nearby dog-friendly lodgings, as do some sleepover camps for those who want slightly more comfort than they offer.
Children Rules vary from camp to camp, so while many don't allow kids, others may allow children thirteen to seventeen, while 4H camps are specifically for kids. Most camps allow two dogs per person (sometimes with an extra fee for the second dog) and some will reluctantly permit a third dog per human camper. Some camps specialize in puppies.

Do your homework Some questions you should ask include issues you might not consider. How structured is the day? Does the camp have a "theory" or philosophy? What size is the camp (they can range from ten per session to 250) and how large are the individual classes? The answer to both affects you differently if individual attention matters to you and what you want to get out of the experience. Also, once you get there, is there a limit on how many dogs can do any particular class or activity?

Expenses The cost is relative, because if you are going to compare camps, you need to find out what is included in the fee. Is room and board included? Are there any extra charges or equipment you'll need? How much will it cost you to travel there? You cannot know which camp is best for you or offers the best value until you consider all the variables.

Other Things to Consider. Practical suggestions from veteran campers are to choose a low-key camp for your first stay, because it can be an overwhelming experience for many people and dogs. Also, make camp reservations as soon as possible, since many summer programs are booked by January. Many camps also offer a discount for enrolling early and a discount for more than one dog camper.

SUPPLIES FOR TRAVELING DOGS

Even if your dog is really well-behaved at home, she may behave differently in a strange environment. Prepare for this possibility by planning "damage control" ahead of time and you won't be shocked or disappointed. There are things you should take with you when you travel with your pooch—which depends, of course, on how you intend to get there and what your plans are once you arrive.

◆ A Portable Crate
There are several portable crates on the market, one of which stands out as a superior product. The Cabana Crate by DoggoneGood!, a company in San Jose, California, is not inexpensive—it ranges from $100 to $200, depending on size—but it is considered well-constructed and is very easily assembled. To find out more, go to www.doggonegood.com, or call (800) 660-2665.

Bringing your dog's collapsible crate can be really helpful: it will feel safe and familiar to the dog and can prevent mistakes or damage.

◆ A Good Collar
Make sure that your dog's collar fits so that it cannot come off over her head. Do not leave home unless you have your cell-phone number on that tag—not your home phone number. If your dog does get loose, he needs to be wearing your portable number so you can be located.

◆ An Extra Leash
It's a good safety precaution to bring an extra leash in case something happens to yours. Even though there are stores where you can buy an extra leash on the road, you never know what situation you might find yourself in. Also, you might want to bring an extendable and retractable leash, in case there are opportunities to take a walk with more freedom for your dog than an ordinary leash allows.

✦ Microchip

If you are going to be traveling in the United States, consider having a microchip implanted in your dog (see page 209). It's the closest you can get to a guarantee that you will be reunited with your dog if she gets lost.

✦ Food and Bowls

If you're traveling by car, it's fairly easy to bring along an appropriate-sized bag and/or cans of your dog's usual food. You don't want to change brands when traveling, since a change of diet can upset a dog's stomach and give him diarrhea (and that's without even figuring in the stress of travel). If you are flying to a place where your dog's food is available, then you can buy it when you arrive. In that case, you can bring a baggie with a couple of days' worth of kibble and a few cans. You'll need a bowl for water and one for food. There are now travel dog meals—freeze-dried meals and other kinds of dog food that can be reconstituted with hot water on the road.

✦ Plastic Jug of Water from Home

For dogs with sensitive stomachs, unfamiliar water can give them diarrhea or make them vomit. If you'll be gone for more than a day or two, and your dog has a delicate tummy you will probably do fine just getting purified jug water from a local supermarket.

✦ Water Bowl for the Car

You can bring a collapsible canvas bowl made for traveling, or a plastic bowl is just as easy.

✦ Old Towels

You will find numerous uses for old towels, from covering the backseat of the car to covering furniture wherever you are going, and to wipe up any mess or dry the dog.

✦ Cleaning/Deodorizing Spray, Paper Towels

It's likely that somewhere on your trip there are going to be dog fluids (vomit, urine, feces, blood) to clean up. If you have a product like Simple Solution with you, cleanup is quick and reliable, saving you from embarrassing or costly dog stains.

✦ Plastic Bags

Bring some bags with you and save any plastic bags you get with purchases while you're on the road. You should clean up anywhere that your dog makes a "deposit," regardless of local laws. You can never have enough plastic bags, because such occasions are frequent and we should all take responsibility for our dog's leavings.

THE LOGISTICS OF STAYING IN HOTELS

✦ Feeding Your Dog

Use the bathroom or a hardwood floor for the food and water bowls. Even if your dog is not a dribbly drinker or messy eater, it is still easiest to keep those hard floors clean. You can also put a bath towel underneath the whole feeding area, since hotels expect to wash dirty towels every day anyway.

◆ Leaving Your Dog in the Room

This may not be advisable for a few reasons. The most basic reason is that anyone coming in to service the room could startle the dog and elicit protective behavior. Second, the dog might run out when the door is opened and then you have a real nightmare on your hands when you come back and learn that your dog is lost in a strange town. Finally, when you are gone your dog may whine from anxiety or bark at strange noises or people passing outside the door. This could disturb other guests and get you tossed out.

If you must leave the dog in the room, put a "Do Not Disturb" sign on the door and let the housekeeper or front desk know that the dog is in there and to wait to clean the room until you take the dog out.

However, if you travel with a crate—and a collapsible crate is even easier—then bring it into the room so that the dog and hotel staff are both safe when you go out. This only works if your dog is accustomed to being crated and feels secure in there.

◆ Extra Thank-yous for the Maid

Give a nice tip to the housekeeper, because even the cleanest dog will create extra housekeeping chores. And if you have a long-haired dog or one that creates any special cleaning chores, tip even more generously.

◆ Good-faith Damage Deposit

If the hotel doesn't require a security deposit for having a dog in the room, then you may want to offer to give such a deposit (especially if there's no chance your dog will do any damage, anyway). This keeps you from being put in a defensive posture and may assure your dog a better welcome.

CANINES IN CARS

◆ Avoid Problems by Starting Young

Take a young dog out in the car as often as you can—and make the destinations fun. So many owners only take their dog in the car when she has to go to the vet or the groomer—so that's the association that the dog makes with car travel. No wonder she's not thrilled. Take the dog on as many fun, short, interesting outings as you possibly can.

Take the dog out of the car at some destinations while other times you should get out and leave her in the car (with the windows down approximately six inches—see "Warnings" page 505). This way she gets used to either option when the car arrives at a new location.

- ❏ As in any situation where a dog is anxious, panting or nervously whining, do not try to soothe him with words and gestures. Ignore it.
- ❏ Bring paper towels or a towel for excess salivation—many dogs salivate heavily in the car. This nervousness usually wears off as they spend more time in the car.
- ❏ Make outings fun and brief—if the travel is fun, that can override the nervousness.
- ❏ Going somewhere other than the vet in the car can make car travel something the dog(s) are psyched to do. Take them to a park, dog run or beach in the car as often as possible.
- ❏ Some dogs do better if they can't see out the window. Pull the front passenger seat forward so the dog can stand on the floor in the area where the backseat passenger's feet would be.
- ❏ Other dogs do best if crated in the car. The crate confines them in a comforting way.
- ❏ The more car trips a dog makes, the more she should settle down.
- ❏ If the dog paces/whines/drools, she is anxious about something. You may be able to get her over it by placing an arm over her shoulders while the car is moving (obviously someone else should be driving). The arm functions as a hug of sorts to settle her down during the trip. You don't have to say anything, just use your arm as a reassuring force—a kind of "reset button"—by adding gentle pressure on her shoulders each time she displays anxiety. Have someone drive around past whatever elicits anxious behavior from the dog, and as soon as she begins acting up apply a firm gentle pressure on her shoulders. This may have a comforting, calming effect.

◆ Car Sickness

Most puppies grow out of motion sickness, which is usually from fear, not the actual motion. The more car trips your dog makes, the more comfortable she'll feel.

Dogs who get sick often benefit from traveling in a crate (the more enclosed, plastic-sided kind) in the back. Pad the crate to keep it from sliding around.

You may not realize that your dog is carsick, because dogs do not always vomit when they are nauseated. Some drool a great deal or get wet all around their mouth; their eyes may show queasiness. Pay attention to these symptoms of nausea so you can help your dog overcome the problem.

Avoid heavy stop-and-go traffic, or a stick-shift car that makes rough transitions between gears. Both of these stop-and-start sensations can increase a dog's tendency to become nauseated in a moving vehicle.

◆ Feeding Before Car Travel

Some experts say not to feed the pup for four to five hours before car travel, that it will not harm her to skip a meal (just like most of us). Other experts say not to feed for twelve hours before a car trip. And still others say that eating can settle a dog's stomach, so they recommend traveling on a full stomach as the best solution. What this tells us is that there is no one answer to motion sickness because dogs are individuals: what works for one may not work for another. Experiment with your dog and see what gives the best result.

Some professionals advocate giving a dog that is prone to car sickness some form of sugar before travel, such as a small piece of candy (anything but chocolate, which in a very pure form can be toxic to dogs—see page 320 in the "Dangers to Dogs" chart). If your dog throws up in the car, don't worry. A fair number of pooches do vomit in the beginning when they are first adjusting to the strange thrill of car travel, but they're bound to eventually look forward to any chance to get in the car.

◆ Assistance from Motion-sickness Medicine

Consult with your vet before trying anything on your carsick dog. Some doctors like to use Dramamine, which works in dogs as it does in people who get nauseated when traveling. Dramamine can help with the motion sickness but can make the dog drowsy—there are non-drowsy versions of the drug, but you'd have to ask your own vet how she feels about these products.

Other vets favor Benadryl, which is sold over the counter. For a healthy small dog, a vet would typically prescribe one quarter of a twenty-five-milligram tablet an hour before traveling—for a larger dog, half a tablet. In both cases, check first with your vet.

◆ Maybe Try a "Non-medicine"?

This is an idea to run by your vet, especially if your doctor is open-minded about alternative therapies and theories. You may want to experiment with ginger for car sickness. Ginger has been shown to work in both people and pets as a preventative for motion sickness. There have been studies that have proven the efficacy of ginger in preventing motion sickness, nausea, dizziness and vomiting.

Ginger comes in pills or capsules, but there is also a fair amount of ginger in good-quality gingersnaps and in candied ginger. Large amounts of ginger can irritate the stomach as well as the mouth in people, but it's unclear what effect it might have on the canine mouth and stomach.

"CURING" SERIOUS CAR SICKNESS

- ❏ Dogs prone to car sickness have to be exposed slowly to being in the car.
- ❏ You want to have the dog in the car in stages. If your dog has a really bad problem, you can follow the steps below and take a week before moving on to the next step. If the dog gets carsick at any point, drop back to the previous step and move ahead more slowly.
- ❏ Get in the car with the dog, but don't turn it on. Have a favorite toy in there.
- ❏ Next time, get in the car with it running, but don't drive.
- ❏ Get in and drive a few feet. Then back up to where you were.
- ❏ Drive around the block—if that makes the dog sick, make it shorter and stay at that distance until the dog is fine.
- ❏ Take the car a short distance with a few stops and starts along the way.
- ❏ Plan a longer outing, based on how your dog is feeling.

◆ Head Out of the Window

Many people say not to let your dog do what she most adores—sticking her head out the window while you're driving. Cautious people say you may get road debris hurled up at the dog's face at forty-five miles per hour or more, which can injure her eyes or nose. There's no doubt that this can happen—even a bug can hit her eye at high speeds—but if you've ever had a dog who lives for the wind ruffling through her ears and her nose catching every message on the wind, then you'll know it's nearly impossible to deny her that joy. My sweetest of all dogs, Yogi Bear, had his black-button-nose out in a snowstorm at 60 mph on an expressway late at night, when I picked him up from a specialty vet hospital. He could barely stand up because of the bone cancer that had just been diagnosed but it must have been worth it to him. The temperature was about thirty-five degrees in that car despite the heater but there was no way I was going to deny him that pleasure.

Many vets are opposed to allowing dogs to keep their heads out, especially at high speeds—they've obviously had to deal with the unlucky dogs who did get hit by debris. But if you have a dog like The Bear, who would prefer "windsurfing" to a steak dinner, my personal preference is to make the pup happy while being as careful as possible. If you're driving over a road you don't know well, or you can see dirt or dust being kicked up, then close the window over that portion of road.

If your dog adores having her head out but you worry about the flying-debris scenario, get a pair of "Doggles" (www.doggles.com) which are like peoples' motorcycle goggles. See whether your dog will tolerate wearing them while his head is out the window. Then everybody will be satisfied.

◆ Dogs Jump Out of Open Windows.

Yes, dogs can jump out of cars—even those going thirty-five, if they see something to chase. When a dog's "chase instinct" is triggered, there's no stopping to figure out the consequences of an action. The easy fix for this is to keep the window height up by the dog's shoulder level so that she can't get a foot up on the edge of the window to propel herself out.

◆ Jumping Out of an SUV Can Cause Skeletal Damage.

Big dogs who routinely leap in and out of high SUVs risk damaging their spine or joints. The impact of the hard landing on the ground—or of propelling themselves back up into the SUV with a skidding arrival—can cause serious long-term injuries. See page 192 under "Necessities for Canine Care" for suggestions on risk-free aids for SUV access, such as the Twistep and ramps.

◆ Brake Hard and Lose Your Dog

Once again, do not keep the back window so far down that if you were to stop short the momentum could fling your dog right out the window. Sudden braking can eject a dog if the window is open lower than chest height.

◆ Do Not Put a Small Dog in Your Lap.

Letting a small dog ride on your lap when you are driving is dangerous for both of you. The danger to you is that a dog reacting to the world outside the car—squirming, barking, scratching—is a distraction when you need to be focused on the road. The danger to the little dog is even greater, because if you drive with your window partway down she can be thrown out if you are forced to stop short or you are hit. Another dangerous prospect that could be equally fatal is that if you have a front-end impact, even at a low speed, it can be enough to deploy the airbag, and the force of the bag could crush a little dog.

GENERAL CAR SAFETY

- ❑ Never let a dog—no matter how small—ride in your lap. It's dangerous for both of you.
- ❑ Don't interact with your dog while driving: it is too distracting.
- ❑ Do not get your dog in the habit of being paid attention to—expect her to sit quietly, and she will.
- ❑ You can praise your dog for being a good girl, but do it quietly and briefly so it doesn't stir her up.
- ❑ Never leave your keys in the car, because a dog can step on the automatic door-lock button and lock you out.
- ❑ Always keep the child safety window lock in the locked position, so that a dog cannot inadvertently step on the electric window button and trap her own head in the window. This is horrible to contemplate, but it has happened. And since in the moment of yelping panic neither the dog nor you knows what has happened, you cannot undo it—especially if the dog's paw is still on the button.
- ❑ *Consider a Dog Seat Belt:* This safety item fits onto the car's own seat belt, and for some dogs provides the semi-confinement they need to be safe.
- ❑ *Consider a Crate:* A very active dog who cannot settle down may be better off in a crate, for his sake and yours. Unfortunately, crates do not fit in many cars, but if you have a station wagon or an SUV, there should be plenty of room in the far back for a collapsible wire crate. There is a soft-sided portable crate that travels well, too, but it can only be used with dogs accustomed to crates, because unless he accepts being crated, the dog can quickly chew or claw his way out of this container (for more on portable crates, go to page 218).
- ❑ *Consider a Barrier:* Many SUVs and station wagons have a wire or heavy-plastic barrier made for that model that can be installed to segregate the dog in the far back of the vehicle. This allows him more freedom than a cage might, and it doesn't interfere with your use of the far back when the dog isn't there (see "Make a Barrier of Your Own," below).

◆ Make a Barrier of Your Own.

Most commercial barriers cost upward of $100 and can interfere somewhat with your rear view. They can also use up a portion of the far-back area with their support structure. You can create a

THE DOG BIBLE

simple barrier yourself that will contain your dog, as long as he is fairly large, while giving him the freedom to put his head over the backseat.

Get an adjustable metal shower rod—the cheap, spring-loaded kind that you wedge between two walls in a bathtub—and open the rod so that it stretches across the top of the backseat, just above the headrests. You want it to run from window to window, pressing against the fixed windows that are behind the ones that open. The rubber or plastic-tipped ends should touch the glass. Duct tape over the adjustable part of the rod in the middle to keep it in that position. Now that the rod cannot close and fills the length of the back from window to window, you'll need to secure the bar in place. The goal is to separate the far back where the dog rides from the backseat—with the bar just high enough above the backseat so that there is no room for the dog to climb over.

You're going to anchor the pole onto the backseat headrests with a bungee cord. Get a medium-length bungee cord that you loop over itself in the middle of the rod so that it is anchored there. The two hook ends of the cord should be hanging down off the middle of the rod, over the back of the backseat. Now hook one end of the bungee cord onto the metal bar holding the headrest—raise the headrests if necessary to get access to the metal bar that attaches it to the seat back. Now hook the other end onto the other headrest. Make sure there is enough tension on the bungee cord to hold the rod in position, with the ends touching the fixed glass panels. By raising the bar up on top of the headrests, a large dog will not be able to climb over, but you can see out the back without the barrier blocking your view. (Now if there was only something you could do about your darling dog's big hairy head, which fills your entire rearview mirror.)

WARNINGS ABOUT LEAVING A DOG IN A HOT CAR

- ❑ Never leave a dog in a car for even a few minutes on a hot day—or even a very warm one.
- ❑ Even cloudy days in warm weather or warm climates can KILL a dog.
- ❑ A car works like a greenhouse: heat builds up very quickly to a level that is lethal to dogs. Even in temperatures in the high seventies or low eighties—and even with the windows rolled down—a dog can die a terrible death while you are running some errands.
- ❑ Even if it doesn't seem that hot outside, if the sun is out you should put a reflective sunshield against the inside of the windshield to deflect the significant heat that the sun blasts through the (heat-magnifying) windshield. If you're parked in such a way that the sun is pouring in a side window, organize the sunshield so that you can hook it up on the side windows if necessary.
- ❑ Have your windows tinted darker to block some sun if you'll have the dog in the car frequently.
- ❑ Park in the shade—check that as the sun moves, its light won't hit your car.
- ❑ Vans and minivans stay cooler than cars and have more windows that open.
- ❑ Check on the dog periodically for any signs of distress.
- ❑ Keep a plastic bottle of water in the car and offer a small bowl of water when you check on the dog. Don't let him drink too much at once—this can cause vomiting.

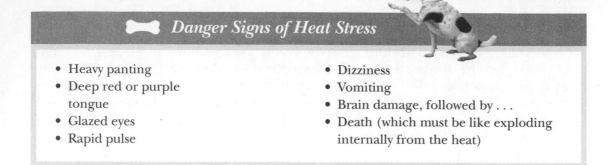

Danger Signs of Heat Stress

- Heavy panting
- Deep red or purple tongue
- Glazed eyes
- Rapid pulse

- Dizziness
- Vomiting
- Brain damage, followed by . . .
- Death (which must be like exploding internally from the heat)

WARNING OTHERS ABOUT DOGS IN CARS

Have you been alarmed or frustrated by seeing dogs left inside cars in hot weather? Have you wanted to warn those owners that they may find their dog dead, but haven't known how to go about it? Instead of trying to write a note to put under the offender's windshield (while watching the panting dog baking inside), you can keep flyers from the Humane Society of the United States (HSUS) in your glove compartment. They are printed for people to use in this way, to alert other dog owners that the dog they have left in the hot car is in jeopardy of dying. To receive these free pamphlets, send a stamped, self-addressed, business-sized envelope to "Hot Car," HSUS, 2100 L Street, N.W., Washington, D.C. 20037.

Airplane Travel

Before I launch into some pretty scary facts and statistics about dogs flying in planes, I have to tell you that—unaware of all these problems—I flew many dogs thousands of miles without mishap. Granted, I knew enough to be nervous from the moment they went into the crate until I could finally open it on the other end, but I still brought my dogs with me all over the place—Roma, my Golden Retriever, and Amalfi, a huge Cocker Spaniel, even traveled twice a year for nearly a decade from Los Angeles to Rome via New York. This isn't to brag about my dog's passports (in those days they did not exist—see page 510 about passports), but only to say that air travel is fraught with potential mishaps—so if you're going to be away for a length of time to a location that is good for dogs, then follow your own heart in making the decision. My dogs cohabit so closely with me that discomfort is better than leaving them behind.

THE DANGERS OF AIRPLANE TRAVEL

The Humane Society of the United States (HSUS) recommends that people not transport pets in cargo areas unless it is absolutely necessary. The agency contends that you are better off not flying with your animals if you can help it. It is considered "Russian roulette" by the ASPCA: your dog either arrives fine . . . or not at all. The facts are laid out below.

◆ Statistics about the Safety of Airplane Travel

The airline industry says that ninety-nine percent of the 500,000 animals that fly each year (note they say "animals," not dogs specifically) arrive fine at their destinations. That sounds pretty good, unless you calculate what that statistic means: *5,000 animals die, get injured or lost.* Now that's a worrisome number, right?

The Federal Aviation Authority (FAA) has recently adopted a rule requiring airlines to submit monthly reports on the loss, injury or death of traveling pets. For the first time, these results will be published in the monthly reports with all other airline complaints and problems. No statistics have ever been compiled before, so there has been no way of knowing how pets actually fare during transport.

NOTE: *Do keep in mind that the airlines have no reason to be less than forthright in their reporting of the facts and conditions of animals they transport. There is no big economic gain in flying pet dogs—it's relatively inexpensive and quite a lot of extra work for them, so it's hard to believe that the airlines have much of anything to gain on the "bottom line" from lobbying for or being less than honest about the facts.*

◆ The American Kennel Club (AKC) and Airplane Travel

The American Kennel Club and the airlines themselves were opposed to the statistical reporting demanded by the FAA, saying it would be too time-consuming. What? *The AKC was opposed?!* Does that make sense—that an organization devoted to dogs would be against a closer look at and tighter regulation of safe airline travel for those dogs? The fact that the AKC was against this safety reporting is really worth noting, because it shows the true function of this organization in a bright light. The AKC is about dog-showing, which can require quite a lot of airplane travel for some dogs. If this travel were to be curtailed for safety reasons, or become more costly, it isn't immediately apparent how that would interfere in the operation and revenue of dog shows. Apparently the AKC, or its lobby, must believe there would be negative ramifications aside from the safety issues involved—otherwise, the AKC would not have come out against the reporting.

What the AKC position *does* clarify is that the American Kennel Club is not an organization out there working for a better world from a dog's point of view. It's important that all dog owners understand that the AKC is not a watchdog organization for how breeding operations are run—it does not police the accuracy and honesty of information submitted to it for official documentation of dogs; nor, apparently, does it lobby for safety reports or safety measures for dogs on airplanes, even though thousands of them must travel thousands of miles a year to get to AKC-sanctioned shows. The AKC is a for-profit business and must never be mistaken for the Humane Society of the United States (HSUS) or the American Society for the Prevention of Cruelty to Animals (ASPCA).

◆ Bad Things That Can Happen to Dogs on Planes

Overheating or freezing, suffocation, being mishandled by rough transport of the crate, crates getting lost in airports, crates opening so the dog is suddenly loose in the compartment of the plane—all of these are possibilities.

Oversedation is to blame for half the animal deaths aboard airplanes. (See "Tranquilizers," page 514.) Environmental stress causes many deaths, especially in snub-nosed breeds, which have some difficulties breathing anyway. The recommendation is for flat-faced dogs not to be transported as cargo. Other deaths occurred due to respiratory illnesses that were not detected beforehand.

THE LOGISTICS OF AIRPLANE TRAVEL

◆ Where Are the Crates Located During Flight?
Animal containers are put in the baggage hold of the plane. The area where the dogs travel is pressurized, but it can be dark and noisy, especially when the aircraft is on the ground waiting for takeoff or for connecting flights.

◆ Reserve the Dog's Flight, Too.
Make a reservation for the dog when you make your own booking. Reconfirm twenty-four to forty-eight hours before departure that you are bringing the dog, whether it's as checked baggage or inside the plane. You want to make sure that your dog is expected, since each flight can only transport a limited number of animals in either location.

Most airlines restrict the number of dogs per flight, due to limitations on the amount of space available in the pressurized portion of the cargo hold where the animals travel.

◆ Airline Policies Differ
- ❏ Many "no-frills" airlines don't take animals at all. Check with each airline for its policies on flying dogs in the cargo area.
- ❏ Find out the airline's rule for preflight check-in times. Also get clear instructions ahead of time (you may be rushed or anxious on the travel day) as to where they want the dog presented, so there's no panic (or just less panic) on the actual day.
- ❏ Curbside check-in is not allowed, so leave yourself at least an extra thirty minutes when traveling with a dog. You have to go inside to check in—ask whether there is a designated area for animal check-in.
- ❏ Ask where the dog crate will be brought on your arrival at your destination. Some airlines have an "oversized luggage" location, others use a special freight elevator for the dogs, while others might have a baggage handler deliver the crate. Knowing how the airline's system works and what to expect can make arrival less stressful.
- ❏ Some examples of airline requirements follow, but know that airlines go in and out of business and their rules can change periodically. What follows is just a random sampling of airlines. Be sure to check and double-check, since one agent may tell you different rules than another at the same airline.
- ❏ **Alitalia**: Will fly you your dog to Milan on a six-seater cargo plane with room for a crate. Contact Mersant International (718) 978-8200 to book.
- ❏ **America West**: No animals in baggage or cargo holds. One small dog per passenger in cabin as carry-on, $50 fee.
- ❏ **Continental**: Small dogs can be carried on, and are not counted as luggage. $50 fee.

- ❏ **Southwest**: No animals on planes except assistance dogs.
- ❏ **United**: Cargo-shipping only from professional animal shippers registered with the FAA. No cargo-shipping of pets when ground temperature on any part of the trip is forecast to be higher than eighty-five degrees.

◆ Travel as "Accompanied Baggage"

This is the term used for pets that go in the checked baggage area of the plane. This is the same area that is used when pets fly unaccompanied, which is referred to as being transported "as cargo" (see below). Where the crate goes is the same, it's just a question of whether the shipper (you) is on the same plane or not.

Buying or renting a crate. If you do not have your own crate, some airlines will sell or rent you one, but you must verify this on the phone ahead of time. Just to be extra safe, call to reconfirm the availability of a crate for lease or purchase, because if you get to the airport and the airline doesn't have a crate, then you won't be traveling (see "The Traveling Crate," p. 512, for more).

◆ Travel as "Cargo"

This is the phrase used for shipping a dog unaccompanied by a passenger on the same plane. Many airlines have developed a specially expedited delivery service for animals, rather than using the regular cargo channels. Obviously this is extremely important, because if the airline is paying special attention to the live animal making a trip, the animal is less likely to get stuck for extra hours in the crate if there are delays or schedule changes.

GENERAL RULES ABOUT AIRLINE TRAVEL

◆ Dogs Are Subject to Outside Temperatures.

Because of temperature issues on the ground and in the air, most airlines will not allow dogs to fly during very hot months.

Delta and American will not ship between May 15 and September 15, when the heat can be extreme. Furthermore, they will not ship a dog if the temperature is forecast to drop below forty-five degrees at the destination. United will not ship dogs when the temperature is forecast to exceed eighty-five degrees or to drop below freezing. US Airways will place an embargo on animals flying anytime due to extreme heat.

Some airlines will make an exception to the freezing-temperature rule if you can bring a letter from your veterinarian dated within ten days of travel that states that your dog can withstand temperatures lower than forty-five degrees for a prolonged period of time.

Individual airports may have their own temperature restrictions on animal travel. Contact your airline's freight department a day before you depart and again on the day of departure to check on their weather forecast. A heat wave or cold spell at either end would automatically cancel your dog's trip.

◆ Documents and Other Requirements

❏ *Health Certificate*: Some airlines require a health certificate issued by your vet within ten days of travel. If your stay will be longer than ten days, you would presumably need another certificate on the other end because yours would have expired.

❏ *Pet Passport*: For international travel to Europe, the European Union recently introduced a required passport for pets (dogs, cats and ferrets) showing that they have been vaccinated. The passport will be the only document required in all member countries except Ireland, Malta, Sweden and Britain, where stricter criteria apply.

❏ *Proof of Dog's Age*: No airline will fly a puppy younger than eight weeks.

❏ *One Dog per Crate*: If you have more than one dog, you'd think they would feel more secure traveling together in the same crate, but this is not allowed. Two—but no more than two—puppies can travel together if they are no older than six months and weigh less than twenty pounds each.

❏ *The Cost*: Most airlines charge $75 to $100 for transporting a dog in the hold—the same as an extra piece of baggage. Other airlines, such as Continental, charge by weight, so that it can cost from $100 to more than $300. In the case of Continental, the higher fees cover their special "Pet Safe" program, which offers personal handling on crates in climate-controlled vehicles and a twenty-four-hour animal help line for information about and the tracking of traveling animals.

WHICH AIRLINE IS BEST?

Some airlines have a long history of specializing in animal transport. For example, where shipping horses abroad is concerned, Lufthansa is known as the premier airline in providing safe, knowledgeable and humane transport, which is not to say that there are not many other highly competent international animal carriers.

Where dog airline travel is concerned, there is no airline that emerges as the clear-cut leader, because FAA rules have changed about the comfort and safety of flying dogs. I had an excellent experience flying a dog from Los Angeles to New York through the Delta cargo system, but I am sure there must be many other good carriers. The airline cargo department of every airline has specialists in animal transport who can answer your concerns about how your dog will be treated at every stage of the journey. If you find a representative who makes you feel more comfortable, and you feel secure about the service that that company provides to pets, then by all means try to use that airline.

SCHEDULING

❏ "Direct" flights are those that make at least one stop but do not require you to change planes. People often mistake the word "direct" to mean "nonstop," but a direct flight always means a stop somewhere, which always makes the travel time longer and also means more crate-time for the dog—more people handling the crate, and more chances for things to go wrong. When planning your itinerary, choose flights that are nonstop. Stopovers are often where pets suffer from being left in their crates in the hot cargo area of the plane or outside in the heat or cold. Even if you favor a particular airline, switch to another airline on the same route if it has a better schedule for you.

- Try to stay with one airline if you have a connecting flight. If your trip involves more than one airline, you will have to claim your animal at the connecting stop and re-check him with the second airline. If you use one airline for the changeover to another flight, that company will be able to make the transfer of the crate.
- Pick a schedule that avoids temperature extremes or variations. During the summer months in which the airlines permit travel, choose evening travel. In cold weather, plan daytime trips.
- Take the same flight as your dog. Avoid sending your dog on a plane that you're not on—being there gives you the best chance of staying on top of the dog's trip. From the moment you get to the airport, try to win the heart of any employee of the airline who's involved in your flight. Tell them that your beloved dog is on the flight and you are a nervous wreck. Appeal to people's best nature and they will usually not disappoint you. Ask to watch your dog actually being loaded on the plane. With the new security restrictions there may be no way that they can do that, but it might be possible through the windows of the terminal, if they face your aircraft.

If there are extended delays or layovers, you can ask that your dog's crate be taken out of the cargo hold or taken off the tarmac if it has been placed there. Again, it may not be possible to relay these requests or to honor them, due to security measures and possibly limited personnel. Also, if your dog were to be taken off the plane, you'd have to worry about whether she had been put back on board.

Once you've gotten on the plane, don't feel bashful about bugging the flight crew to make sure your dog got on okay. Ask an attendant to have someone radio down to the ground baggage crew and ask whether your dog is on board yet and how she is doing. Just say you're a nervous Nellie—it will usually make people more sympathetic. If you don't do this, you may wind up having a pretty miserable flight, worrying the whole time whether your dog made it on board and what kind of shape she's in. Don't fret about being a bit of a pain in the neck to the flight attendants. Isn't it better to "hover" a little than to risk your dog's itinerary going wrong?

PRIVATE-COMPANY AIR TRAVEL

Companion Air has been flying limited shuttles carrying owners and pets on the East Coast, with occasional trips to the West. The small, single-engine turboprop airplanes work well for both small and large airports. The aircraft can carry up to six passengers and ten to fifteen dogs, cats or other small pets. The pets ride in kennels in the cabin and are allowed out one at a time between takeoffs and landings.

If the pet flies without the owners on the plane, there is an onboard attendant to care for the pet traveler on the ground and in flight. Some flights will make stops along the way until such time that volume builds and more nonstop flights are possible.

Fares are based on distance and your flexibility. Sample fares from New York to D.C. are around $500 for the owner and $100 for the pet. The standard fare includes a three-day "window," so if your reservation is for Tuesday, your flight might be Monday, Tuesday or Wednesday.

Sample fare: with a fourteen-day advance purchase, the fare from San Diego to San Jose, California, is $310 for a dog and $250 for the person accompanying him. But if you and your dog can fly anytime within a thirty-day period, you can take advantage of the "Casual Comfort" fares, which are $155 per dog and $125 per person for the same route.

Visit their Web site at www.companionair.com, or call (561) 470-0970. One would hope that such a specialized service will succeed, but it's not clear whether they can generate enough revenue to stay in business.

INTERNATIONAL TRAVEL

For new European Union requirements on pet passports, see page 510 in this section, under "Documents and Other Requirements."

International rates for shipping differ, as do restrictions on the animal's entry into the country you are going to and its reentry into the United States. Check with the embassy of your destination country well ahead of time to learn their regulations and what paperwork they require.

Check with the agriculture department in your home state or the state into which you will be arriving when you return to the United States to learn what regulations may exist about your reentry into the country.

England and most countries affiliated with it (now or in the past) used to require a six-month quarantine of dogs to protect against rabies being introduced into an island where the disease does not exist. However, the great news for travelers to Great Britain is that as of July 2002, England lifted the quarantine on dogs from North America.

THE TRAVELING CRATE

NOTE: *Double-check all the following information with the airline(s) you'll be using. The USDA, which regulates airplane travel for animals, leaves all responsibility for the crate to the individual airlines.*

✦ Should You Buy or Rent a Crate?

Some airlines will rent or sell you a crate at the airport. This seems like less trouble than buying a crate yourself and having to haul it along to the airport, but it's not as easy as it sounds. First of all, it's not a sure thing that the airline will have the correct-size carrier for your dog at the airport. What if you get there and, despite having checked ahead of time, they don't have a crate? Or they don't have one large enough to fit your dog? And what about the same concerns for the return trip? Once you buy a crate, you'll always have it. It can also be the same crate you used for house-training, assuming that the dog still fits.

- ❑ Size: The crate has to be USDA-approved for shipping. It should be large enough for your dog to stand, sit up and turn around in.
- ❑ Lock: No locks are allowed on pet cages. The door must close securely with a mechanism that can be used without any special tools.
- ❑ Labels/markings: The outside of the crate must have arrows or other markings indicating the top of the crate—that is, which way is "up." Write your dog's name and destination

and your cell-phone number in permanent waterproof marker on the outside of the crate. A phone number at the destination address is also good. Write directly on the crate, because an address sticker can get smeared or rip off.

❑ Bedding or bed: The regulations call for absorbent material or bedding, by which they may mean newspaper. Some people put a towel in the bottom of the crate, but this is fairly useless, because it can get balled up and slide around and give the dog no comfort. It is infinitely more comfortable for a traveling pet to have bedding that gives him some cushioning on the cold, hard, slippery crate floor. The important thing is to have something thick and padded that fully fits the bottom of the crate—it's almost better if it's a little too wide and comes up a little on the inside walls for more cushioning. This way, when the crate is moved around—sent up and down conveyor belts, passed hand-to-hand and loaded on and off motorized carts—the dog is not slipping around like a peanut in a jar.

If you happen to have a flat, rectangular dog bed that fits inside the crate, that's great, because then the dog has his own familiar smell and feel in there with him. Otherwise, the best way to pad the bottom of the crate is to buy a flat dog bed with a cover that is almost exactly the size of the cage floor. If you cannot find a bed that is a good fit, then buy a piece of corrugated foam (such as that used for bedridden patients so they don't get bedsores) and cut it to fit the crate floor. Wrap a towel or blanket securely around the foam so that it can't come loose during travel.

❑ Feeding cups: Two, not one, plastic dishes (made especially for crates) must be secured on the inside of the crate door. These dishes are required by the USDA and are supposed to be there for later feeding and watering (although neither is a very good idea for the pet's comfort while traveling, and the cups are so small that any good-sized dog can barely fit a tongue in there anyway). The dog will not be accepted for travel without the cups.

The airlines require that you attach the little plastic water cup to the door of the crate. Filling the cup is out of the question: the first time the crate is tilted, out goes the water. It doesn't really make sense to put anything in the cups—it will just spill and possibly make the dog's trip uncomfortable.

Some people suggest freezing the cup with water in it the night before travel and then attaching the cup to the cage door when leaving home. First of all, the ice will melt at some point, and quickly if the weather is warm when you're traveling. That little cake of ice is probably going to melt in the car going to the airport and leave a big wet puddle somewhere. A worse risk is that in the confusion of going to the airport you will forget the water dish entirely in your freezer and someone at the airport may give you a hard time about not having it. Since the water dish is strictly required—empty or full—it seems more prudent to just keep that cup attached to the crate. Your dog will probably be too nervous to drink anyway.

◆ Tranquilizers for the Dog

Experts now all agree that you should *not* tranquilize your dog. They have found that most dogs handle the physical stress of the trip better without medication. The high altitude and limited oxygen are already a strain on your dog's system. In addition, the effect of tranquilizers is unpredictable at higher altitudes. Sedation is advised against for all dogs.

If you have a pet you feel is too nervous to fly, then you should probably not put the dog on an airplane, anyway. Discuss tranquilizers with your vet if your dog is naturally an anxious creature, but in this case also discuss whether airplane travel is worth the stress that it will cause your dog. A dog with that temperament might be better off staying on the ground, unless you are making a permanent move that is too far away to use other methods of transportation.

◆ Feeding Before Travel

There are two issues here: what is best for your dog and what the regulations require. The rules exist on the theory that if a dog is on a very long trip—or is greatly delayed—she will need food. However a dog is not going to starve by missing a meal—and stimulating her digestive system with food or water would be cruel while she is still confined to the crate.

The truth It is not comfortable for a dog to have food or water in her system before travel. She will be nervous, and the less she has in her, the less there is to upset her digestive tract or stimulate her to need to go to the bathroom. Ask your vet's advice about this, but unless your dog has special health considerations (in which case maybe she shouldn't be flying), it is best not to give her anything to eat or drink after midnight if you travel in the morning. If your travel is late afternoon or evening, then breakfast is all right, but that's it, and make sure the dog has emptied her bowels and bladder before you go to the airport. If the weather is quite warm, give a little bit of water a few hours before travel—just a few sips—especially if your dog has been panting a lot on the way.

The "white lie" The USDA requires that you sign a statement that your pet has been offered food and water within four hours before check-in with the airline. The reason for this is that on a very long trip, the airline is supposed to offer food and water after a certain number of hours of travel. You have to specify the time your dog was "last offered food and water." I do not feel uncomfortable signing that statement and putting down a time within four hours of check-in because nowhere does it state *how* the offer was made to the dog. If I make a *verbal* offer to the dog—"Hey, Scooby Doo, would you like something to eat or drink?"—that's good enough for me. And your dog would thank you if she could for not putting anything into her that could pressure her bowels or bladder.

Rules for Travel in the Plane with You

- You have to make a reservation to bring the dog on board.
- No dogs are allowed loose in the cabin or on your lap.
- You cannot remove the pet from the crate during the flight.
- The dog's container has to fit beneath the seat. Maximum size for a carrier on board is twenty-three inches by fourteen inches by nine inches.
- Being allowed in the cabin applies to small dogs only, because the rules require that a dog be able to stand up in its crate, which generally means a dog of less than twenty pounds. Weight restrictions may vary by airline, however.
- Most airlines (except Southwest, which does not allow them anywhere) allow one to two pets in each cabin (first- and/or business-class cabin(s), and coach). Some airlines don't allow pets in the cabin on transatlantic flights, presumably because of the length of the trip and possible "elimination issues."

LARGE DOGS IN THE PLANE WITH YOU

The only large dogs allowed in the passenger area of a commercial plane are service dogs, such as a Seeing Eye dog.

There was actually one commercial flight where it used to be possible to have your dog walk right on board with you. Unfortunately, the Air France Concorde no longer flies. Merely for the price of a ticket ($5,000 one way, at the time) a dog of practically any size could have his own seat. Too bad you missed that great opportunity, huh?

The only other way to have your large or medium-sized dog in the cabin with you is to fly on a private plane or a pet plane service (see page 511 for information about Companion Air).

AIRPLANE SAFETY PRECAUTIONS

◆ ID Tag Your Dog

Have an ID tag on the dog's collar with a phone number where you can be reached in an emergency. Your home number is rarely useful if you are traveling with the dog.

The dog's collar is a safety issue—it could get caught on the cage door—but you can't really take it off, because the dog would then have no information attached to him if he somehow got out of the crate. So the safest measure is to keep the collar snug.

Dogs are not allowed to fly until seen. The airlines will not guarantee acceptance of an animal for travel until they see it themselves at check-in. Since the airlines cannot ship a violent or dangerous animal, it is understandable that they want to see the health and temperament of the dog beforehand. There will be fewer questions if your health certificate is thoroughly filled out.

So-called "dangerous breeds" Certain dogs—many of the same ones singled out and considered "potentially dangerous" by home insurance companies—are not permitted on some airlines. American Staffordshire Terriers, Bull Terriers, Doberman Pinschers and Rottweilers are the most commonly refused breeds. If you have one of the so-called dangerous breeds, ask the airline(s) if their policy would be flexible if you brought a letter from the dog's vet attesting to the dog's good temperament.

Short-nosed breeds Dogs with the potential for breathing problems—such as Pugs, Boxers, Bulldogs, French Bulldogs, Pekingese and Boston Terriers—have more stringent weather restrictions placed on their travel, for health reasons.

Dogs Who Should Not Travel in Planes

Very old
Not in good health
Nervous or unpredictable in new
    situations

Pug-nosed breeds who don't
    breathe easily
    (Boxers, Pugs, Shih Tzus, etc.)

HAVE A VET CHECKUP BEFORE FLYING

❒ If your dog is older than seven, ask your vet whether it would be a good idea to run a full blood panel on your dog, especially one that checks her kidney and liver functions. Flying can be a physical and emotional strain, so you want to make sure your dog is up to it.

❒ Inoculations and the vet checkup are often required within ten days of travel. Each airline has its own rules—find out beforehand. It would be a shame to have all the proper documentation but have gotten it too soon before traveling.

❒ Make sure the dog's rabies tag is not scheduled to expire before you return home. If that is the case, get the dog revaccinated before leaving.

WHAT TO TAKE WITH YOU FOR THE DOG

◆ Leash

Make sure you have a leash in your carry-on luggage, so as soon as you retrieve the crate at your destination you can get your pooch out for a well-deserved walk. For safety's sake, don't leave the leash in the crate or tied to it—keep it with you.

◆ Bowl and Water

One thing your dog will probably be is really thirsty. I can't tell you what a terrible feeling it is to see no water fountains in the arrivals area and to have nothing with which to offer him the water, anyway. Put a plastic bowl in your carry-on luggage, along with a bottle of water.

◆ Dog Biscuits

Your dog might be famished on arrival—depending on how long it's been since his last meal and how he feels after the trip—but a handful of biscuits in your purse might be well appreciated until you get somewhere to offer him a proper meal.

BOAT TRAVEL

You can take a dog to Europe or anywhere the Cunard Line goes with the *QE2*. There are kennels on board, but you can only walk your dog in that area of the ship.

TRAIN TRAVEL

Even though Amtrak will only allow assistance dogs on board their trains, there are a number of train lines that do allow them. Inform yourself of railroad options before you make other travel plans.

LONG-DISTANCE GROUND TRANSPORT

If you don't want to fly with your dog, there are services that will drive him anywhere that you want him to join you. Although I have not had any personal or secondhand experience with them, there is a company called Professional Pet Transports, which advertises in the back of *Dog Fancy* magazine. They are licensed, insured and bonded, and they offer nationwide door-to-door service. Contact them at (866) ARE-PETS, or www.pro-pet-transports.com.

FOOD AND WATER FOR YOUR DOG ON THE ROAD

◆ Freeze-dried Food Pouches

Several dog-food companies have come out with alternatives to food in a can. For example, Breeder's Choice has come out with a freeze dried dog meal called Perfect Servings. You only have to empty the contents (or a portion of the contents for a small dog) into a bowl, mix with warm water and serve after two minutes. The ingredients are listed as real chicken, vegetables and pasta. This is great way to bring good-quality food on a trip without the bulk and weight of cans. These come in twelve serving pouches, each one equivalent to one 13.2-ounce can of dog food. For about $15 you can have convenience and affordability.

TRAVEL BEDS

There are a number of well-designed roll-up travel beds that are good for a hiking dog to sleep out in the rough with his master. Some will do double-duty: there's one travel bed that is equally suited to camping or use indoors as a plush bed for a room-service-only kind of traveling dog. The Rollover Travel Pack & Bed comes in many sizes, which range in price from $60 to $100. (541) 547-3464

Ruff Wear is a company that makes a lot of outdoor equipment for dogs. They have the Mt. Bachelor Pad outdoor traveling dog bed. It's about $40 and is lighter, easier to pack and somewhat less plush than the Rollover. Contact them at www.ruffwear.com.

Leaving Your Dog Behind When You Travel

It's important to have a plan about where you could take your dog if you have to travel or are hospitalized.

Checking out the choices (a boarding kennel, a veterinarian's facility or a paid pet-sitter) before you actually need them may give you peace of mind.

Information to Leave Behind with the Caregiver

- Dog's name, breed, sex and age (caregiver may not know, or may panic in emergency).
- Existing medical problems and medications—how much to give, and when.
- Vet's name, phone number and address, and directions to his office.
- A DNR ("Do Not Resuscitate") or other letter outlining your wishes regarding the extent of medical care desired.
- Name and phone number of a close friend who knows the dog and can give assistance or support.
- Quirks your dog has that might concern someone else, such as coughing from laryngeal paralysis, snoring, asthma, noisy dreaming or chronic lameness.

PLACES WHERE DOGS AREN'T ALLOWED

There are a few geographical places in the world where dogs cannot travel with you, because those countries demand that dogs be held in a long quarantine. Hawaii is one of those places. The list used to include England, Scotland and Ireland, but at least in England the quarantine has been lifted. Many of the countries and islands that were at one time under control of the British Empire still have quarantine laws, but you should check destinations, since the laws are constantly being revamped. Dogs can come and go freely throughout the rest of Europe without being quarantined.

LEAVE THE DOG WITH A FRIEND, COWORKER OR RELATIVE.

Many dog owners would be happiest if they knew of an individual who could handle taking the dog to their house or coming to stay with the dog—a neighbor, for example, or a fellow dog owner who wants to swap duties so that when they go away, you'll watch *their* dog.

Trade duties with them when they travel—if they don't travel, then just offer to dog-sit for few hours when they go out.

PAID PET-SITTER

There are many individuals who have made a business out of being dog-sitters. Either they come to live in your house until you return or they make a couple of visits to the house every day to feed, exercise and keep the dog company.

Get names of pet-sitters from friends, the vet's bulletin board or a local newspaper. Don't just take someone else's word for a pet-sitter: talk to and meet potential pet-sitters and form your own opinion. There are Internet-based services such as www.petsitters.com and www.pctsit.com, but I have no information about who their members are or how well these systems serve people.

THE ORIGINAL BREEDER

If the breeder of your dog happens to be nearby, you might ask whether he would consider boarding your dog. However, just because there will be many cousins for your dog to play with, it doesn't mean that you will be comfortable with the breeder's setup. You certainly don't want your dog confined to a crate, which breeders often do, and you don't want so many dogs that it is a zoo-like setting without much human interaction.

DOG SPAS (YOU'LL WISH THEY TOOK HUMANS!)

Believe it or not, there are now dog spas that rival those that people go to, at prices (a lot more affordable than the human ones) of about $20 to $60 a day (often with discounts for extended stays of more than twenty days and for multiple dogs). These luxury dog spas offer individualized pampering from massage to swimming and home-cooked meals.

The Golden Paw canine resort and spa in San Diego (www.thegoldenpaw.net) and Canyon View Training Ranch for Dogs (www.canyonviewdogs.com) in Topanga Canyon, California (near Malibu) are among the luxury country clubs that seem to be opening everywhere.

BOARDING AT THE VET'S

For an older or sick dog, this is a really good option, if your vet has facilities. The staff knows your dog and you know the staff, so it's a double comfort factor. Obviously, any medical condition will be noticed and treated promptly.

Be clear about instructions on how much medical intervention you would want done, depending on the nature of the emergency. For a really old and infirm dog, you might want to talk about a DNR ("Do Not Resuscitate") order, like that for people who are very old or terminally ill. What this means is that if your ailing dog were to stop breathing, no extraordinary measures would be taken to revive him. Any other kind of medical situation, however, would be dealt with.

◆ A Pet Medical Emergency While You're Away

Strangely, dogs seem to get sick when their owners go away. It may be that the dog is mildly—but not noticeably—sick when the people leave. Then the stress of the owner's departure and a new person taking care of her at home or in a new place (the kennel) puts her over the top. This can happen with older dogs not accustomed to being left alone.

If the dog gets sick while you are out of town, it's important that everyone involved be aware of what your desires are. Have a clear discussion with the vet or her front-office staff about what you do and do not want to authorize to be done in the way of lifesaving care. Of course, you need to make the same clear emergency plan with the pet-sitter, or valuable treatment time will be lost while people are trying to locate you to get permission for specific medical interventions.

By leaving a credit-card number with the vet's office, you can ensure that they are "prepaid" for any procedure that might be necessary in an emergency.

◆ **Stay in Touch with Home.**

If you have an older dog who takes medication daily for heart disease, or who has an underlying medical condition, plan on calling home or to the vet's once a day (depending on where the dog is staying, of course). Carry a cell phone and keep it charged and turned on. The dog's caretaker should feel free to call you at any time of the day or night if there is concern or uncertainty about anything. You would never want to find out later that the caretaker was debating whether to call you—maybe even for days—when your feedback would have made a constructive difference.

BOARDING FACILITY

Don't assume that being in a boarding kennel would necessarily be difficult for your dog—it may be a very nice place with other dogs for company and distraction.

Well in advance of going away and leaving your dog for an extended period of time, go and look at all the possible options for kenneling your dog. Visit to see if she would be happy enough there—and, just as importantly, if you would feel okay about leaving her there.

Don't even consider a kennel facility that is not diligent about requiring a vaccination record from your vet. If they aren't being careful about your dog, then she is in jeopardy from all the other dogs who haven't been checked out, either.

If you want to experiment, leave your dog at the chosen kennel for a day or overnight. Let the kennel staff tell you how she handled it.

THINGS TO LOOK FOR IN A KENNEL

- ❏ Do they require up-to-date vaccinations? (See "Controversy," page 521.)
- ❏ Are there individual runs for each dog or each pair of sibling dogs?
- ❏ Are dogs kept in crates for much of the day? You don't want that.
- ❏ Are dogs played with or allowed out into a fenced area? This is desirable.
- ❏ Are runs clean—only fresh poop, if any?
- ❏ Are there clean water bowls? Are food bowls left out all day, attracting bugs?
- ❏ Will they feed the diet you want for your dog if you bring food?
- ❏ Will they take a toy or two and a piece of your worn clothing to keep the dog company?
- ❏ Do they bathe the dogs before the owner picks them up? Some facilities do this automatically, free of charge, while others do so on request and charge for it—but a dog can get pretty grungy in a run or out running around with other dogs, so a bath can be a "necessary luxury."

CONTROVERSY ABOUT KENNEL COUGH (BORDATELLA)

"Kennel cough" is the general term for a cold in dogs—an upper-respiratory infection that is as infectious in a kennel setting as a runny nose is in kindergarten.

Bordatella does not come only from kennels, but your dog can catch it there, just as he can from walking in a park, playing in a dog run, being groomed, going to the vet's—anywhere there are other dogs. Bordatella is the one of the most common causes of kennel cough—and is the name of the vaccination against that strain of kennel cough. However, there are many different causes for canine cough for which vaccines haven't even been found.

Most boarding kennels require proof of a bordatella vaccination—but this isn't something you should leave until the last minute, since the vaccine is given in two doses, about two weeks apart. This means you have to plan ahead if you'll need to board the dog where a bordatella is required. However, see if you can't convince the facility of the better option, which would be to accept a blood test showing that your dog has a high level of immunity in his system against the illness. See page 301 for a full explanation of pros and cons of this vaccine.

♦ Educate about Over-vaccination.

Try to explain to the boarding facility that over-vaccinating a dog can be dangerous and pointless. Ask if they will accept a blood titer level showing that your dog has been immunized and still has a high level of immunity.

♦ Boarding a Puppy

A really young puppy should not be boarded—certainly not before sixteen weeks. It isn't safe for a young pup to be around other dogs until he has had his full course of vaccinations, or as many as you choose to give (the controversy about vaccinations is on page TK.) The chance is just too great that he will get sick around a lot of other dogs.

Also, being in a kennel is too hard emotionally for a puppy, who is being separated from the new family/pack he is bonding with—*yours.*

♦ Practice Going to a Kennel.

Preparation for your dog being separated from you at a kennel is something that makes your eventual departures less stressful for the dog.

Dogs who have never been away from their people or never had an "overnight" away from home can be disturbed by your absence. Dogs can stop eating, be unable to rest, go into a depression. Or alternately they can have various G.I. disturbances, such as vomiting or diarrhea, in part because of unfamiliar food and also because of anxiety. Many kennels allow or encourage you to bring the food your dog is used to eating at home (it's in their best interest, after all).

There are ways to soften the blow of your absence and relieve some of your dog's anxiety. Ask the kennel if you can bring along your dog's bed or blanket and a shirt or other piece of clothing that you've worn, with your scent for comfort.

◆ Human Medical Emergencies

Even if you don't plan to be a traveler, you never know when you might have to be away from home because of a medical emergency—or to go take care of someone close to you. So at some point in your dog's life, prepare him for the possibility of being left with someone.

PRACTICE FOR YOUR ABSENCE

- ❐ Short stays and unemotional partings from you set up a positive kennel experience.
- ❐ Have a friend—or someone the dog has never met—stick around your house for fifteen minutes and let you know how the dog handled your absence and the presence of a stranger.
- ❐ Take him to the kennel you might one day use and leave him there if they'll permit it while you run an errand (or just sit in the car) for ten or fifteen minutes.
- ❐ When you do leave your dog there, don't make any fuss about your departure. No tears, no drama, just a simple "adios amigo" and off you go. The less fuss you make about it, the easier it will be for your dog.

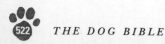

Chapter 16

PROBLEMS GREAT AND SMALL

This chapter covers as many problems, great and small, as I could gather. Some problems are practical and can be solved just by changing the way you do certain things. Some problems may be problems of perception on your part. What bothers you may be natural to dogs—so it's more a question of understanding dogs rather than judging or trying to change them. The problems are arranged alphabetically. In this chapter you will find:

- ❏ A general note on problems
- ❏ Aggression—understanding and dealing with it
- ❏ Anxiety, stress
- ❏ Barking
- ❏ Biting (people)
- ❏ Chasing
- ❏ Chewing
- ❏ Coprophagy (eating feces—yuck!)
- ❏ Emotional/psychological issues
- ❏ Escape artists
- ❏ Destructiveness
- ❏ Fearful personality
- ❏ Furniture (getting up on it)
- ❏ Garbage raiding
- ❏ House soiling
- ❏ Jumping up
- ❏ Licking (themselves or people)

- ❑ Nose nudging
- ❑ Obsessive/compulsive behaviors
- ❑ Possessiveness
- ❑ Separation anxiety
- ❑ Stealing (food or objects)
- ❑ Temperament (depression, high-strung)
- ❑ Territoriality
- ❑ Thunderstorm phobia
- ❑ Visitors (behavior around)
- ❑ Whining

If there is anything I missed—any problem with your dog that isn't covered here, please let me know at www.thedogbible.com so I can answer your concerns and include them in the eventual revised edition of the book (with an acknowledgment to you and your pooch, if you wish!).

A General Note about Dog Problems

Please go to www.thedogbible.com for additional ideas and concepts that have evolved in understanding and correcting behavior and communication issues between people and their dogs.

If people understood better what makes dogs tick and how simple it can be to turn problems around, there would be many more happy owners and dogs, and a lot fewer dogs would die unnecessarily. That may sound overly dramatic, but you might be surprised to know that many of the dogs given up to shelters, or just abandoned, wind up there because their owners were unprepared for the responsibilities of dog ownership or didn't know how to handle house-training or normal canine activities such as jumping up, chewing and digging. Dogs who get no guidance can wind up being labeled as "problem" dogs and/or put to sleep.

People often buy a puppy on impulse, without learning about the characteristics of the breed, how it will influence the dog's personality and behavior, and whether that will work in their human family. Some statistics show that about a quarter of the dogs given up to shelters are there because of some behavior the owner didn't like or know how to handle. These dogs "released" to shelters represent an estimated 1.5 million of the dogs put to sleep in the U.S. every year. That means that three times more dogs are killed because of behavior issues than die just from cancer every year. We can do better than this. Help educate other owners and potential owners. Encourage them to learn about dogs and to seek out obedience or other classes that will get them more in touch with their dogs. And while you're at it, do the same yourself.

WHAT'S NORMAL FOR A DOG

Many of the behaviors that we humans find objectionable, irritating or disgusting in dogs are natural and instinctual to them. So when you are upset that your dog is barking, licking, crotch-sniffing, digging, jumping, whining, etc., just imagine how hard it must be for her to have to repress so many normal impulses and follow people's rules about what she can't do. It doesn't hurt to consider her perspective.

Aggression is the most frequent problem that people report. By the time those dogs reach the shelter or emergency intervention by a trainer their aggression (which might have been nipped in the bud) has erupted into such a dangerous situation that they must be euthanized. The saddest thing is that any dog could potentially wind up in that predicament: often the dogs being killed just needed a different upbringing to become beloved members of a family. People need to learn how to cope with the early signs of an issue so that it won't escalate into a problem that's too large to solve.

WHO'S IN CHARGE HERE?

In general, dogs can be overwhelmed because they perceive that no one is in charge, no one has taken the alpha-dog space in their lives. Many of the obsessive, nervous, even self-mutilating behaviors of dogs are an expression of generalized anxiety at having taken on leadership of the pack because no one else (their owner) was doing it. Nature abhors a vacuum, and dogs really feel it. A dog cannot stand being leaderless, so she will jump into that void and take over, even if it is not a "job" she wants. Tail-chasing, toenail-biting or flinching at the sound of a ringing phone or a clattering pot can all possibly result from not being at ease in the self-appointed role of peacemaker.

Dogs do not mind being number two or number three—as long as they know where they stand and someone is number one. Once the person in the household takes his rightful place as the alpha, everything else should fall into place. There is the (fortunately) rare canine individual who won't settle for anything but being number one herself. This is obviously not going to be easy to live with and probably requires a trained professional for some serious assistance.

◆ YOU Be Leader of the Pack.

Before dealing with any specific problem areas, there is a fairly astounding new line of thinking about human/dog interaction that can revolutionize our thinking and cohabitation with dogs. This wolf-based understanding of dogs evolved fairly recently, and it's based on the idea that dogs' behavior is affected by their descent from wolves. From observing inter-wolf dynamics, people have found ways to use their "language" to interact in effortless harmony with our dogs.

Quite a few trainers have interpreted wolf behavior as it pertains to dogs, but the book I found the most compelling and useful was *The Dog Listener* by Jan Fennell. While I can summarize some of her ideas and those of her colleagues, if you are interested in going into greater depth, Fennell's book is fascinating. It seems clear that the results of these wolf studies have such dramatic success because they enable us to plug right into the dog's brain.

It's especially exciting to put Fennell's theories to work. In my case, it took a mere twenty-four hours (and nothing more from me than ignoring my dogs the way the "alpha wolf" ignores his pack when returning to the wolf den) for my three dogs to stop jumping/barking/clothes-pulling when I returned home or greeted visitors at the door.

◆ What "Alpha" Really Means in Wolf Packs

Wolf packs have an "alpha pair," the highest ranking male and female. The alphas are in charge of life within the pack: they protect the pack from danger, lead the hunt and are the only ones who breed. The rest of the pack is content to be subordinate, as long as they know their own rank within the group. The other wolves are actually more relaxed knowing who is in charge, assuring their safety. This power equilibrium is essential to the health and wellness of the pack. All dog owners will benefit from instituting this redistribution of responsibilities, so that their dogs do not interpret human behavior to mean that the dog herself has to make decisions or take command.

Alphas in the wolf pack get privileges in return for the responsibilities they assume—sort of like "noblesse oblige" in people, the privileges of the ruling class. Now we—the human heads-of-family—have to demand these same courtesies from our dogs, in order to tie in with their wolf-imprinted expectations of us as the alpha. The areas are few but absolute.

THE ALPHA MUST ALWAYS . . .

- ❏ Get first crack at eating.
- ❏ Stand up against danger to the pack.
- ❏ Exit the den first to lead the hunting party.
- ❏ Have his space respected after returning from outside the den.

THE ALPHA WOLF RULES WHEN THE PACK . . .

- ❏ Reunites after a separation.
- ❏ Fears danger from an intruder.
- ❏ Needs a leader when going out to hunt.
- ❏ Is ready to eat, but only after the alpha.

PREVENTIVE "CURES" FOR ALL PROBLEMS

Before going into each of the problems that dogs can exhibit, keep in mind that there are two ways to reduce the severity of or eliminate many problems: exercise the dog until he's tired, and don't put him in a position to misbehave.

◆ Exercise

The simplest advice you'll ever get is that a tired dog is a happier, better companion. A dog with pent-up energy is like a racehorse kept in the stall—he's bursting with energy that has to get released somehow. If he gets regular and generous exercise, he's much less likely to exhibit many of the annoying habits that dogs can get into, such as chewing, barking, whining and jumping.

◆ Reduce the Amount of Protein in His Food.

Excessive protein has been shown to increase behavior problems in general. This is why dogs with problems are sometimes put on low-protein diets. Also, feeding excessive amounts of food in general is considered a contributor to undesirable behavior in some dogs.

◆ **Remove the Opportunity.**

Actually, this is the simplest advice you will ever get about your dog: do not give him the opportunity to misbehave. Do not put your dog is a position in which he is able to do something that you would not want him to do—it is much easier to not give a dog the opportunity to misbehave (especially when he is young and still learning) than it is to try and correct the problem you have allowed to happen. If a dog who chases is never let free outside, then he will not get a chance to chase. If there is no food left out on counters, then a dog who steals food will not be able to practice his well-rewarded skill of "counter-surfing."

Keep in mind that any time a dog does something you don't want, you've given him a chance to rehearse it and be rewarded for it. Most dog behavior that is a problem for us is its own reward for the dog. Every chance he gets to do it is a reinforcement of that behavior. If you anticipate bad behavior and eliminate the dog's chance to engage in it, you have gone a long way to solving any problem.

Remove temptation. Limit the dog's access to forbidden stuff. This may sound ridiculously easy, but put away any item you feel is a target, or keep the dog out of that area.

Substitution of a permitted item This is the other side of the "temptation" coin. When the dog wants an object that is forbidden, give him something in its place. This reinforces for him which objects are acceptable, without having to get harsh over the ones you want to be out of bounds.

GUIDING CONCEPTS FOR DOG PROBLEMS

There are a few basic concepts about problems that can help you handle them as they arise. When you get these ideas firmly planted, there is very little you can't cope with and conquer in a dog's behavior.

◆ **Be as Kind to the Dog as You Would Be to a Child.**

Many times we get furious at our dogs for misbehaving and we lose our temper—I remember feeling like my head was going to blow off when I came home and found that Billy Blue got into the pantry and dragged the pancake mix and popcorn kernels through several rooms. One way to keep your temper from rising is to realize that dogs are generally just doing what comes naturally to them—they're not *trying* to be "bad," and they often don't even know that you'll react negatively. Think of dogs with the same generosity that you would a small child: you wouldn't yell at a toddler who spilled or scribbled when you were out of the room.

A dog is not as vulnerable and impressionable as a child, but it's a good perspective to take on correcting problems with your dog and teaching new habits. Dogs, like children, feel more secure when they know someone is in charge. I am not suggesting that you treat a dog like a human child—that's actually not fair to them—and this isn't about thinking that a dog is just like a child. It is a suggestion about the kindness and firmness you need to bring to interactions with your dog. The point here is to show a dog the same patience and acceptance you would a child.

- Would I scream at a small child for making a mistake?
- Would I knee a child in the chest for jumping on me?
- Would I hit the child in the face with a rolled-up newspaper?

(By the way, if you answered "yes" to any of those questions, you probably aren't a good candidate for parenthood *or* dog ownership!)

Do not make a big deal of mistakes. Do not make a big deal about desired behavior. Do not yell. Do not use physical force or punishment.

BEHAVIOR THAT IS INAPPROPRIATE TO DOGS

If your dog is behaving in ways that seem inappropriate for a dog, consider that you may be the cause of it. Dogs often mimic the behavior of the people they live with. So consider the neurotic things we are prone to do—eating disorders, psychosomatic illnesses, sibling (or other inter-family) rivalries. Dogs have exhibited those problems and many more, and none of them is natural for a dog. Or there may be something in your attitude and interaction with your dog that has caused his unhealthy attitude or behavior—something as simple as your reluctance to enforce rules and boundaries for the dog.

TECHNIQUES FOR HANDLING PROBLEM BEHAVIOR

"Aversion techniques" is the catchphrase for a few different ways of stopping a dog from doing something you don't like. These training techniques are passive on your part—you don't do anything when the dog is exhibiting the unwanted behavior. This is good because it doesn't make you "the heavy"—it doesn't attract the dog's attention to you when you really want it on the behavior itself, and it also doesn't require that you be there when the dog is misbehaving.

Aversion techniques involve booby-trapping the object of the dog's misbehavior. You put something unpleasant in or on the forbidden place or thing, then let the dog spring the trap on himself. You might think these methods are "dirty pool"—pulling a sneak attack on your own pooch. And for sensitive or high-strung dogs—toy breeds and even big breeds like Weimaraners—it's possible that these "scare tactics" could wind up making the dog neurotic and jumpy. But maybe you'll want to try some of them. If this style of teaching appeals to you—or seems like something your dog will respond to—give it a try.

◆ **The Desired Object Should Taste Terrible.**

(Test a small area before trying any of these tactics on valuable objects or materials.)

- Black pepper should dissuade your dog stealing, especially from your garbage can. When he's not around, cover the surface of the garbage with a generous layer of ground black pepper. The dog then sneaks in to rummage in the trash and gets a faceful of pepper.
- Tabasco sauce sprinkled on the objects he loves to gnaw on—such as the tassels of a rug (check first for discoloration)—can make those pretty unappealing.
- Bitter apple is a product made especially to deter dogs from mouthing or chewing any object or area on which it is sprayed.

◆ Frighten the Dog Away with a "Balloon Scarecrow."

A "balloon scarecrow" can be used in a variety of situations in which you want to keep the dog away from something. The technique begins with "pre-frightening" the dog to balloons by blowing one up and then popping it right in the dog's face. If your dog freaks out, that's the point: to make balloons a boogeyman. Then you can tie a couple of balloons anywhere you don't want the dog to be: on the furniture, near a bird cage, in the cat litter, on the kitchen counter, on the sofa, on your bed. Because the previously popped balloon was really scary, the dog will presumably avoid being near a balloon at all costs. Some people find that drawing two big eyes and a mouth with a felt tip pen can make the "scarecrow" even scarier.

◆ Shake-can Surprise

The can involves another aversion tactic that is like setting a mousetrap, this one with a noisy shock. The theory is that it's more effective if *you* are not the one constantly scolding the dog—that he brings it on himself. Fill a soda can with ten pennies and tape the opening shut. Attach a length of string to the can with a piece of duct tape, then attach the other end to the forbidden object the dog has been taking—if it's food, you could use a chicken wing (which has enough odor to attract the dog and can be tied on to without falling apart when it hits the ground). Now put that object on whatever surface it has been on previously—such as the kitchen counter—and leave the room.

However, you have to stick around waiting for the trap to be sprung, because if the dog pulls down the food, he'll be scared by the can that comes noisily down with it, but he'll eventually find a way to eat the chicken, which would backfire by reinforcing the food stealing.

I know of a Beagle who can open the fridge and help himself to whatever is on the lower shelves. The owner tried this aversion technique, with the "pennycans" propped against the inside of the refrigerator door. It actually worked: he was so startled it ended his raids on the refrigerator.

◆ Training Techniques No Longer Used on Dogs

Just as corporal punishment used to be the norm in schools—and just as beating your wife was considered a normal and even recommended principle not so very long ago—there was a period of time in dog training when it was believed that a variety of aggressive, painful actions against a dog would "put him in his place" or "teach him who was boss." These methods are now considered archaic, cruel, inhumane and ineffectual—and they'll often backfire, too.

THE FOLLOWING HAVE BEEN DISCARDED AS METHODS OF TRAINING

- ☐ *Standing on a dog's toes (jumping up)*
- ☐ *Kneeing or kicking in the chest (jumping up)*
- ☐ *Hitting with a rolled-up newspaper (soiling)*
- ☐ *Pushing the dog's face in pee or poop (soiling)*
- ☐ *Spraying the face with lemon juice (barking)*
- ☐ *Hanging the dog by the neck (dominance/aggression)*
- ☐ *Lifting up a dog by its jowls (dominance)*
- ☐ *"Helicopter" whirling a dog in circles by the neck/leash (unwanted behavior)*
- ☐ *Rolling a dog over and pinning it by the neck (aggression)*
- ☐ *Biting or mock-biting a dog (aggression)*

REASONS FOR DISOBEDIENCE

There are different explanations for why a dog might disobey your commands.

◆ Confusion

There can be times when a dog does not respond because she doesn't understand what you want, or is fearful. This lack of reaction is something you can address.

If you give a command like "come" but don't wait for the dog to come, and repeat yourself, you are actually teaching her NOT to come. If you come for her (go to her) you are teaching her not to come to you on her own. This is confusing and contradictory.

◆ Fearfulness

If a dog is afraid of coming or performing tasks, you have to change your personal style. Change the message you are sending to the dog. Even if you feel cranky or angry with your dog, you have to control your reaction. It is your personal style and tone of voice that are frightening the dog. You can rattle a sensitive dog by reprimanding harshly; you can frighten a gentle dog with a loud voice or angry body language; you can get a strong-willed dog to become even more so by backing him into a corner. For example, if you get frustrated and raise your voice, repeating "Come!" in an angry tone, you will make coming to you too scary and unpleasant. So instead you'll get a dog who does nothing because he is paralyzed with doubt and fear.

◆ Genetic Tendencies

There are inborn inclinations in some breeds to exhibit certain behavior, qualities bred into a dog that need an outlet. When dogs bred to accomplish a task find themselves in homes where there is little exercise and no focus for their strong drive to work, they can melt down.

- ☐ Sheep-herding breeds can have predatory behavior—going after other animals like small dogs, puppies, cats and kittens, etc.
- ☐ Old English Sheepdogs can become nervous and jumpy—they'll do better if you trim their bangs so they can see what is around them or who is approaching.

- Chesapeake Bay Retrievers and Dalmatians can be overenthusiastic guarders.
- Retrievers of any kind can become neurotic and begin compulsively retrieving objects—which can often be personal belongings of yours.
- Guarding dogs such as Rottweilers and Pit Bulls have a built-in desire to be protective. You need to make it clear from puppyhood what that means to you—and that *you* will be the judge of when and how they can exhibit their inbred tendencies.

◆ Natural-born Delinquents

As with humans, there are dogs who seem to relish acting up and acting out. The more serious way in which a dog can be disobedient is that he has been trained enough to understand perfectly what you want—and he blows you off. It's fair to conclude that he does not *want* to obey you—but we often make the mistake of projecting human qualities onto any dog and imagining that he *enjoys* being disrespectful. That misperception of a dog who acts out is what can wind up getting him abandoned at a shelter. There is probably a key to that dog's personality that a sensitive and savvy trainer can help you to find.

- As with a trouble-prone human child, you need to "ground" the dog: a "time out" with freedom curtailed.
- You could try a head collar such as the Gentle Leader—to put a lid on his delinquent attitude (although each dog responds differently to this tool, and it won't be a good idea for a dog who totally freaks out with it on).
- You must put a leash on him whenever he leaves the house. No running around or running away; at least for the time being there won't be any off-leash activity. Just as a person does, the dog has to earn back his freedoms and indulgences with good behavior, by showing that he can be trusted.

An Alphabetical Listing of Problems

Aggression

(Also read the section on "Dominance," page 98 and "Aggression Between Dogs," page 540)

THE DIFFERENCE BETWEEN DOMINANCE AND AGGRESSION

"Dominance" where dogs are concerned is generally misunderstood, because people think of it in human terms. In our world, dominance implies a power struggle, a win/lose situation, whereas with dogs it is a word that relates to a natural, harmless aspect of body language in encounters between dogs. However, if people do not understand what canine body language is conveying when it occurs in *dog-human interchanges,* the person's response will not put the dog with dominant tendencies "in his place." Often, just the opposite happens—either because the person didn't understand the dog's body language or because it was just easier to go along with whatever the dog wanted. In a dog who already has an inflated sense of his own importance, that can lead to an escalation in his attempts to exert power.

This may sound kind of silly—unless you see it from a canine perspective. When questions about acceptable behavior arise—and you don't make it clear to your dog (especially a large-breed dog with big teeth and strong muscles) who is in charge of the when/where/how in your house—you will be sending that dog down the road to becoming demanding, aggressive . . . and perhaps dangerous. When a dog does the natural thing and uses his teeth to stake out his "rightful claim" to supremacy in the household, this is an entitlement that you have mistakenly given him. It may lead to someone being bitten. It may lead to the dog being put down. And all of it is preventable by you.

Signs of Dominant Behavior

- Toy-guarding: snaps, growls or bites when you come close.
- Food-guarding: snarls, snaps or chases you away from his bowl.
- Furniture-guarding: claims one or more pieces of furniture, or spots on them, and won't get off when asked, resistance that may include growling, lip curling and snapping.
- Attention-demanding: begs, whines, paws or barks at you, and you can't stop him.
- Dinner-interrupting: barks, whines or paws when you're at the table and won't stop when told. May even try to take food from you.

If your dog has any of the issues mentioned, the sooner you nip them in the bud, the more pleasurable your dog will be to be around—and he *will* be around. It is really important that dog owners make a clear-eyed appraisal of their dog's behavior. No excuses.

◆ Making Excuses for Bad Behavior

You're playing with fire if you indulge your dog's dubious behavior by making excuses for her. It may be that you really feel sorry for her, or maybe you feel badly that you aren't around as much as you'd like to be, but guess what: there is no excuse for a dog to stake claim in a human context.

It is vitally important that you and those around you are clear that there is *no excuse* for aggressive behavior from a dog to a human. Sometimes people are in denial about their dog's nasty actions—or they just don't want to deal with it. So when the dog gets up on the couch and won't get down, or is on the person's bed and growls as her owner tries to move her aside, these owners will excuse what can never be excusable, instead of firmly taking charge and ending the nastiness right then and there. You may have heard people "explaining": "Poor thing—she's tired/cold/lonely/doesn't like holidays/her arthritis is acting up/etc." These people may do the same thing about poor behavior from their children or spouse—but keep in mind that the behavior of those *people* doesn't usually end with them biting somebody.

HOW AGGRESSION ESCALATES

What follows is a chart of the signs of aggression, which become more serious as they progress—and make no mistake, aggression *does* worsen. Every time the dog gets away with his display of aggression and has opportunities to "rehearse" the aggressive behavior, it becomes an even more ingrained habit.

This shows you how a fairly small issue of disobedience or willfulness can escalate into full-blown aggression. If any of the elements here apply to your dog, then correct the problem ASAP with obedience work. And remember that, especially for an aggressive dog, you should try to make obedience sessions fun, *without any punitive component*. If you work with a professional trainer, be sure to pick one who takes a gentle, kind, accentuate-the-positive attitude toward the dog.

THE ESCALATION OF AGGRESSIVE BODY LANGUAGE

- ❐ A "dirty look"—a mean or tough expression
- ❐ A direct stare right at your eyes (see below)
- ❐ A rigid body
- ❐ Moving stiffly, very slowly
- ❐ Snarling
- ❐ Growling from the throat (the least serious growl)
- ❐ Growling from the chest
- ❐ Growling from deep in the belly (the most serious growl)
- ❐ A half-snap—biting the air near you
- ❐ A bruising bite (leaves a red mark or bruise, but doesn't break skin)
- ❐ A hard bite that punctures skin, drawing blood

1) Disobedience

First the dog stubbornly refuses to do what you ask. Or the dog (or older puppy) who has been obedient suddenly stops responding. This is passive aggression. If you let it pass instead of pressing on with unemotional, firm resolve, you are paving the road to hell.

2) Staring

The dog may give you a direct stare—which is viewed as highly aggressive coming from some dogs, yet there are some breeds that have what is called "a lot of eye" because they watch human faces for information. Some breeds known to have a lot of eye are Border Collies, Jack Russell Terriers and Pit Bulls, and their staring has to do with picking up clues from studying your face. However, there are dogs who do have a very aggressive stare, often accompanied by being motionless while staring, which is even more threatening in dog body language. This dog may be ready to do you harm. You need a professional to help you before that happens.

3) Growling

The dog tries to back you off with the first level of growling, a "throat growl." If left unchecked, this can escalate to a chest growl, and lastly, a belly growl.

You must not back down. If you back down, the dog is satisfied with his strength: his position is solidified. (Compare this to not sticking to your guns with a petulant human teenager: if she can get away with backtalk, then next time her behavior will be even worse.) See "Tips for Dealing with Aggressive Dogs" on page 539 later in this section.

Hold your ground, but do not corner the dog. Do not escalate a confrontation.

Don't make excuses for the dog. Demand obedience firmly. But it's not adversarial—just boss and underling. You remain calm, waiting for compliance.

Avoid being harsh when you correct a growl, because that form of communication can be a valuable warning from a dog that he needs some space. If you react too strongly to a dog's growling, you could stop the behavior but lose the message the dog is sending. Removing the growl from a dog's vocabulary leaves him with no way to give a warning before he reacts more aggressively.

WHY A DOG ACTS AGGRESSIVELY

All dogs, from the gigantic Neapolitan Mastiff to the smallest Pomeranian, are capable of aggression and all of them are potential biters. Aggression is a natural canine response in some situations. Dogs have that mouthful of sharp teeth for both offensive and defensive purposes. You have to train a dog not to bite. Our job as dog owners is to integrate our dogs into our world and suppress their natural instinct to use their teeth.

◆ Aggression Can Be Inherited.

Aggression is considered an inherited trait, although a dog's environment can create aggressive behavior just as reliably. If you pick a puppy from the litter that is bullying the others and already "top dog," then it is in his personality. Aggressive leanings are pretty easy to correct at the beginning—but later, if the habits have been allowed to develop, aggression becomes nearly impossible to extinguish.

Many of the large working breeds need a lot of training and exercise, although some enormous dogs like the English Mastiff are couch potatoes by nature. You have to work to socialize any dog properly and to take responsibility for guarding against inborn aggressive tendencies. If you choose a breed that was developed for fighting, like a Pit Bull, or one bred for guarding, like a Doberman Pinscher, Rottweiler or Akita, then the aggressive tendency lies within them and may need attention.

◆ Things That Increase Aggressiveness

Aggression and biting start in puppyhood. If a dog was taken from his family before eight weeks, he has missed an important lesson about bite pressure (see page 112 in Chapter Five, "Raising a

Great Puppy"). So we have to decrease the puppy's tendency to mouth and bite us. We have to train a puppy to use less force when he bites.

- ❑ Puppies or adult dogs who have been isolated from other dogs and people, or been teased or taunted by them, carry the seeds of aggressive behavior.
- ❑ Owners who hit dogs, kick them or yell at them can also trigger the problem: dogs can become aggressive because they have to defend themselves.
- ❑ Playing inappropriate games such as play-fighting and wrestling (see more on "Dogs Playing with People," page 160) is another way in which people can stimulate aggression.
- ❑ Encouraging "protective" behavior in a dog can backfire—teaching a dog to bark at people or menace them creates a ticking bomb. Training a "guard" or a "watch" dog is a job that should be left to professionals.

◆ Other Reasons Dogs Become Aggressive

The dog is in pain. Ruling out a medical reason for aggression should be the first thing you do. Take an aggressive dog to the vet so you can make sure the dog isn't in pain and being aggressive because of it. Keep track of what circumstances have triggered your dog's aggression—this may be a clue for the vet. Note everything from the time of day to what he's eaten to what the weather was like, to what he was doing prior to the aggression.

Hypothyroidism has been linked to aggression. A thyroid gland that doesn't produce enough thyroxine doesn't trigger aggression, but it can make an already aggressive dog more irritable. Ask the vet to include a thyroid-function test in his diagnostic checkup if he doesn't mention it.

Medications Certain medications can trigger aggression or increase a natural tendency. Prednisone (cortisone pills) is often given for skin problems, and is one of the drugs linked to aggression in dogs. Talk to your vet about other options if your dog is on this medication, and be sure to let the doctor know if any medicine the dog is taking seems to have an effect on his personality.

WARNING THREATS, NOT AGGRESSION

"Aggression" should only be used to describe biting or behavior that will do actual harm. People make the mistake of labeling *defensive communication* from a dog as "aggression," simply because they don't understand the basically passive intention of the behavior. These behaviors—barking, growling, baring teeth, staring—are intended to communicate to the recipient to stop or to go away. These behaviors are not aggressive by *our* definition of the word, because the signals are not intended to harm, just to send a warning message. Other dogs all know what these facial or body-language signs mean: if the dog who receives these messages heeds them, they actually *prevent* aggression from occurring. The dog backs off and there's nothing to report.

◆ Growling Is a Warning of Impending Aggression.

You have to take growling very seriously. In any circumstance where the dog has signaled his displeasure with a growl, it adds up to no good. You can't make excuses for growling or hope it was a one-time thing. It is a part of an escalating aggressive pattern that will have a terrible ending if you don't nip it in the bud.

("Play growling" is something else, which you can learn to distinguish in the few dogs who do it. When I'm playing with Jazzy, and her tail is wagging, toys are flying and balls are rolling, she has a growl that I think of as a very loud version of a cat's purr of happiness. To take that away from her would be to lose half the fun.)

◆ Barking Can Also Be a Warning Signal.

If a dog is barking right at you, and has assumed a stance with all four feet planted, the body leaning toward you and the tail held high and perhaps wagging slowly, that is aggressive body language (see below). If you (or another dog) do not back off or leave as a response to that barking, the dog may escalate the aggression level to get his displeasure across more clearly.

◆ Warning Body Language

The dog will be leaning slightly forward, ears forward, standing tall on the front legs. He'll have a fixed, steely expression in his eyes. His hackles—the hair above the shoulder blades—will be raised. The bark may be a low, throaty one, or it can even be shrill—but if it's accompanied by a menacing show of front teeth, it's the real deal.

Do not confront a dog exhibiting any of these behaviors—do not put him on the defensive by reprimanding him, and certainly do not literally back him into a corner, because he will come out swinging with a mouthful of very sharp teeth.

◆ Striking or Threatening a Dog with Aggressive Tendencies

Hitting any dog can bring out defensive aggression in him—with an already aggressive dog, it can push him over the edge to action with his teeth.

◆ Know Your Own Dog's Signs.

Get in the habit of paying attention to your dog's personal idiosyncrasies and the signals he sends. For example, what if he gets nervous around toddlers? That means that if a small child is running and screaming around him, the dog might growl or freeze or curl his lip defensively, but *you* have to pick up on that information and separate him from that child.

MYTH: A DOG BIT "OUT OF NOWHERE"

When the tragic circumstance of a dog biting a human happens, people often say that it was not provoked, that there was no warning, that "it came out of nowhere," but a dog does not lash out without warning unless he's in extreme pain. The people sharing that dog's life paid no attention to the signals he was giving, or they did not understand what they were seeing. Dogs give a series of escalating warning signs that they are reaching their own personal limit. There are always warning signs of impending aggression that owners need to look for and understand. Then they need to diffuse the situation. A dog who bites has *always* signaled that he is being pushed to his ultimate resource—his teeth—but someone has to see and interpret those messages.

COLD TRUTHS ABOUT AGGRESSION

☐ Aggression is not something a dog grows out of—on the contrary, it is something that grows in a dog.

☐ Aggression never improves or stops of its own accord. It is dangerous, and it only gets worse over time if you don't deal with it.

☐ Aggression gets progressively worse. The more times a dog gets to "practice" doing it, the more it becomes a reinforced habit.

☐ Aggression is sometimes not fixable. You need to be open to this horrible possibility—because an aggressive dog who cannot be defused is one who will wind up being kept forever in a shelter "prison" with no chance of escape, or being put to sleep (usually after causing serious injury to a person).

♦ Do Not Be Fooled by Aggression That Seems to Get Better.

If your dog's aggressive behavior appears to be lessening—without any trainer or intervention— it is actually a sign that things are probably worse than you realize. The only reason an aggressive dog would back off is because he has become so sure of his alpha status over everyone in the family that he doesn't have any need to show his aggression. Unless an assertive dog's position is challenged, he doesn't need to do anything to maintain his high position. Let's say your dog is on the sofa or your bed and you don't want him there. But it's easier to leave him sleeping peacefully than to make him move, so you accommodate him: maybe you go sit on a different piece of furniture, or you squeeze into your own bed rather than disturb him. Your compliance in confirming his high position does him a terrible disservice, because one day someone is going to push him aside or just wake him, and that's where the "bite from nowhere" will have come from—you demanded no respect or obedience from him, treated him like a king and taught him to expect that from everyone.

AGGRESSION REQUIRES PROFESSIONAL HELP.

You cannot even begin to solve aggression problems yourself. You MUST find a trainer who has experience, is humane and seems confident about addressing the problem. This is true especially if you are small and the dog is large and powerful.

If you don't have a professional trainer working with you and you challenge the dog—even without realizing it—he will probably come at you, frighten you, and you'll back down. But every time the dog gets that result, it solidifies his "superiority complex" and the freedom to display aggressive behavior.

- Dog bites hard enough to break your skin.
- You feel scared—he growls when you approach him, glares at you.
- He guards objects, won't let you near.
- He lunges at people when you're walking him.

◆ Food-guarding

Some dogs have "issues" about people coming near them when they are eating. This problem comes from improper handling of a puppy when she is small, and then not addressing the "food-guarding" as she grows. It is natural for a dog to defend her food from another dog, but for practical purposes, people must be able to put down a dog's dish and pick it up at any point without any complaint—much less aggression—from her.

There are different degrees of food-guarding. Depending on how intent your dog is, you will know how much work you'll need to put into her reeducation. The mildest sign of food-guarding is a dog whose body tenses as you come near her while she's eating: she may seem to freeze, perhaps cast a sideways glance, but may still wag her tail. Just remember that tail-wagging is not always a happy sign: if a dog accompanies a low-wagging tail with body tension, and the wagging becomes more rapid when you approach, that can be a warning sign of the dog's mounting discomfort with your presence.

A dog's warning is more dangerous when it comes when you aren't even close to her bowl. Other signs that escalate in seriousness are an increase in eating speed, a warning glare right at you, a lifted lip, bared teeth or a low growl that escalates to a deeper growl. The most serious level is a dog who guards her food to the extent of snapping at you, followed by the most serious action of all: an actual bite. For any of these more serious behaviors, you would be safest and get the best results if you have a professional work with the dog.

If you have never seen a dog with serious food-guarding issues, you cannot appreciate the danger a dog poses to you and other people. It can be a Jekyll and Hyde behavior in an otherwise pleasant dog who shows this side of his temperament only around food. It can be *very* serious, with a follow-through that can be a full-strength attack. The reason you need a professional in this situation is because you do not want to punish the dog for growling—you need to counter-condition the growl and modify the behavior.

You can train a dog to accept you near her food dish. To reduce food-guarding, you need to be the dispenser of food (a fact that should already make you Top Dog in your home). Your goal is for her to eat with you there, eventually realizing that you are not a threat to her dinner—in fact, that you are the one who makes it happen. First ask the dog to sit, put down her bowl and then release her with an "okay." Do not leave when she goes to the bowl: stay by her side in a non-challenging way. If her guarding behavior has been mild, she will eat anyway, even though she's uncomfortable with you there. Quietly say something reassuring—praise her in a calming tone for being a good girl. Maybe touch her lightly on the back, near the tail, praising her for submitting to this while she's trying to eat.

If the food-guarding is more pronounced, stand above her bowl and feed her by dropping kibble into it, one piece at a time. This may seem tedious, but it desensitizes the dog to your presence and reasserts your complete control over what she wants. If she growls, take the bowl away (push it away with your foot, drag it with a stick or a long umbrella handle, if need be) and wait five minutes before offering the food by hand again, dropping it in kibble by kibble. She needs to learn that when she growls it does not make you go away—it means her food will disappear. When she has come to accept this amount of your direct involvement with her meals, you can graduate to the lower-key "hanging out" mentioned above.

TIPS FOR DEALING WITH AGGRESSIVE DOGS

◆ Neuter the Dog.

Neutering will lessen a dog's aggression level. He will no longer smell like a threat, so other dogs will stop reacting to him as though he is a threat.

And don't worry about a neutered dog becoming fat—like most of us, pounds stay off with more exercise and a little less dinner (see page 391 on the effects of neutering).

Spaying will usually not lessen the aggression level of a fighting female.

◆ Don't Allow a Male Dog to Lift His Leg Everywhere.

If you walk your dog on a leash and he marks everything on his block, he will then think of it as his territory. When dogs believe an area belongs to them, they are compelled to defend it after they have marked it. By keeping a dog from marking every object he passes, you are cutting down the likelihood that he'll challenge other dogs for that territory.

◆ A Stitch in Time (*Not Literally, I Hope*)

As soon as you see aggression developing in your dog, DO SOMETHING! But that something has to come from the advice and participation of a professional—a gentle, kind one—because an aggressive dog is too frightening and dangerous for you to try to rehabilitate on your own. The suggestions below are some ideas that a dog trainer may suggest to you. Or you can ask him whether any of these tactics might be appropriate for your dog.

Get the dog down off your level. Banish him from any furniture and off your lap, or from anywhere he was able to give you threatening eye contact.

Do not allow your dog on your bed. Keep the dog out of your bedroom so he can't get up on your bed in the first place.

Drop a slip leash over your dog's head. A slip leash is the kind they use in the vet's office—it's just a length of nylon with a ring at the end that you can form into a collar. It only costs a couple of dollars, so you can keep several of them in different spots around the house. This will help you safely move him where you want. While holding the end of this leash, you can then make a growling (or teeth-baring or otherwise threatening) dog get off a piece of furniture or follow whatever command he was unwilling to carry out.

Switch to a low-protein food. Various behavior problems seem to improve in some dogs who are fed a lower-protein diet. You can experiment with this by eliminating any fresh or canned meat for a while and seeing if it seems to make a difference.

Keep control over all food. Feeding is an issue in the wolf ancestry of dogs, and you need to maintain a definite alpha position about it. Keep strict mealtimes on a schedule that you choose. Make the dog sit before you put down his bowl. Remove any uneaten food after fifteen minutes.

Stop picking up your small dog. And never carry the dog. Little dogs can be as dangerously aggressive as large ones. Pampering little dogs and catering to their whims is one of the things that their owners often enjoy, but you cannot indulge in this if your dog is exhibiting any aggressive behavior.

Give less attention—and give it on your ***terms when you do.*** Ignore the dog more until his behavior improves. We know from the wolf-pack model that being given a cold shoulder really means something to a dog—that it shows him that the one giving the brush-off is the alpha. Also, do not respond to a dog's nose-nudging, pawing or whining to get affection. Remember, in dog body language, these are controlling behaviors, and if you respond, you are granting the dog control, even if that is not what it means to you.

No kissing the dog! If you are a kisser (as I am—I just love to smooch my dogs) this may feel as though it's depriving *you* of a pleasure, but there are two reasons for this rule: you need to back off on the heavy affection, and there is the implicit danger of being bitten in the face. Do not underestimate the damage done to peoples' faces by their aggressive dogs, whom they loved more than feared.

Have a plan to defend yourself. While you're trying to figure out your dog, he may turn on you without warning. You need to have a defensive retaliation plan ready. The equivalent of mace for a dog would be a squirt-bottle of water with a little lemon juice in it, or a strong propellant breath-spray such as Binaca (this contradicts the earlier dismissal of the lemon-juice trick as unkind, but here we are talking about self-defense, and if you have a dog that you're scared of, you need a valid weapon). If you're in the kitchen, a squirt of water from the sink hose—or a squeeze in the kisser from a sports-top bottle of plain cold water (or even a pot of cold water in the face)—can have a good deterrent effect.

AGGRESSION BETWEEN DOGS

◆ Why Are Some Dogs Fighters?

Some degree of aggression is a necessary part of survival in dog packs, to get and keep food, mates, etc. In multi-dog households, there are dominance issues. Which of them is going to be king of the castle, getting first dibs on food, toys, beds and human affection? Each dog has issues that can trigger an aggressive response, although in many dogs you will never see it (for more on this topic see the "Dog to Dog Aggression" section on page 541). It is often the circumstances surrounding a dog that set in motion a natural tendency to be a bully, or to refuse to be bullied—it's possible that if the dog had not been placed in a position requiring that inborn response, the button might never have been pushed.

AGGRESSION TOWARD OTHER DOGS

If your dog is aggressive toward other dogs, you can use the training technique of keeping the dog at enough distance from other dogs so that yours does not start exhibiting her usual aggressive behavior. Then, shower her with delicious treats so she associates seeing another dog with something yummy.

You would benefit from a gentle dog trainer who might even be able to bring along another dog to help desensitize yours.

Use happy words and an "ain't-life-grand" attitude. This will help you avoid the usual menacing phrase *"Be niiiiice . . . ,"* which people tend to say in a tense, threatening tone of voice—which only alerts the dog to be on guard instead of relaxed.

◆ Handling Dogfights

1. Stay out of it. A good way to get badly hurt is to try to break up a fight. You can be the victim of a bite intended for the other dog if you get between them. More serious is if one dog turns on you. Now you have a much bigger problem (see "Dominance" in Chapter Four).

2. NEVER reach between them and try to separate them by their collars. People know this, but their instinct for self-preservation seems to get lost in the horrible sights and sounds of a dogfight. Your hands and arms have no chance against two sets of canine teeth in an adrenalized fury.

3. Grab the rear legs of the dog fighting hardest—lift up, then back. Or take hold of the base of the tail and pull straight back. A dog can't fight while he's being held up like a wheelbarrow racer or being pulled backward by his tail. And he can't get at you, either, because you're not at the biting end. However, only attempt this if you feel you have the height and strength to accomplish it and hang on.

   NOTE: *You should also only attempt this in a dire emergency, because it puts you at risk. Another downside of this maneuver is that once the more dominant fighter is incapacitated by you, the other dog may see his chance to come back at his aggressor and raise the stakes.*

4. Water is a great equalizer. Depending on what you are close to when a fight breaks out, grab the dogs' water bowl and heave the contents right at their heads. If you're in the kitchen, pull the sink sprayer out and aim right for their mouths. Use any handy liquid (except hot or chemical, obviously) that can drench and startle them. If you're outside and near a garden hose, grab it and shoot water right in their faces—this will make them let go, but keep the water coming to keep them apart, because with the adrenaline still pumping they may try to go at it again if you stop soaking them.

5. Throw a blanket over the dog—preferably one blanket over each one of the fighters. Being cut off from sensory input around them may confuse them or lower their aggressive drive. Blankets are useful because it becomes possible to reach in and separate the blanketed dogs with less risk of getting accidentally bitten.

6. Aversive sprays work well, and they're portable and practical. One spray you can purchase is called Direct Stop, which is a harmless citronella spray that is an effective tool for interrupting a dogfight. (Animal Behavior Systems, (800) 627-9447, or Premier Pet Products, (888) 640-8840) Halt! Dog Repellent is a pepper spray (ARI, [800] 241-5064). Direct Stop is safer. Pepper sprays are more harmful and can affect other dogs or people—and in some states, users of pepper sprays have to take a training course and carry a permit. But you can also make your own sprays if you're so inclined, as mentioned before: a squirt bottle of water with some lemon juice in it, or Binaca breath spray.

◆ Post-traumatic Fears After a Dogfight

After a dogfight, you or your dog (or both) may be jumpy and defensive around other dogs. *You may be more affected.* Often, the dog who was attacked or was in a fight with another dog doesn't hang on to the memory the way a person who witnessed it does. You, however, may feel anxious and tighten up on the leash when any dog approaches. Your dog—who may not even have been feeling any anxiety at the sight of another dog—picks up your tension and can be either nervous or threatening toward the other dog.

Practice positive experiences. Any dogfight can be pretty scary, but one that involves your own dog can be particularly intense. Set up encounters with other dogs that are guaranteed to be pleasant. Find someone who has a dog that is always friendly to other dogs. Make a plan to have that dog, on a leash, meet you on a walk. This should restore your confidence and put you at ease about encountering strange dogs while walking yours.

SOCIALIZE HIM

Take the dog with you everywhere you can and familiarize him with people, sounds, etc. However, no matter what you do, an aggressive dog will probably in all likelihood not be safe to train and then let out into the world. He probably can't play freely with other dogs—he's too hypersensitive to signals from other dogs to be able to play with them safely.

◆ Encountering Another Dog (or Another Person, If Your Dog Behaves Poorly Around Strange People)

1. Do not panic. You may feel panicky when you're confronted with another dog. Fake being calm, if you have to, because your dog will pick up on your anxiety and become tense himself.

2. Start to give obedience commands to your dog as soon as you spot another dog. Move away from the stimulus, do turns and get the dog's focus on you instead of the other dog. This reinforces your position above him while distracting him from the other dog. If you ignore the other dog and focus on what you are doing, it will encourage your dog to do the same.

3. Keep that leash loose—if you hold it tightly when you see another dog, this communicates your anxiety to your dog, puts him on alert and makes him protective. When an owner pulls on the leash, it alerts a dog that there's something to worry about and increases his tension.

4. Use a relaxed tone of voice with your dog when you see a situation developing. You can even say aloud, "Oh, come on, we don't care about that," because just by saying it you may believe it. If a person yells at a dog, or raises the tension level in some other way, the situation escalates. A dog can pick up a lot from what we say and how we say it.

5. Position friends along the route you will take with your dog. Give the friend(s) cut up bits of cheese or hot dog. Make sure the people stay still as you appear—dogs are less threatened when they are the ones making the approach. Your volunteer(s) should not look right at the dog (too threatening)—they should turn sideways to the dog's approach.

   When the dog notices the person, start talking to the dog in a happy tone of voice and stop near the person. What you'll do next is called "classical conditioning," like Pavlov's famous experiments with dogs. Basically, you want to pair something positive with what has been a negative stimulus—the dog needs a new association. Have your decoy drop little bits of treat when the dog gets close. Even if the dog is growling, the person should still drop several treats. This does not reinforce growling, it reduces the dog's need to growl because the treats make him feel better about a strange person. With each treat dropped, the dog should become less tense, less offensive toward the person and more focused on the goodies. What you want the dog to get is the association of person-cookies, then once again person-cookies.

OBEDIENCE CLASSES—AND THEN MORE OBEDIENCE CLASSES

There are classes designed especially for aggressive dogs. Some places call them "Growl" classes, while others call them "Feisty Fido" classes, but they're both smaller classes with a higher instructor-to-student ratio. What matters the most for your dog is to get professional guidance. If there are no specialty classes in your area, talk to the teacher about joining a regular obedience class. Take a class, take another class. Practice commands as part of your daily routine.

An aggressive dog needs to know his commands and follow them without question. Work especially on "leave it" and "let's go"—then practice it when you encounter another dog. Following the command "leave it" makes your dog break eye contact with the other dog, which is crucial to the buildup of tension that occurs before aggression takes place.

To have a fight you need eye contact, which leads to a challenge and then to the fight.

KEEP HIM ON A LEASH AT HOME AROUND PEOPLE.

When you have guests, it's a good time to practice your dog's level of responsiveness to you. Have him wear a head collar with a "grab piece" attached (see "Equipment" on page 266). The head collar can be used as a training tool to be phased out. It can encourage him to be submissive because of the pressure of the strap at the top of his head, which is reminiscent of being carried by the scruff of his neck by his mother as a puppy. He can also drag a short leash off the head collar or a regular collar, but the calming effect of the former on some dogs makes it valuable for a dog with aggression issues.

To desensitize a nervous dog to being around company, it's best if you're not holding the leash. Instead, you should have a spot for the dog's bed out of the main foot traffic and tether him. Attach a short leash to the leg of a heavy piece of furniture, or you could put an eyebolt in the baseboard and clip the leash to it.

Aggressive dogs are frequently unpredictable with people in the house, on their turf: Keep the leash on the whole time. Don't get sloppy about this and let it slide. Instead of letting him display any aggression, avoid the problem by putting him in a "sit" or "down, stay" when the guests arrive. When they leave, do it again—or else the dog may try to nip at someone as they go. Praise the heck out of him for any obedience—but make sure he gave what you asked for so that his submission is a choice you have both made.

◆ Do Not Put Him on a Time Out.
You may hear a suggestion to use social isolation as a deterrent to aggression, often advising putting the dog in a bathroom with a bowl of water for half an hour or more. This is wrongheaded advice. Banishment and withdrawal of attention are a powerful correction, but aggression cannot be affected because it does not put the dog in the aggression-triggering situation.

MEDICATIONS FOR AGGRESSION
In some cases, your vet may want to try one of the drugs that can help relax an aggressive dog (see below) while you make plans to work on the problem with a behaviorist. There are no miracle pills, but pharmaceutical intervention can help a dog relax while you and a trainer deal with the problem. Any drug therapy must be discussed carefully with your vet ahead of time and monitored closely.

Medications are usually administered for six to twelve months, but never alone—they must accompany a training program to desensitize a dog, make environmental changes or whatever the specific situation calls for. Once the training is complete, your vet will guide you through stopping the medication. When the drugs have worn off, you will discover whether the training program helped make a lasting change and improvement in the dog.

◆ Prozac
This raises the brain levels of serotonin, which often stabilizes the dog's mood and increases his confidence. But Prozac costs $2 a day for a forty-pound dog and $5 a day for a large one, although fluoxetine, a very inexpensive generic version, is now available.

NOTE: *Some of these drugs can also turn into disinhibitors, which you do not want. It means that if your dog does get aggressive, he will bite quicker and harder. You need to discuss this possibility with your vet before making a decision about medications.*

✦ Antipredatory Drugs

Dogs who exhibit a strong drive to "hunt down" small animals—or who respond to babies and/or children as potential prey—become a danger in a household or neighborhood.

Significant daily exercise to tire out such a dog is the first step in curbing the problem. "Predatory behavior" is a strong instinctual drive in some dogs that can be lessened with medication. Talk to your vet about the medications that have measurable antipredatory effects. These are the antidepressant amitriptyline and the anxiety-reducing drug buspirone.

You can't just give the medication and expect a miraculous change. These medications have to be used along with a trainer to modify the dog's behavior.

HOMEOWNER'S INSURANCE

(See "Dogs and the Law" on page 644 in Chapter Seventeen and "Insurance" in Chapter Eleven for more on this topic.)

Your homeowner's policy will be cancelled if your dog bites someone and that person makes a claim against you. There are millions of dog bites and insurance settlements every year; you don't want to become a statistic and find you don't have insurance on your house, either.

GIVING UP ON AN AGGRESSIVE DOG

What's tough about a dangerously aggressive dog is that the majority of the time he's fun, sweet and playful like any other dog—but when things don't go his way, what does he resort to? Growling? Showing his teeth?

You cannot ethically give a dog away or take him to a shelter without reporting the biting or other bad behavior. In most shelters it is grounds for euthanasia in situations where a dog has bitten anyone.

Putting a dog to sleep for dangerous behavior is one of the toughest decisions an owner needs to make, but it's usually the correct one (see more comments on this under "Get a Second Professional Opinion" on the following page).

Do NOT try to place the dog in a different home if he has a specific aggression—for example, don't try to keep him away from children if his aggression was toward children. That will not solve his problems, because even if there aren't kids living in his new home, the dog is going to come into contact with little people at some point. A child could get killed or scarred for life if the dog is passed along to people who know nothing of his aggression.

People fool themselves if they have a dangerous dog and keep saying the solution is right around the corner—a trainer who "finally understands" the dog or a book that will provide the key to curing him. This is magical thinking, and it is dangerous.

When You Know a Dog Can't Be Rehabilitated

- ☐ Your dog has bitten seriously more than once (one time is actually enough).
- ☐ His aggression is unpredictable.
- ☐ He is getting worse no matter what you do.
- ☐ You've discussed the situation with your vet and a good dog trainer with no solution.

GET A SECOND PROFESSIONAL OPINION

If your dog has not reached the "point of no return" (above) but is a fearful/aggressive type of dog, you may not be the right owner for him. But there may be someone else who can enjoy him and give him a good home. An owner who is not in denial about the seriousness of their dog's behavior will take responsibility for making a permanent decision about his future. By getting a second trainer's evaluation of any dog's problem, it may be possible to determine whether a dog who is untrustworthy in his current situation might make a good pet in another person's life.

A second opinion from a trained professional will help clarify whether your dog can be turned around to live safely with you, or whether re-homing the dog with a specifically chosen individual is the best course of action. Of course, there is always the possibility that both trainers will feel that your dog cannot be rehabilitated: this leaves you in the unenviable position of deciding to end your dog's life before he ends someone else's. It is not a decision you can make on your own: getting a second opinion from a dog trainer is highly recommended.

◆ What "Kind" of Aggression Does Your Dog Have?

There is a trend to divide aggressive dogs into different categories: those who behave this way because they are frightened, have been abused, have a superiority complex, are inbred, etc. When things reach a certain point with a dog's aggressiveness, it tends not to matter much why he is out of control. A lot of time and money can be spent consulting with canine specialists trying to determine a dog's "kind" of aggression. No matter what any vet, behaviorist, pet psychic or psychologist tells you, it doesn't really matter what kind of aggression pushed a dog over that boundary. In good conscience you can't keep a dog who will bite.

OTHER PEOPLE'S DANGEROUS DOGS

This is about reporting and dealing with dangerous dogs. If anything in this section applies to your own dog, you really have no choice but to have him euthanized. There is rarely (never?) a good excuse for keeping that dog in society with people and other dogs. The risks to others are too great, the rewards too selfish on your part. No exceptions. With all the millions of beautiful, kind, loving dogs on this planet, there is no place for the few sad creatures whose actions are those of a violent criminal. Of course you love your dog and will be angry or sad about putting that dog to sleep, but the dog will not suffer at all. Yes, you have to deal with your heartbreak, but if you keep that dog around there is a good chance you'll feel a lot worse when someone else has to go to a funeral, or raise a disfigured child, or grieve a possible fatal attack by your vicious dog on theirs.

WHAT IS CONSIDERED A DANGEROUS DOG?

The breed and size of the dog are not relevant: this is about behavior. A dangerous dog can have some or all of the characteristics below, listed in increasing order of severity.

◆ A Loose Dog or Pack of Dogs

These will chase, threaten or stalk other animals or people in the neighborhood.

◆ Aggression Warning Signs

A hard direct stare; stiff body language (leaning forward, ears erect, tail rigid, growling, perhaps with hackles—hair—raised); challenging barks; snarling, snapping and/or baring teeth.

◆ A Leashed Dog Trying to Attack

Lunging aggressively toward other dogs or people with the owner barely holding on, not in control.

◆ During a Dogfight, Puncturing or Lacerating the Other Dog or the Person Trying to Break It Up.

This is different from a scuffle in which no blood is drawn, because the dog has good bite inhibition and does not injure her opponent. In the same altercation, a dangerous dog causes injuries with her teeth.

◆ A Dog Who Bites a Person or Other Animal

If you or your dog are seriously frightened by or attacked by another dog, REPORT IT IMMEDIATELY to the police and/or local animal control agency. Only by creating a "paper trail" about a dog can you help make sure the dog will be removed from the community if necessary.

If you learn that other neighbors have had bad experiences with the dog—or witnessed those encounters—encourage them to make a report to the authorities. Multiple complaints have weight in determining a dangerous dog's fate.

Don't worry about the owner being angry or vengeful—in most communities, animal-control complaints are anonymous. You must give your name to the investigator, but they keep it confidential. Keep a written record (handwritten notes are fine) of all calls and contacts you make.

Don't hesitate to take action because you feel bad that you might be signing a dog's "death warrant." How will you feel if children are mauled by that dog because no one cared enough to do anything about it? Make follow-up calls to see whether police or animal-control reports were filed and what action was taken.

PROBLEMS WITH A NEIGHBOR'S LOOSE DOG

Dogs that are allowed to roam a neighborhood can become aggressive. Generally, dogs shouldn't be out unsupervised because of the danger they pose to themselves and others.

1. First let the neighbor know that her dog has been loose and exhibiting aggressive or otherwise frightening behavior to you or your children. Be friendly, not offensive or accusatory. Try to include the owner in the solution rather than put her on the defensive. What you want is for her dog to be contained.

2. If the dog is loose and aggressive again after you've spoken to the owner, you can follow it up with another visit or phone call if you feel the owner really means well and is receptive. Tell her that she may not be aware that her dog was out again and behaving in a frightening manner: you are really worried and she has to do something. Or you can skip the second contact with the owner and go right to the step below.

3. Contact animal-control authorities. Be specific with a description of the dog, the date, time and details of the incident; the name and address of the owner; photos or videos of the dog in action (very useful); and suggestions of when the owner is usually home so the officials don't take a wasted trip.

Barking

Barking is a dog's way of communicating. It is the way a dog uses her voice to express a wide range of feelings—boredom, warnings, hunger, wanting to play or eat, fear, etc. Trying to understand why your dog barks—and learning her different barking tones and what they mean—will go a long way toward having her barking under your control. If there is a lot of barking, you'll be able to make changes as needed in the dog's environment.

As the chart page 549 shows, there are many reasons why a dog may bark—many of them are legitimate and can serve as ways to deepen your understanding of her communication. There are also dogs who bark in ways and at times that you may find unsuitable for your lifestyle or temperament. A dog on a 2,000-acre ranch in Montana will have different stimuli that inspire barking and follow different "etiquette guidelines" about sounding off than a pooch in a two-bedroom apartment in a Chicago high-rise. The picture changes even further when you have a multiple-dog household—because dogs inspire vocalization in each other.

Each dog/human family has to find a happy medium that ultimately puts the person in charge of when and how their dog barks, while at the same time respecting a dog's entitlement to speak up. Every dog is quite different about barking, and each one has a range of barking tones that may be more or less appealing to your ears.

Some Reasons for Barking

- Just enjoys doing it (some breeds in particular)
- Hears something (and feels frightened or fierce)
- Warning someone is near the house/something is unusual
- Boredom, loneliness
- Sees another animal
- Wants a biscuit
- Reminding you it's dinnertime
- Toy is out of reach
- Excitement about going out for a walk
- Excitement that you've come home
- Wants you (or another dog) to play (especially herding breeds)
- Needs to go out
- Is confused (Canine Cognitive Dysfunction, CCD, see page 590)

You can choose to view it as a positive thing when a dog has the desire and ability to communicate with her people (barking being a dog's version of talking). Of course, there can also be "too much of a good thing"—and when that applies you'll need some remedies.

YOUR ATTITUDE ABOUT BARKING

Many trainers and books seem to treat barking as some terrible, irritating behavior that dogs visit on us and that we have to "bully" them out of. These experts advocate fairly harsh disciplinary reactions to a dog's barking, whenever it occurs. But if you stop to consider "all-barking-is-bad" as a basic principle of training, you'll see how it can be so judgmental that it puts a toxic spin on your interaction with your dog. You may also miss the point that a dog is often trying to make a connection by barking—which isn't all bad.

Of course there will be times when a strong negative reaction to barking is called for. But it also seems fair to suggest that if the mere sound of barking is too horrible for you—if you can't tolerate *any* quantity of dog-generated noise—then it's not really fair to the pooch. After all, if total silence was your ideal quality in a pet you would have picked a goldfish, right?

There's another way to look at barking: don't view the dog as an adversary who must be quieted at any cost. Instead, look at her as a companion trying to converse with you. Naturally, some of the times she picks to make this attempt will be inconvenient—but in order to handle it well for household harmony, I think a positive perspective makes a big difference.

Books and trainers that criticize a barking dog by saying that he's "only doing it to get your attention" may be right in their assessment of the facts, but wrong about being so negative about it. Looked at differently, isn't "trying to get your attention" a positive thing? Isn't being tuned into each other part of the pleasure of sharing your life with an animal? Isn't that cross-species attempt to connect part of what draws people and dogs together?

So really the focus needs to be *why* and *how* does your particular dog bark, and what do you want to do about it?

PREVENTING BARKING

There are some things you can do to lessen the likelihood of barking becoming a habit, because the first thing on the agenda is to eliminate as many triggers for barking as possible.

◆ Don't Reward Any Barking.

When your dog barks to get what he wants, ignore him. Don't pay any attention, verbalize or give a treat when he vocalizes. Don't respond no matter how cute he is.

◆ Discourage a Puppy from Protective Barking.

Territorial barking usually begins between six and nine months of age (although some puppies start even earlier) and can begin as late as three years old. Do not try to encourage any young dog to bark, or you could be teaching something you'll regret.

◆ Keep the Dog Happy and Keep Him Company.

Don't leave a young dog home alone for long periods of time, and make sure a dog of any age gets lots of exercise to tire him. Round out his life with people, toys, games and other dogs to amuse and stimulate him.

◆ Praise Quiet.

When the dog does *not* bark at something, praise and reward him.

DIFFERENT TONES AND TYPES OF BARKING

◆ Territorial/Protective

This is a common type of barking, usually accompanied by the dog in an offensive stance—leaning forward, tail high, kind of "daring" the person, car or animal to come any closer. In fact, as that intruder gets closer, the barking usually increases in tone and frequency. The sound of a doorbell (even on TV) or knocking on the door can set off this same protective stance. For most people, this kind of "barking to alert" is fine in moderation. However, if there is more barking than you or your neighbors would like, you can reduce the visual stimuli that's inspiring the barking. Reduce what your dog can see by changing a fence to solid wood, or denying her access to any glass or screen doors she was looking through.

◆ Boredom/Loneliness

Dogs who have no companions and are left alone for long periods of time may bark part or all of that time, often a monotonous bark in a persistent, measured monotone. Some dogs can stand being alone with nothing to do, but it makes most of them miserable. A dog in this situation needs your help to improve her life. If she's been left outside most of the time, it's only fair to try to find a way to include her in your household; if she's left alone at home all day, she needs someone to take her for a walk and/or spend time with her. You might consider doggie day care.

◆ Fear/Being Startled

A dog barking from fear can be a spooky dog who is shocked by any object she's never seen before (Scooby Doo is a scaredy-cat like that, crouching with raised hackles when he turns a corner and sees a new garbage can, an umbrella or a cement statue). These dogs may just have fearful personalities (see page 572 later in this chapter) or they may not have been properly socialized and introduced to new sights and sounds as puppies. Fearful dogs can also startle easily, so sightings of "monsters" they see from a house or car window can set off shrill alarm barking.

◆ Excitement/Play

This is happy barking that is an expression of joy, often when a dog greets you or another family member or wants to play with you or another dog. Play-barking is often an instinctual expression for dogs—particularly the herding breeds—so it can be hard to change in them. The same is true of the way they nip at other dogs' back legs when playing, just as they would while working a flock or herd.

◆ Attention-getting/"Me Too"

There are two ways of looking at this kind of barking: that the dog is being rude and pushy, or the dog is initiating a conversation with you. Personally, I prefer the second point of view: when Billy Blue tap-dances around the kitchen and whines plaintively as the lunch hour approaches, Scooby-Doo barks to alert me (and to get himself in on the deal). I appreciate the dialogue, as well as my ability to shut it off fairly quickly by sending them to their beds if it's a false alarm and lunch won't be served for another hour. When friends come to visit and we get into animated conversations with raised voices and laughter, Scooby has a whole range of throaty yips and barks that he uses to insert himself into the social festivities. I used to get annoyed and reprimand him, until I responded by talking *to* him and including him verbally—at which point he stopped barking. So I discovered that what he wanted was verbal interaction, the same as I was having with people—it was "me too-ism." So I ask friends who visit to just say a few words to the dog: no need to pat or give him anything, just make eye contact and speak directly to him (which has actually expanded his repertoire of barking sounds). After they do, he settles down.

WAYS TO HANDLE BARKING

Raising your voice only stimulates him to bark more and louder. We have all screamed "SHUUT UPPPP!" at our dog(s) who are barking hysterically at the door—we're not proud of it, and it didn't stop their noise. If you yell at a barking dog, he thinks you are joining in, so what you get is even more vigorous barking.

◆ Teach Your Dog *to* Bark

If you have a noisy dog who just naturally loves to bark, one way to channel this energy is to teach him to bark on command. By teaching barking, you take charge of a situation that has been out of your control and redirect the dog's attention to you. The bonus is that once you have taught a bark command, you can use it as a safety measure if you want the dog to bark to deter possible intruders.

What you want to do is encourage your dog to bark so that you can give him a signal and teach him to bark on command—then you'll practice stopping him. Set up a situation that usually makes the dog bark—a ringing doorbell, a car pulling up in front of your house—and as soon as he barks, use a hand signal with two fingers going up and down against the thumb (as if to mimic talking) and praise him with "Bark! Good boy, bark!" Set up the bark-inducing situation again and use the "bark" hand signal as soon as he starts to vocalize. Praise and reward him.

Training a dog to stop barking usually is quite simple. Acknowledge the dog's voice by saying "Okay" or even "Thank you" as you go to the dog. That is enough time for him to have gotten a few good barks out. Now place your hand on top of his nose and tell him "Enough" or "Quiet" (in a deep, firm tone of voice). The moment the dog stops barking, give him immediate and festive praise and possibly a treat. Now, every time he barks, allow him a handful of barks, tell him "Quiet" or "Enough" in a firm but pleasant voice and give him a reward *the moment* he stops.

A DOG WHO BARKS WHEN LEFT ALONE

♦ **Tire Out the Dog Beforehand.**
Before anything else, try increasing how much time or how vigorously your dog plays or exercises—a tired dog is generally a quiet one.

♦ **Leave without Drama.**
When you leave and come back, put no emotion into either. Just walk out. Then just walk back in. No big greeting. If he is crated, release him from the crate as though it's no big deal.

♦ **Use a Crate to Desensitize the Dog.**
Prepare the dog to be left by putting him in his crate with a piece of your worn clothing for comfort. Turn on the television to something pleasant and chatty (many books say turn on a radio, but a TV has a nice realistic mixture of voices, songs and sounds).

♦ **Leave the Dog for Five Minutes at First.**
Try another left-alone session later. Keep increasing the amount of time you're gone until it's at least an hour. After a while you can practice the left-alone routine without the crate. If she has no destructive drive, then she can be loose in the house while waiting for you to return. The best thing you can do for a dog is to teach her how to tolerate being alone, little by little.

♦ **If the Dog Does Not Bark When You Leave. . .**
Give her a treat as soon as you return. If the dog barks when you leave but stops when you say "Quiet—that's enough," give her *two* treats!

* **Neighbors Complain the Dog Barks When You're Out.**

If your dog doesn't bark right when you leave and you don't hear it, then you can't correct the problem—you can't reward the quiet. To find out what's really going on, you can start a tape recorder when you go out—or any kind of video camera that could be left on remote and show you how your dog behaves when you are gone.

BARKING AT NOISES

When your dog barks, praise him and then call him to you. Now tell him "Quiet" in a firm soft voice—then ask for a "sit" or a "down." It's important for success if you give him something else to do instead of barking, such as lying down or sitting.

If he barks again, tell him "Quiet" in the same firm, soft voice. The moment that he stops barking—if only for an instant—praise him and give him a treat as quickly as you can so it is clear you're rewarding the quiet—not the barking.

* **Barking at the Doorbell**

The doorbell is just another sound the dog is reacting to, so the rules above apply here, too. There is added excitement for the dog in this situation, because a new person is usually on the other side of that doorbell sound.

The sound of the doorbell can be startling to a dog so you need to react quickly—because the dog will! Be prepared to call the dog, praise him for barking, then say "Quiet." Praise him/treat him once he stops barking, then have him sit. If he starts barking again, say "Quiet"—always in a calm firm voice—then "Down."

Always praise the very minute he's quiet. Give him a treat for quieting when you are first teaching, then affectionate praise later, once he's learned what you wanted.

BARKING WHILE RUNNING BACK AND FORTH ALONG A FENCE

This problem usually occurs if you have a dog that is outside much of the time or has a dog door that allows him to exit whenever he wants. These dogs have an even greater territorial defense mechanism than dogs that are inside most of the time or do most of their walking on a leash or off your property. This can become a nightmarish neighbor problem—the kind that has otherwise sane people fuming.

The problem will be worse if there is a fence separating your property from your neighbors, you have more than one dog yourself (pack mentality) and *especially* if those neighbors have a dog or are outside playing or gardening . . . or they have children who run and scream when playing . . . or they have machinery such as leaf blowers and lawn mowers running . . . or they entertain outside with music and groups of people. In these cases, you can EXPECT your dog to run back and forth along that fence every time, barking his head off. The dog is doing what comes naturally and makes total "dog sense": he is protecting his territory against possible interlopers.

+ **You Have Several Choices to Deal with the Situation.**
  - ☐ When you won't be home, bring the dog indoors and close off any dog door.
  - ☐ If you know your neighbors' schedule, then take the dog inside while they are out there, or take him inside at the first warning bark from him. This means that you must be home, must be listening and must act quickly, because as with any dog behavior, the more the dog practices it, the more ingrained it becomes. And as with any of us, once something has become a habit, it's that much tougher to change.
  - ☐ Introduce your dog to everyone in the neighbor's family so that these people are no longer strangers to your dog. Generally a dog barks to alert you to a stranger: so turn them into friends. Tell them your dog's name so that when he begins barking at them they can call out his name (you'll want to see his expression when these apparently dangerous humans suddenly know his name!). This may quiet him right down. Give some treats to the neighbors so they can feed the dog through the fence.
  - ☐ Neighbors will have every right to be miffed at the cacophony coming from your side of the fence. Do not delude yourself that your dog will soon stop because he'll get bored or tired, or because he'll realize there's no reason for his high-alert alarm. He's going to keep at it unless you stop him.

ANTI-BARKING EQUIPMENT

+ **Passive Punishing Collars**

There are a series of passive collars (requiring no involvement from you) that do something aversive when a dog barks. The reason these are effective is because it takes the person out of the equation. Instead of you being involved, the dog gets an immediate nonhuman reaction to his barking. There is a collar that squirts citronella spray into a dog's face when he barks. This was thought to be a more humane barking correction, except that since citronella spray collars are triggered by a microphone, other noises than barking can set it off and spray the dog when he is not barking. Some trainers are opposed to anti-bark collars that give a mild shock; however, they are actually the most reliable way of correcting a "rehearsed barker" (a dog who automatically goes into bark mode and carries on for long stretches). The shock collars are vibration-sensored; a high-quality product like the ones from Tritronics can even tell you the number of times the dog barked when you were gone. There is another collar that emits a high-pitched sound when the dog barks, a sound that irritates dogs' sensitive ears.

+ **Shock Punishment That You Give**

When the dog starts barking, give the "quiet" command you've chosen to stop the barking ("enough" or "quiet"). Say the word calmly and low. If the pup doesn't zip it immediately, keep the lemon water squirt bottle as hidden as you can and give him a quick squirt on the head—try to keep him from seeing that it's *you* who's creating the shock-squirt. You can also do the squirt-bottle *without* the stinging lemon, which may be all that's required to get your point across, anyway.

DEBARKING—A DRASTIC MEASURE

Debarking is major surgery, under anesthesia, in which the vocal cords are altered. The dog will still be able to bark, but the sound will be greatly diminished. The bark winds up sounding like a bark with laryngitis, or a very sore throat. There is no way to determine what the actual volume or tone of the altered vocal chords will be, since it will vary for each dog.

Having your dog debarked surgically is sort of the "Ultimate Solution": it sounds pretty drastic, and it certainly is. You should consider this option only as a last resort with a dog that barks so incessantly that it gives you and/or your neighbors no peace, and no trainer has been able to improve the situation. The only possible defense for debarking might be the rare situation in which a dog's bark is so awful and incessant that it is his death sentence: he would have to be put to sleep without this intervention.

Biting People

There are disturbing statistics about how many dog bites there are in the United States every year, and even more distressing is that a large percentage of the attacks involve children. There's no point in dragging out those numbers, since statistics about any topic are so often mind-numbing, almost as if they absolve people from thinking about what those numbers represent. What you need to know about dogs and biting is that the two go together more than most people realize: biting is part of what dogs do naturally, just like barking and digging. It's up to us to re-orient their impulses so they express them in a way that is more suited to sharing their every waking hour with our species, which does not use teeth, except to eat (and chew gum).

DOG BITES CAN BE AVOIDED

Dog bites are almost never "out of the blue"—the dog has usually given several noticeable indicators of his state of mind. A situation in which a dog bites a person can almost always be avoided, if people learn the dog's pre-biting body language. We also need to know how a dog interprets our actions and reactions, so we're aware of how we are affecting his behavior.

We also have to teach our children how to read and respond to the dog's body language (see page 472 in Chapter Fourteen, "Dogs and Children").

READING A DOG'S BODY LANGUAGE

We can use our knowledge of dog-to-dog greetings to understand dogs better and to learn how they are interpreting our body language.

◆ Different Tail Wags as Greeting Are Not a Problem.

Just as people can have a personal style of shaking hands (from knuckle-crushing to weak and wet), the general intention of a polite, friendly greeting is unchanged. Tail-wagging can be the canine equivalent. For example, a dog with a low, wide "sloppy" tail wag is generally issuing a friendly message, even if his hackles are raised. A dog who has a high, tight, vibrating tail wag is not necessarily exhibiting aggression, he may just be tense or excited.

◆ A Relaxed Greeting

This means that the ears, tail and facial expression are all neutral.

◆ A Fearful Greeting

This indicates that the dog is insecure. His body language could be trembling, slinking against walls, avoidance and a low posture. This fearfulness can escalate to biting if the other dog or a person continues to advance toward the fearful dog.

◆ A Dominant Greeting

This is one in which the dog carries himself to look bigger: a high head and tail carriage, stiffened legs and ears, and raised hackles; he will also often stare at the other dog. This can escalate to a dogfight if the other dog responds the same way.

◆ A Submissive Greeting

A dog does this to calm the dominant dog. The head and tail are held low, and he keeps a low posture when approaching the other dog in a sideways approach. Other submissive behavior is muzzle-licking, avoidance of eye contact, blinking and yawning. All of this indicates "I am no threat."

BASIC SAFETY RULES

Much of what we know comes from observing dogs with each other. It can be especially hard to read a dog that has "altered communication mechanisms," such as cropped tail and/or ears, or a long coat that covers her eyes and ears.

An unknown dog is an unpredictable dog. Assume *nothing*.

Never put your face near the face of ANY dog you meet, no matter how friendly she seems. Putting your face right up to a dog's face is an aggressive act in dog body language, almost like daring the dog to do something.

Reasons Dogs Bite People (Not in Order of Importance)

- Dominance issues are the most frequent reason: the dog thought he was challenged.
- A dog can get overexcited during play: a person winds up getting stitches.
- Defensive: a fearful dog can feel threatened by the victim, but a *timid* one will retreat (unless the avenue of escape is closed, and then he might bite).
- A dog may be in pain or ill.
- Territorial: a dog may feel he must protect his human guardian.
- Stress of any kind—pain, fear, anxiety, arousal—can trigger biting.
- A toddler or child may prod or poke at a dog who is in her safe place.

DIFFERENT DEGREES OF BITES

Just as people can misunderstand dominant behavior or warning behavior in dogs and call it aggression, so can biting be misinterpreted, because all biting is NOT the same. The dog trainer, author and veterinarian Ian Dunbar came up with a system to divide dog bites into six levels of severity, for clarity when discussing biting behavior. The following is based on his idea.

✦ First-degree Bite: "Air-biting"

When a dog snaps or bares his teeth and makes a biting motion, this is intentionally an "almost bite." The dog does not intend to put his teeth on the object of his aggression, nor does he. Don't think the dog was trying to bite and was just clumsy about it: if a dog wants to bite a person or another dog, he is hardwired to be able to connect his teeth to flesh. Therefore, what we know about "air-bites" is that 1) there were probably other warnings (growling, staring, freezing, etc.) that the dog gave first and that were ignored, and/or 2) whatever was going on at the time was such a strong stress or fear trigger for the dog that he went right to the air-bite.

If a dog does air-bite, don't land all over him, punish him or otherwise overreact. Respect the warning, give him his space. Get professional help to determine what set him off, then loosen that stress if possible or work on desensitizing him to it.

✦ Second-degree Bite: Contact with Skin without Puncturing It

This is a very serious warning from a dog. He purposely did not use any bite pressure and therefore did not break the skin. However, a bite like this makes it clear that he needs to make his displeasure known and have it heeded.

✦ Third-degree Bite: Punctures the Skin but Not Deep

You get the drift by now of where this classification idea is going: here the dog used enough pressure to break through the skin but the punctures are few and shallow. There is no bruising (which will come with a heavier bite).

✦ Fourth-degree Bite and Higher

As the biting becomes more ferocious, there are more punctures that are deeper, with bruising and slashed skin from the dog biting and shaking his head. The furthest end point is biting to kill the victim. Generally bites as vicious as these high degrees may be nearly impossible to extinguish or modify. There is no doubt this level of biting is a death knell for the dog.

FEAR-BITERS

Scientific study has shown that if aggression is rooted in fear or anxiety, the use of punishment will compound it.

✦ Biting in Panic

A dog who bites out of fear will lash out in panic, a moment of terror (often over an everyday thing). He's biting to stop you—he's really scared. He's panicky and not making good decisions.

* **Move Slowly, Don't Reach Out to the Dog.**

Don't try to force him to do anything. If the dog is hiding under or behind something like furniture, do not try to move him.

* **Do Not Punish a Fear-biter for Biting.**

If you raise your voice it will increase his fear. Raising your hand to threaten to strike—or actually hitting him—will cause the fearful dog to be even more afraid, especially of fast movements with your hands.

OUTDOOR DOG BITES ARE DIFFERENT

Most "attack and bite" behavior from dogs happens to people outdoors, when they are cycling, running or skateboarding in large, open areas. These types of movements can trigger a "chase response" in a dog. This response comes from predatory instincts.

DO NOT FIGHT AGGRESSION WITH AGGRESSION

The worst thing you can do with a dog who growls is to react in kind: if you come down hard on him, you are punishing him for using his "valuable warning." You may be teaching him that next time, in a similar situation, he shouldn't growl—he should just bite.

WHAT YOU CAN DO ABOUT A BITER

You need an experienced canine behaviorist. You can't just go to any dog trainer, especially one who might mistakenly tell you to overpower or violently discipline a dog who has bitten. Generally speaking, the dog's aggression will worsen if you take a rough approach. A savvy professional should be able to identify what triggers your dog's biting response, help you reduce the dog's exposure to those situations and develop a plan to counter-condition the aggressive reaction.

You have to be willing to make a serious commitment to reorganizing your dog's life so that he never, ever, has the opportunity to bite. Do not delude yourself that the situation in which your dog bit was a one-time thing—it never is. Once a dog has bitten, there is a high probability that he will do it again under the same or similar circumstances. To prevent it, you may have to confine him at certain times, use a muzzle or follow suggestions from a dog trainer experienced with aggressive dogs.

If you can't make the commitment to doing those things, then you have to start looking for someone who will adopt the dog and make that commitment. Frankly, someone else wanting the dog is highly unlikely, since you have to disclose the biting incident. However, if you have a big dog who is in good health—especially a German Shepherd type or Labrador—it may be that a dog who has bitten could be used in law enforcement in the police K-9 unit or in bomb or drug detection. Start calling your local law enforcement agency and work your way up from there.

Failing these options, the dog should be euthanized. If you can't manage and modify your dog's aggression, then the kindest thing—although clearly a hard choice for you—would be to put the dog down. I know that sounds cold and it will be sad, but not half as sad as a child or anyone else being bitten by the dog. If you need to further justify it, consider what kind of life a dangerous dog will have to lead. Depending on the circumstances, what quality of life will your dog have if he must be muzzled, kept in a dog run or shut behind a door?

AVOIDING A BITE FROM AN AGGRESSIVE DOG

Whenever you come upon a dog you don't know—whether inside or outdoors in a public place—there are "rules of disengagement" that you should follow. Be like a submissive dog. Read the description (page 137 of Chapter Six) of what a lower-ranking dog does when approaching a dominant dog: he waits for the dominant dog to lose interest, then backs away slowly.

There is another school of thought that maintains that some aggressive dogs will attack submissive ones anyway, even if the victim is completely unthreatening. So maybe a more neutral posture of quiet confidence is best. If you want to display more self-assurance you can give the aggressive dog a verbalized "woof." A little verbal challenge from you can reveal a canine bully who is actually frightened. He may recoil and even take off when you bark at him.

1. **Stay Back.** By maintaining a distance between you and the dog, you decrease the chance of an encounter—and therefore lower the possibility that you will be bitten.

2. **Stay Calm.** If the dog approaches, be calm and quiet. Do not yell or scream or run away or make jerky movements. Do not stare at the dog or look directly into his eyes. This could provoke an attack.

3. **Stay Still.** If the dominant dog lunges at you, don't run. Push an object toward him that he can bite (instead of you)—offer your purse, backpack, bottle of water, newspaper.

4. **Stay Small.** If you are knocked down, get onto your stomach or curl up in a fetal position. Fold your arms over your head to protect your face.

Chasing

Most dogs like to chase things that move or that you throw. Of course the cat (or chipmunk or rabbit) is more fun since it is self-propelled, but the natural instinct is the same. This is especially true of a dog from any of the hunting breeds (sight hounds, retrievers or terriers) and any dog who is "high-drive" (highly energetic and motivated to action, whether it is in work or play). The breed for which this is especially true is the Border Collie, who lives and breathes to chase and herd.

Chasing people who are on bicycles or jogging happens because the dog has identified the fast-moving person as prey and is just following his instinct by chasing. What a person being chased needs to do is stop, turn around and face the dog, then speak to the dog in a normal tone of voice.

For these reasons, you need to have realistic expectations about managing your dog's desire to chase after fast-moving objects. You cannot teach a dog to not *want* to chase, to ignore her deeply ingrained automatic response. You can't extinguish the lust for the chase in her, which would be like asking her to renounce some part of her "dogness." And there's no way to train a dog to "not chase" when she's on her own the way you can teach her not to get on furniture in your absence. All you can do when you're not around is to remove her physical ability to chase. When you are there, you can use a leash or your voice, if her obedience training is secure enough in the "wait" or "come" commands.

AGGRESSIVE CHASING

The problem changes when a dog who chases wants to get his teeth into his prey, when aggression is part of it. The old gene pool from which dogs are descended included the need to chase to kill and eat to survive; in certain high-drive dogs this inclination is still alive. This does not make them bad dogs, or aggressive dogs. Any dog chasing a runner, bike or other animal can turn predatory—it's a natural progression for a dog, but it can cause accidents if the person is startled and falls. If the dog gets a chance to sink his teeth into a leg, then his future and perhaps his very life are ruined because he has done the unacceptable and caused bodily harm.

If you find that your dog's chase drive borders on aggression, or even if it just makes you nervous, probably the wisest thing would be for you to find a place where you can walk where those temptations are not available him, or never allow him the freedom in the first place.

MULTI-DOG HOUSEHOLDS HAVE A BIGGER PROBLEM

If you have two dogs, the jeopardy increases when they take off together to chase a deer, chipmunk or skateboarder. Some breeds—including herding, sporting, terriers and hounds—like it more, although individuals of any breed or mixed breed can "get their blood up" for a chase.

Once you get three or more dogs, they will operate as a pack—and then all bets are off. The intensity of their chase response and the possible danger to the object of their chase increases again.

CAR CHASING

Set up a remedial situation: have someone drive past slowly and throw out shake-cans tied together or else a balloon filled with water hurled right at the dog.

Even when you are doing this aversive exercise, have the dog on a long line. Never let a chaser have freedom—always have her outdoors on a long line so that you have some control.

WAYS TO MANAGE CHASING PROBLEMS

Remember that your training goal with any problem is to deny your dog the chance to practice the undesirable behavior. This is particularly true of chasing, since the action is its own reinforcement.

◆ Never Encourage Chasing.

Do not egg on a dog, increasing his natural tendency by saying, "Where is it?" in a taunting way; never say, "Go get 'em, Buster." (He really might, and then where will you be?)

♦ Change Your Property Fencing.

If you live in a house and your dog chases at the fence line—or at anything beyond the fence—you can stop that behavior. If you have invisible fencing, this is the most difficult for a chasing dog, because there isn't even a physical boundary to help him curb his passion for the chase—although if you have any kind of actual fence he can see through, that's pretty tempting, too. Solid fences are best: your dog will have no inspiration to chase if you install fence that is sufficiently high that he can't see over it.

♦ Keep Him Inside.

Your dog needs to be confined indoors unless he is with you and directly under your supervision. When you go outdoors, either he has to wear a leash or you must be able to control him perfectly with obedience commands.

♦ Leash and Long-line When Outside with You.

See the "Teaching Manners" chapter for more on the function of a long line. It is a thin, clothesline-type of rope that your dog drags along behind him. If your dog is not responding to a command or just takes off, you can step on the line, making it the ideal solution for thwarting the chase response, because it literally brings him up short when he reaches the end. Not only does this interrupt the chase behavior, but the next time that you call "Wait" or "Come" when he takes off, he may hesitate and consider complying, rather than getting his neck yanked by the line.

Chewing and Other Destructiveness

"DESTRUCTIVE" CHEWING

A fragment complaint about dogs is that they destroy things. People blame a dog for chewing their expensive personal belongings; they assume there must be something wrong with the dog if she is a "destructive" chewer. But "destructive" chewing is a redundancy—chewing *always* destroys something; that's the whole point of a dog having a mouthful of powerful, sharp teeth. What we're referring to is "inappropriate chewing," when the objects going into the dog's mouth do not belong there from our perspective.

♦ Why Dogs Destroy Things

There seems to be a general misunderstanding about why dogs chew in the first place. Dogs don't chew to be destructive—they have no concept of the result of following a natural desire to chew, any more than they would think that scratching an itch is bad—but when they go after your possessions it may be that they chew as an outlet for emotions such as separation anxiety, to get your attention if they feel ignored or because they have too much energy and not enough exercise.

Separation anxiety This fairly common phenomenon is explored in-depth later in this chapter on page 594. Where inappropriate chewing is concerned, the generous-minded assumption is that a dog who destroys your property when you go out—something he never does when you're home—is actually getting some comfort or serenity from doing so. You need to address the separation anxiety, which can cause some dogs profound suffering, but do not ascribe a motive like "vindictiveness" to your dog, since dogs are not wired that way—they do not plot revenge the anysome people do.

Getting your negative attention Just as children who feel ignored or neglected learn how to get their parents' attention with misbehavior (negative attention is better than none at all), so do dogs. But with dogs, people actually *teach* them how to get their human's attention by being destructive. Of course the owners don't realize they are doing this, but it's vital for inter-species living to see that dogs don't do things in a vacuum. We all influence each other. So if you live with a dog that you barely acknowledge—a few pats, a bowl of dry food, leaving her alone most of the time—and then you make a big fuss over her if she rips up a sofa cushion, you have taught a lonely, bored social animal how to get you to pay attention to her.

◆ Attacking Toilet Paper

A roll of toilet paper is a great treat for a puppy. It's usually a form of self-entertainment that puppies engage in when you're not around. It can be pretty annoying to come home and find a roll of toilet paper unraveled in drifts. The easiest cure for a puppy who has found this delightful pastime is to scare the daylights out of her. Place a "shake-can" on top of the roll of toilet paper (see Chapter Ten, "Teaching Manners"). When the puppy starts to mess with the toilet paper, the shake-can will fall down—on her head is just fine—and give her a jolt. As with any correction, it is most effective when it seems *not* to come from you, but seems to be generated by the puppy's own activity.

TOYS AND OTHER "LEGAL" OBJECTS TO CHEW

The best investment you can make for your dog—and especially your puppy—is a fabulous selection of chewable toys. With "legal" outlets for her chewing, there is less chance that your belongings will be targeted. The act of chewing is the most natural thing in the world for a dog. It is pleasurable and self-reinforcing. It's a way to express excitement, to burn off nervous energy, to calm anxiety. Most dogs are grateful to have a basket of "chewables" available for those moments when nothing can satisfy like a good chew.

◆ Make the Toys Available and Tantalizing.

Get some low-sided woven baskets or shallow boxes to be the dog's toy box—that way, the dog knows where to go to grab a chewable, and you have somewhere to toss them when you're tidying up.

You can make chew toys more appealing by putting your smell on them. Rub your hands over each toy before you offer it to the dog.

◆ Rotate the Toys.

Every couple of days put away the toys that have been out and replace them with others, rotating toys so that there's always something new to distract the dog. Get as many as ten or more toys and chewables—get a variety of rubber or latex toys (the former are harder and tougher, the latex are softer but more destructible) with squeakies in them, some cow hooves, various forms of rawhide, balls of every size and material, whatever appeals to you. But only put out a few toys at a time.

WHY DOGS CHEW

There are experts who claim dogs chew from anxiety, stress, boredom or a lack of exercise, as though it is only for negative reasons. That may be true in theory, but from my experience I think it's also about the individual dog's need for chewing as a pleasurable pastime. All the dogs I've had are rarely if ever without people or other dogs around, and they get mountains of affection and attention and huge amounts of exercise and outings in the car. While some of them have shown no interest in chewing, others can't seem can't get enough of it and gnaw from morning to night.

My sense is that some dogs simply are not big chewers—it just doesn't appeal to them as an activity—while others have the drive to chew for many of their waking hours. It seems to relieve tension for them, help pass the time or just feels satisfying. If you realize you have a dog like this, then it makes sense to supply her with a number of good chewable items.

THE DESTRUCTION OF DOG TOYS

The total destruction of rubber squeakie toys poses an interesting dilemma about dog toys: you spend a fair amount on a cute squeak toy that is a big rubber hamburger with lettuce and tomato. This is a toy you probably imagine your dog having months of fun running around with in her mouth—except that within mere minutes of receiving this prize, the dog has extracted the squeaker from the middle and proceeds to gnaw off little bits of the rubber, chewing them like gum before spitting them out in a pile.

I hope you wouldn't even *think* about disciplining the dog for destroying the toy. That would be truly terrible. First of all, it is her toy to do with as she wishes, just as you can't dictate what a person will do with a present you give to them. No matter what plans you had for that toy, or how much it cost, or the time it took to pick it out—at the end of the day, you gave it to the dog, and her idea of what to do with a rubber hamburger may be quite different from yours. Just remember: the alternative is your favorite sandals.

CHOICES IN CHEWABLES

Some people worry about the possibility of choking or intestinal blockage from chewing rawhide, pig's ears or cow's hooves. There isn't much proof of any danger, although it is often mentioned anecdotally. The key is to prevent ingestion. Get oversized rawhide so that the dog is chewing and gnawing and worrying the leather, rather than swallowing it. Also, see "Rawhide Chews" on page 459 in the "Treats" section of Chapter Thirteen. You might ask your vet and the breeder or rescue person where you got your dog what their thoughts are about these treats, since there are many opinions about them.

◆ Rawhide Chews

These come in a vast array of shapes, sizes and even materials. Some are the thin twisted sticks of a yellowish, transparent rawhide, which get soft and gummy as the dog chews them. Another type of rawhide that is tougher to chew through is knotted at the ends and made of thick, bleached white material. Then there are the ones made of pressed rawhide (sometimes colored) that has been ground up and pressed into sticks or various shapes. These crumble when chewed and are easy to chew, even for youngsters or old-timers with diminished tooth power.

✦ Marrow Bones Are Great.

Keep a supply of these bones on hand in the freezer. Just buy a couple of pounds of marrow bones that have been cut into pieces about two inches thick at the supermarket or butcher. At home you can bake the bones in a 300°F oven for about fifteen minutes to get rid of the rawness, or boil them if they are cut so thin that they might become brittle and break if baked. When they are cool, give your dog one and freeze the others. You can take them out for special occasions—either defrost or give to her frozen. It should keep her happy for hours as she chews and licks out the marrow and any bits of gristle attached to the bone. For days afterward she will probably return to the empty bone and chew it for hours more.

✦ Chew Hoofs

These are also great for mega-chewers, because they rarely finish one off at a sitting, and the hoof can still be appealing for another chew on another day. These treats are the "toes" of a cow hoof. They come in random colors, either black or variations on white, and are curved and flat with low sides.

✦ Synthetic Bones

Gumabones and other synthetic bones have a varying degree of desirability to different dogs. These come in shapes, flavors and degrees of hardness. It depends on which ones are satisfying to your individual dog. You can experiment by buying one at a time and seeing which ones appeal to her.

Kongs are hollow toys of a heavy rubber, with ridges on the outside that make them bounce crazily when thrown, which is how they were designed. There are many books that recommend stuffing Kongs with cheese or peanut butter as a long-lasting toy for a dog who suffers from separation anxiety when you're leaving the house. I have to wonder how messy your carpet or dog beds would get—and also how chubby your dogs might get. But even without stuffing them, there are dogs who actually love to chew on the pliable, tough rubber. Although they are purported to be indestructible, my adorable Yogi Bear could chew his way through the outer rim of a Kong in about twenty minutes, leaving a pile of rubber debris scattered around him and a look of great satisfaction on his smiling face.

✦ Toys Made of Lengths of Rope

Rope toys are intriguing to some dogs—some like the bleached white rope, others the multicolored nylon ones. They seem to like to gnaw on the big knots in the ropes. Other dogs like to worry the fringe or tassel on the ends. These are also pull toys, and in a multi-dog family they can pull these between them or with you.

♦ Homemade Toys Are Also Great—Sometimes Even More So.

One of the easiest is a cardboard box—every time you get a box, whether from the postman or from a purchase, give it to your dog. Encourage her to attack the box. Even if she is inhibited, you can shake the box and praise her for taking it in her teeth. It won't be long before she has pulled the box apart. It may leave a scattering of cardboard bits to clean up, but it's an ideal toy because it's free, your dog gets her ya-ya's out and it saves you from having to fold up the cardboard for the garbage.

Another toy is a stick—break it into smaller pieces so it isn't long enough to scratch the walls of your house as the dog proudly parades it throughout. Once again there will be a shredding of wood material to collect and throw away, but it's still better than buying a pricey toy that she doesn't even like.

A rolled-up square of towel with duct tape wrapped twice around makes a perfect throw/tug toy. I call them towel burritos, and I keep a wooden bucket of them at both doors to my house.

Empty plastic milk cartons and water bottles are fun for dogs to chase around, bite and eventually gnaw on. You'll need to keep an eye on an aggressive chewer and take the bottle away when he destroys enough of it that he can bite off pieces and possibly swallow them. Putting a bone inside these bottles is an added bonus: the challenge of getting to that inner treat.

Compulsiveness

(See "Obsessive/Compulsive" on page 590.)

Coprophagy (Eating Feces)

Coprophagy is such an odd-sounding word, but it applies to the equally odd habit that some dogs have of eating feces. If your dog has this (revolting!) habit of ingesting his own or another's stool, there are several explanations for it and several solutions.

DOG EATS HIS OWN DROPPINGS

Only some dogs develop this totally gross habit. Not much is known about why dogs do it—whether it is some nutritional need or even something in their genes. Just as little is known about why they often grow out of it.

♦ There Are Several Ways to Stop This Habit:

❏ Sprinkling Accent (MSG), Adolph's Meat Tenderizer or a product sold by vets called For-Bid on the dog's food (or the food of whichever animal's stool is being ingested) is supposed to make the feces taste really bad. They say that this method can take up to three days to work, but that if you haven't seen improvement in that time, it's not going to work.

❏ Putting pineapple or zucchini into the dog's food is a natural remedy—it also apparently makes a dog's feces especially unappetizing.

- Changing the diet to a less rich food is a suggestion that has limited success.
- Spray the poop with Bitter Apple or bug spray immediately after the dog defecates.
- Prevention is the best solution. As with so many bad habits and problems, picking up after your dog, even in your own yard, is the surest, simplest way to avoid the problem. You're going to pick up the poop eventually, so it might as well be right away to remove the "temptation" from her.
- Ease up on house-training: coming down hard on some dogs during house-training can drive them to ingest the evidence.
- Change the dog's environment for a while. Don't let the dog use his own yard for elimination for a couple of weeks, and walk him away from there—this may break the habit.
- Increase exercise, especially mental exercise, by taking the dog on more outings with you. Occupying his mind can help a dog to burn off excess energy as much as physical outings. Take him with you whenever possible, and include him in your life as much as you can.

REASONS FOR COPROPHAGY

◆ Digestive Problems
Talk to your vet, who may suggest testing the dog's stool to determine if his digestion is functioning well. If this is the problem, the vet may recommend a twice-daily diet that is high-protein, low-carbohydrate and includes added oil.

◆ Boredom
If your dog is left alone most of the day—either paper-trained indoors or in a dog run or a fenced yard outside—he may eat stool because there is nothing else to do.

DOG EATING FROM A CAT'S LITTER BOX
For most dogs, there are no more delicious snacks than the ones in the cat's litter box. For us, nothing seems more disgusting than our dog's breath being . . . well, never mind.

The only way to solve this is to make the cat's box inaccessible to the dog. Depending on your household setup, there are a number of possibilities. If you live in a house with a basement, you can keep the litter box in the basement and keep the basement door open just enough to allow the cat to go through (a nail in the door molding and a string that attaches it to the doorknob can work). You can do the same thing with a bathroom door, although that can be awkward for human use—unless you happen to have an extra bathroom that is rarely used. Putting the litter box inside a bathtub works for some situations, although if the tub is low and the dog is tall, he might find a way to just lean over the tub edge and into the "snack bin."

The litter boxes that have lids on them, with only an opening for the cat, may be a very good solution. Get a model with clamps on either side that hold the lid on, in case the dog is so highly motivated that he'll keep looking for a way to get into the box.

DOG EATS HUMAN FECES

No one likes to admit that this goes on, but you'll see it happen if you take your dogs on long walks in the woods or trails where people have jogged or biked—or if you come upon a construction location where workers may have relieved themselves outside. If you see a pile of crumpled toilet paper or tissue that your dog makes a beeline for, that's probably what is attracting her.

From what I have seen, human feces are even more tantalizing to dogs than cat feces. And doubly gross for us to contemplate, I venture to say. It seems to be a natural desire for the dog, so keep your dog leashed anywhere that you suspect this enticement might be available. If it's an area where you go often with your dog, such as a park or hiking trail, you can try contacting whatever local officials might have jurisdiction and ask them where and how people relieve themselves publicly. You might also want to consider putting up a notice to the offending humans pointing out that they're not out there alone.

Destructive Behavior

(See "Chewing," page 561.)

Digging

The dogs who dig do it because they love it, while other dogs have no interest at all. They say that Terriers and Nordic breeds have a genetic predisposition to dig, but it seems to be just as much an individual leaning.

FILL THE HOLE WITH "DETERRENT."

One of the most reliable and readily available deterrents you can use to keep a dog from digging or redigging in an area is dog poop. For the vast majority of dogs, the presence of canine feces will stop them from excavating that area. This wouldn't work for those dogs who exhibit coprophagy (see page 565 in this section, about dogs who eat dog droppings), but otherwise it's pretty effective.

Put some scooped dog poop in any hole your dog has already begun and cover it over with dirt—she won't go back there to continue her work. This helps in places the dog has already been digging, since it goes into the hole, but it's doubtful you'd want to use this solution for a large area of your property, since you'd have to cover it with dog poop.

PREVENT THE PROBLEM.

Not allowing the dog to be unsupervised in the yard is the only surefire way to avoid the problem. No access means no destruction.

TIRE OUT YOUR DOG.

The fix that addresses the larger issue would be to spend more time tiring out your dog's mind and body—sometimes digging is just a way to burn off steam. If you give your dog plenty of running, walking and chasing, she'll be less inclined to dig to China. Play games with your dog, engage her mind as well as her body, and you may find less excavation work.

DESIGNATE A DIG ZONE

Give your dog some portion of your land that is okay to dig in. You can bring in a few bags of sand or chips or whatever you think will appeal to your dog's desire to dig. Dogs can learn to respect boundaries and understand fairly complex ideas about what you allow where, just as a dog can have one piece of furniture she gets up on, while all the rest are off limits.

Escape Artists/Running Away

This section is going to be full of tips and tricks to escape-proof your property, and recommendations on how to tire and amuse your dog so that she won't want to pull a Houdini. But let me start with the story of a dog with unstoppable wanderlust: Lulu was a Weimaraner I adopted from a "Weim" rescue. I was told she had been adopted and then returned because she was an escape artist who could leap over a six-foot chain-link fence. I figured she must have hated the life those people offered her and was just looking for a better deal, which I felt certain I could provide. My dear Lulu got a dog's paradise with me: she had two male companion dogs (who would do anything the Queen commanded and follow her anywhere she went); there was always someone at home; she lived on two woodsy, fenced acres; the dogs all got twice-daily off-leash runs in the adjoining woods, rain or shine; and she went on many outings a week in the car. Does it get any better than that for a dog? Yet she would persistently find ways to wriggle out under the fence and take marathon hikes well past dark, often in the dead cold, causing us hours of driving around, calling her name with stomachaches, rapid heartbeats and throbbing headaches, fearing the worst. I go into this detail so that you will not be too discouraged or blame yourself if you have a vagabond of your own.

REASONS THAT DOGS RUN AWAY

◆ **Some Breeds Are Prone.**
Certain breeds have the genetic drive to take off—Siberian Huskies, Samoyeds, Border Collies, Irish Setters and Pointers are some that are known to have the high-energy desire to move. Some were bred to pull, others to herd sheep or to travel with hunters.

    Toy breeds pose little risk of running away.

◆ **Sex Drive**
If you have an intact male or a female who comes into heat, those hormones will often propel the dog right out the door.

Spaying and neutering are highly recommended for all pet dogs, anyway—pretty much without any reservation—but with a "runabout," it's one of the most reliable remedies.

◆ Boredom, Loneliness
Dogs are social animals who seek out companionship. Spending lots of time with the dog and giving her exercise and stimulation with new sights and other people and pets will go a long way toward satisfying her drive for adventure and interaction.

RUNNING OUT THE DOOR
Does your dog run off when you open the car door or the door of your house? An untrained puppy will often run off at the first opportunity, but then so can an eager adult dog, especially one that hasn't had enough exercise or is really headstrong. The obvious (and necessary) fix to prevent dashing off is to never open any door around a dog like this, unless he is on a leash.

◆ Create an Enthusiastic Recall.
The word "come" must ALWAYS be the best word in a dog's vocabulary. One problem may be that when you called him in the past, your tone was harsh and scary. The recall must ALWAYS be in a cheery tone with an up-inflection. If need be, there should also sometimes be a treat waiting.

◆ Never, Ever Trick a Dog Who's Responding to a "Come."
You cannot adopt an "all's forgiven, Mommy loves you" tone of voice, only to follow it with curses and punishment. "Come" has to be a command that always sounds welcoming, and obedience must always be praised (even when you are truthfully fuming or frustrated because of the dog's attitude about his delayed return).

◆ More Exercise
"Exercise your dog more" is the refrain you hear about many behavior problems, but with runaways it can be especially relevant. Some escape artists crave exercise and freedom so much that they have to seek it out because it's not being given to them.

DOG RUNS OFF WHEN YOU UNDO THE LEASH

◆ Teach the Dog to Wait to Be Released.
The fix for this problem is super-simple: behave as though you're going to unhook the dog's leash—except don't actually do it. Give the command "Wait" firmly yet softly (if your dog hasn't learned "wait" yet, it would be a good thing to add to his vocabulary—see page 264 in Chapter Ten, "Teaching Manners").

◆ Desensitize the Dog to Having His Leash Unhooked.
Use your finger on the hook end of the leash to make the clicking or snapping noise that releasing the leash makes. Every time the dog hears that sound and wants to bolt, you say "Waaait"

and pat him, if you have a free hand. Praise him for the self-control he shows by not immediately bolting.

Don't ever undo the leash after making the clicking or snapping noise if there's any chance the dog will take off. Besides being dangerous, every time the dog manages to bolt and gets away with it, his delinquent behavior is being reinforced. Don't give him that opportunity.

You need to teach the dog a release word like "okay" (see page 261) so that he knows when he can finish the "restraining behavior" and be free.

RUNNING AWAY FROM HOME

Some dogs want to see the world, and because of that they are really good at finding an exit. Because leaving home is dangerous for an unaccompanied dog, you have to make sure there is absolutely no way the dog can free himself. Keep in mind for the rest of your shared life with your dog that if you don't give him an opportunity to do what you consider "wrong," then he'll never do it.

◆ Keep the Dog Inside When You're Away from Home.

By leaving your dog outside when you go out, you're giving him way too much opportunity to make his escape. With time, a motivated dog will figure out ways to propel himself over or dig under any fence around your property. When you are gone, it may make your dog bored and anxious—so it's only a matter of time before he makes an escape route if you give him the chance.

THE FENCE ITSELF

The first step in protecting a dog that has an inner drive to flee is to tighten up your perimeter.

◆ Fence Before a Dog Ever Joins Your Household.

Before you get your dog, protect his future and your peace of mind by preparing your property with an escape-proof fence (just as *all* dog owners should). Do this even before you have a chance to learn whether your dog is a Houdini, which would make all these fencing issues even more pressing.

◆ Fence Height

The height of the fencing depends somewhat on whether you have an over-and-out jumping dog or a digging dog. You may not know this until the dog has lived with you for a while. Even if your dog is a jumper, some say that making a fence higher is not as important as bending the top inward at a forty-five-degree angle. The point is to make it impossible for the dog to get up and over.

Some say that a five-foot-high fence is the least you need for a small dog—and maybe an even higher one for a really athletic dog like a Jack Russell Terrier—while six feet is the minimum for a medium-sized dog. When you go to buy the fencing, remember that you're going to lose some height with a couple of inches draped on the ground or in a trench. However, when I got Lulu and was told she had gone over a six-foot chain-link fence, I found that if I used a looser (and much less expensive) kind of fencing such as plastic-covered "turkey" wire, even five feet was enough because the fence was not firm and strong enough to hold her weight. A dog trying to climb over has to get some sort of leverage on the fence, and a style of fencing that is more loosely installed than chain-link is actually a deterrent to jumping, in my experience.

♦ Chicken Wire on Top of the Fence
If you put lightweight chicken wire on top of the fence, the dog cannot get a good hold because it is flexible and bends under her weight.

♦ Add a Bar of PVC Pipe on Top
If you have a dog who tries to jump up over the fence and uses the top of it to scramble over, PVC plastic pipe will act like a roller on top. A piece of large PVC pipe on the top of the fence will spin when the dog tries to get a hold and will not allow her to get a grip to boost herself over.

♦ Trench Below the Fence
If the fencing is tall enough, dig a trench beneath the fence that the fence will sit in, with dirt packed back around the base. By burying a couple of inches of fencing inside the trench, it's harder for the dog to dig far enough beneath it to get out. If you have the resources, you could pour a foot of cement or bury cinderblocks (or bricks, large stones—whatever you can come up with) in the trench, so that the area beneath the fence is solid and undiggable.

♦ Fortifying the Base of the Fence
If you cannot put a solid trench beneath the fence, you can place heavy material at the bottom of the fence—both inside and outside, if possible—to discourage digging. Since I live in the woods, I have lots of natural material available—I drag dead tree trunks of various lengths and lay them down on either side of the fence. If you don't have natural options, you can get heavy pieces of wood and do the same thing. While you're protecting the base of the fence, just make sure that what you place there isn't something the dog can stand on and use to boost herself *over* the fence.

♦ Installing the Fence
To give true security, a fence should be high enough not to be able to jump over, and close enough to the ground that a dog can't dig under it. You can use very high, heavy plastic-mesh fencing (the kind often used to keep out deer) or some kind of wire fence, but you have to set the posts so that the bottom of the fence will be flush to the ground. Even better, if it's possible, you could bury a couple of inches in a trench at the time you set the fence. If you can't dig a trench, you can set the fence so that the bottom drapes a couple of inches on the ground toward the *inside* of the fence. You may be able to find the hard-plastic fastener stakes intended to anchor the bottom of the fence into the ground. There is a hook at the top of the stake, so after you hammer the pointed end into the ground, the hook will catch on the bottom wire or plastic of the fence, so that a dog can't push his way under and out.

♦ Gate Latches
A clever dog who is good with her "hands" can figure out how to open many types of gate latches—but you don't want to find this out after she has escaped. Even if you have a latch that

requires an opposable thumb to open, the dog may not be able to open it, but people *will* be using it. You don't want to live in dread of strangers or workmen opening the latch and letting her out in the street. When you hear stories of people losing their dogs, "someone leaving the gate open" seems to be a common reason for the avoidable tragedy. Consider putting a combination padlock on the gate—I did that with Lulu—so that people coming in and out are aware of their responsibility to close the gate carefully. I gave the combination to people who needed to get onto the property, then put a sign on both sides of the gate alerting them to be careful entering and exiting.

SUGGESTIONS ON HOW TO DISCOURAGE ESCAPES

◆ Check Your Perimeter Regularly.

Patrol your fenced-in area on a regular basis. A dog can create gaps and holes and displace logs or rocks you had originally placed to cover up where the fence wasn't properly installed. Branches can fall and affect the fence. Gate hinges can get old or out of alignment.

◆ Don't Leave a Dog Outside for Hours.

Being outside, especially alone, can seem like a punishment to a dog who is bored and lonely. If there are any weather issues—hot, cold, buggy—that just increases the feeling of wanting to escape. So if the dog is left outside without any way of getting indoors, he may be motivated to run away.

◆ Make the Outdoors Appealing and Fun.

The space inside the fence should be pleasant and appealing. Make sure there is a cool, shaded area and fresh water in a tip-proof bowl (put a rock in there, if necessary). If it's summertime, fill a kiddie pool with water so the dog can splash around in it when he gets hot. Make a sandbox area to dig in and even bury some bones in there to inspire a treasure-hunt dig—as an alternative to an under-the-fence dig.

Fearful Personality and Phobias

(This section on fearfulness pertains to all the phobias a dog might have, except the specific "thunderstorm phobia," which is covered in this section on page 610.)

FEARFUL DOGS: BORN OR MADE?

◆ Born Shy: A Fearful Personality in the Genes

Just like every aspect of a dog's personality, the tendency to be fearful or shy can run in the family. If a dog is born with a tendency to be shy, then you have to work doubly hard to help him overcome his instinctive fears. When you're picking a puppy from a litter, do not get sentimental and feel sorry for the timid, cowering-in-the-corner little pup who pushes all your "oh-poor-thing" buttons. A fearful dog is a burden—he can be hard work to socialize and can even turn out to be an aggressive dog.

THE PUPPY "FEAR IMPRINT PERIOD"

All dogs have a fear imprint period at about eight weeks of age, and then there's a longer fear period during adolescence. If a dog has a big scare in either period and it is not dealt with, the result may be a lifelong phobia. The dog may develop a sudden fear of children, certain objects or noises, or even other dogs. The fear can focus on one individual person or a type of dog—a very tall, very small or very hairy one—and that fear may be long-lasting.

Knowing this should help you to be realistic in your expectations of your dog. Do not be impatient or have a timetable of when a dog "should" get over his fears. It will happen when it happens . . . *if* it happens.

DEALING WITH A FEARFUL DOG

Fearful dogs are often misunderstood. If you can see that fear is driving many of your dog's reactions, you can understand him better and be supportive of slow change. Also, accept the fact that this is your dog's personality. As with people, basic character does not change—it may improve, but as the great philosopher Popeye said, "I yam what I yam."

◆ Remain Calm Yourself.

If you react with anxiety in any situation, it can trigger your dog's fearfulness. If you get tense it will show in your body language, your tone of voice, your hand tightening on his leash. When this happens, realize that you're sending a message to the dog that there really may be something to worry about. You need to stay loose.

◆ Don't Feed into His Fears and Doubts.

Don't coddle, soothe or pat a fearful dog while he is exhibiting fear, because you'll just reinforce and confirm his fearfulness, convincing him that he has good reason to be frightened. The best way to handle a scaredy-cat dog is to pat him briskly and behave as though everything is fine. Show him leadership: when he sees you behaving as though all is well, he will start to believe it, too.

◆ Use Positive Techniques.

Be as jolly as you can around the person or thing that's scaring him. If you are upbeat, even laughing, it can have a relaxing effect on the dog.

Have treats or a toy with you whenever you might be dealing with a new situation.

A good way to handle fearful reactions is to put the dog on a "sit, stay" and let the scary thing go by.

◆ Anxiety Medication

If the dog is fearful enough that the fear gets in the way of his being able to enjoy a normal life, talk to your vet about anxiety-reducing or antidepressant drugs, which have been used effectively in dogs. Beta blockers such as propranolol (the generic for Inderal) can also be effective.

THE BURDEN OF A SHY OR FEARFUL DOG

People who don't have much experience with dogs might think that a shy puppy is sweet and a fearful dog is kind of cute and lovable, but that dog is suffering. Imagine what it would feel like to be scared out of your wits by anything unusual that crosses your path. A fearful dog has to be handled with special care or that fear can turn into aggression, creating a potentially dangerous situation. A dog who is scared may shock her owners by developing into a dog who will attack and bite because she is so terrified.

◆ Handling the Shy/Fearful Dog

- ❑ Socialize the dog as much as possible. Put him in agility and obedience classes, and take him with you anywhere you can. The more he sees and experiences, the less he will be worried by new things. Also, it reinforces you as the leader. He will feel there is less to worry about if you are in charge.
- ❑ Do not make many demands on a fearful dog—he can go into "overload." Do not react: do not reprimand the dog and certainly do not shower him with affection which would reinforce his fear.
- ❑ Do not try to force him to deal with anything that spooks him—even if it seems ridiculous to you. Do not press him to confront the feared object.
- ❑ Things may be going too fast if he gets *more* scared after being introduced to something new. If so, back it up a notch. But don't insulate or isolate him, just keep inching him forward into the scary unknown. Take his progress in baby steps.

THINGS FEARFUL DOGS CAN BE AFRAID OF AND WAYS TO DESENSITIZE THEM

◆ Anything Unfamiliar

Anything a dog has not seen before can frighten him—depending on his personality. You'll know what he's feeling because when dogs are frightened, they usually bark defensively. If he's scared of strangers or people with objects he doesn't know—such as a walker or umbrella or tool belt—you want to desensitize him to that thing. Coax him to sniff the object. Ask the person who has it if he can spend more time with you, or if you can borrow it or use a similar object for a day or a whole week. If the dog is still afraid of the object despite being around it, try sitting on the floor with the object and giving the dog biscuits just for coming close. You can also place the object next to his food bowl to give it a positive association.

◆ New people

- ❑ Men and children are the two groups of people most often feared by fearful dogs. Men who are feared often have intimidating characteristics like being tall and/or having beards, hats, big boots and deep voices (and some dogs may have had a bad experience with a man before who had one of those characteristics).
- ❑ Let the dog approach people or things that frighten him—rather than having them come over to him.

- ❑ Do not crowd or corner a dog with these issues, because he may bite for fear that he is trapped with the frightening person. Even if the dog is off-leash and in the open, there is a possibility that he will bite defensively from fear.
- ❑ Give him positive attention for being brave. When he's fearful don't respond in any way: do nothing at all.
- ❑ Give special delicious treats to strangers and let them dispense them. You may want to teach the command "say hello" as a way of reassuring the dog that all is well, giving permission to the dog to go ahead and check out the scary stranger.

◆ Garbage Trucks

Try to take the dog to an area where there are a lot of garbage or other large trucks, first from a distance. These are the same two techniques used together to overcome *all* undesirable dog behavior: desensitization and counter-conditioning. Use a ball or his favorite toy to take his mind off the trucks while accustoming him to the sound (desensitization), and then give him something delicious at the same time he is experiencing the thing he fears (counterconditioning). Then move increasingly closer to the trucks, distracting and rewarding the dog for being near his most dreaded object and not acting up. Eventually you can change his mind about the scary thing.

◆ Loud Noises

Re-create the noises that make him jump. Feed him in a metal bowl, bang the spoon, make noise in general. Desensitize him to loud or sharp noises by being noisy with all objects.

◆ Going through Double Doors or into an Elevator

A glass door followed by a glass door can be scary to a dog because it may look like he'll get trapped between the two. In an elevator, a dog may have gotten scared if the doors ever began to close on him or his paw or tail ever got caught in the doors. No matter what happened to spook him, if you live in an apartment building, the dog has to overcome his phobia.

With a cheery, upbeat voice, just say "Let's go, come on" and praise the dog for following you into the elevator or through the doors. If he won't do that, then you have to use pressure on the leash and just forge ahead. If you pause and wait for him to go, he'll pause and that will be the end of it. You have to exhibit confidence and carry on.

◆ Vacuum Cleaners

Many dogs are afraid of vacuums. Leave the machine out in the open. Give treats to the dog just for being willing to come near the scary thing.

Every time the machine is turned on and the dog barks, offer him a special toy to distract him, then give him a treat when he stops barking. This may take weeks or months.

Garbage-picking

(See "Stealing" on page 600 in this section.)

Getting Up on Furniture

SMALL DOGS ARE ALLOWED.

A dog being up on furniture is only a problem if you think it is. Many owners of small dogs actually *expect* them to jump up onto furniture, so they can be closer for petting and lap-sitting. Many of these same owners like to carry their small dogs around and then set them down beside them when they sit. This is rarely a problem, because most small dogs don't run around outside and get all muddy and then transfer the dirt to the furniture or the person beside them. The worst that might happen is that they'll shed on the furniture.

People with small, hairy dogs such as Maltese or Shih Tzus may want to place dog-hair removers around the house so that when people stand up they can immediately run those masking-tape rollers up and down their legs. For many people, having a lap dog may mean the end of a basic black wardrobe—they often switch to clothes that don't show the hair as much.

Many people own large, hairy, muddy pooches that are not welcome on the furniture . . . and yet, Rottweilers may want to be up there beside you as much as the smallest Pomeranian. Even if the big dogs were always clean as a whistle, the really big ones stretch out and take up most of a couch, leaving both you and your guests to fend for yourselves.

BE CONSISTENT: YES OR NO ON THE FURNITURE.

You cannot let the dog up on the couch one day and then be furious to find her up there the next day. Put a comfortable dog bed near the sofa so she has an alternative to the couch. When you stop her in the act of getting up on the furniture by saying "Off," you can point at the dog bed and tell her in a pleasant voice, "Go to your bed."

This works the way the bait and switch does with a young dog, when you offer an appropriate toy as soon as she lets go of a forbidden shoe. When changing a dog's behavior, it is always good to be positive and give her something to do *instead* of what is being taken away.

Several of the high-end gadget catalogs feature battery-operated "dog-off alarms," which you place on the off-limits object to repel the dog. These alarms have a motion detector inside them, and they emit a high-pitched, siren-type noise when the dog moves in front of them.

WHEN YOU ARE IN THE ROOM

If a dog begins to get up on a piece of furniture while you are there, don't overreact by shouting. There are better ways to handle this, which are actually effective.

◆ **Catch Him in the Act.**

Try to catch the dog in the process of getting up before he gets settled. Say his name to get his attention, and then not just the word "No" but a command for him to do something else instead, such as "Get off" and then perhaps "Lie down" in another spot.

◆ **If You Can't Catch Him in the Act**

If the dog is already on the couch, stand near the dog and say "No, off" in a friendly way (*not* in a murderous tone because you just had the couch steam-cleaned). Point away from the couch to emphasize the "off" command. (Don't say "Down," because that is a specific command that designates lying down and should not be used here, or when a dog is jumping up on you. That would be another occasion for the word "off." Even if your dog has not learned the word "off" before, he will get the picture if you're calm and patient.) Don't repeat what you said ("No" or "Off"), just stand there with your finger pointing to the ground. If the dog stops climbing up and even begins to put his feet back on the ground, give him verbal praise. As soon as all four feet are back on the floor make a fuss over him. If he starts right back up on the sofa repeat the command of "no, off" and point to the floor again.

VERBAL REINFORCEMENT

If you're in the room and the dog starts up onto furniture, interrupt him immediately with the ever-useful "unh-uh" grunt that means "Don't even think about it" to a dog. Somehow, most dogs understand the ominous warning in our tone—they stop what they are doing and look up at us. At that point you have their attention and can redirect their intentions. You can call the dog over to you and give her lots of scratches and pats, or you can direct her to her bed or "allowed furniture" and then give her lots of praise.

STUBBORNNESS

If your dog refuses to get down when you say "Off" and point to the floor, take his collar and gently pull him off. Then pat and praise him for having his feet off the furniture, although not with the same genuine appreciation that you would show if he had done it on his own. Impress upon him that being off the furniture brings him positive feedback.

If he has already settled in, he may not even lift his head, probably just look up at you with his eyes only and give you a "Surely you jest?" look.

In this case, don't hesitate to take him by the collar and pull him slowly but surely off the edge of the couch. You can repeat "off," but make sure there is no rancor or other emotion in your voice. Try to avoid the sense that the dog is being reprimanded for being a bad dog. The message needs to be simple and clear: the *dog* is not bad, he is in a *bad place*, a place where dogs are not supposed to be.

SEND THE DOG TO HER OWN SPOT

For some dogs, it really helps to send them to their own bed at this juncture. The message the dog should be getting is: get off our furniture and onto your own, where you will get lots of loving.

Keep a dog bed in the living room, or anywhere you spend time, so that the dog has a comfortable alternative to his first choice, which would be the sofa or chair.

◆ Set Aside a Chair.

You could also designate a sofa or chair as "dog permissible," depending on the condition of your furniture, and send the dog there as a compromise. Just point down to the floor when you say "No, off," and then point to the acceptable furniture and say "Okay," even patting the furniture and saying "Up!" to make it clear.

Some trainers claim that dogs cannot differentiate between a permissible piece of furniture and all the other inanimate objects in the house that have four legs—chairs, sofas, tables, beds. I have not had trouble with any dog understanding this concept perfectly: that is yours, all the rest of the sitting-on objects are ours. I often put a synthetic lambskin throw blanket on the acceptable furniture, both to keep it clean and to earmark it for the dog. If the dog is feeling excited or anxious, it also gives her something to chew on (in the case of Lulu, who must have been removed from her mother too young, these blankets became like a baby's "blankie" to *suck* on).

There may be a couple of misfires as the dog attempts to get back on your furniture and you have to go through the drill again, but it should be pretty easy to get him straightened out so that he knows his place, furniture-wise.

AVERSION TRICKS FOR WHEN YOU ARE NOT AROUND

There are several ways to booby-trap your furniture so that your dog will not even try to get up when you are out, or will try and get a nasty scare.

◆ Mousetraps

Buy some old-fashioned mousetraps at the hardware store—one each for chairs and one for each seat cushion area of a couch, depending on the length. Your intention here is not to catch some part of your dog's anatomy in a mousetrap, but to scare him with the snapping sound of the trap, making him paranoid about getting up on the furniture.

Set the traps and place one on each chair or seating area. Then take several big sheets of newspaper and gently cover each trap. Use some masking tape to secure the edges and corners of the newspaper onto the furniture—you don't want the paper to fall off the cushion. If the mousetraps were exposed you would run the risk of actually hurting the pooch.

If the dog tries to get up on the furniture when you're out, he will set off the mousetrap(s) beneath the newspaper and scare the dickens out of himself. Any dog with half a brain will not be going near a newspaper-covered sofa anytime soon.

This is only a training tool—presumably after a week a dog will have learned to stay off the furniture. But a really smart dog might learn to only avoid furniture with newspaper on it, and help himself to the couch again as soon as you get tired of booby-trapping "his" couch.

◆ Balloons

(NOTE: *Do not try this if you have a timid, shy dog—it could be too much for him.*)

This method works similarly to the mousetraps in that it involves making the furniture scary to a dog. Mousetraps rely on the surprise shock effect. With balloons, you first make them scary to a dog, and then cover the couch with them.

Blow up a couple of balloons and bring them over to the dog. Let her sniff and touch a balloon, then suddenly stick a pin in it so it explodes. The loud noise scares dogs. If your dog was really frightened, then one balloon is enough—if she doesn't seem that rattled, do it a second time. Blow up about ten balloons and tape or tie them to the furniture you want to protect from the dog. If the dog was properly scared by the popping balloon, she will not approach the couch or chair that is covered by them.

Do this for a week. Once again, if you have a sly fox of a dog, she may wait until the balloons are gone before settling herself back among your sofa cushions.

◆ Aluminum Foil

This is possibly the best booby-trapping technique for a mild-mannered dog. If you think your dog's personality is sensitive, then try this aversion technique before the more explosive versions above.

Cover the cushions of the furniture with long sheets of aluminum foil, taping the edges down onto the material so that the foil stays in place and doesn't float off. If the dog tries to get up on that furniture, she will be repelled by the shiny surface, the crinkly sound of the foil and the slippery feel of it under her paws. As with the other two techniques, try this for a week and see if it cures your dog of getting up on the furniture after the leaves of aluminum foil are no longer there.

House-soiling

(See also Chapter Nine, "House-training," page 215.)

WHY IS YOUR DOG ELIMINATING IN THE HOUSE?

◆ Medical Reasons for Soiling

There are several reasons that previously house-trained dogs will begin soiling in the house. Most of them are medical, so if your dog does begin eliminating inappropriately in the house, assume that there is a physical cause for it and take her to the vet.

◆ Behavioral Reasons for Soiling

You can only consider other motivations for soiling *after* you have eliminated medical reasons

House-soiling from Medical Conditions (Urine or Stool)

- Bladder infection (urine)
- Diabetes (urine)
- Bladder stones (urine)
- Kidney disease (urine)
- Low-calorie, high-fiber diet (stool)
- Irritation of intestinal or urinary tract (either)
- Hormonal urinary incontinence (urine)
- Arthritis (can't get outside quickly/if spinal, loss of nerve control) (either)
- Obesity (can't get outside quickly enough) (either)
- Steroids (prednisone, etc.) (urine)
- Diuretics (water pills) (urine)
- CCD (canine cognitive dysfunction) (either)

with your vet. After you have done that, there are numerous possibilities to consider, from separation anxiety, to other anxieties and temperamental issues. A number of these problems are covered later in this chapter. But there is no easy slot in which to put house-soiling, since each dog is unique. So to solve your dog's house-soiling, you need to pay attention to when and where she soils and—without being angry or critical of her—try to figure out what is generating this behavior.

Dogs do not soil out of "spite" or "revenge" These are not considered canine emotions. However, you do hear anecdotal information about dogs, especially small ones, jumping up and eliminating on their owners' beds and pillows when left alone. Although it does humanize the little pooches to think that they are "getting back at their owners," a more likely reason might be that the dogs *are* suffering from separation anxiety and are somehow comforted by "marking" the place that has the strongest odor of you.

✦ Changes in the Daily Routine

If your schedule changes, it will usually affect your dog's daily rhythms, too: her mealtimes change, and/or the amount of time she is left alone, the hours that she gets walked, even the length of those walks. All the adjustments can affect her digestive and urinary system, as well as her emotional state.

✦ Changes in the Weather

Many dogs cannot stand to go out in the rain, and even if they are willing to brave the wet they don't want to do their business out there. The only solution to this is to get your dog to accept the discomfort. That means that *you* have to brave it, too—put on your foul-weather gear and take her out for as long as it takes. If you get your dog as a puppy, start walking her in the rain, wind and snow (if these occur where you live) when she's young, so that she accepts weather changes as a part of life.

- ❑ Try a coat if she is small, short-coated or frail: try a rain slicker on her and see if that makes it more bearable for her to walk outside. For some dogs, however, the sensation of wearing a coat makes it even less likely that they'll relieve themselves.
- ❑ Carry a large umbrella so you can both fit under it. If the dog senses that there's less precipitation falling on her if she sticks close to you, she'll be able to benefit from your shelter. Some dogs really do take advantage of this.

◆ **Territorial Reasons for House-soiling**

Many male dogs are territorial, even ones who have been neutered. Once in a while you'll find a female who has a strong drive to mark her territory, too.

- ❑ If another dog comes into your house, there is a chance that your dog may feel compelled to mark his turf. You certainly don't want another dog to come inside who might lift his leg, or you'll have the start of a real pee-a-thon! But for some really territorial dogs, even just the odor of another dog inside his house can inspire marking.
- ❑ If your dog sees another dog outside on your property it can cause him to lift his leg and mark his turf *inside.* So if your dog sees another dog on your land—and you're not home or do not witness it—then you may think he has lost his mind if you find he's left a marker somewhere. But he's actually just following his deepest instincts, and your damask sofa is the closest place to express himself.

TOTALLY CLEAN THE SOILED AREA

Dogs will go back to wherever they have soiled before and repeat the offense. The way to fix this is to thoroughly clean the area and then "redesignate" the function of the area in canine terms. The chapter on house-training describes all of this in detail, but basically, you need to first clean the area well with an enzymatic cleaner.

After that, there are several ways to redefine the function of that part of your house. Depending on where the area is, you will decide which of the following techniques is right for you.

WAYS TO CHANGE AN AREA'S FUNCTION

- ❑ Move the dog's food and water bowl there.
- ❑ Groom the dog there.
- ❑ Play with the dog there.
- ❑ Put his bed over the area.
- ❑ Sit there and read or work yourself.

Jumping Up on People

(For more on this topic, see "Off" on page 261 in Chapter Ten, "Training Manners.")

CONSISTENCY IS ESSENTIAL

Jumping up is a common problem, which is made worse by people being inconsistent in what they allow their dog to do. In addition, they are not consistent with the command they use to stop the behavior. Instead of the word "off," they'll say "Down" one time, "Get down" another, or "No, get off." This lack of consistency doesn't give the dog a chance to understand what behavior you are reprimanding or what you want him to do instead.

You have to decide as a household that jumping will *never* ever be okay—and everyone who lives in your house or comes there frequently must agree to stick to a plan. Otherwise, if you *sometimes* allow a dog to jump, it's really unfair to him. A dog can't tell the difference between your good clothes and work clothes, between you feeling playful or being distracted by other concerns, and he certainly cannot learn whether there are some people he can jump on and others that he cannot.

REPLACE "JUMP" WITH "SIT."

Not all dogs have a strong desire to jump up, but the ones who do need to have that enthusiasm redirected. Take the energy the dog puts into wanting to jump and instead tell him to "Sit," then praise the heck out of him for making that switch. You are basically telling him what you want—it's something active he can do. You're not just saying "No!" and sounding hysterical when he jumps; you're calmly commanding "Off," then quietly commanding "Sit" and giving him a special treat.

Believe it or not, some dogs get this after three tries and never jump again.

PRACTICE WITH A FRIEND AS "GUINEA PIG."

Once you've practiced "off" with family members, you need be able to have the same control when a guest comes. You need a friend to volunteer to ring your doorbell and be a visitor. Give the friend some extra-delicious dog treats to keep in her pocket, which will be your dog's reward for not jumping up. When your friend comes to the door and enters, you should already have a leash on your dog for the practice session.

◆ Timing Is Everything.

As soon as the dog begins to jump up, say "Off." At *the same moment* give the leash a jerk to the side or—depending on the dog's size relative to yours—give a body-block (to a large dog) to knock him off course. You don't want to hurt or punish him, just stop that upward motion and get him off balance.

Here's the important part: the MOMENT that all four of his feet hit the ground, praise the heck out of him. Then ask him for a "sit" instead. Cue your friend to give the dog a treat at the moment that he sits himself down.

OTHER CORRECTIONS FOR JUMPING UP

There are a number of theories about how to correct a jumping dog, but many of them evolved in an era when painful aversion tactics were often used. Those ideas in all dog training have been mostly replaced by more humane ideas. This method—interrupting the jump and rewarding the "sit"—works so well that there's no point confusing the dog with other exercises. But if this does not work for you, you obviously should try anything else you learn about from a trainer or elsewhere. (If you find something that's more effective and easier, please let me know at www.thedog bible.com.)

The maneuvers on the list that follows were all part of old-fashioned methods of keeping a dog from jumping up. People may still attempt them without realizing that at worst they are hurting a dog, and at best, they're not doing anything that will effectively achieve their goal.

WHAT NOT TO DO ABOUT JUMPING

❏ Do *not* try to punch your knee into a dog's chest as he jumps (you can hurt his leg, or *your* leg; if you knee him higher, you can hurt his torso or gut).

❏ Do *not* try to catch hold of the dog's front feet and squeeze the paws painfully until he pulls to get down.

❏ Do *not* try to catch hold of the front feet and spread his front legs apart until he struggles to get down.

❏ Do *not* try to grab the front feet and then try to step on his back feet (this makes for a particularly ridiculous dance with a large dog, who weighs a ton to hold up while you stomp around underneath, trying to land on his foot).

Licking (People and Themselves)

This friendly (and generally submissive) gesture that dogs use with each other can get out of control with a dog that is very pushy and just doesn't want to stop licking. One thing that's important to note is that dogs will usually not tolerate a prolonged amount of licking from another dog—so why would you want to encourage an unnatural behavior in your dog? It will be work for you to stop once it becomes a nuisance.

Some dogs lick your legs, feet and hands, especially if you have some kind of lotion on. You need to firmly say "No," ignore the dog and break eye contact. Then make the dog sit, and give her lots of praise when she does.

WHY ENCOURAGE SOMETHING YOU'LL REGRET?

You may think it's sweet at first to have your dog lick you, but what if *her* idea of "how much and how often" is quite different from yours? There are so many ways for dogs and people to express their affection for one another—why create the problem of a heavy-licking dog by encouraging her? How will you stop her, and how will you keep her from bugging other people with her enthusiastic tongue? Most people abhor being licked in the face by a dog—I've noticed them recoil and turn their heads aside when my dogs sniff near their faces. The people relax as soon as I tell them that my dogs are trained not to lick, that they're just curious, "in case someone had eggs for breakfast and they were left out." The visitor inevitably relaxes, knowing they're not going to get a tongue-bath.

IT JUST TAKES A LITTLE DISCOURAGEMENT TO STOP A DOG'S LICKING.

With many dogs it's actually pretty easy to stop them from licking: ignore the dog the moment her tongue connects with your flesh. Get up and leave whenever she starts to lick.

You can set this in motion by sitting down next to the dog and putting your face near the dog's face. If she starts to lick, say "No"—firmly but quietly. Turn your face away, removing your attention. No big dramatic reaction, just the withdrawal of your affection. Then you can pat and even kiss the dog. If she starts to lick you, all it takes is removing your attention again: take your hands off her, turn your face away and say "No!" with a tone of disgust and disbelief that she's still trying to lick you.

DON'T LET OTHER PEOPLE ENCOURAGE LICKING.

Some people really want to be kissed on the face, especially on the lips, by a dog. They don't seem to be interested in respecting your desires about your dog's conduct. Other people can encourage your dog to lick them—you have to keep an eye on this and stop them, or it can undo the no-licking rules you've established. You don't want your dog corrupted into a behavior you don't approve of, any more than you'd let people teach your dog to jump on the sofa or eat off the dining-room table.

(I've actually tried to deter some lick-happy friends with the reminder that the last thing my dog licked was her own private parts—but even that didn't serve as the immediate deterrent I had hoped.)

DOGS LICKING THEMSELVES
("Lick granuloma," also known as "acral lick dermatitis (ALD)";
see under "Skin, Lick Dermatitis" on page 389 in the health chapter.)

It is normal for dogs to lick themselves. This is a natural grooming technique to clean their limbs and genital area and to remove parasites. Dogs who groom much more intensely and for longer than a normal dog does may suffer from a disorder called "lick dermatitis," in which they lick until they have licked off the top layers of hair and skin and created a deep, infected wound. A dog suffering from this medical condition may lick repetitively at one spot, usually on the wrist area of the front leg, although the back leg can also be the chosen spot. It is a compulsive disorder.

✦ Why Some Dogs Develop Licking Compulsions

Genetics are thought to play some part in this disorder, both in terms of the basic underlying anxiety that a dog may be born with, and the fact that the licking behavior has become the coping mechanism of choice. Anxiety is considered the most likely cause of the lick compulsion.

Large breeds are usually the ones affected—Golden Retrievers, Labrador Retrievers, German Shepherds, Great Danes and Dobermans—any of which may be at an increased risk for developing acral lick granuloma. The dog's size is relevant because it's sort of mechanical: when a large dog lies down, her forelegs and the hocks of her back legs are the closest part of herself to lick. In a small dog, her legs are short and she can reach her nails—and nail-biting is most common in small dogs, who bite their nails out of anxiety, just as people do.

WHAT TO DO ABOUT THE PROBLEM

♦ Do Not Use Bitter Products.
An obsession with licking cannot be stopped by spraying the affected area with a product like Bitter Apple or applying cayenne pepper or other physical deterrents. A dog will lick right through and past the bad taste, so save that effort for something that it might help.

♦ Have a Vet Examine the Dog.
Sometimes, dogs lick when they feel nauseated. Some signs of nausea include not accepting treats from you, rejecting meals or eating them tentatively. Another medical reason a dog can lick is if her joints are sore, which a vet can also help determine.

♦ Reduce Stress in the Dog's Environment.
Any behavior disorders can be the result of a dog's experience of stress in her life. It may sound ludicrous, but in fact there can be various elements of a domestic dog's lifestyle that contribute to tension and the resulting inappropriate behavior. If you recognize any of the environmental issues here, see what you might be able to do to make a change in your dog's surroundings or routine. Each dog is an individual, so factors in the environment that might have no effect on one dog can cause another to go over the edge.

If a dog is experiencing conflict—for example, "sibling rivalry" with another pet, or feeling jealousy or displacement from a new member of the family (whether it is an in-law that has come to stay or a new infant)—this can show up as compulsive licking.
Loneliness If a dog is left home alone all day, she may get anxious and bored and turn to licking herself out of loneliness and frustration. The amount of time you can leave a dog home alone before trouble begins varies with the individual dog.
An unpredictable routine If your dog has a schedule she can count on—so she knows when you will come and go, and when to expect meals—it can lower her anxiety level.

♦ Get Her Tired Out, Keep Her Mind Engaged.
Generally, the best treatment is to get the dog's mind off her obsessive licking. This is usually best achieved by keeping the dog active. A stressed dog needs lots of exercise, lots of diversion. This can mean taking the dog with you in the car or on foot as much as possible to stimulate her body *and* mind.

⬥ Give Her Engaging Toys.

See the section on "Toys," page 193, to learn more about the many mind-stimulating toys that are available, such as a Kong stuffed with cheese or a cube toy that dispenses treats. Also, remember not to leave out too many toys: just give a couple of toys at once. When she seems bored by them, put those away and bring out a couple of new toys to catch her interest.

⬥ Get Canine Company for Her.

If your dog does well around other dogs, a "play date" with other dogs or doggie day care is a good solution.

IF THE LICKING PROBLEM PERSISTS

⬥ The Area Can Get Infected.

If an infection occurs where the dog licks (which is often the case), be sure to see the vet, who may prescribe antibiotics. Even if the raw, ulcerated wound starts to heal without getting infected, there is a good chance that the dog will return to compulsively licking it, reopening the wound and increasing the chance of infection.

⬥ Medications Can Help.

If the dog cannot stop licking, there are medications that your vet may suggest to control this compulsive behavior. If your doctor is not familiar with these drugs for treatment, ask her to recommend a vet who may specialize in these problems.

Human drugs such as Prozac or clomipramine (Anafranil) may help with compulsions. Other human antidepressants and anti-obsessional medications can also be effective, such as Zoloft, Paxil and Luvox.

Drugs alone cannot perform magic. Medicine generally cannot work in a vacuum—you have to combine it with some of the activities and environmental changes mentioned above. However, these medications are really intended to assist in lowering cortisol levels in the dog so that learning can then take place. It is very rare to have any medicine completely extinguish the compulsive activity. In fact, medical treatments must go hand-in-hand with a behavior modification program or else you wind up with long-term reliance on medication without full satisfaction.

Drugs take time. The medicated dog can take quite a long time to show any improvement. After four months, if the medicine is going to work for your pet, she'll probably show an eighty percent to ninety percent improvement. It is very rare to have the medicine completely extinguish the compulsive activity.

⬥ Natural Remedies Can Work for Some Dogs.

There are a number of homeopathic substances that can lessen anxiety. A product called Rescue Remedy (sold in health food stores) is used to reduce nervousness with a few drops in the dog's water—some dog owners and medical practitioners have gotten good results with this. Melatonin (a natural substance often recommended for human jet lag) can also reduce anxiety in some dogs. Lavender oil sprinkled on the dog's bedding as aroma therapy is also credited with having a calming effect. Some of these homeopathic remedies have a short duration if they do work, but many people prefer using these natural substances.

◆ Acupuncture Can Help.

Although acupuncture has treatment sites that respond specifically to lick granuloma, acupuncturists have found that many owners do not want to take the time and incur the expense of $80 to $100 or more for each treatment just for obsessive licking.

Nose-nudging (Crotch-sniffing)

There are several irritating places that dogs can nudge people with their noses: the person's hand (to get some patting), the person's elbow when they are sitting at the table (to get some food or attention) and the person's crotch when they first come in—to do what? Embarrass them? Actually, crotch-sniffing is probably just the dog doing to a person what dogs do to each other as a way to get more sensory information.

The good news is that you can keep nose-nudging from starting, and it's not that hard to stop. By the way, the same rules apply to a dog who paws at you for any of the same reasons.

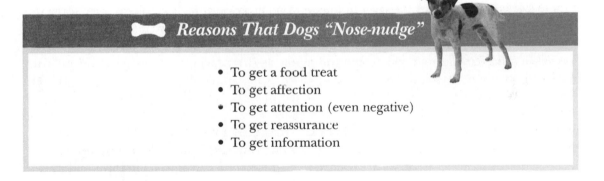

Reasons That Dogs "Nose-nudge"

- To get a food treat
- To get affection
- To get attention (even negative)
- To get reassurance
- To get information

NUDGING FOR ATTENTION

You can stop a dog from the unpleasant habit of trying to engage you with his nose by refusing to acknowledge it *in any way*. This is an important distinction in our overall relationship with our dogs that's not easy to fully grasp: *anything at all* that you do or say to your dog is giving him something. If he has *demanded* that interchange with nose-nudging (or pawing, whining, etc.), then you have fulfilled his request by giving him something back, and you have reinforced whatever he did to get it. It doesn't matter whether your response is positive or negative. Even if you yell or glare or push him away, you have increased the likelihood that he will do it again *because he got you to respond.*

Totally ignoring a dog means precisely that. Turn your back. Turn your head away. No eye contact. No voice contact. No physical contact. It sounds simple, but it's remarkable how infrequently we actually achieve it.

✦ Any Acknowledgment By You Is Good Enough for Him.

Most dogs aren't that fussy or sensitive to how you respond to their needs. It's hard for us to believe that if we snap at our dog and say, "No, damn you!" with a snarling glare and push him away with our foot that he won't have his feelings hurt all day. If it were us we'd be crushed. Not only do dogs not really understand human language, if they want attention badly enough they'll take any feedback, even cranky.

✦ The Cold Shoulder

Giving your dog "the arctic freeze" is the kindest thing you can do. It is what works every time with dogs. It instantly conveys your displeasure, he gets the point and changes his tune. Neither of you has to go through a long, drawn out debate about nudging or pawing. If you feel you can't do it—if you feel that a chilly response is antithetical to your nature—then consider it a skill you should work to develop. It's a big part of dog-human communication—and you'd be surprised how useful it can be in certain human interactions, too.

✦ It's Worse to React Later, After Ignoring Him.

The worst thing you can do with nose-nudging is to give in to it after you've hung tough and ignored him. If your dog is nudging you and you successfully ignore him half a dozen times, pretty soon he's going to give up. If you remain consistent in not responding when he makes this kind of demand, then before long you will have extinguished the behavior entirely. UNLESS YOU GIVE IN. If, on the seventh nudge, you get sick of the nudging, or "feel sorry" for the dog and so much as touch him, you have now taught him to be a *marathon* "nose-nudger." You've taught him that persistence pays off, that he'll need to hit you with at least six nudges to get what he wants. In classical conditioning terms (like Pavlov's famous dog), by delaying your response you have reinforced the dog's activity more than if you had just given right in to it.

NUDGING AS PART OF MEALTIME BEGGING

One of the most pleasant good manners that any dog can have is to *not* hang around the table when people are eating. It can be annoying and distracting for a dog to stand there and stare at you, nudge or paw you, or otherwise demand your attention.

✦ Does It Work to Feed the Dog Before You Eat?

This is advice that otherwise reliable trainers may recommend, but it seems impractical to me. People eat at least three meals a day and dogs eat two—and these may not even be timed in such a way that they fall right before a human mealtime. Also, there are other times that people may sit down for a cup of tea or snack, so any of these occasions at the table can elicit nose-nudging that would not be addressed by feeding the dog first.

Also, assuaging a dog's hunger before your own contradicts the idea that the "alpha" in the pack eats first and the rest of the pack waits. Since wolf-based thinking has been so helpful in understanding dogs and modifying our interactions with them, why would we not be consistent in applying those concepts to our dinner table, too?

• Send the Dog to His Bed.

As soon as you're going to sit down to a meal, send your dog to his bed. It should be fairly close to the table—I keep beds right in the kitchen near the table, so that the dogs are included in the household event of the meal, but not in the actual proceedings. As soon as he goes to his bed, praise him, give him a biscuit and tell him to stay with a calming pat. Most dogs will learn to go right to sleep while you're eating, content to just be in a relaxing environment, in your presence.

• Give the Dog a Slow-to-eat Treat While You're Eating.

If you have a real table pest who tries to work the nose-nudge angle whenever you sit down, try this idea for a while until he gets used to being on his bed. Give him a good-sized rawhide, a baked marrow bone or some special chewable he doesn't get any other time. You wouldn't want to give him one of those cubes he has to roll around to extract the kibble, because the rattling would not make for a peaceful mealtime for you. Also, I would not suggest you do it if your dog is pretty laid-back at mealtimes, or you'll teach him to *expect* something spectacular, when he was fairly content to lie down with nothing, not even a paltry biscuit.

• Save the Treat Until Dinner Is Over.

This is my personal favorite, and it works like a dream: you teach the dogs that after you finish eating and stand up from the table, they'll get a little taste of something delicious. My dogs lie asleep through an entire meal, and when I get up to clear the table they dash into the kitchen with wide eyes. Depending on what dinner was, they may get to lick the (nearly empty) plates—which are going into the boiling hot dishwasher anyway—or I give them some bits of leftovers. If there was no dog-friendly ingredient in the meal, I'll give them a snippet of cheese instead.

CROTCH-SNIFFING: THE ULTIMATE NOSE-NUDGING

If your dog greets everyone with a flip of his nose where it doesn't belong, you might think it would be hard to cure, but it shouldn't be. You need to keep the dog from fulfilling his mission, and give him another task in its place.

• Turn Your Back on the Dog.

When your dog goes for the groin area on you or someone else, turn around. Don't say anything—no sharp negative command, no pushing or yanking his collar in a physical correction. When you turn your back on him, your position keeps the dog from gaining the physical information he wanted, and your cold shoulder denies him the attention he wanted.

• Tell the Dog to Sit When People Come In.

Before the dog has a chance to jump on or nose-nudge a visitor, tell him to sit, because a dog who is sitting cannot get to anyone's groin. Give the dog a treat for sitting. Even ask the guest to give him a treat.

Obsessive/Compulsive Behavior

Compulsive repetitive behavior that appears pointless may be CCD, canine compulsive dysfunction, the canine version of obsessive compulsive disorder (OCD) in humans. If your dog engages in any of these behaviors, seek out medical attention immediately, because early intervention seems to be important in getting the condition under control. The doctor needs to rule out any medical condition such as a seizure disorder (epilepsy).

The cause for CCD is presumed to be that the dog experiences a frustrating situation or conflict and has to adapt to it—which is normal. The CCD arises when the original problems are resolved but the behavior remains as the dog's default response to any stress or excitement.

Obsessive Behaviors

- Eating feces
- Light-chasing
- Nonstop barking
- Pica (ingesting rocks and other objects)
- Self-biting and licking
- Snapping at the air
- Spinning
- Staring
- Sucking fabric
- Sucking at his sides
- Tail-chasing or biting
- Tennis ball and toy fixation

In order to determine your dog's level of compulsiveness, make some notes on how it affects his daily life. Does your dog engage in the behavior for more than an hour a day? Does he insist on continuing it when you try to stop him? Does it get in the way of a normal day's activities? Does he become obsessive when you leave the house? That would mean he is exhibiting separation anxiety (see page 594 later in this section).

BREEDS AT RISK FOR CCD

There is some genetic component to obsessive conduct, because certain breeds are more prone to it. And different breeds exhibit different compulsive behavior.

- ❏ Bull Terriers and German Shepherds are known to tail-chase. Tests have shown an association with seizure activity in Bull Terrier brains.
- ❏ Cavalier King Charles Spaniels are a breed linked with "fly-snapping" (snapping at imaginary insects in the air).
- ❏ Doberman Pinschers, Golden Retrievers, Labradors and German Shepherds are prone to excessive licking (acral lick dermatitis).
- ❏ Dobermans are also known for flank-sucking.

❒ Consult with vet ASAP.

❒ Use medication if prescribed.

❒ Increase exercise and attention.

❒ Decrease stress.

❒ Identify and remove triggers.

❒ Countercondition to another response.

MEDICATIONS FOR CCD

The cause of CCD is still unclear, but serotonin seems to play some part. Drugs that address this have been successful in treating CCD. Serotonin-related antidepressant drugs such as clomipramine and fluoxetine (Prozac) are now considered better than the phenobarbital that was previously used. But drug therapy must be used in conjunction with a trainer and your vet.

If your vet runs tests on the dog that seem to confirm CCD, she may try the dog on anticonvulsant medication (such as phenobarbital) or an anti-obsessional medication such as Prozac (generic name, fluoxetine hydrochloride).

Possessiveness

It is natural and instinctive for a dog to defend his toys or food bowl from others. Some dogs are just more naturally possessive about their toys and treats, but you can counter condition a dog to "barter": to give up one prized possession for another.

If your dog does *not* growl when you come near or touch him when he has a treasure in his mouth, then keep on approaching and touching him when he has valued items in his mouth. You want to make him less worried and intense when he has a treat, so that he doesn't become possessive and neurotic about his favorite items.

FOOD BOWL GUARDING

Dogs who are possessive are obviously more prone to guard their food. You cannot allow a dog to growl when you or someone else comes near his bowl at mealtimes.

◆ **Some Ways to De-emphasize Food-guarding**

1. Don't feed in a corner where the dog might feel trapped.

2. Put only a small amount of his dinner in his bowl. Let him finish it—maybe he'll let you pat his back while he's eating, to relax him. When the bowl is empty, pick it up and refill it. Put it down again and praise and pat.

3. The next time you feed him, give only a little food again, but this time refill the bowl on the floor by slowly pouring kibble and/or putting big spoonfuls of canned food into the bowl. Talk to the dog in a relaxed tone.

Two commands you'll need to teach a dog with guarding issues are "leave it" and "out" (see Chapter Ten, "Teaching Manners").

AVOID CONFLICT BY ELIMINATING THE TRIGGERS.

The possessiveness problem can be tackled with much less work by employing some basic avoidance techniques. You really don't want to spend your life having power struggles and contests of will with your dog (unless you want to do it as practice for when you have a teenager).

Rather than suggestions on how to "win" a battle for possession of a rawhide bone, the larger suggestion is to just eliminate from your household those items that your dog thinks are worth fighting for. Bones and rawhide chews can bring out growling, guarding behavior—you can try to correct it by using the techniques below, but if it doesn't feel right to you, then why pick a fight. Many dogs live a full life without ever having a rawhide bone—your dog will now join their ranks.

DISCOURAGING POSSESSIVENESS

Practice handing the dog the item that causes her to be possessive—and then take it away. Say "Out" and try to remove it slowly and gently from her mouth—don't grab it fast or with too much pressure, both of which could trigger a guarding/grabbing reaction from her. If she still holds on to it but seems to be having second thoughts about letting go, you can say encouraging things such as, "Come on, good girl, that's it." If she seems to be considering letting go, repeat "Out" firmly but kindly. Take one end of her treasured item and try again to pull it gently so she will release it.

• Praise Her for Any Amount of Jaw Pressure That You Feel Her Give Up.

The moment that she gives it up to you—however reluctantly—take it, and then praise her to the skies. Make a big fuss over her, give her a treat for letting go and *give the treasure right back to her.* Let her keep it, patting her head and neck. As long as she doesn't growl when you are that near and touching her face, you can call it a day.

• You Might Repeat This over a Period of a Few Days.

Every time you take the object gently away, you can increase the number of times you take the item and then return it to her, until you can do it three times in a row. You can phase out the treats and just rely on the praise to reinforce her compliance. Of course, returning the item to her is the most important reward. Always end the last exchange so that the dog keeps the item. What she learns is that by going along with your demands, she suffers no ultimate loss and even gets some extra loving.

• Don't Get into a Tug-of-war.

If you don't get some feeling of compliance from the dog, *do not fight with him.* You do not want to create a power play with a dominant dog. You may get bitten if you get tough and try to crack down. If he is standing over something, guarding it and growling with frozen body posture, this is not the time to train. Just ignore the treasure. Distract him by calling him, then work on "come" and "down."

If at any point the dog gives you a scary growl, or you feel threatened, immediately stop this exercise. Pick up the leash, or clip on a leash, and start to do some basic obedience commands, such as sit, down, stay, etc. Totally ignore the treat in her mouth. As she complies with your training refresher, she may even drop the item, but don't make a lunge for it and wind up in a renewed battle for the toy. The point of it all is just that she needs to do what you want, when you want it—period. No questions asked.

Rage Syndrome

Called "rage syndrome" or "Jekyll and Hyde syndrome," this is the violent, uncontrollable aggression that is seemingly brought on by no outside stimulus. Dogs with this disorder can awaken and lash out and attack whatever is there, either an object or a living thing. After this instantaneous fierce aggression, the dog can just as suddenly go back to a normally sweet nature.

This aggression syndrome is considered most frequent in English Springer Spaniels—so much so that it is called "Springer rage" by some. Cocker Spaniels and Bull Terriers are two other breeds in which the syndrome has been seen, but Springers have become the most notorious for it. All three of these breeds are known for having high levels of dominant behavior—certain of the breeding lines in these breeds are supposed to produce offspring that are highly dominant or aggressive. In the U.K., the question was raised as to whether rage syndrome could be related to the red coat color in red Golden Retrievers (since some Goldens did become vicious in England—although this could also have been inbreeding).

CONTROVERSY OVER THE VALIDITY OF RAGE SYNDROME

There are two schools of thought about whether rage syndrome exists. This contradiction will only be cleared up when it is understood what is at the bottom of this extreme form of explosive canine aggression.

One school believes that rage syndrome does exists but that it's so rare that most trainers will never even encounter it. This group believes that most cases of rage are actually extremes of dominance-related aggression. The other point of view defines rage syndrome differently—the interpretation becomes so liberal that it includes all kinds of violent canine aggression.

IS IT "LOCALIZED EPILEPSY"?

New thinking has raised questions about whether rage syndrome could actually be a form of seizure-related aggression. It seems that these outbursts of rage may be some form of seizures.

There is usually a mood change before the aggressive episodes—it may last for hours or only minutes—and afterward there is a depression, a dissociated slump common to seizures.

Dogs treated with a single daily dose of an anticonvulsant like phenobarbital usually stop having these episodes. However, you still have to watch the dog closely and monitor the dosage of medication with your vet.

LONG-TERM DANGER TO YOUR FAMILY

A dog who has had one or more of these rage outbursts is a danger to everyone in the household. You have to be super-alert to any symptoms that an attack is imminent. Since total cures are rare—even with medication—if there are children in your household the danger of them being attacked is high.

Everyone in the household has to be taught to look out for signs of an impending attack. It is essential that everyone be taught to proceed with extreme caution when dealing with an affected dog—especially when she is behaving strangely, which may signal an attack is coming.

Putting a dog with this condition to sleep is sometimes the most prudent, although very sad alternative, and this is something to discuss with your veterinarian.

Separation Anxiety

No dog likes being left alone—but some like it a lot less than others. Dogs are social animals and pack animals, so being completely alone is not natural for them. When you leave a dog she has no idea where you went or when you'll be back, which can cause varying degrees of anxiety in dogs.

SOME DOGS SUFFER MORE.

For some dogs, your leaving the house can be an emotional trauma every time, while others learn to take your departures and reappearances in stride. There is no clear answer to whether dogs are born with a tendency to suffer from separation anxiety, or whether it is a product of their experience. However, there is agreement that a dog who exhibits extreme separation anxiety is much like a dysfunctional person. These dogs are products of their early environments: they seem to be insecure and have low self-confidence, and then they become completely dependent on their owners, whom they doggedly (no pun intended) worship and adore.

ARE YOU MAKING IT WORSE?

Generally speaking, whether they are aware of it or not, the owners of a dog that is neurotic about departures are themselves active in this tango—it does take two. For an emotionally needy person, a clingy, adoring dog can seem like a great companion: the two become—to use an overused phrase—codependent.

There are some suggested remedies listed below, but it is generally agreed that the *least* helpful attitude to take, believe it or not, is to be really empathetic with a crying dog. "Feeling your dog's pain" and wanting to make her feel better probably validates it, which reinforces her unhappiness.

◆ **What NOT to Do.**
   ❒ Do not act sympathetically toward your dog's suffering. If you show that you feel sorry for her, you'll be giving the wrong message.
   ❒ Do NOT pat the dog if she cries, whines, trembles, etc. The worst thing you can do is say soothingly, "It's okay, good dog." You may think you are calming her down, but the mes-

sage she actually gets validates that she *should* be worrying, because you seem to be sharing her anxiety with your words and actions.

❏ Do not coddle the dog—it will only make her more worried that she has something to be anxious about. If you ignore her carrying on, she will get over it (eventually, anyway).

CAUSES OF SEPARATION ANXIETY

◆ Too-early Weaning

Weaning a puppy too early can cause psychological trauma and lay the groundwork for later separation anxiety. "Puppy mill" puppies are virtually *always* taken away from their mothers and littermates too young (for more on "Pet Stores and Puppy Mills," see page 26). Puppies "produced" in breeding farm environments are often removed from their mothers when only four or five weeks old. The very young pups are then transported long distances to pet stores across the country, a journey that could be frightening and disorienting to any dog, much less a puppy.

Puppies in pet stores are typically sold at around three to five months (twelve to twenty weeks), during which time they are often kept in isolation in a cage, or with one other puppy, in cramped conditions. They will have been handled by a constantly changing assortment of store workers and customers, which can be confusing. However, even the puppies sold right away are ultimately prone to separation anxiety and all the problems that come with it.

Weaning too young even takes place with some individual breeders who remove puppies from their siblings and mother before the recommended eight weeks of age. Supposedly reputable breeders have been known to give puppies to their new owners at six and seven weeks: they claim this is good for the puppy's ability to bond to people, a misconception if there ever was one. Cynically speaking, early delivery of puppies means a monetary gain to the breeder, who has to give two weeks less of feeding, poop cleanup and puppy shots, and gets the buyer's money that much sooner. This can be a significant savings with breeds like Golden Retrievers and Labs, which often have eight puppies per litter. The only thing early weaning benefits is the breeder's convenience and bank account: it deprives the puppies of the social skills they need with other dogs, and often contributes to separation anxiety.

Pups taken away too young lose up to a month of developmental time with their littermates. Pet-store puppies can miss out on perhaps the most critical period in their development, because they have not been socialized to individual people and handled with gentle patience that enhances bonding with humans. Depending on how you socialize a dog with this early trauma, it can erupt into emotional suffering for the dog and major destruction for the homeowner, unless the problem is understood for what it is.

◆ Genetic Predisposition

There are a few breeds that have been identified as being prone to being insecure or unhappy when their owner is absent. Although this would be a weak excuse not to buy a certain breed, you might want to think about it if you will be away from the dog for much of the day. (By the same token, there are very few dogs of any breed whose quality of life adds up to much if their owners are absent much more than they are present: eventually, separation anxiety would seem to be an unavoidable reaction.)

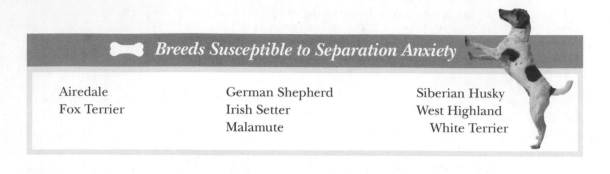

Breeds Susceptible to Separation Anxiety

Airedale	German Shepherd	Siberian Husky
Fox Terrier	Irish Setter	West Highland
	Malamute	White Terrier

ANXIETY IN ADOPTED DOGS
(Also see section on Second-chance Dogs on page 40.)

You can never be certain what sort of life a dog from a shelter or breed-rescue has had—but you can bet that loneliness was probably part of it. It may take him longer to develop trust in you. Abandoned dogs are usually young adults who have already lost a home, or have even been through multiple homes. They have good reason to worry: one minute the family pack was intact, the next they were gone forever.

When they have to separate from you, their new loving caregiver, it can make them more nervous than a well-adjusted dog, because a foundling dog's heart may already have been broken by losing his original people.

◆ Neglected in the Past
If a young pup was owned by people who did not have enough time for him, he probably spent too much time in isolation. Just as with children, mistreatment does not have to take the form of aggressive abuse. Damage can be done by passive neglect.

SYMPTOMS OF SEPARATION ANXIETY
Dogs suffering separation anxiety can show it in many ways. Some symptoms are normal behavior, except that they happen immediately after the owner leaves or occur in a magnified form. The dog may appear anxious as you are preparing to leave and then become increasingly distraught from the moment you leave—what begins with whimpering and whining can escalate to barking and become incessant barking, all within a few minutes.

SIGNS OF SEPARATION ANXIETY

- ❏ Digging
- ❏ Chewing
- ❏ Excess salivation (puddles of saliva wherever the dog waits for you)
- ❏ Anxiety-related urinating or defecating inside (reprimanding increases anxiety)

- ❏ Anorexia (refusal to eat until you return; the dog may then chow down hungrily)
- ❏ Follows you around the house, never loses sight of you, wants to touch you
- ❏ Big greeting displays when you return

✦ Separation Anxiety and Noise Phobia Go Together.
Seventy percent of dogs with separation anxiety issues also suffer from noise phobia. See "Thunderstorm Phobia" (on page 623) later in this chapter.

WAYS TO HANDLE AND REDUCE THE DOG'S ANXIETY
There are ways to handle the anxiety, which can also lessen it and thereby reduce the dog's stress and destructiveness. Eventually your pet may even learn how to calm himself.

✦ Tips on Calming an Anxious Dog
- ❏ Give the dog tons of exercise—let him get all worn out before you depart.
- ❏ Crate or confine in a small space a highly anxious dog who goes on a destructive rampage when left alone. Some dogs are actually calmed by being in confinement. However, if the dog is showing physical symptoms of anxiety, you cannot do this without medication.
- ❏ Leave a piece of clothing you have worn recently—your scent can be soothing.
- ❏ Leave a radio station (soothing classical station—no heavy metal bands, please!) or the television on, preferably with programs that feature people talking.

✦ Encourage Her Independence.
In order for the dog to better tolerate your going out and leaving her behind, she has to become more comfortable with having some measure of separation from you when you are both at home. This is called "independence training," and in the long run it can make your cohabitation smoother and less emotionally charged.

Many anxious dogs follow their owners around from room to room. This clingy following behavior can be a sign of separation anxiety. Try to discourage this habit.

✦ Command Her to Do Something Else Instead.
Send her to her bed to lie down. But it's no use to just say "No" when she begins following you—she needs another command. If she goes to her bed but just pops up again the moment you leave the area, try giving her a rawhide or other chew as a reward for getting on her bed and staying there when you go elsewhere in the house. Maybe the chewing activity can relieve some of her stress and at the same time give her something positive to associate with having some distance from you.

✦ Insist on Her Distance from You.
If you have a dog that is attached to you at the hip, so to speak, then you need to create some air space between you for a few weeks. If she is used to spending the better part of the day—or many hours of it—right by your side, this is going to be rough for her. But for her sake, insist on detachment whenever possible.

- Be patient, be kind. This is not intended as a punishment, and you must not have a negative tone to your voice. Think of this as building character for your dog, aiding her in developing the self-confidence and courage to develop a sense of herself separate from her attachment to you.
- Discipline yourself to keep some physical distance from your dog for approximately a month. You need to consider that you may actually enjoy her intense attachment to you, that it meets both of your needs—except for the dog's suffering at the point at which you exit without her.
- You cannot allow your dog to sleep on your bed. It's perfectly fine, however, for her to be next to your bed or in the bedroom—it's even desirable, so that she can get a good, *passive* dose of bonding with you.
- While you're moving around your house, you also have to send her away from your ankles, where she may have been virtually attached until now. Give her less physical contact with you. As she hovers near you, direct her to go to her bed, which you will have placed in another part of the room. Then praise her for going there—even if she drags her heels about it and adopts an expression of woe at the idea of being even slightly apart from you, encourage her verbally.
- Practice having her sit or lie down while you move around a room. Eventually, she may be able to tolerate your leaving the room. You may have to talk her through it in a quiet, soothing voice—"Waaait, Maisy, good girl, you waaait." And then go back to where she is sitting or lying and, in a low-key way, pat and praise her for her supreme self-restraint and growing bravery in being able to withstand your distance from her.

◆ **Desensitize Departures by Practicing Leaving.**

Dogs notice many "predeparture" cues you give that you are about to go out. Pay attention to your own minor activities on your next exit from home and notice what you do before leaving like putting on different clothes with different-sounding shoes, putting on outerwear, getting car keys or door keys, a purse or a briefcase etc.

- Start the desensitization by practicing just one of those departure behaviors every few minutes. It might be to touch or turn the door handle or to put on an outdoor coat—and then sit back down. Do that for a day or two until the dog does not react.

  Then practice more than one departure behavior, but still don't leave. When you string together a few departure actions, the dog will probably become agitated. You need not react to this. Ignore the dog's agitation. Do what you're doing and don't leave afterward until the dog does not react anymore. This might take four tries or four days of tries, but eventually it's going to be worth the effort.
- Practice coming and going for small amounts of time. Make no fuss over the dog either before or after your exits or re-entries until she barely reacts to either. Start with five minutes and increase it in five-minute increments up to twenty minutes. The first twenty minutes of separation are thought to be the hardest for dogs who suffer from separation

anxiety. Make no big deal about your leaving and returning—treat both as everyday occurrences and they will become that.

❏ For fifteen minutes before you go out and again when you come back, pay no special attention to the dog. The more you downplay your comings and goings, the more she will accept them as part of normal life.

❏ Take some responsibility for your dog's reaction, since you may be one of those people who reinforce a dog's anxiety by indulging in long, intense greetings and good-byes.

◆ **Tips for Positive Rewards on Your Exit**
❏ Give a really great rawhide or pig's ear right before you leave.
❏ Stuff peanut butter or cheese into the hollow of a big marrow bone.
❏ A Kong rubber chew toy can also be stuffed and can provide a smokescreen for your comings and goings.
❏ Feed the dog her meal about fifteen minutes before you leave, followed by a quick post-digestion walk. Dogs normally want to sleep after they eat, so food should have a calming effect.
❏ Give a large bone about fifteen or twenty minutes before you leave. The bone will keep her busy during your preparations to leave and the departure itself.

◆ **Experiment with a Crate for Security.**
A crate is not generally recommended for dogs with separation anxiety, since many dogs who suffer from separation anxiety tend to panic in close confinement.

However, there are dogs who were successfully crate-trained and think of their crates as a safe haven from the hectic world around them.

Even dogs who have not been raised with a crate will benefit from getting comfortable in one. A crate with solid sides and "windows" up high may give the dog a greater sense of security and a safe den. To get a grown dog used to a crate, use the same techniques you would use to accustom a puppy to one (see page 218 in Chapter Nine, "House-training").

MEDICATIONS FOR EXTREME CASES

Once a dog is in a state of panic, no medication can stop the attack, but you can medicate in anticipation of an event. Talk to your vet about trying antianxiety or antidepressant medications, both of which can help in cases of separation anxiety where nothing else does. Clomicalm is a tricyclic antidepressant that is FDA-approved for veterinary use in treating separation anxiety: the less expensive generic is clomipramine, which is actually the exact same drug made by the same company for human use under the name Anafranil. Amitriptyline is another well-known antidepressant also used for veterinary purposes. Other medications that seem to be effective in calming anxious dogs are alprazolam (which is the generic for Xanax, the brand name antianxiety drug), and in some cases, diazepam (Valium). However, many dogs have the opposite reaction to Valium and get more wound up, and many of these drugs elicit such a poor response from the dog that his symptoms get worse.

Your vet will make the choice of which is most appropriate for your situation; the process may take some time because she also may have to experiment with dosage amounts until she gets the right dosage of the most effective drug for your dog. Obviously, you cannot and should not try to embark on this program except under the close guidance of a vet (i.e., do not even *think* of "borrowing" a friend's medication). In time, reduce and then stop using these medications once the dog has learned to tolerate your departure and absence. These medications are intended as a tool to accomplish the job, with the goal being to wean her from them eventually.

THE MOTIVATION FOR DESTRUCTIVENESS

When dogs express their anxiety by being destructive around the house, this is a function of nerves, of desperation. Do not project human motives on a dog: he is NOT "getting back at you." Human emotions such as revenge do not exist in the canine heart or head.

◆ Coming Home to Destructive Behavior
(See page 567 in this chapter under "Destructive Behavior.")

When you get home and the dog has ruined something, DO NOT react to what you have found. Do not punish him (it's after the fact anyway, so there's no lesson he could learn). Any punishment will only increase his anxiety.

People often project human motives onto canine behavior and think the dog is being vengeful, that he is mad to have been left home.

If the destructive behavior is not related to anxiety, then you still want to ignore the mess and carry on with whatever you need to do. However, if the dog returns to the mess for more chewing gratification, at that point you are catching him "in the act."

Stealing

Some dogs are quicker and bolder than others in jumping up on a counter to purloin food. Some dogs have more interest than others in the contents of your trash and laundry hamper. But all dogs tend to snatch what isn't theirs. Count yourself lucky if your dog isn't active in this department, but you should know that all of our food and belongings are potential snacks and toys for our dogs, even if the better-behaved among them don't act out their impulses.

YELLING DOESN'T WORK.

Screaming at your dog after he's rearranged a leg of lamb on your kitchen floor has no deterrent effect on future food-stealing. Losing your temper at your dog when you find him with your food teaches him one thing only: to be more crafty in how and when he steals, so that you don't interrupt his feast the next time.

If you want to have an impact on your dog's thievery, you need to deter him *during* the act of stealing the food—without you even present if possible, so you won't seem to have caused the punishment. This means "booby-trapping" the area (see page 602).

DON'T PROVIDE OPPORTUNITIES.

You've heard the legal term "attractive nuisance"? That's when someone has a swimming pool without a fence that other people can fall into—and the pool owner is then liable for having left an attractive danger accessible. Applied to canine thievery, this means that if you leave items that are attractive to a dog in plain view and he steals them, you have no one to blame but yourself. If there was a *Judge Fido* television program, you would surely be deemed an accessory to the dog's crime.

◆ Think of It as Childproofing a House.

Put anything that is an attractive nuisance out of harm's way. The best way to prevent the turkey dinner from being pulled onto the floor or your favorite clothes or shoes from being destroyed is to *not leave these things where a dog can get at them*. It's really not that hard to figure out: don't make your tasty stuff accessible.

Childproof kitchen cabinets and cupboards. Put latches in the inside of any drawer or door that a dog could open—because some of them are as resourceful as raccoons.

◆ Each Successful Theft Encourages the Thief.

Every time a dog gets a crack at food left unattended, his dreams are realized. He is reinforced in his drive to hunt for it and is reaffirmed in his belief that he can accomplish the mission. This is actually true of anything your dog does that you disapprove of: every time he gets a chance to jump on someone it reinforces that experience; every time he gets to run off without a leash it cements his belief that lots of fun can be had out there; and every time you leave shrimp on the cocktail table, or a sandwich on the counter and he gets a mouthful, you can be sure he'll be looking for that treat again soon.

Do not leave any food somewhere that's vulnerable to a dog's paws or teeth. If you want to leave food out of the refrigerator or cupboard, put it in a safe place: inside the cold stove is perfect (but make sure you check what's in there before preheating the oven the next time). For smaller items, the toaster ovens and bread boxes make good "food safes." You can also put nonperishable things way up high in a cupboard.

DO NOT UNDERESTIMATE A DOG'S SENSE OF SMELL.

Never underestimate your dog's drive to get your goodies. Don't think that because meat/fish/chicken is frozen solid and wrapped in double plastic, a dog doesn't smell it—because she does. My favorite example of food I *never* thought could be a target for a canine heist was frozen mushroom soup that I took out of the deep freeze. I put the big plastic container filled with five pounds of rock-solid soup into a deep sink to defrost. My Weimaraner Billy Blue—who lives for food and whose biggest pleasure in life is found at mealtimes—managed to stand on the counter edge, lift that heavy plastic container up and out of the sink (with his teeth gripping only a narrow plastic edge with all that weight) and carry it out the dog-door flap, where he pried off the vacuum-sealed lid and gnawed through six portions of creamed porcini mushroom soup. But his accomplishment might be a toss-up with my friend's Great Dane, who ate through a three-layer strawberry cake that was on top of a cupboard in as many minutes. In any case, you get the point: no food item is safe from a determined dog's snout.

GARBAGE CAN RAIDING

Have you ever been to a dog owner's house and seen one of those tall, metal step-on garbage cans—which often have strange dents in one edge of the nice, shiny lid? Look closer: they're probably teeth marks. A garbage can is a highly tempting repository of delights for a dog.

Keep the bin out of sight and smell in an inaccessible place such as a closed garage, inside a pantry or under the sink.

Put nothing too fragrantly odiferous in the can. This might sound ridiculous—garbage cans are for garbage, right?—but in a dog household, smelly garbage is something else. If you put delicious food remains in an accessible garbage can, you are running the risk that they may wind up strewn across the kitchen floor.

BOOBY-TRAPPING

This is considered a good way to scare your dog in the act of stealing food, and might be effective for training him not to jump up on your kitchen counters in search of food. However, it takes time and effort on your part, and it might just scare the living daylights out of a dog. What's the point of being sadistic, setting out bait for a dog that is going to frighten him?

An alternative to trying any of the booby-trapping methods, consider this: wouldn't it be a kinder solution to just plan ahead, know the mischief your dog likes to get into and make sure you don't create an opportunity for trouble?

Stress and Anxiety

The way we live in the so-called modern world—the way people dash around with barely enough time for all their "multitasks"—has an effect on the emotional state of the dogs who share our lives. There may be individual dogs who are more laid-back and live alongside our raised voices, frustrated phone conversations and high-speed comings and goings without being affected, but many dogs are sponges or magnets for our emotional states, and they pay a price for what we put ourselves through. Of course, the humans pay their own price for rushing and stress, but (theoretically, at least) the humans have some choice in the matter. The dogs are hapless victims, trapped on our carousel—for our sake and theirs, we should probably take a minute to reevaluate the pace and attitude with which many of us dash through our days.

While it is universally accepted that stress causes physical and emotional problems in people, we rarely consider the cost of our lifestyle on our animal companions.

CANINE STRESS FACTORS

- ☐ Speedy human lifestyle
- ☐ Lack of mental stimulation
- ☐ Insufficient physical exercise
- ☐ Loneliness
- ☐ Discord between/among human family members

- Sudden family changes
- Hyperactivity from being crated or ignored

PEOPLE CAN CREATE HYPERACTIVE DOGS.

If you have a dog who is kept in a crate a great deal of the day, that dog can develop what's known as a "cratey" personality. The dog can act cratey when the owner gets home at the end of the day—and if the person then ignores or reprimands the dog for being so wound up, it only makes it worse. A dog like this is not naturally hyperactive—it is a condition caused by the stress of being left alone and locked up.

UPHEAVAL IN THE HUMAN FAMILY

Big changes in the human household—death, divorce, a child going away to school, a relative coming to live in—cause tension that the dog feels. Emotional problems in the human family—quiet anger, unresolved tension or yelling and screaming—can put the dog in the middle as a sort of buffer between the people. This emotional strain can lead to house-soiling in the dog.

If there are loud or extremely tense problems in the marital relationship, it has an impact on everyone in the household. Very sensitive dogs have been known to exhibit specific reactions to this stress, such as defecating on the warring couple's bed. (One would imagine this would be incentive enough to go to a couples therapist to deal with the issues, rather than having it spill over onto the rest of the family.)

SIGNS OF STRESS IN DOGS

- Licking (self, floor, walls, furniture)
- Tail-chasing
- Pacing
- Running back and forth along a fence
- Panting or drooling excessively
- Lying flat, completely still
- Excessive hair loss
- Pooping symbolically (owners' bed, middle of living room)

There are also more subtle signs of anxiety in a dog that are good to keep an eye on, because that way you can address the early stress before it becomes a full-blown problem.

Panting, drooling	Tongue-flicking
Yawning	Opening and closing mouth rapidly
Pacing	Head held below shoulders

THE TTOUCH MASSAGE SYSTEM

This system of therapeutically touching animals to relieve tension is called TTouch, after Linda Tellington-Jones, the woman who developed it using Chinese acupuncture and acupressure points. I have no experience with this—or any—formalized dog massage. I rub my hands all over my dogs all the time, for my pleasure as much as theirs. TTouch books, videos and a directory of practitioners of this system are available through www.lindatellingtonjones.com.

DON'T FORGET THE OLD STANDBYS.

Never lose sight of the benefits of increasing exercise and reducing protein in the food to improve a dog's temperament.

PRODUCTS TO RELIEVE STRESS

Anxiety Wrap is a product that uses the principle of applied pressure to put a sort of bodysuit around a dog's middle that can be comforting and soothing. It works on the principle behind swaddling an infant to calm her. Information about this ACE-type bandage is available at www.anxietywrap.com.

Comfort Zone is a room-atomizer that emits a substance the manufacturer calls "dog-appeasing pheromone" ("DAP" for short). The company claims that DAP releases a natural stress-reducing hormone similar to what a mother dog emits while nursing her puppies. It has reportedly been used successfully in Europe for some time to reduce or eliminate stress-related barking, destructiveness, whimpering and whining, urination and defecation, etc.

The Comfort Zone atomizer plugs into an electrical socket the way a room deodorizer does and releases the DAP substance, which is supposed to cover an area of 500 to 650 square feet for about a month. The substance is deemed safe for puppies and dogs and has had no reported affect on people. Anecdotal evidence suggests that if you keep your dog(s) in proximity to this remarkable little gizmo, you could be one of the lucky ones that the DAP may help with arousal barking, thunder phobia, separation anxiety, noise phobia, aggression, etc.

If your dog has stress-related personality issues, it seems well worth it to spend $25 and give it a try. Personally, my experiment with car-travel anxiety and spray DAP showed no improvement in Jazzy's nervousness.

NOTE: *If you try the Comfort Zone and your dog's behavior or stress gets worse, it's obviously not a product for you. Unplug the DAP as soon as you realize this and either throw it away or give it to a friend to try with her dog, since so many people's dogs have had a good response to it.*

Temperament/Psychological Problems

If your dog has a difficult temperament, that can be the reason for a variety of problems that seem to relate to *aggression,* the primary personality component that causes problems in dogs (see page 531 for that part of this chapter). Fear of people, attempts to bite them, fear of other dogs, and picking fights with them are fundamental behaviors that can make life difficult with a dog like this.

SOCIALIZE YOUR DOG AT ANY AGE.

Dog-to-dog issues related to temperament can be solved simply by giving your puppy lots of chances to interact with other dogs (see Chapter Five). You can also do this with a dog that's past puppyhood—you just have to keep the situation as low-key as possible. It is usually helpful to have the dogs meet on neutral ground (neither one will feel territorial) and not to be on-leash, since being attached to a person seems to make dogs behave less well with each other than they do when they are loose. Dogs seem to do best with other dogs if humans aren't in the way.

• Social Maturity Begins at Eighteen to Twenty-Four Months.

Puppies are youngsters for a very long time, especially puppies of large breeds, so you don't have to worry that you've missed the chance to socialize your dog if he is more than a few months old. Reaching social adulthood can range from twelve to thirty-six months of age, depending on the size of the dog. Larger dogs take longer to mature—usually not before they are two years old. Dogs fine-tune their skills with people and other dogs during this period, so the more opportunities you offer, the greater the chance that temperament issues will improve.

DOGS' PERSONALITIES CHANGE IN NEW SITUATIONS.

It is rare among dogs or humans for an individual to have a personality that remains consistent in all situations. Most dogs are not always the same—many things in their environment are potential influences on their actions and reactions.

- ❏ A dog's personality can be affected if he's tired, frustrated, angry or frightened.
- ❏ In a new setting, things may change radically—your dog may not even follow simple commands.
- ❏ Cut the dog some slack when you go to a new physical environment, so that he can adapt.
- ❏ Be calm and encouraging to a dog in a new environment, until he settles down and is "himself" again.

HANDLING A NERVOUS OR HYPERACTIVE DOG

You'll know whether your dog falls into this category if he is in perpetual motion, rarely still and sometimes gets so wound up that he seems wild.

This can be one of the most troublesome temperaments. General fear and anxiety, in differing degrees, are the engine that drives this type of dog, and he will rarely be still. These dogs rest only when they are sleeping—and they do *that* with one eye open.

You have to stay totally calm and neutral when dealing with a hyperactive dog. The louder and more upset you get, the more wound up she'll get. Some dogs become nervous and anxiety-ridden because their masters have that sort of personality.

• Only Mental Stimulation and Physical Exercise Will Help.

It is pointless to try to change a dog like this or to train him into submission. The only thing you can do is to harness some of his energy by directing his actions. To get a picture of what is going on in the minds of dogs like these, I recall a great analogy that Aimee Sadler (the training expert on this book) made about Lulu, my first rescued Weimaraner, who was so alert and reacted to everything around her with intensity. Aimee watched Lulu for a while and said, "The inside of her head is like a vacuum chamber: Ping-Pong balls are bouncing off the wall." So Amy proceeded to teach Lulu a series of tricks, using subtly different hand signals that the dog had to watch carefully to distinguish between one trick or another. I was truly amazed that after a mere fifteen minutes of trick training (during which my brilliant escape artist learned half a dozen new tricks), the dog was so mellow that after Aimee left, Lulu had a long nap for the first time. Lulu finally burned off some of that excess nervous energy, proving the "mental stimulation" theory.

To help a dog like Lulu focus and settle down, you need to give her boundaries by practicing obedience commands as a constant part of everyday life. Ask for a sit before going out a door, or ask for a paw-shake before giving a treat.

Give precise tasks, such as fetching a particular toy you have named and bringing it to a place next to you when you're at the table or lying down.

"Down, stay" is good to help the dog settle down, but not for any length of time which would be unrealistic given her energy level.

Being too rigid and harsh will backfire—your intensity can make her become even more wound up. Do not overcorrect or demand unreasonable levels of obedience from a dog who is already "tightly wound."

• Rescued Dogs Often Have Nervous Temperaments.

Rescued dogs can become nervous and unsettled because some of them have been re-homed several times. Each new home has its own set of habits and rules, and each new owner commands them in different ways, all of which can be confusing.

• Early Trauma Can Shape Personality.

A shock at the impressionable "fear imprint" stage of puppyhood can also render a dog frightened and anxious—for example, a thunderstorm, gunshot or vehicle backfire during those critical weeks can leave him fearful for life.

DOG "SHRINKS"

Animal behaviorists are a subspecialty in the dog-training world, and while many dog owners may need trainers, they are often embarrassed to seek one out. People are often self-conscious about their dog's neurotic behavior, which may be a reflection of their own problems.

To clarify what a behaviorist is: there are medically trained veterinarians who specialize in dog behavior, and there are certified dog trainers who can go on to get a second certification as a "behaviorist." These specialists in dog behavior and problem correction are quite possessive of their "title" and do not appreciate it being appropriated by trainers who have not earned it.

Getting help for your dog from a "dog shrink" can be embarrassing for some people, the way some people used to be (and some still are) gun-shy, for a variety of reasons, about going to a psychologist themselves.

A consultation with a behaviorist means only that she will gather information about your dog (from you, from observing the dog and sometimes from blood work) and then come up with a diagnosis. After that, she gives you advice about how to treat the situation. That advice typically revolves around making alterations in the dog's diet and exercise routine, and maybe suggesting some brief retraining exercises. Such a visit can give you information about the dog you love, and reassurance about whether you are handling her well.

IT COULD BE IN THE GENES.

There may be specific odd things that dogs from a breed do which that are part of their normal behavior. Breeders have been selecting for certain qualities in their dogs for a century or more. Not every breeder will be honest about these quirks and idiosyncrasies, but in the short lifetime of one dog, it's not likely that you are going to make much of a dent in the dog's inborn behavior or inclination, so go with the flow. A dog behaviorist can clue you in about what attributes your kind of dog "comes with."

Don't blame yourself for whatever may be off-the-wall about your dog's behavior. For example, you can't consider it your fault if your Springer Spaniel displays the breed typical rage syndrome. If your Dachshund indulges in blanket-sucking, it's unlikely that you made him insecure and in need of a "blankie:" it runs in the breed. Afghans can have anxiety attacks, while Golden Retrievers and Labradors can both be obsessive-compulsive.

MEDICATIONS FOR EMOTIONAL AND BEHAVIOR ISSUES

Modern psychoactive drugs have a place with dogs, which is a new concept. Anti-obsessional drugs, tricyclic antidepressants and anxiety-relieving medications are becoming common practice with some behaviorists and vets. These medications give relief from emotional problems for dogs and their owners, who were suffering without any other solution. Initially, people laughed when the human antidepressant Prozac was first used on dogs with obsessive-compulsive disorder and aggression problems. Another drug that vets use to treat aggression and obsessive-compulsive disorders such as tail-chasing is Clomicalm (the less costly generic is clomipramine)—which, by the way, is exactly the same as the drug called Anafranil, which is FDA-approved for human use. However, there have been excellent results in some cases, especially those where behavior modification (training) had made no difference.

◆ Dog's Emotions Aren't So Different from Ours.

Dogs have mental disturbances that are quite similar to the ones that affect people. There are many differences between the two species, but there are also biological similarities in the structure and function of the brain. In fact, there are behavior problems in animals that will be studied to learn more about human psychiatric problems—which means the treatment, medications and research will come full circle when dogs benefit from the medications.

◆ Better to Use Drugs with a Behaviorist.

Just as the use of these drugs by humans is best combined with talk therapy with a professional, so are the medications for dogs best combined with a behavior-modification plan drawn up by a professional.

DEPRESSION

Any dog can become depressed. The death of a companion pet, the death or departure of a family member, the arrival of a new baby (and loss of time for the dog), a prolonged stay in a boarding kennel or even just a big change in his daily routine can be disturbing enough that a dog gets the blues.

Signs of Depression

Lethargy	Anxiety
No interest in previously enjoyed activities	Change in sleep habits
Mood swings	Aggression
Loss of appetite	Attention-seeking behavior

THINGS YOU CAN DO FOR DEPRESSION

If you notice a big change in your dog's mood or behavior, don't ignore it.

◆ Consult Your Vet about Possible Underlying Illness.

Your dog's mood change could be a medical problem, or it could be the beginning of depression, but in either case it should be addressed. There are a number of medical conditions that can cause a fairly content dog to have an unpleasant attitude, which can be unfairly attributed to his having a bad personality. Ear infections, skin rashes, impacted anal glands, etc., can all make a dog as irritable as they would make you. They can also cause a dog to snap or bite when the affected area is inadvertently touched.

Have your vet give the dog a thorough physical to see if there is a medical explanation for his change in personality. Needless to say, whatever physiological issues turn up need to be addressed—and then see whether the dog's mood doesn't improve as soon as he feels better.

If there is no medical explanation for what's bothering your dog, it's reasonable to wait three to six weeks for her to come out of her funk.

INCREASE EXERCISE.

As with people, physical exertion in dogs releases endorphins and raises their levels of serotonin, the body's own natural mood enhancer. Going for walks provides visual stimulation and circulation. Playing ball or other games with him may also lift his spirits.

BOOST HIS SOCIAL LIFE.

Take your dog to a park or dog run where he can interact with other canines—they can be so much more fun to play with than people. If your dog is gloomy because he has lost a canine brother or sister, consider whether getting him a new companion will work for you and/or him.

MEDICATIONS AND DIET CAN INFLUENCE A DOG'S BEHAVIOR.

A hyperactive dog should come off puppy food by six months, which is when most dogs should switch to adult food, anyway.

A diet high in fat and protein may be too much for a dog who is already wound up. Many behavior modification plans for "problem dogs" begin with instructions to feed the dog a low-protein food. This is something you can experiment with after you speak to the vet about whether that is appropriate for your dog.

Territorial Problems

(*See also "Fearful Personality" on page 572, because fear is often at the bottom of territorial displays of aggression.*)

This is a situation in which a dog shows aggression toward strangers when they enter what she considers her territory. There are several locations that cause some dogs to be aggressively territorial: the house, the yard, the surrounding neighborhood and, often most of all, the car. Dogs are more confident on their own turf—and the car is an extension of that turf.

WHY DOGS EXHIBIT THIS BEHAVIOR

Dogs are often possessive about their turf not out of bravery, but just the opposite: fear of strangers, intruders, anything new. This is partly genetic—it's an inborn tendency in German Shepherds and other guarding or herding breeds—but it's also a sign of improper socialization in the first three months, so that anything that is unusual to the dog automatically becomes a threat. You cannot completely eliminate the trait in a dog, but you can certainly minimize and modify it so that the reactions are not so great.

UNIFORMED VISITORS

The mailman is always a prime target—and one with whom the dog's territoriality is constantly reinforced. The dog barks like mad and the mailman always leaves, so the dog thinks she has accomplished great things. She feels emboldened to do even more next time. Any uniformed visitor (UPS, FedEx, gas deliverymen) gets the business from her, and they all leave fairly quickly, which only reinforces her sense of power.

◆ Desensitization Counterconditioning

You want to change your dog's perception of visitors, especially ones in uniform. Explain that you need their help in making your dog more welcoming. Give each visitor a few treats. The first step should be through food—no eye contact from the person. Put your dog on a leash with a head collar so that you can nip any nipping in the bud—and then have the strangers reward the dog for coming over to them quietly. Let the dog go to the scary person, not vice versa, to build her confidence. Praise her for being brave and calm. Eventually, one visitor at a time, she may become a better hostess.

CAR TERRITORIALITY

Put a head collar on the dog, with leash attached, that you can hold. Some say you should run a long leash under the front seat before starting out, so that the dog has to stay lying down in the backseat. Decide for yourself if you feel this would distract you while driving and whether you might not be better off just holding the leash between the front two seats so you have some physical control if she really loses it and lunges at the windows.

If the dog does not settle down with a quick tug on the head collar, then keep a shake-can (see page 280 in the "Equipment" section) in the car. For sensitive dogs, sometimes just holding up the dreaded can in warning is enough. I've tried a water pistol in the car but I always missed my target "shooting blind" behind my shoulder!

MEDICATION

There are some dogs whose fear-based territoriality can be retrained better and more easily if the dog receives some medication first.

There are drugs like Inderal (propranolol) that reduce anxiety and aggression without causing sedation. This medication is used for people with heart conditions, because it reduces anxiety and prevents sudden increases in heart rate and blood pressure. It is used in humans for stage fright, fear of public speaking and performance anxiety. It has been used to treat aggression in people. Talk to your vet about the pros and cons, since it has a significant cardiac effect.

LOW-PROTEIN DIET

There is some evidence that fearful dogs may improve their behavior if put on a low-protein diet. If you feed a dry kibble, it should contain about eighteen percent protein. Check first with your vet since it is not advisable for dogs, who are young, pregnant or have certain medical conditions.

Thunderstorm Phobia

Many dogs are disturbed by thunderstorms, but we're talking about full-blown terror: a dog that is afflicted by this fear can go to extremes. The dog may be super-clingy with you. Many of them seek out a small, den-like place to hunker down until the storm passes.

Other dogs have extreme physical reactions to thunderstorms, including panting, drooling, vomiting and even losing control of their bladder or bowels.

If you're not home when there is a thunderstorm, a phobic dog may go one step further and become destructive, wreaking havoc in the house, perhaps trying to "get away" from the thunder that so terrifies him.

WHAT CAUSES THUNDER PHOBIA TO BEGIN?

Normally it takes years for this fear to develop, and no one knows why. Many people have a dog who has not had any reaction to thunderstorms, and then suddenly one day becomes agitated and then unglued when there is thunder and lightning. The average age at which thunderstorm phobia begins is seven years old. Some dogs suffering from a fear of thunderstorms are also prone to being anxious in other situations.

◆ Which Dogs Suffer the Most?

Some breeds are more prone than others to experience terror around thunderstorms. Northern breeds such as Huskies and Samoyeds, and some of the larger breeds such as Labradors, Retrievers and German Shepherds are prone to the phobia. No one knows why.

◆ What Causes the Terror?

- ❑ Acute hearing is one theory about why this phenomenon happens to some dogs: that the sound of thunder may be painful or uncomfortable to very sensitive ears.
- ❑ Muted hearing is another theory, and this one contradicts the preceding one. This idea is that dogs that don't generally hear well become phobic because they are shocked by the sound of thunder entering their fairly silent world.

   These "hearing theories" don't make good sense, because many thunder-phobic dogs do not react in any special way to other very loud booming sounds, such a car backfiring or gunshots or fireworks—while other dogs can anxiously pant and tremble from *all* of the above sounds.

- ❑ Changes in atmospheric pressure seems like the best guess at what makes a dog phobic about thunder. Many dogs pace, pant and seek refuge in the closet or bathroom long before a storm actually starts. Changes in barometric pressure and other indications of a storm reach a dog's superior sensory capabilities long before we are aware of them.

WHAT YOU CAN DO ABOUT IT

If your dog's reaction to thunder is to pant, tremble, refuse food or water and/or seek a hiding place, there are some things you can do and others you should avoid.

◆ The Worst Thing You Can Do Is to Show Pity.

If you show concern during the storm—even if the concern is about how your frightened dog is doing—it will make the dog even more anxious. It may not make sense to you, but in the dog's mind you are validating his worry and fear. The more compassion you show, the worse it makes it for the dog.

◆ The Best Thing You Can Do Is Show Leadership and Give Him Direction.

The best way to deal with a dog suffering from a phobia is to give the impression of confidence and take the dog's attention off the storm by giving him direction. Instead of showing affection in the form of patting and chatting (which increases a dog's anxiety), you want to give him clear direction with some obedience commands, or try coaxing him to play his favorite games. A really scared dog is not going to want to chase a ball or even gnaw on a rawhide chew, but if you offer them with an upbeat attitude, the dog will be helped even by that.

Whatever you do, maintain a confident air: the dog will gain confidence if his leader shows no reaction to the storm.

TIPS FOR HANDLING THUNDERSTORMS

- ❏ Exercise your dog several hours before the storm is expected.
- ❏ Do not leave your dog outside. Her fear of the storm could drive her to try to dig out or jump out of the yard, and she might hurt herself.
- ❏ Lock any dog door to prevent her from running outside in a panic.
- ❏ Put a piece of your worn clothing in whatever "safe room" the dog usually chooses (generally a closet or bathroom) to give her more comfort.
- ❏ Muffle the sounds of the storm by putting on music, TV, an air conditioner or an air purifier. If you have no other way to cover the sounds of the storm, turn on the noisy fan over your stove or in the bathroom if the dog hides in there.
- ❏ Try to get her to play an indoor game with you.
- ❏ Give her a very favorite treat, such as a Kong stuffed with cheese or peanut butter or a baked marrow bone.

"DESENSITIZATION" OR "BEHAVIOR MODIFICATION"

For dogs whose phobia is really terrible, it is possible to embark on an elaborate system of exposing the dog in stages to tape-recordings of thunder. The reason this technique is not included here is because it could become a full-time job. This behavior modification is a labor-intensive task with a number of critical decisions and transitions to make. The step-by-step instructions involve finding or making a storm recording that is realistic (without it being so intense that it freaks the dog out right away) and then very slowly making the dog listen to it while doing pleasurable things to him.

This desensitization to thunder has to be done in different rooms and areas of the house, or it will have no effect. It takes a professional to know when to go up to the next level of intensity on the recording and when to back off. Another problem is that all of the work you will have done can be erased if one real thunderstorm happens during the counter-conditioning process.

MEDICATIONS FOR SEVERE THUNDERSTORM PHOBIAS

Medications have a place in severe phobic reactions in dogs. The most commonly used medication for this condition is acepromozine, a tranquilizer that has been around for years. (It was the tranquilizer used for years on show horses to make them more mellow, until regulations forbade it and urine tests were instituted to rule it out.)

If for some reason Ace, as it is called, does not work on your dog's phobia, there are many other anxiety-reducing medications you can discuss with your vet. Buspirone is one of the type of medications known as "smart drugs," so called because they target specific receptors in the brain. They have minimal side effects while getting maximum results in affecting behavior, although exactly how they function isn't fully understood by doctors.

Another prescription drug known as Xanax (alprazolam) is used for anxiety disorders in people. It is a Valium-type drug that apparently works best for thunder phobia in dogs when you give it on the day of the storm, or when the dog shows the initial signs of anxiety.

There are some vets who view thunderstorm phobias differently, and feel that the dog should be medicated all the time, viewing the condition as though it were arthritis or diabetes. They suggest beginning a treatment with clomipramine or preferably amitriptyline for several weeks before the thunderstorm season begins where you live, with daily medication until the risk of thunderstorms has passed. The thinking behind the season-long theory is that the longer-acting drugs take weeks to change how the brain actually works—they have to be present in the body before the stormy weather begins.

Visitors (and Poor Behavior)

(Also see "Territorial Problems" on page 609 in this section for related information.)

Many dogs get all worked up and their worst old habits come right out when you have company—whether it's the UPS man or Uncle Marvin.

USE THE HEAD COLLAR.

The head collar (see page 269 in the "Teaching Manners" chapter about the product Gentle Leader) works like a dream for some dogs. Put it on in anticipation of a visitor, or slip it on when unexpected visitors arrive at the door. You can attach the leash, but after a while, just putting on the head collar can calm some dogs. In fact, you can take it off within a minute or two—it's often just the initial rush of adrenaline toward strangers that's the problem. I use it this way for Scooby Doo to help him chill out. In fact, if you leave it on for long, the dog may try to rub her face against you (or probably the new arrival) to scratch his face and/or try to rub the collar off.

THE "COLD SHOULDER" CONQUERS AGAIN.

Tell everyone who comes to your house to totally ignore the dog(s) for the first few minutes. Do not touch. Do not talk. Do not make eye contact. Tell them to turn their back if the dog insists on making contact, nudging with his nose or anything similar.

This will be hardest for dog lovers and owners—they think it's cruel, rude, whatever. Just tell them they have to do it, period. The consistency in the cold-shoulder approach is very important, because each and every human has to be perceived by the dog as alpha.

You'll be amazed at how a normally jump-up, barking, mouthy dog will just go right to his bed and chill out when he's snubbed. By now you know that in dog terms it has to do with the alpha issue, the hierarchy. What ignoring a dog says is this: I am in charge, I have come in and you don't have to check me out or figure out where I am in the scheme of things. I am above you, that's all you have to know." And so the dog shrugs and says to himself, "Fine by me. I can go catch a few winks instead of worrying myself sick trying to take charge of everything around here."

PUT THE DOG AWAY.

Placing the dog in his crate or behind a dog gate is a lot easier than trying to monitor, excuse and correct his behavior while guests are just coming in the door. Depending on how informal your occasion is, who your guests are and how dog-friendly they may be, you can let the dog out (wearing a head collar and leash for full control) after everyone has settled in.

Don't lock the dog away behind a closed door, however. This can cause high anxiety and even panic attacks in some dogs—they need to see what's going on and feel part of it, even at a distance.

Whining

A dog's whining can be so irritating to us, but a dog is rarely even aware that she's doing it. In most dogs, the whining generally isn't even under their control. The dog's anxiety and excitement tighten up his throat so that the air comes out in a high-pitched, whiny sound.

Reasons That Dogs Whine

Nervousness/anxiety
Excited anticipation
Frustration
Stress
Low self-confidence

THREE THINGS TO NEVER DO WITH WHINING

1. Do not react verbally to the whining, especially in a comforting voice. The dog perceives any sympathetic platitudes from you such as, "Don't worry, it's okay," as being a reward for the way she is behaving.

2. Do not pat or stroke the dog to comfort him when he's whining, because that will seem like a reward to him.

3. Do not reprimand or correct the dog, because that will just make her more nervous.

◆ **Just Ignore the Whining.**
Go about your business as though everything is normal. Give the dog other things to do—try simple obedience commands, or even toss a toy to distract him.

Chapter 17

A LITTLE OF THIS AND THAT

This is a mixed chapter, filled with miscellaneous topics that didn't quite fit elsewhere. However, just because they are here in a sort of grab bag doesn't mean they aren't just as important and useful as anything else in the book. For example, the section on "Senior Dogs" is vitally important to all dog owners, because our dogs will all be seniors at some point.

In this chapter you'll find:

- ❏ Large dogs
- ❏ Small dogs
- ❏ Multi-dog households
- ❏ Dogs and cats
- ❏ Blind, deaf, handicapped dogs
- ❏ Dogs and the law
- ❏ Senior dogs
- ❏ Euthanasia
- ❏ The grieving process
- ❏ Emergency preparedness

Large Dogs

I expected that there would be more information and equipment specific to larger breeds, but oddly enough there are really just two diseases that affect only large dogs. The important issue of how to feed a large dog is already covered on page 455 of Chapter Thirteen, "Nutrition." Otherwise, all you need to know is that large dogs have a shorter life expectancy—so love your big dog twice as much, because you'll probably have less time with him.

BONE DISEASE IN GROWING PUPPIES (HOD)

"Growing pains" is the simple name for hypertrophic osteodystrophy (HOD), which is an inflammation in the growth plates of the long bones of a large-breed puppy. The long bones are undergoing rapid growth, and the growth plates become inflamed and painful.

◆ Which Dogs Are at Risk?

This is a young dog's disorder that usually surfaces when the pup is three to four months old. Any dog that will be heavier than sixty pounds when fully grown is a candidate for this painful growth period, but HOD is most frequently seen in Labrador Retrievers, Great Danes, Boxers and Setters.

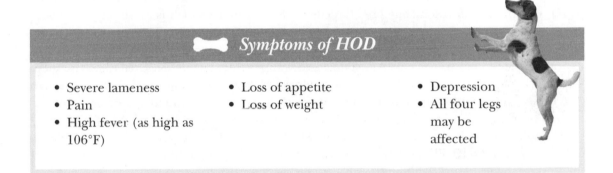

Symptoms of HOD

- Severe lameness
- Pain
- High fever (as high as 106°F)
- Loss of appetite
- Loss of weight
- Depression
- All four legs may be affected

◆ What You Can Do for the Puppy

Go to the vet with any dog displaying these symptoms, both to rule out any less-common bone disease and to allow the doctor to give you some pain relief for the pup. Painkillers are important, because this can be a really painful condition for a puppy, but which drug to use is a decision to be made very carefully with your vet. (See page 375 in Chapter Eleven under "Medications" for information and warnings on Rimadyl, Deramaxx and other medications.)

HOD and panosteitis (see below) will disappear over time, but giving supportive care and pain relief to the puppy is important. Cutting back on exercise will minimize lameness. Keeping the dog lean, without excess fat, should be easy in a growing puppy, and it may also help with discomfort.

PANOSTEITIS

Like HOD, this condition occurs in large-breed puppies and is characterized by lameness and pain in the mid-portion of a bone. The puppy will react to pressure on the middle of a front leg, for example, but there will be no joint pain. The reasons for this syndrome are unknown.

This condition tends to occur when the puppy is four or five months old and lasts for only a few months before disappearing. Any dog that will grow to more than sixty pounds can be affected, but the breeds most at risk are Setters, German Shepherds and Great Danes.

Small Dogs

More than a third of the dogs in America are small breeds. It is obvious why they are so popular. They are portable, adorable companions who often have big personalities and make devoted pets. It is really a shame that so many people who buy toy breeds get them from pet stores, which is the absolute *worst* environment for these precious, delicate little dogs. As you will see below, these little creatures should stay much longer with their mother and littermates, and when they do join the human world, it should be with careful attention to their health, which is at great risk in their early months.

Pet stores don't want to frighten away customers, so they rarely tell people the truth about these dogs' fragility (one exception being the store Puppy Love, mentioned on the following page). Generally, unless someone buys directly from a breeder—which is more important with toy breeds than others—the buyer will not know how extremely fragile these tiny puppies are, and how much vigilant care they require for their feeding and warmth. Any breeder will want to educate you and help you give their tiny dogs the best possible start in life. Even as adults, these little breeds can be quite delicate and prone to illness. Make sure you have the time and desire to give these dogs the attention they need so that your happiness—and their well-being—are not marred by tragedy.

The information in this section pertains to all small-breed dogs, but the chart lists the tiniest breeds. These are dogs who, when fully grown, weigh less than fifteen pounds and are no taller than twelve inches. The breeds below will always need your special attention.

The Smallest Breeds

Affenpinscher	English Toy Spaniel	Pekingese
Bichon Frise	Havanese	Pomeranian
Bolognese	Italian Greyhound	Pug
Brussels Griffon	Japanese Chin	Schipperke
Cavalier King Charles Spaniel	Maltese	Shih Tzu
Chihuahua	Manchester Terrier	Silky Terrier
Chinese Crested	Miniature Pinscher	Toy Poodle
	Papillon	Yorkshire Terrier

SMALL BREEDS ARE HIGH-RISK PUPPIES

Toy breeds are so tiny as infants and so fragile that they require a level of care and attention that is entirely different from "regular" puppies. Small breeds present a high maintenance situation that people should know about when choosing a toy breed, and they should consider carefully before buying.

If you've never heard any of this before and wonder whether I'm a worrywart, well guess what—I'd never heard any of it, either, until I began my research. You might ask why pet shops (which sell millions of toy dogs, especially in cities) and breeders don't warn people, and the answer is economics, of course: if everyone knew how much care and kid-glove treatment little dogs need, they might not buy so many of them. If you wonder why you don't hear of toy dogs getting very sick and dying, it may be that most pet shops give a guarantee with their puppies: if one is sick, the store will often just replace it, considering the fact that they may lose some "product" just a cost of doing business. I learned a lot from the dedicated couple who own Puppy Love, a pet store in Ridgefield, Connecticut. Despite my misgivings about the canine misery that goes into the mass production of dogs on Midwestern puppy farms, many people are still going to get their purebred dogs from a pet store. One would hope that the puppies would at least get some personal attention at the "distribution end" of the dog business. At Puppy Love they educate potential buyers about the fragility of toy puppies (and they interview potential buyers of "dangerous" breeds such as Rottweilers before they consider selling to them). They also isolate puppies who seem to be getting ill—particularly the small breeds—segregating and medicating them until they are well enough to return to the general population in the store.

AGE THAT SMALL-BREED PUPS CAN LEAVE THE LITTER

The smallest breeds cannot be taken away from their litter at the commonly presumed age of eight to twelve weeks. If these dogs are removed at the age considered appropriate for larger dogs, the little ones would be sickened by the stress and trauma of being separated from their littermates. If you see a toy dog in a pet store younger than twelve weeks, do not get involved: that puppy is going to have an uphill battle, physically and emotionally.

RISKS FOR TOY PUPPIES

Toy-breed puppies are at an increased risk for parvovirus, coronavirus and skin conditions. They get colds and coughs more easily than larger breeds. Even playing too hard or too long can be dangerous for their health. But the greatest danger for small puppies is how easily they can develop low blood sugar, or hypoglycemia.

◆ What Is Hypoglycemia?

This medical condition is pretty much the same as in humans: the blood sugar falls. The most common form is "transient juvenile hypoglycemia." Puppies of all breeds are more prone to hypoglycemia than adults because their livers are smaller in proportion to their bodies than their brains are. The brain is using more glucose than the body is producing. But in toy breeds, these imbalances are more noticeable, and low blood sugar can develop very quickly, even overnight.

The cure for hypoglycemia varies depending on the severity of the symptoms. In mild cases all it takes is a meal of readily digested and metabolized fuel. Ask the breeder or your vet what they would recommend, but having jars of baby food meats on hand is probably a good idea. Otherwise, you must take the pup to the vet (usually for a an IV dextrose solution) because repeated hypoglycemic episodes can lead to more severe complications.

🦴 Symptoms of Hypoglycemia

(Keep puppy warm and call the vet, even for mild symptoms.)

Eyes rolled back	Seizures
White gums	Comatose
Depressed attitude	

PREVENTING HYPOGLYCEMIA

- ❏ For the first month at home, put light Karo syrup in the puppy's water (one tablespoon to one cup of water).
- ❏ Frequently feed high-carbohydrate, high-protein or high-fat foods.
- ❏ Keep puppy warm—getting chilled can set it off.
- ❏ Monitor play—both how long and with what vigor.
- ❏ Don't pass puppy from hand to hand: too much stimulation, chance of poking or squeezing.
- ❏ Give puppy plenty of rest time—and "time outs" if play gets too vigorous.

SAFETY TIPS FOR TOY PUPPIES

If any of the following rules for toy puppies sounds too cautious to you, talk to your veterinarian about the risks and what precautions she feels you should follow. The fragility of small dogs has never been properly explained to most people, but it is better to be safe than sorry. Every one of these warnings applies equally to these little dogs as adults. Each owner will use the following advice to suit his own situation; the point is to raise awareness.

- ❏ Keep her under constant supervision to prevent falls from furniture or stairs. Any fall or compression of her body can cause serious injury.
- ❏ Monitor her the whole time she is outside the crate, even after she is house-trained. You always need to know where she is, since anything can be a danger—larger animals, children, even adults who don't see her and can kick, step or sit on her (this may sound ludicrous, but it really happens). The crate is quite literally her safe haven.

- ☐ Put cozy little beds in every room to discourage her from hanging out on chairs or sofas: this habit can end her life if someone accidentally sits on her.
- ☐ Make sure the puppy doesn't get dropped, squeezed or poked when lifted.
- ☐ *Do not allow any child to handle a toy puppy.* This may sound harsh, but it's a rule you must follow to protect your pet. Not only should a child not hold a toy puppy, you really shouldn't let a child play with her unattended: even the slightest roughness risks bruising her internally. If a very tiny puppy is dropped (accidents happen) it can be devastating: physically to the animal and emotionally to the child. Some breeders will not sell their dogs to anyone with a child younger than seven.
- ☐ Toy dogs need quiet time. They cannot take overstimulation. Long-term personality changes and health problems may result from overhandling. Rest time is as important to toys as their frequent meals.
- ☐ If you already have a large dog, be super-vigilant in how he relates to the toy puppy. Rough play with a larger dog can break her bones. Also, many dogs—even friendly ones—adopt hunting behavior with tiny breeds. Some breeders will not sell to a household with larger dogs.
- ☐ Always have the dog on a leash outdoors because she can dart into traffic or get into an altercation, especially with a bigger dog she may have antagonized (little dogs are renowned for not knowing their limitations and can come on with fearless assertiveness to dogs of any size).
- ☐ When traveling in a car, she should always be in a cage that is padded and secured. Any short stop, sudden turn or accident could propel a small, unrestrained dog around the interior or out a window.
- ☐ Don't let your puppy play for too long and lower her energy stores. Running and playing too hard can wipe out a toy puppy's reserve of energy; she should always have some "in the bank" for later use.
- ☐ Maintain a constant warm temperature—getting chilled is dangerous.
- ☐ Toy puppies **must** have four meals a day if they are under four pounds and younger than twelve weeks. After that, these puppies need three to four meals a day. They are prone to hypoglycemia—low blood sugar—which can be very serious. They cannot eat less frequently than that; they cannot miss a meal.

FEEDING INSTRUCTIONS FOR TOY PUPPIES

Toy puppies need to eat every single one of their three to four meals a day. It's not an option for them to skip a meal because of the risk of their blood sugar dropping. So the instructions that follow are all about getting food into that little puppy, whatever it takes.

◆ How to Feed

Mix one-quarter cup premium dry puppy food with one to two tablespoons of canned or fresh cooked meat. If you can make it warm, so much the better. If the puppy isn't hungry, remove her dish and try again in fifteen minutes. Try sitting with her so she has company when she eats, which is stimulating or comforting to some dogs. But if the puppy shows no interest in the second offering of her meal, try the food tricks below.

✦ Not Wanting to Eat
If a toy puppy misses two meals in a row, she is at risk for transient juvenile diabetes (this is diabetes that can be reversed). You will have to do ANYTHING you can to stimulate her appetite. Follow the suggestions below until your puppy eats.

TIPS TO STIMULATE A LITTLE DOG'S APPETITE

- ❏ Mix warm beef or chicken broth (canned is okay, low sodium is best).
- ❏ Add small bits of cooked chicken, beef or fish.
- ❏ Try small pieces of any cooked (never raw) meat you have.
- ❏ Canned cat food is really appealing.

If the puppy doesn't eat despite these enticements, it's a good idea to take her to the vet to be evaluated. A tiny puppy cannot go very long without nutrition before she gets weak, and once her blood sugar drops you have another set of problems to deal with.

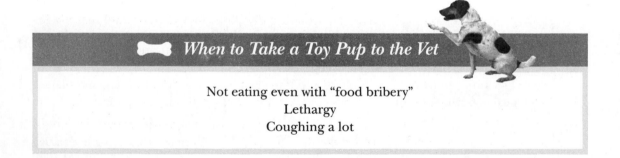

When to Take a Toy Pup to the Vet

Not eating even with "food bribery"
Lethargy
Coughing a lot

TRAINING ISSUES WITH SMALL-BREED DOGS

✦ Special Considerations about Equipment
You can't use a choke chain or slip collar because of the risk of trachea problems—neck and throat injuries—that occur in toy breeds such as Pomeranians, Chihuahuas, Toy Poodles and Yorkshire Terriers. You can't do obedience training with a halter, but a plain dog collar should work just fine.

✦ Growling When Picked Up
Some small dogs feel threatened when people loom over them like giants to scoop them up. If you have a small dog that growls or acts threatening when you try to lift her up, don't start judging or pigeonholing the dog as "aggressive" or "mean." She may just feel frightened or threatened by a huge human bearing down on her. Don't get started comparing your dog negatively to

other small dogs who are happy to be swept off their feet. Just as some people love roller coasters, others view them with dread. So try to respect your dog's way of communicating to you that she is not comfortable when you reach down to pick her up.

Solving Bad Reactions to Being Lifted

- Avoid the situation that triggers the growl response.
- Avoid body postures that a small dog could view as threatening—avoid direct eye contact and avoid facing her head on
- Try crouching down into a squatting position before lifting her up.
- Teach her to jump up onto something—a chair, couch, etc.—before being lifted.

LITTER-TRAINING A SMALL DOG

The idea of litter boxes for puppies and small dogs is fairly new, but it's so logical (it's really just another form of paper-training) that you have to wonder why no one thought of it until recently. Purina has come out with a litter-training system called secondnature, with a specially designed pan, training guide and a litter made from super-absorbent pellets of recyled newspaper and wood pulp. The litter doesn't stain or track on paws, has odor control and is environmentally friendly.

◆ Start Young
Research into the litter box showed that adult dogs would not use it, and even puppies of four or five months would not use it readily, either. However, ten-week-old puppies used it just like paper, proving that the key to litter training is to start young.

This is confirmed by earlier research that demonstrated the age at which dogs develop preferences for where they will eliminate: 8½ weeks. This is the same age at which puppies develop physical control of their bladders, and also the age when their brains are primed to learn and remember, all of which taken together makes it the prime time to house-train.

◆ Using a Litter Box for Life
Whereas people used to use paper-training and "wee-wee pads" temporarily to house-train, now the owners of small dogs are using this system permanently. The owners may not want to make many trips outside from an apartment building in all types of weather, and a small dog's tiny bladder and active metabolism do require many more "pit stops" in a day.

Just remember that if you turn to litter boxes or the equivalent for your dog to relieve herself, that does not mean that she should be kept inside all the time. Toy dogs need fresh air, exercise and the chance to interact with other dogs and see the world—don't forget that they need to go on walks for reasons other than elimination.

Multi-dog Households

(See "Dog Body Language" on page 134 for more on this.)

Indulge me while I pass on a few personal observations about living with multiple dogs, which may be helpful to you since I have lived with three dogs—sadly, not always the *same* three—for many years. There are a few nuggets of wisdom I've gathered in these multi-dog years. The first is that two dogs are a pair. Any more than that, and you have a pack: they'll be more wound up, even offensive, in their behavior toward interlopers on the property and, in my case, especially where cats are concerned. When I had two dogs, they cohabited peacefully with the two cats— but when I added a third dog to the household, they began to hunt, chase and then attack the cats. I had to give my beloved kitties away to save their lives. It was hard not to feel angry at those dogs, even though I knew they were only heeding their wolf-pack instincts, emboldened by each other.

I grew up as a one-dog girl, with Pango as my first sibling until my little human sister Holly came along. I didn't begin having a multi-dog life until years later, when my dear Golden Retriever Roma fell head over heels for Marmaduke, the handsome Golden of an acquaintance. They were so crazy for each other that we owners sheepishly arranged play dates and sleepovers for them! The pure joy of their running, wrestling and hunting together made me think how selfish it was not to give Roma someone of her own species to pal around with. I didn't think I could accommodate two large dogs, so (based on my then-sweetheart's soft spot for Cocker Spaniels) I wound up with Amalfi, who was sweet and funny and stunningly un-doglike. How was I to know that Cockers can be visitors from another planet, marching to drummers only they can hear? Poor Roma, what a comedown from the bounding Marmaduke, to the Louis IV cocker who preferred a satin pillow to the ground.

Without digressing any further, I'd just like say that while you might think you have a good reason for getting a second (or third) dog, there is no way to predict how those dogs will interact. You fantasize that a second dog will be good company for your perhaps lonely or bored dog—but it can wind up that a second dog expects you to be her "everything." In my life, with three big outdoor dogs living on more than two acres in a deep pine forest, I thought they'd be outside living it up all day. The reality is that I have three dogs who shadow me, who jump up and follow me with wagging tails and expressions of "Great, boss, where are we going now?" every time I get up for a cup of tea.

On a logistical note, when three dogs all want patting and you only have two hands, you develop new skills with your feet, elbows, etc. I am tremendously fortunate that I have a schedule and a location that are conducive to getting the most pleasure from my dogs and giving them the best life imaginable, but if I had a traditional job or lived in a city or had school-age children, I'd feel quite differently about having three dogs to dry after rainy walks, three bodies to check for ticks, and sixty-six toenails to cut each time. (The dewclaws were surgically removed on the Weimeraners as puppies, or I'd have sixty-eight.)

DOES YOUR DOG REALLY WANT A COMPANION?

Before you jump in and present your dog with another pooch, stop to figure out whether or not it's a good idea. There are a number of issues to consider from your point of view and your dog's before you make an impulsive decision that you'll be stuck with for a long time.

◆ Are You Really Prepared for Another Dog?

Sometimes, very busy people feel guilty that they don't spend enough time with their dogs—and they get the idea to "give" that dog a companion. But if you don't have enough time and energy to give to one dog, then you have to consider whether you might be shortchanging *two* dogs and *doubling* your guilt if you get another. Beyond the question of time, there are the issues of space, cost and affection, *all* of which are necessary to include another dog in your life.

◆ Is Your Dog Ready for a Companion?

Is your dog used to being around other dogs? If he's never lived with another dog, what is he like when he's around other dogs? Is he mellow and cheerful, or tense and fearful? Does he generally get along well with other dogs—or are there only one or two dogs he likes? If you aren't sure where he stands on strange dogs, then take him somewhere that dogs congregate, such as a park or a dog run, and evaluate his comfort and confidence levels, as well as how sociable he is around his own species.

◆ Not All Dogs Get Along.

This is something to keep in mind as you are making introductions: some dogs are just not a good match for each other. Although you can work with a trainer to get two incompatible dogs to like each other more, that becomes a burden and an expense with an uncertain outcome. Don't try to force something that does not appear to come naturally: be ready and willing to pass up the prospective new dog and wait for another opportunity for a better match. You'll be doing yourself and both dogs a favor.

CHOOSING A NEW DOG

Generally, it's a good idea to introduce a potential new canine member of your family to the existing dog(s) to get a sense of whether things will work out between them. This "personality test" is less important with a puppy, since all puppies behave submissively to older dogs. Most breeders won't allow dogs to visit their litters (see following page) but most will probably tell you to get a puppy of the opposite sex from the one you currently have. Of course, if you already have two dogs of opposite sexes, this becomes a fifty-fifty gamble as to whether you have picked the "right" opposite sex to mesh well with the others!

◆ Choose a Dog Similar to Yours.

Your odds of making a harmonious match increase if you try to find a dog like your own. You want a personality that complements your dog's; if your dog is still on the young side, look for a second dog of about the same age and size. Dogs play better when their heights and weights are close—their chasing and wrestling are matched, and there's less risk of either getting hurt.

At least get a similar breed, so that when the puppy grows, the sizes of the two will be compatible.

However, if the existing dog is getting on in years, you may think that a bouncy young pup will perk him up (as well as serve as a bridge for the people into the years ahead when the old timer will be gone). If the older dog is physically weak or slowed down so much that he sleeps a lot of the time, then a puppy might be too revved up and just a nuisance to the older dog. Optimally, you'd like to see them synchronize their energy levels so they can do some things together. If your older dog is only middle-aged, then a puppy may bring him the proverbial "new lease on life"; if the older guy doesn't feel well, then it's not fair to subject him to a puppy's shenanigans. However, the good thing about a puppy is that he will not challenge the senior adult's position, since all a youngster wants is to be accepted and have someone to play with.

◆ Getting a Puppy from a Breeder

If you are getting a purebred puppy from a breeder, you should tell the breeder about the dog you already have. Unfortunately, you can't let your dog and the puppy meet ahead of time, because a breeder wouldn't want your current dog to come with you to visit the litter: the mother wouldn't like it. Besides, the puppies shouldn't be exposed to any dogs until they are about sixteen weeks old and have had all their shots. It's different if you bring a new puppy home and your dog is healthy and inoculated.

◆ Getting the New Dog from a Shelter or Breed-rescue

Introducing the newcomer to your resident dog will be encouraged by most breed-rescue organizations. A general animal shelter would be wise to insist that you bring any existing family dog(s) with you to their facility. The staff can help determine if the dog you are considering adopting may be a problem with the dog(s) you already have. Even though you know your current dog better than anyone, the employees of a shelter or the volunteers of the breed-rescue have been present for a lot of "first meetings": they know how to evaluate the introduction of the two dogs as a predictor of how things are likely to turn out. What you'll be looking for in a new dog is one who will accept the older dog as the number one, or at least won't challenge his position.

◆ What Type of Dog to Look For

Some breeds tend to be more feisty and prone to fight, including Pit Bulls, Terriers and herding-dog breeds. People have bred these dogs to have a low tolerance for members of their own species. On the other hand, there are breed groups such as hounds and sporting dogs that are genetically predisposed to be comfortable and work in harmony with other dogs, including Beagles, Basset Hounds, Foxhounds, Coonhounds, Bloodhounds, Labradors and Golden Retrievers.

❒ Avoid a dominant personality, because it's not fair to the older gent to introduce a mature dog who will challenge the "incumbent" and try to push the older dog aside. A dog who has spent most of his life being the main event in your life (in an animal sense)

should not have to duel with a younger dog to maintain the position that has historically been his.

❑ Get a dog of the opposite sex. If the older dog is a male, then a new female would immediately defer to him; an older female will generally defer to a male newcomer.

❑ Keep competition to a minimum. A senior dog's status should be maintained by you. That means feed him first, pat him first, show the newcomer that the older dog is a senior member of your "firm" and deserves deference and respect. Designate separate feeding areas so mealtimes are not competitive, and have separate food and water bowls so there is no jockeying for position.

✦ Older Dogs May Be Upset by Another Dog.

If you have a mature dog who is used to being the only dog in the household, the transition to sharing that position may be more unpleasant for him than you'd expect. Also, if you spent a lot of time alone with your older dog and/or he goes "everywhere" with you, then sharing you with a new dog may be a source of jealousy and discomfort for him. No matter what the eventual outcome of bringing another dog home, it will probably be stressful and confusing to the older dog during the settling-in period, so give him some extra support.

HOW TO ORCHESTRATE THE INTRODUCTION

One way to introduce two dogs that aren't puppies is to meet on-leash at a neutral outdoor spot—that way, neither dog can feel territorial. Have someone come with you to hold the new dog while you hold the leash of your resident dog. However, as mentioned elsewhere, just being on a leash can create a more aggressive or defensive posture in a dog, so keep this in mind before coming to a conclusion about whether their temperaments are compatible.

❑ Keep the leashes loose. If you tighten the leash, it telegraphs your nervousness and a sense of jeopardy to the dog.

❑ Have a large fenced area where they can interact off-leash once you feel comfortable allowing them to interact freely. If you have doubts about the reliability of either dog, you can leave their leashes on while they are getting to know one another—this gives you something to grab, if necessary.

❑ When the dogs are first sniffing, encourage them with a happy voice, tell them how good they're being, etc. Set an upbeat tone and they will be influenced by it.

❑ Watch their body language for signs of incipient aggression or displeasure. See the chart on page 135 with the different meanings of head and tail carriage, eye contact and other indicators of a dog's stress level. If need be, before you conduct this introductory experiment with the dogs, check with the chart of "Signs of Dominance" and "Signs of Submissiveness" (on page 138). By learning or reminding yourself how to interpret a dog's body language, you can figure out pretty quickly what hierarchy the dogs are negotiating and which of them is going to be the one in charge. It will also alert you to the possibility of ugliness between the dogs, which you could interrupt.

(See the section on "Dog Body Language" in Chapter 6, page 134 for more on this topic.)

The social standing/status negotiations between dogs are often misunderstood by us. When dogs are figuring out their pecking order, it has no relationship to human ideas of fairness or comportment.

◆ The Fundamentals of Rank within the Pack

Nearly ninety percent of what dogs do is connected to their wolf heritage, especially when it comes to interactions with other dogs. An essential component of that genetic "hardwiring" is about rank within the pack. Rank works very simply: a dog respects, obeys and follows those *above* him—and just the opposite toward those *beneath* his rank. Among themselves, dogs develop a sense of who is king of the hill. Rank is about who gets what privileges. The dominant dog gets to decide what/when/how he wants it vis-à-vis the other dog(s). However, this is not an across-the-board ranking in every area of life. In a multi-dog household, for example, no one is king forever, and every issue does not have equal importance. One dog eats first. Another dog gets the bed he chooses. Another goes outdoors first. Not everything has equal importance, or is consistent with our human way of thinking.

Not all dogs are interested in being on top. Do you want to be the chief/boss/president of everything? (And even if you do, rest assured that not everybody does, whether it be a person or a dog.)

◆ What Exactly Is Going on When Two Dogs Meet?

The body language of two dogs approaching each other establishes their rank immediately—and often imperceptibly to us. The dog holding his head higher as they approach each other is the higher-ranked—if the other dog lowers his head and does not make eye contact. But if the second dog does *not* submit in this way but also keeps his head high and makes direct eye contact, then you have a standoff that will lead to a dogfight unless one of the two backs down. All this can happen within seconds and without any visible aggression or dramatics.

Dogs will rarely fight unless humans get in the way of their initial dance and communication. But if people are in the middle of things and do not understand how dogs communicate with their body language, fights can erupt from dog-to-dog misunderstandings. For example, if a person has the submissive dog on a leash and tightens it up when he sees another dog, this can lift up his dog's head, putting it into an aggressive, "I'm not backing down" position that the dog would never choose on her own. The approaching dog—if he is the more assertive one—is expecting the submissive one on the leash to acknowledge her lower rank and submit with lowered head and averted eyes. The assertive dog does not know that it is the human's leash holding his actually meek adversary's head up in that offensive posture, so the more dominant dog keeps on coming, perhaps finally physically challenging the leashed dog, who would like nothing better at that point than to turn and run!

SERIOUS BEHAVIOR PROBLEMS AND DOMINANCE ISSUES

Many of the serious problems that dogs have come directly from their misconception about their rank within your family pack. The people may have let the dog feel dominant (see Chapter Seven, page 148) or, if there is more than one dog, the humans may have interfered in the power balance between the dogs and reinforced or "propped up" the position of one dog over the other, creating a false leader.

♦ People May Crown One Dog "King."
Sometimes a dog's people lead him to think he is the alpha in the family. This burden forces the dog by its very nature (the wolf heritage) to protect against all intruders or perceived threats. This burden is unwanted by many dogs, and those who want to be on top will profit unfairly because of human intervention. As soon as the dog's ranking is put back into a more manageable place, the tension should dissipate.

♦ Aggressive Behavior
Biting people, chasing joggers, going after bicycles and attacking other dogs are all symptoms of a dog who has been led to believe that she is the leader of her pack, and she is therefore indiscriminately wielding power that is not rightly hers.

    If the dogs in a multi-dog household start fighting with each other, you need a professional trainer to immediately evaluate what's triggering their hostility and whether it can be defused.

OTHER WAYS THAT DOGS COMMUNICATE PHYSICALLY

♦ Playing with a Sibling
- ❑ Playing with an object shows rank, because whichever dog ultimately winds up with the toy is the higher-ranking dog. Even if it all seems in good fun—without any growling or bared teeth—the unequivocal result is: "to the victor go the spoils."
- ❑ Mounting another dog is about social position, not sex (unless a dog is in heat), even though the mounting is often accompanied by a "humping" motion that appears sexual to people. In multi-dog households, there may be one dog who always mounts the other, or they may take turns.
- ❑ Over-peeing another dog's urine is status, too. Last one to pee is highest in the pecking order. If you have a clear Top Dog, you will see that dog determined to over-pee any time he sees one of his pack peeing.
- ❑ Going through narrow openings is an indicator of a dog's position: if a higher-ranked dog occupies a doorway (lying down or standing), then lower-ranked canines won't approach until the passageway is clear.
- ❑ Playing can get too intense, and that's something that the owner has to keep an eye on. Two dogs who are nuts about each other can start playing so hard that their adrenaline flows, they can start to be too rough with each other. At this point, you should intercede by calling the dogs' names, offering a toy or biscuit and separating them for a few minutes, just long enough for their adrenaline levels to even out. Then they can go back to playing if they feel like it.

Dogs and Cats

Dogs and cats can coexist quite well and share the same home and the same humans. What these animals from different species have in common is that people provide for their every need and have domesticated them into a sort of parent-child relationship. Despite enormous differences in their natural behavior and in their wild ancestors, dogs and cats can live together harmoniously and even form bonds as strong as those they each have with their human caretakers.

THE DIFFERENCE BETWEEN DOGS AND CATS

Cats and dogs are not natural enemies, but they aren't natural friends, either. When living under the same roof, they are in competition for food and water, territory and the affection of the people. If the two animals live together over several years, they come to an understanding and learn to respect the different issues that are important to each of them.

◆ Start Young.

The most successful relationships between dogs and cats are those that begin when both animals are young—introduced as puppies and kittens, they can grow up together and figure each other out. If you don't have a youngster of both species, then know that a young kitten can adapt to a grown dog more easily than a young dog can imprint on a grown cat. However, a lot depends on the personalities on both sides—and for every rule there will be exceptions. There are contradictions, too. You may find your dog is a cat-hater—he seems to detest the whole species and will go after strays—yet he'll develop a loving relationship with the family cat.

◆ Territoriality

Dogs can be territorial about specific locations and objects—especially dominant males of terrier breeds and working breeds, although females can exhibit these same reactions. Dogs can get vicious about things like food and water bowls, special areas of a room, their beds and people of whom they're especially fond.

Cats can also prize locations and objects, but they'll rarely fight over them and even then not with a dog—maybe with another cat. What does makes cats fiercely assertive are: *pathways* leading to those favorite locations, *attention* from favorite people, *play objects* (especially catnip) and *special food treats*.

◆ Differences in the Social Order of the Two Species

While dog and cat behavior is quite different, both species have a dominant/subordinate order—the difference being that, with cats, the issue of top cat/bottom cat is constantly fluctuating. Cats do not have a social order that is easily understood. In the wild, most cats are solitary creatures that come together and stay together to mate and raise their young. Otherwise the males and females live separately within their own territories (the only cat this is *not* true of is a lion, who lives in a pride, which is itself a kind of pack).

The solitary feline lifestyle in the wild gives clues about the origin of independence in domestic cats, who give the impression of being aloof about human attention. But now that cats have been pampered by humans who cater to their every need (just as we do with dogs), cats have learned to crave the affection, grooming, scheduled fancy meals and affection lavished on them by their people. You could say this is something they have developed in common with dogs—a shared dependence on humans.

GUIDELINES FOR DOGS AND CATS SHARING YOUR LIFE

- ❒ Bring animals together when they are young.
- ❒ Dogs and cats rarely compete for the same thing because they usually don't want what is important to the other—a big part of what makes peaceful cohabitation possible.
- ❒ Establish separate areas for each animal, with their sleeping "dens" as far apart as possible and with the cat's lair higher up.
- ❒ The cat's food and water should be up on a counter or sink area and her sleeping den should be somewhere the dog cannot reach or does not go, such as the second floor if you live in a house.
- ❒ Feed the pets at different times and in different places.
- ❒ Any special attention or grooming you give to one pet should be done when the other one is not around to see and get jealous.

CATS IN MULTIPLE-DOG HOUSEHOLDS

For the most part it is not advisable to bring a cat or kitten into a home that has more than two dogs, since three dogs become a pack. Each dog is fine on his own with cats, and two dogs usually won't chase a cat, either—but put three dogs together and that cat had better have a good climbing tree ready.

Although it is possible to desensitize your dog pack to cats, it's probably not worth the effort and residual worry.

INTRODUCING THE TWO SPECIES

"Let's just put them together and see what happens" is sure to be a recipe for disaster. The goal for introductions is keep all the animals as relaxed as possible.

When the time comes (see below), you'll need to have the dog on a leash. The cat needs to be able to escape without being chased.

✦ Give It Lots of Time.

The introductory period generally takes anywhere from two weeks to two months, but it really needs to be done in stages to slowly desensitize the animals to each other.

Patience on your part may be hard—you want two animals you love to love each other, but in each household it will take as long as it takes. You can't set any timetable if you want long-lasting success.

BEFORE YOU EVER BRING A DOG HOME

Before a dog ever steps on the premises, your cat has to have established safe havens and escape routes that she is familiar with and can readily use. As you will see from the instructions below, it can take quite a few days or even weeks to lay this groundwork; you can't rush into this introduction.

◆ Escape Routes: Catwalks, Perches, Cat Doors, Baby Gates

The cat needs places out of a dog's reach where she can go when she feels threatened.

Perches and catwalks can give a cat real security, although not every house or apartment has places to install them. If you can, purchase or build escapes for her wherever you can reasonably do so.

Get the cat used to the perches or they'll be of no use. Your preparatory work is not done until the cat knows where her "bolt holes" are and she is used to jumping up on them. To entice her to use them you need to bait these spots—put something delicious such as her favorite food or catnip crumbs up there and sweet-talk her into jumping up to get her treat.

The cat needs to understand that she can jump right over a baby gate and that the dog cannot follow her over. First acclimate her to the gate by teaching her to jump over it—with you on the opposite side offering sweet talk and treats.

Cat doors can be so helpful, even if your cat does not go outdoors. You can also install a door like this in the door to your basement or another room such as the laundry room by cutting it into the bottom of the door. You can teach the cat how to go through the door by showing her how the flap lifts up; get her used to the feeling of it coming down behind her on her body. Hold up the flap—you should be on the opposite side of the door from her—and entice her through with more sweet talk and treats. Little by little, most cats will jump through easily, and as you let the flap down gradually they will understand how to push the flap with their heads.

If your cat is really reluctant, there are a few things you can try for further encouragement. You can duct-tape the flap open for a few days so she only has to deal with going through the opening. Feed her meals on the far side of the door from where she usually is, so that she has added incentive. And if you want her to be more responsive to your calling her through, have her favorite treat waiting for her.

Once your cat is familiar with all her possible escape routes, it's time to see how it will go with a dog in the picture.

◆ The Cat's Necessities Have to Be Up High.

The cat's food, water and toys should be up on a countertop or table. If you haven't had them up high before you bring the dog home—and you know ahead of time you'll be getting a dog—then move the dishes onto a tabletop weeks before the dog arrives so that the cat knows where her belongings are and doesn't have too much to adjust to all at once when the dog does come.

The litter box needs to be somewhere the dog cannot get to it—perhaps the basement or a laundry room or extra bathroom where you can tie or wedge the door so that only the cat can get through.

BEFORE THE FIRST MEETING

The first thing is to let each of them get used to the other's odor. Desensitizing the animals to each other starts with scent. To do this, rub a towel or small blanket on each of them and place the towel near a place of positive association—under the other animal's food dish, on your cat's favorite nesting place (including spreading the doggie towel on your own lap) and on the dog's bed.

Cats will often avoid the dog-scented towel at first. If you find this to be true, you can be sure that if your cat wants no part of the dog's smell, he will certainly want to avoid the actual dog if he sees her.

A cat that slashes his tail at the smell of the dog is upset. Continue switching the towels between the two until you no longer get tail-slashing from the cat.

A dog who is highly aroused may bark or whine at the smell of the cat; keep those towels and blankets coming until the dog doesn't react much anymore.

When the dog is no longer acting too interested in the cat's scent, and the cat is no longer avoiding the dog's scent—you can rub the towels on the animals a few more times to keep the scent strong—then it's time to try the introduction.

THE "PRE" INTRODUCTION

The bringing together of a dog and a cat is a slow process that has to be done in stages. In this step, they don't yet see each other—they get used to each other from either side of a closed door.

One goal that you should keep in mind in all phases of this introduction is to create as many good associations and feelings around the other species as you can—it should seem to the animals that positive things happen when the other one is around. So on either side of a closed door—you on one side with an animal and someone familiar with the other animal on the other—let the animals sniff under the door and give them special tummy rubs, treats, toys, whatever you know will make them happy. Try to sit right next to the door, but if the animals don't want to get that close, encourage them to get as close as they can stand while you make a big fuss over them.

GETTING CLOSER

• **Start Small.**

When the dog and cat are relaxed with each other on either side of the door, have the dog on a leash and prop the door open just an inch or two with a heavy doorstop on each side (even a big chair on the dog's side, if needed). The leash is there in case the dog decides to take matters into his own hands. Practice this until both parties are comfortable with being able to see each other a little bit and smell each other directly.

• **Next Step: the Baby Gate**

The next step is to set up a baby/pet gate between the two rooms—you might still want to keep the dog on a leash in case he seems eager to scale the gate. Stay with this arrangement until the cat doesn't run away and the dog isn't too excited as they sniff each other through the gate.

MEETING WITHOUT A BARRIER

After all this preparation, the animals are ready for a freer meeting. You still want to keep things calm, so eliminate any distractions that could escalate the tension level; keep your own energy and voice cool.

◆ First Create an Escape Route for the Cat.

Before the actual meeting, create a "safe zone" for the cat that is out of the dog's range. Often, upstairs for the cat and downstairs for the dog works. You need to make sure that the cat has a "bolt hole" somewhere up high if she wants to bail out (see "Escape Routes," page 632). Keep a long leash or long line on your dog so that if the cat takes off and his instinct to chase takes over, you can always grab or step on his leash.

INCHING TOWARD COHABITATION

Once you have gone through all the steps above and reached a place of mutual acceptance between them, it should be safe to leave the animals loose in the house together *when you are there*. However, when you leave you should confine one of the animals or erect a secure barrier between them. You never know what outside provocation or inner instincts could trigger the cat to run and the dog to chase—with possible bad consequences for one of them.

The final outcome of the dog/cat relationship is that they will eventually live in cozy harmony or peaceful neutrality. If, after several weeks of slow exposure to each other, there is still a low-boil of tension or overt hostility between the animals, you'd be well-advised to consult with a professional animal behaviorist/trainer to help you solve it, or even to help determine if it can be worked out at all.

HOW THE CAT AND DOG REACT

◆ The Cat Takes Much Longer to Warm Up.

If your cat has not had a dog in the house before, expect the cat to have a meltdown when the dog arrives, and don't be surprised if it lasts a fairly long time.

Most cats take months to adjust to having a dog in the house—and there's not really anything you can do to speed the process along. As long as the cat has high places to jump up onto, away from the dog, there's no danger of serious harm coming to her.

Normal defensive behaviors for a cat: hissing, swatting.

◆ How the Dog Reacts

Most dogs are curious and have the instinct to chase a cat. Some cats will stand their ground, hiss, arch their backs, growl and swipe out with their paws—but many times a cat will do the opposite and take off and run. The cat's flight is what triggers the "prey drive" in a dog—the instinct to chase a small moving object. This must be discouraged.

If the dog starts to lunge or to run after the cat, give a quick tug on his collar with a firm "No" and calmly tell him to "Sit." If the dog's desire to chase is really strong (if he's pulling and his eyes are bugging out of his head and he's practically drooling with desire to bolt after the cat), then the reward you give him for restraining himself needs to be a really big reward (such as a delicious piece of cheese).

Just as they say the punishment should fit the crime, so should the reward fit the accomplishment. If the dog considers going after the cat but is easily dissuaded by your correction, then the reward can fit the effort he had to make to control his impulses.

DOGS AND OTHER SMALL HOUSEHOLD PETS

You cannot leave your dog loose in your house or yard with any small pet (rabbits, ferrets, birds, potbellied pigs, snakes). Some dogs view any smaller animal as prey and would go after it in a flash.

Don't think that because your dog has had one or more neutral encounters with other pets that there is no jeopardy—all it takes is something to trigger that hunting impulse in the dog, and tragedy will follow.

Blind, Deaf and Handicapped Dogs

BLIND DOGS

Blindness may actually be easier to work with than deafness, because dogs respond well to verbal commands and want to stay close to their owners. A blind dog can have a happy life as long as you make accommodations in certain aspects of your home. One reason that a blind dog's quality of life is pretty good is because his sense of smell is crucial to his perception of the world, and at least he hasn't lost that. His loss of vision is not as devastating as we might imagine, because a dog's ability to communicate is based on smelling pheromone, the hormone-like substance emitted by many animals. A blind dog is still able to get information about other dogs, people and his surroundings.

◆ No Surprises, Please.

Getting around is the hardest thing for a blind dog. The dog has to know where furniture or any other obstacle is in order to feel safe and secure in navigating your home and yard. A basic rule to follow is to avoid changes in his environment: predictability makes life easier for him. The dog's physical environment has to remain constant and predictable: imagine how frightening it would be to try to navigate all alone and encounter objects you weren't expecting. Below is an overview of safety tips for blind dogs: further explanation, where necessary, follows.

GUIDELINES FOR LIVING WITH A BLIND DOG

- ❏ Don't move furniture.
- ❏ Don't move the dog's food or water bowls.
- ❏ If you don't have a second dog, consider getting a companion.
- ❏ Encourage exercise to keep the dog from becoming sedentary and putting on weight.

- ❏ Teach him to walk on a harness or leash (if he's not accustomed).
- ❏ Buy toys that have a noisy squeaker or a recognizable odor, including balls with bells or scent.
- ❏ Avoid very loud noises or sudden startling movements.
- ❏ Ask visitors to speak gently when approaching and before touching him, so that he isn't shocked by being touched out of the blue.

✦ Navigating Inside the House.

There are a number of ways you can help your dog move around comfortably in the house. Use whatever seems useful to you, depending on the layout of your house or apartment and your dog's own adaptability.

People have to be careful to keep the house uncluttered. The people in a household with a blind dog must be thoughtful about this: don't let anyone in the family leave things on the floor such as bicycles, bags, briefcases, backpacks, toys, packages or anything else the dog might bump into. It's unfair and can make life miserable for him. Needless to say, do not move any of your furniture around—or when you do, take time to reorient the dog to its location (see "furniture marking" below). A potential problem is when people get up from the table and don't push their chairs back in: the chairs left sticking out from the kitchen or dining-room table can be painful for a blind dog to crash into.

Make a "smell path" for him. To help make your dog's life easier, create a smell path to guide him around pieces of furniture—the most significant obstacles in any house—and through doorways. Spray the legs of furniture and the sides of doorways with a mildly scented perfume, room deodorant or more natural scents such as citrus or vanilla (test any piece of furniture first in an inconspicuous spot to make sure it doesn't stain). Keep in mind that with a dog's keen sense of smell, you only have to spray *very lightly*—a dog's nose is incredibly sensitive. If you can barely smell it at all, that's perfect—because the odor will be potent for him.

Tape steps and stairs. You can use a wide painter's tape such as masking tape or the wide blue kind (which doesn't hurt the paint or flooring) to mark the edges of steps and stairs. The dog will feel the texture of the tape on his feet and can also smell it: he will learn that the tape means he is on the edge of a step.

Make a path with hall runners. If you want to be really kind to your blind dog, you can make an actual tactile path for him using any carpet runners you want, or just the clear plastic runners used during inclement weather to protect flooring. He will feel the difference between the runner and the floor around it and will stick to the runner for easy navigation. If you want to mark doorways or the top of steps or stairs, you can put a doormat of some kind there so that he can feel the informational marker.

He may get disoriented once in a while. If your dog seems to lose his way every so often, guide him back to his food and water bowls. From his feeding area he can get his bearings and set out again.

All dogs have a skill called "cognitive mapping," which helps them to find their way home from a distance and to find bones that they've buried. Blind dogs use this ability to get a mental map of the inside of the house and garden so they can get around quite easily. If they temporarily lose their "coordinates" on that mental map, they can reorient themselves by going back to a central spot.

A "Seeing-eye pet companion" If you don't already have another dog in your home, or even a cat (if your blind dog would tolerate one), consider getting an animal companion for your blind dog. It can make life much easier for a dog who has another animal's sound and scent to follow around and can be guided by his senses of hearing and smell.

If you do have other animals, it is helpful to put little bells on their collars—unless their tags are already noisy—so that the blind dog can know where the other creatures are in the house.

♦ Walking Outdoors

When going for walks, you will become a "seeing-eye person" for your blind dog, and he will learn to trust you to take care of him. The best favor you can do for your dog is to give him cues to let him know what's coming underfoot so he can feel secure going out with you. Be conscious of your footwork. Think about where the dog will be walking next to you, and get in the habit of preparing him verbally for changes in the terrain. For example, when you put his leash on and start off on a walk saying "Let's go," always step with the foot closest to him. Then, when you come to a flight of stairs, slow down and say "Stairs," and do the same when coming to a curb on the sidewalk—say "Curb." He will soon learn what this means and can prepare himself for the change underfoot.

Mark pathways with mulch. Depending of the size of your property, you can make paths for your dog even in a modest backyard. Get some wood chips or cedar mulch and lay down a path leading to where your dog usually eliminates. This will give him the confidence to go trotting right out there without worry.

Fence an exercise area. If your dog seems reluctant to go outside, you may need to give him the security of a small, enclosed space where he can get some fresh air and relieve himself. At least until the dog feels more comfortable in his condition, fence a fairly small exercise area for him and don't make any changes to it.

Block access to all water. You have to take the risk of drowning quite seriously with a blind dog. If he were to fall into any body of water—whether it's a pool, a pond or a lily pond—he would be unable to see any potential exit and could just thrash around until exhausted. It may help if you think of a blind dog's vulnerability in this area as being similar to a toddler and water: all water is unsafe, and if it is not completely inaccessible, you have to watch him every minute.

CAUSES OF BLINDNESS

♦ Sudden Blindness

If your dog becomes suddenly blind (usually from an accident), she may exhibit equally sudden changes in her disposition: fearfulness, depression, aggression. Everyone in the family should talk about any change in her personality so that no one, especially children, does anything to provoke negative, fear-based behavior from the dog.

♦ Blindness from Cataracts

If your dog's blindness is the result of cataracts, you should be inspecting his eyes every day, looking for changes that could be symptoms of glaucoma or other problems. The changes to look for include:

RESOURCES FOR BLIND DOGS

There is a book that is widely recommended for owners of blind dogs called *Living with Blind Dogs* by Caroline D. Levin, RN (Lantern Publications, 1998, $29.95), which is an often-quoted resource guide for cohabitating with and training a blind dog. In addition:

❑ www.blinddogs.com (for owners of blind dogs)
❑ www.blinddog.info/blinddoghelp.htm (information about blind dogs)
❑ http://groups.yahoo.com/group/blinddogs (e-mail list)

Deafness

REASONS FOR DEAFNESS

A few dogs become deaf due to ear infection, injury, exposure to loud noise or old age. However, the most common cause of deafness is genetic—and in most cases, this deafness is linked to large amounts of white fur in the dogs, which comes from a gene that is linked to hearing defects. These genes are even more likely to cause deafness if the dog also has blue eyes. There is also a second kind of inherited deafness that can happen to dogs of any color.

Some breeds tend toward being deaf. Dalmatians are a well-known example—and of course, they're predominantly white. There is so much known deafness in the Dalmatian gene pool that the Dalmatian Club of America has a code of ethics to give serious consideration to deafness in their breeding programs, and there are Dalmatian breeders who have accomplished a near zero deafness rate in their breeding program. Here is a list of breeds that are genetically at risk for deafness:

Breeds with Congenital Deafness

Australian Cattle Dog	Boxer	Dalmatian
Australian Shepherd	Bull Terrier	English Cocker Spaniel
Border Collie	Catahoula Leopard Dog	English Setter

RISKS FOR DEAF DOGS

A deaf dog must always be on a leash, unless she is in a fenced yard or you are hiking in an area completely isolated from roadways. There are very few risks that are specific to deaf dogs except the chance that they may run after something and cross a road. If something catches her attention—and a deaf dog's eyesight is even sharper than a hearing dog's—she can take off, and you'll have no way to call her back. She won't be able to hear you call her back, or to hear approaching cars.

THE MYTH ABOUT DEAF DOGS BEING AGGRESSIVE

Nobody seems to know where this misinformation was first hatched, but there are some breed and rescue groups that recommend killing all deaf puppies in the mistaken belief that they will become aggressive dogs. It is commonly known that aggression comes from a genetic predisposition and from the way a dog is raised and socialized. Deafness does not cause aggression.

The Deaf Dog Education Action Fund (DDEAF) has not seen any correlation between deafness and aggression. The director of the organization has organized six Florida deaf dog picnics in public off-leash parks, and they have had every kind of dog, including Pit Bulls, as well as other breeds prone to deafness: Australian Shepherds, Border Collies, Boxers and Dalmatians, without ever having so much as a scuffle between dogs.

✦ "Startle a Deaf Dog and She Will Bite."

This is another misunderstanding about aggressiveness in deaf dogs: the fact is, if you take any dog by surprise she may act aggressively. Not all dogs respond with aggression, but some may go on the offensive. The saying "Let sleeping dogs lie" refers to the fact that if a dog is rudely awakened, her first impulse may be to protect herself—but this saying has nothing to do with deaf dogs.

✦ Practice Startling Your Deaf Dog.

Deaf dogs (or any dog, really) can be "conditioned" not only to tolerate being startled but to actually like it. Set up surprises when you come upon your deaf dog from in front and behind, armed with her favorite treat. Right at the moment that she looks alarmed or jumps up, give her the treat and a pat. Some dogs actually learn to look forward to being surprised.

DEAFNESS AND DALMATIANS

There is a controversy about how to handle Dalmatian puppies that are born totally deaf. The Dalmatian Club's code of ethics includes euthanizing all puppies that are bilaterally deaf (both ears). While adherents to this rule concede that it may seem cruel to eliminate an otherwise healthy puppy just because it cannot hear, they claim that these deaf puppies apparently suffer from high anxiety and general fearfulness before they are even eight weeks old.

Those opposed to the practice of killing deaf puppies say these pups don't even know they're deaf, that they are smart companion animals who can be trained and that it is we who have to learn how to communicate with them (see "Hand Signals," page 641).

FIGURING OUT IF YOUR DOG IS (OR IS BECOMING) DEAF

If you are wondering whether your dog is deaf or going deaf, be sure to consult your vet, because there may be something you can do about it.

One sign of deafness is that your dog doesn't come to the door to welcome you home. If you stamp your foot on the floor and she suddenly runs to you—having felt the vibration—then you can be pretty sure she could not hear you.

TEACHING DEAF DOGS

You can teach a deaf dog basic commands using hand signals modified from those you'd use with a hearing dog. There are also signals modified from the sign language used by hearing-impaired humans. Contact www.handspeak.com to get that book. But you can go way beyond basic commands: a deaf dog can learn as many commands and tricks as any other dog.

◆ Sensitivity to Visual Stimuli

Deaf dogs are especially sensitive to visual stimulation—as with any sensory loss, the other senses compensate by becoming more pronounced. This can make things both more difficult and easier at the same time. Since the deaf dog is often distracted by anything moving, you need to begin training in a setting in which there's nothing for him to look at but you. However, because of that same visual sensitivity, the deaf dog will notice your attempts to get her attention by waving or otherwise signaling her, and then the hand signals themselves can become small and subtle after the initial learning phase.

The main issue is being able to get the dog's attention on you so that she can see the visual commands (see below). Also, deaf dogs have a hard time keeping their focus, so in the beginning it's helpful to use food treats when training; later on you may want to offer food rewards randomly from time to time (which is actually considered a more powerful reinforcement for learning than giving a treat every single time—see page 241 under "Teaching Manners").

◆ Different Ways to Get a Deaf Dog's Attention

❏ The "watch me" signal is quite easy to teach: hold a treat in your fingers, pass it near your dog's nose and then bring your hand right up to your face, sort of at your nose so the dog is looking you in the eyes. As soon as the dog looks at your face, give him the thumbs-up sign (see below) with the other hand and feed him the treat.

Do a lot of repetitions of "watch me" with the treat, and then try a few without the treat in your hand. Pass your hand in front of the dog's nose with the fingers pinched together, continue your hand up to your face, and when the dog looks you in the face, give him the thumbs-up sign and then feed a treat, even though you didn't have one to bait your attention-getting hand this time.

Keep playing and practicing, working for a long period of eye contact—at least one minute while you're teaching it, which may seem like an eternity to both of you. Don't give the thumbs-up sign and treat until the dog has been looking at you for as long as you wanted.

- A tap on the shoulder or on the rear end is an easy cue to look at your face. You can start by giving a light tap on your dog's shoulder or rump: as soon as she looks up at your face, give a thumbs-up and a treat.
- Vibrating collars are sold by manufacturers listed on the Web site of the Deaf Dog Education Action Fund (www.deafdogs.org). These collars work with a remote control and are not intended to teach anything, just to gently get the dog's attention. But if you send a signal to the collar and the dog looks at you, a thumbs-up and great treat should follow. It won't take long for her to learn to look at you when she feels the vibration—and it's a great tool if you go on walks with your dog on a beach, park or trail in which there's some distance between you.
- A laser light can get a dog's attention when you flash it on the ground in front of her (never directly into her face, as it could damage her eyes). A flashlight can be used for the same effect in most situations. Once again, as soon as the dog looks up to your face, give her the thumbs-up sign and a treat.
- Flicking a light switch can work indoors, but it's not as specific as a light shined right in front of the dog.
- Stamping on the floor is used by some people to summon their dog's attention. In many situations the dog can feel the vibration, but there are surfaces that will not vibrate, or the vibration could be masked by other activity. It seems the least dependable attention-getting method, because it hinges on how the ground reacts to your stamping, which would also depend on what shoes you have on, if any at all. For example, if you were barefoot and outdoors in the summer it would be quite useless.

✦ The "Thumbs-up" Becomes the Reward Marker.

Since you can't use your voice to encourage your dog, or to let her know that she has done exactly what you wanted, you need to use this signal to mark the moment that she has succeeded. Some people clap their hands and smile, but the dog can't hear the clapping, and applause seems like a huge gesture for something you'll use many times a day. Just turn your thumb up—either hand is fine—and perhaps smile or nod, since dogs are quite used to checking our facial expressions. Remember how important it is to always use the reinforcement of the thumbs-up, since you have no other way to give instant praise. Use it the way you would "good girl" anytime the dog gives you the response you wanted.

HAND SIGNALS FOR TRAINING

The main hand signals you'll have to develop (after "watch me") are for "come," "sit," "stay" and "down." Deaf dogs communicate by watching your face and body language. In the early stages of training, you need to get comfortable using large, dramatic gestures, exaggerating the command. Once the dog has learned what you mean, you can dial it back to a more subtle version of the command.

• Try Out Different Hand Signals to Get Comfortable.
You can experiment with motions and gestures that you're comfortable with, keeping in mind that the gestures should be recognizably different from each other so the dog is not confused.

• You Can Use Any Part of Your Body.
You don't have to limit your signals to your hands. Experiment with what works for you, especially if your hands are often full with chores, laundry, gardening tools or little children. There is a limitless number of motions you can choose from to give your commands: you can tap your toe for "down," you can shrug your shoulders, bow your head, raise your eyebrows, tilt your head or even stick out your tongue, if you're so inclined.

• Keep the Gesture Small and Subtle.
We tend to overdo the scope of our hand signals with any dog, but deaf dogs are especially tuned in to our body language and, therefore, require even less of a motion to understand us. For example, when people are giving the "down" signal to a dog, they often raise their entire arm stiffly from the shoulder and make a huge sweeping motion downward with their palm facing the ground. This is the equivalent in physical signals to screaming at the top of your lungs while giving a verbal command. A dog, with or without hearing, can learn to lie down perfectly well from a signal as small as closing your hand into a fist facing the floor and just bending your wrist downward.

An example of the most dramatically simple physical signal I've ever seen: Aimee Sadler, the training consultant on this book, came to visit Jazzy, the Collie-mix I had just adopted from the shelter where Aimee was the consultant. She hadn't spent time teaching this dog anything special, but I told her how smart and super-responsive Jazzy was, even quicker than Lulu, whom Aimee had taught tricks to years before. So Aimee decided to experiment to see if she could get the dog to roll over. She got Jazzy's full attention by holding a treat in her hands, which she held together up against her chest, so that Jazzy's eyes were on Aimee's face. Aimee made the simple motion of bending her chin down to her chest, staring right at the dog. Jazzy hesitated, then melted down into a "down." Aimee smiled and said "Goood" quietly. Then Aimee cocked the side of her head down toward her shoulder—she didn't repeat the motion, she didn't elaborate on it, she just waited. Jazzy stared and stared as if she was reading an instruction manual, and I'll be darned if that dog didn't roll onto her side.

The "release" command This is the physical equivalent of the word "okay," used to tell the dog that the lesson or command is over and she is released. You need to give the physical equivalent of "game over" to give the dog permission to stop paying attention—in fact, to command her to leave you alone, that she is "off duty." You do not want the idea of "watch me" to become a clinging way of life, but simply the response to a command that then ends. You can choose the signal that suits you best, but a dismissive sideways wave of your hand that might imply "go away" can work. But you must pair the command with the entire removal of your attention from the dog— turn your back, put her out of your mind. If you read the "Cold Shoulder" (in Chapter Sixteen, page 613), you will understand why a cold shoulder from you will cause her to go calmly lie down.

Showing displeasure To show your displeasure or disapproval, you can wag your finger as you would with a child for "no, no, no."

"Come": With the back of your hand facing the dog, crook your index finger at the dog and gesture it toward you; or face your palm toward your stomach and beckon with all four fingers.

"Down": Motion toward the floor with your hand open flat, palm down. Or just point your finger to the ground while you look down at the ground.

"Stay": Same as for any dog—make a "stop" motion by pushing your hand at the dog, with the palm facing flat toward her.

"Sit": Same as for any dog—hold your hand up in a fist close to your body and raise your index finger; or bend your elbow with your open hand palm-out toward your dog (the way Indians said "How" in old Western movies).

"Walk/Heel": Pat the side of your leg next to the dog and step forward.

"Off/Leave It": Cross your hands on top of each other in front of you—palms toward you—then move them apart in a motion like a baseball umpire indicating that a runner is "safe" at the base.

RESOURCES FOR DEAF DOGS

There are several Web sites that are sources of information and support about deafness in dogs. You'll need to check them out to see which, if any, are helpful to you.

www.deafdogs.com (the Deaf Dog Education Action Fund)

www.thedca.org (Dalmatian Club of America)

www.handspeak.com (Sign Language Dictionary, includes signing for animals)

There are also some e-mail lists, which like any such resource can be really supportive and helpful or a ridiculous waste of time, depending on your needs and tolerance level.

groups.yahoo.com/group/deafdogs

groups.yahoo.com/group/DeafDalmatians

groups.yahoo.com/group/parentsofdeafdogs

OTHER PHYSICAL HANDICAPS

♦ Wheelchairs for Paralyzed Dogs

❏ Dewey's Wheelchairs for Dogs (877) 312-2122; www.wheelchairsfordogs.com

❏ Doggon' Wheels (888) 736-4466; www.doggon.com

❏ Eddie's Wheels for Pets (888) 211-2700; www.eddieswheels.com

- Four Flags Over Aspen (800) 222-9263; www.fourflags.com
- K-9 Carts (800) 578-6960; www.k9carts.com
- Surgi-Sox (877) 787-4479; www.surgi-sox.com
- Walkabout (800) 779-0439; www.walkaboutharnesses.com

DOG AMPUTEES

If your dog is missing a limb, you will not need to baby him or even feel sorry for him. Dogs have lost a front or back leg to cancer, accidents or other causes and still managed to lead a full and happy life. Dogs are able to compensate wonderfully for this loss: they can usually jump into the back of a car, climb stairs and swim.

In order to train a dog with a missing limb, gauge how quickly and how well he can respond to your commands by watching him around the house. Unless you observe him having great difficulty with certain movements, there is nothing that should keep him from being able to handle a "sit," "down" or anything else. However, do keep in mind that leg stumps can be tender or sensitive, so do any training on a soft, carpeted surface, especially when teaching and practicing commands such as "down."

RESOURCES FOR AMPUTEE DOGS INCLUDE:

- Pets with disabilities: www.petswithdisabilities.org; (410) 257-3141
- Handicapped pets: www.handicappedpets.com
- Limb amputation: www.petplace.com/articles/artShow.asp?art1D=52

Dogs and the Law

TRUSTS AND WILLS PROVIDING FOR DOGS

Fewer than thirty percent of Americans have provided for their pets in their wills—but what is going to happen to your dog if you die? The local animal shelter? Euthansia for an older dog?

There are differences between trusts and wills, the latter taking effect only once you die, while a living trust can be put into effect immediately if you are disabled. Only about half the states in the U.S. enforce pet trusts.

◆ Get Professional Advice.

There are specific laws in every state about all the legal issues affecting dogs, and planning for the death of a pet owner is one of them. There is nothing I could tell you here that would be correct in every situation or geographical location, so you're going to have to do some homework.

Get advice on estate planning from a professional, but before contacting an expensive lawyer (who may not even know much about dogs and the law) there are two books you might want to look at. *All My Children Wear Fur Coats* is by a Florida lawyer named Peggy Hoyt, and *Dog Law* is written by another lawyer, Mary Randolph, and covers everything to do with dogs and the law in the U.S. These books are a gold mine for someone wanting to make sure they are making watertight provisions for their dogs, since a will or a trust for a pet has to be written defensively, taking into account the potential heirs who might want to fight provisions you've made for an animal over them.

The Humane Society of the United States (HSUS) will send you a free estate planning kit. Call (202) 452-1100 or visit www.hsus.org/petsinwills.

◆ Pets Are Property.

The problem with trying to provide for your dog after your death in any state is that dogs are viewed as property. You can make provisions for your dog in your will but it is much trickier than you might imagine. You can't leave anything directly to your dog—legally, you can't leave property to *other* property—and even if you leave someone in charge of the dog(s), there are only certain ways you can leave money to that person.

◆ How Much Does a Dog Need to Survive?

Some legal advisors say that the more money you leave for the pet the more likely it will be challenged by angry relatives. It is not unusual for people you leave behind to feel they are more entitled to your estate than your dog—and they will challenge the will, holding things up in ways that may endanger your dog's welfare.

Some legal experts suggest leaving an amount appropriate to the actual needs of a dog, which in 2005 has been estimated at $900 to $1,600 a year. (I don't know where medical emergencies and procedures are considered in that number, since even with pet insurance just one serious medical episode costs more than the supposed year's allowance.) There are many sophisticated ways to legally protect the financial welfare of your dogs *and* the kind person who has agreed to be their guardian should you die—but every case is an individual one. So read those books, and once you've gotten the drift of the legal ins and outs of taking care of a pet in your will, then consult with a local lawyer, preferably specializing in trusts and wills, and recommended by someone you trust.

RETIREMENT HOMES

There are pet retirement homes such as Pet Estates near Albany, New York, which can give lifetime care for pets when owners can no longer care for them because of death or disability.

You name the home in your will or trust and your estate pays the necessary costs. But it doesn't come cheaply: at Pet Estates, for example, that can run from $7,500 a year to well over $20,000. So you may want to reconsider and find someone you'd trust to look after your dog(s)—in the hope that that person would be willing to take on the responsibility—and then protect that person financially in your will.

DIVORCE AND THE DOG

A dog who has been part of a human couple's relationship can take on a childlike role between them. When the couple's relationship is going to be terminated, they may have an understanding about how they want to treat the dog, but it is something they have to agree upon in writing.

◆ Dogs Are Not Children Under the Law.

Dogs are property, under the law. So the court will not consider dog "custody" issues such as joint custody, visitation rights and support payments unless you have a written agreement on these issues beforehand. Otherwise, the court will treat the dog as property to be given to one or the other of you.

◆ The Dissolution Agreement

You can specify dog-related issues in your dissolution agreement; the final divorce decree can include that provision, and the court can enforce it.

Senior Dogs

LIFE EXPECTANCY

The larger the dog, the shorter the life span, usually. What geriatric experts know is that small dogs age more slowly than large ones. Nearly forty percent of small breeds live longer than ten years, while only thirteen percent of the giant dogs live that long. So far, vets cannot find a reason for this disparity. So the average fifty-pound dog lives ten to twelve years—which means that a small Yorkie or Chihuahua can live to fifteen and beyond, while a giant breed like a Great Dane or a Deerhound rarely reaches its eighth birthday. Half of all senior dogs, generally those over age seven, will die from cancer. This is obviously a disturbing statistic, given that we'd do anything to keep our pets from dying a horrible death (for more on "Cancer," see page 334 in Chapter Eleven).

◆ Calculating Your Dog's Age in Human Terms

There used to be a saying that every year in a dog's life was equal to seven human years, in terms of development and life expectancy. But medical care and other advancements have extended the lives of dogs, and now there is a more sophisticated formula to equate dog years to human ones. Personally speaking, I don't know how or why this cross-species comparison idea even began. What does it really mean? Dogs live a completely different life than we do on this planet; other than our love for each other, our two species have very little in common. If I look at the chart it seems ludicrous to me: Billy Blue, at seventy-five pounds and nearly twelve years of age, is supposedly equal to a ninety-four-year-old man. But as Mr. Blue canters through the woods and gnaws a thick slab of rawhide every day, he doesn't remind me of any ninety-four-year-old I've ever seen, except for the white hairs on his chin! Nevertheless, people have come to expect this "dog years/human years" formula, so what follows is a further refinement of the calculations.

In the chart that follows, the age on the left is the dog's actual age; the right side shows the human equivalent of the average medium-sized dog of twenty to fifty pounds. To figure out small dogs (under twenty pounds) subtract about five years at each of those human age breaks—and for large dogs (fifty to 120 pounds) add approximately ten to the human years at each age break. For giant breeds (more than 120 pounds), you have to add nearly twenty more years to each of the human equivalents.

A Dog's "Human" Age

DOG'S ACTUAL AGE	EQUIVALENT HUMAN AGE
8 months	13 years
1 year	16 years
2 years	24 years
3 years	30 years
5 years	40 years
7 years	50 years
9 years	60 years
11 years	70 years
13 years	80 years
15 years	90 years

◆ Don't Treat Your Old-Timer As Though His Days Are Numbered.

Dogs don't have any concept that they will die some day; fortunately, they don't realize that deafness, blindness, incontinence, etc., are all signs of the end coming nearer. Keep a positive, upbeat attitude with your senior dog—he will take his cue about how things are from you. Don't exclude him from walks or other activities: just because he moves slower or is a little lame from arthritis or runs out of breath or steam sooner doesn't mean he doesn't enjoy outings. Being included is good for his mind and body; going on walks may even maintain his health and extend his life, just as it would for older humans.

◆ You Can Help Keep Your Older Dog Young.

A recent study of how to maintain the youthfulness of older Beagles was done in the interest of studying the process of aging in humans. The reason dogs were chosen for the study is that they have similar brain structures to ours and develop brain pathologies similar to those in people; scientists also consider that dogs live in a similar environment to ours and have similar nutritive requirements.

The study found that with an enriched diet and intellectual stimulation the dogs acted younger and smarter. Those Beagles who received a diet fortified with vitamins E, C and other antioxidants had better outcomes than the dogs without enriched diets—and those dogs who were given a mentally stimulating environment with kennel mates, exercise and mental challenges had less decline in the two-year study. However, those dogs who were enriched with a combination of both the correct diet and intellectual challenge had the highest mental functioning in the study. As might be expected, dogs who were not given either enrichment showed deterioration.

Many people are aware that as humans get older and retire, it can be often bring on a rapid physical and intellectual decline that is not evident in people who remain mentally and socially active into their later years. This study of Beagles helps to confirm some of those ideas for humans—yet the value for dog lovers is to give us important information about how to keep our elder canine statesmen sharp and lively, prolonging their quality of life and ours with it.

TIPS TO MAKE LIFE MORE COMFORTABLE

The physical comforts mentioned on the next couple of pages would be nice for any older dog, not just one with the aches of arthritis. So whatever your dog's condition, try and implement as many of the following niceties as you can.

⬩ Avoid Changes in His Environment.

Change is stressful to some dogs as they age—they get set in their ways, as some people do. Many dogs get less adjustable as they get older, so any change in their routine can be difficult. Knowing this, the nicest thing you can do for your dog is to keep as much of an even keel as you can in his life: no big changes, no surprises.

⬩ Be Prepared That Your Older Dog May Get Ill If You Go Away.

No one is certain why older dogs tend to get sick when their owners go away, but it seems that the dogs may suffer depression or stress from the absence of "their people." You need to know that this is a possible response to your going away so that you don't unfairly blame the kennel or dog-sitter.

Make clear provisions for how to reach the vet and what sort of decisions you would make if you were there (assuming that you can't be reached or there is an emergency that doesn't allow time for anyone to contact you).

Avoid putting an older dog in a kennel—even a super-nice one—if you go away. A kennel environment can be more stressful on an old-timer than on a younger dog: it would be a lot easier on him to have someone stay at your place with him.

⬩ Arthritis Causes a Lot of Aches and Pains.

Many of a dog's problems in the golden years are related to the normal aches and pains often caused by mild arthritis. Along with arthritis you can also get some instability and reduced muscle strength, all of which make getting around a bit tougher. Your dog may need a helping hand in some of the everyday aspects of life. There is more on arthritis later in the "Medical" part of this section, but what follow are some practical everyday adjustments that your dog will be grateful for.
Warmth can be a great relief. Heat therapy can be applied for ten minutes two to four times a day on the areas that you know are painful—and before and after a walk or other activity. The heat

source can be from a hot-water bottle or the kind of bead-filled microwaveable pads that create damp heat. You can also make your own heating pads by dampening a cloth or paper towel, putting it in a Ziplock bag and then microwaving it, but watch out—make it a short heating time, because the bag heats up quickly. **Warning**: *NEVER put anything hot on a dog's skin: the heat should be no warmer than what your own skin can comfortably tolerate.*

Elevate the food and water dishes. Use any stable low table or bench, or invest in one of the "feeding stations" that has a platform on legs for the dishes. It's much easier on the dog's back and neck not to have to bend all the way down (there is controversy about bloat and raising a dog's bowl).

Add traction to the surfaces the dog usually travels. If possible, it makes life easier on the senior citizen if you cover some portion of a slippery floor. Try carpet runners going up stairs and down hallways, and a nonslip area rug in tiled spaces such as kitchens, where a dog can slip and slide. This includes adding rubber-backed carpets (or carpet pads underneath throw rugs that slide around) in rooms with wooden floors.

Put several water bowls around the house. Drinking sufficient water is important to a dog's health, but he may get lazy about it as he ages. Make it easy on him by having a few bowls of water (preferably elevated) around the house, especially near his favorite resting spots so he doesn't have to walk long distances to quench his thirst.

Try a ramp for getting into and out of the car. Commercially made ramps and steps can be a big help to a dog struggling to get up onto furniture (if allowed) or into a car. But maybe before you buy or order one of these ramps, you can borrow one from a friend (or rig a stable but temporary ramp similar to the advertised products) to find out whether your dog is one of those dogs who is simply not willing to go up one. Also see "Twistep," page 192.

Give a helping hand to hind-end problems. Your senior dog can be shaky or painful in the spine or hip area. It can make walking a lot more comfortable if you give some support—especially going up and down stairs or when he first gets up to go outside for a walk. You can buy a padded sling with strap handles so you can give support to a dog who is a little wobbly on his feet when he first gets up from lying down. This belly sling is a strip of material that you slip under the dog's stomach just in front of his hind legs. Then you hold on with the cloth handle on either side and help support his weight. A stabilizing device of this kind is what veterinarians usually send a post-operative dog home with, especially after orthopedic (bone) surgery.

There are a number of good products (which you can check out on the various dog-supply Web sites and catalogs in the index). One of them is the Lift-n-Aid, which is especially good for large dogs because you can maneuver the dog without lifting his entire weight. This product is available at surfingrhino.com, or call (513) 984-5590.

Instead of spending money on a sling, you can also just improvise by using a towel or sheet that you slip under the dog's belly and then grab hold of the sides or ends. However, you're better off with two people doing it this way because a towel or sheet is unwieldy and you need a person on either side for stability. If your dog isn't too large, you can also fashion your own lifter: you can make a sling with handles for yourself in just a couple of minutes. Just take any old canvas or cloth carry bag and, holding it by the handles, cut down the seam on either side so that you wind up with a rectangle of canvas with a handle on the two short ends. You slip one handle under the dog's belly, wrap the canvas around his torso from beneath, then bring the two handles together above the dog's back.

Put comfortable beds around the house. A beanbag style of bed, or the orthopedic foam ones made especially for older dogs, are good. Keep the bed soft, low to the ground and warm, especially in cold climates. Even if your dog hasn't used a bed before, now is the time to offer her one. But don't use one that she has to climb in and out of—that can be hard on arthritic limbs. Anywhere that you or other family members spend a lot of time should have some kind of bed available for the older dog—even just an old quilt folded over.

Leave him alone if he gives you signals that he needs privacy. Your older dog may not be able to handle the situations he once could, such as kids running around or loud groups of people. So respect that change and protect his need for quiet time.

MODIFICATIONS IN EXERCISE

◆ Moderation Will Be the Operative Word as Your Pooch Grows Older.

Ease up on the exercise your dog has been accustomed to. Make it less strenuous, shorter in duration. Keep him moving every day, but maybe go out more frequently on shorter outings. Don't exhaust him or let him get overheated, since his body is less able to rebound as he ages. Let the dog determine the pace. He'll be following his instincts.

◆ If Your Dog Was a Ball-chaser

Don't throw the ball so far anymore—modify the game.

Toss the ball underhanded to the dog's mouth. He'll learn to catch it if he doesn't already know how. This is a fun game for him that doesn't involve the wear and tear on his body of running full tilt after a ball.

Play "hide the toy." Tell your dog to "Sit," then "Stay." Then hide a toy as he watches. Release him with a command to "Find it!" and make a big fuss over him when he goes to its hiding spot. As he learns the idea of the game, you can hide the toy in increasingly more difficult spots for him to find. This keeps him mentally alert.

◆ The Beach Can Be a Problem for Elderly Dogs.

If you are accustomed to taking your dog to the beach, you may find that he comes up lame or moves with stiffness or pain later that day or the next morning. Walking or running on the soft, uneven sand is especially difficult for dogs—or people—if they already have aches and pains in joints. You may not want to give up the joy of beach walks with your dog, but you should consider making shorter outings on the sand and/or limiting any running or chasing for him. The other possibility is to talk to your vet about giving your dog a pain reliever or anti-inflammatory either just before or after physically challenging exercise such as going to the beach.

CHANGES IN DIET

Dogs tend to get fatter as they get older—this is usually because their metabolism slows down while they are eating the same amount and often getting less exercise.

◆ **Keep Your Dog on a Diet, If Necessary.**

Dogs will eat way past the feeling of hunger—which means you are the one who has to show self-control in how much you feed the dog and what you offer. Obesity is a big problem for aging dogs, because it puts a strain on their joints and on the functioning of their organs. He should be slim enough that you can easily feel his ribs and/or hip bones without pressing hard.

◆ **Diet and Chronic Health Problems**

Chronic health problems such as heart and kidney conditions—which are not uncommon in older dogs—are often treated by feeding foods prescribed and sold by veterinarians. Your older dog may be fussy about eating these foods, since they can be less tasty than what she's used to, but you can talk to your vet about what you may be able to add in the way of homemade, salt-free chicken broth or cooked vegetables to make the food tastier.

PHYSICAL/MEDICAL CONDITIONS (ALPHABETICAL)

◆ **Make Vet Visits Twice a Year.**

By going more frequently to the vet as your dog ages, there are a number of common health conditions that affect older dogs that you can catch before they have a chance to become more serious. Even if your vet has several other doctors in her practice, you might want to try and stick with one individual as your dog ages. Your dog will feel at ease and you will have a professional pair of eyes to identify any decline.

◆ **Arthritis, Lameness, Stiffness**

Arthritis strikes many older dogs in their joints and spine, making even simple movements painful, especially when he first gets up and during cold, damp weather. In the previous section you'll find tips on making your dog's life more comfortable.

Go to the vet and get a thorough physical examination for your dog to determine whether the soreness may be from strained muscles. If it is joint pain, it is probably from arthritis, which affects older pooches.

Weight control Carrying too much weight puts stress on the joints. If your dog has arthritis and is even somewhat overweight, the pain is not likely to go away until the dog slims down. Increase exercise and reduce calories—a simple formula that works to shed pounds.

Warm bed(s) Arthritic dogs do poorly when they get cold, so keep yours warm. A warm bed can really make a difference—there are orthopedic beds with heating elements inside and various kinds of electrically heated pet beds. Check them out at your favorite dog catalog or Internet shopping site.

Relief for arthritis pain See page 374 in Chapter Eleven, and talk to your vet about the many possible ways to get pain relief. There are food supplements such as glucosamine and chondroitin, medications such as buffered aspirin or anti-inflammatory (Advil type) medications such as Rimadyl, Etogesic and Deramaxx. (***Caution about Rimadyl:*** *This medication puts extra stress on the dog's liver. A dog on Rimadyl must have a blood test every six weeks to check on liver function. This dangerous side effect is rare but occurs most often in Labrador Retrievers.*)

Adequan injections may also give relief (see page 376), although you need to commit to a monthly shot.

For many dogs, an extraordinary food supplement called Platinum Performance can put the spring back in the step of a dog who is moving slowly and painfully. See pages 453–54 for more on this amazing product.

♦ "Cognitive Dysfunction Syndrome" (Canine Cognitive Dysfunction)

Until recently, dogs were simply called "senile" as they got older and periodically became disoriented, wandered aimlessly, stared blankly at walls or didn't seem to recognize their masters. This syndrome of changes in senior dogs is now known to be a progressive degeneration of the brain comparable to Alzheimer's in humans. Studies have shown that about thirty percent of dogs between the ages of eleven and twelve, and nearly seventy percent of dogs between fifteen and sixteen years of age have at least one sign of cognitive dysfunction.

The resulting behavioral changes are often difficult to accept and deal with for those taking care of the aging dog (or human, for that matter). The canine form of these brain changes often goes by the acronym DISH, the letters of which represent the following four syndromes:

Symptoms of DISH

Disorientation (wanders around like a confused, lost soul)
Interaction Reduction (doesn't respond to his name, doesn't respond to your comings and goings, wanders away when getting attention)
Sleep Difficulties (sleeps more during the day, wakes in the middle of the night and barks or howls pointlessly)
House-soiling (pees or poops inside, even after being outdoors)

Once you are aware of the DISH acronym—and especially if your dog is seven years or older—you may want to look out for the longer list of behaviors on the chart below so you can keep track of changes in his behavior.

SIGNS OF COGNITIVE DYSFUNCTION SYNDROME

- ❒ Soiling in the house
- ❒ Staring at walls or into space
- ❒ Pacing or wandering without destination
- ❒ Getting "trapped" in corners or behind walls
- ❒ Getting "lost" in the yard or house
- ❒ Sleeping more during the day and less at night

- ❏ Wanting less petting and interaction with people
- ❏ Not recognizing family members
- ❏ Not responding to her name
- ❏ Ignoring known commands, no response
- ❏ Not able to learn new commands or routes
- ❏ Frequent trembling or shaking
- ❏ Altered appetite or thirst

As your dog ages into the higher-risk age group, see how many symptoms apply to your pet. You and your vet need to decide whether you're dealing with what some call "doggie Alzheimer's," and then decide if you want to try to alleviate the effects with medication. You might wonder, why not just let the dog age and get doddery in one area or another? Certainly for dog owners that's a perfectly fine option. However, as you can see from the long list of symptoms that befall dogs as they develop cognitive dysfunction syndrome, it is a progressive disease that can affect the quality of life, just as for people with Alzheimer's.

The way a vet makes a diagnosis of cognitive dysfunction is through a process of elimination. First you want to rule out other medical problems that share many of the same symptoms. For example, a dog that is losing his sight or hearing, or is suffering the pains and stiffness of arthritis or is developing heart problems might exhibit some of the symptoms above—but not because she is developing canine cognitive dysfunction. If tests for these other medical problems are negative, then it is presumed that a dog has CCD, for which your vet may try the medications DHEA or Anipryl. The latter can alleviate some signs of senility, especially memory loss. Anipryl changes neurotransmitters in the brain in seventy-five percent of cases—which means that there are some dogs who get no benefit from it. However, for the majority of dogs, Anipryl improves their interaction with their humans and may slow degenerative changes in the brain. A vet will generally keep a dog on Anipryl permanently, or until the drug stops working. Note that Anipryl cannot be used in conjunction with some other drugs, and that diarrhea and vomiting are possible side effects.

◆ Cold Intolerance

An old dog has less tolerance to cold. He needs to wear a sweater in cold weather and he can't stay outdoors for long in extreme conditions. The reason for his intolerance to cold is that the dog's production of the thyroid hormone drops thirty percent between the ages of three and eleven—and the thyroid has a major role in a dog's metabolism.

◆ Hearing Loss

If you suspect that your older pup may be losing his hearing, clap your hands behind his head to see whether he reacts.

If you sense that his hearing is diminishing, it could be a good idea to start teaching him the hand signals for deaf dogs now (see page 641). You still have the advantage of some hearing, and by starting communication now with sign language it will make his transition to deafness much smoother.

◆ Incontinence (Leaking Urine)

As dogs get older, they can lose bladder control. This is especially true of spayed females, although neutered males can suffer from it, too. You may begin to find puddles around the house. Take your dog to the vet and see if there is a diet change that can help. There might be an underlying infection or other problem. In the case of older spayed females who begin leaking, there is a medication that can be given daily that helps in many cases. Her hormone levels may have dropped so much that the dog has lost muscle tone. This is a treatable problem.

Do not reprimand your dog for these mistakes: she can do nothing about it. This is a physical problem over which she has no control. You will make life easier on your dog if you can walk her more often. You may also find you need to confine her to the kitchen or a bathroom where you can put her bed and some papers on the floor—just like when she was a puppy.

Leaking urine while sleeping is quite common in older dogs. You can protect his sleeping areas by putting down a terry bath mat that has a rubber backing or placing a rubberized sheet (like you'd use for a bed-wetting child) over the bed area for protection. These washable coverings can also be used to protect other surfaces where the dog lies.

◆ Pain Relief

You might want to talk to your vet about prescribing one of the anti-inflammatory/analgesics that are sort of like Advil, especially following strenuous exercise. On page 375 there is a full description of the effects (and dangers) of Rimadyl and Deramaxx, an even newer pain-reliever and anti-inflammatory. Another choice that your vet might prefer is nonprescription buffered aspirin, or Ecotrin, an aspirin that does not dissolve in the stomach and therefore minimizes the chance of causing gastric problems.

◆ Lumps and Bumps

The bumps and lumps that may appear under your dog's skin are usually fatty tumors and nothing to worry about. These tumors are usually benign (not cancerous) when they are round, soft, have well-defined edges and don't feel tightly attached beneath the skin. You can move them and get your fingers nearly around them.

However, it is always best to have your vet check any lumps or bumps that crop up. As in humans, *changes* in skin conditions are the warning sign.

Any changes in the size or shape of a bump—especially if it happens over a short period of time—means the vet should check it. This is not something to ignore. Prompt attention to skin changes can mean the difference between a fairly routine procedure and your dog's death. Imagine how you'd feel if you procrastinated about a strange growth or lump on your dog and it turned out to be cancer that had had a chance to spread because it wasn't caught in time?

If your vet is suspicious of a lump—because of what it looks like or where it's located—he may want to biopsy it. This usually involves just an injection of a local anesthetic and the removal of a small amount of the growth to be studied in a laboratory, similar to what would be done for a person. Depending on what the lab findings are, the lump can be left alone, or it may need to be surgically removed if it has cancerous or pre-cancerous cells.

◆ Nighttime Anxiety

Some aging dogs begin to show anxiety, which usually happens at night after you have gone to bed. The dog may whine, pace the room, pant, make noises, paw at you, try to get attention however she can. An owner would naturally assume that this behavior is about the dog needing to relieve herself, but she will typically show no interest in going outside or will continue the behavior once she has come back inside and you are comfortably under the covers again. It is worrisome, because you can see that your old dog is upset, and you want to make her feel better, but you have no idea what the fuss is all about.

This nighttime display may be a form of separation anxiety. As a dog gets older, and perhaps somewhat senile or disoriented, he may feel that he has lost contact with his people, who have disappeared into sleep in the dark. The dog may show all the symptoms of thunder phobia (see page 610) or separation anxiety (see page 594), even though the dog may have never exhibited any of those problems earlier in his life.

During the day these dogs usually do not seem to exhibit any out-of-the-ordinary behavior, although some do display anxiety when separated from their people. A few of these dogs may have had a touch of separation anxiety in their younger days but it never got out of hand.

Your veterinarian might consider prescribing a mild antianxiety medication such as buspirone, which relieves anxiety symptoms in many dogs. Another drug that also has analgesic (pain-relief) qualities along with a calming effect is amitriptyline. The latter is an antidepressant that is often used to treat chronic pain in humans, although it takes a few days to kick in.

Undiagnosed disease can be a possible reason for these nighttime anxieties. Unexplained and fairly sudden behavioral changes in a dog are often due to underlying physiological problems that can be difficult or impossible to find. Blood tests and other routine tests often don't show potentially serious medical conditions; even extensive medical testing (if you want to spend the money and put the dog through it) may not turn up a diagnosis.

◆ Vision

Some dogs do experience a loss of sight as they age, and some go blind. But you need not feel too sad if this happens to your dog, because dogs can usually adjust to the loss of this sense quite easily (see page 635 earlier in this chapter). Sight is not the primary sense for a dog, who relies more on his sense of smell. There may be some exception to this with the breeds known as "sight hounds," which hunt or chase based on sight, but even *they* depend most on their sense of smell for everyday life.

You have to protect the older blind dog from dangers that she may not be able to see, so either she gets walked on a leash or can walk herself in a fenced yard that she knows well (so there are no nasty surprise bushes or benches to bump into).

You may be amazed to see that your blind dog doesn't bump into things—she has a good memory of where objects are. Obviously, it would be unkind to move furniture, but if you need to do so, then bring your dog over to "introduce" her to it and try to orient her to the new configuration.

Cataracts and glaucoma in dogs can often be treated surgically by specialists, as they are in humans. However, the cost is just as steep.

◆ Toenail-clipping

Older dogs don't run around as much, so their nails get longer quicker than they did when they were younger. You will need to take the dog into the vet for this, or clip them more often yourself (see page 428).

◆ Teeth-cleaning

(For more on dental care, see page 424.)

Vets and owners are learning to care for the teeth of older dogs. Eating can be painful or difficult for a dog with dental problems; infections in the gums cause pain, and eventually these bacteria make their way into the rest of your dog's body and can weaken her immune system and make her sick. Bacteria that enter her bloodstream through the infection in her mouth can actually reach her heart and infect the valves (this dangerous possibility is why some people take antibiotics when they have any dental work done).

To keep your dog's teeth clean and healthy, you can actually brush them. There is dog toothpaste (liver-flavored). Never use people's toothpaste or baking soda to brush, because they are too high in sodium (salt) for dogs. You can use a "finger toothbrush," which is a plastic brush on a short hollow stem that fits over your finger and allows you to reach into your dog's mouth and scrub his teeth using your finger. You can also wrap gauze bandage around the tip of your finger or around a toothbrush (whichever gets the best reaction from the dog) and wipe the dog's teeth that way.

Your vet may want to give your dog a thorough teeth-cleaning if there are problems. This involves general anesthesia and takes less than an hour. The teeth are cleaned but also checked for decay and loose or broken teeth.

When the Time Comes to "Let Go"

Putting a dog to sleep is a painful and difficult decision, but one that most dog owners have to face at some time. However, your dog does not suffer the emotional turmoil you do—she doesn't have any idea what you are considering, so don't *imagine* that she knows anything when she gives you a long look. Neither will she suffer physically when the time comes, since euthanasia is a painless procedure that takes very little time—the dog is unconscious within seconds from the first shot and after that his heart stops within a minute.

Euthanasia is the medical word for what we usually refer to as "putting a dog to sleep." And the dog does just close his eyes and seem to go to sleep. As difficult a decision and experience as it is for us, it is actually a gift to an ailing, suffering pet. It is our final act of selflessness and love.

MODERN MEDICINE CAN MAKE IT HARDER.

Modern advances in veterinary care can make the difficult decision about putting a dog to sleep even more difficult. More procedures and medications make it possible to prolong the life of an old dog—even a very sick one. Almost every medical intervention available to people—from cancer treatments to pacemakers—is now available to pets.

◆ Does the Medical Care Enhance Quality of Life?

Is prolonging his life good for the dog? Even though there are all of these advanced medical techniques and treatments available, it does not mean that every owner should necessarily be trying to get them for her dog. What if your dog can only gain a few weeks or months of life from some procedure that will take a great deal of your time, emotion and money? You have to hope that you have someone on your "team"—whether it's a family member or a medical provider—who will help you find a proper perspective that takes into account your dog's physical and emotional state, as well as your own. You have to ask yourself the tough question: "Am I doing this for me, because I cannot stand the idea of letting the dog go, or do I believe it will result in some more wonderful months for him?"

What about your quality of life? Complex medical treatments cost a great deal of money (even pet insurance only goes so far) and can involve days and days of dropping off and picking up the dog and handling his reaction to the treatment. Ask yourself whether you can handle the emotion, time and money demanded of you in such a situation. If you have a human family who needs you, a job you have been neglecting or other demands on your resources, please give them the weight they deserve in your decision-making process. Just because you are *willing* to go into debt to pay for some special treatment for your dog doesn't mean you should do it if it will only buy some less-than-great time for your sick dog.

Do not feel guilty or defensive about your decision. If you have a really sick dog, or one with a terminal disease, more often than not it is a blessing to be able to offer your pet the privilege of leaving this world on a good day, or at least to be able to shorten the number of bad days.

Will medical intervention just prolong suffering? Even if money or your time were of no consequence, in any medical situation with an older dog you have to question whether you are doing the right thing to put your dog through radiation, chemotherapy, dialysis or operations. The trauma, pain and perhaps long confinement or repeated hospital visits should be weighed against a peaceful existence at home with you, in some cases with suffering that may be alleviated with medication. Sometimes the most humane and loving thing to do is to allow your dog to live out his life with dignity and your attentive affection.

HOW TO KNOW WHEN THE TIME HAS COME

"Playing God" is a burden, and deciding when it is time to euthanize your dog is really a big responsibility. There is no perfect time.

◆ It's a Deeply Personal Decision.

Each owner will have her own guidelines and conscience to guide her to make the best possible decision. Don't let anyone push you either way, but you may need to talk it through to feel at peace with your decision. Be aware that the experience of your dog's illness (or just advancing age) may trigger complicated and painful memories of a *person* in your life who was once at a similar juncture. Dealing with your dog's imminent death, especially death preceded by pain and suffering, may stir up your feelings about that person. To the best of your ability, try to make decisions for your dog that are separate from those intense memories.

Only you know what is right for you and for your dog—and if you aren't sure, then talk it through with your vet or any person close to you who will give you feedback based on respect for your situation and your outlook on life.

◆ More Bad Days than Good

Many people try to decide when the time for euthanasia has come by determining whether their dog has reached the point of having more bad days than good. Is she having more pain than pleasure? Can she do any of the things that she loves (walks, fetching, swimming, car rides)? Is she suffering from physical pain or a loss of dignity (because of incontinence, not being able to climb stairs or falling down, for example)?

"She still wags her tail," some people say, figuring that they should delay euthanasia because of this sign. However, a dog who loves you or recognizes where she is will wag automatically to signal her pleasure at seeing you or a familiar place. Whether a dog wags her tail is not a valuable yardstick of her state of mind, or even whether she is suffering.

"She'll still eat," other people say, thinking they cannot justify ending the life of a sick or old pet who is still eating. A dog continuing to eat doesn't necessarily mean she's feeling good or has a good quality of life—it is just a survival instinct. If you wait until your dog will no longer eat and don't take other things into consideration to decide the "moment of truth," you may have waited past the point of significant suffering.

WHERE AND HOW SHOULD THE END COME?

◆ Staying Beside the Dog

Being with your dog when she is put to sleep depends on your feelings. It is a quick, simple and painless process for the dog. You can be prepared for anything unusual that might happen by looking at the list later in this section.

Certainly your dog would feel more relaxed and comforted to have you by her side, but if you feel you cannot stand being there then you have to follow your instincts. Also, if you feel you might break down uncontrollably and become really emotionally distressed before she is gone, then you don't want her to pick up on your anxiety and become agitated, also.

◆ Euthanasia at the Vet's Office

Most veterinary offices have a lot of experience with putting pets to sleep, so they are well aware of the emotional intensity it creates for owners and their families.

You may fear that you will break down when you are putting your dog to sleep—but that is natural and normal, and your vet and the staff understand. Or, if you are the kind of person who keeps it all in and doesn't show any emotion, you may be concerned that the staff will think you don't care. It is understandable to feel self-conscious about how you will handle it. Vets have seen many kinds of reactions. They know how much people's dogs mean to them and they will not judge the ways that people deal with their grief.

Some animal clinics have a euthanasia room that allows you privacy and the chance to make your dog's passing a personalized, spiritual experience. Some people light candles or incense, play music or have others present.

Done with the help of a compassionate veterinarian, euthanasia can be an almost spiritual emotional event, and/or a peaceful relief for you if your aging dog has been ill or suffering. Even in a regular room at the vet's, you can personalize the experience in whatever way makes it more bearable for you.

◆ Euthanasia at Home

You may feel more comfortable having your dog put to sleep at home. This may be because you want the privacy or because your dog is really anxious about going to the vet under any circumstances and you don't want his final moments to be frightening.

Most veterinarians will make arrangements to come to your home before or after hours if your dog has been a longtime patient. If your vet cannot assist you because you live too far away or there are other practical impediments, the doctor should be able to inform you of a mobile vet whose practice is based on home visits.

Some people fear having the memory of the dog's death in their house. They worry that they will always look at the spot where it took place and be emotionally haunted by it. The decision of where to end your pet's life is one that only you can make.

BEFORE THE CHOSEN DAY COMES

Assuming that your dog is well enough, you might want to plan a special farewell time together with your dog. Depending on where you live, what your dog's pleasures usually are and her condition, you might want to go for a drive, for a swim, to the beach or park or some approximation of these things, depending on how weak she is. You could even just share a hot dog, macaroni and cheese or a bowl of ice cream, anything that feels like a special farewell, even if it makes you sad.

THE PROCEDURE ITSELF

If you have made an appointment ahead of time to have your pet euthanized, most veterinary hospitals will not expect you to go in the main door and sit in the waiting room. If they do not inform you ahead of time of an alternate entrance, ask them where it is so you can bypass the other dogs and people out front and be shown right into a room.

◆ Your Dog's Size Determines Where to Lie Her Down.

If your dog is large, it will probably be best to have her lie on a blanket on the floor, where she can be put to sleep with you sitting or kneeling next to her. So you should wear clothes that allow you to sit comfortably on the floor beside her.

If you have a smaller dog she can lie down on the examination table and you can stand beside her. If being up on the table makes her anxious, you might prefer to get down on the floor with her. Your vet will undoubtedly accommodate your wishes.

♦ **Bring a Blanket or Ask If They Will Provide One for You.**
Some vet offices will provide a blanket or bedding for your dog, which they can use to lift and wrap the body afterward, if you are going to transport it. You may want to bring a familiar blanket or quilt for her to lie on—one that you would want her to be wrapped in afterward if you plan on taking the body home. However, if you are going to leave her body for cremation, burial or disposal, the blanket should be one you are willing to forfeit.

WHAT HAPPENS DURING THE PROCEDURE ITSELF

♦ **First an Injection of Sedative is Given.**
Once you are settled in with your dog—whether you cradle her head, or just stay near by stroking and perhaps speaking to her—the doctor will give the dog a shot of tranquilizer. It helps when the doctor tells you what she is going to do and reminds you what effect it will have. Some vets insert an I.V. catheter before beginning so that all the medication goes into the vein.

This shot may sting a little and get a pain reaction from your dog, but that's the worst that will happen. Within moments, your dog will be heavy-lidded and groggy, and she may close her eyes. Vets say this is a nice mental zone for the dog to be in.

Sometimes the dog gives a big sigh (of what may seem to us to be relief) at this point as the tranquilizer relaxes her.

Some dogs may appear to be agitated or excited (this is called "involuntary excitement, during which the dog can't control her reflexes), but it is a very rare reaction. The sedative affects the brain: the dog may look agitated but is not experiencing any distress.

♦ **Say Your Good-byes Now.**
The next thing the doctor will do is administer anesthesia in the dog's vein, from which she will drift away very quickly. So before that medication is injected, you'll have a final moment in which she'll still be conscious (even though she is groggy and super-relaxed) if you want to say any last words to her.

♦ **The Overdose of Anesthesia Is Injected.**
(If an I.V. catheter was placed this preparation is not necessary.) First the doctor will prepare the dog's front leg, where she will be injecting. She will place a tourniquet or press a finger against the bone high up on the leg and may shave a small patch of hair below it if necessary. Then she will slide the needle directly into the vein—the dog does not suffer; she may even already be asleep at this point from the sedative—and the anesthetic medication will take your dog out of her suffering forever.

The dog looks like she is in a very deep "sleep": she is completely unconscious at this point, perhaps still breathing very slowly, although generally it is only seconds before it reaches first her heart and then her brain.

The doctor will listen to the dog's heart with a stethoscope to be sure it has stopped. The dog's brain and feeling are already gone at that point (which is what they mean by "brain dead") but the heart muscle may continue a little past that point. The doctor will often say something like "She is gone now." My old vet said to Yogi Bear, "Go find Lulu," which was so sweet it made me cry even more.

◆ **Alone Time with the Body**

You may want to spend some time with your dog's body. For some people the lifeless body may seem gruesome, for others it is an important first step in beginning the grieving process. This is not entirely different from some of the feelings and realities that people have to grapple with when a person they love dies. If you are afraid of what your dog will look like, be assured that it is a peaceful way to go and that your dog's body will reflect that.

◆ **Odd Things to Expect During Euthanasia**

Some unsettling things may happen at different points during the euthanasia process, and it can be reassuring to know ahead of time what they might be. These physical events are simply the body letting go, since whatever you may think of as the spirit or soul is gone by then.

PHYSICAL EFFECTS OF EUTHANASIA

- ❐ At the end the dog may have spasms, twitches or tremors.
- ❐ Her tongue may protrude way out of her mouth.
- ❐ Her eyes may open partially and seem to be rolled back into the sockets.
- ❐ She may exhale all the air left in her lungs with what seems to be a sigh (but at this point the dog is completely dead and feels nothing).
- ❐ The dog may make a "last gasp," the final contraction of the chest muscle (but she's completely unconscious and not experiencing distress or anything else).
- ❐ The bowels may evacuate or the bladder empty (the body releases everything).
- ❐ The abdominal contents may gurgle.
- ❐ Fluid or blood might drip from the nose or mouth (depends on the dog's illness).
- ❐ Some breaths may continue past brain death (the last part of the brain to go regulates breathing).

WHAT TO DO WITH THE REMAINS

There are several ways that people can deal with a dog's body, and it is a good idea to consider the options and make a decision ahead of time. You will probably be too emotional to think very clearly after the dog is put to sleep, and it will be a relief to have this plan made beforehand.

◆ **You Can Leave the Dog's Body at the Vet Clinic.**

If burial at home is not allowed where you live or is not practical, your vet can arrange for the body to be picked up and disposed of. In the case of a very large dog, this is probably the most realistic choice, which does not exclude the possibility of having a memorial without the body (see the following page).

♦ You Can Take the Dog's Body Home for Burial.
Every local area has its own rules about whether burial is allowed on residential land. If it's not allowed where you live, you may know someone in a more rural setting who would let you bury your dog or her ashes there.

♦ Cremation costs around $200 and is arranged by the vet.

♦ Pet Cemeteries
There are also pet cemeteries at various locations throughout the country; if it is geographically feasible you can arrange for full burial and funeral services. You can also arrange to bury your dog's ashes at a pet cemetery (the "grief hotlines" in the next section may have some suggestions about burial options in your area).

♦ Remembering Your Dog
You may want to set aside an area and plant something special as a tribute to your dog. You can also order one of the memorial markers engraved with your pet's name and dates and a message—there are many of these available on the Internet or through advertisements in the back of dog magazines such as *Dog Fancy*.

You can make a contribution in her memory to a local animal rescue group or shelter. Another way to remember your dog is to make a gift in your pet's name to the veterinary school that your veterinarian attended—most of these schools have provisions to take contributions in this way. This allows you not only to celebrate the life of your pet but also to further research to help other animals, while showing gratitude to the doctor who cared for her during her life.

Grief over Losing Your Dog

You may be surprised at how intensely you, or others around you, react to the loss of your dog. If you weren't expecting such a depth of feeling, you may be uncomfortable about it, perhaps self-conscious to have been that attached to an animal. Some people experience grief over their dog more profound than for people they have lost, and that can be disturbing.

It may give you a better understanding of this intense emotion when you realize that for many of us, what we feel when we lose a dog is the end of that whole era of our lives the dog lived through with us. So we aren't just mourning the loss of our devoted pooches, we are also grieving for all those years we lived through with them—and all those personal and professional ups and downs—during which they were by our sides.

Accept your grief as a testament to the depth of your feeling for your dog; the profound way in which she enhanced your life is commensurate with the depth of your sadness in losing her.

THE SIX STAGES OF GRIEF

If you have ever suffered a profound personal loss before, you may be familiar with what psychologists have named the six stages that people go through when they are grieving. Everyone does not necessarily experience all of these emotions, and they don't always appear in this order:

◆ Denial

This reaction can begin to happen while your dog is still alive—you may be in disbelief when you are told he is injured or has a disease that may take his life.

If the dog's death is sudden and you had little or no time to prepare yourself for the loss, a natural reaction is to question your veterinarian's competence. You may voice doubts about whether your vet is right in her diagnosis, made good choices in care or gave you good information. You may "doctor shop" the way terminally ill people are known to do, looking for a more optimistic evaluation of your dog's condition. This is an example of being in denial about the prognosis for your pet.

You may seek out alternative therapies in non-Western medicine fields—drawn only by stories of "miracle" cures—but you will probably be better off if you stop to question the logic of these stories. If it were really true that herbal-type medicines could cure cancer, you can be pretty sure people would be using it for themselves.

◆ Guilt

Depending on the circumstances of your dog's death, it's common to feel guilty about it. For example, "If only I'd taken him to the vet sooner . . ." is a feeling that many of us have had when our dog is finally diagnosed with a deadly illness. Even if an earlier diagnosis would not have saved his life, it is natural to wonder if our tardiness in seeking medical attention allowed the disease to flourish.

Or say your dog is killed by a car through a person's carelessness with a gate, fence or door—you may feel guilty about that (or angry at whomever was careless).

Deciding to euthanize a dog can provoke guilt in owners, too—it can make the guilt worse depending on the circumstances of the dog's death and whatever part human choices played in the death.

◆ Anger/Blame

There may be no logical explanation for the angry feelings you may have as part of the grief process, but you may place blame all over the place—caregivers, family members, friends—anyone who was part of the end of your dog's life, whether it was someone driving a car that hit the dog or the way an assistant at the vet's office handed you back your dog's leash after euthanasia.

◆ Bargaining

This is another stage of grief that some people experience when they have dogs who are gravely ill. It is a primitive sort of superstitious "deal" that you might make with yourself that if your dog recovers you'll promise to do something specific (give up some personal pleasure, or make a contribution to a charity) or effect some sort of change in general (pay more attention to your dog, be nicer to people at work.)

◆ Depression

When the reality of your dog's death settles in—which for some people will be soon after the death and for others may be months later after experiencing other stages of grief—then the sadness will take over. The depression people feel about their lost pets can be every bit as intense as for the loss of a loved person: crying, eating disturbance, withdrawing from previous activities, lethargy, sleeping too much.

Some people may feel that life has no meaning, that there is no reason to go on living without their beloved dog. Feelings this intense and possibly dangerous need to be dealt with by a professional. Sometimes, thoughts of suicide enter the picture and must be taken seriously, whether or not other people respect that the loss of a loved animal might drive someone to end his own life. This phase of grief, when depression sets in, is when people often seek out professional help—not just because of how much pain they are feeling, but also because they're having trouble dealing with day-to-day life.

◆ Acceptance

The final stage of grief is the part where the pain has lessened but, although sadness about your dog may come in waves for a long time, you can resume most aspects of your everyday life. All of the feelings mentioned so far can still surface, but usually with less intensity and for a shorter amount of time.

You may cry about your dog for weeks or years to come—and your sadness about losing her may hit you when you least expect it. Allow yourself these feelings—don't judge yourself, don't try to repress these sentiments—because they are normal and healthy. It might make your intense sadness easier to accept if you view it as an expression of how deeply you loved your dog.

RITUALS AND GRIEF

There is a social reason for many of the rituals surrounding death in human society. Just as rituals help when a person dies, they can help people coping with a dog's death. You might want to consider whether having such structured expressions of grief would make you feel more at peace and satisfy a need to celebrate your dog's place in your life and heart.

There are any number of ways to ritualize your loss: funerals with caskets; ashes that you can bury, scatter, or keep in specialized urns (see page 665); memorial services; charitable donations in your pet's name to animal rescue organizations such as the ASPCA (www.aspca.org, (212) 876-7700) or the Humane Society of the United States (www.hsus.org, (202) 452-1100) or to a veterinary research program (such as those at Cornell or Tufts), or to the Morris Animal Foundation (www.morrisanimalfoundation.org, (800) 243-2345), which funds veterinary research programs; a tree planted (www.treegivers.com, (800) 862-8733) or public bench donated in the dog's memory.

• Some Resources for Pet Memorials, Urns, Commemorative Keepsakes

All Pets Crematory & Remembrances, Stamford, CT (203) 967-4949, (toll-free, [866] 334-PETS), www.allpetscrematory.com

OldYeller.net Pet Memorials, San Francisco, CA (415) 558-9977, www.oldyeller.net

Rock-It Creations, Council, ID (toll-free (866) Z-ROCK-IT), www.rockitcreations.com

Personal Creations, Burr Ridge, IL (toll-free [800] 326-6626), www.personalcreations.com

Whisper in the Heart, Antioch, California (925) 755-WITH, whisperintheheart.com

Forever Pets, Inc., St. Paul, Minnesota (toll-free [888] 450-7727), www.foreverpets.com

My Cherished Pet, Henderson, Kentucky (888) 830-6412, www.mycherishedpet.com

The Pooka, Ulen, Minnesota (218) 596-8360, www.thepooka.com

RoxAnn's Glass House, Commack, New York (631) 266-3167, www.glassbyrox.com

• Find a Sympathetic Ear.

Seek out friends who understand the importance of your pet's love and your loss. It may be that your best company will be other pet owners—in particular, those who may have lost a pet not long ago and can be particularly empathetic to what you are experiencing.

Don't belittle your own grief. Your dog was a member of your family; your loss is very real; your sadness is legitimate.

Don't let anyone else belittle the pain you are feeling because it's "only" about an animal—non-dog-owning friends can fail to recognize that what they're referring to is an animal who may have been your constant companion, or even closest friend, for years. They don't mean to sound callous and insensitive—but they are nonetheless!

• Pet-loss Support Groups and Hotlines

Petloss.com started in 1992 as an online pet bulletin board designed to pay tribute to departed pals and share solace and advice. That Web site has attracted hundreds of thousand of visitors, but there are now dozens of other Web addresses devoted to pet loss. Over the past decade, counseling hotlines have emerged, and with them comes the social validation that the death of a beloved animal can be as heartrending for people as the loss of a human family member.

Reaching out for compassion and guidance is an excellent way to cope with grief and get support. For many people, the symbiotic relationship they had with their deceased dog—or the intensity with which they loved—is not always understood or respected by those who either do not have dogs in their family, or have not yet suffered the loss of one they felt connected to.

Telephone hotlines—and in some cases e-mail hotlines—are part of a growing social recognition that it isn't "just an animal" that people lose when their dog dies: the human-animal bond is being taken seriously and people's grief is being shown respect and compassion.

Several veterinary colleges have hotlines that are manned at no charge by volunteers who receive special education in grief counseling. Most of the hotlines are staffed by nonprofessional counselors who are students in veterinary medicine. In theory, this means not only that grieving people are helped, but that the next generation of vets will be that much more capable of dealing with the emotional needs of their human "patients." The professionals-to-be learn important interpersonal skills and insights, gaining valuable experience for the future while helping pet owners at a dark time.

Here are the phone numbers of established hotlines. Except for the twenty-four-hour service offered by Pet Grief Support Service in Arizona (see below) the phones are generally manned only from 6:00 to 9:00 PM (local time)—if you leave a message and number, expect a call back collect. You can take your pick of any number—you'll probably feel better just by reaching out to someone who understands what you're going through. It does not have to be in your geographic area.

PET LOSS SUPPORT LINES

- ❏ Chicago Veterinary Medical College (630) 603-3994
- ❏ Colorado State University (970) 491-4143
- ❏ Cornell University (607) 253-3932
- ❏ Grief Recovery Hotline (800) 445-4808
- ❏ Iams Company Pet Loss Support Hotline (888) 332-7738
- ❏ Iowa State University (888) 478-7574
- ❏ Michigan State University (517) 432-2696
- ❏ Ohio State University (614) 292-1823
- ❏ Pet Grief Support Service (Arizona) (602) 995-5885
- ❏ Tufts University (508) 839-7966
- ❏ University of California at Davis (800) 565-1526, (530) 752-4200
- ❏ University of Florida (800) 798-6196, (352) 392-4700
- ❏ University of Illinois (877) 394-2273, (217) 333-2760
- ❏ University of Minnesota (612) 624-4747
- ❏ University of Pennsylvania (215) 898-4529
- ❏ Virginia-Maryland Regional College of Veterinary Medicine (540) 231-8038
- ❏ Washington State University (509) 335-5704

Pet Loss Grief Counseling on the Web:

- ❏ The American Veterinary Medical Association Web site is: www.avma.org, and they have grief counseling under "Goodbye My Friend."
- ❏ Animal Love and Loss Network is an organization of pet loss counselors: www.alln.org.
- ❏ The Delta Society has information about counselors and links to support groups: (425) 226-7357, or www.deltasociety.org.

Dogs and Their Grieving

Dogs do grieve over the loss of a close family member—human or animal. In addition to death, this also includes other human disappearances such as a divorce, a child going off to school, etc. We don't know whether dogs have a concept of a person or animal never returning, or whether it is just the upset in the household routine. But they can be profoundly affected. If the dog loses a person with whom he was closely bonded, it can be months before the dog is totally himself again. But dogs can generally snap out of it within a week, reflecting an inborn ability to bounce back from personal loss, which is part of what makes dogs able to form attachments to new people after losing their previous ones.

THE SURVIVING DOG(S) AND EUTHANASIA

A theory has floated around that the dogs left behind after a pack-mate is euthanized should stay with the dead dog's body for hours or overnight. Advocates say that the other dog(s) will be scared, fascinated, disinterested, but eventually it may help them to pay their last respects. Go with your own instinct. Don't do it if the idea of a dead body around the house freaks you out—your other dog(s) may not even be among these who "need" the dead body to grieve and move on.

There are some advocates of having your other dog(s) present for the euthanasia itself, but most agree that would be macabre and even cruel to the dog(s) left behind. Having canine company at that point isn't going to make any real difference for the dog who is being put to sleep, while it may be distressing and even traumatic for the dog witnessing it. Obviously we cannot know what—if anything—death means to a dog, but why risk doing the wrong thing?

Dogs are individuals with reactions that are not always predictable: should another dog die in the house, word has it that a companion dog may not react to his departed pal's death. Yet another dog may be devastated when his pack-mate dies, and go into a deep depression and stop eating. So you could say that on some level, dogs are as varied about experiencing and expressing grief as we are.

EASING YOUR DOG'S GRIEF

Dogs need help to get through their grieving process. What follows are suggestions of ways to support and understand your dog as he goes through this difficult transition.

Give the dog more time and attention than you ordinarily would. However, don't overdo it and focus so much emotion on her that she adopts the grief-related behavior as a permanent habit.

Keep the surviving dog's schedule as consistent as you can—it is a comfort to her to stick to the routines she had before in mealtimes, exercise and grooming.

Add some new elements into the dog's life to give him something new to focus on. This can be joining an agility or companion-dog class, going to a dog park, going out places with you or having a play-date with a friend's dog.

Keep your dog on the go, doing things with you—don't let her lie around depressed.

If your dog has lost her appetite, go ahead and indulge her with some tasty additions to her food (or, if you've been feeding two dogs kibble all this time, why not treat her and try switching to a premium canned food.)

If you have two surviving dogs, there is the possibility that they may have some rearranging of power positions to work out. Whatever the power balance was with the dog who died, it will now be altered, so expect some rumbles as the hierarchy shifts, and let them work it out between themselves.

Do not get a new dog right away. A dog who is grieving the loss of a family member—person or dog—needs time to get over his loss, as do you. Your surviving dog will not necessarily welcome a new dog while he is still grieving.

ACKNOWLEDGMENTS

ALL MY FRIENDS HAVE BEEN SO SUPPORTIVE and encouraging through the many long years of preparing this book, and rather than boring all of you (and inadvertently forgetting someone) I'd just like to say THANK YOU SO MUCH for putting up with all those nights I left dinner at nine o'clock to get back to the book.

Two friends were especially devoted to this book: Loring Bolger, a fellow multi-dog/-cat owner, who generously offered to help me with research in the early days (and wisely bailed out when it was clear that only a brain as tightly wound as mine would be able to gather and separate all the necessary strands!). And my childhood pal Carolyn Arnold, who even with no dog of her own was my personal clipping service, sending me every dog-related article she came across.

Dr. Dawn Stelling is a warm, wonderful veterinarian, whose early enthusiasm for this book meant a great deal, as did her loving care of my dogs. I will always be grateful for her deeply compassionate help in sending two of them to Puppy Heaven.

Aimee Sadler is a private trainer who has worked across the country, developing and implementing training and behavior modification programs for shelter animals. She is a proud member of the International Association of Canine professionals (IACP). Aimee checked every part of this book related to training and canine behavior. She has guided much of my personal understanding of dogs: without her insight and involvement through my adult years of dog ownership I could never have controlled nor enjoyed my nutty dogs as much. Aimee has worked closely with the renowned trainer/author Brian Kilcommons (*Good Owners, Great Dogs*). Ms. Sadler recently relocated to Boulder, Colorado, to work with countyshelter dogs there. She lives with five rescued cats, four rescued dogs, a husband and three adorable sons (the latter four are almost as well trained as the former nine).

And as for those boys, my dog Scooby Doo would like to thank the Sadler brothers for helping him with his fear of children. Kodi, Kian and Willan are some pretty cool guys, who offered themselves as "guinea pigs" to help stop Scooby from chasing, barking at and jumping on children. The brothers were smart and brave because Scooby weighed more than all three boys put together—and he was taller than any of them, too. Even Kodi, the oldest brother, was only six when they helped Scooby. The boys accomplished Scooby's transformation in part by following "Scooby Doo's Twenty-five Rules for Kids" (page 487, Chapter Fourteen), which helps kids live safely and happily together with dogs.

And then there is the unique contribution of my friend Bob, who solved a historical problem in people's bond with their dogs. Owners are often frustrated trying to describe on which side their animal is hurt. They get confused about whether to refer to "right" or "left" from the dog's point of view or from the human perspective: Bob solved this by declaring, "It's simple: it's either on the driver's side or the passenger side."

Robert Lescher, who has been my agent for twenty-five years, helped shape the presentation for this book. Then he brought it straight to the most perfect home it could have had. I hope he and I will have *another* quarter-century of book-making together.

And what a home it has been: Gotham Books is an author's dream. As though we were still living in the good old days of publishing, imagine my gratitude to be in a small company with one smart publisher, free to act on his instincts and passion, surrounded by a few excellent people dedicated to bringing a book to its potential. I say this not because They bribed me—nor to make other writers envious—but so everyone who loves books will not lose heart or lose hope (as so much of the publishing industry has already done) for the book business.

Finally, to the best thing about Gotham Books: my editor, the utterly lovely Erin Moore. What could be more amazing than a smart, fun, creative editor whose father as well as his father before him just happened to be *veterinarians*?! Erin steered me and cheered me over the mountain of material I had to scale. Part of me wishes that she'd been my first editor years ago, but I also realize that she would have spoiled me for all the ensuing years and books, which would have been disappointing experiences by comparison. It's kind of wonderful that I have enough experience to fully appreciate her intelligence, humanity, humility and diplomacy.

And last of all (it won't hurt their feelings since they *still* have not learned to read) are my dog companions, Billy Blue, Scooby Doo and Miss Jazzy. You really couldn't ask for a better gang. I would never take the time to enjoy every mushroom, chipmunk and clump of moss in my wild woods, if it were not for my pack needing to get out there twice a day, in every weather. I rarely get to leave my house without three stowaways aboard; and if I ever do, I can never slip back into the house without fireworks of raucous joy exploding around my return. Their endless hijinks provide all the entertainment you could want, along with a constant reminder to enjoy every moment in life. Naming my house after them was a small tribute to the pleasure and companionship they give me (of course, they still can't read the sign on the gate, either).

The funniest thing people say to me (as twelve hairy legs supporting 300 total pounds of dog leap around me) is: "You mean you live *all alone* out here in that white-pine forest by *yourself*?" Hardly. . . .

THE MOST GRATEFUL ACKNOWLEDGMENT OF ALL

May all your dogs find a medical caretaker as warm, wise and careful as Dr. Barry Browning. He was just the voice of reason, wisdom and balance that I had hoped to find for the medical and nutritional aspects of this book. Over the years, I have known and befriended a number of small-animal and equine vets, so I know how hard it is for a veterinarian to keep up on evolving medications and procedures, to be able to conduct thorough, hands-on physical examinations and to also come up with ideas for health management and problem-solving based on a nonaggressive or invasive philosophy. Dr. Browning is that doctor, the first one I've known with a BVM & S (Bachelor of Veterinary Medicine & Surgery), by the way. His degree from the Royal College of Surgeons followed his veterinary training at the University of Edinburgh in Scotland. Just pure luck that he would wind up in a solo veterinary practice only steps from a little beach beside a bucolic boat marina in Sag Harbor (New York State–licensed, of course) and a few minutes from where I live. Dr. Browning gave an enormous amount of thought and time to steering me in the right direction with the medical aspects of this book. It is a mystery to me how he managed to find time to meticulously "vet out" the medical information in this book while juggling a beautiful wife and two small children, handling all his pet patients without a veterinary partner (but with a great all-female staff of his "vet tech," Marie Steffens, Meredith Greene and Kim O'Brien), even returning all after-hours calls from his patients (or their people) himself. And that's not even counting finding time for his beloved cranky terrier, Haggis, who is a Corgi/Australian Terrier mix. A thousand leaps and licks of gratitude to him (Barry, that is, not Haggis).

INDEX

stifle area
  location of, 168
  stroking/petting, 168–69
stings. *See* insect stings/bites
stool sample, 118–19, 121, 333
strangers. *See* visitors
stray dogs, finding owners, 53
stressed dogs. *See* anxiety
stroking/patting
  to assert authority, 159
  guidelines for, 168–69, 241
  head, avoiding, 12, 167, 168
  massage, 402–3
  puppy preparation for grooming,
    123, 409
  Scooby's Twenty-five Rules for
    Kids, 488
stubborn dog, on furniture, 577
subaortic stenosis (SAS), 56
submissive dogs
  behaviors related-to alpha, 133,
    153
  body language of, 135–38, 556
  and dog fights, 98–100
  dog-to-dog communication of,
    71, 135–38
  licking by, 165
  in multiple dog households, 98,
    133–34
  overly shy dogs, 74
  puppy behaviors, 67, 70–71, 74
  submissive peeing, 67, 71, 233–34
submissive peeing, 67, 71, 233–34
  solutions to, 234
sunburn, 335–38
  at-risk breeds, 337
  nose, 337
  prevention of, 329, 336
  in snowy areas, 337, 413
  ultraviolet damage, signs of, 337
supplements, 451–54
  Platinum Performance Plus,
    453–54, 652
  vitamins/minerals, 452–53
  zinc, 453
surgery, 397–99
  altering. *see* spaying/neutering
  anal gland removal, 332–33
  anesthesia cautions, 397
  cancer treatment, 343
  cardiac pacemaker, 359–60
  for cruciate ligament tears,
    372–73
  debarking, 555
  ear canal ablation, 355
  kidney transplant, 370
  pain control, 397–98
  spinal-disk, 396–97
  wound-licking prevention, 398–99
Surgi-Sox, 390

swimming
  hot weather exercise, 201
  in open waters, 204
  precautions, 202–5, 329–30
  water-borne disease, 330
swimming emergency
  cardiopulmonary resuscitation
    (CPR), 312
  out-of-water position of dog, 317
  potential problems, 203
swimming pools
  alarms, 205
  precautions, 329–30

table scraps, avoiding, 125, 227,
  443, 446
tail, docking, 164, 399
tail-chasing, 142
tail wagging
  breed differences, 164
  messages of, 136, 138, 489,
    555–56
  position and dominance, 71, 164,
    556
  position and submissive dogs, 71,
    164, 556
tapeworms, 121, 333, 387
tar, removing from fur, 414
taste
  preferences of dogs, 131
  sense of, 129–30
Tattle Tale, 279
tattoo ID, 214
Tavist, 389
teacup-sized dogs, breeding issues,
  32
tear-staining syndrome, 415
Teaser Balls, 194
teeth
  care of. *See* dental care
  dominance, gesture of, 71, 136,
    153
  of healthy puppy, 66
  submission, gesture of, 71, 136
  teething, 117
  undershot bite, 67
teletherapy, 344
Temeril, 389
temperament
  adopted/shelter dogs, 43–44
  dog-ownership decisions, 12,
    66–67
  nature-nurture question, 21
  puppy personality change, 107
  Volhard personality testing, 66–69
temperament issues, 605–9
  depression, 349–50, 608–9
  hyperactivity, 606–8
  and invisible fence, 187

temperature of dogs
  normal reading, 119, 315, 360
  taking the temperature, 315
  See also fever
tennis balls, avoiding, 194
terriers
  breeds of, 17
  general characteristics, 17
territorialism, 609–10
  and barking, 550, 553–54
  in car, 610
  and cats, 630
  desensitization for, 610
  and house-soiling, 232, 581
  medications for, 610
  and new dog introductions,
    95–96, 98
  overpeeing. *See* urine marking
  pack behavior, 216
  and uniformed visitors, 609
tethers
  outdoors, avoiding, 184
  as training tool, 281–82
thunderstorm phobia, 610–13
  at-risk breeds, 611
  desensitization, 611–12
  medications for, 612–13
thyroid problems
  hypothyroidism, 57
  testing for, 57
tibial plateau leveling osteotomy
    (TPLO), 372
tick-borne diseases, 386–87
  Lyme disease, 384, 386
  Rocky Mountain spotted fever
    (RMSF), 386
ticks
  checking for, 303
  tick repellents, 380
  types of, 386
time, dog awareness of, 197
time-out
  and aggressive dogs, 544
  guidelines for use, 126, 242–43
  puppy training, 126
titer testing, 298–99
toddlers and dogs, 481–84
toenails, cutting. *See* nail-trimming
tongue flicking, 136, 165
top dog. *See* dominance
towel burritos, 193, 565
toxic substances. *See* poisoning
toy dogs
  breeds of, 18
  and children, warnings, 470, 621
  general characteristics, 18
  see also small dogs
toys, 193–95
  cardboard box as, 193, 565
  for chewing. *See* chew treats/toys

in crate, 221
destroying, 563
Frisbee substitute, 16, 193, 195
homemade toys, 565
Jolly Ball, 194
Kong toy, 194, 220, 564
retrieving, 69
rope toys, 194, 564
sticks as, 565
swallowing, 195, 305
towel burritos, 193, 565
toy-guarding, 155, 469, 532
as training aid, 125
treat dispensers, 194
warnings about, 194–95
trachea, collapsed, 347, 622
training, 236–82
and age of dog, 238–39
aggressive dogs, 240
and breed of dog, 15–18
and child-dog household, 477–78
classes, 237–38
commands. *See* training commands
consistency, 123, 244, 582
correcting dog. *See* training corrections
devices. *See* training equipment
human-issues, 236–40
mounting trainer, 145
puppies. *See* puppy training
rewards. *See* training rewards
small dogs, 239, 622
training commands
bark, 551–52
come, 249–55, 643
deaf dogs, hand signals, 641–43
down, 258–60, 643
enough, 260
go to bed, 261, 576
leave it, 104, 643
no, 246–47
off, 262, 576–77, 643
pre-feeding, 156
quiet, 553–54
release command, 261, 265, 570, 642
sit, 256–58, 643
stay, 262–64, 643
voice in, 126, 217, 244–48
wait, 264–65
walk or *heel,* 643
words/practices to avoid, 246–48
See also specific commands
training corrections, 242–44
aversion techniques, 242, 269, 528–29
counterconditioning, 255
guidelines/sequence for, 244

ignoring as. *See* ignoring dog
practices to avoid, 246–48, 529–30
puppies, 126
spraying water, 126, 243–44
squirt bottle/gun in, 126
time-out, 126, 242–43
training equipment
collars, 266–68
halters, 269–75
harnesses, 275
leashes, 276–78
muzzles, 279–80
shake-can, 280–81, 529
spraying water, 126, 243–44
tethers, 281–82
training rewards
affection, 241–42
food treats, 241
importance of, 239
praise, 159, 242, 244, 247, 253, 263
train travel, 517
tranquilizers
airplane travel, 508, 514
groomer use, 412
thunderstorm phobia, 612–13
trauma emergencies, 305
travel, 492–522
airplane, 506–16
boat, 517
car travel, 500–506
with crate, 218
dog beds, 513
foods and feeding, 499, 517
ground transport services, 517
heartworm risk, 383
hiking/camping, 495–98
hotels/motels, dog friendly, 212, 493–94
leaving dogs behind, 518–22
quarantine laws, 518
supplies for, 498–99
train, 517
See also specific travel methods
Travis Fund, 296
treat(s)
burying, 145
for chewing. *See* chew treats/toys
child-offered, 484
dietetic, 458
homebaked, 441, 457–59
nose-nudging for, 587
peanut butter, 113–14
as reward. *See* treat rewards
treat dispenser toy, 194
treat rewards
house-training, 223, 224
and new dog introductions, 95, 99, 104
training tips, 241, 247, 249

when meeting new people, 113–14
trusts, legal, providing for dogs, 644–45
TTouch System, 142–43, 604
tugging games, avoiding, 161, 195
turf. *See* territorialism
Twistep, 319, 649
Tylenol, toxicity, 318, 378

uniformed persons, 609
United Kennel Club (UKC), 19, 30
University of Pennsylvania Hip Improvement Program, 54
unknown dogs
attacks by, 540–42, 547
avoiding bite, 490, 559
danger, signs of, 547
introducing. *See* new dog introductions
ununited anconeal process (UAP), 55
urinary incontinence, 399–400
diagnostic questions, 400
medication for, 400
and senior dogs, 654
sphincter incompetence, 400
and urinary-tract infections, 230, 400
urinary-tract disorders
bladder stones, 400, 449
and diabetic dogs, 352
emergencies, 307
and incontinence. *See* urinary incontinence
infections, 230, 352, 400
urination
accidents. *See* house-soiling; urinary incontinence
marking behavior. *See* urine marking
training. *See* crate; house-training
urination, excessive
and diabetes, 350
polydipsia/polyuria, 234
urine marking
and aggressive dogs, 539
inside house, 232, 581
and new dog introductions, 100–101
and ranked order, 139, 144, 216, 629
urine sniffing, 139

vaccinations, 296–304
adverse reactions, 297, 303–4
AVMA recommendations, 297
by breeders, 121

Tracie Hotchner is the author of the million-copy best-seller *Pregnancy & Childbirth*, which was nominated for the American Book Award, as well as three other books on pregnancy. She has appeared on national talk shows, including *The Today Show* and *Oprah*. She lives with her three dogs, Jazzy, Billy Blue and Scooby Doo, in East Hampton, New York, where she is also a volunteer Emergency Medical Technician and driver with East Hampton Village Ambulance Association.

Please Let Me Hear from You!

I really hope you like this book and that it's made a positive difference in your life and your dog's—but please don't be a stranger. I genuinely want to know how you feel about this book—whether topics were missing that you looked for, whether certain recommendations were successful or disappointing and especially if you have ideas or information that you want to share with others. Even though the book is done and in your hands, I consider it a work in progress. I'd like to think that this book stimulates dialogue and change in some of the ways that we interact with our dogs, but the only way I'll know for sure is if people stay in touch with me.

In researching *The Dog Bible* I did as thorough a job as I could, but there's always something you miss—plus ideas, services and products change all the time. I intend to constantly keep on top of all aspects of our lives with dogs but I can't do it alone: I need the input of people whose connection to their dogs means enough to them to take the time to get involved. I will be grateful for the feedback and contributions of people who love their dogs and want to optimize the canine portion of their lives for themselves and other dog lovers.

Please consider this an invitation to get in touch with me by sending your comments and questions to my Web site, www.thedogbible.com. I cannot answer people personally but I will try to reply on the Web site—with the help of Aimee Sadler for training and behavioral questions and Barry Browning for medical ones—so that even more people can benefit from the answers. I will also collect all new ideas and suggestions and will give you credit for the ones that I use in organizing an eventual revised edition of the book.

I thank you . . . and I know your dog thanks you, too.